Kristan Stoddart

Russia's Hybrid Warfare Offensive Against the West

De Gruyter Contemporary
Social Sciences

Volume 55

Kristan Stoddart

Russia's Hybrid Warfare Offensive Against the West

DE GRUYTER

ISBN 978-3-11-158299-3
e-ISBN (PDF) 978-3-11-158346-4
e-ISBN (EPUB) 978-3-11-158391-4
ISSN 2747-5689
eISSN: 2747-5697

Library of Congress Control Number: 2025943704

Bibliographic information published by the Deutsche Nationalbibliothek
The Deutsche Nationalbibliothek lists this publication in the Deutsche Nationalbibliografie; detailed bibliographic data are available on the internet at http://dnb.dnb.de.

Cover image: Gwengoat / iStock / Getty Images Plus
Printing and binding: CPI books GmbH, Leck

www.degruyterbrill.com
Questions about General Product Safety Regulation:
productsafety@degruyterbrill.com

Acknowledgments

I am grateful to be able to reproduce under a Creative Commons Attribution license material from the excellent study by Philip Howard, Bharath Ganesh, Dimitra Liotsiou, John Kelly, and Camille François, "The IRA, Social Media and Political Polarization in the United States, 2012–2018," Computational Propaganda Research Project, University of Oxford (2018).[1] I am also grateful to be able to reproduce material from commissioned by the U.S. Senate Select Committee on Intelligence, in particular, New Knowledge's report, "The Tactics & Tropes of the Internet Research Agency."

I owe a huge debt of gratitude to my friend and former colleague, Professor Emeritus Len Scott, who read most parts of this when it was a larger two-volume study and then as a separate completed draft. This book is dedicated to Len, not only as a thank you for his excellent comments and searching questions but more importantly for two decades of friendship, support, loyalty, and collegiality. Additionally, my long-term collaborator and friend, Professor Emeritus John Baylis, supported and aided me in some fundamental discussions.

Whilst the content I have used produced by United States government agencies is in the public domain I am grateful to be able to reproduce materials from a number of U.S. government agencies. These are the White House, National Security Council, United States Congress and United States Senate, the Department of Energy, Department of Homeland Security, Department of Justice, Federal Aviation Authority, Federal Bureau of Investigation, Federal Emergency Management Agency, the National Institute of Standards and Technology (NIST)/Department of Commerce. This is in addition to the Department of Defense and branches of the DOD including the National Security Agency, Central Intelligence Agency, Defense Intelligence Agency, Office of the Director of National Intelligence, U.S. Cybercommand, the Office of the Director of National Intelligence, the Defense Advanced Research Projects Agency, and the Joint Chiefs of Staff. I am also grateful to NATO's Cooperative Cyber Defence Centre of Excellence (CCDCOE) for permission to quote from a selection of sources. While best efforts have been made to trace and acknowledge all copyright holders, I would like to apologize should there have been any errors or omissions.

This book was begun during a career break in the summer of 2018. I began to learn that I needed to separately discuss cyberespionage after completing my 2022 book *Cyberwarfare: Threats to Critical Infrastructure.* As my knowledge (and hopefully my understanding) grew further as I thought about the fundamental issues

1 https://creativecommons.org/licenses/by-sa/4.0/deed.en.

https://doi.org/10.1515/9783111583464-001

of cyberwar(fare) and then thought in tandem about the myriad of cyberespionage cases and activities I knew of or came to encounter I realized more still. This second, more evolved realization was that not only was separation necessary and that some acts of cyberespionage were also part of the debate/continuum surrounding cyberwarfare, but that Russia's related and broader and deeper sets of nefarious active measures, strategized and undertaken now for more than a decade, is better thought of and conceptualized as hybrid warfare. I hope I have done these subjects justice.

On a more substantive point, if time had permitted as this book progressed towards publication (and as I learned more still), sections of the book (probably in Chapter 1 on Active Measures) would have been devoted to Russia's FSB and Russia's Spetsnaz units. These are contained instead in the Introduction and Chapter 1. The spread and depth of the Kremlin's multi-level activities and the highly active nature of them means this has been a difficult book to research and write. Whilst I made my best efforts over the past seven years, the time and resources currently afforded me have not allowed me to do be as thorough and systematic I would have liked as my knowledge has grown. In addition, whilst I have done my level best to reach out to colleagues and organizations who know more than me on specific issues (including dedicated experts on Russia who have my great respect and admiration) I cannot help but feel I could have done more still. Nevertheless, the proofing stages alone have reminded me of the complex dynamics at work and the moving pieces and that I have done my level best. This matters to me. Russian activities are persistent and have real world consequences, not least for Ukraine and its people.

In shedding further light on these issues, I owe a debt of gratitude to all at De Gruyter who brought what you are reading to fruition with consummate professionalism and support from commissioning this book (and my book on China) through to publication. These are André Borges, Anett Rehner, Antonia Mittelbach, Michaela Göbels, and Liz Nichols my excellent and engaged copy-editor. Michaela in particular was incredibly supportive and understood what a major undertaking it was for me to complete two books for De Gruyter at the same time (alongside editing a third book on hybrid warfare for the U.S. Marine Corps University Press).

Contents

List of abbreviations and concepts

Access privileges	Technical barriers exist which limit access privileges to systems and data.
Active measures	(see also Covert Action) Conducted by state intelligence agencies, active measures include forgeries, propaganda, destabilization, forgery, assassination, acts of terrorism, hacking political parties, election interference, and dis/misinformation campaigns for political effect.
Agent	A person unofficially employed by an intelligence service, often as a source of information.
APT28	Known by a variety of names the most common of which is "Fancy Bear." APT28 is a Russian cyberespionage actor run by the GRU.
APT29	Also known by a variety of names or monikers the most common being "Cozy Bear." They too are a Russian cyberespionage actor run by the SVR.
Backdoor	A way in purposefully left or discovered.
Bots/Botnets	Taken from the word robot, these are automated applications that are (amongst other things) used to generate or spread mis- and disinformation.
CERT	Computer Emergency Response Team.
CI	Critical infrastructure – includes public utilities such as electric power generation and distribution, water supplies and water treatment, natural gas and oil production and pipelines, shipping and maritime traffic, hydroelectric dams, traffic lights and train switching systems.
CIA	(Central Intelligence Agency) The main U.S. foreign intelligence gathering service.
CIS	Commonwealth of Independent States
CISA	The U.S. Cybersecurity Information Sharing Act (2015)/Agency.
Counterintelligence	The business of thwarting the efforts of foreign intelligence services/agencies. This includes information gathered and activities conducted to counter foreign intelligence threats. This includes but is not limited to spy-catching.
Counterterrorism	Preventing and deterring terrorist threats through all available and permissible means.
Covert action	A wide range of activities which rely on plausible deniability by the perpetrator. This can include an operation designed to affect foreign affairs including the use of lethal force.
Cybersecurity	A term that encompasses computer or chip-based technology and its security.
Cyberspace	A generic term which has various meanings encompassing the Internet, intranets, and other computer-based networks and devices.
Cyberwar	A contested term. Throughout the book this refers to acts defined under international law and the Tallinn Manuals as cyber capabilities capable of critically degrading a nations capacity to respond to cyber acts and capable of causing physical destruction qualifying as "armed attack."

https://doi.org/10.1515/9783111583464-002

Cyberwarfare	Directly related to cyberwar. Acts of state-on-state war which may standalone or be used in conjunction with cyberespionage or the use of military force.
Cyber privateer/proxy	These are hackers who are frequently part of collectives who are used by states for their benefit. They can also be proxy forces.
"Dark Net"	(see also TOR) Part of the Internet that has access privileges and is inaccessible from search engines like Google and requires a TOR browser.
DHS	The U.S. Department of Homeland Security founded after 9/11.
Disinformation	Information that is known to be false, purposely designed to influence and deceive the target.
DNI	Director of National Intelligence (U.S.).
DOJ	Department of Justice (U.S.)
Espionage	Espionage includes obtaining military, political, commercial, and other secret information through spying (often described as the world's second oldest profession after prostitution), infiltration, or through monitoring devices. It is used for intelligence gathering and is illegal under domestic law but an accepted customary norm in international law.
EU	European Union.
Fake news	Mis and disinformation which is knowingly or unwittingly sown or repeated. It has become a politicized term carrying different meanings.
False flag	A tactic used by one group to blame another.
Fancy Bear	(see APT28).
FBI	Federal Bureau of Investigation. The U.S. domestic counterintelligence service and federal law enforcement agency.
Five Eyes	An intelligence sharing partnership between the United States, United Kingdom, Canada, Australia, and New Zealand facilitated by a series of treaties.
FSB	(*Federal'naya Sluzhba Bezopasnosti*/Federal Security Service) Russia's civilian intelligence service founded in 1995 tasked with domestic and (increasingly) foreign operations.
Gray zone	A concept beneath the threshold of war that sees diplomacy, economic coercion, media manipulation, cyberattacks (including misinformation and disinformation) utilized against a target state. This can include the use of paramilitaries and proxy forces.
GRU	(*Glavnoye Razvedovatel'noye Upravlenie*) Russian military intelligence.
Hacktivist/hacktivism	Hacking for a political or social cause.
HUMINT	(Human Intelligence) Intelligence collected from human sources. It is said that HUMINT consists of case officers, support personnel, and field agents operating under a designated cover. Some have official legal (diplomatic) cover and status, others Non-Official Cover (NOC), whilst others operate as "Illegals" with no official connection to a government. Whilst recruits into government service are encouraged they also carry risks. This includes the potential for double agents or increased exposure.
Hybrid warfare	Mostly associated with Russia (where it is known as *gibridnaya voina*) but with antecedents that stretch back to antiquity. Hybrid warfare can combine information, influence, legal disputes (lawfare), and economic opera-

	tions, as well as the use of military and paramilitary force and increasing cyber operations.
IC	(Intelligence Community) Often used singularly or to describe the interactions between national intelligence agencies like the Central Intelligence Agency and National Security Agency. Intelligence communities relate to these as a broad international series of organizations and how national agencies like the CIA interact transnationally and internationally.
ICS	(Industrial Control Systems).
ICT	Information Communications Technology. A global term to describe software and hardware related to these areas.
Illegal	KGB/GRU/SVR operatives infiltrated into a target country without the protection of diplomatic immunity, having assumed new identities.
Internet	A global decentralized and interconnected network of computer systems and information.
IoT	Internet of Things (see also SMART). All devices that use Internet protocols. This includes everything from home computers and tablets to Internet connected machinery, wearable technology and monitoring or sensor-based devices such as electricity meters.
IT	Information Technology.
KGB	(*Komitet Gosudarstvennoy Bezopasnosti*) The Soviet Union's all-powerful intelligence and security service during the Cold War.
Malware	(Malicious software) Widely referred to as computer viruses.
MI6	The British foreign intelligence service; officially known as Secret Intelligence Service (SIS).
Misinformation	(see also Disinformation) Information that is not known to be demonstrably false, and where individuals and groups can be unknowingly misinformed in making or supporting claims. Neither misinformation or disinformation are clearly defined as separate or related terms. Both terms continue to generate debate.
Mole	An agent of one organization sent to penetrate an organization or intelligence agency by gaining employment; a term popularized by John Le Carré.
MVD	*Ministerstvo Vnutrennikh Del* (Russia's Ministry of Internal Affairs).
NATO	North Atlantic Treaty Organization.
NSA	National Security Agency. A branch of the U.S. Department of Defense responsible for ensuring the security of American communications and for breaking into the communications of other nations.
NSC	National Security Council (U.S.).
OPCW	Organisation for the Prohibition of Chemical Weapons.
Operational Technology	(OT) This is used to control physical processes and devices across industry and throughout critical infrastructure. OT include Industrial Control Systems (ICS) and Supervisory Control and Data Acquisition (SCADA) systems.
OSINT	Open source intelligence. Intelligence information derived from publicly available sources.
Phishing	(see also spear phishing) Contact by email, telephone, or text message by someone posing as a legitimate to obtain sensitive information. This

	can include directing an end user via e-mail to click on a link hosting malware designed to extract information.
Ransomware	Encrypting files to extort money from organizations and individuals.
SCADA	Systems Control and Data Acquisition. SCADA systems enable the management and remote access of on-site control devices, or field devices through a central system. They are the underlying control system of most critical infrastructures.
Server	A computer used in a network which provides a service/s to a client computer/s (which are requesting data held by servers). Servers usually have more processing power, memory, and storage than clients.
SIGINT	Signals intelligence; consists of COMINT (communications intelligence) and ELINT (electronic intelligence). Platforms for Russian SIGINT collection include ground-based stations within Russia and a small number abroad. Embassies and consulates are also used for SIGINT. Russia also maintains seaborne and maritime assets for SIGINT as well as airborne and space-based (satellite) platforms. The GRU also maintains mobile ground-based SIGINT vehicles and drones. Russia's intelligence agencies also continue to employ close-access SIGINT capabilities in addition to their massive and pervasive use of cyber.
Siloviki	Russian for "strong men." Those from a security services background who hold power in Russia.
Spear phishing	(see also Social engineering) A targeted and tailored cyberattack through e-mail or electronic communications (phish/scam) tailored towards a specific individual and/or organization with the aim of defrauding the target, extracting information for malicious purpose, to install malware, and/or to provide a gateway for deeper activity towards individuals and their associates or organizations. Social engineering is being increasingly used in spear phishing.
SVR	*Sluzhba Vneshnei Razvedki* (Russia's Foreign Intelligence Service).
TOR	(The Onion Router) TOR is an encryption technology that routes data through multiple layers. It was originally developed by the U.S. Navy and Defense Advanced Research Projects Agency (DARPA) in the 1990s before becoming open source in 2004. It is now run by a nonprofit organization but it is still funded by U.S. government agencies. It offers anonymity to its users and 'hides' U.S. military users in a sea of other TOR users. Users also include cybercriminals, other state actors and whistle-blowers. Anyone can use a TOR browser and gain access to the 'Dark Net'.
Tradecraft	Methods developed by intelligence operatives to conduct their operations.
Trojan	(see also Malware) In cybersecurity, a Trojan horse or Trojan is a type of malware that is disguised as legitimate to infect a host.
UN	United Nations.
US-CERT	United States Cyber Emergency Response Team.
USCYBERCOM	United States Cyber Command is primarily run out of the NSA in Fort Meade but has capabilities across the U.S. military for offensive and defensive cyber operations.

VPN	Virtual Private Networks are designed to be secure, encrypted tunnels for online data between systems. As in most other areas of encryption, VPNs add a layer of security but do not guarantee anonymity or complete protection.
Wikileaks	An Internet repository for leaked information founded by Julian Assange.
Wiper	A wiper is a form of malware designed to delete information from computer systems.

Introduction

On February 24, 2022 Russia invaded Ukraine. The Kremlin frames this as a "special military operation" to protect pro-Russian/Russian speaking factions in Ukraine, especially in Crimea and the Donbas in Ukraine's east, and to "demilitarize" and "de-nazify" Ukraine. Russian president Vladimir Putin stands at the center of the decision-making process.[1] This book will detail why Putin was emboldened to take these actions. It will also detail the nature of his regime, and how Russian cyberespionage, at times in coordination with traditional espionage, has been effective against the West, the former Soviet space of Russia's near abroad, and into Africa and even further afield.

But for a four-year interregnum, which saw him revert to Prime Minister in a "castling move" which saw Dmitry Medvedev becoming President, Putin has been President of the Russian Federation since 2000. Putin was reelected unimpeded by serious opposition for another six-year term in March 2024.[2] In the quarter centu-

1 Niklas Masuhr and Benno Zogg, 'The War in Ukraine: First Lessons', CSS Analyses in Security Policy, No. 301 (April 2022), https://www.research-collection.ethz.ch/bitstream/handle/20.500.11850/540121/2/CSSAnalyse301-EN.pdf, James Risen, 'U.S. Intelligence says Putin made a last-minute decision to invade Ukraine' (March 11 2022), https://theintercept.com/2022/03/11/russia-putin-ukraine-invasion-us-intelligence/. Both accessed 9 March 2023. See also Tor Bukkvoll, 'Why Putin went to war: ideology, interests and decision-making in the Russian use of force in Crimea and Donbas', *Contemporary Politics*, Vol. 22, Issue 3 (June 2016), pp. 273–279. Leonid E. Grinin, "The Role of an Individual in History: A Reconsideration," *Social Evolution & History*, Vol. 9, No. 2 (September 2010), pp. 95–136.

2 Kevin P. Riehle, *The Russian FSB A Concise History of the Federal Security Service* (Washington, DC: Georgetown University Press, 2024), p. 82. Anonymous, "Putin claims victory in election with no serious competition" (March 17, 2024), https://www.dw.com/en/putin-claims-victory-in-election-with-no-serious-competition/a-68597661, accessed 21 March 2024. This article by Deutsche Welle (Germany's international broadcaster) is an example where a journalist(s) from a mainstream news organization have chosen not to sign their name(s) and remain anonymous. One can speculate why but as you will read below mainstream journalists, and many others from accredited news organizations, have been targeted. Many have been killed, including in Russian strikes on hotels in Ukraine. Others, including international journalists and the organizations they work for have been harassed. An unknown number of journalists and the organizations they work for have also experienced cyber intrusions and breaches. Russian agents working under the cover of journalists such as the GRU agent Pablo González (aka Pavel Rubtsov) have also been discovered. For more information see Reporters Without Borders, "In a new report, RSF and Truth Hounds reveal Russian strategy of bombing Ukrainian hotels to silence the press", https://rsf.org/en/new-report-rsf-and-truth-hounds-reveal-russian-strategy-bombing-ukrainian-hotels-silence-press and the Committee to Protect Journalists, https://cpj.org/europe/russia/. Both accessed 26 July 2025.

https://doi.org/10.1515/9783111583464-003

ry since his first (more authentic) election in 2000, Russia has reasserted itself on the geopolitical stage. It has done so by violating the territorial integrity and political independence in parts of its near abroad and by sowing division and seeking influence over its perceived adversaries in Europe and the United States. Russia has also engaged in politico-military interventions in Syria, Libya, the Central African Republic (CAR), Sudan, Libya, Mozambique, and Mali. Many of these interventions were through its paramilitary proxy, the Wagner Group, led by the late Yevgeny Prigozhin.[3]

President Putin is said to be a student of history and in 2021 penned an essay which decried Ukrainian statehood and pronounced on a number of themes.[4] Two themes are relevant to this book. The first is what he called "deliberate efforts by ... forces ... to undermine ... unity. The formula ... divide and rule ... [and] sow discord among people, the overarching goal being to divide and then to pit the parts of a single people against one another." Second, Putin also spoke of the actions of "both the official authorities and local oligarchs, who robbed the people of Ukraine and kept their stolen money in Western banks, ready to sell their motherland for the sake of preserving their capital."[5]

Both arguments are profoundly ironic. Domestically, Russia's renationalized natural wealth in hydrocarbons, especially oil and gas, has not been reinvested into infrastructure projects or elevated the standard of living for most Russians. Instead, it has brought great wealth to Russian government officials and enabled the same system of oligarchs that Putin describes in Ukraine.[6] Russia has also systematically attempted to undermine the unity of Ukraine and sought to divide Western nations to further Kremlin policies. These activities are detailed in this book as part of a suite of active measures/hybrid warfare campaigns combining misinformation, disinformation and mal-information which have mined socio-po-

---

3 On their activities see Digital Forensic Research Lab, "Yevgeny Prigozhin: A History of Violence and Propaganda Around the World" (June 28, 2023), https://dfrlab.org/2023/06/28/yevgeny-prigozhin-a-history-of-violence-and-propaganda-around-the-world/, accessed 2 July 2023.

4 en.kremlin.ru/events/president/news/66181, accessed 3 April 2022.

5 en.kremlin.ru/events/president/news/66181, accessed 3 April 2022.

6 Mark Galeotti, *The Vory: Russia's Super Mafia* (New Haven, CT: Yale University Press, 2018). Liz Campbell and Nick Lord, "Following the Money: Illicit Financial Flows and SDG," in Jarrett Blaustein, Kate Fitz-Gibbon, Nathan W. Pino, and Rob White (eds.), *The Emerald Handbook on Crime, Justice and Sustainable Development* (Bingley UK: Emerald Group Publishing, 2020), pp. 355–377. The author is grateful to Professor Lord for highlighting this chapter. Laura Solanko, "Where do Russia's mobilized soldiers come from? Evidence from bank deposits," BOFIT [Bank of Finland Institute for Emerging Economies] Policy Brief 2024 No. 1 (February 21, 2024), https://publications.bof.fi/bitstream/handle/10024/53281/bpb124.pdf?sequence=1&isAllowed=y, accessed 18 March 2024.

litical fault lines on issues including identity politics and nationalism, liberalism, immigration, and globalization.

As set out in the preceding list of abbreviations and concepts, misinformation is information or knowledge that stems from being misinformed but is not demonstrably false or communicated with malign intent. Disinformation is false, falsified or contestable and is designed to influence and deceive target audiences. Relatedly, malinformation is purposefully designed for influence and deception campaigns with malicious intent. Each of these terms and the use of them can be contested (and they can also be hyphenated as mis-, dis-, and mal-information).

More importantly, whether one perceives information (especially on social media) as falling into one or more of these categories, debating the terms and the boundaries between them can become politically and socially charged (sometimes invoking the label or dismissive charge of "fake news"). Instead, the use of these terms and contestations need to be understood alongside issue areas that include confirmation bias, media literacy, and critical thinking skills. Using terms like these can also box or silo the way we think of issues, depictions, and events whilst investing time and energy into debating meanings or contextualizing. This too is part of Kremlin designs that sees and uses social media and wider mass media and mass messaging as a globalized information space ripe for manipulation and exploitation. The aim is to influence internal politics, social discourse, national cohesion, and international relations of far distant societies and nations that it perceives it can effect (and has effected) for political and strategic ends. As Carl Miller suggests, these definitions are a distraction but for good or for ill the one "word that has really struck is disinformation".[7] Russia's campaigns have also utilized their intelligence agencies (also referred to as "Special Services") and criminal and cybercriminal fraternity in a series of business deals, political pacts, and cyberespionage campaigns that appear financially motivated, but with underlying politico-military dimensions. This is in addition to suspected sabotage and assassination operations.[8]

7 Carl Miller, "Directing Responses Against Illicit Influence Operations (D-RAIL)" (August 2024), p. 1., https://www.disinfo.eu/wp-content/uploads/2024/08/20240818_D-RAIL.pdf, accessed 31 July 2025. See also, Esma Aimeur, Sabrine Amri, & Giles Bassard, "Fake news, disinformation and misinformation in social media: a review", *Social Media Analysis and Mining*, Vol. 13, Article No. 30 (2023), pp. 1–36. Samuel C. Wooley and Philip N. Howard (eds.), *Computational Propaganda: Political Parties, Politicians, and Political Manipulation on Social Media* (New York: Oxford University Press, 2019).

8 Assassinations are also sometimes euphemistically described as wetwork/wet work (*mokrie dela*) or *delo* (affairs) as in having bloody hands or getting your hands bloody. Targeted assassi-

With Russia's System for Operative Investigative Activities (SORM), designed for the surveillance of domestic Internet traffic, allowing the FSB (*Federal'naya Sluzhba Bezopasnosti*) to directly collect this traffic "without the knowledge or co-operation of the service provider," Russian cybercriminals would have to circumvent this system to bypass government surveillance.[9] Russia's counterterrorist-directed Yarovaya Law of 2018, described as Russia's "Big Brother" Law, adds another layer of domestic surveillance.[10] These means of domestic control echo those of the KGB and the days of the Soviet-era.

1 The fall of a superpower

As the Soviet Union was collapsing, NATO estimated its military at over 4 million personnel organized in 200 plus army divisions, with four naval fleets, and an arsenal of strategic nuclear weapons supplemented by tactical nuclear weapons. Its substantial presence in the Warsaw Pact states of Eastern Europe helped maintain Soviet dominance over its conquests in World War II as well as providing a buffer zone between Soviet Russia and NATO forces stationed in Western Europe. Offers of military assistance through its two main intelligence agencies, the KGB and GRU, also provided a conduit to spread Soviet influence into what was then described as the Third World through arms sales, military advisors, and periodic interventions.[11] The cost of the arms race with the United States and NATO Europe whilst maintaining a military and security apparatus at an unaffordable scale are two of the main underlying reasons for the collapse of the Soviet Union and end of the Cold War.

After the Soviet Union collapsed in 1991, Russia's first president Boris Yeltsin implemented a radical series of economic and political reforms. State industry was privatized with the adoption of free-market capitalism and a multi-party system with the promise of democracy. Economically, this meant "By mid-1994, al-

nations are authorized under Russia's Federal Law No. 35-FZ (2006) focused on counterterrorism. "Federal Law No. 35-FZ on counteraction against terrorism, 2006", https://ihl-databases.icrc.org/en/national-practice/federal-law-no-35-fz-counteraction-against-terrorism-2006, accessed 14 August 2025. Riehle, *The Russian FSB*, p. 85.

9 James A. Lewis, "Reference Note on Russian Communications Surveillance" (April 18, 2014), https://www.csis.org/analysis/reference-note-russian-communications-surveillance, accessed 30 June 2019.

10 "Russia's 'Big Brother' Law Enters Into Force" (July 1, 2018), https://www.themoscowtimes.com/2018/07/01/russias-big-brother-law-enters-into-force-a62066, accessed 30 June 2019.

11 1991 Military Forces in Transition, https://archives.nato.int/uploads/r/null/1/3/137881/0300_Military_forces_in_transition_1991_ENG.pdf, accessed 18 August 2025.

most 70 percent of the Russian economy was in private hands."[12] Russia's large hydrocarbon fields, the natural wealth behind the economic boom years of 1999–2008, led to the rise of series of oligarchs – a class of businessmen who became wealthy and powerful through privatization and ruthless business deals.[13] These policies also saw mass unemployment and grinding poverty for the majority of Russians and "By the turn of the century, Russia had come to be viewed as a disastrous failure and the 1990s as a decade of catastrophe for its people."[14] This was felt personally by Vladimir Putin, who was stationed as an intelligence officer for the KGB in Dresden, East Germany when the Berlin Wall fell in November 1989. Towards the end of the 1990s, whilst working for St. Petersburg's Mayor (after resigning from the KGB following the 1991 coup which brought Yeltsin to power), he was moonlighting as a taxi driver to make ends meet.[15]

Richard Sakwa outlines that "In the 1990s Russia endured one of the greatest economic depressions in peacetime in modern world history." Sakwa adds, "Russia exercised the attributes of a world power, with a permanent seat in the United Nations Security Council and the second largest nuclear arsenal, but its weakened economic status opened up a contradiction between aspiration and capacity."[16] Russia's economic collapse in August 1998, when it defaulted on its national debt and devalued the ruble, was the nadir. This saw savings wiped out and saw the domestic banking sector come close to bankruptcy, alongside a period of high inflation that still lives long in the collective memory.[17] The opening up of Russia to foreign investors and rising levels of foreign debt left Russia with little option but to accommodate the West at a time when the European Union (EU) and

---

12 Andrei Shleifer and Daniel Treisman, "A Normal Country: Russia After Communism," *Journal of Economic Perspectives*, Vol. 19, No. 1 (Winter 2005), p. 153.

13 See for example Mikael Wigell and Antto Vihma, "Geopolitics versus Geoeconomics: The Case of Russia's Geostrategy and Its Effects on the EU," *International Affairs*, Vol. 92, Issue 3 (May 2016), pp. 605–627 and Clifford Krauss, "Russia Uses Its Oil Giant, Rosneft, as a Foreign Policy Tool" (October 29, 2017), https://www.nytimes.com/2017/10/29/business/energy-environment/russia-venezula-oil-rosneft.html, accessed November 18 2017.

14 Shleifer and Treisman, "A Normal Country," pp. 151–153.

15 Anonymous, "Vladimir Putin: I moonlighted as a taxi driver in the 1990s" (December 12, 2021), https://www.bbc.co.uk/news/world-europe-59629670, accessed 26 June 2023. This was widely reported at the time as it was mentioned by Putin himself in a documentary on Russian state television entitled "Russia. Recent History". This was not disputed or denied by the Kremlin.

16 Richard Sakwa, "'New Cold War' or Twenty Years' Crisis? Russia and International Politics," *International Affairs*, Vol. 84, No. 2 (2008), p. 242.

17 Niko Gobbin and Bruno Merlevede, "The Russian Crisis: A Debt Perspective," *Post-Communist Economies*, Vol. 12, Issue 2 (2000), pp. 141–163. Ivor Bennett, "'Panic' in Russia as rouble slips to symbolic mark against US dollar" (November 28, 2024), https://news.sky.com/story/panic-in-russia-as-rouble-slips-to-symbolic-mark-against-us-dollar-13262344, accessed 4 December 2024.

NATO were expanding to its borders through the accession of former Soviet and Eastern European republics.[18]

The perilous state of the economy also impacted on Russia's military with a downsizing of operational capabilities and front-line strength, endemic problems in combat-readiness, and reduced military expenditure across the defense sector.[19] There also remained concerns, evident since the dissolution of the Soviet Union, of some of the large number of former Soviet scientists and technicians becoming security risks as severe financial pressure bit hard on them. This was particularly evident in the civil and military nuclear fields.[20] In Yeltsin's final term of office (1996–1999), Russia remained in sharp decline with little hope of resisting Western encroachment into the former Soviet space.[21] This encroachment into lands that have periodically been Russian or under Russian imperial influence since the forging of modern Russia under Ivan IV (Ivan the Terrible) in the 16th century, which Putin's 2021 essay drew on, is also a reflection of *smuta* (Russian for periods of turmoil or malaise).[22]

Putin, who succeeded Yeltsin as President in a peaceful transfer of power in 1999–2000, began to arrest this decline with increasingly authoritarian and kleptocratic moves to bring Russia's major economic assets back under state control.[23] Under Putin, *siloviki* ("strong men" from a KGB or military background) simultaneously rose prominently to great wealth and political power through renationalization.[24] In 2023, Russia was the world's eleventh largest economy with a Gross

---

18 Gerhard Mangott, "Farewell to Russia: The Decay of a Superpower," in Heinz Gärtner, Adrian Hyde-Price, and Erich Reiter (eds.), *Europe's New Security Challenges* (Boulder: Lynne Rienner, 2001), pp. 381–385.

19 Mangott, "Farewell to Russia," pp. 385–388.

20 Siegfried S. Hecker, *Doomed to Cooperate: How American and Russian Scientists Joined Forces to Avert Some of the Greatest Post-Cold War Nuclear Dangers* (Los Alamos: Bathtub Row Press, 2016).

21 Margarita M. Balmaceda, *Energy Dependency, Politics and Corruption in the Former Soviet Union: Russia's Power, Oligarchs' Profits and Ukraine's Missing Energy Policy, 1995–2006* (Abingdon: Routledge, 2007).

22 Danica Jenkins, "How Russian history and the concept of 'smuta' (turmoil) sheds light on Putin and Prigozhin – and the dangers of dissent" (August 28 2023), https://theconversation.com/how-russian-history-and-the-concept-of-smuta-turmoil-sheds-light-on-putin-and-prigozhin-and-the-dangers-of-dissent-210289, accessed 27 August 2025.

23 Simeon Djankov, "Russia's Economy under Putin: From Crony Capitalism to State Capitalism," Peterson Institute for International Economics, Policy Briefs 15–18 (September 2015), https://www.piie.com/publications/policy-briefs/russias-economy-under-putin-crony-capitalism-state-capitalism, p. 3.

24 Alena V. Ledeneva, *How Russia Really Works: The Informal Practices That Shaped Post-Soviet Politics and Business* (Ithaca: Cornell University Press, 2006), pp. 86 and 90, Ian Bremmer and

Domestic Product (GDP) of $1,778 billion (the same size as Italy). Oil and gas dominate Russia's exports.[25] Russia's wealth resides mainly with the oligarchs and *siloviki* headed by Putin. This relationship is characterized by "chaotic profiteering and tribalism."[26]

Whether Russia was ever a democracy in the Western sense is debatable but the rise of United Russia out of the 1999 presidential elections saw it become the dominant political party in Russia's parliament, the *Duma*. It is to this party that Putin aligned himself as power passed from Boris Yeltsin to him.[27] The 1990s had embedded corruption and self-aggrandizement, already evident from Soviet days when communist party affiliation bought favor, goods, and services, turning Russia into a kleptocracy. It has since also become an authoritarian state, but Russia under Putin is not the Soviet Union 2.0 with a one-party communist system and state ownership founded on a political ideology.[28]

2 Russian nationalism and regional security

The centrifugal forces of Russia and Marxist-Leninism had not prevented the Soviet Union from unraveling rapidly. Between 1990 and 1991, declarations of independence were made by the three Baltic states of Estonia, Latvia, and Lithuania. They were followed in rapid succession by the twelve other republics: Armenia, Azerbaijan, Belarus, Georgia, Kazakhstan, Kyrgyzstan, Moldova, Tajikistan, Turkmenistan, Ukraine, Uzbekistan, and lastly Russia itself in December 1991. At the

---

Samuel Charap, "The Siloviki in Putin's Russia: Who They Are and What They Want," *The Washington Quarterly*, Vol. 30, Issue 1 (Winter 2006/7), pp. 83–92 and Mark Galeotti, "Putin's Spies and Security Men: His Strongest Allies, His Greatest Weakness", *Russian Analytical Digest*, No. 173, (October 12, 2015), pp. 8–11.

25 Rebecca M. Nelson, *The Economic Impact of Russia Sanctions* (December 13, 2022), Congressional Research Service, https://crsreports.congress.gov/product/pdf/IF/IF12092. Andres B. Schwarzenberg, *Russia's Trade and Investment Role in the Global Economy* (updated January 17, 2023), https://crsreports.congress.gov/product/pdf/IF/IF12066. Both accessed 11 November 2023.

26 Joss I. Meakins, "Squabbling Siloviki: Factionalism Within Russia's Security Services," *International Journal of Intelligence and CounterIntelligence*, Vol. 31, Issue 2 (March 2018), p. 245.

27 Ora John Reuter and Thomas F. Remington, "Dominant Party Regimes and the Commitment Problem: The Case of United Russia," *Comparative Political Studies*, Vol. 42, No. 4 (April 2009), pp. 501–526. Putin's Asymmetric Assault on Democracy in Russia and Europe: Implications for U.S. National Security. A Minority Staff Report, Committee on Foreign Relations United States Senate, January 10, 2018, pp. 191–192. https://www.foreign.senate.gov/imo/media/doc/FinalRR.pdf, accessed 5 November 2019.

28 Taras Kuzio, "Nationalism and Authoritarianism in Russia: Introduction to the Special Issue," *Communist and Post-Communist Studies*, Vol. 49, Issue 1 (March 2016), pp. 1–11.

time "two-thirds of the Russian people, and ... the majority of democratic politicians," viewed the dissolution "as a tragic mistake, something that must somehow be undone."[29] Putin was among them, and this bitterness has become a major driver for Russia's revanchist foreign and security policies. Russia's current leadership sees these developments through a strictly realist, zero-sum, post-imperialist lens.[30]

The dissolution of the Union of Soviet Socialist Republics also left a legacy of disputed territories and ethnic tensions in a number of its regions, some of which have spilled into conflict (often stoked or pacified by Russia).[31] This includes in Transnistria, a breakaway northeastern province of Moldova, South Ossetia and Abkhazia in Georgia (which led to Russian intervention in 2008), Nagorno-Karabakh involving Armenia and Azerbaijan, and Chechnya in the North Caucasus.[32]

Aside from trying to manage relations with the former Soviet states, separatist movements and acts of terrorism in trouble spots like majority-Islamist Chechnya and the wider North Caucasus threatened the unity of Russia. Acts of terrorism, and the questionable responses of Russian counterterrorist teams, included the Budennovsk hospital hostage crisis in Stavropol in June 1995 where Chechen terrorists took 1,500 hostage in a five-day stand-off that saw 129 killed, the October 2002 Dubrovka Theater siege in Moscow (which saw 912 hostages taken, again by Chechen terrorists, and 125 people, including 10 children, die with five others executed by militants), and most infamously Beslan. The Beslan school siege of 1–3 September 2004 in North Ossetia on the eastern border of Chechnya saw 326 people die, including 159 children attending school on their first day of term. This upsurge in terrorist attacks saw Putin vow to re-form the Ministry for Regions and Ethnicities (subsequently recreated as the Ministry of Regional Development) whose antecedents stretch to the Russian Revolution of 1917. It also saw threats from the head of the Russian General Staff to "take all measures

29 Zbigniew Brzezinski, "The Premature Partnership," *Foreign Affairs*, Vol. 73, No. 2 (March–April 1994), p. 72.

30 Keir Giles, *Russia's War on Everybody and What It Means For You* (London: Bloomsbury, 2024), pp. 9–15.

31 Jeffrey Mankoff, "Russia's Latest Land Grab: How Putin Won Crimea and Lost Ukraine," *Foreign Affairs*, Vol. 93, No. 3 (May/June 2014), pp. 60–68.

32 Ali Askerov, Stefan Brooks, and Lasha Tchantouridzé, *Post-Soviet Conflicts: The Thirty Years' Crisis* (London: Lexington Books, 2020). Hanna Smith, "Russia as a Great Power: Status Inconsistency and the Two Chechen Wars," *Communist and Post-Communist Studies*, Vol. 47, Issues 3–4 (September–December 2014), pp. 355–363 Riehle, *The Russian FSB*, pp. 112–113.

to liquidate terrorists in any region of the world".[33] According to Dov Lynch, "for Putin, Russia's rebirth was to start in Chechnya".[34]

Managing a vast multiethnic nation like Russia, built on historical conquest, has long been challenging and devolving power to the republics has been seen as empowering local elites (even if it inhibits regional development, especially in economically or strategically important regions). What has been favored are varying degrees of regional autonomy centrally managed by the Kremlin.[35] As Stalin understood, the autonomy of Russia's regions needed limits to mitigate the risks of Russia unravelling from the outside in. This is also reflected in the ministries now overseeing the regions.[36]

What is also apparent is migration from more rural areas to urban centers since the early 2000s which increases pressures on urban infrastructure, including housing demands with around 73 million (over half of Russia's population) now living in 40 of the largest urban centers. Growing urbanization has also contributed to an excess of "improperly planned housing construction" lacking much needed transport and social infrastructure and drawing resources away from the regions.[37] In Siberia and elsewhere in Russia's Far East, "a large number of settlements do not have a year-round transport connection with the nearest large city".[38] Climate change is also being felt across these northerly regions further effecting social and economic development. Climate change has seen parts of Russia's permafrost melt, badly affecting the Arctic, Siberia and Far East. This has also contributed to regional planning (traditionally based on Soviet-era military districts), which now increasingly has to factor in interregional economic relations, and ethnonationalist tensions.[39]

33 Lynch, Dov Lynch, "'The enemy is at the gate': Russia after Beslan", *International Affairs*, Vol. 80, Issue 1 (2005), p. 142.

34 Lynch, "'The enemy is at the gate'", p. 143. Supporting evidence can also be found in Riehle, *The Russian FSB*, pp. 37, 84, 108.

35 Alexander Libman & Andrei Yakovlev, "A Centralist Approach to Regional Development: The Case of the Russian Ministry for the Development of the Far East", *Europe-Asia Studies*, Vol. 73, No. 6 (July 2021), pp. 1125–1148.

36 Paul Goble, "'No Regions, No Problems' – Putin Downgrades Regional and Ethnic Issues" (September 8 2014), https://www.interpretermag.com/no-regions-no-problems-putin-downgrades-regional-and-ethnic-issues/, accessed 23 August 2025. Libman & Yakovlev, "A Centralist Approach," pp. 1125–1148.

37 Kanat Makhanov, "The New Spatial Development Strategy of Russia" (undated, 2025), https://www.eurasian-research.org/publication/the-new-spatial-development-strategy-of-russia/, accessed 22 August 2025.

38 Makhanov, "The New Spatial Development Strategy of Russia".

39 Makhanov, "The New Spatial Development Strategy of Russia".

A number of these regions now contain Russian peacekeepers and other forces (giving Russia a foothold). Most of these missions are mandated by the United Nations (UN) and others by the Organization for Security and Co-operation in Europe (OSCE) and/or European Union (EU) and continue to harbor ethnic conflict.[40] As early as 1993, there were concerns that the continuing post-imperial presence of Russians and Russian business interests were providing justifications for intervention in the Caucasus and Central Asia.[41]

In December 1991 the Commonwealth of Independent States (CIS) was also founded as "an organisation designed to manage the Soviet breakup and preserve many of the pre-existing economic, political, and military ties among the Soviet republics."[42] Armenia, Azerbaijan, Belarus, Kazakhstan, Kyrgyzstan, Moldova, Tajikistan, and Uzbekistan are current members alongside Russia. Ukraine formally left in 2018, having been *in absentia* following the Revolution of Dignity/Euromaidan revolt in 2014, with Georgia having left in 2008 after the Russo-Georgian War. Through to 2023, the CIS is a collective that "has survived rather than flourished."[43] As Kubiek describes, "Much of the problem was that the major security threat to CIS states came from either within their own states (for example civil conflict in Tajikistan) or from within the CIS itself, which, in most cases, meant from Russia."[44]

The Eurasian Collective Security Treaty Organization (CSTO), comprising Armenia, Belarus, Kazakhstan, Kyrgyzstan, Tajikistan, and Russia, formed in 1992, operates alongside the CIS. In 2000 the Eurasian Economic Community/Union (EEC/EEU)[45] was founded. From Belarus in Europe to Armenia in the Caucasus, through the capitals of the ancient Silk Road in Central Asia, they were attempts at "integration fora seeking to bind states from the post-Soviet space to Russia."[46] Meanwhile, Russia, Kazakhstan, and Kyrgyzstan were also "cooperating with

---

40 Frederick M. Burkle, Krzysztof Goniewicz, and Amir Khorram-Manesh, "Bastardizing Peacekeeping and the Birth of Hybrid Warfare," *Prehospital and Disaster Medicine*, Vol. 37, No. 2 (April 2022), pp. 147–149. Conflict Prevention and Resolution, https://www.osce.org/conflict-prevention-and-resolution, accessed 13 March 2023.

41 Brzezinski, "The Premature Partnership," p. 76.

42 Paul Kubicek, "The Commonwealth of Independent States: An Example of Failed Regionalism?" *Review of International Studies*, Vol. 35, Issue 1 (February 2009), p. 237.

43 Richard Sakwa and Mark Webber, "The Commonwealth of Independent States, 1991–1998: Stagnation and Survival," *Europe-Asia Studies*, Vol. 51, No. 3 (1999), p. 379.

44 Kubicek, "The Commonwealth of Independent States" p. 242.

45 Also referred to by the acronym EAEU.

46 Marie Raquel Freire, "The Russia Factor in European Security: Back to the Future" (August 2017), p. 2, CES Policy Brief, https://carleton.ca/ces/wp-content/uploads/Raquel-Freire-Policy-Brief_Russia-and-European-security-08-01-2017.docx.pdf.

China through the Shanghai Cooperation Organization (SCO) – a political, economic, and military alliance founded in 2003 – before the foundation of the EEU [Eurasian Economic Union]."[47]

Since 1991 Russia, a state comprised of 193 different ethnic groups and distinctive regions, has also had to contend with the potential Balkanization of its territory, as happened in the former Yugoslavia during the 1990s, as well as guarding against perceived external threats.[48] During the 1990s there was already disquiet in the former Soviet states of the Caucasus and Central Asia that Russian expatriates, settlers, and business interests were being used "as a justification for claiming the right to intervene."[49] Zbigniew Brzezinski, a former National Security Advisor to U.S. President Jimmy Carter, cautioned in a prescient 1994 article "Insurance is needed against the possibility – one might even argue the probability – that the weight of history will not soon permit Russia to stabilize as a democracy, and that the single-minded cultivation of a partnership with Russia, while downgrading other interests, will simply accelerate the reemergence of an ominously familiar imperial challenge to Europe's security."[50]

Brzezinski warned that imperialist designs and maintaining a sphere of influence were still a factor in Russian foreign policy. He also worried that "President Yeltsin's inclination toward authoritarianism has transformed the new constitution for a democratic Russia into a document that can be easily used to legitimize arbitrary personal rule."[51] He also posed a longstanding question, "Is Russia primarily a nation-state or is it a multinational empire?" For Brzezinski, "The bottom line ... is a simple but compelling axiom: Russia can be either an empire or a democracy, but it cannot be both ... the imperial impulse remains strong ... in the effort to retain or regain control over the old Soviet empire."[52] These leitmotifs are evident in the work of Keir Giles and Sergey Radchenko three decades later.[53]

---

47 Kataryna Wolczuk, Rilka Dragneva, and Jon Wallace, "What is the Eurasian Economic Union?" (July 15, 2022), https://www.chathamhouse.org/2022/07/what-eurasian-economic-union, accessed 6 January 2023.

48 https://minorityrights.org/country/russian-federation/, accessed 6 January 2023.

49 In a similar way Hitler had used the same rationale in Czechoslovakia's Sudetenland in 1938.

50 Brzezinski, "The Premature Partnership," pp. 76, 79.

51 Brzezinski, "The Premature Partnership," p. 71.

52 Brzezinski, "The Premature Partnership," pp. 71–72.

53 Keir Giles, *Moscow Rules. What Drives Russia to Confront the West?* (Washington DC: Brookings, 2019), pp. 1–68, 103–124 (and a theme throughout). Sergey Radchenko, *To Run the World: The Kremlin's Cold War Bid for Global Power* (Cambridge: Cambridge University Press, 2024).

Two Russian theorists are noteworthy in these respects and in terms of Kremlin policies, approaches, and narratives.[54] The first is Russian/Eurasian nationalist ideology given voice by Aleksandr Dugin (most infamously in his 1997 book *The Foundations of Geopolitics*).[55] Dugin draws on ideas of nationalism and Eurasian ethnocentrism to advance ideas of Russian revanchism of former Soviet territories and expansionism beyond alliances.[56] Among many disparate sources Dugin leans on are the writings of Carl Schmidt and Samuel Huntingdon's "Clash of Civilizations." Dugin has been influencing the nationalist right in Russia since its publication.[57] By the mid-2000s he had "become one of the most fashionable thinkers of the day… disseminating the myth of Russian great power, accompanied by imperialist, racialist, Aryanist and occultist beliefs."[58] In August 2022, he narrowly escaped an assassination attempt which claimed his daughter's life.[59]

By 2000, *The Foundations of Geopolitics* had been reprinted four times "and had become a major political pamphlet, enjoying a large readership in academic and political circles."[60] In it, "He offered them a certain vision of international politics colored by an 'isolationism that only serves to disguise a project of expansion and conquest.'"[61] Indeed, "Influenced and motivated by Dugin's Eurasian theories," Putin has been seeding the ground gradually over two decades ideologically, politically, economically, and militarily for a "Eurasian project" "to unite the former Soviet states … into one reborn Russian empire."[62]

The second theoretician is Major-General Vladimir Slipchenko. Shortly before his death in 2005, Slipchenko began to refine ideas of what he saw as "sixth gen-

---

54 Others have been influential including Sergey Bogdanov, Sergey Chekinov, and Andrey Kartapolov (Russia's former Chief of Main Directorate for Political-Military Affairs of the Russian Armed Forces). Alina Polyakova and Mathieu Boulègue, "The Evolution of Russian Hybrid Warfare: Executive Summary" (January 29, 2021), https://cepa.org/comprehensive-reports/the-evolution-of-russian-hybrid-warfare-executive-summary/, accessed 26 July 2023.

55 Aleksandr Dugin, *The Foundations of Geopolitics: Russia's Geopolitical Future* (Moscow: Arktogeya, 1997). Marlene Laruelle, "Aleksandr Dugin: A Russian Version of the European Radical Right?" Kennan Institute, Occasional Paper #294 (undated), p. 22, https://www.files.ethz.ch/isn/20571/OP294.pdf, accessed 5 April 2019.

56 Dugin, *The Foundations of Geopolitics.*

57 Taras Kuzio, "Imperial Nationalism as the Driver Behind Russia's Invasion of Ukraine," *Nations and Nationalism*, Vol. 29, Issue 1 (January 2023), pp. 35–36.

58 Laruelle, "Aleksandr Dugin," p. 22.

59 Anonymous, "Darya Dugina: Daughter of Putin ally killed in Moscow blast (August 21, 2023), https://www.bbc.co.uk/news/world-europe-62621509, accessed 5 July 2023.

60 Laruelle, "Aleksandr Dugin," p. 3.

61 Laruelle, "Aleksandr Dugin," p. 3.

62 Vira Ratsiborynska, "When Hybrid Warfare Supports Ideology: Russia Today," Research Paper, NATO Defense College, Rome, No. 133 (November 2016), pp. 9–10.

eration" warfare (the fifth for him being the development of nuclear weapons). This included ideas of "information superiority" (which were very much in the vanguard of Chinese thinking); "information confrontation"; next generation warfare; and concepts of new generation "noncontact warfare."[63] "Hybrid warfare" is a significant component of Slipchenko's theories.[64] These theories will be returned to later. How they have been operationalized is seeded throughout the book.

3 Russia's "New Nobility": the oligarchs, *siloviki*, and society

Reflective of their thinking is Russia's political system. This has become increasingly authoritarian with widespread reporting of vote-rigging, opposition repression, corruption, systematic clampdowns on press freedoms, freedom of speech and assembly, state censorship, and Kremlin propaganda.[65] It embraced the capitalist model and has seen its natural wealth benefit the few, not the many. A culture of cronyism has developed as the *siloviki* and oligarchs became increasingly embedded throughout Russian society including government agencies and businesses. This cronyism and kleptocracy became institutionalized with "personal connections ... used to dole out favors and [where] no one is truly clean."[66] The *siloviki* have "used these perches to observe, control, and build their power, often in cooperation with organized-crime networks."[67]

This has led to a "network of former KGB officers surrounding Putin" which "has established de facto ownership of the entire Russian economy, with all property rights effectively conditional on the regime's goodwill."[68] Russia was characterized as a "mafia state" in leaked U.S. diplomatic cables provided by U.S. corpo-

---

63 Timothy L. Thomas, *Dragon Bytes Chinese Information Warfare Theory and Practice* (Fort Leavenworth, KS: Foreign Military Studies Office, 2004).

64 Ratsiborynska, "When Hybrid Warfare Supports Ideology," p. 16.

65 Timothy Frye and Ekaterina Borisova, "Elections, Protest and Trust in Government: A Natural Experiment from Russia," BOFIT Discussion Papers 9 (2016), https://helda.helsinki.fi/bof/bitstream/handle/123456789/14319/dp0916.pdf?sequence=1&isAllowed=y, "Russia," https://freedomhouse.org/report/freedom-world/2019/russia. Both accessed 25 February 2020.

66 Peter Hobson, "How Europe Became a Russian Gangster Playground" (May 12, 2016), https://www.themoscowtimes.com/2016/05/12/how-europe-became-a-russian-gangster-playground-a52842, accessed 12 November 2019.

67 Hobson, "How Europe Became a Russian Gangster Playground."

68 Miriam Lanskoy and Dylan Myles-Primakoff, "Power and Plunder in Putin's Russia," *Journal of Democracy*, Vol. 29, No. 1 (January 2018), p. 77.

ral Bradley Manning to Wikileaks.[69] In exchange for support and protection the Kremlin utilize "organized crime groups to do whatever the government of Russia cannot acceptably do" and these operate "'hand-in-hand' with the state."[70]

Whilst Putin and his fellow *siloviki*, (as well as supportive oligarchs) have personally benefited, renationalization was also used to arrest Russia's geopolitical decline and regional influence backed by booming oil and gas prices and exports to European markets.[71] The rise of Gazprom and Rosneft in particular as major oil and gas exporters has buttressed Russia's domestic economy. Russia's economy largely rests on its vast, and increasingly accessible and transportable, hydrocarbon base. Russia's natural resources in oil and gas make it an energy giant. Russia has the largest hydrocarbon resource base in the world and is the biggest global producer of oil and gas combined. Its closest rivals are Saudi Arabia, Venezuela, and Iran. Two thirds of Arctic resources are in Russian waters and climate change, and new extraction technologies, are making it possible to plan extraction in East and West Siberia. Further deposits are located in the Black Sea and the Caspian Sea east of the Caucasus.[72] Currently, approximately 70 percent of the oil produced in Russia comes from the West Siberian Basin.[73] This was one of the reasons behind the development of the Nord Stream pipelines into Western Europe that were mysteriously sabotaged to make them inoperable.[74]

By the 2010s this had also enabled Russia to periodically use energy security and supplies as political and economic weapons.[75] Until the imposition of the major series of Western sanctions and exodus of Western companies resulting

---

69 Now Chelsea Manning following gender reassignment. David Leigh and Luke Harding, *Wikileaks: Inside Julian Assange's War on Secrecy* (London: Guardian Books, 2013), pp. 216–219.

70 Hobson, "How Europe Became a Russian Gangster Playground." Insights are also found in Giles, *Russia's War on Everybody*, pp. 191–209.

71 Putin's Asymmetric Assault, pp. 54–58. This includes the Nord Stream 2 oil pipeline. "A European Pipeline Energy infrastructure for the future," https://www.nord-stream2.com/, accessed 29 February 2020.

72 James Henderson and Alastair Ferguson, *International Partnership in Russia: Conclusions from the Oil and Gas Industry* (London: Palgrave Macmillan, 2014), p. 2.

73 "West Siberian Oil Basin," http://petroneft.com/operations/west-siberian-oil-basin/, accessed 5 November 2018.

74 László Á. Kóczy, Dávid Csercsik, and Balázs R. Sziklai, "Nord Stream 2: A Prelude to War," *Energy Strategy Reviews*, Vol. 44 (November 2022), pp. 1–9.

75 See for example Wigell and Vihma, "Geopolitics Versus Geoeconomics." Krauss, "Russia Uses Its Oil Giant, Rosneft, as a Foreign Policy Tool." Anna Mikulska and Robert Hamilton, "Nord Stream 2: Energy Security For Europe Or Prelude To Russian Aggression In The Baltic?" https://www.forbes.com/sites/thebakersinstitute/2019/09/03/nord-stream-2-energy-security-for-europe-or-prelude-to-russian-aggression-in-the-baltic/ (September 3, 2019). Both accessed 1 March 2020.

from the full-scale invasion of Ukraine, the wealth of Russia's "new nobility" was demonstrably visible within Russia and well beyond. This included through acquisitions of foreign companies, property, and displays of opulence. Domestically this includes redevelopment in major cities like Moscow, St. Petersburg, and Sochi, the "Russian Riviera" on the Black Sea where the 2014 Winter Olympics were held immediately prior to the annexation of nearby Crimea. Elsewhere, "pitifully little has been built or repaired."[76]

Wealth inequality has remained a pronounced feature of Russian society since the 1990s. Relative to the size of its economy, Russia has more billionaires than any other comparable nation. 75 percent of their wealth is estimated to be hidden offshore. Meanwhile, as of 2023, 22 low-income Russian republics (semi–autonomous regions subordinate to Moscow rule) required subsidies to cover their budgets. This includes many republics in the Caucuses, as well as the Mari El republic (400 miles east of Moscow – home to the minority Finno-Ugric Mari people – at the mid-point of the Volga, Europe's longest river at 2,200 miles). It also includes the vast but sparsely populated Republic of Tuva (annexed by Russia in 1944 – historically part of Outer Mongolia and Qing dynasty China) in Southern Siberia. These regions experience relative poverty and marked inequalities within the Russian Federation. At the same time, they have long become part of Russia although many of their peoples cherish their cultural and religious heritage whilst maintaining their own distinctive languages and regional dialects. In the Caucuses this has included fighting for their independence from Russia.

Wealth and employment prospects are largely centered in Russia's main business, trade, and industrial centers. These range from the highly developed major cities of Moscow and St. Petersburg in Western Russia to oil and gas-rich regions including Western Siberia in Russia's far east, the central city and wider administrative oblast (region) of Ryazan and city and oblast of Volgograd (formerly Stalingrad) on the West bank of the Volga in Southern Russia and south to Astrakhan near to where the Volga drains into the Caspian Sea.[77] To give an example of Russia's diversity, the Yamalo-Nenets Autonomous Okrug (district) forms part of the 1.2 million miles^2 West Siberian basin. This is Russia's richest source of income

76 Edward Lucas, *Deception: The Untold Story of East-West Espionage Today* (New York: Bloomsbury, 2012), p. 74. Shleifer and Treisman, "A Normal Country," pp. 151–174 shows the promise of the mid-2000s.

77 Socioeconomic inequality in Russia (2018), https://www.europarl.europa.eu/RegData/etudes/ATAG/2018/620225/EPRS_ATA(2018)620225_EN.pdf, accessed 27 July 2025.

from hydrocarbons.[78] It is also home to the 10,000 strong animistic, Polar Bear hunting, and reindeer herding, Yamal-Nenet people whose nomadic way of life in Russia's Arctic region is a far cry from life in Moscow and has been under threat since the discovery of oil and gas in the 1970s.[79]

Contrastingly in Southern Russia, republics in the Caucasus through into Central Asia have high unemployment and poor job prospects. They too have regional identities distinct from Russia. Not only are they unsettled, they are also areas where the highest proportions of men have been conscripted or incentivized to fight for Russia in Ukraine. Even with state subsidies, the unemployment rates in these regions ranged from a pre-war average of 41.6 percent (2000 – 2020) in the Republic of Ingushetia to over 10 percent in the Republic of Dagestan, North Ossetia, and the Chechen Republic. These and similarly deprived regions, have not only seen the highest proportions of conscripts and volunteers but also the highest proportion of deaths and casualties.

Whilst overall unemployment in Russia has decreased since Putin assumed the presidency (averaging 6.7 percent between 2000 – 2020), the average annual salary of Russia's 76 million strong labor force was $14,250 (USD) in 2023 (with marked regional disparities).[80] Less senior staff working for Russia's "Special Services" are paid only $4,800 – $12,000 per annum ($400 – $1,000 a month). They are also required to vacation within Russia and are forbidden from traveling abroad for ten years after they leave government service. This is combined with a lack of comradeship and distrust.[81] In other parts of Russia, conscription has contributed to shortages in the labor market. Meanwhile, right across Russia, the public healthcare system is under-funded, poorly-equipped, with long waits for treatment. Where Russia outperforms most other OECD nations is in access to university education.[82]

---

78 Gregory F. Ulmishek, "Petroleum Geology and Resources of the West Siberian Basin, Russia", U.S. Geological Survey Bulletin 2201-G (2003), https://pubs.usgs.gov/bul/2201/G/B2201-G.pdf, accessed 27 July 2025.

79 BBC "Tribe" series, https://www.bbc.co.uk/tribe/tribes/nenets/, accessed 27 July 2025.

80 Stanislav Boiko, Olena Davlikanova, Vadym Fedchyshyn, Maria Kucherenko, Dmytro Lyvch, Lesia Ogryzko, Yuliia Pavytska, Yaroslav Yashchenko, "Russia 2032 Scenarios: A Decade Post Full-Scale Invasion of Ukraine Perspectives from A Neighbor Who Knows Too Well" (May 2025), Sahaidachnyi Security Center, https://sahasec.org/wp-content/uploads/2025/04/russia-Scenarious_10-4-2025-new.pdf, accessed 27 July 2025.

81 Riehle, *Russian Intelligence*, p. 266.

82 Boiko et al, "Russia 2032 Scenarios:" accessed 27 July 2025.

4 Regime loyalty, energy security, and political assassinations

After he succeeded Yeltsin as President in 1999–2000, Putin began renationalizing Russia's major companies. This included Yukos, TNK-BP, and Sibneft. Their owners included Mikhail Khodorkovsky (Yukos), Leonard Blavatnik (TNK-BP), and Boris Berezovsky and Roman Abramovich (Sibneft).[83] The renationalization of Yukos "marked the start of political raiding of private companies in Russia" and sent a warning to the oligarchs and political opponents.[84] The beneficiaries of this raid, which began as a purported criminal case of tax evasion in 2003, were figures associated with the *siloviki* and President Putin. This raiding has seen the Putin regime use the FSB and domestic lawfare "to redistribute local economic resources to favored clans, meet public demands to fight corruption, and ensure political loyalty from regional officials".[85] These "ownership changes in 2004–2005 involved moving fundamental control from the oil oligarchs and ex-soviet bureaucrats to the Kremlin's allies."[86] Wresting control from private hands led to Khodorkovsky, Blavatnik, and Abramovich living in exile through to 2022 when they were compelled to return after further sanctions were imposed as a result of Russia's invasion of Ukraine.[87] In addition, Khodorkovsky "spent 10 years in custody for tax evasion and theft after funding opposition parties."[88]

---

83 Graham Ruddick, "Should Oxford and the V&A take millions from Ukrainian-born billionaire Len Blavatnik?" (September 3, 2017), https://www.theguardian.com/business/2017/sep/03/len-blavatnik-oligarch-controversy-philanthropy-resignation-oxford-professor, Kirsten Korosec, "Meet the Russian Billionaires That Took on BP and Won" (May 18, 2011), https://www.cbsnews.com/news/meet-the-russian-billionaires-that-took-on-bp-and-won/. Both accessed 23 February 2020. The FSB confers military titles and ranks as did the KGB.

84 The Dossier Center, "Lubyanka federation: How the FSB determines the politics and economics of Russia" (October 5 2020), https://www.atlanticcouncil.org/in-depth-research-reports/report/lubyanka-federation/, accessed 22 August 2025.

85 The Dossier Center, "Lubyanka federation".

86 And "Once Rosneft swallowed up the biggest private oil company (Yukos) and Gazprom bought Sibneft, the Kremlin gained control over a substantial portion of Russia's oil reserves (30 %), and almost all of Russia's gas reserves and pipelines." Nadejda Makarova Victor, "Gazprom: Gas Giant Under Strain," Working Paper #71, Program on Energy and Sustainable Development at Stanford University, pp. 51–52, https://www.researchgate.net/profile/Nadejda_Victor/publication/287215359_Gazprom_Gas_Giant_Under_Strain/links/567429da08aebcdda0de1ec2/Gazprom-Gas-Giant-Under-Strain.pdf, accessed 23 February 2020.

87 https://khodorkovsky.com/; Ilya V. Ponomarev, "In Exile, but Ready to Save Russia" (April 15, 2015), https://www.nytimes.com/2015/04/16/opinion/in-exile-but-ready-to-save-russia.html; Andrew Roth, "Chelsea owner Roman Abramovich is without a UK visa" (May 20, 2018), https://www.the

Berezovsky too fell afoul of the regime, later becoming a fierce critic, and fell out with his former business partner Abramovich.[89] After Berezovsky's chauffeur's head was blown off by a car bomb in 1994 intended for his employer, Berezovsky met 32-year-old lieutenant colonel Alexander Litvinenko. Litvinenko, having joined the army in 1980, and then the MVD, had transferred to the KGB in 1988, and by the time he was assigned to investigate the case he had become a senior figure in the FSB's organized-crime unit.

Officially known as the Economic Counterintelligence Service (*Sluzhba Ekonomicheskoy Bezopasnosti*, SEB) or "Fourth Service", the SEB is putatively focused on serious, organized, and financially motivated crimes. However, its real focus has become protecting those in power and the financial interests of the ruling elite whilst policing Russia's competing "clans". When it was known as the Department of Economic Security (DEB), it was headed by Nikolai Patrushev. When the reins of power were passing to Putin, Patrushev replaced the president-elect as director of the FSB. The DEB also contained sub-divisions that dealt with specific sectors with directorates dealing with crime types that include counterfeiting, smuggling, and narcotics.[90] Against this background, and after becoming close to Berezovsky, in late December 1997 Litvinenko would claim that he had been personally requested to kill him.[91] Instead, in November 1998 Litvinenko publicly called out corruption in the upper echelons of the FSB, headed at the time by Vladimir Putin.[92] This saw Litvinenko arrested on corruption charges.

---

guardian.com/world/2018/may/20/chelsea-owner-roman-abramovich-is-without-a-uk-visa, all accessed 23 February 2020.

88 Anonymous, "Profile: Mikhail Khodorkovsky" (December 22, 2013), https://www.bbc.co.uk/news/world-europe-12082222, accessed 23 February 2020. See also Richard Sakwa, *Putin and the Oligarch: The Khodorkovsky-Yukos Affair* (London: IB Tauris, 2014), pp. 64–65, 118, 123–124.

89 Anonymous, "Boris Berezovsky" (March 24, 2013), https://www.telegraph.co.uk/news/worldnews/europe/russia/9950088/Boris-Berezovsky.html, Will Stewart, "Exiled oligarch Boris Berezovsky was murdered because he was about to hand Putin evidence of a coup plot, claims former head of security" (March 25, 2015), https://www.dailymail.co.uk/news/article-3011021/Exiled-oligarch-Boris-Berezovsky-murdered-hand-Putin-evidence-coup-plot-claims-former-head-security.html. Both accessed 23 February 2020.

90 Riehle, *The Russian FSB*, p. 43.

91 "Alexander Litvinenko's videotape transcript: protection of organized crime by FSB, part 1" (August 1, 2022), https://tbcarchives.org/alexander-litvinenkos-videotape-transcript-protection-of-organized-crime-by-fsb/, accessed 26 April 2025. See also Riehle, *The Russian FSB*, p. 114 (who has slightly different timelines and slightly differing details on Litvinenko's career).

92 He later wrote two books reflecting on his time in the FSB. Alexander Litvinenko, *Lubyanka Criminal Group* (Dnìpropetrovs'k: Grani, 2002) and Yuri Felshtinsky and Alexander Litvinenko, *Blowing Up Russia: Terror From Within* (London: Gibson Square Books, 2007).

Two years later Litvinenko exiled himself to London when Putin became president and went on to work for Berezovsky (later allegedly working with Britain's Secret Intelligence Service, MI6), and himself becoming a fierce critic of Putin's regime.[93] In exile he was investigating Spanish links to the Russian mafia as well as the assassination of the investigative journalist Anna Politkovskaya, when he too was assassinated with highly radioactive polonium-210 in London in 2006.[94] Berezovsky also died in exile in London in 2013 in mysterious circumstances aged 67 after his "close protection team of former French foreign legionaries" "had been whittled down to a single bodyguard."[95]

Berezovsky was one of seven businessmen key to the privatization of Russia's state sector "securing the lion's share of the spoils for themselves."[96] When renationalization was instituted, it led to "merger mania" in Russia which saw the Kremlin also retake control of "Surgutneftegas, Slavneft, at least half of TNK-BP, and the remains of Yukos, using the state giants Rosneft and Gazprom as the vehicles for consolidation."[97] This was chiefly limited to four sectors: energy (oil, gas, and electricity), banking, transportation, and the defense industry. This saw state corporations become "a mechanism of political control and rent extraction in Putin's system of vertical power by enriching allies and neutralizing any opposition."[98]

This embedded a political regime "whose legitimacy in many respects rested on the promise to not allow a return to the 'wild 90s,'" to become "in practice a hostage to the worldview and methods of that decade, in which financial prosper-

93 Litvinenko claimed to have been ordered to assassinate Berezovsky. He separately claimed Putin "had links to organised crime in his earlier career" when deputy mayor of St. Petersburg. Litvinenko feared "he would soon be killed or arrested." After Berezovsky stopped payments, his widow Marine told the inquiry into his death, Litvinenko became a "paid consultant" for Britain's Secret Intelligence Service MI6. Anonymous, "Alexander Litvinenko was 'a paid consultant' for MI6" (February 2, 2015), https://www.bbc.co.uk/news/uk-31096849, accessed 25 February 2020. This was also suspected by the FSB. The Litvinenko Inquiry Report into the Death of Alexander Litvinenko [January 2016], pp. 20, 54, 63–67. https://assets.publishing.service.gov.uk/government/uploads/system/uploads/attachment_data/file/493860/The-Litvinenko-Inquiry-H-C-695-web.pdf, accessed 30 June 2023.

94 Litvinenko was also "being paid by the British secret service MI6." Anonymous, "Alexander Litvinenko: Profile of murdered Russian spy" (January 21, 2016), https://www.bbc.co.uk/news/uk-19647226, accessed 23 February 2020.

95 Anonymous, "Boris Berezovsky"; Stewart, "Exiled oligarch Boris Berezovsky was murdered."

96 Anonymous, "Boris Berezovsky"; Stewart, "Exiled oligarch Boris Berezovsky was murdered."

97 Victor, "Gazprom: Gas Giant Under Strain," p. 51.

98 F. Joseph Dresen, "The Role of State Corporations in the Russian Economy" (undated), https://www.wilsoncenter.org/publication/the-role-state-corporations-the-russian-economy, accessed 23 February 2020. See also Giles, *Russia's War on Everybody*, pp. 46–59.

ity depended on your proximity to the throne."[99] Although oligarchy power diminished, they still retained an influential role in Russian political life. Renationalization has fueled Russia's economy since 2004/5, especially when the price of oil is high. Periodically, Russia's energy suppliers (Gazprom and Rosneft in particular), have been used as political and economic weapons in Russia's near abroad and in EU countries.

Energy security has become a powerful tool. Reducing reliance on Russian gas and oil has since been felt across Europe in price rises after Russian businesses were further sanctioned after the Ukraine invasion (having first been sanctioned for the annexation of Crimea and then after the attempted assassination of Sergei Skripal in England in March 2018).[100] This was intended to serve as a warning to others and as revenge on Skripal and his daughter (Skripal was a double agent for British intelligence whilst a GRU officer).[101] It was the latest of a series of political assassination attempts on foreign soil as well as within Russia. Many have been successful.[102] These are designed to be covert operations.[103] The exposure of these operations is likely a sign of poor tradecraft, but they also serve as a signal and message to other would-be foreign agents, defectors, dissidents, and organizations.[104] Indeed, for defectors like Skripal, a number of nonconforming oligarchs, dissidents, journalists, human rights activists, and others who make enemies in Russia their lives frequently do not end well.[105]

---

99 Yury Saprykin, "20 Years of Vladimir Putin: How Russian Society Has Changed" (August 20, 2019), https://www.themoscowtimes.com/2019/08/20/20-years-of-vladimir-putin-how-russian-society-has-changed-a66930, accessed 23 February 2020.

100 Putin's Asymmetric Assault, pp. 54–58; Wigell and Vihma, "Geopolitics versus Geoeconomics," pp. 605–627 and Krauss, "Russia Uses Its Oil Giant, Rosneft, as a Foreign Policy Tool." Matúš Mišík, "The EU Needs To Improve Its External Energy Security," *Energy Policy*, Vol. 165 (June 2022), pp. 1–5.

101 Skripal, codenamed *Forthwith*, was exposed in the early 2000s and was arrested by the FSB in December 2004. In 2010 he was traded in a spy swap with the 2010 Illegals.

102 David V. Gioe, Michael S. Goodman, and David S. Frey, "Unforgiven: Russian Intelligence Vengeance as Political Theater and Strategic Messaging," *Intelligence and National Security*, Vol. 34, No. 4 (March 2019), pp. 561–575.

103 Riehle, *Russian Intelligence*, p. 205.

104 Dave Aitel, Sophia d'Antoine, Thomas Garwin, Ian Roos, Nicholas Rostow, Justin Sherman, and Abraham Wagner, "Russia's Cyber Operations. A Threat to American National Security" (2022), pp. 22–23, https://margin.re/content/files/2023/01/Russia-s-Cyber-Operations---Full-Report.pdf, accessed 7 August 2023. Riehle, *Russian Intelligence*, p. 206.

105 Daniil Turovsky, "What is the GRU? Who gets recruited to be a spy? Why are they exposed so often? Here are the most important things you should know about Russia's intelligence community" (November 6, 2018), https://meduza.io/en/feature/2018/11/06/what-is-the-gru-who-gets-recruited-to-be-a-spy-why-are-they-exposed-so-often, accessed 26 December 2018. Putin's Asym-

Assassinations have also involved the use of Russian *Spetsnaz* (Special Forces). To take one example, Vympel and Alpha are *Spetsnaz* that form part of the FSB's Special Purpose Center. Alpha is Russia's dedicated counterterrorist *Spetsnaz* unit whilst Vympel conducts foreign operations. This includes sabotage, assassinations, and covert surveillance.[106] Vympel/Directorate S officers were implicated in the assassination of the Chechen-Georgian radical, Zelimkhan ("Tornike") Khangoshvili at Berlin's Kleiner Tiergarten in August 2019 (including supplying his cover documents for entry into Germany). FSB officer Vadim Krasikov, who was born in Kazakhstan in 1965, had shot Khangoshvili three times with a Glock pistol fitted with a silencer which he then threw into the River Spree after cycling up behind him. He was arrested (after having removed his disguise and changed clothes) as he tried to flee the scene. He was given a life sentence for murder in 2021. Bellingcat had helped identify him through his tattoos which included a demon wearing a crown and a snake. The German government subsequently expelled 101 diplomats from Russia's extensive Berlin embassy. Krasikov would spend three years behind bars before a complex multinational prisoner exchange agreement was struck with Russia. Krasikov was greeted personally by President Putin when he landed.[107]

Krasikov had been aided by someone travelling under the identity of Roman Davydov. "Davydov" too had connections to the FSB. Alongside Krasikov, "Davydov" was also connected to the assassination of another Chechen national in Istanbul in 2015. Bellingcat has indicated that several more FSB field agents were active and had helped assist the "Tornike" assassination in Berlin. It is also reported by Bellingcat that both these murders were tied to a kill list of 19 Chechens born during Soviet times. One of those on the list was Abdulvakhid Edilgeriev. Edilgeriev was assassinated in Istanbul in November 2015. Travelling with his young niece, Edilgeriev's car was rammed from behind and a gunman then

---

metric Assault, pp. 187–189, 193–194. Anonymous, "Litvinenko poisoning and a journalist gunned down: The critics of Vladimir Putin who met untimely deaths" (August 27, 2023), https://news.sky.com/story/litvinenko-poisoning-and-a-journalist-gunned-down-the-critics-of-vladimir-putin-who-met-untimely-deaths-12946525, accessed 29 August 2023.

106 Andrew S. Bowen, Russian Military Intelligence: Background and Issues for Congress, Updated November 15 2021, p. 13, https://www.congress.gov/crs_external_products/R/PDF/R46616/R46616.7.pdf, accessed 26 August 2025.

107 Tucker Reals, "U.S.-Russia prisoner exchange includes Vadim Krasikov, Russian assassin serving a life sentence in Germany" (August 1 2024), https://www.cbsnews.com/news/us-russia-prisoner-swap-russians-released-include-vadim-krasikov-murder-germany/. Thomas Escritt, "Who is Vadim Krasikov, Russian hitman freed from German jail in prisoner swap?" (August 1 2024), https://www.reuters.com/world/europe/vadim-krasikov-russian-hitman-sprung-german-jail-prisoner-swap-2024-08-01/. Both accessed 14 August 2025. Riehle, *The Russian FSB*, pp. 85–86.

tried to shoot him in the car. Edilgeriev ran but this did not save him. He was found dead having been shot five times and stabbed in the neck multiple times. This too had been planned and executed by a hit team. That team had also been implicated in the assassination of a Uzbek cleric named Abdullah Bukhari who was shot in the back whilst entering a madrassah in Istanbul in 2014. The FSB had also tried to co-opt local contract killers for a fee of $300,000. Both cases were linked to the FSB's Vympel *Spetsnaz* who had tried to raise a false flag by leaking links to Chechen organized crime.[108]

Krasikov was also implicated in the death of Alexey Zhalo, the son of the deputy director of FSB's "Second Service" and head of the FSB's Directorate for Protection of Constitutional Order, General Alexey Zhalo, at the Russian embassy in Berlin. Alexey Zhalo (who shared the same name as his father) was found dead after seemingly falling from the top floors of the Russian embassy. Russia repatriated his body, and no autopsy was performed as the entire incident took place on embassy grounds. He was officially a second secretary at the embassy but according to Christo Grozev, was in reality an undercover FSB officer. The reason for the hit is unclear, but officers from General Zhalo's directorate were part of the team behind the failed assassination of Alexey Navalny in 2020 and the suspected poisoning of other Kremlin opposition figureheads including Vladimir Kara-Murza.[109] Around 21 Chechen-affiliated people have been assassinated or targeted for assassination. This includes Mamikhan Umarov who was killed in Austria in 2020 and the attempted assassination of Mokhmad Abdurakhmanov (also in 2020) on suspected orders from Chechen president Ramzan Kadyrov.[110] The assassination of Boris Nemtsov in 2015 and the attempted assassination of Alexei Navalny in 2020 were likely organized by the FSB's UBTPE sub-unit with support from the Science and Technology Service. The chemicals (and/or their means of delivery) used to poison Navalny might have been manufactured through the FSB's two scientific research units, NII-1 and NII-2.[111] The FSB's growing role beyond Russia now increasingly resembles KGB activities of the Cold War-era.

---

108 Bellingcat, "FSB's Magnificent Seven: New Links between Berlin and Istanbul Assassinations" (June 29 2020), https://www.bellingcat.com/news/uk-and-europe/2020/06/29/fsbs-magnificent-seven-new-links-between-berlin-and-istanbul-assassinations/, accessed 27 August 2025.

109 Christo Grozev, "Russian Diplomat Who Died at Berlin Embassy is Senior Intelligence Figure's Son" (November 5 2021), https://www.bellingcat.com/news/2021/11/05/russian-diplomat-who-died-at-berlin-embassy-is-senior-intelligence-figures-son/, accessed 14 August 2025.

110 Riehle, *The Russian FSB*, pp. 85 – 86.

111 Riehle, *The Russian FSB*, pp. 82, 99 – 101.

5 Russian intelligence from Yeltsin to Putin: division, competition, opportunism and the rise of the FSB

From the outset through to its demise in 1991, the Soviet Union was an extraordinarily capable and well-resourced actor using any and all means to gather and exploit the intelligence it felt it required as a superpower alongside the United States. Their intelligence services, the *Komitet Gosudarstvennoi Bezopasnosti* (KGB) and military intelligence, the *Glavnoye Razvedovatel'noye Upravlenie* (GRU), mounted a wide range of operations, including using covert means and active measures including propaganda, destabilization campaigns, and political assassinations.[112] They gathered intelligence of all types from all sources, including political and industrial espionage.

Active measures were a key tool of the Soviet state through the KGB and GRU. Whilst it is claimed that the Russian Federation now employs the term "measures of support" it remains a clandestine equivalent.[113] The KGB, where Putin rose to be Lieutenant Colonel before entering politics in 1991, was the prime organization responsible for intelligence gathering and for conducting operations domestically and externally. As secret police surveilling its own people within the Soviet Union and its Eastern European satellites, it also conducted covert operations and espionage abroad (mainly in the West). The KGB, which numbered as many as 620,000 members as the USSR fell in 1991, was described by a visiting journalist in the fragmenting Soviet Union as more than just a spy agency. It was the Central Intelligence Agency (CIA), the Federal Bureau of Investigation (FBI), and the National Security Agency (NSA) combined. It was also part of Border Patrol and "To the Soviet people, it was the jackboot on the stairs, the instrument of terror that could, in an instant, pluck people from the safety of their homes and send them to some Siberian gulag."[114]

Their clandestine activities continued after the collapse of the Soviet Union in 1991 despite major cutbacks in their budgets and scope of operations. In these early post-Cold War years, and with diminished resources, their main intelligence

---

112 Christopher Mark Davies, "The Ukraine Conflict, Economic–Military Power Balances and Economic Sanctions," *Post-Communist Economies*, Vol. 28, Issue 2 (March 2016), p. 183. Michael S. Goodman, David Frey, and David Gioe, "Alexei Navalny poisoning: what theatrical assassination attempts reveal about Vladimir Putin's grip on power in Russia" (September 9, 2020), https://theconversation.com/alexei-navalny-poisoning-what-theatrical-assassination-attempts-reveal-about-vladimir-putins-grip-on-power-in-russia-145664, accessed 30 September 2023.

113 Riehle, *Russian Intelligence*, pp. 190–191.

114 David Wise, "Closing Down the K.G.B." (November 24, 1991), https://www.nytimes.com/1991/11/24/magazine/closing-down-the-kgb.html, accessed 6 October 2018.

focus switched from military objectives to economic and industrial targets.[115] Early plans were to "dismember the KGB." However, facing political opposition and resistance from KGB veterans, Boris Yeltsin had to scale back wholesale reforms.[116] The KGB was instead reformed as the *Federalnaya Sluzhba Kontrrazvedki* (FSK). In 1995 the FSK was reorganized as the *Federal'naya Sluzhba Bezopasnosti* (FSB) with a separate service, the SVR (*Sluzhba Vneshnei Razvedki*) designated Russia's Foreign Intelligence Service (FIS).

Predating the formation of the FSB was the Federal Agency for Government Communications and Information (FAPSI). FAPSI had been formed in 1993 from the KGB's Eighth Chief Directorate overseeing information security and Sixteenth Chief Directorate responsible for SIGINT. This was the only time that Russia has had a separate, dedicated SIGINT organization (including during the Soviet-era).[117] It lasted until government reforms in 2003 which saw the FSB take control of most of FAPSI's remit and functions (as well as Russia's Border Guard Service). This included FAPSI's Center for Information Security (TsIB) which was focused on monitoring domestic Internet use and Internet users as a means of checking dissent and criticism. TsIB was also designed as a guard against foreign influence on Russia's population and electorate or what General Markomenko of FAPSI called "information warfare" at home and abroad on issues that included democracy promotion, social equality and patriotism.[118] When FAPSI was dissolved in 2003, its 3rd Main Department (responsible for SIGINT) was folded into the FSB and became the basis of Center 16 (detailed below).[119] Responsibility for military SIGINT still resides with the GRU. In addition to various sites throughout Russia, this includes ground-based long-distance early warning radar sites for air defense and

115 Hedieh Nasheri, *Economic Espionage and Industrial Spying* (Cambridge: Cambridge University Press, 2005), pp. 8–9, 11 which, in part, she attributes to the low barriers to entry in computing.

116 Mark Galeotti, "Putin's Hydra: Inside Russia's Intelligence Services," p. 2, https://www.ecfr.eu/page/-/ECFR_169_-_PUTINS_HYDRA_INSIDE_THE_RUSSIAN_INTELLIGENCE_SERVICES_1513.pdf, accessed 2 January 2018.

117 Riehle, *Russian Intelligence*, p. 239.

118 Timothy L. Thomas, "Russia's Information Warfare Structure: Understanding the Roles of the Security Council, FAPSI, the State Technical Commission and the Military", *European Security*, Vol. 7, No. 1 (Spring 1998), pp. 156–172. Riehle, *The Russian FSB*, pp. 20–21, 34, 48–49.

119 Russia's FSB malign activity: factsheet (Updated 7 December 2023), https://www.gov.uk/government/publications/russias-fsb-malign-cyber-activity-factsheet/russias-fsb-malign-activity-factsheet, accessed 18 August 2025.

airspace monitoring in Armenia, Belarus, one in occupied Crimea, and another space surveillance facility in Tajikistan.[120]

The FSB is headquartered in Lubyanka in the same building that housed the KGB, a short walk from Red Square and the Kremlin complex. It is purported to have a 300,000 strong staff.[121] This is said to make them "the largest security service in Europe."[122] The senior leadership and leadership structure of the FSB are outlined in Riehle's 2024 book *The Russian FSB*. Whilst indicating gaps in public knowledge about those involved in Russia's intelligence services, Riehle indicates that eight of its sixteen most senior leaders began their careers in the Cold War KGB with its leadership structure formed in 2004. Its leadership, almost all from a KGB background, is aging. The next generation are neither as well trained nor well-educated as their Soviet-era predecessors, despite it becoming a mirror to the KGB-era and the fear that instilled in ordinary Russians (and many in the West). The FSB is now built to protect Putin's regime from real or perceived threats. Moreover, the endemic corruption within its ranks means investigating these cases alone would need the resources of the entire FSB.[123] The SVR, which is headquartered in Yasenevo on the Moscow Ring Road, has been growing since 2007, but in contrast was said to number 13,000 in 2010. but could employ between 10–15,000 (with a quarter of them stationed abroad).[124]

The director of the FSB is General of the Army, Alexander Bortnikov. He is served by two first deputy directors and two deputy directors and, as head of the FSB, he is mandated to serve the president who is the primary decision-maker of Russian state security under the FSB's establishing statute. One of the FSB's first deputies also serves as head of Russia's Border Guard with another deputy in charge of the National Counterterrorism Center.[125] The Border Guard Service (*Pogranichnaya Sluzhba*, PS) contains around 212,500 staff monitoring Russia' 22,000 km long land border and 36,000 km coastline. The FSB also operates 99 regional directorates or "mini-FSB's" across Russia. This includes 42 border direc-

120 Riehle, *Russian Intelligence*, pp. 239–244. Riehle, *The Russian FSB*, pp. 5–28 also insightfully covers this entire period of time.

121 Lucas, *Deception*, p. 68.

122 Robert W. Pringle, *Historical Dictionary of Russian and Soviet Intelligence* (Lanham, MA: Scarecrow Press, 2006), p. 88.

123 Riehle, *The Russian FSB*, pp. 105–128. These gaps are also indicated in the introduction to Riehle, *Russian Intelligence*, pp. 7–18.

124 Steven Aftergood, "Russia Foreign Intelligence Service Expands" (July 13, 2016), https://fas.org/publication/svr-expands/. Anonymous, "Profile: Russia's SVR intelligence agency" (June 29, 2010), https://www.bbc.co.uk/news/10447308. Both accessed 3 May 2025. Riehle, *Russian Intelligence*, pp. 61–62.

125 Riehle, *The Russian FSB*, p. 105.

torates, 16 of which are in areas near to republics with separatist elements (including the North Caucasus and Crimea). The two most powerful are in Moscow and St. Petersburg. Many of their regional directorates are focused on missions associated with their locations. This includes regional offices in the North Caucasus dealing with counterterrorism, and those in the Far East focused on China. In Western oblasts, those close to NATO member states and Ukraine are geared towards counterintelligence. The FSB's "Fifth Service" and elements of the Border Guard (performing both policing and military functions) are also thought complicit in identifying and (at times) facilitating smuggling operations. Many low-paid rank-and-file members of the FSB and Border Guards serve out their careers at these regional directorates but for the leaderships it is a pathway to promotion. Promotion is the gateway to corrupt financial rewards.[126]

Bortnikov has been in post since he succeeded his patron Nikolai Patrushev in 2008. Patrushev, another former KGB officer and Kremlin hawk, went onto become Secretary of Russia's Security Council through to May 2024 (when Putin made his close ally an aide).[127] Putin and Patrushev are reportedly good friends. Both are close in age, joined the KGB around the same time, and worked together in Leningrad during the 1970s and 80s.[128] Bortnikov meanwhile is believed to suffer from ill-health and has passed official retirement age. His "anointed successor" is said to be Sergei Korolev (who is a decade younger and described as a "ruthless and ambitious operator").[129] Bortnikov had been Deputy Director of the FSB, and head of the Economic Security Service. In this role he would have known of Alexander Litvinenko. In January 2016, a British government inquiry would conclude that Litvinenko was assassinated at the direction of the FSB. In his deathbed statement, Litvinenko would claim (as would many other witnesses who gave ev-

126 In March 2022, the names and personal information of 620 FSB members were published by the Ukrainian government. A quarter were women, and over three-fourths were born before the Soviet Union collapsed. The vast majority of the senior and operational staff were men over 40. Riehle, *The Russian FSB*, pp. 51–53, 62–65, 89–95, 125, 147–152.

127 Mark Galeotti, "Russia's Security Council: Where Policy, Personality, and Process Meet," *Security Insights*, No. 41, October 2019, George C. Marshall Center for Security Studies, https://www.marshallcenter.org/en/publications/security-insights/russias-security-council-where-policy-personality-and-process-meet-0, accessed 30 June 2023.

128 Riehle, *The Russian FSB*, p. 112.

129 Mark Galeotti, "Siloviki at War: The Russian Security Community Since February 2022", *Russian Analytical Digest*, No. 323 (January 2025), p. 9, https://css.ethz.ch/content/dam/ethz/special-interest/gess/cis/center-for-securities-studies/pdfs/russiananalyticaldigest-323.pdf, accessed 27 April 2025.

idence before a UK government inquiry) that confirmation for the hit could only have come from Vladimir Putin (in an operation sanctioned by Patrushev).[130]

Bortnikov joined the KGB in what was then Leningrad in the 1970s.[131] It is now again St. Petersburg. It is Putin's birthplace and where he made his political reputation after leaving the KGB and entering local politics. It is where Putin first forged his political connections. From Russia's second city, many others have followed Putin in his ascent to power.[132] Like Putin, they come from the *siloviki* that first emerged in the early 1990s, in tandem with Russian organized crime and corruption. Competition between these groups also saw a hard-fought power play between Russia's security services. Out of this Darwinian process the FSB, with backing from President Putin, became the strongest of the three competing agencies around 2014.[133]

This includes those operated by Center 16 (Unit 71330) and Center 18 (Unit 64829). These five number designations (in this case 71330 and 64829) are military unit codes "consistent with Russia's intelligence and security services."[134] Center 16 (also known as the Center for Radio-Electronic Intelligence by Means of Communication/TsRRSS) is home to the FSB's SIGINT capabilities which include message interception, decryption, and processing (which it inherited from the 16th Directorate of the KGB in 2003). Evidence suggests Center 16 could be comprised of at least 10 departments and have regional sub-units (each employing the same five number designation used for concealment), each staffed by around 560 employees. These regional sub-units are spread across Russia with some facilities said to be decades old, whilst others (particularly near sensitive border regions like those of sub-Unit 03110 located close to Sochi) have been modernized. Their radomes and antennas are designed to collect and decipher satellite communica-

130 The Litvinenko Inquiry, pp. 241–244. Riehle, *The Russian FSB*, pp. 114–115.

131 Anonymous, "Bortnikov Alexander" (undated), https://www.spisok-putina.org/en/personas/bortnikov-2/, accessed 30 June 2023. His background is well covered in Riehle, *The Russian FSB*, pp. 107–108.

132 Anders Åslund, "How Vladimir Putin Rose to the Top," *The International Economy*, Spring 2019, http://www.international-economy.com/TIE_Sp19_Aslund.pdf. Tatiana Stanovaya, "The Putin Regime Cracks" (May 2020), Carnegie Moscow Center, https://carnegieendowment.org/files/Stanovaya_Putin_Elite-Final.pdf. Both accessed 30 June 2023.

133 Meakins, "Squabbling Siloviki," p. 237, Alexander Klimburg, "Mobilising Cyber Power," *Survival*, Vol. 53, No. 1 (February–March 2011), p. 49, Alexander Klimburg, *The Darkening Web: The War for Cyberspace* (New York: Penguin 2017), pp. 225–242.

134 CheckFirst, "Unveiling FSB's 16th Center SIGINT Capabilities (2025), https://checkfirst.network/decoding-secrets-through-symbols-how-military-insignia-revealed-russias-hidden-sigint-network/, accessed 8 August 2025.

tions (SATCOM) and radio signals.[135] With the FSB also focusing on internal security, Russian émigrés have been among its targets.

According to the UK's Foreign, Commonwealth & Development Office, Center 16's cyberspace operations began before or around 2010. Among its operations are the cyber threat actors with the monikers: "Dragonfly," "Berzerk Bear," "Energetic Bear," and "Crouching Yeti". Meanwhile, Center 18 (Unit 64829 aka Center for Information Security/TsIB) is suspected of running "Star Blizzard," and "Callisto Group" (with further threat actors also potentially linked to them). Center 18 is part of the Counter-Intelligence Service of the FSB ("First Service"). Its former deputy director, FSB Colonel Sergei Mikhailov, and Mikhailov's deputy, Dmitry Dokuchayev (a former hacker heavily implicated in cybercrime), were tried in a military court in Moscow in early 2019 for passing classified information to Western intelligence agencies. Mikhailov received a 22-year sentence, whilst Dokuchayev made a plea deal in return for evidence used to convict Mikhailov. The GRU had conducted the investigation which also involved Russian multiple cybercriminal hackers operating internationally. It was a case tied also into U.S. election interference in 2016 (chapter 4), and there was an element of score settling but it also draws attention to a longer-term trend that has seen figures from Russia's cybercriminal underworld being enlisted into the FSB for active measures campaigns on behalf of the Russian state.

Both Centers have reportedly targeted healthcare, finance, energy, education, and government sectors as well as Russian expatriates including dissidents and political opponents. Members of Center 16 have also been charged by the U.S. Department of Justice with hacking industrial control systems of private sector companies in electricity generation and distribution. Meanwhile, Center 18 controls and coordinates domestic surveillance and provides information security as well as conducting external cyber operations.[136] Center 16 cooperates with Center 18 (which is subordinate to the FSB's Counterintelligence Service) in what appear to be (multiple) separate cyberspionage campaigns. More broadly, whilst also competing with the GRU in cyberespionage campaigns, the FSB has progressively reaccumulated roles and responsibilities previously splintered across multiple organizations following the Soviet Union's dissolution. As it has regrown these remits and capabilities

135 CheckFirst, "Unveiling FSB's 16th Center SIGINT Capabilities (2025).

136 Aitel et al., "Russia's Cyber Operations," pp. 19 – 21, 24. Russia's FSB malign activity: factsheet (Updated 7 December 2023), https://www.gov.uk/government/publications/russias-fsb-malign-cyber-activity-factsheet/russias-fsb-malign-activity-factsheet. Mike Eckel, "In Moscow Treason Trial, A Major Scandal For Russian Security Agency" (February 27 2019), https://www.rferl.org/a/russia-hacker-mikhailov-stoyanov-fsb-scandal-for-russian-security-agency/29794092.html. Both accessed 8 August 2025.

(many of which trace their lineage back directly to the KGB), this has led to overlapping responsibilities with rival agencies including the MVD.[137]

The GRU survived the breakup of the Soviet Union. Officially the Main Intelligence Directorate, they were founded in 1918 (but with origins dating back to the early nineteenth century). It is now officially military intelligence (GU), but is still more widely known by its old acronym, GRU.[138] It survived large-scale reform unlike the KGB because it had a degree of protection from political infighting as part of the Defense Ministry and for its role in World War II (known and lauded in Russia as the Great Patriotic War). Its primary Cold War mission also survived: to provide strategic warnings of attack. It is headquartered in northwest Moscow – a metro ride away from the FSB in Lubyanka in a building dubbed the "Aquarium."[139] This "sports a swimming pool, a spa, multiple saunas, tennis courts, basketball and volleyball courts, and a winter garden."[140] The size of its workforce is unknown but the Congressional Research Service describes it as large and expansive, and whilst it survived intact, the GRU's capacity and capabilities were reduced during the turbulent 1990s. It is believed to have 15 Directorates. Four are regional. Nine are mission specific.

Table 1: The GRU's internal structure. Source: Andrew S. Bowen, Russian Military Intelligence: Background and Issues for Congress (updated November 15, 2021), https://crsreports.congress.gov/product/pdf/R/R46616/7.

Regional Directorates (4)	Mission-Specific Directorates (11)
(1) First Directorate: European Union	(5) Fifth Directorate: Operational Intelligence[141]
(2) Second Directorate: North and South America, United Kingdom, Australia, New Zealand	(6) Sixth Directorate: Electronic/Signals Intelligence
	(7) Seventh Directorate: NATO
	(8) Eighth Directorate: Spetsnaz
(3) Third Directorate: Asia	(9) Ninth Directorate: Military Technology
(4) Fourth Directorate: Africa	(10) Tenth Directorate: Military Economy
	(11) Eleventh Directorate: Strategic Doctrine
	(12) Twelfth Directorate: Information Operations
	(13) Space Intelligence Directorate
	(14) Operational and Technical Directorate
	(15) External Relations Department

137 The gradual expansion of the FSB's remit has been accompanied by changes in Russian legislation from its establishment in 1995. Riehle, *The Russian FSB*, pp. 29, 60–61, 92–94.

138 The old acronym GRU is used throughout for clarity.

139 Lucas, *Deception*, pp. 6–7, 113–114. Turovsky, "What is the GRU?'

140 Turovsky, "What is the GRU?"

141 Responsible for the deep cover "Illegals" program.

The GRU operates under the command of the Ministry of Defense and is headed by Admiral Igor Kostyukov (the longest serving military intelligence chief since the collapse of the Soviet Union). Kostyukov reported to Sergei Shoigu, who until May 2024 was Russia's Minister of Defense. The GRU's standing benefited from a decade of successful military operations up to the 2022 invasion of Ukraine. This included the "pacification" of the Caucusus region (typified by the Chechen conflict during the 1990s and into the 2000s), engagement in Ukraine, and the 2014 annexation of Crimea, as well as key interventions in the Syrian civil war in support of President Bashar al-Assad (where, until al-Assad's ousting as President in December 2024, Kostyukov was said to have played a key role).[142] His deputy, Lieutenant General Andrei Averyanov, is said to control all other all active measures outside Ukraine.[143] The GRU's Ukrainian operations have been controlled by Lieutenant General Vladimir Alekseyev, the First Deputy Director, following the invasion of Ukraine.[144] Favorable access to President Putin depends to a degree on whether or not the GRU, and its head, has been deemed successful with access to decision-making thought to be a sign of favor, not a right.[145]

All three main intelligence agencies, the FSB, GRU, and SVR compete with one another (though this might be giving way to grudging cooperation).[146] This rivalry has been mirrored in competition between the oligarchs and compliance with, or displeasure from, the Kremlin. This is visible in Russian cyberespionage campaigns and in their use and protection of Russia's organized crime networks. The GRU in particular is described as having an "aggressive and risk-taking culture" which "reflects its military background and its broad portfolio of assets."[147] This includes important strategic assets such as satellite and battlefield reconnaissance capabilities through electronic intelligence (ELINT) systems. It also includes its own dedicated *Spetsnaz* (special forces) units.

---

142 Bowen, Russian Military Intelligence: Background and Issues for Congress. Lucas, *Deception*, pp. 54, 57, 114–115, 176. Alexis A. Blanc, Alyssa Demus, Sandra Kay Evans, Michelle Grisé, Mark Hvizda, Marta Keep, Natasha Lander, and Krystyna Marcinek, "The Russian General Staff Understanding the Military's Decisionmaking Role in a 'Besieged Fortress,'" (2023), Rand Corporation, p. 23, https://www.rand.org/content/dam/rand/pubs/research_reports/RRA1200/RRA1233-7/RAND_RRA1233-7.pdf, accessed 30 June 2023.

143 Seth G. Jones, "Russia's Shadow War Against the West" (March 2025), p. 5, https://www.csis.org/analysis/russias-shadow-war-against-west, accessed 5 May 2025.

144 Anonymous, "Putin Gives GRU Boosted Role in Ukraine – Report" (May 11, 2022), https://www.themoscowtimes.com/2022/05/11/putin-elevates-gru-in-ukraine-intelligence-gathering-report-a77632, accessed 5 May 2025.

145 Bowen, Russian Military Intelligence, p. 5.

146 Galeotti, "Siloviki at War", p. 9.

147 Galeotti, "Putin's Hydra," p. 2.

There are variances between Russia's *Spetsnaz* units (including airborne and maritime or marine roles) but they still share commonalities. The Russian army, navy, and air force all have dedicated *Spetsnaz.* The Russian Navy alone has four assigned to the Northern Fleet, Pacific Fleet, Baltic Fleet and what remains of the Baltic Fleet. They have demonstrated multiple times in multiple locations (in geographies varying between Artic weather and desert terrain to cities and urban areas) their ability to operate behind enemy lines, with missions that include surveillance and reconnaissance or they can be used as a spearhead using guile, stealth, speed, and surprise where needed. One of their primary missions is counterinsurgency (COIN).

There is also the semi-independent Unit 35690 (or Special Purposes Center (TsSN) which is the FSB's dedicated *Spetsnaz* unit designed primarily to combat terrorist incidents including hostage taking and hijackings.[148] It is believed their deployments have included Afghanistan, Chechnya, Crimea, Syria, and Ukraine, and include Chechen and Ingush among their number to disguise their official government origins.[149] Russia's (then pivotal) entry into the Syrian Civil War in 2015, led the FSB to become more involved in foreign intelligence and international operations. This saw Center 16 and Center 18 increasingly engage in external operations. This led to overlap with the GRU and SVR and this became another source of factional rivalry.[150]

The GRU, like the SVR, also run deep cover "Illegals." This includes an infiltration and spying network in Ukraine, Belarus, and Poland exposed in 2022/23 as part of a wider series of operations.[151] Another spy ring of Bulgarian nationals who were target spotting individuals was also prosecuted by the UK in 2025.[152]

---

148 Riehle, *The Russian FSB*, pp. 39–41.

149 Ben Smith, "Russian intelligence services and special forces" House of Commons Library, Briefing Paper Number CBP 8430, 30 October 2018, pp. 10–11, https://researchbriefings.files.parliament.uk/documents/CBP-8430/CBP-8430.pdf, accessed 18 August 2025.

150 Andrew S. Bowen, Russian Military Intelligence: Background and Issues for Congress, Updated November 15 2021, pp. 5, 13, https://www.congress.gov/crs_external_products/R/PDF/R46616/R46616.7.pdf,. Oscar Rosengren, "The FSB: Russia's Federal Security Service" (October 9 2024, https://greydynamics.com/the-fsb-russias-federal-security-service/. Mark Galeotti, "The Three Faces of Russian Spetsnaz in Syria" (March 21 2016), https://warontherocks.com/2016/03/the-three-faces-of-russian-spetsnaz-in-syria/. All accessed 26 August 2025.

151 Andrzej Rybałt, "GRU spy Andrii Derkach and his "acquaintances" in Poland: report" (June 27, 2022), https://www.polskieradio.pl/395/9766/Artykul/2988956,GRU-spy-Andrii-Derkach-and-his-%E2%80%9Cacquaintances-in-Poland-report. Jamie Dettmer, "Russian spies rebound in Europe. Critical infrastructure is a key target for Russia's intelligence gathering, the priority being to monitor 'the production and supply of Western arms to Ukraine.'" (April 4, 2023), https://www.politico.eu/article/russia-spy-rebound-europe/. Both accessed 4 August 2023.

The GRU remains highly active and "enjoys a degree of operational autonomy."[153] There is also strong evidence that the GRU has found itself in ruthless competition with the FSB, including in cybersecurity and foreign "offensive information operations of every kind."[154] The FSB, GRU, and SVR are also known to contract out to Russian private cybersecurity firms.[155] This has been revealed through hacking, whilst others have experienced internal leaks which have yielded valuable information/intelligence.[156]

The FSB and SVR are at least as potent and combative as the GRU. Their leaderships covet domestic power and international influence and are well funded, highly active, and aggressive. They are "granted considerable latitude in their methods, unconstrained by the concerns of diplomats or the scrutiny of legislators."[157] It is within this competing domestic context that CrowdStrike identified the lack of de-confliction between competing "hack and leak" espionage operations of "Fancy Bear" (APT28) run by the GRU and the SVR's "Cozy Bear" (APT29) during the presidential election of 2016 (the subject of Chapter 4).[158]

APT28 and APT29, as all other known APT groups, are also (unhelpfully) widely referred to by other monikers given to them by the cybersecurity industry. Nevertheless, these aliases are also indications of the difficulties in identifying threat actors through their tactics/targets, techniques, and procedures.[159] This is even more difficult in relation to Russia because of the intermingling between state-intelligence, sub-state cybercriminals, and "patriotic" hackers, as well as non-state

---

152 "Bulgarian trio convicted of conspiring to spy for Russia" (March 7, 2025), https://www.cps.gov.uk/cps/news/bulgarian-trio-convicted-conspiring-spy-russia, accessed 1 May 2025.

153 Galeotti, "Putin's Hydra," p.2. Blanc et al., "The Russian General Staff," pp. 22–23.

154 Galeotti, "Putin's Hydra," p. 2.

155 It is unclear whether the same is true of the SVR.

156 This includes SyTech and NTC Vulkan. Zak Doffman, "Russia's Secret Intelligence Agency Hacked: 'Largest Data Breach In Its History'" (July 20, 2019), https://www.forbes.com/sites/zakdoffman/2019/07/20/russian-intelligence-has-been-hacked-with-social-media-and-tor-projects-exposed/?sh=3bed6c3e6b11. Luke Harding, Stiliyana Simeonova, Manisha Ganguly, and Dan Sabbagh, "'Vulkan files' leak reveals Putin's global and domestic cyberwarfare tactics" (March 30, 2023), https://www.theguardian.com/technology/2023/mar/30/vulkan-files-leak-reveals-putins-global-and-domestic-cyberwarfare-tactics, accessed 15 July 2023.

157 Galeotti, "Putin's Hydra," pp. 1–2.

158 Dmitri Alperovitch, "Bears in the Midst: Intrusion into the Democratic National Committee," https://www.crowdstrike.com/blog/bears-midst-intrusion-democratic-national-committee/, accessed 13 October 2016. Andrew S. Bowen, Russian Cyber Units (updated February 2, 2022), https://crsreports.congress.gov/product/pdf/IF/IF11718, accessed 1 July 2023.

159 M-Trends 2023, p. 102, https://mandiant.widen.net/s/dlzgn6w26n/m-trends-2023, https://attack.mitre.org/versions/v7/, both accessed 3 August 2023.

cybercriminals abroad acting as proxies.[160] Reporting from the cybersecurity industry indicates APT28 was operating as early as 2004.[161] APT29 since at least 2008.[162]

Writing in 2011 Klimburg argued, "The rise of the *siloviki* marks the end of a process ongoing since the early 1990s" which featured "a vicious power struggle between the various security services and establishment of strong links between them and criminal elements."[163] From this power play, the FSB emerged as the clear winner. According to Galeotti, these "Silovik wars" "raged on-and-off since 2004" through "competitive intelligence ... but with a strong admixture of bloody-fanged social Darwinism." This has led to "blurring of boundaries [that] encourages regular direct and indirect turf wars, and not just over the usual bureaucratic prizes of responsibilities, funding, and access to the leadership but also business opportunities for officers, and sometimes outright survival."[164] This competition emerged forcefully during the renationalization of key industries sold off during the 1990s.

6 Russian intelligence failures and operational security

Russia's system places stress on accurate and actionable intelligence especially in localized information-challenged or information-denied environments. Each of these elements is a contributor to Clausewitzian friction.[165] That the decision to

160 For APT28 this includes Sofacy, STRONTIUM, Pawn Storm, IRON TWILIGHT, SNAKEMACKEREL, Swallowtail, Group 74, Sednit, Tsar Team, Threat Group-4127, TG-4127 as well as Fancy Bear. APT29's monikers include ATK 7, IRON RITUAL, IRON HEMLOCK, Group 100, Yttrium, NobleBaron, Dark Halo, StellarParticle, Minidionis, CloudLook, NOBELIUM, UNC2452, YTTRIUM, The Dukes, CozyDuke, SolarStorm, Blue Kitsune, Cloaked Ursa, Grizzly Steppe, as well as Cozy Bear. Electronic Transactions Development Agency (formerly Thailand's government Computer Emergency Response Team), "Threat Group Cards: A Threat Actor Encyclopedia APT group: APT 29, Cozy Bear, The Dukes," https://apt.etda.or.th/cgi-bin/showcard.cgi?g=APT%2029%2C%20Cozy%20Bear%2C%20The%20Dukes&n=1 and "APT28," https://attack.mitre.org/groups/G0007/, "APT29," https://attack.mitre.org/groups/G0016/. All accessed 19 July 2023.

161 "APT28."

162 APT group: APT 29, Cozy Bear, The Dukes, https://apt.etda.or.th/cgi-bin/showcard.cgi?g=APT%2029%2C%20Cozy%20Bear%2C%20The%20Dukes&n=1, accessed 10 October 2023.

163 Klimburg, "Mobilising Cyber Power," p. 49. Klimburg, *The Darkening Web*, pp. 225–242.

164 Galeotti, "Putin's Hydra," p. 4.

165 Blanc et al., "The Russian General Staff," pp. 43–44. Friction is the impediment to battle plans encompassing anything that can go wrong and elements such as weather, and much else that is dynamic and unpredictable. Here each part of the war effort, down to the role of individuals, are contributors to friction and interact to increase and create chance and uncertainty. Carl von

invade Ukraine was shrouded in secrecy and public denials after weeks of troop deployments and training exercises harmed operational and tactical planning, preparedness, and execution of Russia's war plans.[166] Sleeper agents, proxies, and collaborators (some inside Ukraine's own security service, the SBU) also told their Russian intelligence handlers (who paid them handsomely for their services) that Ukraine was weak.[167]

Decision-making in the Kremlin, centered around the Presidential Administration and Security Council (*Sovet Bezopasnosti*), appears difficult to penetrate and as a former KGB officer now at the center of power, Putin makes exceptional precautions knowing that foreign intelligence services have their eyes and ears on him and his inner circle. This sees intelligence and orders restricted to a small number of close confidantes. They are trained to be guarded in their operational security (OPSEC), including their use of communications devices. This includes landlines, cellphones, computers, and any other devices that could be penetrated or compromised.[168]

The same cannot be said of Russian forces in Ukraine. Electronic interception and jamming combined with deficient numbers of secure military communications equipment, as well as the disorder of Russia's rank-and-file soldiers have

---

Clausewitz, *On War*, edited and translated by Michael Howard and Peter Paret (Oxford: Oxford University Press, 1997), pp. 65–68.

166 Blanc et al., "The Russian General Staff," p. 98. Robert Dalsjö, Michael Jonsson, and Johan Norberg, "A Brutal Examination: Russian Military Capability in Light of the Ukraine War," *Survival*, Vol. 64, No. 3 (June–July 2022), pp. 7–28. Faith and trust in subordinates to carry out orders carries further uncertainty. Loyalty and clear rules of engagement (RoE) also play a part and, in the case of Russian forces in Ukraine, that sub-ordinates in the chain-of-command can follow, trust, and have faith in the orders issued from above. Carl von Clausewitz, *Principles of War*, translated by Hans Wilhelm Gatkze (Harrisburg PA: Military Service Publishing (1942), p. 27.

167 As well as overstating their importance and influence. Mari Saito and Maria Tsvetkova, "The Enemy Within" (July 28, 2022), https://www.reuters.com/investigates/special-report/ukraine-crisis-russia-saboteurs/, Mick Krever, "Ukraine's security service hunts the spies selling information to Russia" (May 17, 2022), https://edition.cnn.com/2022/05/16/europe/ukraine-sbu-russian-spies-intl/index.html. Both accessed 11 April 2023. See also the insightful article by Huw Dylan, David V. Gioe, and Elena Grossfeld, "The Autocrat's Intelligence Paradox: Vladimir Putin's (Mis)Management of Russian Strategic Assessment in the Ukraine War," *British Journal of Politics and International Relations*, Vol. 25, Issue 3 (August 2023), pp. 385–404.

168 Greg Miller, "As Russia reasserts itself, U.S. intelligence agencies focus anew on the Kremlin" (September 14, 2016), https://www.washingtonpost.com/world/national-security/as-russia-reasserts-itself-us-intelligence-agencies-focus-anew-on-the-kremlin/2016/09/14/cc212c62-78f0-11e6-ac8e-cf8e0dd91dc7_story.html, accessed 17 June 2019. Dara Massicot, "What Russia Got Wrong. Can Moscow Learn from Its Failures in Ukraine?" (March/April 2023), https://www.foreignaffairs.com/ukraine/what-russia-got-wrong-moscow-failures-in-ukraine-dara-massicot, accessed 2 July 2023.

each contributed.[169] Their personal cellphones, as well as captured or stolen ones, have seen insecure communications on commercial networks intercepted and widely leaked on the Internet.[170] Alongside other sources and methods, this provides significant and actionable real-time intelligence including real-time geolocation and other metadata useful to Ukrainian forces.

After cultivating a public image of machismo during the previous twenty years Putin has seldom visited Ukraine and never publicly visited the frontlines.[171] Yevgeny Prigozhin, when leading the Wagner Group, by contrast had been highly visible and vocal from the frontlines and within Russia. This contributed to his popularity in Russian military circles.[172] During the COVID-19 pandemic it was reported that Putin became increasingly isolated. Even before further travel restrictions were imposed prior to the invasion of Ukraine, he notably began to meet Western leaders and his own government officials a long table length apart. Since the annexation of Crimea in 2014 it is also reported he travels mainly by armored train within Russia.[173]

Recruiting sources inside Putin's inner circle, and the presidential administration inside the Kremlin more generally, is extremely difficult. Those tasked with protecting him have been richly rewarded.[174] Alongside rigorous operational secu-

---

169 Daniel Ong, "Russian General Brutally Dies In Ukraine: 'Collected His Guts ... Back In His Belly'" (April 27, 2022), https://www.ibtimes.com/russian-general-brutally-dies-ukraine-collected-his-gutsback-his-belly-3488076, accessed 23 May 2022.

170 Including on Ukraine's SBU channel on YouTube.

171 Lidia Kelly and Mark Trevelyan, "Putin visits Russian-occupied Mariupol after ICC issues arrest warrant" (March 19, 2023), https://www.reuters.com/world/europe/putin-makes-surprise-trip-mariupol-first-occupied-donbas-ukraine-2023-03-19/, accessed 2 July 2023.

172 Ivan Fomin, Milana Mazaeva, Elina Beketova, and Pavel Luzin, "The Prigozhin Uprising, the Aftermath, and What Comes Next" (June 25, 2023), https://cepa.org/article/the-prigozhin-uprising-the-aftermath-and-what-comes-next/, accessed 2 July 2023.

173 This has led to speculation regarding his mental and physical health. Anonymous, "Antler baths and isolation. As Putin approaches 70, investigative journalists look into the state of his health" (April 1, 2022), https://meduza.io/en/feature/2022/04/01/antler-baths-and-isolation. Anonymous, "That extra-heavy load. Instead of flying, Vladimir Putin prefers to travel around Russia by armored train (allegedly for fear of Ukrainian attack) (February 13, 2023), https://meduza.io/en/feature/2023/02/13/that-extra-heavy-load, "CNN gets rare glimpse inside Putin's secret train," https://edition.cnn.com/videos/world/2023/07/10/putin-luxury-train-matthew-chance-pkg-ac360-intl-ldn-vpx.cnn. All accessed 30 June 2023. Magdalena Kaltseis, "Cold and Distant or Hearty and Human? The Visual Portrayal of Vladimir Putin on Russian Television," *Media Literacy and Research*, Vol. 2, Issue 2 (2019), pp. 6–33.

174 Roman Anin, "Putin's Bodyguards Rewarded with Land and Power" (November 19, 2018), https://www.occrp.org/en/investigations/8922-putin-s-bodyguards-rewarded-with-land-and-power, accessed 18 August 2023.

rity, Putin "confides in only a small group of people" which makes penetration and exfiltration of intelligence problematic.[175] Putin was schooled in this world and mindset both as a former KGB officer (mainly stationed in East Germany) and then as director of the FSB for thirteen months between 1998 and 1999 after being handpicked by Yeltsin after he protected Yeltsin's family from corruption charges.[176] According to Mark Galeotti, he was not chosen because of outstanding abilities, but because he was loyal and reliable and would cover up embarrassing misdeeds. Indeed, he was unused to working at this level and been out of the service for seven years whilst in St. Petersburg's city government.

He has since surrounded himself with a small cadre of former intelligence professionals including Sergei Ivanov, his former chief of staff (and former KGB), Deputy Prime Minister Dmitry Kozak (ex-GRU), Rosneft chairman and "*silovarch*" Igor Sechin (suspected to be a former GRU officer and a close ally whose relationship with Putin dates back to the 1990s in St. Petersburg),[177] and the secretary of Russia's Security Council (until May 2024), Nikolai Patrushev. Almost all invariably tell him what he wants to hear rather than what he needs to know and do not work in concert. They instead provide politicized intelligence in competition with one another.[178] Domestically, Russia's security services have been instrumental for "building a 'regime of repression' to fix elections and cripple political opponents" as well as for "blackmail, bribery, arrest, and … assassination."[179]

Putin and other high-ranking officials are protected by the Federal Guard Service (*Federal'naya Sluzhba Okhrany*, FSO) whose director is Colonel-General Dmitriy Kochnev (2016–date). It is charged with protecting the Russian president and around 40 other senior government officials whilst also securing official high-level government communications. The FSO is also in charge of the underground command centers and subterranean metro system spread around Moscow connecting

---

175 Julian E. Barnes, Adam Goldman, and David E. Sanger, "C.I.A. Informant Extracted from Russia Had Sent Secrets to U.S. for Decades" (September 9, 2019), https://www.nytimes.com/2019/09/09/us/politics/cia-informant-russia.html?action=click&module=Top%20Stories&pgtype=Homepage, accessed 10 September 2019.

176 Riehle, *The Russian FSB*, pp. 110–111.

177 A portmanteau of siloviki and oligarch. Daniel Triesman, "Putin's Silovarchs," *Orbis*, Vol. 51, Issue 1 (Winter 2007), pp. 141–153. Mark Galeotti, "The Intelligence and Security Services and Strategic Decision-Making," *Security Insights*, No. 30 (May 2019), George C. Marshall Center for Security Studies, https://www.marshallcenter.org/sites/default/files/files/2019-09/SecurityInsights_30_Galeotti_May2019.pdf, accessed 29 June 2023. Riehle, *The Russian FSB*, p. 100.

178 Mark Galeotti, "Spooks in the Kremlin: The Dangers of Putin's Unhealthy Reliance on Russian Intelligence," *Foreign Policy*, No. 232 (Spring 2019), pp. 17–19.

179 Meakins, "Squabbling Siloviki," p. 253. See also Brian Taylor, *State Building in Putin's Russia: Policing and Coercion After Communism* (New York: Cambridge University Press, 2011).

key government facilities. The FSO also protects aircraft flying high-ranking government officials and Putin's armored train. There is also a failsafe provided for by the Main Directorate of Special Programmes of the President of the Russian Federation (GUSP).[180]

There is a degree of monitoring of the infighting through the Federal Protective Service (FSO), which is "broadly comparable to the American Secret Service." However, this is designed to protect Putin from the inner circle by "watching for signs of unrest or revolution," not as a check on the intelligence services.[181] This small decision-making inner circle centered around Putin, variously described as Russia's "new nobility" and "institutionalized competition," has become an "informal network of governance behind the formal state."[182] It is a potential source of strength as well as a potential weakness.[183]

7 Decision-making in Russia

According to a 2023 RAND study, there is a wider variety of actors influencing Russian national security policymaking. These include members of the Ministry of Defense (MoD), Ministry of Foreign Affairs, Presidential Administration, Security Council, the oligarchs, and other groups. Senior members are connected with wider networks through a power vertical. However, only "an increasingly small circle of individuals" wield "national-level decisionmaking power" although "individuals outside this small circle have agency."[184] With President Putin head of the Security Council, it is "the pinnacle of power" in the Kremlin.[185] Some even describe it as Politburo 2.0.[186]

180 Smith, "Russian intelligence services and special forces" , pp. 5–6. Riehle, *Russian Intelligence*, pp. 69–71.

181 Meakins, "Squabbling Siloviki," pp. 235, 237. Nikolai Petrov, "The Elite New Wine into Old Bottles?" *Russian Politics & Law*, Vol. 55, Issue 2 (March 2017), pp. 115–132.

182 Samuel A. Greene, "Editor's Introduction," *Russian Politics & Law*, Vol. 55, Issue 2 (March 2017), p. 60.

183 Fiona Hill, "Putin: The One-Man Show the West Doesn't Understand," *Bulletin of the Atomic Scientists*, Vol. 72, No. 3 (April 2016), pp. 140–144.

184 Blanc et al., "The Russian General Staff," p. 4.

185 Åslund, "How Vladimir Putin Rose to the Top." See also Anders Åslund, *Russia's Crony Capitalism: The Path from Market Economy to Kleptocracy* (New Haven, CT: Yale University Press, 2019).

186 Martin Kragh and Andreas Umland, "Putinism beyond Putin: The Political Ideas of Nikolai Patrushev and Sergei Naryshkin in 2006–20," *Post-Soviet Affairs*, Vol. 39, Issue 5 (September 2023), pp. 366–389.

From 2008 to 2024 the Security Council was headed by Nikolai Patrushev. Patrushev ran the secretariat and oversaw its day-to-day business. In May 2024, Patrushev was demoted to oversee Russia's shipbuilding industry. His son, Dmitry, was made Deputy Prime Minister in charge of agriculture. The Prime Minister is Mikhail Mishustin. Mishustin is described as a technocrat with a low-profile. He has no background in the security services and is not a member of the *siloviki*. When he replaced Dmitry Medvedev in June 2020, he arrived in office as the decade-long head of the federal tax service. He was reappointed Prime Minister in May 2024. Although he is first in line to take over as acting president under the Russian constitution, he is not one of the main power holders. That might change but his current role is more of a government administrator than a Prime Minister in the Western sense.[187] As a further part of the post-2024 election reshuffle Alexei Dyumin, Putin's former bodyguard and a former deputy head of the GRU, became Secretary of the State Council (an advisory body containing the heads of Russia's oblasts).[188] Beneath the Security Council, "the security community in Russia is characterised by division, duplication, and deep institutional rivalry."[189]

This is partly by design. A series of Russia experts point to a system of government characterized by ambition and rivalry. Sergey Radchenko points to imperial ambition evident from the time of Peter the Great (1682–1725) that extended to the Soviet era (1917–91).[190] Keir Giles argues along very similar lines. For Giles

---

187 Reuters, "Who is Russia's Mikhail Mishustin?" (May 10 2025), https://www.reuters.com/world/europe/who-is-russias-mikhail-mishustin-2024-05-10/. Anonymous, "Putin reappoints his prime minister, a technocrat who has kept a low political profile" (May 10 2024), https://apnews.com/article/russia-cabinet-appointment-putin-5915b06308d722e17a875892a6d1bdb5. Both accessed 23 August 2025.

188 As part of Putin's post 2024 election reshuffle, Maxim Oreshkin, 41, was raised to Deputy Chief of Staff. There was also continuity. Anton Vaino, 52, remained as Chief of Staff. Alexei Gromov, 63, and Sergei Kiriyenko, 61, also remained as First Deputy Chiefs of Staff. Denis Manturov, 55, was handed the role of First Deputy Prime Minister (specializing in industry) with Alexander Novak, 52, staying as Deputy Prime Minister (administering energy). Both Novak and Oreshkin are expected to work closely to tackle Russia's sanctioned economy. Institute for the Study of War, "Russian Offensive Campaign Assessment" (May 29, 2024), https://www.understandingwar.org/backgrounder/russian-offensive-campaign-assessment-may-29-2024, Guy Faulconbridge and Andrew Osborn, "Putin demotes Cold War warrior Patrushev and raises two younger allies" (May 14, 2024), https://www.reuters.com/world/europe/putin-appoints-patrushev-dyumin-kremlin-aides-2024-05-14/. Andrew Osborn, "Putin names ex-bodyguard Alexei Dyumin, a potential successor, to senior role" (May 29, 2024), https://www.reuters.com/world/europe/putin-makes-former-bodyguard-alexei-dyumin-secretary-state-council-says-kremlin-2024-05-29/. All accessed 30 May 2024.

189 Galeotti, "Putin's Hydra," p. 3.

190 Radchenko, *To Run the World*.

the system of government is founded on a hierarchical relationship between ruler (be they Tsar, General Secretary or President), the state, and subjects.[191]

Russia's General Staff, which dates back to the time of Peter the Great, is the senior decision-making body of the MoD responsible for the operational control of Russia's armed forces. It is headed by the Chief of the General Staff, Valerii Gerasimov, a 1977 graduate of the Soviet army's tank corps who rose through the ranks before becoming Chief in 2012. He is the longest serving Chief of the General Staff since the Russian Revolution and third longest in 200 years. With a secondary role as the First Deputy Minister of Defense, he commands an estimated 1–1.2 million military personnel alongside the Minister of Defense, Sergei Shoigu (November 2012–May 2024).[192] Gerasimov was subordinate to Shoigu in a symbiotic relationship. Their roles needed to be mutually supportive in the Russian system of governance. Because of Russia's use of its armed forces as a foreign policy tool, including operations in Ukraine and Syria, Gerasimov's political influence has grown.[193] How (and whether) that might change with the replacement of Shoigu with former deputy prime minister Andrei Belousov remains to be seen.[194]

Gerasimov and his General Staff report to the President, who is the Supreme Commander in Chief of Russia's Armed Forces. The General Staff is the conduit to carry out the orders of these three men: Putin, Shoigu, and Gerasimov. That was the case for almost twelve years. With Belousov replacing Shoigu, and Shoigu replacing Nikolai Patrushev as head of Russia's Security Council it remains to be seen if these changes amount to more than a reshuffle of power holders beneath Putin.[195] Though at some point there will inevitably have to be generational changes, this aging leadership constitutes a top-down, centralized decision-making process designed to promote micromanagement from Moscow. This reduces the tactical role of local commanders to executing orders issued down the chain-of-command. Bottom-up feedback is not fostered, even with units of the General Staff embedded in theater headquarters. This approach discourages adap-

191 Giles, *Moscow Rules*, pp. 71–99.

192 There are plans for a 30 percent rise to 1.5 million through conscription. Around 250,000 are conscripts. Some are able to avoid being drafted. Those who are conscripted are frequently "poor and unconnected." During the Ukraine War, many who were eligible for the draft fled Russia when they were able. Elisabeth Braw, "Wagner's Revolt May Weaken Russia's Draft" (June 26, 2023), https://foreignpolicy.com/2023/06/26/wagner-revolt-russia-conscription-ukraine-war/, accessed 2 July 2023

193 Blanc et al., "The Russian General Staff," pp. 10–19, 95.

194 Galeotti, "Siloviki at War," p. 9.

195 Guy Faulconbridge and Andrew Osborn, "Putin taps civilian economist to run defense, replacing Shoigu in surprise move" (May 13, 2024), https://www.reuters.com/world/europe/putin-proposes-sacking-defence-minister-shoigu-parliament-says-2024-05-12/, accessed 13 May 2024.

tivity, creativity, and flexibility in carrying out orders and in the conduct of operations. Moreover, in-theater commanders are personally accountable for the actions of their subordinates which also inhibits battlefield initiative and a failure to receive orders from above risks paralyzing forces in the field (as it has periodically in Ukraine).[196]

Russia's military tradition "places a significant amount of personal responsibility on commanders. The importance of commanding roles in the Russian military cannot be overstated. The Chief of the Russian General Staff holds *personal* responsibility for the success of the tasks assigned to the General Staff" and is a personal appointment of the President with no term limit.[197] This provides clear means for Putin to exercise influence on military decision-making and "to exert control over the Armed Forces."[198] Foreign policy is dictated by the Kremlin. Despite Russia having an experienced Foreign Minister in Sergei Lavrov, he is an outsider at court. Lavrov, who has been in post since 2004, is described as a pragmatist. He is the diplomatic face of Russian foreign policy and has been a frequent public defender of Russian security and foreign policy in the United Nations and other forums.[199]

8 Does Russia have a decision-advantage?

According to a July 2020 British government Intelligence and Security Committee (ISC) report on Russia, for good or for ill "Putin's inner circle appear to be willing and able to make and enact major decisions (for example, on the deployment of troops) within days." The ISC also assessed the inner circle retains "tight command and control over the whole government infrastructure – which can be put in the service of Russia's foreign policy goals at a moment's notice."[200]

However, in late June 2023, Prigozhin took a contingent of Wagner fighters and armored vehicles and seized control of the southern Russian city of Rostov unopposed. They then rapidly moved north and took control of Voronezh before heading northeast towards Moscow. Over a period of 24 hours a truce was then

196 Blanc et al., "The Russian General Staff," pp. 27–28, 43–45. Dalsjö, Jonsson, and Norberg, "A Brutal Examination," pp. 7–28.

197 Blanc et al., "The Russian General Staff," pp. 17–18.

198 Blanc et al., "The Russian General Staff," p. 18.

199 Corneliu Bjola, "Diplomatic Leadership in Times of International Crisis: The Maverick, the Congregator and the Pragmatist," *The Hague Journal of Diplomacy*, Vol. 10, Issue 1 (January 2015), pp. 4–9.

200 Russia HC 632, 21 July 2020, p. 29.

brokered.[201] Putin spoke of being stabbed in the back and betrayal. SVR chief, Sergei Naryshkin, described it as an "attempted armed rebellion."[202] This had been anticipated as a growing possibility by Western intelligence, but it was not anticipated by Putin and his inner circle, including his Minister of Defense, Sergei Shoigu, or Chief of the General Staff Gerasimov.[203]

Instead, they had let Wagner off the leash in Ukraine and with it had let a second center of military power grow and break the Russian state's monopoly of force. Prigozhin did not long survive this rebellion and was killed alongside his number two in a possible missile strike on a chartered aircraft in August 2023.[204] The ISC had assessed that "Putin appears to value surprise and the unexpected."[205] Prigozhin's rebellion was not the kind of unexpected surprise Putin intended. Since then, the Wagner Group has had its wings clipped. In Ukraine, its members have either been made to join the regular army or the Expeditionary Volunteer Assault Corps (which is subordinate to the army). In Africa, they are being kept on a leash by General Andrei Averyanov (sanctioned in 2020 over Russian involvement in Libya). Averyanov, a former head of Unit 29155 (a Military Unit that which will feature later in this book) and now deputy head of the GRU, has overseen the Wagner Group being absorbed into an Africa Corps (also being styled as the African Initiative) run by Russian military intelligence. Inside the GRU, Averyanov is also in charge of a newly created Service for Special Activities.[206]

In contrast, against the West Putin has "consciously retained and cultivated this 'decision-advantage' as a way of outmanoeuvring adversaries." Resultantly Western governments took time to comprehend "the pace of Russian decision-

---

201 CNN, "'Fishy': Former DNI on Prigozhin deal with Russia" (June 26, 2023), https://www.youtube.com/watch?v=JLLZ-nb_9qk, accessed 26 June 2023.

202 Helen Regan, Andrew Raine, Sophie Tanno, Hafsa Khalil, Tori B. Powell, Adrienne Vogt, and Kaanita Iyer, CNN, "June 24, 2023 – Wagner head says group standing down" (June 25, 2023), https://edition.cnn.com/europe/live-news/russia-ukraine-war-news-06-24-23/h_4fba079bda68626873593a71edc1a43a, accessed 26 June 2023.

203 Ellen Nakashima and Shane Harris, "U.S. spies learned in mid-June Prigozhin was planning armed action in Russia. The intelligence fed concerns about whether Vladimir Putin would remain in power and what any instability could mean for control of Russia's nuclear arsenal" (June 24, 2023), https://www.washingtonpost.com/national-security/2023/06/24/us-intelligence-prigozhin-putin/, accessed 26 June 2023.

204 Victoria Bisset and Miriam Berger, "Prigozhin is confirmed dead. What happened to Putin's other rivals?" (August 24, 2023), https://www.washingtonpost.com/world/2023/08/24/russia-vladimir-putin-yevgeniy-prigozhin-foes/, accessed 1 October 2023.

205 Russia HC 632, 21 July 2020, p. 29.

206 Galeotti, "Siloviki at War," p. 8.

making" and this hampered their individual and collective "ability to respond effectively to Russian aggressions" including "the annexation of Crimea in 2014."[207] However, the rapidity of this centralized decision-making process meant orders and planning were poorly communicated down the chain of command when the decision was made to invade Ukraine.[208] This contributed to strategic failure in the early weeks of the war with structural military weaknesses also affecting Russia's stuttering military "successes" and setbacks.[209] This included the blunting of a major cyber offensive that was only prevented with allied support and support from private industry and could qualify as attempted cyberwar in its own right.[210] Despite this notable setback, cyberespionage and traditional espionage are where they have seen success (as well as exposure). Under Putin, the KGB's successors (the FSB, SVR, and GRU) have again become well-resourced agencies with a renewed focus.[211]

The FSB is very active in more traditional Cold War style spycraft and counterintelligence as well as cyberespionage.[212] It also maintains "inner access" to President Putin and his inner circle.[213] Meanwhile, the SVR is headed by the aforementioned Sergei Naryshkin who, at a meeting of the Security Council on February 21, 2022, was publicly berated by Putin over his seeming indecision whether to recognize the independence of the secessionist "People's Republics" of Donetsk and Luhansk. Before being appointed to lead the SVR, he was Chief of the Presidential Administration from 2008 to 2011 and then Chairman of the Russian State Duma through to 2016. During Soviet times, he was another former KGB officer. Naryshkin is described more a pragmatic hawk than ideologue and (perhaps wisely) given his treatment by Putin in the televised meeting of Russia's Security Council, is another who appears unlikely or unwilling to bring Putin unwelcome news.[214] He has been described as a "permanent stand-in" whose "authority has never fully recovered from the mauling Putin gave him" and said to be looking

207 Russia HC 632, 21 July 2020, p. 29.

208 Herb Lin, "Russian Cyber Operations in the Invasion of Ukraine," *Cyber Defense Review*, Vol. 7, No. 4 (Fall 2022), pp. 37–38.

209 "Ukraine Conflict Updates," https://www.understandingwar.org/backgrounder/ukraine-conflict-updates, accessed 26 June 2023.

210 Kristan Stoddart, "Russia's Cyber Campaigns and the Ukraine War: From the 'Gray Zone' to the 'Red Zone', Applied Cybersecurity & Internet Governance, Vol. 3, No. 1 (June 2024), pp. 1–33.

211 Lucas Kello, *The Virtual Weapon and International Order* (New Haven, CT: Yale University Press, 2017), pp. 212–228.

212 David Gioe, "Cyber Operations and Useful Fools: The Approach of Russian Hybrid Intelligence," *Intelligence and National Security*, Vol. 33, No. 7 (December 2019), pp. 954–973.

213 Bowen, Russian Military Intelligence, p. 5.

214 Kragh and Umland, "Putinism beyond Putin," p. 368, 379–381.

towards retirement and devoting more time to chairing the Russian Historical Society.[215]

Moreover, among the FSB's shadowy sub-divisions and directorates is the "Fifth Service" (the Service of Operative Information and International Ties/Sluzhba Operativnoy Informatsii i Mezhdunarodnykh Svyazey, SOIiMS). SOIiMS (the "Fifth Service") has at least four directorates and it was during Putin's directorship of the FSB in 1998 and 1999, alongside his deputy Sergey Ivanov, that saw the FSB take on a foreign intelligence role. Ivanov, who Yeltsin would promote to Secretary of the Security Council (before becoming Minister of Defense from 2001–2007 under Putin whilst remaining on the Security Council), would be replaced by Colonel-General Sergei Beseda. Beseda, who features in Chapter 1, is another *siloviki* who had risen through the ranks after starting out as an intelligence officer in the KGB.[216] The "Fifth Service" (SoliMS) now oversees FSB operations abroad (using all available means) and is especially concerned with former Soviet and Warsaw Pact states. After a domestic focus during the 1990s, "Putin's internal and foreign policies have become increasingly hybrid" and more so after the invasion of Ukraine.[217]

According to Jack Watling of Britain's Royal United Services Institute, this intermix (whether coordinated or competing) sees the FSB provide *rezidents* for Russia's embassies, consulates, and international institutions.[218] Foreign embassies and people with connections to them have also become targets for the FSB.[219] This would have been a KGB responsibility for large parts of the Cold War alongside the GRU.[220] As the GRU also provided rezidents during the Cold

215 Galeotti, 'Siloviki at War'. For more on Naryshkin see Riehle, *Russian Intelligence*, pp. 65, 69, 222.

216 Kateryna Denisova, "Who is Sergey Beseda, Russian spy handler leading talks with US?" (March 24 2025), https://kyivindependent.com/sergey-beseda-russias-negotiator-in-saudi-arabia-and-his-role-in-ukraines-war/, accessed 26 August 2025.

217 Irina Borogan and Andrei Soldatov, "You Broke it, You Fix it — The Kremlin's Spooky Ukraine Negotiator" (March 25, 2025), https://cepa.org/article/you-broke-it-you-fix-it-the-kremlins-spooky-ukraine-negotiator/, accessed 29 April 2025.

218 Jack Watling, "The Kaleidoscopic Campaigning of Russia's Special Services" (September 20, 2022), https://www.rusi.org/explore-our-research/publications/commentary/kaleidoscopic-campaigning-russias-special-services, accessed 29 April 2025. FSB embassy staff are likely provided for by the International Cooperation Directorate (UMS) of the FSB's "Fifth Service" (SOIiMS). This is also responsible for postings to international organizations. Riehle, *The Russian FSB*, pp. 47–48, 72.

219 Riehle, *Russian Intelligence*, pp. 88–91.

220 Pringle, *Historical Dictionary of Russian and Soviet Intelligence*, pp. 4–9, 16, 26, 28–29, 49, 56, 61–62, 68–71, 76–77, 81–83, 86, 98–101, 107–108, 112–115, 120–123, 128, 135–142, 147, 161–162, 186, 192–205, 214, 221–224, 229, 236–241, 254–257, 264, 268, 278, 282–286, 295–299. On the structure and organization of Rezidentura please see Riehle, *Russian Intelligence*, pp. 231–234.

War, it appears plausible this was continued or reinstituted under Putin so Watling's reading might not be entirely accurate. But a combination of the increasingly hybridized intermix of internal security with domestic and foreign policy, alongside the FSB's growing primacy among the "Special Services" and extension of its remit from the near abroad to further afield has become reflective of changes in Putin's Russia and his loyalty to the FSB.

There (among the FSB's other duties that include counterterrorism and counterintelligence and undermining or influencing nations), they can exploit diplomatic cover and diplomatic bags and give instructions to agent handlers alongside the SVR and GRU. This targets those hostile to Russia or nations with friendly or pro-Russian factions.[221] As a mainline or sideline, this also includes setting up safe houses, arranging dead drops, and creating shell companies and obfuscated financial structures.[222] FSB training and tradecraft development is provided through a variety of training centers, including centers in St. Petersburg, Novosibirsk, Yekaterinburg, and Nizhniy Novgorod. There are also two specialized train-

---

221 Another branch of the FSB is worthy of note, in respect to counterterrorism and counterintelligence and Russia's near abroad. This is the Service for the Defense of the Constitutional Order and Combating Terrorism (SZKSiBT). Whilst this "Second Service" has antecedents in the Soviet-era it is also designed to combat genuine and significant systematic terrorist attacks stemming from separatist movements. The SZKSiBT is as concerned with separatists, dissent and opposition groups. Domestic lawfare is used to brand and prosecute separatists, dissenters, and opposition groups who threaten regional and federal stability. An indication of this can be found in the work of two sub-organizations of the SZKSiBT. The first is designed to protect the constitutional order (UKZS), and another (closely related) for combating terrorism and political extremism (UBTPE). They have investigated ultranationalist neo-Nazi's, but they have also been mobilized against civil society groups seen as dissidents. This includes quelling politically-inspired secessionist unrest and acts of terrorism in the troubled Caucasus Republic of Ingushetia. A separate FSB sub-organization, the DVKR, is responsible for preventing foreign penetration of Russia's military and ensuring its regime loyalty. The DVKR is headed by Colonel General Nikolay Yuryev, a career military officer, who later joined military counterintelligence. Yuryev replaced Aleksandr Bezverkhniy in 2015 who had been in post since 2002 which at the time made him the longest-serving chief of military counterintelligence in Russian and Soviet history. Riehle, *The Russian FSB*, pp. 35, 38–39, 41–43, 76–78, 117, 120. Mark Galeotti, "The Law Enforcement Agencies: Russian Domestic Security and International Implications", Marshall Center Security Insights, Number 045 (February 2020), https://www.marshallcenter.org/en/publications/security-insights/law-enforcement-agencies-russian-domestic-security-and-international-implications-0. Simon Shuster, "The Russian General Who Stands to Gain Most From Wagner's Mutiny" (June 27 2023), https://time.com/6290766/zolotov-putin-prigozhin-russia-wagner/. Alec Bertina, "The Rosgvardia (National Guard of Russia): Russia's Internal Guard" (December 15 2024), https://greydynamics.com/the-rosgvardia-national-guard-of-russia-russias-internal-guard/. All accessed 29 August 2025.

222 Watling, "The Kaleidoscopic Campaigning of Russia's Special Services."

ing centers in Moscow: the Institute of Cryptography, Communications, and Informatics (IKSiL) and the Moscow Institute of New Information Technologies (MINIT).[223] The FSB and FPS (Border Guards) also operate their own dedicated aircraft. Its Aviation Directorate (UA) has its own fleet of low-noise fixed-wing aircraft and helicopters, unmanned aerial vehicles (UAVs) and dirigibles (which communicate geolocations and video footage). Most are used for the FSB's *Spetsnaz* units.

Moreover, if Russia's attempted occupation of Ukraine had succeeded the FSB would have been key to establishing the administration of the occupation. When operations do not go as planned, as in Ukraine, even senior members of the FSB can fall from favor. This happened to the aforementioned Colonel-General Sergei Beseda, the head of the FSB's "Fifth Service" through to summer 2024. His directorate was widely blamed for the over-optimistic assessments of Ukraine's willingness to assist, resist, and withstand Russia's February 2022 *blitzkrieg* (including by Russia's military leadership). Whilst publicly accused of embezzling cash out of the funds earmarked for the invasion and occupation of Ukraine, he was placed under house arrest and imprisonment before his partial rehabilitation into government service in Spring 2025.[224] Beseda was reported to be behind the attacks on the protesters in Maidan (Independence Square) and was on scene in Kyiv in 2014.[225]

The FSB also has significant domestic influence. This includes through the Investigative Committee and General Prosecutor's Office which have become tools of prosecution or protection. For those holding power and influence, the FSB is said to operate a "clan" system of patronage interlaced with protection of favored officials and businessmen. This includes protecting or prosecuting business interests (an intermix between personal aggrandizement and state ownership), and sidelines that include arms and drugs trafficking, kickbacks, and embezzlement.[226] The "clan" system also leads to intra-agency rivalries, including between the SEB and Department K.[227]

223 Riehle, *The Russian FSB*, pp. 58–60.

224 Watling, "The Kaleidoscopic Campaigning of Russia's Special Services." Riehle, *The Russian FSB*, pp. 45–48, 97, 121–122.

225 Denisova, "Who is Sergey Beseda". Contained within the FSB's "Fifth Service" is the Operational Information Department (DOI). They are primarily responsible for intelligence operations in the former Soviet states. Riehle, *The Russian FSB*, pp. 45–48, 97, 121–122.

226 Seconded or temporarily reassigned FSB officers working with other agencies or Russian firms are managed by a Seconded Personnel Section (APS) connected to SOKR. These are referred to as "APSniks". Riehle, *The Russian FSB*, pp. 56–57.

227 The Dossier Center, "Lubyanka federation".

Evident from the early 1990s (and into Soviet times), this system is stratified from the top-down in symbiosis with organized crime. This symbiosis was buttressed in 2003–4 when the FSB's "Fourth Service" for Economic Security (SEB) and its Department K (which monitors Russia's financial services sector), having first elbowed the Interior Ministry aside, replaced them in investigating organized crime and responsibility for witness protection (expanding further the FSB's longstanding portfolio). Their power was extended in the second half of the 2010s through a series of high-profile arrests of regional governors, following growing public discontent with endemic corruption since the beginning of Vladimir Putin's third term in 2012. Whilst portrayed as a fight against corruption, it was really designed to quell protests by excerpting power from the center to intimidate regional administrations.

Rather than stymie corruption, this move was instead used by the center (the Kremlin) to redistribute economic interests to dominant clans and to reward loyalty to regional elites who were rowing in behind (and politically strengthening) the federal center. This led to a mass purge of regional governors, many of whom had been arrested before. Coverage of the anti-corruption fight by pro-Kremlin media and national television stations placed the FSB in the vanguard of this fight beginning with the arrest of the regional governor of Sakhalin Island, Alexander Khoroshavin, on bribery charges in March 2015. This series of operations was largely carried out by the head of the FSB's "Sixth Service" (the Internal Security Directorate), Ivan Tkachev, and in July 2016, Tkachev was rewarded with his transfer to head the SEB's Department K.

These arrests had been planned for months with the FSB receiving their orders from above with regular show trials designed to pacify complainers and dissenters in a further demonstration of manufacturing consent. Meanwhile, Department M (a department buffeted by internecine strife) is meant to provide counterintelligence support for law enforcement agencies as "the police of the police" (Internal Affairs), instead it is right at the center of organized crime and the power struggles between clans.[228] This process has seen the FSB become a key agency working for the Putin regime whilst mirroring or reflecting earlier intelligence and state security incarnations like the Cheka, *Narodnyy Komissariat Vnutrennikh Del* (NKVD), and KGB.[229] This "chekist mindset" sees internal dissent

---

228 The Dossier Center, "Governors' Affairs" (undated), https://fsb.dossier.center/gubernators/, and The Dossier Center, "Lubyanka federation". Both accessed 28 August 2025.

229 The Dossier Center/Atlantic Council, "Lubyanka Federation How the FSB determines the politics and economics of Russia" (October 5 2020), https://www.atlanticcouncil.org/wp-content/uploads/2020/10/FSB-Report-Printed-Final.pdf, accessed 29 April 2025.

stoked from abroad, justifying internal (and external) agencies of repression, as this protects Russians from foreign threats.[230]

9 Manufacturing consent

With opposition politicians, parties, and organizations stifled and silenced, United Russia's grip on the *Duma* has tightened. In 2016 it gained 76 percent of the vote, with another landslide victory in September 2021 seeing over two-thirds support.[231] This was despite economic stagnation, high inflation, and cronyism. Consent has been manufactured through systematic and long-term suppression of opposition politicians, including jail terms for high profile opposition figures like Aleksei Navalny, buttressed by Russian state media.[232] Navalny's work included documenting cases of FSB corruption, unfavorable exposés of FSB operations (including his own attempted assassination), and a television documentary on Putin's vast wealth and how his own corruption is protected by the FSB. These have drawn millions of viewers, including many within Russia. Corruption within the FSB has also been highlighted by the website kompromat.ru. The most infamous and well known of these cases is the "Three Whales" (*Tri Kita*) but it is by no means the worst.[233] For Navalny, having had suspended sentences previously imposed on him, this was to be his final time in prison. After being recognized as a Prisoner of Conscience by Amnesty International, he died in February 2024 in a remote penal colony in the Arctic Circle in mysterious circumstances. He had made the decision to return to Russia following months of medical treatment in Germany after being poisoned with the nerve agent Novichok in August 2020.[234]

The maintenance of power has also included accusations of voter manipulation and outright fraud.[235] The extent of opposition suppression means "the num-

230 Riehle, *Russian Intelligence* pp. 56–58.

231 Shuhei Mizoguchi, "The Stability and Vulnerability of the Putin Administration in the 2021 Russian State Duma Elections," pp. 1–6. Research Group on "Russia in an Era of Great Power Competition," Japan Institute of International Affairs, www.jiia.or.jp/en/column/2022/02/02/ENG_russia-fy2021-05.pdf, accessed 18 June 2023.

232 Giles, *Moscow Rules*, pp. 127–157. Giles, *Russia's War on Everybody*, pp. 43–46.

233 Riehle, *The Russian FSB*, pp. 147–152.

234 Nadezhda Beliakova and Zhanna Timofeeva, "Religious Symbolism and Political Resistance: Navalny's Martyr Narrative in the Russian Opposition", *Religions*, Vol. 16, Issue 1 (January 2025), article 40.

235 Regina Smyth, *Elections, Protest, and Authoritarian Regime Stability: Russia 2008–2020* (Cambridge: Cambridge University Press, 2020). Regina Smyth, "Vladimir Putin plans to win Russia's parliamentary election no matter how unpopular his party is" (August 16, 2021), https://

ber of seats currently held by liberal opposition has been reduced to zero" and at home and abroad "brazenness and brutality have grown over time."[236] According to a U.S. Senate report:

> Putin's regime has harassed and killed whistleblowers and human rights activists; crafted laws to hamstring democratic institutions; honed and amplified anti-Western propaganda; curbed media that deviate from a pro-government line; beefed up internal security agencies to surveil and harass human rights activists and journalists; directed judicial prosecutions and verdicts; cultivated the loyalties of oligarchs through corrupt handouts; and ordered violent crackdowns against protesters and purported enemies. This laundry list reflects not just governance tactics in the abstract, but tangible, regrettable impacts on lives and prosperity. Some cases in point: an estimated $24 billion dollars has been amassed by Putin's inner circle through the pilfering of state resources.[237]

Russia's independent media organizations have also been systematically pressurized (or become willing participants) into adopting the Kremlin line. What remains have become propaganda outlets including the television channels RT (formerly Russia Today), Zvezda TV, REN TV, and NTV, the newspapers *Izvestiya*, *Kommersant*, and *Komsomolskaya Pravda*, and radio and online news outlets like Sputnik. These, described as "firehoses of falsehoods," are highly relevant to Chapters 3 and 4.[238] Television is the main source of news for over 80 percent of Russians, but the messaging application Telegram is also popular, especially for Russia's military blogging communities as well as for dissenters.[239]

One of a small number of influential female power holders in Putin's Russia is Margarita Simonyan; RT's editor-in-chief. Described by the U.S. State Department as one of the "main faces of propaganda and disinformation, both internationally and inside Russia … serving up lies as truths … with a smile," Simonyan and those close to her, have found this a lucrative business.[240] Those who have opposed or

---

theconversation.com/vladimir-putin-plans-to-win-russias-parliamentary-election-no-matter-how-unpopular-his-party-is-160078, accessed 18 June 2023. Edward S. Herman and Noam Chomsky, *Manufacturing Consent: The Political Economy of the Mass Media* (London: Vintage Books, 1994).

236 Putin's Asymmetric Assault, p. 15.

237 Putin's Asymmetric Assault, p. 15.

238 Christopher Paul and Miriam Matthews, "The Russian 'Firehose of Falsehood' Propaganda Model: Why It Might Work and Options to Counter It," https://www.rand.org/pubs/perspectives/PE198.html, accessed 4 July 2023, Dinara Tokbaeva, "Media Entrepreneurs and Market Dynamics: Case of Russian Media Markets," *Journal of Media Management and Entrepreneurship*, Vol. 1, Issue 1 (January–June 2019), pp. 40–56.

239 Sam Farbman, "Telegram, 'Milbloggers' and the Russian State," *Survival*, Vol. 65, No. 3 (June–July 2023), pp. 107–128. Giles, *Russia's War on Everybody*, pp. 27–59.

240 Faces of Kremlin Propaganda: Margarita Simonyan (Press Release, August 31, 2022), https://www.state.gov/disarming-disinformation/faces-of-kremlin-propaganda-margarita-simonyan/. This

investigated Russian policies and misdeeds have fared less well. According to the Committee to Protect Journalists, as of 2023, 59 Russian journalists had been killed, 7 are missing, and 19 imprisoned since 1992. Many more have left or been exiled.[241]

10 The law and policing: Living and dying in Putin's Russia

Non-governmental organizations (NGOs) campaigning for human rights and democracy face a battery of legal restrictions and freedom of assembly. Protestors against Putin's rule have faced police crackdowns.[242] The police in turn are obligated to enforce Russian law and face many problems.[243] After Putin returned to the presidency in 2012, amid a short wave of protests, laws were enacted by the *Duma* which forced Russian NGOs to register as "foreign agents" (*inostrannye agenty*). This was especially if they were in receipt of foreign funding and were engaging in activities deemed political. Registration is with the Ministry of Justice.[244] This is a situation made worse by Russia's invasion of Ukraine.[245]

Amendments to Russia's Criminal Code (Federal Law No. 32-FZ) in March 2022 criminalized disseminating "false information" about the Russian military. Henceforward, journalists are made to comply with how the Russian military describes the conflict. This is not "war" or an invasion but a "special military operation." Breaching these laws could lead to "prison terms of up to 15 years for … disseminating 'fake news' or any information that Russian authorities deemed to be

---

is part of a wider body of State Department work through its Global Engagement Center, https://www.state.gov/wp-content/uploads/2022/01/Kremlin-Funded-Media_January_update-19.pdf. Both accessed 4 July 2023. See also Bo Petersson and Emil Petersson, "Coveted, Detested and Unattainable? Images of the US Superpower Role and Self-Images of Russia in Russian Print Media Discourse," *International Journal of Cultural Studies*, Vol. 14, Issue 1 (January 2011), pp. 71–89

241 https://cpj.org/europe/russia/, accessed 4 July 2023.

242 Putin's Asymmetric Assault, pp. 18–23. "Russia Events of 2018," https://www.hrw.org/world-report/2019/country-chapters/russia; Andrew Osborn and Maria Tsvetkova, "Russian police detain over 800 in opposition crackdown in Moscow" (August 3, 2019), https://uk.reuters.com/article/uk-russia-politics-protests/russian-police-detain-over-800-in-opposition-crackdown-in-moscow-idUKKCN1US2MB. Both accessed 11 November 2019.

243 Olesya Gerasimenko, "Russia police crisis: Burned out, disappointed and demoralised" (October 1, 2023), https://www.bbc.co.uk/news/world-europe-66924404, accessed 1 October 2023.

244 Freek van der Vet, "'When They Come for You': Legal Mobilization in New Authoritarian Russia," *Law & Society Review*, Vol. 52, Issue 2 (June 2018), pp. 291–554.

245 Taras Kuzio, *Russian Nationalism and the Russian-Ukrainian War: Autocracy-Orthodoxy-Nationality* (Abingdon: Routledge, 2022).

false."[246] Roskomnadzor, Russia's media regulator, censored dozens of established media outlets on this basis. This included TV Rain, Radio Free Europe/Radio Liberty (RFE/RL), and Echo of Moscow. Others, including *Novaya Gazeta* opted to self-censor by suspending war-related reporting.[247]

These laws have led to multiple prosecutions and a further stifling or closing down of a series of independent media, anti-corruption, civic activism organizations, and independent writers or bloggers.[248] "Knowingly false information" is redefined under these amendments from information that is "objectively untrue" to that which does not conform with "Russian official sources."[249] Echoing George Orwell's novel *1984*, this also means Western organizations, including Google and Wikipedia, have been fined alongside Russian social media companies. China's TikTok also falls within these amendments.[250] In an attempt to counter the Kremlin's domestic narrative, Russian state media has been blocked in the EU. This includes Russian government-owned and pro-government media outlets including Sputnik, RT, RIA Novosti, Zvezda, and Lenta.ru and Gazeta.ru.[251]

---

246 "Understanding the laws relating to 'fake news' in Russia," https://cpj.org/wp-content/uploads/2022/07/Guide-to-Understanding-the-Laws-Relating-to-Fake-News-in-Russia.pdf, pp. 1–2, accessed 25 March 2023.

247 International Press Institute, "Will Russia's independent journalism survive the Kremlin's crackdown?" (March 10, 2022), https://ipi.media/events/will-russias-independent-journalism-survive-the-kremlins-crackdown-march-10-2022/, "One year on, Russian media survive mass repression" (March 10, 2023), https://ipi.media/ipimedia/one-year-on-russian-online-media-survive-mass-repression/. Both accessed 21 June 2023.

248 This includes "BBC Russian Service, Deutsche Welle, Radio Liberty and its regional projects, Meduza, Mediazona and others. Russian regional media outlets like TV Station TV-2 in Tomsk, Znak.com in the Urals, Pskovskaya Gubernia from Pskov and "7x7" from Syktyvkar have also been blocked. Online access to the popular radio station Echo Moskvy was blocked on 1 March, after it was taken off air and then liquidated. Some other independent media outlets, like TV Rain and Znak.com, also announced that they had to suspend their work due to censorship and restrictions. Other media, like *Novaya Gazeta,* chose to continue their work but had to delete materials covering the armed conflict in Ukraine as a precaution against possible penalties, while others like The Bell decided to explicitly state that they would stop covering the situation." EUR 46/5345/2022, https://www.amnesty.org/en/wp-content/uploads/2022/03/EUR4653452022ENGLISH.pdf, p. 3. See also Maria Lipma, "How Putin Silences Dissent Inside the Kremlin's Crackdown," *Foreign Affairs*, Vol. 95, No. 3 (May/June 2016), pp. 38–46.

249 "Understanding the laws relating to 'fake news' in Russia," pp. 3–5.

250 "Understanding the laws relating to 'fake news' in Russia," pp. 5–13.

251 EU imposes sanctions on state-owned outlets RT/Russia Today and Sputnik's broadcasting in the EU, https://www.consilium.europa.eu/en/press/press-releases/2022/03/02/eu-imposes-sanctions-on-state-owned-outlets-rt-russia-today-and-sputnik-s-broadcasting-in-the-eu/, accessed 25 March 2023.

Immediately after the March 2022 laws, Amnesty International was reporting how "Anti-war demonstrations to protest against Russia's invasion of Ukraine have been routinely dispersed, often with the use of unnecessary and excessive force." This has seen "peaceful protesters, including women, being brutally beaten by police with batons and electrocuted with stun guns, punched, kicked, dragged and otherwise ill-treated." For those taken into custody Amnesty also recorded "reports of torture or other ill-treatment of people held in some police stations ... detention in cruel, inhuman and degrading conditions, unlawful fingerprinting and photographing for a police database, confiscation of mobile phones" and delays or denials of access to lawyers.[252]

Alongside Alexei Navalny, many other opposition figures and activists have either left Russia, been imprisoned, or died. This also includes Boris Nemtsov who led protests after widespread allegations of fraud in the 2011 parliamentary elections. He worked with Navalny "to expose massive corruption schemes orchestrated by Putin and his cronies" until he was assassinated in February 2015.[253] He was shot and killed on the Bolshoy Moskvoretsky Bridge near the Kremlin two days before he was due to take part in a rally against Russia's involvement in Ukraine. He was 55.[254]

Amended treason and espionage laws in December 2022 extended the designation of "foreign agents" and "undesirable organizations." This has seen an increasing number of Russians come under investigation by the police and FSB.[255] Russia uses these authoritarian laws and the *Ministerstvo Vnutrennikh Del* (MVD, Ministry of Internal Affairs) to police domestic order. It is a system where "Police officers view themselves as a part of the state that they often personify as President Putin."[256] However, the Interior Minister is General (Police) Vladimir Kolokoltsev. Kolokoltsev is described as another "technocrat" who has been a career police officer since 1982. He replaced the unpopular KGB and FSB veteran Rashid Nurgaliev in 2012. As a "policeman's policeman" who believes in

252 EUR 46/5345/2022, p. 3.

253 Michael McFaul, "Russia's Road to Autocracy," *Journal of Democracy*, Volume 32, No. 4 (October 2021), p. 21.

254 Andre Mommen, "Boris Nemtsov, 1959–2015 The Rise and Fall of a Provincial Democrat," *Demokratizatsiya: The Journal of Post-Soviet Democratization*, Volume 24, No. 1 (Winter 2016), pp. 5–28.

255 van der Vet, ""When They Come for You"", pp. 302, 312–313, 320–329.

256 Olga Semukhina, "The Evolution of Policing in Post-Soviet Russia: Paternalism versus Service in Police Officers' Understanding of their Role," *Communist and Post-Communist Studies*, Vol. 51, Issue 3 (September 2018), p. 225. Claire Bigg, "Russian Police Force To Change Its Name, But Not Its Ways" (February 27, 2011), https://www.rferl.org/a/russia_police_change_name_not_ways/2322433.html, accessed 27 February 2020.

public order and the Rule of Law, Kolokoltsev is one of the rare leaders who seeks to police effectively and tries to stay clear of the political infighting. This is part of the reason why the MVD has seen its remit and resources reallocated to other agencies. He is aided by another so-called technocrat who has risen through the ranks, General (Justice) Igor Krasnov, the Prosecutor General. Krasnov was appointed in 2020 as part of a reshuffle, having developed a reputation for following a case wherever it leads, regardless of the political dynamics. In 2015, he was removed from the investigation of Boris Nemtsov when he began to uncover links to Chechen leader Ramzan Kadyrov.[257]

The MVD's most bitter rival is said to be the FSB, which it has consistently grown capabilities that now overlap with the MVD and Russia's other agencies with security responsibilities including those of the Federal Customs Service and Federal Drug Control Service.[258] This includes the Investigative Committee (*Sledstvennyi Komitet Rossiiskoi Federatsii*, SKRF), headed by Putin's former university classmate and close aide Alexender Bastrykin (who failed to investigate Sergei Magnitsky's alleged mistreatment and subsequent death in custody), and General Prosecutor's Office (*General'naya prokuratura Rossiiskoi Federatsii*, GPRF). Bastrykin is reliant on Putin's support for his career progression and his very survival, having burned other political bridges in his time with no political power base or other patrons. This sees Bastrykin and *Rosgvardiya's* head General Viktor Zolotov overegging the scale and nature of domestic opposition and color revolutionary threats. Like many others in positions of power, both are close in age to Putin, and this might well portend generational change at some point.[259]

---

257 Mark Galeotti, "The Law Enforcement Agencies". Maxim Solopov, "'An investigation loves silence' What little we know about Igor Krasnov, Russia's next attorney general" (January 20 2020), https://meduza.io/en/feature/2020/01/21/an-investigation-loves-silence., accessed 23 August 2025.

258 Riehle, *The Russian FSB*, pp. 54–56, 71–73, 106–107. Zolotov is one of Putin's longtime bodyguards and a regime loyalist who in 2018 publicly threated to pound Alexei Navalny into a "juicy slab of meat" having previously challenged him to a dual. His rise to power began in the KGB before his transfer to the Federal Protection Service where he became a close-protection officer to President Yeltsin and then Putin. He received praise from Putin for defending Moscow during Prigozhin's rebellion whilst trumpeting the well-established line that it had been orchestrated by the West. Galeotti, "The Law Enforcement Agencies". Shuster, "The Russian General Who Stands to Gain Most".

259 The SKRF was part of the GPRF and tasked with investigating serious crimes and inspecting government agencies. In 2011 it was made a stand-alone agency in what was generally regarded as a power grab by Bastrykin with the GPRF taking on prosecutions and preliminary investigations with the Prosecutor General (a very generalized equivalent of the U.S. Attorney General). Mark Galeotti, "The Law Enforcement Agencies". "Alexander Bastrykin Head of Russia's Investigative

Regime stability, including the ability to quell protests, is also tasked to the National Guard (*Rosgvardiya*) created in 2016. Drawn from the MVDs approximate ranks of 1.4 million police, *Rosgvardiya* is estimated to number 320,000–430,000. This includes the "Interior Troops, all OMON[260] (riot police) and SOBR[261] (SWAT) units, and several special units." As with *Rosgvardiya*, the MVD is led by Viktor Zolotov, who previously headed the presidential bodyguard, an elite Presidential Regiment of 5,500 personnel with its own dedicated intelligence unit (a unit of the FSO), and is former KGB.[262] The MVD, like Russia's armed forces, centrally directs policing from Moscow, and MVD officials and serving police officers continue to be implicated in protection rackets.[263]

This has seen the police and judiciary mete out sentences against political opponents of the Kremlin. Any cases against law enforcement personnel and state officials are treated leniently or never reach court. Instead, most potential criminal cases against these groups or those further up the system remain almost immune from the scrutiny of the criminal justice system aided by shoddy and under-resourced policing. The majority of cases instead affect those towards the bottom rungs of Russian society. Sometimes police and judiciary work with the FSB, Russia's domestic intelligence agency which increasingly has a growing footprint at home and abroad.[264]

Whilst *Rosgvardiya's* primary responsibility is to preserve public order and regime security, it also takes part in Russia's military exercises as a rear guard, sometimes described as a "Praetorian Guard".[265] In this role it is deployed in exercises against imagined foreign special forces aiding domestic "insurgents" bent on separatism or Color Revolutionary regime change. In this light this could be why *Rosgvardiya* are also suspected of running double-agents. It too has its own Spetsnaz unit. In addition, they are publicly tasked with rooting out corruption

---

Committee" (undated), https://www.occrp.org/interactives/russian-asset-tracker/en/person/15/alexander-bastrykin. Both accessed 23 August 2025.

260 *Otryad Mobil'niy Osobogo Naznacheniya*, Special Purpose Mobile Unit.

261 *Spetsial'niy Otryad Bystrovo Reagirovaniya*, Special Quick Response Unit.

262 Meakins, "Squabbling Siloviki," pp. 238–240.

263 Serguei Cheloukhine, Nesibeli Kalkayeva, Tima Khvedelidze, and A. R. Bizhanova, "Corruption in Russian Law Enforcement," *Communist and Post-Communist Studies*, Vol. 53, No. 1 (March 2020), pp. 117–134.

264 Ella Paneyakh, "Faking Performance Together: Systems of Performance Evaluation in Russian Enforcement Agencies and Production of Bias and Privilege," *Post-Soviet Affairs*, Vol. 30, Nos. 2–3 (March 2014), pp. 115–136. It has also become also the main point of liaison with the security services of Russia's friends and allies. Riehle, *The Russian FSB*, p. 2.

265 Meakins, "Squabbling Siloviki", p. 238. Mark Galeotti, *Russian Security, and Paramilitary Forces since 1991* (Osprey, 2013), p. 3.

in the defense industry and military as well as investigating the narcotics trade, organized crime and corruption, the illegal arms trade, and "illegal military formations" such as Prigozhin's (including domestic terrorism and coup attempts). Clearly, these responsibilities overlap with the MVD, and organizational units of the FSB but this is by-design. This too reflects the engineered competition and rivalry that characterizes Russia's security services.[266]

To a large extent Russia's legal system and policing within Russia are used by the Kremlin as tools of power and system maintenance with primacy accorded to state interests and those of its power holders. This has seen especially strong connections develop between domestic law enforcement and external security.[267] The FSB operates throughout Russia enforcing Russian law whilst conducting physical and electronic surveillance with few restraints.[268] Internal conflict and rivalry between Russia's powerful security services are seen by Putin as a way to maintain a balance of power between them and to prevent any one agency and its leadership becoming too powerful. In playing them off against one another, confrontation is seen "not an unwanted by-product of corruption but an essential element of Putin's rule".[269]

11 The scale and use of Russian mis and disinformation

Externally, Russian disinformation campaigns in Europe are, according to a 2018 U.S. Committee on Foreign Relations report, seen in a wide number of semi-consolidated democracies and transitional governments.[270] This includes Ukraine.[271] These campaigns stretch to many other areas of their near abroad. These include the former Soviet or Warsaw Pact states of Georgia, Montenegro, Serbia, Bulgaria, and Hungary, and many others in central Asia and Transcaucasia. Russian intelligence and proxy organizations have also been active in consolidated democracies including the former Soviet-ruled Baltic states of Estonia, Latvia, and Lithua-

266 Galeotti, "The Law Enforcement Agencies", Shuster, "The Russian General Who Stands to Gain Most". Bertina, "The Rosgvardia". Riehle, The Russian FSB, pp. 41–43, 76–78.]
267 Galeotti, "The Law Enforcement Agencies".
268 Riehle, *The Russian FSB*, p. 1.
269 Meakins, "Squabbling Siloviki", p. 238.
270 Putin's Asymmetric Assault, pp. 65–97.
271 Putin's Asymmetric Assault, pp. 67–72. Council of the EU Press release 28 July 2023, Information manipulation in Russia's war of aggression against Ukraine: EU lists seven individuals and five entities – Consilium, https://www.consilium.europa.eu/en/press/press-releases/2023/07/28/information-manipulation-in-russia-s-war-of-aggression-against-ukraine-eu-lists-seven-individuals-and-five-entities/, accessed 29 July 2023.

nia, the Nordic states of Sweden, Denmark, Norway, and Finland, and The Netherlands. They have also been active in the five largest Western European states – the United Kingdom, France, Germany, Spain, and Italy. Since 2004, at least 27 European and North American countries have experienced Russian influence campaigns.[272]

According to a UK parliamentary Select Committee report at least ten African countries have seen non-military interventions, including disinformation campaigns. This includes Burkina Faso, Cameroon, Chad, Democratic Republic of the Congo, Madagascar, South Africa, Zambia, and Zimbabwe. Outside Africa, it includes Afghanistan and Serbia.[273] Russia has also funded majority buy-outs of local news outlets which then air pro-Russian content.[274] In Africa, Russia's interventions have propped up authoritarian regimes and led to "atrocities, corruption and the plunder of natural resources."[275] In addition, disinformation and propaganda campaigns have been seen as far afield as South Africa and India. It is a global operation. In particular, the Internet Research Agency (IRA), a "private" firm often described as a "troll farm" based in St. Petersburg run by Yevgeny Prigozhin (who subsequently found fame and notoriety as head of the Wagner Group), was being employed by the Kremlin as a proxy actor.[276]

Under Putin, the security services, Russia's mainstream media, public and private companies, organized criminal groups, as well as religious organizations have spread purposeful disinformation, sown distrust in state institutions, fueled corruption, threatened energy security, and most importantly interfered in elections. They have also been used to discredit domestic and foreign opposition. They have also tried to discredit investigations into systematic Russian doping in sport by the World Anti-Doping Agency (WADA) and created false narratives around Russia's political assassinations. All the while Russian cybercriminals have been protected

272 Putin's Asymmetric Assault, pp. 65–97, 99–139.
273 House of Commons Foreign Affairs Committee, Guns for gold: The Wagner Network exposed, Seventh Report of Session 2022–23, 18 July 2023, pp. 9–16, 69–70, 74–75, https://committees.parliament.uk/publications/41073/documents/200048/default/. See also Guns for gold: the Wagner Network exposed, https://committees.parliament.uk/committee/78/foreign-affairs-committee/news/196695/guns-for-gold-the-wagner-network-exposed/. Both accessed 26 July 2023.
274 Elena Cryst, "Stoking Conflict by Keystroke" (December 15, 2020), https://cyber.fsi.stanford.edu/io/news/africa-takedown-december-2020, accessed 11 November 2020.
275 This has included the alleged murder of investigative journalists in these conflict zones. Guns for gold, pp. 3, 6.
276 UK exposes sick Russian troll factory plaguing social media with Kremlin propaganda (May 1, 2022), https://www.gov.uk/government/news/uk-exposes-sick-russian-troll-factory-plaguing-social-media-with-kremlin-propaganda, accessed 11 November 2023.

and exploited.[277] This has been used to undermine states and international organizations, combined with a thin veil of plausibly deniability, beginning with the coordinated denial-of-service attacks against Estonia in 2007 (described by some as the first cyberwar).[278] These have measurable objectives and effects.

This includes the use, *en masse*, of trolls and automated botnets (bots) on the Internet to sow and spread mis and disinformation. It includes "false reports in genuine media outlets."[279] Bots are then used by groups with fake accounts to promote, like, and post content in sync.[280] This strategy is set in the context of "Russia's long-standing, overall foreign policy objective ... to weaken adversaries, particularly countries on its periphery, those in NATO, and the United States, by any means available" including using "information warfare" to target "social cohesion and political systems."[281] NATO itself is also a target.[282] Their use, combined with military interventions in Ukraine and Syria (Russia's first major foray outside of its near abroad) are "examples of Russia implementing its long-standing intent to challenge the West" when it felt "strong enough to do so."[283]

Information warfare forms one of the elements of Russian active measures and its foreign and security policy and plays its part in suppressing domestic opposition. These are designed to obscure realities or confuse the target. For David Gioe, these combinations of information warfare, hacking, and use of agents of influence (*agent vliyaniya*) is better conceived as hybrid intelligence than hybrid warfare with its basis in intelligence-led active measures.[284] However, for nations

---

277 Putin's Asymmetric Assault, pp. 1, 38, 65–140, 171–179.

278 Eneken Tikk, Kadri Kaska and Liis Vihul, International Cyber Incidents: Legal Considerations, NATO Cooperative Cyber Defence Centre of Excellence, 2010, https://ccdcoe.org/sites/default/files/multimedia/pdf/legalconsiderations_0.pdf, accessed 15 August 2017.

279 Keir Giles, "Countering Russian Information Operations in the Age of Social Media" (November 21, 2017), https://www.cfr.org/report/countering-russian-information-operations-age-social-media; Anonymous, "How Russian bots appear in your timeline" (November 14, 2017), https://www.bbc.co.uk/news/technology-41982569, both accessed 25 October 2019.

280 Bob Abeshouse, "Troll factories, bots and fake news: Inside the Wild West of social media" (February 8, 2018), https://www.aljazeera.com/blogs/americas/2018/02/troll-factories-bots-fake-news-wild-west-social-media-180207061815575.html, accessed 12 November 2019.

281 Giles, "Countering Russian Information Operations."

282 Veronika Špalková, "Influence of Russian disinformation operation: Specific examples in data and numbers," Kremlin Watch Program (2018), p. 15, https://www.europeanvalues.net/wp-content/uploads/2019/02/Influence-of-Russian-Disinformation-Operations-Specific-examples-in-data-and-numbers.pdf, accessed 4 November 2019.

283 Keir Giles, "Russia's 'New' Tools for Confronting the West: Continuity and Innovation in Moscow's Exercise of Power" (March 2016), p. 3, https://www.chathamhouse.org/sites/default/files/publications/2016-03-russia-new-tools-giles.pdf, accessed 26 October 2019).

284 Gioe, "Cyber Operations and Useful Fools," p. 955.

like Ukraine that have experienced Russian military (as well as non-military) intervention, how we conceptualize and potentially counter Russian actions and activities matters much less than the reality and outcomes.

12 Human Rights violations and the Law of Armed Conflict

Having withdrawn from the Council of Europe on March 15, 2022, Europe's primary human rights organization, Russia was suspended from the UN's Human Rights Council following a vote called in the UN General Assembly (UNGA) through a special emergency session on the war in Ukraine. This followed reports of human rights violations committed by Russian forces in Ukraine. The UNGA was told this included, "disturbing photos ... from the city of Bucha" where "hundreds of civilian bodies were found in the streets and in mass graves following Russia's withdrawal from the area."[285]

Forced deportations (as well as offers of sanctuary to those fleeing the war) to Russia from Ukrainian regions (oblasts) controlled or occupied by Russian forces administered by Russian-affiliated officials, were also reported by Human Rights Watch (HRW). According to HRW, these are violations of the Law of Armed Conflict (LOAC) "amounting to a war crime and a potential crime against humanity."[286] Amnesty International's 2022/23 report also lists human rights cases within Russia resulting in restrictions on freedom of expression, assembly, and association. Amnesty also listed domestic cases of torture and other ill-treatment, enforced disappearances, unfair trials, and further clampdowns on "non-traditional sexual relations" aimed at the LGTBQ community (as well as deportations from Eastern Ukraine).[287] Russia disputes and denies these as false claims or disinformation designed to discredit Russia's military.[288]

---

285 UN General Assembly votes to suspend Russia from the Human Rights Council (April 7, 2022), https://news.un.org/en/story/2022/04/1115782, accessed 21 June 2023.

286 Human Rights Watch, "We Had No Choice." "Filtration" and the Crime of Forcibly Transferring Ukrainian Civilians to Russia (September 1, 2022), https://www.hrw.org/report/2022/09/01/we-had-no-choice/filtration-and-crime-forcibly-transferring-ukrainian-civilians, accessed 22 June 2023.

287 Amnesty International, The State of the World's Human Rights Report 2022/23, pp. 307–312, https://www.amnesty.org/en/documents/pol10/5670/2023/en/, accessed 21 June 2023.

288 Jade McGlynn and Ian Garner, "Russia's War Crime Denials Are Fuel for More Atrocities. In Moscow's myths, Russia is always the victim" (April 23, 2022), https://foreignpolicy.com/2022/04/23/propaganda-russia-atrocity-bucha/. "Ukraine: Apparent War Crimes in Russia-Controlled Areas Summary Executions, Other Grave Abuses by Russian Forces" (April 3, 2022), https://www.hrw.org/

13 Russia's armed forces

Russia's armed forces numbered around 881,000 personnel prior to the Ukraine war. There were 394,000 regular contract soldiers, 267,000 conscripts (serving 12 months), and 220,000 officers.[289] In October 2022, 300,000 additional reservists were ordered to be conscripted. On hearing the news, many fled to neighboring states. Many others could not leave but did not want to serve.[290] 185,000 have enlisted. 109,000 of these are in the reserve with the remaining 76,000 contract soldiers enlisted to make up for manpower losses in Ukraine.[291] Russia is believed to have seen half of its pre-war land forces destroyed, degraded, or depleted in Ukraine.[292] More conscriptions are planned. June 2025 estimates indicate Russia has around 15,000 tanks (some of Cold War vintage) in various conditions of combat readiness, but which have experienced significant losses in Ukraine. They also possess 6,000 artillery pieces and 1,500 combat aircraft. As Russia is operating a war economy and actively engaged in Ukraine at the time of writing, these numbers are subject to active change.[293]

Early on Russian forces invading south from Belarus towards Kyiv were soon bogged down by Ukrainian guerrilla attacks, further hampered by poor logistical support. Even when they occupied Hostomel Airport, rather than it becoming a key staging post pointing towards Kyiv and a base to resupply and land Russian aircraft it instead became isolated. This made it a target, not the intended beachhead. Close-air support also proved problematic with Russian pilots forced to conduct low-level sorties making them vulnerable to man-portable surface-to-air missiles aided by Ukraine's (much more limited) air force. They have also lost aircraft

---

news/2022/04/03/ukraine-apparent-war-crimes-russia-controlled-areas. Both accessed 1 October 2023.

289 Johan Norberg, Ismail Khan, and Jonas Kjellén, "Attrition and Regeneration: Russia's Armed Forces at War," in Maria Engqvist and Emil Wannheden (eds.), Russia's War Against Ukraine and the West: The First Year, Swedish Defence Research Agency, FOI-R–5479–SE June 2023, pp. 65–76, https://www.foi.se/en/foi/reports/report-summary.html?reportNo=FOI-R--5479--SE, accessed 9 July 2023.

290 Anonymous, "Russia's Medvedev: 185,000 new contract soldiers have joined armed forces this year" (July 4, 2023), https://www.reuters.com/world/europe/russias-medvedev-185000-new-contract-soldiers-have-joined-armed-forces-this-year-2023-07-04/, accessed 10 July 2023.

291 Anonymous, "Russia's Medvedev: 185,000 new contract soldiers."

292 Hans M. Kristensen, Matt Korda, and Eliana Reynolds, "Russian Nuclear Weapons, 2023," *Bulletin of the Atomic Scientists*, Vol. 79, No. 3 (May 2023), p. 175.

293 Molly Carlough and Benjamin Harris, "Comparing the Size and Capabilities of the Russian and Ukrainian Militaries" (June 3 2025), https://www.cfr.org/in-brief/comparing-size-and-capabilities-russian-and-ukrainian-militaries, accessed 19 August 2025.

through Western-supplied anti-aircraft and air defense systems. Russian tanks fared little better. Over 500 were destroyed in these early stages, amounting to 20 percent of their mobilized armor inventory.[294] More losses of armor and tens (potentially hundreds) of thousands of combat troops have followed in what has been described as a "meat grinder".[295]

Russia's navy has had a more limited role but through its Black Sea Fleet it has engaged southern targets in Ukraine surged from its main base of Sevastopol in Crimea. Once an important construction base for large naval vessels, when Ukraine ceded from the Soviet Union and became independent again in 1991, Russia's capacity to build, maintain, and modernize its Black Sea Fleet was greatly diminished. Although Russia had negotiated naval basing rights in Crimea prior to the 2022 invasion, this is one of the reasons why Russia tried to seize Mykolaiv and cities along the Black Sea from Kherson to Odessa in the early months of the invasion in February-March 2022. Repelling these attacks in the land battles that followed also involved (eventually) neutralizing Russian naval attacks in order to limit missile strikes from the Black Sea to the south and to forestall or defeat amphibious and airborne landings. This included the recapture of Kherson in November 2022 and the staging ground on Snake Island in June 2022. In January 2025, following the collapse of the Assad regime, Russia also lost basing rights in Tartus, Syria and was forced to withdraw.[296] It was also strangling civilian shipments of Ukrainian grain until agreement was brokered by Turkey.[297] In between it also lost the flagship of the Black Sea Fleet, the *Moskva*, in April 2022.[298]

In December 2015, it was estimated that the Russian navy had 160 surface vessels and 58 submarines. Numbers will vary over time and not all are optional at the same time. They are divided between the Northern Fleet, Baltic Fleet, Black Sea Fleet, the Pacific Fleet, and the Caspian Flotilla.[299] Russia's surface vessels include nuclear-powered Kirov-class cruisers, Gorshkov-class frigates, and a single

294 Dalsjö, Jonsson, and Norberg, "A Brutal Examination," pp. 7–28.
295 Russia's defense ministry declines to provide figures of combat losses.
296 Andrew Latham, "The Russian Navy Is a Spent Force" (April 1 2025), https://www.19fortyfive.com/2025/04/the-russian-navy-is-a-spent-force/, accessed 18 August 2025.
297 The Black Sea Grain Initiative: What it is, and why it's important for the world (September 16, 2022), https://news.un.org/en/story/2022/09/1126811, accessed 10 July 2023.
298 Kristensen, Korda, and Reynolds, "Russian Nuclear Weapons," p. 175.
299 Office of Naval Intelligence, The Russian Navy: A Historic Transition, December 2015, xiii, https://www.oni.navy.mil/Portals/12/Intel%20agencies/russia/Russia%202015print.pdf?ver=2015-12-14-082038-923, accessed 9 July 2023.

aircraft carrier, the *Admiral Kuznetsov.*[300] Although China is catching fast, Russia's total submarine fleet (including those undergoing repairs or upgrades) is second only to the United States in size and capabilities with 64 submarines in its inventory (like all navies seagoing vessels have to port periodically for refit and crew changes).[301] Its submarine fleet consists of 11 nuclear-powered ballistic missile submarines (SSBNs); 17 nuclear-powered attack submarines (SSNs); 21 diesel-electric attack submarines (SSKs); and 9 nuclear-powered cruise missile submarines (SSGNs).

Among its fleet of fast-attack SSNs (hunter-killers) is the advanced nuclear-powered Yasen-class (Project 885-M), upgraded Antey-class (Oscar II) carrying cruise missiles including the much-vaunted Kalibr alongside Tsakara, Vodopad and Granit anti-ship cruise missiles, Schuka-B (Project 971) and Sierra classes (Project 945 and Project 945 A/Sierra I and II), and conventional diesel-electric Kilo-class (Project 877 and updated Project 636) submarines. The diesel-electric fleet is armed with anti-ship, anti-submarine, and land attack cruise missiles (LACMs) as well as torpedoes. During their patrols they have intelligence gathering and espionage missions that form part of Russia's capabilities to conduct active measures/hybrid warfare. Russia's submarine fleet remains both capable and useful (including against undersea cables and other sea-lines-of-communication, interdiction, and for escort duties), even as Russia is engaged in the biggest land war Europe has seen since WWII.[302] Whilst Russia no longer possesses the blue water capabilities of the Soviet era, the Northern fleet remains potent enough to exploit or contest the climate-effected Arctic region.[303]

The Russian Federation inherited an aging fleet from the Soviet Union. Modernization was long overdue, but this has been beset by delays. This includes delays to the Borei-class replacements for Russia's massive Delta IV Typhoon-class SSBNs (two new Borei-K-class submarines are also capable of carrying cruise missiles). Two are operational with the second Borei-class ship, the *Generalissimo Suvorov*, entering service in the Northern Fleet in late 2022. Meanwhile, their Antey-class SSGN submarines have had their service life extended by 20 years but are planned to be fitted with new "Kalibr" cruise missiles. "Kalibr" are dual-capable

---

300 Sidharth Kaushal, "The Death of Gorshkov's Navy: The Future of the Russian Surface Fleet" (June 1, 2022), https://www.rusi.org/explore-our-research/publications/commentary/death-gorshkovs-navy-future-russian-surface-fleet, accessed 9 July 2023.

301 One, the *Chelyabinsk*, has been out of service for over fifteen years.

302 Brent M. Eastwood, "Russia's Nuclear Submarine Fleet Explained In 4 Simple Words" (March 13 2025), https://www.19fortyfive.com/2025/03/russias-nuclear-submarine-fleet-explained-in-4-simple-words/, accessed 18 August 2025.

303 Latham, "The Russian Navy Is a Spent Force".

meaning they can carry either nuclear or conventional warheads, however just a single Antey-class has seen this upgrade (the *Irkutsk*). In this modernization program is the Project 9852 *Belgorod* and sister-ship, the Project 09851 *Khabarovsk*. These submarines are designed to carry Russia's much vaunted long-range nuclear-powered torpedo, the Status-6 "Poseidon"/"Kanyon." This is designed to generate a radioactive tsunami and, alongside their hypersonic sea-launched "Kalibr," has been publicly trumpeted as part of Russian nuclear saber-rattling.[304]

Another hypersonic missile, and another Russia proclaims to be undefendable, is the "Kinzhal." It too is dual-capable and air-launched. It has an estimated range of 1,500–2,000 km and although primarily designed to hit land targets, it might also be envisaged as an anti-ship missile. As a hypersonic missile, it might be possible to reach Mach 10. This high Mach speed combined with an erratic flight path and maneuverability makes it difficult to defend against in theory, including by ship-borne defenses. It is believed to be carried by a squadron of MiG-31K "Foxhounds" (the first of the Soviet Union's fourth-generation aircraft, which entered service in 1981). "Kinzhals" were first used in combat to attack a munitions depot near the town of Deliatyn in southwestern Ukraine in March 2022.[305] Over most of Ukraine however, Russia has failed to achieve air superiority let alone air dominance, or the suppression of Ukrainian air defenses. Instead, Russian air power has been labeled a Potemkin Village (a façade intended to impress but with nothing behind it).[306] Similar comparisons have been made of Russian armed forces more widely.

Putin and his supporters have consistently projected an image of military readiness and modernization across its spectrum of capabilities in official announcements and information, buttressed by Russian state media and displays in Red Square. However, there is a discrepancy between claims made and the reality (a reality evident in Ukraine). Weapons, including the new Armata main battle tanks and fifth-generation Su-57 "Felon" multirole aircraft, have both been beset by delays into operational service.[307] As stocks of modern weapons have been depleted, Russia has resorted to firing repurposed anti-ship missiles at

304 Kristensen, Korda, and Reynolds, "Russian Nuclear Weapons," pp. 174–199.
305 "Kh-47M2 Kinzhal" (updated March 19, 2022), https://missilethreat.csis.org/missile/kinzhal/, accessed 9 July 2023.
306 Sean M. Wiswesser, "Potemkin on the Dnieper: The Failure of Russian Airpower in the Ukraine War," *Small Wars & Insurgencies*, Vol. 34, Issue 7 (November 2023), pp. 1205–1234.
307 Siemon T. Wezeman, "Russia's military spending: Frequently asked questions" (April 27, 2020), https://www.sipri.org/commentary/topical-backgrounder/2020/russias-military-spending-frequently-asked-questions, accessed 9 July 2023.

ground targets and have been dipping into their stockpiles of Cold War-era cruise missiles as the war in Ukraine drags on.[308]

As of early 2025, the Russians were reported to have had seen around 8,000 tanks and armored vehicles destroyed or damaged in 2023 and 2024 (mainly by coordinated and adaptive drone attacks and counter-battery fire).[309] This included armored personnel carriers and artillery pieces, whilst also experiencing a shortage of spare parts. This saw Russia refurbish and deploy Cold War-era stocks whilst trying to ramp up production of new equipment. The International Institute of Strategic Studies estimated in February 2025 the number destroyed included around 1,400 main battle tanks (approximately four divisions), and around 3,700 infantry fighting vehicles (and still more armored personnel carriers). Even by dipping into Soviet-era stocks like the T-72 main battle tank, there is ever diminishing availability with what remained of existing Cold War-era and current stocks likely only fit for cannibalization to repair existing equipment. Burning through field equipment of this type and at this rate saw Russia adapt its tactics. Without this change, it was estimated by the IISS and Institute for the Study of War that this rate of losses could only be sustained until February 2026/7.[310]

Prior to the invasion, Ukraine's inclusion into Russia's "sphere of influence" and commitments to never join NATO or the EU were the primary goals. Despite its many successes, when they could not accomplish this through hybrid warfare (including the malicious use of cyberspace for cyberespionage and active measures campaigns) Putin may have seen the chance to stamp his mark on Russian history. Whether characterized as a "hot peace," non-linear war, a new Cold War, or a "gray zone" between war and peace, in this and other operations, the use and perceived usefulness of Russia's intelligence organizations for politico-military ends would have been familiar to those who lived through the Soviet-era.

---

308 Kristensen, Korda, and Reynolds, "Russian Nuclear Weapons," p. 175. A different take on Russian military strength and capabilities can be found in Giles, *Russia's War on Everybody*, pp. 103–110.

309 Russia's embrace of drone technology, including for Information, Surveillance, and Reconnaissance (ISR) was also in earlier evidence in Syria for situational awareness and real-time targeting. Riehle, *Russian Intelligence*, p. 173.

310 Christina Harward, "Russia's Weakness Offers Leverage" (February 19 2025), https://understandingwar.org/backgrounder/russias-weakness-offers-leverage, accessed 27 July 2025.

14 Conventional overmatch: From the "gray zone" to the "red zone" and Russian nuclear threats

Russia is overmatched by the West in every category of power, except nuclear weapons and in its uses of cyberespionage and cyber influence campaigns as a force multiplying, extremely potent, and cost-effective facet of modern hybrid warfare.[311] Most importantly, Russia remains a nuclear superpower. Under the New Strategic Arms Reduction Treaty (New START) of 2010, it is treaty bound not to deploy more than 1,550 strategic warheads. Its nonstrategic stockpile is estimated at 1,816 warheads.[312] These are often referred to as tactical, although as the former West German Chancellor Helmut Schmidt once articulated: "any 'tactical' or 'so-called battlefield' nuclear which hits people of German soil for the German nation is a strategic event."[313] Russian noncompliance with New START began in April 2020, during the COVID-19 pandemic, when they first refused to allow on-site inspections on health grounds. These are a bedrock of the treaty and why "trust but verify" is a mantra in the arms control community. Russian grievances relating to Western arming of Ukraine following sanctions were catalytic contributors for Russia to "suspend participation" in New START in February 2023 whilst technically remaining treaty compliant.[314]

When Russia invaded Ukraine exactly a year before, nuclear signaling was used in an attempt to deter the United States and NATO from intervening in Ukraine. Announcing the "special military operation," Putin asserted "no matter who tries to stand in our way or … create threats for our country and our people, they must know that Russia will respond immediately, and the consequences will be such as you have never seen in your entire history." Putin ominously added, "We are ready for any development of events. All necessary decisions in this regard have been made. I hope that I will be heard."[315] He then turned to Defense Minister, Sergey Shoigu, and Chief of the General Staff, Valerii Gerasimov and pub-

---

311 Andrew S. Bowen, Russian Armed Forces: Capabilities (June 30, 2020), https://crsreports.congress.gov/product/details?prodcode=IF11589, accessed 9 July 2023.

312 Russia also has around 1,400 retired but intact warheads waiting to be dismantled. This brings their total inventory to approximately 5,889 operationally deployable warheads. Kristensen, Korda, and Reynolds, "Russian Nuclear Weapons," p. 175.

313 "War and Peace in the Nuclear Age; Zero Hour; Interview with Helmut Schmidt, 1987," https://openvault.wgbh.org/catalog/V_55D8B7AC02BD4D7CA6D1E705F68A0604, accessed 10 July 2023.

314 Kristensen, Korda, and Reynolds, "Russian Nuclear Weapons," pp. 176–177.

315 Address by the President of the Russian Federation, February 24, 2022, http://en.kremlin.ru/events/president/news/67843, accessed 10 July 2023.

licly ordered them to place Russia's "deterrence forces" on "high combat alert."[316] In September 2022, he repeated "that the territorial integrity of our Motherland, our independence and freedom will be defended – I repeat – by all the systems available to us ... This is not a bluff."[317]

Whilst nuclear signaling/saber rattling is part of Russia's hybrid warfare strategy, any potential use of nuclear weapons (with the attendant risks of miscalculation and nuclear escalation) focuses minds.[318] It did not deter Western support for Ukraine; but it does raise concerns, and gives room for pause. It also helps explain why support has not been full-throated.[319] This included baulking at an initial supply of tanks and heavy armor and slow-moving support in response to Ukrainian calls for fourth generation F-16 multirole aircraft with the risk of escalation.[320] This is also why discussion of politico-military off-ramps, de-risking, and not backing Russia into a corner, has been prominent in Western debates.[321] Rose Gottemoeller, the chief U.S. negotiator for New START, warned in October 2022 of the potential Putin might "strike back ... in really unpredictable ways that may even involve weapons of mass destruction" including "a nuclear demonstration strike."[322]

Nuclear "saber rattling" also concerned UN Secretary General, António Guterres. In June 2022, he warned that "the once unthinkable prospect of nuclear conflict is now back within the realm of possibility."[323] In September 2022 Guterres

---

316 Anna Clara Arndt and Liviu Horovitz, "Nuclear rhetoric and escalation management in Russia's war against Ukraine: A Chronology," German Institute for International and Security Affairs, WP NR. 03, September 2022, p. 15. https://www.swp-berlin.org/publications/products/arbeitspapiere/Arndt-Horovitz_Working-Paper_Nuclear_rhetoric_and_escalation_management_in_Russia_s_war_against_Ukraine.pdf. See also Putin orders nuclear forces on high alert | AFP (February 27, 2023), https://www.youtube.com/watch?v=R4y_y84nVDO, accessed 19 July 2023.

317 Transcripts President Events President of Russia, September 21, 2022, http://en.kremlin.ru/events/president/transcripts/statements, accessed 19 July 2023.

318 Arndt and Horovitz, "Nuclear rhetoric and escalation management in Russia's war against Ukraine."

319 This is one of the main themes of Keir Giles' *Who Will Defend Europe? An Awakened Russia and a Sleeping Continent* (London: Hurst, 2024) and why this emboldens Russia.

320 Mary Chesnut, "US/NATO-Russian Strategic Stability and the War in Ukraine," CNA Occasional Paper, Russian Studies Program (June 2023), https://www.cna.org/reports/2023/06/US-NATO-Russian-Strategic-Stability-in-Ukraine.pdf, accessed 10 July 2023.

321 Manpreet Sethi, "Nuclear Overtones in the Russia-Ukraine War," *Arms Control Today*, Vol. 52, Issue 5 (June 2022), pp. 12–15.

322 Carol Giacomo and Shannon Bugos, "Putin Calls Up Reservists, Renews Nuclear Threat," *Arms Control Today*, Vol. 52, Issue 8, (October 2022), pp. 28–29.

323 Eliminate nuclear weapons before they eliminate us: UN chief (June 21, 2022), https://news.un.org/en/story/2022/06/1120932, accessed 10 July 2023.

cautioned the General Assembly that "The era of nuclear blackmail must end. The idea that any country could fight and win a nuclear war is deranged. Any use of a nuclear weapon would incite a humanitarian Armageddon. We need to step back."[324] Later that same month President Zelenskyy announced Ukraine's intention to apply for "fast-track" NATO membership. This saw Alexander Venediktov, the deputy secretary of Russia's Security Council, to warn: "Kyiv is well aware that such a step would mean a guaranteed escalation to World War Three. The suicidal nature of such a step is understood by NATO members themselves."[325]

To up the ante, former president Dmitry Medvedev, now deputy chief of Russia's Security Council, publicly suggested the "annexed territories" of Crimea and the Donbas also now fall beneath Russia's nuclear umbrella through extended deterrence. This is despite knowing that these annexations are not recognized under international law.[326] In March 2023, Guterres stated in Kyiv: "The position of the United Nations, which I have consistently expressed, is crystal clear: Russia's invasion of Ukraine is a violation of the UN Charter and international law."[327] From Crimea in 2014 through to the recognition of the self-declared breakaway regions of Donetsk and Luhansk (the DPR and LPR), Russia has driven a coach and horses through the UN Charter, alongside constructed pretexts and denials.[328] Through to February 2022 it did this mainly through hybrid warfare and active measures. When it invaded it moved from the "gray zone" into the "red zone" of armed conflict. Unlike in Crimea, where in 2014 it employed "little green men" without insignias to mask direct military involvement, it did so through a massive deployment of uniformed Russian armed forces.[329]

---

324 UN chief calls for an end to 'nuclear blackmail' and risk of 'humanitarian Armageddon' (September 26, 2022), https://news.un.org/en/story/2022/09/1127961, accessed 10 July 2023.

325 Chesnut, "US/NATO-Russian Strategic Stability and the War in Ukraine," p. 15.

326 Chesnut, "US/NATO-Russian Strategic Stability and the War in Ukraine," pp. 14–16.

327 https://www.un.org/sg/en/content/sg/press-encounter/2023-03-08/secretary-generals-press-encounter-kyiv-ukraine-delivered, accessed 20 March 2023.

328 Roy Allison, "Russian 'Deniable' Intervention in Ukraine," *International Affairs*, Vol. 90, Issue 6 (November 2014), pp. 1260–1263, 1266, 1286.

329 Ukrainian sources suggest the FSB's Organizational and Personnel Service (SOKR) or "Sixth Service" was responsible for contracting, arming, and administering Russian mercenaries recruited from 2014 by FSB offices across Russia. From over 25 Russian regions, 3,300 mercenaries were recruited just from August-December 2014. Riehle, *The Russian FSB*, p. 56.

15 Book structure

Much of the work of the intelligence agencies remains highly classified, whether in Russia or the West. This includes the inner structure of the various agencies. Despite these challenges, a large number of Russian domestic cases and foreign operations have come to light. These help form a better understanding of this classified and clandestine environment. They permit a fuller appreciation both of Russia's present means and aims and what we know about the roles of their intelligence services and operatives. What has not helped is a decline in specialism on Russia outside of the former Soviet bloc. The CIA is addressing this, but it has been slow in coming.[330] At the same time, August 2025 reports that the USIC's Foreign Malign Influence Center (FMIC) will cease to operate as a standalone organization as part of a wider package of reorganizations and cuts put forward by the Office of the Director of National Intelligence (ODNI) is concerning.[331] Another issue is "mirror imaging" which, in relation to Russia, leads to misunderstandings by policymakers and analysts. According to Keir Giles, Russians and their leaders do not see the world through Western eyes (with the same true in reverse).[332] This uniqueness and distinctiveness is a reflection of strategic culture, and alongside mirror imaging, is good to be aware of.[333]

Against this backdrop, the opening chapter, "Espionage and Active Measures: Russia's Use of 'Hybrid Warfare'," begins by discussing human intelligence (HUMINT), and some of the targets and limits of cyberespionage. This makes use of virtual territory that has been mined by Russia's intelligence agencies as well as through proxy actors. These agencies and their scope of operations are analyzed in turn beginning with the FSB, then, GRU, and finally the SVR. The GRU

---

330 CIA Launches Telegram Channel (May 16, 2023), https://www.cia.gov/stories/story/cia-launches-telegram-channel/, U.S. Central Intelligence Agency Director William J Burns, "LIX: A world transformed and the role of intelligence (July 1, 2023), https://www.ditchley.com/programme/past-events/2020-2029/2023/lix-world-transformed-and-role-intelligence. Both accessed 4 July 2023.

331 Beatrice Peterson, "Gabbard announces plan to reorganize her agency, cut staff by half Gabbard wants to create "a leaner, faster, and more agile institution." (August 20 2025), https://abcnews.go.com/Politics/gabbard-slash-director-national-intelligence-staff-50/story?id=124819630. David Salvo, "What Just Happened? Dismantling the Intelligence Community's Foreign Malign Influence Center" (August 28 2025), https://www.justsecurity.org/119653/wjh-dismantling-foreign-malign-influence-center/. Both accessed 1 September 2025.

332 Giles, *Russia's War on Everybody*, pp. 3–9.

333 Originating with Jack Snyder, strategic culture was reinvigorated by Alastair Iain Johnston in the mid-1990s. Jack Snyder, *The Soviet Strategic Culture: Implications for Limited Nuclear Operations* (Santa Monica: Rand, 1977). Alastair Iain Johnston, "Thinking about Strategic Culture," *International Security*, Vol. 19, No. 4 (Spring 1995), pp. 32–64.

and SVR in particular have been highly effective cyberespionage actors. Both have conducted influence operations whose aims are the promotion of external destabilization and the exploitation of divisions in the West and much else besides. It further points to a symbiotic relationship with Russian organized crime. This utilizes elements of *maskirovka* (disguise) to cloud Russian state involvement, where cybercriminals have supported cyberespionage through conducting cybercrime. It then goes onto analyze the reasons Russia has attempted to control the information space within Russia, including through the guise of "net neutrality." It ends by setting the scene for Russian cyberattacks in the context of foreign and domestic policy.

Chapter 2, "Russia: An Advanced Persistent Threat to Critical Infrastructure," begins by looking at cases of major Russian cybercrime, which in the United States alone, run into the hundreds of millions of dollars, and Russia's use of cybercriminals. It questions whether these are amounting to cyber enabled economic warfare? It then moves onto Russian campaigns against critical infrastructure (CI) and their own domestic concerns regarding CI and cyberwarfare. It assesses the extent to which these represent targets of opportunity or design, especially as some of their targets have been authors and journalists, human rights organizations, and other non-governmental organizations as well as political activists. Russian cybercriminal gangs and some state-intelligence run Advanced Persistent Threats (APTs) have also targeted government and military personnel, and supply chains in the defense-industrial base. It then systematically discusses major Russian APT campaigns beginning with Moonlight Maze in the mid-1990s, before chronologically analyzing Red October, Dragonfly, BlackEnergy, "Industroyer" or "CrashOverride," Bugdrop, "Dragonfly 2.0," and finally the Colonial Pipeline and SolarWinds attacks.

Chapter 3 is the first of the two detailed case studies on Russian political influence campaigns. These active measures campaigns have Cold War antecedents. Britain has long been a residence for Russian oligarchs, Russian money, as well as a target of Russian active measures and covert action. These campaigns stretch back to the Cold War and before. National alt-right groups were also on the side of leaving the EU. The UK's referendum for exiting the European Union (EU) was expected to be close, but even late polling was indicating the vote would be to remain. It will show how anti-EU Russian state media messaging, amplified by Russian Internet bots and trolls became highly active in the lead up to the June 2016 vote. Despite four separate investigations and two major government reports, debate since has been *whether* Russia interfered in the 2016 Brexit referendum. That debate needs to move on to *how* the Kremlin interfered and *what effect* it had.

The second case study is "Project Lakhta," Russia's intelligence agency-led Kremlin directed campaign to get then presidential candidate Donald Trump elected over Hillary Clinton. Chapter 4 begins by analyzing two related active measures of hacking and then leaking damaging or embarrassing information from the Democratic Congressional Campaign Committee (DCCC) and Democratic National Committee (DNC) by Russia's GRU and SVR. It then demonstrates how this was allied to a related Russian active measures campaign which included propaganda and dis/misinformation, and destabilization efforts, for election interference. Like the previous chapter, it examines the influence of Russian actors on social media platforms and how social media executives sought to defend the misuse of their platforms. It also examines the roles of Julian Assange and Wikileaks in distributing this hacked information. Russia interference in the 2016 U.S. presidential election started to come to light in mid-2016 and led in 2019 to the two-volume Mueller Report but despite its detail and supporting evidence, including intelligence provided to U.S. agencies by their "Five Eyes" partners, this has become one of the most divisive issues in American domestic politics. The repercussions of Donald Trump's election victory in November 2016 continue to affect America's body politik. Despite multiple indictments and prosecutions, and much attention, there are many more and wider aspects to this and other Russian political influence campaigns. These are reflected on in this chapter.

These and other campaigns have generated a great deal of smoke and mirrors, competing narratives and motivations, and a parallax view of events. This is dissected in the conclusion. The conclusion begins with an overview of the threat posed by Russia. As an essential precursor step to potential cyberwarfare enabled by cyberespionage, it analyzes Russian critical infrastructure vulnerabilities and domestic security, before assessing some of Russia's key internal dynamics and external foreign policy drivers. It then looks back and looks forward at the multi-vectored threats constituted by Russia through its cyberespionage campaigns. It questions the guiderails of the "Gerasimov doctrine," and the extent to which cyberespionage and traditional intelligence operations under Putin have embraced "gray zone" "hybrid warfare." It then discusses Russian use of propaganda to incite or promote division and destabilization, drawing on the two case studies of Brexit and the 2016 U.S. presidential election, but also the wider context provided by more than 40 further cases. In so doing it posits the extent to which social media platforms are being leveraged as part of wider trends first pioneered by "spin doctors" and government advisors for political and electioneering purposes. To what extent Russia has learned from China, and what lessons the Chinese are taking from Russian campaigns and policies are the final set of assessments. The utilization of espionage and cyberespionage for active measures and its uses of hybrid, "gray zone" warfare is the subject of Chapter 1.

Chapter 1
Espionage and active measures: Russia's use of "hybrid warfare"

1 Introduction

Active measures (*aktivnyye meropriyatiya*) form the basis of and are fundamentally interwoven into Russia's "hybrid warfare" strategy to advance the Kremlin's political, military, and economic goals. During the early 1990s these were rebranded as "support measures" (*meropriyatiya sodeistviya*) under Russian federal law. This was originally intended to apply to the SVR but was then expanded to include the FSB under the Law on the Federal Security Service of 2003 as part of an extensive restructuring of Russia's security services. Whether this was just a name change or whether, as time progressed, it heralded an expansion of Soviet-era active measures is not discernible from open sources. However, the types of active measures and their scale is apparent. Importantly, Russian and Soviet defectors have also provided insights. Chief among them is Vasili Mitrokhin, an archivist working for the First Chief Directorate of the KGB who defected to Britain in 1992 after approaching the Secret Intelligence Service (MI6). Mitrokhin later edited a lexicon of KGB terms drawn from KGB documents. In it, active measures were broadly defined as "exerting influence on the foreign policy and the internal political situation of target countries ... [and] weakening the political, military economic and ideological positions of capitalism, undermining its aggressive plans, in order to create conditions favourable to the successful implementation of the Soviet Union's foreign policy".[1]

Externally, as part of Russia's foreign policy toolbox, non-violent and violent means of influencing continue to be apparent. They also appear to be expanding.[2] This has been demonstrated in conflict zones and on the "virtual battlefield" in

1 Vasili Mitrokhin, *KGB lexicon: The Soviet Intelligence Officer's Handbook* (London: Frank Cass, 2002), p. 13. See also Christopher Andrew and Vasili Mitrokhin, *The Mitrokhin Archive The KGB in Europe and the West* (London: Allen Lane/Penguin Press, 1999); Christopher Andrew and Vasili Mitrokhin, *The Mitrokhin Archive II The KGB in the World* (London: Penguin Press, 2018). Eberhard Schneider, "The Russian Federal Security Service under President Putin", in Stephen White (ed.), *Politics and the Ruling Group in Russia* (New York: Palgrave Macmillan, 2008), pp. 42–62.
2 Ivo Juurvee, "Hybrid CoE Strategic Analysis 7 The resurrection of 'active measures': Intelligence services as a part of Russia's influencing toolbox" (April 2018), https://www.hybridcoe.fi/wp-content/uploads/2020/07/Strategic-analysis-7-April.pdf, accessed 1 August 2025.

https://doi.org/10.1515/9783111583464-004

many parts of the world. Under Putin, influence operations have been experienced through information warfare and state-directed or state-sanctioned propaganda, destabilization efforts (including sabotage), assassinations, lawfare, cybercrime, cyberespionage, and cyberwarfare capable of "armed attack."

Some of these can be traced back to the Soviet-era. Others are representative of changes that have taken place since the end of the Cold War which are deepening and accelerating still.[3] Those of the Cold War era include:

- disinformation campaigns (using the media and methods of the times);
- staging insurrections;
- the establishment and use of front organizations or companies;
- backing friendly political or social movements (and supporting individuals);
- orchestrating or suppressing domestic unrest (this included within the Soviet Union itself whilst intervening in Warsaw Pact states);
- Acquiring secret intelligence from the West and beyond.

These were part of a zero-sum mind-set aimed at weakening the West whilst some were also used within the Soviet Union and Warsaw Pact. The roots of these intelligence activities stretch back to tsarist Russia and the subsequent establishment of the Cheka and NKVD (*Narodnyi Komissariat Vnutrennykh Del*) during the Russian Revolution and its aftermath. This included the Russian civil war (1917–22) where Chekism was built to suppress non-conformist counter-revolutionaries and anti-communist forces at home and abroad. This also helped embed a siege mentality that lasted until the rise of Mikhail Gorbachev in the mid-1980s and fall of the Soviet Union. Chekism persisted until then through the KGB and Politburo. The KGB's networks abroad (alongside those of the GRU) subsequently unraveled during the troubled 1990s. They would not begin to reemerge until well into the presidency of Vladimir Putin who rose from the ranks of the FSB in the late-1990s.[4]

The forms of these long-established practices are now combining with new and expanded active measures chiefly enabled by technology, the Internet and changes to information consumption combined with globalization and increased cross-border travel. These are used alongside traditional spycraft and wider tools

---

3 See for example Thomas Rid, *Active Measures The Secret History of Disinformation and Political Warfare* (New York: Farrar, Straus and Giroux, 2020).

4 Mark Galeotti, "Active Measures: Russia's Covert Geopolitical Operations", Marshall Center Security Insight, No. 31, June 2019, https://www.marshallcenter.org/en/publications/security-insights/active-measures-russias-covert-geopolitical-operations-0, accessed 1 August 2025.

of remote warfare.[5] Russia has become the lead user and lead developer of many of these strategies. These developments have led to characterizations of "hybrid warfare."

The concept of hybrid warfare was set-out in *Cyberwarfare: Threats to Critical Infrastructure* and *Hybrid Warfare: Western and non-Western definitions, concepts, and regional case studies.* However, some elements are worth restating. These have been in evidence since antiquity and were described by Thucydides and Sun Tzu on opposite sides of the earth from the fifth century BCE. This includes the use of mercenaries, irregular armies, and fighting local counterinsurgency (COIN) campaigns. These ancient campaigns, and campaigns throughout recorded history, also saw displays of patronage and favor/disfavor among feudal lords, warlords, whilst leveraging traders and trade blocs. Tribalism and nascent nationalism also fueled wars and affected the fighting. By the middle ages, intelligence practices and diplomacy were also studied by (among others) Niccolò Machiavelli in his 16th century treatise, *The Prince.*[6]

Len Scott relatedly discussed in his thought-provoking study of Western covert action that secret intelligence services also conducted clandestine diplomacy and that this was a feature of pre-modern inter-state relations. In the modern world this can be a means of extending "peace feelers" between warring parties that can overlap with interventionist practices (notwithstanding that politico-military agendas and the priorities of intelligence services might not always represent official government policy – including pronouncements over whether any dialogues are taking place). In this light, clandestine diplomacy can also establish or be a conduit for deniable back-channel dialogues. These can also involve third parties. This can also apply in the context of COIN and (for example) was a factor in what eventually became an established peace process in Northern Ireland. Disinformation or misinformation can also be fed into these processes. In addition, clandestine diplomacy can also be (or become) an influence operation and/or overlap

5 This includes the use of drones. Dominika Kunertova, "The War in Ukraine Shows the Game-Changing Effect of Drones Depends on the Game," *Bulletin of the Atomic Scientists*, Vol. 79, No. 2 (March 2023), pp. 95–102. Christian Enemark, *Armed Drones and the Ethics of War: Military Virtue in a Postheroic Age* (Abingdon: Routledge, 2013). On the potential for "drones" to be hacked see Kim Hartmann and Christoph Steup, "The Vulnerability of UAVs to Cyber Attacks – An Approach to the Risk Assessment" in Karlis Podins, Jan Stinissen and Markus Maybaum (eds.), *5th International Conference on Cyber Conflict Proceedings* (Tallinn: CCD COE Publications, 2013), pp. 95–118.

6 Kristan Stoddart, *Cyberwarfare: Threats to Critical Infrastructure* (London: Palgrave/Springer, 2022), pp. 61–65. Kristan Stoddart, "What is hybrid warfare?" in Kristan Stoddart (ed.) with Christian Kaunert and Kiril Avramov, *Hybrid Warfare: Western and non-Western definitions, concepts, and regional case studies* (Quantico, VA: Marine Corps University Press, 2026).

with deception and intelligence gathering. It could steer those involved away from hostilities (including military or terrorist action) and towards political processes but it could also provoke or produce undesirable outcomes. Those involved could also stray beyond their remits or agency. Scott also observed that the relationship between intelligence organizations and the functions they perform has varied over time and location. This included a division and trading of responsibilities between Western agencies during World War II and Cold War. Among the interventionist and influence activities conducted was clandestine (and plausibly deniable) CIA support for paramilitaries in Afghanistan (chief among them the Mujahideen) during the Soviet occupation from 1979–88.[7]

Across wide and deep sets of activities, Russia has pushed the lines of acceptable state behavior and redrawn the borders of active measures into one that is better conceived as hybrid warfare. This has been aided by globalization, increasing free trade, and more open borders meaning cross-border travel is far easier in the post-1991 world than was possible during the Cold War. Examples of these wide and deep sets of activities were detailed in the Introduction. Other related cases further illustrate how the Kremlin has misused cross-border travel and developed extensive influence campaigns that leverage the Internet and social media platforms geared around foreign policy goals and geopolitical aspirations. In 2016, this included a coup attempt in Montenegro, which also reportedly involved an attempted assassination of Montenegro's prime minister during an election campaign centered on NATO membership.[8] In addition, in December 2024 Romania's Constitutional Court canceled its presidential election amid intelligence-led concerns of a successful Russian election influence campaign in support of unheralded far-right nationalist, Călin Georgescu. This followed similar attempts in Moldova and Georgia.[9] These have led to pushback against Russia, most notably in economic, financial, travel, and diplomatic sanctions, but little else (publicly at least).

---

7 Len Scott, "Secret Intelligence, Covert Action and Clandestine Diplomacy," *Intelligence and National Security*, Vol. 19, No. 2 (Summer 2004), pp. 337–338.

8 Putin's Asymmetric Assault on Democracy in Russia and Europe: Implications for U.S. National Security A Minority Staff Report, Committee on Foreign Relations United States Senate, January 10, 2018, pp. 77–80. https://www.foreign.senate.gov/imo/media/doc/FinalRR.pdf, accessed 5 November 2019. Riehle, *Russian Intelligence*, p. 207.

9 Veronica Anghel, "Why Romania Just Canceled Its Presidential Election" (December 2024), https://www.journalofdemocracy.org/online-exclusive/why-romania-just-canceled-its-presidential-election/. Rowan Ings, "The TikTokers accused of triggering an election scandal," https://www.bbc.com/articles/cqx41x3gn5zo. Both accessed 2 May 2025.

In 2016 Mark Galeotti wrote "The West finds itself in a new 'hot peace' in which many consider Russia not just as an irritant or challenge, but as an outright threat ... [through] covert, indirect, and political operations, typically conducted, controlled, or facilitated by the numerous Russian intelligence and security agencies, which strike from every side ..."[10] Against the multi-vectored threats posed by Russia (and other nations and groups), defense in all directions (*tous azimuts*) is impossible.[11] It has been, and remains, increasingly difficult to defend against the multiple pathways of attack engaged by Russia coming from all sides and at a multitude of levels.[12] This needs redressing. In its near abroad, especially against Ukraine, this has included the resort to large-scale military force and outright war. Russia was already more than an irritant, but Galeotti's choice of words was not misguided.

2 Active measures or hybrid warfare?

Those who are skeptical of the term and descriptions of hybrid warfare tend to appear from two schools of thought. The first school is that of small wars and insurgencies, many of them historians. They argue that COIN operations (guerrilla warfare), especially that of the post-World War II-era of decolonization, predates and articulates some or most of what is conceived of as hybrid warfare. The second main school comes from the field of intelligence studies. This sees hybrid warfare through the lens of the spycraft and tradecraft observed in active measures and covert action (or through the updated uses of both in the post-Cold War world).[13] As Galeotti, one of the most active scholars analyzing Russian hybrid warfare contended in 2016, this has led to an "active and sometimes ferocious debate as to whether this is something truly new or not, and whether it is limited to certain specific theatres and contexts, rather than any wider evolution of military art."[14] Indeed, it has sparked a debate which echoes that of Mary Kaldor's well-re-

10 Mark Galeotti, "Putin's Hydra: Inside Russia's Intelligence Services," p. 1, https://www.ecfr.eu/page/-/ECFR_169_-_PUTINS_HYDRA_INSIDE_THE_RUSSIAN_INTELLIGENCE_SERVICES_1513.pdf, accessed 2 January 2018.

11 The concept of *tous azimuts* originates in France with earlier Arabic origins.

12 Keir Giles, *Russia's War on Everybody and What It Means For You* (London: Bloomsbury, 2024), pp. 91–96.

13 See for example Rory Cormac and Richard J. Aldrich, "Grey is the new black: covert action and implausible deniability", *International Affairs*, Vol. 94, Issue 3, pp. 477–494.

14 Mark Galeotti, "Hybrid, ambiguous, and non-linear? How new is Russia's 'new way of war'?", *Small Wars and Insurgencies*, Vol. 27, No. 2 (2016), p. 287.

garded 'new' and 'old' wars thesis that first appeared in 1999.[15] Both approaches are well-reasoned, historically documented, and clear sighted and many of the "old" versus "new" criticisms are valid.[16]

Intelligence gathering can provide forewarning and much else besides and can aid policymakers. It can also mislead them as it did in Kremlin decision-making to invade Ukraine.[17] Espionage has other functions, including for Russia. It is argued that "espionage serves as a form of either arms control or conflict prevention by making aware the capabilities of other states, serving as a mechanism to promote stability and peace."[18] It has been argued by some legal scholars that espionage is permissible under customary international law. The UN Charter does not refer to espionage (but does refer to peace, justice, security, international disputes, and "the progressive development of international law and its codification").[19] Espionage has been termed "a necessary part of statecraft and a means of peremptory self-defense" (particularly by legal scholars of the New Haven School first developed at Yale University in the post-war 1940s).[20] By extension, cyberespionage by states is permissible under international law, even when wrong-

15 Mary Kaldor, *New and Old Wars: Organized Violence in a Global Era Third Edition* (Cambridge: Polity Press, 2012).

16 Rizwan Zeb, "Hybrid or No Hybrid, War is War" in Stoddart et al (eds.), *Hybrid Warfare*, chapter 1. See also Erik Reichborn-Kjennerud & Patrick Cullen, "What is Hybrid Warfare?", Norwegian Institute for International Affairs Policy Brief, 1/2016, https://www.jstor.org/stable/pdf/resrep07978.pdf, accessed 2 August 2025.

17 For example, it can provide accurate intelligence, and accurate intelligence estimates, but it can also inflate capabilities, intentions, and threats. This has led to arms spirals and arms racing as well as real and unfounded fears of capabilities and intentions. Judgment and luck also play their parts. For detailed information on the intelligence cycle see Mark Phythian, *Understanding the Intelligence Cycle* (Abingdon: Routledge, 2013). See also Julian Richards, *The Art and Science of Intelligence Analysis* (Oxford: Oxford University Press, 2011).

18 Darien Pun, "Rethinking Espionage in the Modern Era," *Chicago Journal of Internal Law*, Vol. 18, No. 1 (Summer 2017), p. 363.

19 United Nations Charter (full text), https://www.un.org/en/about-us/un-charter/full-text, accessed 5 August 2025.

20 Pun, "Rethinking Espionage in the Modern Era," p. 363. Another legal scholar simply says "customary international law ... has very little to say about espionage." A. John Radsan, "The Unresolved Equation of Espionage and International Law," *Michigan Journal of International Law*, Vol. 28, Issue 3 (Spring 2007), p. 597. For insights into the New Haven School (often mentioned by the esteemed lawyers involved in drafting NATO's Tallinn Manuals) please see W. Michael Reisman, Siegfried Wiessner & Andrew R. Willard, "The New Haven School: A Brief Introduction", *Yale Journal of International Law*, Vol. 32: 575 (Summer 2007), pp. 575–582 and Rián Derrig, *The New Haven School: American International Law* (Oxford: Oxford University Press, 2025).

ful under national laws.[21] This permissibility has led to violations largely without penalties. This has seen cyberespionage proliferate and increasingly take advantage of technological developments. For Russia, and many other states, this has encouraged wider use. There are no visible signs that any legal course of action, domestically or internationally, has encouraged Russian intelligence agencies to disengage from their activities, which include active measures campaigns of mis and disinformation and destabilization efforts.[22]

As Abrams describes, "With roots in Leninist thinking, over generations the Soviets mastered a range of techniques known as *aktivnyye meropriyatiya*, or 'active measures,' ranging from simple propaganda and forgery to assassination, terrorism and everything in between."[23] This is not unique to the Soviet Union and Russian Federation. Other nations have their own distinct and legally defined practices known as covert action and also (as the name suggests) because their work and working practices are designed to be covert.[24] However, it will be seen below that their ability to stay covert is under renewed challenge in the digitized information age. Also, in democratic nations are legitimate questions concerning accountability and government oversight.[25] The demarcation lines between what state intelligence agencies, and sometimes proxy organizations working with or against them, regard as active measures and covert action can be blurry.[26]

Michael Warner, previously a CIA historian and now the Historian for United States Cyber Command, in his reconsideration of covert action in the era of cyber, offers testament to this blurriness. This sees him describe covert action as "the secret supplement to war and diplomacy, employed at the margins of conflict to

---

21 Michael N. Schmitt (ed.), *Tallinn Manual 2.0 on the International Law Applicable to Cyber Operations* (New York: Cambridge University Press, 2017), pp. 168–176.

22 As Pun remarks, "International law cannot remain stagnant and ignore the enormous benefits brought to information collection by cyber espionage … The ability now to engage in constant wide-reaching surveillance and activities that can be interpreted as offensive operations necessitates new legal reforms that properly reflect the capabilities of modern technology." Pun, "Rethinking Espionage in the Modern Era," pp. 390–391.

23 Steve Abrams, "Beyond Propaganda: Soviet Active Measures in Putin's Russia," *Connections: The Quarterly Journal*, Vol. 15, No. 1 (Winter 2016), p. 7.

24 "Many of the terms used – 'covert action,' 'special operation,' 'special activities,' and 'disruptive action' are used interchangeably though there are also important terminological differences." Scott, "Secret Intelligence," p. 324. See also Mark Stout, "Covert Action in the Age of Social Media," *Georgetown Journal of International Affairs*, Vol. 18, No. 2 (Summer/Fall 2017), pp. 94–103.

25 Peter Gill, "Democratic and Parliamentary Accountability of Intelligence Services After 9/11", in Hans Born and Marina Caparini, *Democratic Control of Intelligence Services: Containing Rogue Elephants* (Abingdon: Routledge, 2007), pp. 195–215.

26 Scott, "Secret Intelligence," pp. 322–341.

shift patterns of trust and allegiance." Officially, it was defined in the 1991 Intelligence Authorization Act as "an activity or activities conducted by, or on behalf and under the control of, an element of the US government to influence political, economic, or military conditions abroad so that the role of the United States is not intended to be apparent or acknowledged publicly."[27]

Warner makes the case that although the purpose of U.S. covert action (distinct from military activities, formal diplomatic channels and "clandestine diplomacy"), is to remain secret and plausibly deniable, cyber is changing this paradigm in several ways. First, covert actions remained small in order to remain hidden but cyber increases the scale and reach of what is possible through covert action. Covert action was also designed to operate within a certain window of time. Cyber can produce instantaneous effects both locally and over a wide area and affect large numbers of people. It can also be rapidly and cost-effectively be scaled-up in ways traditional operations would struggle with. For Warner, "The scope of cyber-enabled efforts like the IRA's [Russia's Internet Research Agency] quite simply dwarfs anything possible before the Internet. Even radio broadcasts to entire countries during the Cold War did not make active, unwitting participants of their audiences ...".[28]

With its low-barriers to entry and ease of use, cyberspace also encourages proliferation and innovation. Warner looks at this through the lens of nation-states, but this applies to a wider spectrum of actors. Importantly, he is acutely aware of the capabilities and capacity of what this book terms cyberespionage to unite people and to divide them which he then applies to foreign regimes hostile to the U.S. Offensively and deniably used, this can "reach directly into a country and turn them against the regime" and part of the reasons why nations including Russia and China champion what they characterize as Internet Sovereignty.[29]

As Warner suggests this blurriness extends to the borders and linkages between covert action, espionage, cyberespionage, and hybrid warfare. These linkages were discussed in *Cyberwarfare: Threats to Critical Infrastructure* (especially

---

27 Michael Warner, "A Matter of Trust: Covert Action Reconsidered", *Studies in Intelligence*, Vol. 63, No. 4 (December 2019), pp. 33–34.

28 Warner: A Matter of Trust, p. 38

29 Warner: A Matter of Trust, pp. 39–40. Stanislaw Budnitsky and Lianrui Jia, "Branding Internet sovereignty: Digital media and the Chinese–Russian cyberalliance", *European Journal of Cultural Studies*, Vol. 21, Issue 5 (2018), pp. 594–613. Alexandra V. Orlova, ""Digital Sovereignty," Anonymity and Freedom of Expression: Russia's Fight to Re-Shape Internet Governance", *UC Davis Journal of International Law & Policy*, Vol. 26, Issue 2 (2019), pp. 225–248.

in relation to Russia).[30] Against critical infrastructure, potential pre-emption is enabled through cyberespionage and traditional espionage. Cyberespionage in particular is a prerequisite to pre-position for pre-emptive attacks against critical infrastructure (CI). This is enabled because of increasing connectivity of devices, systems, and people.

The modern world to large degrees now depends on the Internet. Connectivity takes many forms including wireless signals, and 4G and 5G communications. This enables a wide variety of routes which open previously inaccessible gateways allowing remote access to critical infrastructure sites as well as for political influence campaigns. Critical infrastructure facilities include "public utilities such as electric power generation and distribution, water supplies and water treatment, natural gas and oil production and pipelines, shipping and maritime traffic, hydroelectric dams, traffic lights and train switching systems."[31] These are the backbones of every industrialized state. The most important of all of these sectors is electrical generation and distribution because it powers all other sectors.[32] Holding these facilities and sectors at-risk of attack can simultaneously be a form of deterrence and a means to undercut stability.[33] It is a component piece of the security dilemma where the development of offensive and defensive capabilities is seen as threatening, producing insecurity.[34]

Cyberespionage is not the flip side of the coin. It is the essential precondition that enables kinetic and destructive cyberwarfare.[35] Much like cyberwar(fare), hybrid warfare can be conceptually blurry and almost infinitely extendable in scope and area. Nevertheless, examining active measures through the lens of hybrid warfare also has conceptual value. This is because it helps conceptualize and strategize multi-dimensionally in a world where technology and contestation are increasingly permeating developed and developing nations. Dwight D. Eisenhower once remarked that "Every war is going to astonish you in the way it occurred and the way it is carried out." Strategic innovation is clearly taking place. With it comes surprise and adaptation. Even with knowledge and insights

---

30 Kristan Stoddart, *Cyberwarfare: Threats to Critical Infrastructure* (London: Palgrave/Springer, 2022), pp. 53–146.

31 Stoddart, *Cyberwarfare*, pp. 1–2.

32 Facilities also be accessed "over the fence" or on-site using equipment which can be bought commercially off-the-shelf. Stoddart, *Cyberwarfare*, pp. 1–2, 408–410.

33 Stoddart, *Cyberwarfare*, pp. 53–65.

34 The security dilemma is influenced by regime type, ethnocentrism, worst-case forecasting, and enemy imaging, amongst other things. Shiping Tang, "The Security Dilemma: A Conceptual Analysis," *Security Studies*, Vol. 18, Issue 3 (October 2009), pp. 587–623.

35 Stoddart, *Cyberwarfare*, pp. 106–114.

from the intelligence community, adversarial innovation continues to mean "some surprise is inevitable."[36] Hybrid warfare, and its relationship with active measures/covert action, is both a material and conceptual challenge portending what Krepinevich terms "a disruptive shift … in the character of warfare."[37]

The areas of these shifts, and an illustration of the blurriness and scope, is found in a UK government call seeking to fund research into hybrid warfare. This identified 57 separate "functions" "based on empirical cases in the recent past" which can "achieve more than one intent" or can be "clustered to support a single, particular intent." These "57 functions" include many areas that feature in this book and its two companion volumes, such as agents of influence; cyberespionage and cybercrime; disinformation; energy security; election interference; influence operations; intelligence campaigns; lawfare; the Law of Armed Conflict; and proxy or front organizations. These were categorized under political, military, economic, social, informational, infrastructural, and legal parameters. The research call did not even term this hybrid warfare. Instead, it is nebulously defined as "Sub-Threshold Activities" taking place beneath the level of armed conflict and war.[38]

As Cormac and Aldrich critique, this dearth of clarity is leading to confusion or bewilderment, not only in definitional terms but also in terms of understanding and interpreting dynamics and events in contested and clouded information spaces. Where active measures/covert action is situated in discussions and publications on hybrid warfare is therefore an important consideration as are the parameters of hybrid warfare. This discussion and debate can be extended to cyberwarfare and cyberespionage (originally the primary areas concentrated on in this book and the companion volume on China). Without offering their own definition of hybrid warfare, Cormac and Aldrich suggest "Hybrid warfare forms a timely example of implausibly deniable operations creating exploitable ambiguity. The approach, developed in the United States but now associated with Russia, combines political and military activity with covert action, especially influence operations."[39] Valuably, they also question the connections between covert action and

36 Mark Cancian, "This isn't the surprise you were expecting" (March 2, 2018), https://warontherocks.com/2018/03/isnt-surprise-expecting/, accessed 26 July 2023.

37 Andrew F. Krepinevich, *The Origins of Victory: How Disruptive Military Innovation Determines the Fates of Great Powers* (New Haven CT: Yale University Press, 2023), p. 3.

38 "Sub-Threshold Activities, Intentions, & Indicators: Insights for MSSA in the Information Domain", https://assets.publishing.service.gov.uk/government/uploads/system/uploads/attachment_data/file/1148447/57_Functions_Excerpt_FINAL.pdf, accessed 20 July 2023.

39 Rory Cormac and Richard J. Aldrich, "Grey is the New Black: Covert Action and Implausible Deniability," *International Affairs*, Vol. 94, Issue 3 (May 2018), p. 490.

hybrid warfare. As they explain, "understanding covert action is integral to understanding this wider form of interventionism."[40]

Influence operations and campaigns have been a feature of modern Russian covert action/active measures with a pre-history in the Soviet Union and its "Special Services."[41] So too has been Russian money used to fund, or intended to fund, organizations, pressure groups, political parties, and agents of influence (sometimes characterized as "useful idiots" or "sock puppets").[42] When it comes to Russia's potential to engage in cyberwarfare, the essential precursor steps can only be achieved through persistent cyberespionage (potentially combined with traditional tools of spycraft and recruitment). This was one of the main points demonstrated at length in *Cyberwarfare* and one of the primary reasons why Russian campaigns into critical infrastructure and campaigns which solely constitute active measures/covert action through cyberespionage were treated separately in this book on Russia whilst a separate book on China provides a wider focus still. Russia's intelligence sharing relationship with China "is unclear" as is the relationships with India and Pakistan.[43] There are competing dynamics at work which require delicate balancing. There are few shared regional interests between these major (and nuclear-armed) neighbors who more often compete than cooperate. India and Pakistan's relationship is particularly fractious and has bled into open conflict on several occasions. None are natural or historic allies with Russia.

3 Russia's use of the "gray zone" and "hybrid warfare"

Russian conceptions of "information superiority" and "information confrontation" have been, as in China, built up on ideas of an offense–defense balance and a zero-sum game. Like a number of Chinese strategists, these are conceived as war-fighting tools akin to military employment. What is somewhat new is the idea of "noncontact warfare," envisaged as a suite of cyber warfighting options from "soft kill" *dezinformatsiya* (disinformation) operations to physical damage and destruction of information infrastructure. This includes network attacks

40 Cormac and Aldrich, "Grey is the New Black," p. 493.
41 Stretching back into the days of the Soviet Union.
42 Putin's Asymmetric Assault, pp. v, 2–5, 30–31, 52–58, 79, 102–106, 117–118, 122–123, 128, 134–139. Corruptly acquired Russian money has also been implicated widely in money laundering. Evidence can also be found in the Pandora, Paradise, and Panama Papers leaks. https://offshoreleaks.icij.org/, accessed 20 July 2023.
43 Kevin P. Riehle, *The Russian FSB* A concise history of the Federal Security Service (Washington DC: Georgetown University Press, 2024), p. 134.

and "psychological strikes" or "psychological aggression."[44] These ideas were first proposed in an influential 2005 book *Future War* authored by Major-General Vladimir Slipchenko and Makhmut Gareev – a former head of the Directorate of Military Science of the General Staff.[45]

Jacob W. Kipp notes that "Slipchenko's basic point is that war was not abolished by the end of the Cold War but only is in a process of transformation, a transformation dominated by the shift from industrial to information societies."[46] As with Chinese strategists, Slipchenko saw in the First and Second Gulf Wars how the use of precision guided munitions (PGMs) was heralding an evolutionary change into non-contact wars.[47] Slipchenko lectured in China where his book on "sixth-generation" warfare was translated and where he was influenced by Chinese strategy of non-contact operations against Taiwan.[48]

Gareev also foresaw "indirect means being applied to achieve contemporary political ends – economic sanctions, diplomatic pressure, information warfare – to bring about internal collapse of opposing states."[49] This was placed against a background of unsustainable military expenditure by the Soviet Union and before that, by Russia in Tsarist times. In the context of cyberwar and, in particular cyberattacks on electrical power grids, Peter Pry describes Slipchenko's ideas as "a revolution in military affairs that is deeper, more traumatic and more profound than any other that has preceded it."[50]

Although Galeotti and many others now disagree whether Russia has a doctrine or template, the "Gerasimov doctrine" (discussed below) maps onto patterns of behavior, operations, and cyberespionage campaigns described by Slipchenko.

---

44 Vladimir Slipchenko, "Information Resources and Information Confrontation: their Evolution, Role, and Place in Future War," *Armeyskiy Sbornik* (Army Journal), No. 10 (2013), pp. 52–57 in Timothy Thomas, "Thinking Like A Russian Officer: Basic Factors and Contemporary Thinking on the Nature of War," Foreign Military Studies Office (FMSO) (April 2016), pp. 34–35, https://community.apan.org/wg/tradoc-g2/fmso/m/fmso-monographs/194971, accessed 5 April 2019.

45 Vladimir Slipchenko and Makhmut Gareev, *Budushchaya voyna* (Future War) (Moscow: Polit.ru Ob"edinennoye Gumarnitarnoye Izdatelstvo, 2005).

46 Jacob W. Kipp, "Book Review Vladimir Slipchenko and Makhmut Gareev. *Future War*," *Journal of Slavic Military Studies*, Vol. 20, Issue 1 (April 2007), p. 150.

47 Timothy L. Thomas, *Dragon Bytes: Chinese Information Warfare Theory and Practice* (Fort Leavenworth, KS: Foreign Military Studies Office, 2004). Timothy L. Thomas, *Decoding the Virtual Dragon: Critical Evolutions in the Science and Philosophy of China's Information Operations and Military Strategy* (Fort Leavenworth, KS: Foreign Military Studies Office, 2007).

48 Kipp, "Book Review Slipchenko and Gareev. *Future War*," p. 151.

49 Kipp, "Book Review Slipchenko and Gareev. *Future War*," p. 154.

50 Dr. Peter Pry, "Insights into the Vulnerability of the Power System" (February 7, 2017), http://mackenzieinstitute.com/insights-vulnerability-power-system/, accessed 5 April 2019.

This is described in Western circles as "hybrid warfare."[51] These theoretical constructs have been applied and serve both foreign and domestic political goals as well as revisionist strategic goals. Cyber is the biggest force multiplier in terms of hybrid warfare but hybrid embraces much more than just cyber.

Utilizing longstanding tactics embodied by Sun Zu and Clausewitz, Gerasimov argued: "Among such actions are the use of special operations forces and internal opposition to create a permanently operating front through the entire territory of the enemy state, as well as informational actions, devices, and means that are constantly being perfected."[52] Gerasimov's "doctrine" also talked about the future where Artificial Intelligence (AI) and robotics will play an increased role in military operations. It is also where, "The information space opens wide asymmetrical possibilities for reducing the fighting potential of the enemy."[53] Gerasimov concluded:

> no matter what forces the enemy has, no matter how well-developed his forces and means of armed conflict may be, forms and methods for overcoming them can be found. He will always have vulnerabilities, and that means that adequate means of opposing him exist ... We must not copy foreign experience and chase after leading countries, but we must outstrip them and occupy leading positions ourselves."[54]

Russia's ongoing cyber campaigns, allied to their traditional espionage operations, operate within this framework. It might not be a blueprint for the Russian military and Russia's foreign and security policy, but it is evidenced in their campaigns.

A March 2017 report by Michael Connell and Sarah Vogler of the Arlington-based Center for Naval Analyses illuminates the Kremlin's orchestrated mis and disinformation campaigns and the place of socio-political influence operations and election interference in the context of Gerasimov's "doctrine." They argued, "Russian officials are convinced that Moscow is locked in an ongoing, existential struggle with internal and external forces" and information warfare "is viewed as

---

51 Roger N. McDermott, "Does Russia Have a Gerasimov Doctrine?" *Parameters*, Vol. 46, No. 1 (Spring 2016), pp. 97–105. Victor R. Morris, "Grading Gerasimov: Evaluating Russian Nonlinear War Through Modern Chinese Doctrine" (undated), https://smallwarsjournal.com/jrnl/art/grading-gerasimov-evaluating-russian-nonlinear-war-through-modern-chinese-doctrine, accessed 9 March 2020. Giles, *Russia's War on Everybody*, p. 21.

52 General of the Army Valerii Gerasimov, Chief of the General Staff of the Russian Federation Armed Forces, "The Value of Science Is in the Foresight New Challenges Demand Rethinking the Forms and Methods of Carrying out Combat Operations," *Military Review* (January–February 2016), p. 24.

53 Gerasimov, "The Value of Science Is in the Foresight," p. 27.

54 Gerasimov, "The Value of Science Is in the Foresight," p. 29.

both a threat and an opportunity."[55] Connell and Vogler further argued that neither cyber (*kiber*) or cyberwarfare (*kibervoyna*) are terms used in Russian military discourse, except when commenting on Western operations. Instead, they argue the Kremlin conceptualizes cyberespionage through the lens of information warfare. This includes electronic warfare and psychological operations.[56] These are also functions of active measures and they also claim that the Russian leadership sees these operations as unending. Connell and Vogler also suggest that "like the Chinese, they tend to use the word informatization, thereby conceptualizing cyber operations within the broader rubric of information warfare (*informatsionnaya voyna*)." Specifically:

> cyber is regarded as a mechanism for enabling the state to dominate the information landscape, which is regarded as a warfare domain in its own right. Ideally, it is to be employed as part of a whole of government effort, along with other, more traditional, weapons of information warfare that would be familiar to any student of Russian or Soviet military doctrine, including disinformation operations, PsyOps [psychological operations], electronic warfare, and political subversion.[57]

It might be a "whole of government" effort but evidence presented throughout this book strongly indicates that Russia's campaigns are seldom, if ever, coordinated between agencies leaving their capabilities and capacity fragmented (hitherto at least). More crucially, it is difficult to see how cyberespionage campaigns against critical infrastructure should be consigned to the "information warfare" domain. The results and opportunities these present go beyond information manipulation or exfiltration into acts causing, and capable of causing, highly damaging real world kinetic effects. This is cyberwarfare. These developments could and should have been taken more seriously.

4 Western intelligence priorities: Counterterrorism and "Color Revolutions"

Putin's successive governments addressed the endemic and structural weaknesses Russia experienced domestically and internationally during the 1990s as it sought to locate its place in the new world order heralded by the end of the Cold War and

55 Michael Connell and Sarah Vogler, "Russia's Approach to Cyber Warfare," Center for Naval Analyses, Occasional Paper, March 2017, p. i, https://www.cna.org/cna_files/pdf/DOP-2016-U-014231-1Rev.pdf, accessed 9 January 2018.

56 Connell and Vogler, "Russia's Approach to Cyber Warfare," p. i.

57 Connell and Vogler, "Russia's Approach to Cyber Warfare," p. 3.

the bipolar international system. At the same time Russia slipped down the order of priorities for Western intelligence which gave them time to reorganize. Resultantly, specialists on the Soviet Union known colloquially as "Sovietologists" and "Kremlinologists" atrophied. Russian specialism diminished further in the wake of 9/11 when counterterrorism gained immediate focus.[58] This trend increased with the invasion and occupation of Afghanistan (2001–2021) and then Iraq (2003–2011) as part of the "Global War on Terror" (GWOT). Whilst the CIA has slowly sought to address this deficit, not only was it slowing but, as the Introduction indicated, it is also showing signs of reversal.[59] Russia should become a renewed priority for Western intelligence both over the short-term and for longstanding reasons.[60]

There subsequently followed a series of popular uprisings known as the "Arab Spring" which began in earnest in 2011. This saw repressive authoritarian regimes toppled across the Middle East and North Africa (MENA), beginning with Zine El Abidine Ben Ali in Tunisia, then Colonel Muammar Gaddafi in Libya, and Hosni Mubarak in Egypt. Others, including Syrian President Bashar al-Assad responded by cracking down on the uprisings. Through to his regime's sudden (and somewhat unexpected) downfall in December 2024, his survival depended on Russian military and Wagner Group mercenary support under the twin pressures of Islamic State and organized rebels in the civil war.[61] These series of uprisings generated political turbulence across the MENA region (turbulence that continues to be felt today) and was one of the contributory factors of the rise of the so-called Islamic State which brutally occupied areas of Iraq and Syria between 2014 and 2019/20.

---

58 Intelligence and Security Committee of Parliament, Russia HC 632, July 21, 2020, pp. 15–28, 34–36, http://isc.independent.gov.uk/news-archive/21july2020. Michael J. Sulick, *American Spies: Espionage against the United States from the Cold War to the Present* (Washington: Georgetown University Press, 2013), pp. 183–188, 221–240.

59 CIA Launches Telegram Channel (May 16, 2023), https://www.cia.gov/stories/story/cia-launches-telegram-channel/; U.S. Central Intelligence Agency Director William J. Burns, "LIX: A world transformed and the role of intelligence (July 1, 2023), https://www.ditchley.com/programme/past-events/2020-2029/2023/lix-world-transformed-and-role-intelligence, both accessed 4 July 2023.

60 David Omand, "Understanding Putin's Russia: a continuing challenge for Western intelligence", *Intelligence and National Security*, Vol. 39, No. 3 (2024), pp. 386–399.

61 Tarek Masoud, "The Arab Spring at 10: Kings or People?" *Journal of Democracy*, Vol. 32, No. 1 (January 2021), pp. 139–154. Roy Allison, "Russia and Syria: Explaining Alignment with a Regime in Crisis," *International Affairs*, Vol. 89, No. 4 (July 2013), pp. 795–823. Michael Kofman and Mathew Rojansky, "What Kind of Victory for Russia in Syria?" *Military Review* (March–April 2018), pp. 6–23. Zarar Bin Saleem, Imtiaz Khan, and Zeeshan Khurshid, "The Fall of Bashar al-Assad: Implications for Syria and the Broader Middle East", *Dialogue Social Science Review*, Vol. 2, No. 5 (December 2024), pp. 752–764.

Liberal democracy has not taken root across the MENA region since. Instead, "Despite the demise of many autocracies, the post-Arab Spring states are confronted by deepening fragmentation at the regional, sectarian and tribal levels." This has led to "new breeds of authoritarian Salafist and Jihadist parties" and sporadic but persistent "sectarian warfare between Sunni, Shia, Alawis, and Kurds, with a spill-over in the direction of the already fractured ethno-sectarian regional fabric."[62] It has also increased the threat of domestic terrorism across the West. This in turn is part of the wider set of dynamics addressed by Anne Applebaum in her 2025 book *Autocracy Inc.*[63]

For Putin, the West was responsible for this instability by cultivating these regime changes as well as covertly supporting "color revolutions" in areas of their post-Soviet "near abroad."[64] This included uprisings in Serbia in 2000 that deposed President Slobodan Milošević, Georgia's "Rose Revolution" in 2003, the 2004 "Orange Revolution" in Ukraine, and the 2005 "Tulip Revolution" in Kyrgyzstan.[65] For the Kremlin, the most pivotal was the 2013–14 Revolution of Dignity/Euromaidan revolt which deposed Ukraine's pro-Russian president Victor Yanukovych.[66]

In between, the Arab Spring revolutions of 2011 "reinforced this phobia by producing not just regime change but also much more chaos and conflict than earlier ones in the post-Soviet space."[67] This has led to oft-repeated claims that the West conducts forms of "'hybrid warfare' against Russia in the post-Soviet space" with Russia's 2015 National Security Strategy marking clear policy paths

62 Imad Salamey, "Post-Arab Spring: Changes and Challenges," *Third World Quarterly*, Vol. 36, No. 1 (January 2015), pp. 125–126.

63 Anne Applebaum, *Autocracy, Inc: The Dictators Who Want to Run the World* (New York: Penguin, 2025).

64 Giles, *Russia's War on Everybody*, pp. 9–15.

65 Lucan Way, "The Real Causes of the Color Revolutions," *Journal of Democracy*, Vol. 19, No. 3 (July 2008), pp. 55–69.

66 Mark Galeotti, "(Mis)Understanding Russia's Two 'Hybrid Wars,'" *Critique & Humanism*, Vol. 59, No. 1 (2018), p. 1. Reprinted in https://www.eurozine.com/misunderstanding-russias-two-hybrid-wars/?pdf. See also Mark Galeotti, "I'm Sorry for Creating the "Gerasimov Doctrine,'" *Foreign Policy*, March 5, 2018, https://foreignpolicy.com/2018/03/05/im-sorry-for-creating-the-gerasimov-doctrine/. Both accessed 9 January 2018.

67 Nicolas Bouchet, "Russia's 'Militarization' of Colour Revolutions," *Policy Perspectives*, Vol. 4, No. 2 (January 2016), pp. 1–2. Putin himself commented in 2014 that "There was a whole series of controlled "colour" revolutions. [...] instead of democracy and freedom, there was chaos, outbreaks in violence and a series of upheavals. The Arab Spring turned into the Arab Winter. A similar situation unfolded in Ukraine." V. V. Putin, Address by President of the Russian Federation, 18 March, 15:50. The Kremlin, Moscow, http://en.kremlin.ru/events/president/news/20603. Quoted in Mette Skak, "Russian Strategic Culture: The Role of Today's *Chekisty*," *Contemporary Politics*, Vol. 22, Issue 3 (July 2016), p. 324.

for greater military and hybrid interventions abroad to protect Russia's "spheres of interest."[68] For Galeotti, "The Russians honestly – however wrongly – believe that these were not genuine protests against brutal and corrupt governments, but regime changes orchestrated in Washington, or rather, Langley [home of the CIA]."[69] This belief forms part of the Kremlin's world view. It also informed the controversial "Gerasimov doctrine."

5 "Hybrid warfare" and the "Gerasimov doctrine"

In February 2013 General Valerii Gerasimov, Russia's Chief of the General Staff, discussed the adoption of a set of doctrinal principles for "nonmilitary means of achieving political and strategic goals" which "has grown, and, in many cases … exceeded the power of force or weapons in their effectiveness."[70] This has become known as the "Gerasimov doctrine" but its qualification as a doctrine is controversial. For Galeotti "It doesn't exist" and "I feel I can say that because, to my immense chagrin, I created this term, which has since acquired a destructive life of its own, lumbering clumsily into the world to spread fear and loathing in its wake."[71]

It was seized on as events in Crimea in 2014 were unfolding as "prophetic," but in Galeotti's view Gerasimov is "a tough and effective chief of the general staff but no theoretician."[72] Galeotti instead suggests there is no single Russian "doctrine." Instead, he argues Gerasimov was seeing these principles through the lens of the "color revolutions" and the "Arab Spring" uprisings culminating for Russia in Ukraine's "Maidan revolt." The Kremlin believed these were not popular uprisings but were instead regime changes orchestrated by America's Intelligence Community. Through this lens Gerasimov was looking for ways Russia

---

68 Bouchet, "Russia's 'Militarization' of Colour Revolutions," pp. 1–2. A critique of its utility can be found in Bettina Renz, "Russia and 'Hybrid Warfare,'" *Contemporary Politics*, Vol. 22, Issue 3 (July 2016), pp. 283–300.

69 Galeotti, "I'm Sorry for Creating the 'Gerasimov Doctrine.'"

70 The original Russian version appeared in *Voenno-Promyshlenni Kurier* (VPK) in the February 27–March 5, 2013 issue of under the title "The Value of Science in Prediction." https://vpk-news.ru/sites/default/files/pdf/VPK_08_476.pdf, accessed. The English translation used is from the aforementioned *Military Review* (January–February 2016), p. 24.

71 Galeotti, "I'm Sorry for Creating the 'Gerasimov Doctrine.'" See also Mark Galeotti, "The Mythical 'Gerasimov Doctrine' and the Language of Threat," *Critical Studies on Security*, Vol. 6, No. 1 (February 2018), pp. 1–5.

72 Galeotti, "I'm Sorry for Creating the 'Gerasimov Doctrine.'"

might prevent future foreign interventions at home and abroad.[73] Galeotti is not alone in believing it is not a doctrine and instead a musing on military philosophy, borrowings from China's *Unrestricted Warfare* treatise of 1999 (and other Chinese writings), and lessons learned from the "Color Revolutions" and Arab Spring of 2011.[74] In this light it is a reflection on "unconventional approaches" to warfare mixing hard and soft power, not a fully-fledged theoretical construct.[75]

This is not to say Russia was, and is, on the backfoot or defensive. Galeotti also points out that "There is no denying that the West is facing a multivectored, multi-agency campaign of subversion, division, and covert political 'active measures' by Russia." However, "it is largely opportunistic, fragmented, even sometimes contradictory. Some major operations are coordinated, largely through the presidential administration, but most are not."[76] However, even if they are as opportunistic and fragmented as Galeotti suggests, designs, strategy, and planning are also evident.

Michael Kofman, another Russia watcher, is another of a growing number of well-versed observers who doubt it qualifies as a "doctrine." He argues, "Hybrid warfare has become the Frankenstein of the field of Russia military analysis; it has taken on a life of its own and there is no obvious way to contain it."[77] As a result, it has become a catch-all term. For Kofman, Gerasimov's article "did more damage to Western analysis of Russian military thought than any deception operation could. It was presumed to be a blueprint of Russian military thinking and doctrine."[78]

Without viewing it as a holistic template or as a fully-fledged doctrine it is part of the evolution of Russian politico-military thinking. Much of it is not new and were also responses to Counter-Insurgency (COIN) campaigns and ideas of Fourth Generation Warfare (4GW). These contain formulas and strategies that,

73 Galeotti, "I'm Sorry for Creating the 'Gerasimov Doctrine.'"

74 Qiao Liang and Wang Xiangsui, *Unrestricted Warfare* (Beijing: People's Liberation Army Literature and Arts Publishing House, 1999). See also Yevgeny Messner and his concept of *myatezh voina* ("subversion–war"), and Igor Panarin who developed some of Messner's themes, as well as Aleksandr Dugin. Ofer Fridman, *Russian "Hybrid Warfare": Resurgence and Politicisation* (New York: Oxford University Press, 2018), pp. 60–85.

75 McDermott, "Does Russia Have a Gerasimov Doctrine?" pp. 97–105. Morris, "Grading Gerasimov: Evaluating Russian Nonlinear War Through Modern Chinese Doctrine."

76 Galeotti, "I'm Sorry for Creating the 'Gerasimov Doctrine.'"

77 Michael Kofman, "Russian Hybrid Warfare and Other Dark Arts" (March 11, 2016), https://warontherocks.com/2016/03/russian-hybrid-warfare-and-other-dark-arts/, accessed 9 January 2019.

78 Kofman, "Russian Hybrid Warfare and Other Dark Arts."

like "hybrid warfare" itself, stretch back to antiquity.[79] As Galeotti describes, during the 1990s "Many within the Russian security establishment genuinely understood that the nature of war was changing."[80] In this respect they were drawing on two decades of experiences of revolutions and ethnic tensions that periodically erupted.

In their campaigns the Kremlin also utilizes proxies and "privateers." This is indicated in several high-profile cases which, like in Ukraine, leverage, or accept cybercriminal groups as part of their "hybrid warfare" doctrine. As part of their espionage activities Russia has long been testing NATO in a variety of ways, through to targeting individual soldiers on social media platforms.[81] This extends to individuals from Western media organizations, academia, and embassies. For diplomats this can include "home visits," and harassment (extending to their children and pets).[82] Even in the age of highly successful cyberespionage, Russian tactics also still include cultivating and exploiting human intelligence assets and insiders. This is the case in Ukraine, other parts of Russia's near aboard, areas in Africa where Russia's mercenary Wagner Group operate, and in the West.

6 Russia's use of the gray zone in cyberspace

Since Vladimir Putin returned as President in 2012, after trading places with Prime Minister Dmitry Medvedev (his hawkish close ally) in 2008, Russia has utilized its intelligence agencies to repress domestic protests, political opponents, civil society groups, and opposition to the Ukraine War. They have also been used extensively in external destabilization campaigns.[83] Whether characterized as a "hot peace," non-linear war, a new Cold War, or a "gray zone" between war and peace, Russia's intelligence organizations under Putin are using their intelligence agencies, military, and proxy forces for politico-military ends. This has

---

79 Williamson Murray and Peter R. Mansoor (eds.), *Hybrid Warfare: Fighting Complex Opponents from the Ancient World to the Present* (New York: Cambridge University Press, 2012). See also Frank G. Hoffman, *Conflict in the 21st Century: The Rise of Hybrid Wars* (Arlington VA: Potomac Institute for Policy Studies, 2007), and Martin van Creveld, *The Transformation of War* (New York: Free Press 1991).

80 Galeotti, "(Mis)Understanding Russia's Two 'Hybrid Wars.'" p. 4.

81 Keir Giles, "The Next Phase of Russian Information Warfare," NATO STRATCOM (May 2016), http://www.stratcomcoe.org/next-phase-russian-information-warfare-keir-giles and Anonymous, "Russian military admits significant cyber-war effort," (February 23, 2017), http://www.bbc.co.uk/news/world-europe-39062663, both accessed 27 February 2017.

82 Giles, *Russia's War on Everybody*, pp. 146–157.

83 Galeotti, "Putin's Hydra," p. 2.

seen them reach back to the Soviet-era tactics and methods to gather intelligence and to be coercive and disruptive.[84]

This is one of the characteristics of what has been termed "hybrid warfare." "Hybrid warfare" blurs the distinction between civilian non-combatants (including non or sub-state actors and the use of the term "terrorism" to describe forms of nationalism) and uniformed combatants. For Russia, proxy actors like the Internet Research Agency, and oligarch-controlled businesses are also on these "battlefields," as are terrorists who use violence for political ends. This is part of the dynamic of Clausewitz's remarkable trinity that also plays into the discussions of cyberwar(fare).[85] This is not a pitched battle of two clearly identifiable enemies and state-on-state conflicts and open war.

Viktor Zhora, the Deputy Chairman of Ukraine's State Service of Special Communication and Information Protection (SSSCIP) stated that Ukraine was fighting Russia on two levels: conventionally, and in cyberspace. For Zhora this makes it the first fully hybrid war.[86] As of June 2023 it had attempted to repel 260 million Russian cyberattacks over many years.[87] These fell into three categories: cyberespionage; subversive operations (including influence and information operations incorporating propaganda); and destructive and disruptive cyberwarfare.[88] Russia's ability to successfully mount cyberwarfare operations was being countered

---

84 Brandon Valeriano, Benjamin Jensen, and Ryan C. Maness, *Cyber Strategy: The Evolving Character of Power and Coercion* (New York: Oxford University Press, 2018), pp. 110–142.

85 Stoddart, *Cyberwarfare*, pp. 53–72

86 Joe Tidy, "Ukraine says it is fighting first 'hybrid war'" (March 4, 2022), https://www.bbc.co.uk/news/technology-60622977. Google, "Fog of War How the Ukraine Conflict Transformed the Cyber Threat Landscape" (undated), https://services.google.com/fh/files/blogs/google_fog_of_war_research_report.pdf. Both accessed 18 March 2024.

87 Maxim Tucker, "Still standing after 260 m attacks: Inside Ukraine's cyber warfare squad" (June 2, 2023), https://www.thetimes.co.uk/article/still-standing-after-260m-attacks-inside-ukraines-cyber-warfare-squad-pxkqdp3pt. Jakub Przetacznik with Simona Tarpova, "Briefing Russia's war on Ukraine: Timeline of cyber-attacks," June 2022, https://www.europarl.europa.eu/RegData/etudes/BRIE/2022/733549/EPRS_BRI(2022)733549_EN.pdf. Both accessed 15 July 2023.

88 Royal United Services Institute (RUSI), "Cyber Operations in Ukraine: A Conversation with Victor Zhora," https://www.rusi.org/events/open-to-all/cyber-operations-ukraine-conversation-victor-zhora, Pia Hüsch and Joseph Jarnecki, "All Quiet on the Cyber Front? Explaining Russia's Limited Cyber Effects" (June 1, 2023), https://www.rusi.org/explore-our-research/publications/commentary/all-quiet-cyber-front-explaining-russias-limited-cyber-effects. Ken Proska, John Wolfram, Jared Wilson, Dan Black, Keith Lunden, Daniel Kapellmann Zafra, Nathan Brubaker, Tyler McLellan, and Chris Sistrunk, "Sandworm Disrupts Power in Ukraine Using a Novel Attack Against Operational Technology" (November 9, 2023), https://www.mandiant.com/resources/blog/sandworm-disrupts-power-ukraine-operational-technology. All accessed 15 November 2023.

even before the war began.[89] As a result, Russia has employed traditional kinetic weapons on Ukraine's critical infrastructure. This affects civilian non-combatants (another breach of the Law of Armed Conflict), aimed at undermining Ukrainian morale. Although capacity has been diminished by the "brain drain" of technology professionals from Russia as the war progressed, kinetic attacks and cyberattacks from patriotic hackers remain in evidence.[90]

Prior to the war and more widely, cyberspace is an arena in which inconvenience and discomfort can be created for governments, societies, and economies without escalating their consequences to cross the threshold qualifying as the use of force or armed conflict.[91] It is however a "gray zone" where "Subversion, disinformation, and sabotage" can "prepare the ground for eventual kinetic operations."[92] Russian intelligence and Russian cybercriminals have long been actively exploiting the "gray zone" of cyberspace. In its 2024 annual review, Britain's National Cyber Security Centre warned "Russia is routinely seeking to compromise the systems of NATO states and aiming to shape the information space globally around Ukraine as it erroneously sees itself in conflict with NATO."[93]

This has been seen in the former Soviet republics, especially Ukraine. Extending these operations to sabotaging critical infrastructure through cyber-kinetic operations, especially against a NATO member state, whilst possible, would be a far riskier gambit.[94] Nevertheless it was prudent for "Five Eyes" cybersecurity agencies to issue alerts in the wake of the invasion warning owner-operators of critical infrastructure to put their "shields up" against increased threats that might emerge from "malicious cyber activity from Russian state-sponsored cyber actors or Russian-aligned cybercrime groups."[95] Whether one subscribes to ideas of "hy-

---

89 Stoddart, *Cyberwarfare*, pp. 189–198.

90 RUSI, "Cyber Operations in Ukraine," Hüsch and Jarnecki, "All Quiet on the Cyber Front?" From the perspective of those helping Ukraine see Kim Zetter, "Security Firms Aiding Ukraine During War Could Be Considered Participants in Conflict" (December 7, 2022), https://www.zetter-zeroday.com/security-firms-aiding-ukraine-during/, accessed 18 March 2024. This is an acceleration of a longer-term post-Cold War process making it increasingly difficult for Russia to retain those wishing to leave for political or economic reasons. Riehle, *Russian Intelligence*, pp. 258–260.

91 The Tallinn Manual, https://ccdcoe.org/research/tallinn-manual/, accessed 22 June 2022. Schmitt (ed.), *Tallinn Manual 2.0*, pp. 350–354.

92 Galeotti, "The Mythical 'Gerasimov Doctrine' and the Language of Threat," p. 157.

93 National Cyber Security Centre, Annual Review 2024, p. 24, https://www.ncsc.gov.uk/files/NCSC_Annual_Review_2024.pdf, accessed 4 December 2024.

94 Samuel Charap, "The Ghost of Hybrid War," *Survival*, Vol. 57, No. 6 (December 2015 – January 2016), pp. 51–58.

95 ALERT. Russian State-Sponsored and Criminal Cyber Threats to Critical Infrastructure (April 20, 2022), https://www.cisa.gov/news-events/alerts/2022/04/20/russian-state-sponsored-and-

brid warfare" or not, case studies show that Russia has systematically used its intelligence agencies, sub-state cybercriminals, and organizations as proxies and "privateers" to weaken their perceived adversaries by non-military means.[96] It does not necessarily follow that these are part of a fully orchestrated strategy or demonstrations of the "Gerasimov doctrine" and may instead reflects targets of opportunity.

7 Plausible deniability and the 4Ds of Russian information warfare

Connell and Vogler also accurately record that the Kremlin tries to hide behind a cloak of plausible deniability, especially through proxy criminal actors or front organizations. This can be useful when exfiltrating data or documents used for dis/mis and mal-information campaigns and influence operations being run by the GRU, SVR, or domestically by the FSB. These operations and campaigns can be used for a range of purposes. This includes attempts at discrediting foreign leaders or government institutions, including hacking and leaking to third-party sites like Wikileaks (or their own outlets) to stoke divisive issues.[97]

By 2016, if not before, Russia became adept at amplifying these information/influence operations. By the time cyber forensics has traced the sources back to Russia, this stolen and repurposed information has already seeded. In its wake are smoke and mirrors and denials of responsibility. These are part of the 4Ds of Russian information warfare: dismiss, distort, distract, and dismay directed to "dismiss the critic, distort the facts, distract from the main issue and dismay the audience."[98] To these four needs to be added a fifth – disruption. This is not only in the domain of information warfare but now, alongside a sixth D – destruction, needs setting in the context of hybrid warfare in Ukraine and beyond.

---

criminal-cyber-threats-critical. These continue to be issued. Russia Cyber Threat Overview and Advisories, https://www.cisa.gov/topics/cyber-threats-and-advisories/advanced-persistent-threats/russia. Both accessed 15 July 2023.

96 Michael Kofman and Matthew Rojansky, "A Closer look at Russia's 'Hybrid War,'" Kennan Cable, No. 7 (April 2015), https://www.files.ethz.ch/isn/190090/5-KENNAN%20CABLE-ROJANSKY%20KOFMAN.pdf accessed 28 February 2020, Alexander D. Chekov, Anna V. Makarycheva, Anastasia M. Solomentseva, Maxim A. Suchkov, and Andrey A. Sushentsov, "War of the Future: A View from Russia," *Survival*, Vol. 61, Issue 6 (December 2019–January 2020), pp. 25–48.

97 Connell and Vogler, "Russia's Approach to Cyber Warfare," p. 23.

98 Ben Nimmo, "Anatomy of an Info-War: How Russia's Propaganda Machine Works, and How to Counter It" (May 19, 2015), https://www.stopfake.org/en/anatomy-of-an-info-war-how-russia-s-propaganda-machine-works-and-how-to-counter-it/, accessed 2 April 2023.

These tactics, operations, and operatives can also be useful for cyberespionage causing sabotage as well as for standard Distributed Denial of Service (DDoS) attacks. Third-party sites like Wikileaks, either wittingly or unwittingly, have aided dissemination and the effects and effectiveness of hacking secret and private information with political effects in the minds of the readers/recipients, leading to real world consequences. By "camouflaging the source of the information and concealing the motivations for its release" organs of the Russian state have influenced politics and social cohesion.[99] This leads to difficult to measure effects in terms of cognitive and behavioral changes, including voting intentions and political and social views.

These campaigns of influence are primarily used against foreign nations and supranational bodies seen as rivals or posing problems. Information and influence operations have also been used alongside intimidation, threats, and assassinations against domestic opposition. Externally, the prime target is the United States and liberal Western order. Various NATO member states have experienced orchestrated campaigns as have members of the European Union. Areas of Africa where the Wagner Group has been active have also been subjected to Russian information and influence operations alongside military intervention.

8 The Wagner Group: Hybrid warfare destabilizing Africa and Europe

In regions of Africa, especially contested areas of the vast but unstable areas of the Sahel and into North Africa, the Wagner Group has been invited in by threatened regimes and military juntas. By extension, Russia has gained political influence in these conflict zones. Interventions have not always proved successful. This includes in Libya where civil war and political instability took hold after the 2010/11 "Arab Spring" which deposed the regime of Colonel Muammar Gaddafi where Wagner assist the forces of General Khalifa Haftar.[100] They were also unsuccessful in countering Islamist insurgents in Mozambique.[101]

---

99 Connell and Vogler, "Russia's Approach to Cyber Warfare," p. 23.

100 House of Commons Foreign Affairs Committee, Guns for gold: The Wagner Network exposed, Seventh Report of Session 2022–23, July 18, 2023, pp. 6, 14, 20–25, 45, https://committees.parliament.uk/publications/41073/documents/200048/default/. CIA World Factbook, https://www.cia.gov/the-world-factbook/countries/libya/, accessed 27 July 2023. Yahia H. Zoubir, "The Protracted Civil War in Libya: The Role of Outside Powers," *Insight Turkey*, Vol. 22, No. 4 (Fall 2020), pp. 11–27. Sergey Sukhankin, "Wagner Group in Libya: Weapon of War or Geopolitical Tool?" *Terrorism Monitor*, Vol. 11, Issue 13 (June 2020), pp. 5–6. Sarah Brockmeier, Oliver Stuenkel, and Marcos

In 2022/23 Wagner helped displace UN peacekeeping operations in Central African Republic and Mali.[102] In Mali this included a mal-information campaign targeting French peacekeepers which accused them of staging an atrocity with rumors of mass graves.[103] Reports suggest responsibility instead lay with the Wagner Group.[104] French forces also ended counterterrorism operations in Burkina Faso, following a second military coup in a year, amid concerns Wagner forces were trying to step in.[105] Across the Sahel, a region of sub-Saharan Africa that stretches from Senegal to Eritrea as well as in Libya (part of Africa's northern Maghreb region), Russia's Wagner Group has been highly active.[106] It is an area riven with conflict, failed, failing, and unstable states divided by civil wars, and Islamic terrorist insurgencies. This has led to UN-mandated Western-led interventions, main-

Tourinho, "The Impact of the Libya Intervention Debates on Norms of Protection," *Global Society*, Vol. 30, No. 1 (January 2016), pp. 113–133.

101 Guns for gold, pp. 13–15, 24, 45, 66, 77.

102 For background and operations see United Nations Multidimensional Integrated Stabilization Mission in the Central African Republic (MINUSCA), https://minusca.unmissions.org/en/about; United Nations Multidimensional Integrated Stabilization Mission in Mali (MINUSMA), https://minusma.unmissions.org/en/history. Both accessed 27 July 2023.

103 Amy Mackinnon and Robbie Gramer, "Russian Mercenaries Staged Atrocities in Mali, France Says. The French military watched what appeared to be Wagner operatives attempting a false-flag operation to discredit the West" (April 26, 2022), https://foreignpolicy.com/2022/04/26/russian-mercenaries-staged-atrocities-mali-france-says/, accessed 27 July 2023. See also Giles, *Russia's War on Everybody*, pp. 158–163.

104 Mali: New Atrocities by Malian Army, Apparent Wagner Fighters (July 24, 2023), https://www.hrw.org/news/2023/07/24/mali-new-atrocities-malian-army-apparent-wagner-fighters, accessed 27 July 2023. For background see Nicolas Desgrais, Yvan Guichaoua, and Andrew Lebovich, "Unity is the Exception. Alliance Formation and Deformation Among Armed Actors in Northern Mali," *Small Wars & Insurgencies*, Vol. 29, No. 4 (August 2008), pp. 654–679 and Amir Seyedfarshi, "French Interventionism in the Age of R2P: A Critical Examination of the Case of Mali," *Creighton International and Comparative Law Journal*, Vol. 7, Issue 1 (2016), pp. 2–36.

105 Guns for gold, pp. 16, 29. Cyril Bensimon, Elise Vincent, and Morgane Le Cam, "France's Operation Sabre in Burkina Faso: From a quiet arrival to a bitter withdrawal. At the request of the ruling junta in Ouagadougou, French special forces have withdrawn from the West African country, marking the end of more than 20 years of military presence" (February 25, 2023), https://www.lemonde.fr/en/le-monde-africa/article/2023/02/25/france-s-operation-sabre-in-burkina-faso-from-a-quiet-arrival-to-a-bitter-withdrawal_6017245_124.html, accessed 27 July 2023. CAR, Mali, and Burkina Faso are former French colonies.

106 Anna Naa Adochoo Mensah and Kwesi Aning, "Russia Resurgent? Untangling the Role and Meaning of Moscow's Proxies in West Africa and the Sahel," *Strategic Review for Southern Africa*, Vol. 44, No. 1 (2022), pp. 49–64.

ly for peacekeeping and stability but also to tackle jihadist extremism and attempts to curtail refugee flows to Europe.[107]

Russia has exploited this chaos and in so doing created pressures on the European Union by inserting Wagner forces to militarily support undemocratic regimes and junta leaders. There they have also run dis/mal-information campaigns from their hybrid warfare toolbox to brew instability and help facilitate regime changes.[108] Regional instability has seen over 32 million Africans become internally displaced. Millions of these have become refugees or asylum seekers in neighboring states. These migratory flows increase pressures already faced by neighboring countries, "which themselves may be fragile or conflict-affected."[109]

This has led to migration routes from the Sahel to Maghreb states and illegal migration routes opening from North Africa across the Mediterranean. As asylum seekers and illegal (forced) migration have increased, European governments are finding it difficult to sustain high levels of mass immigration. This was compounded by the Ukraine War and an exodus of Ukrainian civilians seeking refuge and safety. These waves of immigration have generated political pressures across the European Union (EU), European Economic Area (EEA), and for the United Kingdom, where they have become electoral issues.[110] Relatedly, during the war Russia's effective blockade of Ukraine's Black Sea ports has seen supplies of essential grain from Ukraine create or exacerbate food insecurity and drive inflation, especially in Africa and Europe.[111]

---

107 Bruno Charbonneau, "Counter-Insurgency Governance in the Sahel," *International Affairs*, Vol. 97, No. 6 (November 2021), pp. 1805–1823. Morten Bøås and Francesco Strazzari, "Governance, Fragility and Insurgency in the Sahel: A Hybrid Political Order in the Making," *The International Spectator*, Vol. 55, No. 4 (November 2020), pp. 1–17.

108 Alina Polyakova and Mathieu Boulègue, "The Evolution of Russian Hybrid Warfare: Executive Summary" (January 29, 2021), https://cepa.org/comprehensive-reports/the-evolution-of-russian-hybrid-warfare-executive-summary/, accessed 26 July 2023.

109 Guns for gold, p. 29.

110 Norman Sempijja and Ekeminiabasi Eyita-Okon, "Examining the Effectiveness of the EU Security-Development Strategy in Tackling Instability in the Sahel: The Case for an Alternative Strategy?" *South African Journal of International Affairs*, Vol. 29, No. 2 (July 2022), pp. 139–160. Africa Center for Strategic Studies, "32 Million Africans Forcibly Displaced by Conflict and Repression" (June 17, 2021), https://africacenter.org/spotlight/32-million-africans-forcibly-displaced-by-conflict-and-repression/. Teresa Nogueira Pinto, "The EU's imperfect choices on migration from Africa" (March 13, 2023), https://www.gisreportsonline.com/r/eu-africa-migration/. Both accessed 28 July 2023.

111 Carlos Lopes, "The Untamed Impact of a Faraway Shock: Africa and the War in Ukraine," *Strategic Review for Southern Africa*, Vol. 44, No. 1, pp. 9–24. Robert Kappel, "Russia and Africa: The Invasion of Ukraine Leads to the Next Major Crisis," *Strategic Review for Southern Africa*, Vol. 44, No. 1 (2022), pp. 25–35.

Wagner has also brought significant supplies of Russian weaponry into Africa's conflict zones. In exchange they receive money, basing facilities, mining rights for gold and gemstones, and other natural resource extraction deals.[112] Geopolitically, it has seen Russia re-establish old ties, forge new ones, and substitute Western peacekeepers and counterterrorism operations.[113] This sets an important context why Prigozhin remained at liberty for some time after his failed "coup" attempt in June 2023 and why he was part of the Russian-Africa summit in July 2023.[114]

Evidence was also submitted to Britain's Foreign Affairs Committee of Wagner forces operating in Venezuela. Russia has long supplied military equipment to the governments of Hugo Chávez and his successor Nicolás Maduro.[115] In addition, Russia has conducted joint naval exercises and flown intercontinental Tu-160 "Blackjack" bombers over to Venezuela in public displays of support.[116] It described Wagner as "a sprawling, decentralised network of individuals and commercial entities, which is active in several countries and for which the 'membership' is not always clear." It added, "This network ... benefited the personal financial interests of Prigozhin and the interests of Russian political elites" and the "Russian state directly or indirectly."[117] These and other allegations are always

---

112 Guns for gold, pp. 10–11, 24–26, 38, 41, 67–69.

113 Mensah and Aning, "Russia Resurgent?". Saskya Vandoorne and Arnaud Siad, "Macron announces end of France's anti-terror Operation Barkhane in Africa's Sahel region" (June 10, 2021), https://edition.cnn.com/2021/06/10/europe/france-sahel-operation-barkhane-end-intl/index.html, accessed 27 July 2023. Guns for gold, p 32.

114 Kimberly Marten, "Whither Wagner? The Consequences of Prigozhin's Mutiny and Demise," *Survival*, Vol. 65, No. 5 (October–November 2023), pp. 45–64.

115 Written evidence submitted by Professor Mark Galeotti (WGN0005), May 2022, https://committees.parliament.uk/writtenevidence/108294/pdf/, accessed 26 July 2023. Thomas Posado, "From Chávez to Maduro: From Delegative Democracy to De-Democratization," in Alain Dieckhoff, Christophe Jaffrelot, and Elise Massicard (eds.), *Contemporary Populists in Power* (Cham, Switzerland: Palgrave/Springer Nature, 2022), pp. 75–92.

116 Written evidence submitted by Professor Mark Galeotti (WGN0005), May 2022. See also Timothy Frye, Ora John Reuter, and David Szakonyi, "Vote Brokers, Clientelist Appeals, and Voter Turnout: Evidence from Russia and Venezuela," *World Politics*, Vol. 71, No. 4 (October 2019), pp. 710–746. Lynnette Hui Xian Ng, J. D. Moffitt, and Kathleen M. Carley, "Coordinated through a Web of Images: Analysis of Image-based Influence Operations from China, Iran, Russia, and Venezuela," ICWSM-2022 workshop proceedings, https://arxiv.org/pdf/2206.03576.pdf, accessed 26 July 2023. Victor M. Mijares, "Soft Balancing the Titans: Venezuelan Foreign-Policy Strategy Toward the United States, China, and Russia," *Latin American Policy*, Vol. 8, No. 2 (December 2017), pp. 201–231.

117 Guns for gold, pp. 5–6, 37, 54. The committee reported, "Its guiding hand has been the Russian state," p. 52.

met with denials.[118] In many ways, this mirrors Putin's Russia and Russian foreign policy.

Furthermore, early on in Russia's invasion it was reported that there was a "kill list" of 24 Ukrainian officials, including President Zelenskyy, and two separate sabotage groups in Kyiv totaling 400 members. Neither of these were Russian intelligence units. They were instead from Wagner and Chechen special forces who were allegedly exposed by dissident FSB agents.[119] Zelenskyy was offered the chance to evacuate by the Americans and British, accompanied by his family and key officials, and set up a government in exile. Zelenskyy refused to leave Kyiv. Instead, he became a lightning rod for Ukrainian resistance and freedom and self-determination by fervently asserting, "I need ammunition, not a ride."[120]

9 Russia's shifting intelligence priorities and uses of cyberespionage for active measures

The massive growth of cyberspace, growing global and interpersonal connectivity, and explosion in social media also present new problems, opening up new opportunities for grassroots intelligence analysis and leaktivist sites.[121] These developments have seen unaccredited self-styled investigative journalists and websites emerge like the controversial Julian Assange and Wikileaks as well as less controversial (and valuable) groups like Bellingcat.[122] ICT developments have also been a key enabler for Russia's three intelligence agencies, the SVR, GRU, as well as the FSB. This has seen them target Western social media platforms with precision

---

118 Guns for gold, p. 8.

119 Graham Massie, "Anti-war Russian FSB agents have helped thwart three assassination attempts against Zelensky, Ukraine claims" (March 4, 2022), https://www.independent.co.uk/news/world/europe/russia-ukraine-zelensky-assassination-attempts-b2028963.html, accessed 14 April 2023.

120 Jack Dutton, "Russia Nearly Captured Zelensky in First Few Hours of Ukraine Invasion" (April 29, 2022), https://www.newsweek.com/russia-nearly-captured-zelensky-first-few-hours-ukraine-invasion-1702156. Institute for the Study of War, "Ukraine Conflict Updates," https://www.understandingwar.org/backgrounder/ukraine-conflict-updates. Both accessed 6 January 2023.

121 Avi Tal and David Siman-Tov, "HUMINT in the Cybernetic Era: Gaming in Two Worlds," *Military and Strategic Affairs*, Vol. 7, No. 3 (2015), p. 97.

122 Eliot Higgins, *We Are Bellingcat: An Intelligence Agency for the People* (London: Bloomsbury, 2022).

and at scale and to engage as Advanced Persistent Manipulators (APMs) as well as Advanced Persistent Threats (APTs).[123]

In cyberspace, the SVR and GRU in particular have demonstrated they are again capable of mounting long-term espionage campaigns and undertaking active measures. This has seen them become APTs in cyberspace.[124] They have also returned to many Soviet-era policies and methods. In the U.S., analysis by the Office of the Director of National Intelligence (DNI) also pointed to Russia's influence campaigns showing they are opportunistic and built on longstanding practices. They are designed to build Russian influence in Europe and Eurasia through a series of affiliations, including financial support and political connections, to like-minded political parties and non-governmental organizations (NGOs). This sees monetary support used "in combination with other tools of Russian statecraft, including propaganda in local media, direct lobbying by the Russian Government, economic pressure, and military intimidation."[125] As outlined in the opening to this chapter, this remains in evidence.

The U.S. State Department has recognized how the Kremlin has sought to manipulate elections and referendums in Europe. This includes covert and overt support for political parties of both right and left and leveraging front organizations and NGOs. In addition, they make "small, low-profile investments in key economic sectors to build political influence over time" alongside "tactics that focus on exploiting internal discord in an effort to break centrist consensus on the importance of core institutions."[126] The U.S. National Counterintelligence Strategy for 2020–2022 went further. It outlined how Russia's campaigns are designed to sway public opinion and influence government policies and influence or deceive key decision-makers. This includes the use and amplification of conspiracy theories. This then feeds into:

> targeting of our democratic and electoral processes using influence operations that can be long in duration, have broad strategic implications, and include activities that are covert, overt, and illegal. Our adversaries regard deception or manipulation of the views of U.S. ci-

123 "Propaganda in the digital age: How cyber influence operations erode trust" (November 9, 2022), https://www.microsoft.com/en-us/security/business/security-insider/threat-briefs/propaganda-in-the-digital-age/, accessed 10 July 2023.

124 A discussion of some of Russia's cyber capabilities, their organizational structure, and operations can be found in Sergei A. Medvedev, "Offense-defense theory analysis of Russian cyber capability," Monterey, California: Naval Postgraduate School (March 2015). Available from http://calhoun.nps.edu/bitstream/handle/10945/45225/15Mar_Medvedev_Sergei.pdf?sequence=1, accessed 25 March 2017.

125 Putin's Asymmetric Assault, p. 38.

126 Putin's Asymmetric Assault, p. 38.

tizens and policymakers to be an effective, inexpensive, and low-risk method for achieving their strategic objectives.[127]

The construction of the Russian state and the national interest under Putin has directly led to a number of other shifts in focus. These have rolled back the policies of the Yeltsin era which saw a more integrationist and accommodating approach to the West in Russia's foreign and security policy.[128] The expansion of NATO to Russia's borders combined with Russia's relative political, economic, and military decline frame Putin's approach, bolstered by renationalization of state industries.[129] Since switching its main Cold War intelligence focus, Russian cyberespionage has metastasized. This includes the adoption of active measures including hacking political parties and election interference and dis/misinformation campaigns which generate "fake news" stories for political effect. This has been most widely reported in the United States, but America has not been the only target. Far from it.[130]

Some of these changes have also been attributed to the appointment of Sergei Shoigu as Minister of Defense in November 2012 having already served in government roles for over two decades. He was loyal to Yeltsin during the attempted coup in 1991 and threats to his power in 1993. He also stood aside during Putin's presidential run in 1999.[131] Shoigu is described as influential and ambitious and a key member of Putin's inner circle. Until the 2020 COVID-19 pandemic, which has

---

127 National Counterintelligence Strategy of the United States of America 2020–2022, p. 9. https://www.dni.gov/files/NCSC/documents/features/20200205-National_CI_Strategy_2020_2022.pdf, accessed 2 September 2021.

128 Yuri Felshtinky and Alexander Litvinenko, *Blowing Up Russia: Terror from Within* (New York: Encounter Books, 2007), especially pp. xxi–xix.

129 Marcin Kaczmarski, "Domestic Power Relations and Russia's Foreign Policy," *Demokratizatsiya*, Vol. 22, No. 3 (2014), pp. 383–409. Nadejda Makarova Victor, "Gazprom: Gas Giant Under Strain," Working Paper #71 (January 2008), Program on Energy and Sustainable Development at Stanford University. https://pesd.fsi.stanford.edu/sites/default/files/WP71,_Nadja_Victor,_Gazprom,_13Jan08.pdf, accessed 16 September 2017.

130 It is also worthy of mention that the U.S. engaged in election interference itself during the Cold War. For an overview see Timothy Carothers, "Is the U.S. Hypocritical to Criticize Russian Election Meddling?" (March 12, 2018), https://carnegieendowment.org/2018/03/12/is-u.s.-hypocritical-to-criticize-russian-election-meddling-pub-75780, accessed 9 January 2018.

131 Alexis A. Blanc, Alyssa Demus, Sandra Kay Evans, Michelle Grisé, Mark Hvizda, Marta Keep, Natasha Lander, Krystyna Marcinek, "The Russian General Staff Understanding the Military's Decisionmaking Role in a "Besieged Fortress" (2023), Rand Corporation, p. 27, https://www.rand.org/content/dam/rand/pubs/research_reports/RRA1200/RRA1233-7/RAND_RRA1233-7.pdf, accessed 30 June 2023.

seen Putin take fewer and fewer visits outside of Moscow,[132] he was "a frequent companion on Putin's outdoorsy vacations." Strengthened by a "radical shift in Russia's foreign policy since the Ukraine crisis" in 2014, Shoigu also had begun a "big hunt for programmers." This included recruiting students from Russia's universities and funding hacking competitions.[133]

Russia has also sometimes looked to others when reforming from within. When USCYBERCOM was founded in 2010, Shoigu felt this was a command structure that Russia could emulate. Since then, aided by the GRU, Shoigu has helped drive Russia's cyberespionage and cyberwarfare capabilities and capacity.[134] This is also when Russia began looking to their hacker community (including cybercriminals) for recruits.[135] By 2014 a symbiosis had developed where Russia's intelligence agencies were piggybacking on cybercrime operations to cost-effectively gather intelligence.[136] They are also suspected of leveraging entrepreneurial hackers/cybercriminals, Russian technology developers and providers, front companies, academic institutions and think tanks, as well as private military contractors.[137] The head of the GRU reports directly to Shoigu.

Partly for their perceived failure to provide accurate intelligence of Georgian capabilities in the 2008 conflict, in the early 2010s there had been speculation that the GRU might be disbanded with their famed *Spetsnaz* special forces integrated with the regular army and their SIGINT ability passing to the SVR. However, the appointment of Igor Sergun as Director in 2011 revitalized the GRU. Sergun was described as "an able, articulate, and effective champion of his agency's interests

---

132 Anonymous, "'I consider the president a war criminal.' An escaped Federal Guard communications officer speaks about Putin's obsession with secrecy and self-preservation" (April 4, 2023), https://meduza.io/en/feature/2023/04/04/i-consider-the-president-a-war-criminal, accessed 30 June 2023.

133 Christian Esch, "Doing Putin's Dirty Work. The Rise of Russia's GRU Military Intelligence Service" (October 19, 2018), http://www.spiegel.de/international/world/russia-and-the-rise-of-gru-military-intelligence-service-a-1233576.html, accessed 3 January 2018.

134 Daniil Turovsky, "Russian armed cyberforces. How the state creates military detachments of hackers" (November 7, 2016), https://meduza.io/feature/2016/11/07/rossiyskie-vooruzhennye-kibersily, accessed 19 July 2023.

135 This is not an uncommon practice. Both the NSA and Britain's GCHQ also recruit through these methods by turning "poachers into gamekeepers."

136 Putin's Asymmetric Assault, p. 182.

137 Dave Aitel, Sophia d'Antoine, Thomas Garwin, Ian Roos, Nicholas Rostow, Justin Sherman, and Abraham Wagner, "Russia's Cyber Operations A Threat to American National Security" (2022), pp. 19, 25–82, https://margin.re/content/files/2023/01/Russia-s-Cyber-Operations---Full-Report.pdf, accessed 7 August 2023. This source, funded by research from the U.S. Defense Advanced Research Projects Agency (DARPA), contains further details of individuals, their organizations, and their connections to the Russian state and Russian intelligence found elsewhere in this book.

… particularly good at managing relations with Putin and those to whom the president listens."[138] The GRU's position rose significantly under Sergun with the GRU central both to destabilization in the Donbas region of Eastern Ukraine in 2014 and Russia's intervention in the Syrian civil war.[139] Upon his sudden death aged 58 in January 2016 he was succeeded by Igor Korobov, who himself died suddenly in November 2018 at 62.

No cause of death was attributed although Korobov was reported to have suffered from a long-term illness (Sergun is reported to have died from a heart attack).[140] Not all agree. According to one report, "Korobov reportedly started feeling unwell after a severe reprimand from President Putin in mid-September [2018], following the exposure of an apparently bungled GRU operation to assassinate Sergey Skripal in Salisbury, England."[141] Admiral Igor Kostyukov took over as chief of the GRU from Korobov. He is the first to come from the Russian Navy and his role in supporting Russia's ground intervention in Syria was key to his appointment.[142] Kostyukov's predecessors might have died from natural causes but at home and abroad a wide number of former and serving officials have died unex-

138 Amy Knight, "GRU-SOME. This Russian Spy Agency Is in the Middle of Everything" (August 8, 2018), https://www.thedailybeast.com/this-russian-spy-agency-is-in-the-middle-of-everything, accessed 4 January 2018.

139 Mark Galeotti quoted in Knight, "GRU-SOME" (August 8, 2018). Mark Galeotti, "We Don't Know What to Call Russian Military Intelligence and That May Be a Problem" (January 19, 2016), https://warontherocks.com/2016/01/we-dont-know-what-to-call-russian-military-intelligence-and-that-may-be-a-problem/, accessed 1 July 2023. Russia also utilized proxy forces and "other shadowy figures" in the Donbas. Relatedly, the GRU and FSB also overstated Russian sympathies in Eastern Ukraine as well as the fragility of Ukraine's government. Blanc et al., "The Russian General Staff," pp. 77, 99.

140 Nathan Hodge and Laura Smith-Spark, "Igor Korobov, head of Russian military intelligence, dies age 62 – state media" (November 22, 2018), https://edition.cnn.com/2018/11/22/europe/russia-gru-death-intl/index.html, accessed 3 January 2018.

141 Anonymous, "The Real Russia. Today. The head of Russia's GRU is dead, funny Health Ministry promos, and a 'baby murder' controversy" (November 22, 2018), https://meduza.io/en/brief/2018/11/22/the-real-russia-today. Oliver Carroll, "Igor Korobov: Death of Russian GRU chief latest in long line of fatal incidents surrounding agency" (November 22, 2018), https://www.independent.co.uk/news/world/europe/igor-korobov-dead-russia-gru-spy-agency-sergei-skripal-yulia-salisbury-novichok-a8646856.html. Both accessed 4 January 2018. Carroll is one of a number of investigative journalists to suggest his death was natural causes. However, he adds that "revelations about the probable identities of several hundred active agents" through Bellingcat's OSINT investigations into Russian intelligence activities saw Korobov under pressure due to intelligence lapses by field agents responsible for the attempt on the Skripals and the botched hack attempt on the OPCW offices.

142 Anonymous, "Russia's GRU: New Chief, Same Goals" (December 10, 2018), https://warsawinstitute.org/russias-gru-new-chief-goals/, accessed 30 October 2019.

pectedly.[143] Those also include some Russian oligarchs whilst others were forced out, including out of Russia, or retired.[144] The oligarchy system rose during the early 1990s during the early days of privatization and remains a power base in Russia.

10 The limits of cyberespionage: Traditional espionage, HUMINT and "hard targets"

The Kremlin's targets might be of such high value that a covert operation involving trained agents from their intelligence agencies, military, or Special Operations Forces (especially the GRU's *Spetsnaz*) are used. Specific NATO and EU facilities and personnel have been targeted along with International Governmental Organizations (IGOs) including the Organisation for the Prohibition of Chemical Weapons (OPCW) and World Anti-Doping Association (WADA). Non-Governmental Organizations (NGOs) have also been hit.[145] As headquarters for a series of important international organizations including the UN's European HQ and subsidiary bodies like the UN Human Rights Council, UN High Commissioner for Refugees (UNHCR), as well as the World Health Organization (WHO), and World Trade Organization (WTO), traditionally neutral Switzerland has also emerged as a hotbed of Russian intelligence gathering through intelligence officers operating under diplomatic cover.[146] Close-access SIGINT collection has also been discovered in Norway's parliament.[147]

Tal and Siman-Tov characterize three key stages of Human Intelligence (HUMINT). The first locates and selects targets (spotting). Spotting is based on a range of factors. This includes the targets' qualifications, connections, influence, abilities, their current and potential motives, and their accessibility. They need to be accessible to recruit and handle. The next stage is recruitment. This can

143 Marshall Cohen and Jose Pagliery, "Nine months, nine prominent Russians dead" (August 24, 2017), https://edition.cnn.com/2017/03/24/europe/dead-russians/index.html, and Joel Gunter, "Sergei Skripal and the 14 deaths under scrutiny" (March 7, 2018), https://www.bbc.co.uk/news/world-europe-43299598. Both accessed 4 January 2017.

144 Mark Galeotti, *The Vory: Russia's Super Mafia* (New Haven, CT: Yale University Press, 2018), pp. 113–120, 253–271. Serguey Braguinsky, "Postcommunist Oligarchs in Russia: Quantitative Analysis," *The Journal of Law and Economics*, Vol. 52, No. 2 (May 2009), pp. 307–349.

145 Putin's Asymmetric Assault, pp. 1–31, 47–139.

146 Switzerland's Security 2023 – Situation Report of the Federal Intelligence Service, pp. 62–63, https://www.vbs.admin.ch/en/documents/search.detail.document.html/vbs-internet/en/documents/intelligence-service/situation-reports/NDB-Lagebericht-2023-e.pdf.html, accessed 5 July 2023.

147 Riehle, *Russian Intelligence*, pp. 246–247.

be planned, made to appear chance, or they can be "walk-ins" who offer their services of their own accord. The most desirable agents are "walk-ins." Many "walk-ins" have yielded major intelligence successes for the agencies running them. This includes double agents like Robert Hanssen (whose occupation meant he understood the tradecraft, and to avoid exposing his identity he refused meetings with his handlers).[148] The third stage revolves around handling and operational situations. The preferred option remains physical clandestine meetings. This helps establish trust and personal affinity with the agent to be handled. It is also where information and skills can be passed on or developed. Increasing opportunities for remote access between agent and handler is now changing some of these practices.[149]

"Walk-ins," co-opted insiders, and agents of influence ("useful idiots"/*polezni durak*) continue to be nurtured through recruiting and running sources. How Russia has combined its classical tradecraft in HUMINT will be seen below and in subsequent chapters. In Ukraine, this has seen Ukrainians collaborating with Russia for reasons ranging from a promise of high office to corruption and bribery, and in autumn 2023 a Bulgarian cell working for Russian intelligence was uncovered operating in the UK (leading to their 2025 prosecution).[150] For Edward Lucas, Western nations are "astonishingly, almost suicidally, trusting when it comes to real security – protecting our secrets and our decision-making."[151] Despite the openness of Western societies, there are hard targets, including highly protected facilities and systems, whose barriers to entry make them very difficult to

148 Robert Hanssen, https://www.fbi.gov/history/famous-cases/robert-hanssen, accessed 6 March 2020. David Wise, *Spy: The Inside Story of How the FBI's Robert Hanssen Betrayed America* (New York: Random House, 2003).

149 Tal and Siman-Tov, "HUMINT in the Cybernetic Era," p. 94. Moles and Illegals did not form part of their analysis. More broadly still, bearing in mind that "throughout history, the terms "espionage and "spying" have carried varying amounts of pejorative baggage...[HUMINT] subsumes many human collection efforts that are not properly considered espionage". Geoffrey B. Demarest, "Espionage in International Law", *Denver Journal of International Law & Policy*, Vol. 24, No 2 (Spring 1996), p. 324.

150 Mari Saito and Maria Tsvetkova, "The Enemy Within" (undated), https://www.reuters.com/investigates/special-report/ukraine-crisis-russia-saboteurs/. Luke Harding and Matthew Weaver, "Three Bulgarians suspected of spying for Russia charged in UK" (August 15, 2023), https://www.theguardian.com/uk-news/2023/aug/15/three-bulgarians-suspected-of-spying-for-russia-reportedly-charged-in-uk. Daniel De Simone and Amy Walker, "Bulgarians guilty of spying for Russia in the UK" (March 7 2025), https://www.bbc.co.uk/news/articles/cx2gx52xqqpo. All accessed 1 May 2025.

151 Lucas, *Deception*, p. 311. See also Mikael Wigell, "Hybrid Interference as a Wedge Strategy: A Theory of External Interference in Liberal Democracy," *International Affairs*, Vol. 95, Issue 2 (March 2019), pp. 255–275.

breach.[152] However, new avenues of infiltration and exfiltration have been opened up by interconnected cyberspace. The Internet and mobile 4G and 5G technologies have also opened up new ways to recruit and communicate with HUMINT assets as well as reach remote target audiences.

11 Unit 29155: Sergei Skripal, the "drive-by" hacking of the OPCW, and "dirty work"

Direct or physical infiltration of organizations is rare, or at least rarely reported, but there has been one notable Russian case. This was Russia's attempted penetration of the OPCW in a drive-by cyberattack at its headquarters at The Hague in The Netherlands in April 2018. The GRU had already tried and failed at remotely penetrating the OPCW.[153] At the time the OPCW, alongside Britain's Defence and Science Technology Laboratory (DSTL) at Porton Down, were independently analyzing the chemical used against former GRU officer (and former double agent for Britain's Secret Intelligence Service, MI6) Sergey Skripal in March 2018.[154]

This saw the use of the deadly nerve agent Novichok in a public space in Salisbury. This same method had been used on Alexei Navalny prior to boarding a flight from Tomsk to Moscow.[155] There is no doubt that Skripal was an extremely valuable double agent, but he had been "wrung dry under interrogation" during five years in jail "before being released in a trade" for the 2010 U.S. "Illegals" (detailed below). By 2018 he had no more secrets to give up and had settled in Salisbury.[156] The order might have originated within the GRU or by Putin personally.[157] The field operation was conducted by Dr. Alexander Mishkin, a GRU physician,

152 Kyle S. Cunliffe, "Hard Target Espionage in the Information Era: New Challenges for the Second Oldest Profession," *Intelligence and National Security*, Vol. 36, No. 7 (December 2021), pp. 1018–1034.

153 Florian J. Egloff and Max Smeets, "Publicly Attributing Cyber Attacks: A Framework," *Journal of Strategic Studies*, Vol. 46, No. 3 (September 2023), p. 521.

154 Egloff and Smeets, "Publicly Attributing Cyber Attacks: A Framework," p. 521. Mark Urban, *The Skripal Files: Putin, Poison and the New Spy War* (London: Macmillan, 2018).

155 Julia Masterson, "Novichok Used in Russia, OPCW Finds," *Arms Control Today*, Vol. 50, Issue 9 (November 2020), pp. 25–26.

156 Jeff Stein, "From Moscow with Murder: Is Russia Hunting Defectors in America?" (March 31, 2018), https://www.newsweek.com/russian-defectors-america-putin-russia-threat-skripal-868013, accessed 9 March 2020.

157 David V. Gioe, Michael S. Goodman, and David S. Frey, "Unforgiven: Russian Intelligence Vengeance as Political Theater and Strategic Messaging," *Intelligence and National Security*, Vol. 34, No. 4 (March 2019), pp. 562–567.

and Anatoliy Chepiga, a highly decorated GRU colonel. It necessitated a major clean-up operation by chemical weapons experts from nearby DSTL.[158] In 2025, the British government also indicated that X-Agent had been used to compromise the e–mail accounts of Yulia Skripal. This had been carried out by Aleksey Lukashev and Ivan Yermakov. They too were part of Unit 29155.[159]

Like Navalny, Ukrainian president Viktor Yushchenko (who was poisoned with dioxin in 2004), and Alexander Litvinenko's poisoning with polonium-210 in 2006, it was an act of revenge and political theater.[160] The intended audience are traitors and potential traitors from Russian intelligence who spy for the West as well as disaffected government or military officers and officials, or oligarchs thinking about betraying the Kremlin. It was another extraordinarily brazen assassination attempt demonstrating tradecraft which paid scant regard to the consequences (including the casual disposal of the perfume bottle containing the Novichok rather than burying it or throwing it in a river or out to sea).

It likely incapacitated Skripal for life, and almost claimed the life of his daughter Yulia. Four months later it took the life of Dawn Sturgess whose partner had discovered the discarded bottle in nearby Amesbury. Sturgess, who had sprayed what she believed was perfume onto her wrist, started experiencing deadly symptoms within 15 minutes and died eight days later.[161] Others were taken ill, including police Detective Sergeant Nick Bailey, who was contaminated when he touched the door handle of the Skripal home where the Novichok had been sprayed. So dangerous is Novichok, significant swathes of Salisbury had to be cordoned off in the aftermath as investigators on "Operation Verbasco" followed the trail.[162]

A month later, a four man team of GRU officers tried to hack the OPCW offices (a hard target) with equipment concealed in the trunk of their car close to the

---

158 Gioe, Goodman, and Frey, "Unforgiven," pp. 561–575.

159 Policy paper Profile: GRU cyber and hybrid threat operations, https://www.gov.uk/government/publications/profile-gru-cyber-and-hybrid-threat-operations/profile-gru-cyber-and-hybrid-threat-operations (July 18 2025), accessed 20 July 2025.

160 There is also some evidence the two cases are connected. Fiona Hamilton, David Brown, and Deborah Haynes, "Spy mystery: Sergei Skripal's contact with MI6 in Spain suggests links to Litvinenko case" (March 9, 2018), https://www.thetimes.co.uk/article/spy-mystery-sergei-skripal-contact-with-mi6-in-spain-suggests-links-to-litvinenko-case-skripal-putin-poison-g0p2l6ptb, accessed 21 July 2023.

161 Her death is the subject of a public inquiry which is yet to report. Dawn Sturgess Inquiry, https://www.dawnsturgess.independent-inquiry.uk/, accessed 21 July 2023.

162 Anonymous, "Salisbury Novichok-poisoned officer Nick Bailey quits" (October 17, 2020), https://www.bbc.co.uk/news/uk-england-wiltshire-54582981. Tom Symonds, "Dawn Sturgess: 'Rigorous' inquiry into Novichok death" (March 25, 2022), https://www.bbc.co.uk/news/uk-england-wiltshire-60873483. Both accessed 7 October 2023.

main building. Two were hackers, Alexey Morenets and Evgeny Serebryakov. The other two, Oleg Sotnikov and Alexei Minin, were supporting field agents. All four had traveled on diplomatic passports providing them with diplomatic immunity under the 1961 Vienna Convention.[163] They were caught red-handed and expelled from The Netherlands. Bellingcat subsequently revealed they had traveled under their real names and not assumed personas (indicating either poor tradecraft or brazenness).[164] Around this time APT28 (the GRU) was also trying to remotely hack into the systems of the British Foreign and Commonwealth Office (FCO) and DSTL which was conducting analysis both for the Skripal case and recent chemical weapons attacks in Syria, Russia's ally.[165]

DSTL subsequently confirmed that Novichok nerve agent had been used in Salisbury. A British government minister stated: "we now know for certain was carried out by serving GRU officers" and "the officers disrupted in The Hague are part of the same Unit of the GRU – 26165 – which is responsible for APT28."[166] In the aftermath, 150 Russian diplomats and spies were expelled from across the West as a message to Russia. As during the Cold War, Russia also expelled an equal number tit-for-tat.[167] There was also a disinformation campaign launched by the GRU which attempted to distort and distract from Russia's involvement.[168] This included a staged television interview on RT with Mishkin and Chepiga (under their aliases of Alexander Petrov and Ruslan Boshirov) where they claimed to be tourists who had nothing to do with the case despite the strong body of evidence being presented (including CCTV being made public).[169] The previous summer, Chepiga "the tourist" had been an invited

---

163 Radsan, "The Unresolved Equation," pp. 598–599, 621. Julian Borger, "Embassy cables: Where does diplomacy end and spying begin?" (November 28, 2010), https://www.theguardian.com/world/2010/nov/28/where-diplomacy-end-spying-begin, accessed 3 January 2018.

164 "305 Car Registrations May Point to Massive GRU Security Breach" (October 4, 2018), https://www.bellingcat.com/news/2018/10/04/305-car-registrations-may-point-massive-gru-security-breach/, accessed 7 January 2019.

165 UK exposes Russian cyber attacks, October 4, 2018, https://www.gov.uk/government/news/uk-exposes-russian-cyber-attacks, accessed 21 July 2023.

166 Minister for Europe statement: Attempted hacking of the OPCW by Russian military intelligence (October 4, 2018), https://www.gov.uk/government/speeches/minister-for-europe-statement-attempted-hacking-of-the-opcw-by-russian-military-intelligence, accessed 6 January 2019.

167 Russia has also arrested a significant number of foreigners traveling in Russia, some of them on spurious charges, who have subsequently also been used as leverage or exchanged for "spy swops". Some of the more high profile cases include Paul Whelan, a former U.S. Marine attending a wedding and Brittney Griner, an Olympic basketball gold medalist.

168 Gioe, Goodman, and Frey, "Unforgiven," pp. 561–575.

169 Anonymous, "Skripal Suspect Boshirov Identified as GRU Colonel Anatoliy Chepiga" (September 26, 2018), https://www.bellingcat.com/news/uk-and-europe/2018/09/26/skripal-suspect-boshirov-identified-gru-colonel-anatoliy-chepiga/. Anonymous, "Full report: Skripal Poisoning

guest to the daughter of Major General Andrei Averyanov, the head of Unit 29155 where "After dinner and dancing, fireworks lit up the sky."[170]

A third GRU agent, using the cover identity "Sergey Fedotov," was also subsequently identified. He was separately implicated in the poisoning of Bulgarian arms trader, Emilian Gebrev in Sofia. "Fedotov" was named as senior GRU officer, Denis Sergeev, a graduate of Russia's Military Diplomatic Academy and the GRU's Conservatory. Sergeev has also been linked to a series of quickly liquidated sham companies linked to the GRU suspected of being used for money laundering and cover for GRU agents employed through "respectable businesses."[171]

Czech intelligence linked their operation to the shadowy GRU unit, Unit 29155.[172] Unit 29155 was first identified in 2016 and is believed to have been active since at least 2009.[173] However, its history dates back to 1963 with the establishment of the GRU's 161 Center. This worked undercover "and brought together both human intelligence and special forces personnel," leading to Unit 29155 also referred to as 161 Intelligence Specialists Training Centre.[174] According to a former GRU officer, Unit 29155 operates clandestinely and internationally, tasked with "diversionary" missions, "in groups or individually – bombings, murders,

---

Suspect Dr. Alexander Mishkin, Hero of Russia" (October 9, 2018), https://www.bellingcat.com/news/uk-and-europe/2018/10/09/full-report-skripal-poisoning-suspect-dr-alexander-mishkin-hero-russia/. "Skripal Suspects Confirmed as GRU Operatives: Prior European Operations Disclosed" (September 20, 2018), https://www.bellingcat.com/news/uk-and-europe/2018/09/20/skripal-suspects-confirmed-gru-operatives-prior-european-operations-disclosed/. All accessed 7 October 2023.

170 Mark Krutov, Sergei Dobrynin, Mike Eckel, and Carl Schreck, "Russian Wedding Photos Highlight Novichok Suspect's Security Ties" (October 14, 2019), accessed 5 May 2025, https://www.rferl.org/a/member-of-the-wedding-russian-nuptials-highlight-novichok-suspect-s-intelligence-ties/30216231.html.

171 This includes visa applications for foreign travel. Anonymous, "Third Skripal Suspect Linked to 2015 Bulgaria Poisoning" (February 7, 2019), https://www.bellingcat.com/news/uk-and-europe/2019/02/07/third-skripal-suspect-linked-to-2015-bulgaria-poisoning/. Moritz Rakuszitzky, "Third Suspect in Skripal Poisoning Identified as Denis Sergeev, High-Ranking GRU Officer" (February 14, 2023), https://www.bellingcat.com/news/uk-and-europe/2019/02/14/third-suspect-in-skripal-poisoning-identified-as-denis-sergeev-high-ranking-gru-officer/. Both accessed 7 October 2023. See also Riehle, *Russian Intelligence*, p. 210 for more information on why Gebrev was likely targeted.

172 Sébastian Seibt, "Unit 29155, the Russian spies specialising in 'sabotage and assassinations'" (April 20, 2021), https://www.france24.com/en/europe/20210420-unit-29155-the-russian-spies-specialising-in-sabotage-and-assassinations, accessed 7 October 2023.

173 Michael Schwirtz, "Top Secret Russian Unit Seeks to Destabilize Europe, Security Officials Say" (October 8, 2019), https://www.nytimes.com/2019/10/08/world/europe/unit-29155-russia-gru.html, accessed 18 March 2020.

174 Jack Watling, Oleksandr V. Danylyuk, and Nick Reynolds, "The Threat from Russia's Unconventional Warfare Beyond Ukraine, 2022 – 24", February 2024, p. 6, https://static.rusi.org/SR-Russian-Unconventional-Weapons-final-web.pdf, accessed 5 May 2025.

anything."[175] Averyanov went on to succeed Yevgeny Prigozhin as leader of the Wagner Group's African operations (now reconfigured as the Africa Corps).[176] It has been implicated in other operations including a 2014 explosion at a Czech ammunition depot; a 2016 political destabilization campaign in Moldova; the 2016 coup attempt in Montenegro; and the Catalonian independence demonstrations in 2017 (operating through a base of operations in France's rural Savoie region bordering Switzerland). They have also been linked to the mysterious "Havana Syndrome."[177] Unit 29155 has been described as an "elite force," numbering as few as 20 agents, conducting "a concerted program of activity" carrying out the Kremlin's dirty work. Very little is off-limits.[178] After their exposure, the Kremlin sought to expunge the records of Mishkin, Chepiga, and Sergeev as part of an attempted cover-up.[179]

12 Russia and traditional intelligence gathering

The evidence above strongly suggests the Kremlin continues to employ traditional Soviet-era active measures alongside their cyberespionage campaigns. The character and characteristics of these methods reflect KGB practices of the Soviet era

---

175 Another elite unit of the GRU, Unit 99450, is thought to have been involved in the annexation of Crimea in 2014. Schwirtz, "Top Secret Russian Unit Seeks to Destabilize Europe, Security Officials Say".

176 Anonymous, "Yevgeny Prigozhin: Who could become the new Wagner boss?" (August 25, 2023), https://news.sky.com/video/yevgeny-prigozhin-who-could-become-the-new-wagner-boss-12947295. Christo Grozev, "Socialite, Widow, Jeweller, Spy: How a GRU Agent Charmed Her Way Into NATO Circles in Italy" (August 25, 2022), https://www.bellingcat.com/news/2022/08/25/socialite-widow-jeweller-spy-how-a-gru-agent-charmed-her-way-into-nato-circles-in-italy/. Mark Galeotti, "Siloviki at War: The Russian Security Community Since February 2022," *Russian Analytical Digest*, No. 323 (January 2025), p. 8, https://css.ethz.ch/content/dam/ethz/special-interest/gess/cis/center-for-securities-studies/pdfs/russiananalyticaldigest-323.pdf, accessed 27 April 2025. All accessed 3 May 2025.

177 Roman Dobrokhotov, Christo Grozev, and Michael Weiss, "Unraveling Havana Syndrome: New evidence links the GRU's assassination Unit 29155 to mysterious attacks on Americans, at home and abroad" (April 1, 2024), https://theins.ru/en/politics/270425, accessed 1 April 2024. Watling, Danylyuk, and Reynolds, "The Threat from Russia's Unconventional Warfare Beyond Ukraine, 2022–24", pp. 6–8.

178 Seibt, "Unit 29155." See also Daniel De Simone, "Man who spied for Russia in UK 'discussed killing journalist'" (November 28, 2024), https://www.bbc.co.uk/news/articles/c20gvl0x8yyo, accessed 4 December 2024.

179 Rakuszitzky, "Third Suspect in Skripal Poisoning."

and further back to imperial Russia.[180] Both the SVR and GRU employ human intelligence (HUMINT) officers but "There are crucial distinctions in their missions and organisational cultures."[181] Some officers work under diplomatic cover, including through Russia's embassies (with *rezidents* supplied by the FSB's "Fifth Service"), but outside the diplomatic chain of command. Others are operated by the SVR and GRU as "Illegals."[182] The FSB also operates "Illegals." This includes a group of four U.S. nationals convicted in September 2024 for conspiracy to act as unregistered agents of a foreign government whilst leading the African People's Socialist Party (a longstanding Black rights group).[183] Covert officers, or "Illegals" operate under non-official cover (NOC). NOC can vary with the cover provided by legitimate professions or legitimate causes (as in the above case). This can include masquerading as reporters from accredited media outlets, through affiliations with academia, or by representing businesses or organizations. Official cover can include government delegates to international organizations like the Permanent Mission at the United Nations in New York or at the World Bank.[184] They can also be less glamorous.[185]

To this mix can be added those who are recruited from within other foreign intelligence or security services (double agents); "deep-penetration agents" or "moles" who are tasked to join or penetrate an organization; counterintelligence agents and operations (which seek to identify "moles" and expose operations); or "double cross" (where disinformation is deliberately fed to known or suspected intelligence operatives). Russia continues to actively recruit and run these assets and operations in the West.[186] Most, if not all of these activities involve deception and deceit. For those caught spying against Russia, charges of treason or worse follow, including a lifetime of looking over their shoulders after assuming new

---

180 Abrams, "Beyond Propaganda," pp. 18–19.

181 Galeotti, "Putin's Hydra," p. 2.

182 Radsan, "The Unresolved Equation," pp. 620–622. Riehle, *Russian Intelligence*, pp. 225–227.

183 U.S. Citizens Convicted of Conspiring to Act as Illegal Agents of the Russian Government, September 12, 2024, https://www.justice.gov/archives/opa/pr/us-citizens-convicted-conspiring-act-illegal-agents-russian-government, accessed 4 May 2025.

184 An analysis of some of these high profile target organizations and the profile of individuals targeted as well as the close-access employment of SIGINT (including eavesdropping devices) used against them can be found in Riehle, *Russian Intelligence*, pp. 108–111, 113–117 122–124.

185 On the types of cover see Riehle, *Russian Intelligence*, pp. 217–227.

186 Micael Ertl, "Germany charges intelligence 'mole' with treason in Russia spying case" (September 6, 2023), https://www.bbc.co.uk/news/world-europe-66727785, accessed 8 September 2023.

identities under state protection such as in the Skripal case.[187] These field agents are known as "officers," "agents," "assets," or simply spies to most.

Like most other major intelligence agencies, the FSB, GRU, and SVR operate out of local, regional, or national bases of operations. As in Soviet days, these are still called *rezidentura* (Russian for residency).[188] The head of a *rezidentura* is a *rezident* (known as a station chief in the U.S. and Chiefs of Station in the UK). Their subordinates have responsibilities for gathering political, military, or economic intelligence, or for conducting active measures. Many locations are known or suspected of being *rezidentura*/intelligence stations and take counter-surveillance measures. These include vibrating pipes that emit white noise making eavesdropping difficult and using rooms with no telephones or Internet-connected devices.

Among other things, the SVR are suspected of copying documentation from U.S. citizens applying for Russian visas for work or as tourists in these *rezidentura.* This is used to aid "Illegals" seeking cover by adding credence to their background or "legend." This especially applies to those operating under NOC and working for organizations with direct or indirect access to government – including businesses and lobbyists. They have been known to operate for years without diplomatic cover, living under assumed identities.[189] "Illegals" can also act as sleeper agents. "Illegals" are believed to be operated by the GRU and by "Directorate S" of the SVR.[190] The FSB's "Illegals" are likely run out of the FSB's "Fifth Service".

In this clandestine world DNA samples, disguises, and fingerprints continue to play a role. Technologies such as biometrics also play their part.[191] This includes the utilization of facial recognition alongside distinctive human gait characteris-

187 Stein, "From Moscow with Murder."

188 The Western equivalent is "stations."

189 Guy Faulconbridge, "What is Russia's GRU military intelligence agency?" (October 8, 2018), https://uk.reuters.com/article/uk-britain-russia-gru-factbox/what-is-russias-gru-military-intelligence-agency-idUKKCN1MI27F, accessed 6 January 2019.

190 Jim Edwards, "Russia probably has more undercover 'sleeper' agents who can assassinate Western targets today than during the Cold War" (March 6, 2018), https://www.businessinsider.com/illegals-of-directorate-s-russia-undercover-covert-sleeper-agents-2017-12?r=UK&IR=T, accessed 6 January 2019.

191 Ian Brown, "Data Protection: The New Technical and Political Environment," *Computers & Law*, Vol. 20, No. 6 (February 2010), pp. 2–3, Ami Rojkes Dombe, "Espionage in the Era of Biometric Identity" (September 15, 2016), https://www.israeldefense.co.il/en/content/espionage-era-biometric-identity, Caroline Mortimer, "China to take fingerprints of all foreign travellers entering country" (February 9, 2017), https://www.independent.co.uk/news/world/asia/china-fingerprints-tourist-visits-scanning-customs-a7571871.html and https://www.rusemb.org.uk/consnews/29. All accessed 28 June 2019.

tics. Combined, these can help identify intelligence operatives (as well as criminals and terrorists). In addition, social media profiles, posts, or hacked databases can cast doubt upon cover stories.[192] This is how Bellingcat have been able to reveal the true identities of Russian agents.

For some this "digital threat to cover" is a significant challenge to traditional espionage. For the United States and its own intelligence gathering and counterintelligence activities, "digital threat to cover" creates anxieties within the CIA and FBI as well as congressional intelligence committees.[193] However, it also opens opportunities for Western intelligence agencies to recruit in parts of the world like Russia that are difficult to reach or risk exposure.[194] Since 2014 in particular, high levels of counterintelligence protection surrounding the Kremlin leadership have seen the CIA take "a more aggressive approach to recruiting Russian officials to spy for the United States" especially "high-ranking Russians who travel abroad."[195] Walk-ins are actively encouraged.[196]

Within the FSB, counterintelligence is the primary responsibility of the Prosecutor's Office and Investigative Committee (SKR – *Sledstvyennyy Komitet Rossiyskoy*). The SKR was founded in 2004 but its history dates back to 1922 and the end of the Russian Civil War (1917–1922). In turn, there are six sub-organizations of the SKR. These are the:

– Department for Counterintelligence Operations (DKRO – *Departament kontrrazvedyvatel'nyh operacij*);

---

192 Mark Urban, "MI6 set to recruit 1,000 extra staff" (September 21, 2016), https://www.bbc.co.uk/news/uk-37434131, accessed 17 June 2019.

193 Sam Jones, "The spy who liked me: Britain's changing secret service," *Financial Times* (September 29, 2016), https://www.ft.com/content/b239dc22-855c-11e6-a29c-6e7d9515ad15, accessed 17 June 2019.

194 Kyle S. Cunliffe, "Cyber-Enabled Tradecraft and Contemporary Espionage: Assessing the Implications of the Tradecraft Paradox on Agent Recruitment in Russia and China," *Intelligence and National Security*, Vol. 38, No. 7 (2023), pp. 1075–1094. Tony Ingesson and Magnus Andersson, "Clandestine Communications in Cyber-Denied Environments Numbers Stations and Radio in the 21st Century," *Journal of Policing, Intelligence and Counter Terrorism*, Vol. 19, No. 2 (2024), 144–165.

195 Greg Miller, "As Russia reasserts itself, U.S. intelligence agencies focus anew on the Kremlin," *Washington Post* (September 14, 2016), https://www.washingtonpost.com/world/national-security/as-russia-reasserts-itself-us-intelligence-agencies-focus-anew-on-the-kremlin/2016/09/14/cc212c62-78f0-11e6-ac8e-cf8e0dd91dc7_story.html, accessed 17 June 2019.

196 Huw Dylan, David V. Gioe, and Daniela Richterova, "Western Agencies Offer an Open Door for Russian Defectors" (July 26, 2023), https://foreignpolicy.com/2023/07/26/western-intelligence-recruit-russian-defectors/, accessed 8 October 2023.

- Directorate for Coordination of Analysis and Counterintelligence Activities (UKAKD – *Upravlenie Koordinatsii Analiza i Kontrrazvedochnyh Deyatel'nostey*);[197]
- Directorate of Information Support for Operational-Investigative Activities (UIORD – *Upravlenie Informacionnogo obespecheniq Operativno-Sledstvennoy Deqtel'nosti*);
- Center for Information Security (TsIB – *Tsentr dlya Informatsionnoy Bezopasnosti*). TsIB features earlier as Center 18 (Unit 64829). It is also responsible for GosSOPKA. TsIB is led by Sergey Skorokhodov (in post since June 2017 following his promotion from deputy);[198]
- Directorate for Facility Security (DBO – *Direktsiya po bezopasnosti ob'ektov*);
- Directorate of Special Measures (USM – *Upravleniye Spetsial'nykh Mer*).

The DKRO or "First Service" dates to WWII and the invasion of Russia under Operation Barbarossa as well as the secret counterintelligence organization SMERSH ("Death to Spies"). The DKRO is primarily responsible for tackling foreign intelligence services and concentrates on combating NATO governments (especially the Americans and British) as well as Chinese intelligence services. It is said to have sub-units with specific country and regional foci. According to leaked documents from the DKRO, countering intelligence threats from China includes monitoring Central Asia as Russia's intelligence focus shifts Westwards as a result of the Ukraine invasion. Sino-Russian rivalry grows (including through the Belt and Road Initiative) despite the outward and public appearance of increasing economic, diplomatic, and military cooperation.[199]

The DKRO's activities include monitoring and harassing foreign diplomats and foreign journalists whilst liaising with Russia's Ministry of Foreign Affairs (MID). Harassment includes arbitrary police stops and residential break-ins or implicating foreigners or Russian nationals attending protests or gatherings as colluding, spying or inciting unrest (with associated news used for propaganda). This also serves as a tool to stress test embassy, consulate staff and foreign journalists. The DKRO also works to recruit foreign embassy staff at all levels of the diplomatic corps whilst also monitoring the regime loyalty of MID personnel

---

197 Likely established in the late 1990s.

198 Riehle, *The Russian FSB*, pp. 31–35, 95–97.

199 Riehle, *The Russian FSB*, pp. 31–35, 70–75. Joesph Fitsanakis, "Revealed: Little-known Russian counterintelligence unit that targets foreigners" (July 12 2023), https://intelnews.org/2023/07/12/01-3294/. Giuliano Bifolchi, "Friends or Foes: Russia-China Relations and the FSB Intel Leaked Document" (June 10 2025), https://www.specialeurasia.com/2025/06/10/russia-china-fsb-intelligence/. Both accessed 18 August 2025.

(and able to be exploited in case of turf wars or interagency conflict).[200] Little is publicly known about either the Directorate for Facility Security (beyond its name being an obvious signpost) or Directorate of Special Measures (USM) but its portfolio includes counterespionage – including among the ranks of the FSB.[201]

13 The SVR: Non-official cover and "Illegals"

It was reported in 2016 that the SVR had an estimated 150 operatives in the U.S. concentrated in Washington DC, the UN headquarters in New York, and in major cities including San Francisco.[202] The SVR's main role is believed to be political intelligence. The SVR is reported to be "quite traditional, not least in its penchant for long-term, deep-cover spy rings, inherited from the KGB" but "often of questionable cost-effectiveness."[203] They have also continued with NOC operations. One of these operations was exposed in 2014/15.

Evgeny Buryakov (codenamed Zhenya) was employed by the SVR under NOC as a banker for the state-owned Vnesheconombank (VEB), working in Manhattan, New York. His work largely involved economic, not political intelligence (mainly relating to oil, gas, and fracking). However, intelligence gathered by Buryakov was also being passed onto the SVR's MS: Active Measures Directorate.[204] Buryakov was operating in a spy ring alongside two other SVR agents; Igor Sporyshev (Buryakov's handler) and Victor Podobnyy. Podobnyy's name would later reappear in connection to the attempted recruitment of Trump campaign employee, Carter Page, during the period this group was active (discussed in Chapter 4).[205]

---

200 Riehle, *The Russian FSB*, pp. 31–35, 70–75. Marina Miron, "Smersh: why Putin has reinstated Stalin's notorious and much-feared anti-spy unit (January 12 2024), accessed 17 August 2025: https://theconversation.com/smersh-why-putin-has-reinstated-stalins-notorious-and-much-feared-anti-spy-unit-220627.

201 Riehle, *The Russian FSB*, pp. pp. 31–35, 74–75.

202 Miller, "As Russia reasserts itself."

203 Galeotti, "Putin's Hydra," p. 2.

204 "Buryakov Complaint." Conspiracy to Act as an Unregistered Agent of a Foreign Government, January 26, 2015, pp. 21–22, https://www.justice.gov/sites/default/files/opa/press-releases/attachments/2015/01/26/buryakov-complaint.pdf, accessed 25 July 2023. Riehle, *Russian Intelligence*, pp. 151–152.

205 Special Counsel Robert S. Mueller, III, Report on the Investigation into Russian Interference in the 2016 Presidential Election Volume I of II (March 2019), pp. 95–103, https://www.justice.gov/storage/report.pdf, accessed 2 September 2019. Oliver Laughland and Martin Pengelly, "Trump-Russia: FBI believed Carter Page 'collaborated and conspired' with Moscow" (July 22, 2018), https://www.theguardian.com/us-news/2018/jul/22/trump-administration-releases-carter-page-wiretap-documents, accessed 6 July 2019.

Sporyshev's official cover was as a trade representative of the Russian government in New York. Podobnyy was an attaché to the Permanent Mission of the Russian Federation to the United Nations. This meant they had diplomatic immunity. As a NOC agent Buryakov did not enjoy this status. All three worked for Directorate ER, a division of the SVR responsible for economic intelligence.[206] Each shielded their knowledge of one another and communicated via coded messages and other means. Sporyshev would relay SVR requests to Buryakov.[207] Buryakov had been passing on economic intelligence regarding American companies and industries. He was engaged in gathering intelligence on possible U.S. sanctions against Russian banks following the annexation of Crimea as well as economic intelligence on alternative energy sources when he was arrested.[208]

Sporyshev and Podobnyy were simultaneously working as "spotters" and were surveilled trying to recruit "individuals employed by major companies, and several young women with ties to a major [New York] university."[209] Russian spotters are known to befriend targets with knowledge or access at organizations including companies, news outlets, think tanks, and universities, with conferences and trade fairs fertile ground for approaches.[210] In Soviet times, spotters were used for industrial as well as economic espionage. This included the theft of cutting-edge research and designs. These encounters have been used to cultivate long-term relationships as people move and rise through the ranks. These have usually been separate to intelligence officers who approach targets before passing them to a handler which limits potential exposure and allows a degree of remoteness.[211] Moreover, non-official cover officers "sometimes have such 'deep cover' that they are considered too valuable to make a recruitment approach directly, leaving that

206 Podobnyy was recorded complaining to Sporyshev that he should have been operating under an assumed identity and that his day-to-day work as an SVR covert agent was "not even close [to] movies about James Bond." "Buryakov Complaint," pp. 5, 8–9, 23.

207 Russian National Pleads Guilty in Connection with Conspiracy to Work for Russian Intelligence (March 11, 2016), https://www.justice.gov/opa/pr/russian-national-pleads-guilty-connection-conspiracy-work-russian-intelligence, accessed 25 July 2023.

208 Russian Banker Sentenced in Connection with Conspiracy to Work for Russian Intelligence (May 25, 2016), https://www.justice.gov/opa/pr/russian-banker-sentenced-connection-conspiracy-work-russian-intelligence, accessed 4 November 2016.

209 "Buryakov Complaint," p. 11.

210 Giles, *Russia's War on Everybody*, pp. 192–197.

211 Annual Report to Congress on Foreign Economic Collection and Industrial Espionage 2003, Office of the National Counterintelligence Executive, pp. vi, 5–6, https://apps.dtic.mil/sti/pdfs/ADA439091.pdf, accessed 25 July 2023.

work to a cut-out who could more easily disappear if the recruitment pitch is rejected."[212] This may have been part of their undoing.

Their spy ring had operated from 2010 to 2014 until Buryakov, Sporyshev, and Podobnyy were detained by the FBI in a counterintelligence operation in 2015.[213] Buryakov would plead guilty in March 2016 and was sentenced to 30 months in prison in May 2016. He would serve less than a year and was expelled back to Russia in April 2017.[214] Neither Sporyshev nor Podobnyy were prosecuted as they had diplomatic immunity. Instead, they were expelled as *persona non grata* "leaving Buryakov to bear the brunt of the blame."[215] *The Moscow Times* noted, "Under the leadership of President Vladimir Putin, himself a former KGB officer, Russia's Foreign Intelligence Service (SVR) has continued the work of its Soviet predecessors."[216]

It was reported the FBI's investigation began months after the 2010 arrest of another cell of 10 Russian "Illegals."[217] The most famous among them was Anna Chapman (nee Kushchyenko), a Russian national who had dual UK citizenship.[218] Others included Richard and Cynthia Murphy, a low key couple living a suburban family life with their two daughters, who in reality were Vladimir and Lidiya Guryev. They were arrested at their home in New Jersey, the others in Boston, Manhattan, and northern Virginia. All were infiltrating financial and political policy-making circles under deep cover.

---

212 Garrett M. Graff, "China's 5 Steps for Recruiting Spies" (October 31, 2018), https://www.wired.com/story/china-spy-recruitment-us/?verso=true, accessed 28 August 2019.

213 DOJ, Russian Banker Sentenced.

214 DOJ, Russian Banker Sentenced. Brian Ross, Pete Madden, and Michelle McFee, "Russian spy Evgeny Buryakov deported from United States" (April 5, 2017), https://abcnews.go.com/International/russian-spy-evgeny-buryakov-deported-united-states/story?id=46601947, accessed 30 October 2019.

215 Kaja Whitehouse, "Russian spy busted in undercover sting gets light sentence" (May 25, 2016), http://nypost.com/2016/05/25/russian-spy-busted-in-undercover-sting-gets-light-sentence/, accessed 3 April 2017.

216 Mathew Bodner, "Top 3 Successes of Soviet Economic Espionage," November 4, 2016, https://themoscowtimes.com/articles/top-3-successes-of-soviet-economic-espionage-43360, accessed 4 November 2016.

217 Benjamin Weiser, "Bank Employee Pleads Guilty to Conspiring to Work as Secret Russian Agent," March 11, 2016, http://www.nytimes.com/2016/03/12/nyregion/evgeny-buryakov-russian-bank-employee-pleads-guilty-to-conspiring-to-work-as-unregistered-agent.html, accessed 4 November 2016.

218 She married a British national in 2002. They divorced in 2006. Gordon Rayner and Andy Bloxham, "'Russia spy' Anna Chapman's husband: I thought I knew her" (July 2, 2010), http://www.telegraph.co.uk/news/worldnews/europe/russia/7866824/Russia-spy-Anna-Chapmans-husband-I-thought-I-knew-her.html, accessed 29 September 2016.

Their spy ring had been provided with fake documents to establish their identity and citizenship along with an elaborate legend. According to a joint report issued by the FBI, CIA, and NSA their operation was run by the SVR's Directorate S (Illegals) program.[219] Their operation involved the use of codes and cyphers, shortwave radio, encrypted Morse code messages, and the use of radiograms.[220] Their training had included how to create and exploit a cover profession, counter surveillance measures, how to conceal or destroy equipment or materials, and methods of avoiding detection such as "brush passes" and "dead drops."[221]

FBI Counterintelligence Assistant Director Frank Figliuzzi stated how they had been able to wirelessly tap into communications between Chapman and her handler across six locations in New York. She was transmitting and receiving messages within close proximity but not close enough to be seen. Even though these messages were encrypted the FBI was able to break them. This prevented further penetration of U.S. foreign policy circles. Figliuzzi appended that the Russians were in it for "the long haul ... patient enough to wait decades to achieve their objective."[222] The FBI equated the "Chapman ring" with the Cambridge Five. The Five were British nationals spotted at Cambridge University during their studies who rose through the ranks of British intelligence and the Foreign Office. The intent of the "Chapman ring" was the same: to spot and recruit rising talent.[223] This might prove highly valuable long-term but "Running agents as illegals under deep cover requires a huge commitment of resources and time."[224]

---

219 Background to "Assessing the Russian Activities and Intentions in Recent US Elections": The Analytic Process and Cyber Incident Attribution, January 6, 2017, p. 5, https://www.dni.gov/files/documents/ICA_2017_01.pdf, accessed 2 September 2019.

220 Radiograms use a coded burst of data that is able to be received at a pre-determined frequency.

221 As detailed in the DOJ's two complaints. "Ten Alleged Secret Agents Arrested in the United States" (June 28, 2010), https://www.justice.gov/opa/pr/ten-alleged-secret-agents-arrested-united-states, accessed 21 January 2020. A "brush pass" is "where something is passed between a case officer and an agent" and "Dead drops" "where materials, information or money can be left for another party or agent to retrieve." Fred Burton, "Above the Tearline: Brush Passes and Dead Drops" (November 9, 2011), https://worldview.stratfor.com/article/above-tearline-brush-passes-and-dead-drops, accessed 21 January 2020.

222 Pierre Thomas, Jack Cloherty, and Jason Ryan , "How the FBI Busted Anna Chapman and the Russian Spy Ring" (November 1, 2011), http://abcnews.go.com/blogs/politics/2011/11/how-the-fbi-busted-anna-chapman-and-the-russian-spy-ring/, accessed 29 September 2016.

223 Operation Ghost Stories, October 31, 2011, https://www.fbi.gov/news/stories/operation-ghost-stories-inside-the-russian-spy-case, accessed 8 October 2023.

224 Gordon Corera, "Long history of deep-cover 'illegals'" (June 29, 2010), http://www.bbc.co.uk/news/10452384. For more information see Gordon Corera, *Intercept: The Secret History of Computers and Spies* (London: Weidenfeld & Nicolson, 2016).

Training is provided through a network of academies.[225] One of these is dedicated to the GRU.

14 The GRU's "Conservatory": Training, methods, and HUMINT

"The Conservatory" is the name given to the Defense Ministry's Military Academy in Moscow. Training at "The Conservatory" lasts for three years and, like all major intelligence schools, trainees are vetted and subject to rigorous testing in areas such as languages and facial recognition. "The Conservatory" has three departments. The first department trains learners to operate under "official cover" status. Their responsibilities can also include foreign recruitment and running undercover agents. One such officer operating under official cover was a GRU colonel named Viktor Ilyushin whose cover was as a deputy air attaché at the Russian Embassy in Paris.

He was expelled in 2014 after French counterintelligence uncovered him trying to recruit one of French President François Hollande's senior aides. Ilyushin would wine and dine prospective sources and offer them unpublished information on Russia's armed forces. He knew family details and offered gifts before attempting bribery. Ilyushin initially went after "soft" sources including journalists and think tank researchers who work in the world between open and classified sources. Like his SVR counterparts, Ilyushin would also try to recruit those in and around the political center as "useful idiots."[226] In 2020–21 alone, the Congressional Research Service highlighted the cases of a U.S. Special Forces officer, French and Austrian military officers, a Russian spy ring operating in Bulgaria, and an Italian navy officer who had all been caught spying for the GRU.[227] Recruitment and running agents and assets utilizes the tools from the MICE toolbox

---

225 Kazimierz Kraj, "The System of Military Higher Education in the Russian Federation," *Bezpieczeństwo. Teoria i Praktyka*, Yearbook 2019, No. 3, pp. 169–184.

226 Vincent Jauvert, "Faux-diplomates, pseudo-journalistes, barbouzes : l'offensive des espions de Poutine en France," *Le Nouvel Observateur* (now *L'OBS*), July 23, 2014 and John R. Schindler, "Putin's Espionage Offensive Against France" (August 2, 2014), https://20committee.com/2014/08/02/putins-espionage-offensive-against-france/, accessed 1 January 2018.

227 Andrew S. Bowen, Russian Military Intelligence: Background and Issues for Congress (updated November 15 2021), https://crsreports.congress.gov/product/pdf/R/R46616/7, accessed 30 June 2023.

(Money, Ideology, Compromise/Coercion and Ego).[228] Money is often a common denominator.

The second department trains military attachés who work in diplomatic missions whilst serving as members of the armed forces. This includes GRU officers such as Eduard Shishmakov and Vladimir Moiseyev. Using the cover names Eduard Shirokov and Vladimir Popov, they were exposed in the attempted Montenegro coup in 2016.[229] The third department is dedicated to instructing officers for foreign "special operations."[230]

The first year at "The Conservatory" emphasizes language skills and area studies to ensure candidates are culturally versed in the locations they operate. They are also trained in encryption and decryption and how to operate specialized equipment. Training also involves fieldwork in covert intelligence, including evading surveillance and the invention of a backstory (a "legend"). Part of the training involves finding routes and locations for covert meetings and where to place listening devices. Another important aspect is learning to successfully gain valid entry into a secure facility. This includes befriending someone who can provide access.[231] Compromising information (*kompromat*) remains important in running sources and maintaining access.

Many of these methods were used by intelligence agencies across the world during the Cold War, World War II, and further back. Although remote access to people and facilities is now considerably easier thanks to the Internet, cellular/mobile devices, and global connectivity, these practices continue to be valuable against hard targets. Remote operations are also much more cost effective than running double agents (infrequently discovered in NATO, the EU, and national governments, as alluded to above) or trusted insiders who are compromised. This has seen cyberespionage/hybrid intelligence prove its value time and again.

---

228 Giles, *Russia's War on Everybody*, pp. 165–189.

229 Christo Grozev, "Balkan Gambit: Part 2. The Montenegro Zugzwang" (March 25, 2017), https://www.bellingcat.com/news/uk-and-europe/2017/03/25/balkan-gambit-part-2-montenegro-zugzwang/, Moritz Rakuszitzky, "Second GRU Officer Indicted in Montenegro Coup Unmasked" (November 22, 2018), https://www.bellingcat.com/news/uk-and-europe/2018/11/22/second-gru-officer-indicted-montenegro-coup-unmasked/, and Anonymous, "Bellingcat Names Second GRU Agent In Failed Montenegrin Coup" (November 23, 2018), https://www.rferl.org/a/montenegro-bellingcat-coup-/29616265.html, all accessed 1 January 2018.

230 Daniil Turovsky, "What is the GRU? Who gets recruited to be a spy? Why are they exposed so often? Here are the most important things you should know about Russia's intelligence community" (November 6, 2018), https://meduza.io/en/feature/2018/11/06/what-is-the-gru-who-gets-recruited-to-be-a-spy-why-are-they-exposed-so-often, accessed 26 December 2018. These were originally described by Turovsky as divisions.

231 Turovsky, "What is the GRU?"

It has many uses and purposes. This includes harassing foreign diplomats, journalists, and others living and working inside Russia.[232]

The GRU's 85 Main Special Service Center is home to Unit 26165 which among many other things, stands accused of hacking WADA and the investigation into the shooting down of Malaysia Airlines flight MH17 over eastern Ukraine in July 2014. This led to international condemnation, investigations, and denials.[233] Unit 26165 is suspected of being in existence since the 1970s (originally specializing in cryptography), run by the GRU's Sixth Directorate (listed alongside other GRU directorates in the Introduction). This had a broad portfolio including operating listening posts, encryption, and decryption of foreign communications.[234] That portfolio has now widened.

According to the database being compiled by the Center for Strategic and International Studies (CSIS), the GRU has a wide range of targets. This includes transportation, government (military bases and officials), critical infrastructure, and industry. Of its targets, 21 percent have been against critical infrastructure. This includes pipelines, undersea fiber-optic cables, as well as the electricity sector. Underwater operations might involve the secretive Main Directorate for Deep Sea Research (*Glavnoye Upravleniye Glubokovodnykh Issledovaniy* – GUGI/ Military Unit 40056), an agency directly controlled by the Russian Ministry of Defense. This operates submersibles which can damage or destroy a number of types of cable (be they for power, data telecommunications, or gas and oil). Drag anchors are widely used to cut undersea cables.[235]

Relatedly, the GRU has also been key to registering and operating Russia's "shadow fleet" of commercial vessels to evade economic and travel sanctions. Part of this "shadow fleet," which has also been used to transport Russian oil and gas, is the oil tanker *Eagle S.* This sailed under the flag of the Cook Islands (one of many "flags of convenience" used by Russia and other nations and entities) and was used for sabotage by severing undersea cables off Finland. The "shadow fleet" also deploys sonar to map undersea cables and other parts of the seafloor useful to GUGI and the Russian Navy. Telecommunications cables are also vulnerable to subversion through data exfiltration. With around 95 percent of all transat-

---

232 Giles, *Russia's War on Everybody*, pp. 146–157.

233 Esch, "Doing Putin's Dirty Work."

234 Roland Oliphant, "What is Unit 26165, Russia's elite military hacking centre?" (October 4, 2018), https://www.telegraph.co.uk/news/2018/10/04/unit26165-russias-elite-military-hacking-centre/, accessed 28 December 2018.

235 Peter Lobner, "You Need to Know About Russia's Main Directorate of Deep-Sea Research (GUGI)" (May 21, 2018), https://lynceans.org/tag/military-unit-40056/, accessed 10 May 2025.

lantic data traffic routed through undersea cables, they are especially at risk in international waters.[236]

As detailed above, the GRU (and other "Special Services") are also longstanding users of cut-outs (intermediaries between the intelligence agency or operation). This has seen them use local recruits, criminals, diaspora populations, NGOs, and companies. These proxy operations can go rogue and increase the risk of exposure. This has happened with some frequency.[237] Exposure was exacerbated by the "mass expulsions of Russian special services personnel across Europe following the full-scale invasion of Ukraine."[238] This was on top of increasing exposure of their operatives and operations because of cellphone tracking and cyber forensics of geodetic data from the carrier and Internet Service Providers. This is helping expose long-term and shorter-term "Illegals" and foreign agents. Diplomatic expulsions from *rezidentura* have also made handling and running these and other assets more difficult. This has meant having to run more assets and operations remotely. Remote running decreases their reliability, combined with the movement of Russian "Special Services" operatives now being more constrained. This has increasingly contributed to the exposure or failure of operations. Such difficulties began to be addressed in 2020.[239]

Around 2022, new Committees of Special Influence were established under the Presidential Administration. These are headed by First Deputy Chief of Staff, Sergei Kirienko. They are responsible for tasking the "Special Services" and focused on specified target states and operational effectiveness and appear to be part of a top-down attempt at improved coordination. In relation, the GRU's deputy, Andrei Averyanov, also established a Service for Special Activities. This is said to have three components: a headquarters and planning department, the aforementioned Unit 29155, and a new Unit 54654 which was established around 2022/23. Whether it is dedicated to Unit 29155 or part of 161 Center is unclear. It is also said to have three training units, a unit for operational planning and another for financial and logistical support, with a third for supplies. It aims to improve OPSEC whilst also seeking to further leverage deep-cover "Illegals" and the criminal fraternity (including drug cartels). In addition, there may have been a change in political influence campaigns. Instead of focusing on ma-

---

236 Seth G. Jones, "Russia's Shadow War Against the West" (March 2025), pp. 1–8, https://www.csis.org/analysis/russias-shadow-war-against-west, accessed 5 May 2025.

237 Jones, "Russia's Shadow War Against the West," pp. 5–6.

238 Watling, Danylyuk, and Reynolds, "The Threat from Russia's Unconventional Warfare Beyond Ukraine, 2022–24," p. 8.

239 Watling, Danylyuk, and Reynolds, "The Threat from Russia's Unconventional Warfare Beyond Ukraine, 2022–24," p. 9.

jority opinion they instead focus on "elite capture" by empowering potential presidential candidates or favorable politicians.[240] According to a 2024 RUSI study, Unit 54654 focuses on HUMINT and supporting Russia's networks of "Illegals" and also directs the GRU's Expeditionary Corps (aimed at the recruitment of fighters in Ukraine).[241]

Whether as a result of this reorganization, or the product of additional resources and focus, there has been a surge in subversive activities across Europe. This also includes electronic jamming, arson and explosions (sabotage operations), and immigrants being used as political pawns (alongside messaging immigrant threats) in addition to the many other activities already mentioned. Many of these activities link back to European support for Ukraine. This includes targeting major weapons suppliers including BAE Systems, Rheinmetall, German Diehl Group, and EMCO. It is also noteworthy that the chief executive officer of Rheinmetall, Armin Papperger, is one of the only instances of a Western citizen to be targeted for assassination.[242] These operations have manifested across Europe, but there are exceptions. This includes no reported attacks in either Hungary or Serbia (both outlier nations in Europe with respect to perception of Russia). As detailed in the Introduction, this has included the use of *Spetsnaz*. In the meantime, Russian cyberespionage remains a major threat.

15 The GRU's "Fancy Bear": APT28

It has been suggested that APT28 ("Fancy Bear") could operate two sub-units. The first targets militaries and governments. The second, banks and financial institutions.[243] This analysis is too simplistic. In 2014 FireEye released "APT28: A Window into Russia's Cyber Espionage Operations." FireEye's report is one of the most thorough studies made public by the cybersecurity industry on state-run APTs/APMs. Their analysis concluded that in contrast to most Chinese APTs, APT28's pri-

---

240 Jones, "Russia's Shadow War Against the West," pp. 5–6, 8–13.

241 Watling, Danylyuk, and Reynolds, "The Threat from Russia's Unconventional Warfare Beyond Ukraine, 2022–24," pp. 10, 20, 26–32.

242 Riehle claims Russian assassination attempts fall into three categories: political, military, and traitors. At the same time, and given the closeness of organized crime to state activities, revenge, money, and power are significant motivating factors. Riehle, *Russian Intelligence*, pp. 201–212.

243 Elizabeth MacDonald, "New Russian Hacks Target US Banks" (May 14, 2015), http://www.foxbusiness.com/features/2015/05/14/new-russian-hacks-target-us-banks.html, accessed January 21 2018.

mary aims are not intellectual property theft.[244] Instead, APT28 was gathering political and military intelligence (especially defense and geopolitical intelligence) from governments and militaries in locations including Eastern Europe and Georgia, as well as European security organizations "that would only be useful to a government."[245]

FireEye set out their methodology through which they attributed APT28 to the Russian government. This included malware (malicious software) which had Russian language settings with date stamps indicating Russian time zones. These included the major cities of Moscow and St. Petersburg. This was a highly skilled operation that was both long-standing and focused. What they did not reveal were pictures of buildings, people, or personas, and they also did not point to one specific agency.[246] Pictures of buildings, names and personas, and government agencies would come to be revealed by others as will be shown later. More broadly, this level of detail reflects important advancements made in cyber forensics and the development of actionable cyber threat intelligence (CTI).[247] It also indicates that major private companies in the cybersecurity sector were now increasingly prepared to go public.[248] Many of these firms on the front line also publicly acknowledge they work in concert with the U.S. government and other Western governments against threats from Russia and other hostile actors.[249]

Across Europe, the Middle East, and Africa, FireEye also attributed a series of cyberattacks in the telecommunications sector to Russian state-sponsored actors (as well as seeing Chinese and Western actors). The primary goal of Russia's actors was intelligence on the European Union (EU) and the collection of signals intelligence (SIGINT) to benefit Russia's military.[250] In the military realm, Russia has

244 FireEye, "APT28: A Window into Russia's Cyber Espionage Operations" (2014), https://www.fireeye.com/content/dam/fireeye-www/global/en/current-threats/pdfs/rpt-apt28.pdf.

245 FireEye, "APT28," p. 3.

246 FireEye, "APT28," p. 3.

247 Antonia Nisioti, George Loukas, Alexios Mylonas, and Emmanouil Panaousis, "Forensics for Multi-Stage Cyber Incidents: Survey and Future Directions," *Forensic Science International: Digital Investigation*, Vol. 44 (March 2023), pp. 1–16. Ali Dehghantanha, Mauro Conti, and Tooska Dargahi (eds.), *Cyber Threat Intelligence* (Cham, Switzerland: Springer Nature, 2018).

248 The merits of private cybersecurity firms and governments publicly attributing nation-states and their intelligence agencies is discussed in Egloff and Smeets, "Publicly Attributing Cyber Attacks: A Framework," pp. 502–533.

249 Thomas D. Wagner, Khaled Mahbub, Esther Palomar, and Ali E. Abdallah, "Cyber Threat Intelligence Sharing: Survey and Research Directions," *Computers & Security*, Vol. 87 (November 2019), 101589, pp. 1–13.

250 FireEye, "M-Trends 2017. A View From the Front Lines," p. 45. Available from https://www.fireeye.com/current-threats/annual-threat-report/mtrends/rpt-m-trends-2017.html, accessed 31 March 2020.

also continued and revitalized its seaborne ship-based SIGINT capabilities. This includes the deployment of Auxiliary General Intelligence Ships near key ports and bases, maritime chokepoints, and to monitor naval exercises and to shadow military vessels. Russian vessels have also been detected many times near vulnerable undersea cables vital to Western communications (as well as pipelines like Nordstream). SIGINT aircraft near to NATO airspace has also been regularly detected and engaged. This has also been observed in war zones including Syria and Ukraine (where they have also been used for jamming) as well as previous military operations in places like Georgia and the Caucasus. Jamming has also been detected in NATO Europe. This includes jamming a chartered flight of EU President Ursula von der Leyen over Polish airspace in September 2025. SIGINT also utilizes Russian satellites and ground stations. This is all in addition to their pervasive use of cyberespionage.[251]

In December 2017, Kevin Mandia, then FireEye's Chief Executive Officer, testified to the U.S. Senate's Intelligence Committee on Russian interference in the 2016 U.S. presidential elections. He summarized how since 2014 FireEye has seen them hacking into organizations leading to the theft and release of compromising information. This has included using invented hacktivist personas to mask and deny responsibility. These personas have included "Guccifer 2.0," "DC Leaks," "Anonymous Poland," the "Fancy Bears' Hack Team," and "CyberCaliphate." Through appropriating hacktivist personas and ideological brands, Russian intelligence is attempting to muddy the waters, create credibility, and establish plausible deniability.[252] Mandia drew on FireEye's extensive experience and expertise in cybersecurity as a front line provider in identifying several salient points in regard to Russia's wider state goals.

Based on extensive intelligence and analysis collated by FireEye, APT28's *modus operandi* is consistent with Russian government sponsorship and control. This is indicated by the development and deployment of sophisticated malware tools. These needed the resources of a nation-state or state-protected contractor because they required significant financial and personnel resources and assets and there was no clear profit motive or ransom demanded. The organizations and individuals targeted were those where Russian interests were high and the

251 Riehle, Russian Intelligence, pp. 247–260. Siobhan Robbins, "Russia responds to GPS jamming accusations – but such instances are expected to escalate" (2 September 2025), https://news.sky.com/story/russia-responds-to-gps-jamming-accusations-but-such-instances-are-expected-to-escalate-13423288, accessed 2 September 2025.

252 Prepared Statement of Kevin Mandia, CEO of FireEye, Inc. before the United States Senate Select Committee on Intelligence March 30, 2017, p. 3, https://www.intelligence.senate.gov/sites/default/files/documents/os-kmandia-033017.pdf, accessed 1 December 2017.

levels of activities conducted over multiple years are not something seen outside of nation-states. Leaking and not ransoming were aligned with broader propaganda efforts and closely integrated with other cyberattacks and campaigns. Perhaps more importantly, "alternative explanations for APT28's sponsorship ... only appear to be a plausible explanation for one incident at a time and are not credible when considering the totality of APT28's operations."[253] That profit motives were not identified as central to "Fancy Bear's" cyberattacks demonstrates that their goals instead form part of a broader politico-military campaign consistent with "hybrid warfare." Any economic/monetizable benefits are largely a side order effect.

In the wake of Russian interference in the U.S. election, FireEye released a further report, "APT28: At the Center of the Storm" in January 2017. This stated that since 2007 APT28's espionage activities have primarily targeted organizations in in the U.S., Europe, and former Soviet states. This included governments and militaries. Also targeted were media organizations, Russian dissidents, and individuals critical of the Russian government.[254] It was also reported in December 2015 that APT28/"Fancy Bear" had been successfully penetrating air-gapped systems (systems that are configured to have no connection to the Internet) in the defense sector for five months. This was by using costly zero-day (previously unknown) exploits to implant malware. In the year after the annexation of Crimea (2014–15), APT28's activities grew almost tenfold.[255]

These increases and the scope of operations would suggest that assessments of the U.S. Intelligence Community (USIC) might have been behind the curve. In September 2015, James R. Clapper, then Director of National Intelligence (DNI), reported to the Senate. He informed them that Russia's Ministry of Defense (which commands the GRU) was in the process of establishing "its own cyber command" which would be "responsible for conducting offensive cyber activities, including propaganda operations and inserting malware into enemy command and control

253 Prepared Statement of Kevin Mandia, p. 6.

254 FireEye "APT28: At the Center of the Storm Russia Strategically Evolves Its Cyber Operations," January 2017. Available from https://www.fireeye.com/blog/threat-research/2017/01/apt28_at_the_center.html, accessed 2 December 2017.

255 Darren Pauli, "Russian 'Pawn Storm' expands, rains hell on NATO, air-gapped PCs Group cooks zero days, malware modules, and hacks anything it likes" (December 7, 2015), https://www.theregister.co.uk/2015/12/07/op_pawn_storm/, accessed 7 January 2019.

systems" whilst "Russia's armed forces are also establishing a specialized branch for computer network operations."[256]

Computer network operations (CNO) includes, in U.S. parlance, both offensive cyber operations (OCO) and defensive cyber operations (DCO).[257] Reporting suggests this process of improving Russia's cyberespionage and cyberwarfare capabilities and capacity had begun with Sergei Shoigu's appointment as Minister of Defense in November 2012 and was accelerated in 2013. By 2014 the Ministry of Defense (MOD) was employing graduates of technical universities in mathematics, computer science, engineering, and specializations including cryptography as "information operations troops." These were likely placed in newly formed Military Units dedicated to cyber (including those mentioned above), supported by existing research institutes. This was allied to recruits from Russia's underground cybercriminal hacker scene.[258] The USIC was caught off guard by what these developments portended.

16 The SVR's APT29/"Cozy Bear": Dutch intelligence penetration

Running APT28 is the primary role of the GRU's Unit 26165. APT28 is perhaps better known as "Fancy Bear" (a moniker given them by CrowdStrike).[259] "APT28/ "Fancy Bear" is suspected of working in parallel with APT44/"Sandworm" run by Unit 74455. "Sandworm" is described by Mandiant as a dynamic and mature threat actor in its own right and these APT groups are viewed by the Kremlin as serving Russia's foreign and security policy through full spectrum cyber operations from espionage to political influence campaigns (including being the prime cyber threat to Ukraine). This is why Mandiant elevated "Sandworm" to the level of an APT group in April 2024. Both APT28/"Fancy Bear" and APT44/"Sandworm"

---

256 James R. Clapper, Statement for the Record Before the Senate Armed Services Committee, September 29, 2015, http://www.armed-services.senate.gov/imo/media/doc/Clapper_09-29-15.pdf, p. 4, accessed 12 December 2018.
257 Stoddart, *Cyberwarfare*, p. 306.
258 Turovsky, "Russian armed cyberforces."
259 Garrett M. Graff, "Indicting 12 Russian Hackers Could Be Mueller's Biggest Move Yet" (July 13, 2018), https://www.wired.com/story/mueller-indictment-dnc-hack-russia-fancy-bear/, accessed 3 January 2019.

are suspected by Mandiant of being subordinate to a higher GRU Military Unit designated Unit 55111.[260]

The British government relatedly assessed in July 2025 that GRU Units 26165 (APT28/"Fancy Bear") and 74455 (APT44/"Sandworm") present advanced, comprehensive cyber threats that have long targeted Ukraine, European partners, and NATO allies. A further threat is presented by a newly formed arm of Unit 29155 (know as "Cadet Blizzard"). This group, comprised mainly of younger recruits operating under "seasoned handlers", is described as "ill-disciplined and haphazard" leaving it unclear whether it coordinates with Units 26165 and 74455. Despite being previously grouped with APT28/"Fancy Bear", the cyber arm of Unit 29155 ("Cadet Blizzard") is deemed responsible for many "disruptive and destructive cyber operations" in its own right, including Whispergate malware deployed in Ukraine ahead of Russia's 2022 invasion. Unit 29155 are also implicated in wider operations (primarily field operations involving wet work) such as the ammunition warehouse explosions in Vrbětice, Czechia in 2014 and the attempted assassination attempts on Sergei and Yulia Skripal in 2018.[261]

Meanwhile, APT28/"Fancy Bear" (Unit 26165) been implicated in the 2015 cyberattack on TV5 Monde, a cyberrattack on the German Bundestag (also 2015), and using X-Agent to geolocate Ukrainian military hardware in the Donbas (2014–16). "Fancy Bear" is linked directly with the intrusions on organizations investigating the Salisbury attacks which the U.S. Department of Justice also links to Unit 74455. The use of X-Agent also implies their involvement in the DNC and DCCC hacks in 2016 (Chapter 4).

APT28/"Fancy Bear" was also attributed by the French government with hacking and leaking e-mails relating to Emmanuel Macron ahead of the 2017 French presidential election whilst the British government attributed them to a long-term cyberespionage campaign targeting the German Social Democratic Party (SDP) and Czech government institutions. France also linked them to cyberattacks on organizations involved with the 2024 Olympic and Paralympic Games. Unit 74455 (APT44/"Sandworm") had separately attacked the 2018 Winter Olympics held in Pyeongchang, South Korea in 2018. This followed a ban on Russian athletes

---

260 Gabby Roncone, Dan Black, John Wolfram, Tyler McLellan, Nick Simonian, Ryan Hall, Anton Prokopenkov, Dan Perez, Lexie Aytes, Alden Wahlstrom, "APT44: Unearthing Sandworm" (2024), https://services.google.com/fh/files/misc/apt44-unearthing-sandworm.pdf, accessed 19 July 2025.

261 PROFILE: GRU CYBER AND HYBRID THREAT OPERATIONS, https://assets.publishing.service.gov.uk/media/687a0d96a52cca025ef5be89/Profile-GRU-cyber-and-hybrid-threat-operations.pdf, accessed 19 July 2025.

competing at the Olympics as a result of systematic state-sponsored use of performance enhancing drugs.[262]

APT29/"Cozy Bear", is run by the SVR.[263] It is also extremely active alongside APT28/"Fancy Bear". They have been implicated in hacking the Democratic Party during the 2016 U.S. presidential election, the company SolarWinds in 2019, and targeting COVID-19 vaccines during the 2020–22 pandemic.[264] They have also targeted diplomats and government agencies since 2013.[265] This has seen an uptick in activities since Russia began the Ukraine War.[266] They were behind a coordinated series of spear-phishing campaigns of U.S.-based think tanks and non-governmental organizations (NGOs) in 2016, a wide number of European government departments, think tanks, and international organizations in 2021, and NATO-aligned foreign ministries in 2023. They have also targeted Dutch government ministries and police in 2017.[267] At the time they were investigating the 2014 downing of MH17 over Eastern Ukraine carrying 196 Dutch nationals on its way from Amsterdam to Kuala Lumpur.

There is good evidence that Dutch military intelligence, the Militaire Inlichtingen- en Veiligheidsdienst (MIVD) and civilian Algemene Inlichtingen- en Veiligheidsdienst (AIVD), penetrated the SVR's APT29/"Cozy Bear". This was accomplished after the creation of a Joint SIGINT Cyber Unit (JSCU), part of an operation codenamed "Project Symbolon."[268] "Project Symbolon" begun in summer 2014.[269] It

262 PROFILE: GRU CYBER AND HYBRID THREAT OPERATIONS, https://assets.publishing.service.gov.uk/media/687a0d96a52cca025ef5be89/Profile-GRU-cyber-and-hybrid-threat-operations.pdf.

263 Galeotti, "Siloviki at War", p. 7.

264 Advisory: APT29 targets COVID-19 vaccine development, https://media.defense.gov/2020/Jul/16/2002457639/-1/-1/0/NCSC_APT29_ADVISORY-QUAD-OFFICIAL-20200709-1810.PDF, accessed 15 October 2023.

265 Allen Bernard, "Russian hacker group APT29 targeting diplomats" (May 3, 2022), https://www.techrepublic.com/article/russian-hacker-group-apt29-targeting-diplomats/, accessed 15 October 2023.

266 Luke Jenkins, Josh Atkins, and Dan Black, "Backchannel Diplomacy: APT29's Rapidly Evolving Diplomatic Phishing Operations" (September 23, 2023), https://www.mandiant.com/resources/blog/apt29-evolving-diplomatic-phishing, accessed 15 October 2023.

267 APT group: APT 29, Cozy Bear, The Dukes, https://apt.etda.or.th/cgi-bin/showcard.cgi?g=APT%2029%2C%20Cozy%20Bear%2C%20The%20Dukes&n=1, accessed 10 October 2023.

268 Max Smeets, "The Challenges of Military Adaptation to the Cyber Domain: A Case Study of the Netherlands," *Small Wars & Insurgencies*, Vol. 34, Issue 7 (September 2023), p. 1350.

269 This was first reported by *de Volkskrant*, a long established newspaper in The Netherlands and the Dutch television program *Nieuwsuur.* Huib Modderkolk, "Dutch agencies provide crucial intel about Russia's interference in US-elections" (January 25, 2018), https://www.volkskrant.nl/wetenschap/dutch-agencies-provide-crucial-intel-about-russia-s-interference-in-us-elections~b4f8111b/, accessed 9 January 2019. Rick Noack, "How a Dutch intelligence agency secretly hacked

was described as a "goldmine," providing the AIVD with intelligence on Russian targets, methods, and the chain of command through to the highest levels of Russia's security services. Up to this point, even "Specialists from the best intelligence services, among them the British, the Israelis and the Americans" had previously failed despite "hunting … for years, as have analysts from major cybersecurity companies."[270]

They found APT29 operating from a university building near Red Square with an entrance through a curved hallway.[271] The AIVD had managed to gain access to their computer network and the CCTV camera monitoring those entering and leaving the building. Through this, photographs of every visitor were captured. These photographs were analyzed and compared with known or suspected Russian intelligence officers.[272] Based on these images the AIVD assessed that APT29/"Cozy Bear" was operated by the SVR. Further analysis suggested APT29's composition varied, with only around ten people active at any one time.[273]

In November 2014, during the operation, the JSCU discovered that the SVR/APT29 had gained access to one or more unclassified U.S. networks through civil service employees who had been compromised by spear phishing. This began with the State Department, and they moved towards accessing White House servers. Conceivably, this could have given them access to Barack Obama's unclassified e-mails and those of White House staff had they not been stopped in a tense 24-hour period.[274] This was described by Richard Ledgett, the NSA's Deputy Director at the time, as a cyber version of "hand-to-hand combat." The NSA was able to counter, including through the use of their "foreign intelligence capabilities in adversary space" which allowed them to see what APT29 were trying to deploy

---

into the Kremlin's most notorious hacking group" (January 27, 2018), https://www.independent.co.uk/news/world/europe/netherlands-dutch-russia-kremlin-united-states-robert-mueller-intelligence-agencies-cozy-bear-aivd-a8181046.html, accessed 22 July 2023.

270 Modderkolk, "Dutch agencies provide crucial intel." Pierluigi Paganini, "The Dutch intelligence service AIVD 'hacked' Russian Cozy Bear systems for years" (January 26, 2018), https://securityaffairs.co/68241/intelligence/aivd-hacked-cozy-bear.html. Both accessed 9 January 2019.

271 It is more plausible it was one of the research institutes.

272 Modderkolk, "Dutch agencies provide crucial intel."

273 Modderkolk, "Dutch agencies provide crucial intel."

274 Eelco Bosch van Rosenthal, "Dutch intelligence first to alert U.S. about Russian hack of Democratic Party" (January 25, 2018), https://nos.nl/nieuwsuur/artikel/2213767-dutch-intelligence-first-to-alert-u-s-about-russian-hack-of-democratic-party.html, accessed 22 July 2023. See also Dan Goodin, "Russia's hack of State Department was 'hand-to-hand' combat" (April 3, 2017), https://arstechnica.com/tech-policy/2017/04/russias-hack-of-state-department-was-hand-to-hand-combat/, accessed 22 July 2023.

before they could deploy them. This was "a new level of interaction ... a little bit of a game changer."[275]

Later, in the summer of 2015, Dutch intelligence was the first to alert their U.S. counterparts of the breach at the Democratic National Committee (DNC). For Michael N. Schmitt, the lead expert for NATO's two Tallinn Manuals, "The DNC hacks epitomized the grey zone strategy ... a form of 'asymmetrical lawfare.'"[276] This intelligence was reportedly first passed through the NSA-liaison in The Hague. It was subsequently personally communicated at the very highest levels by the then director generals of the AIVD, Rob Bertholee and Pieter Bindt to James Clapper, America's DNI, and National Security Agency and CYBERCOM director Michael Rogers.[277] In return, it is said the Dutch were given technology and intelligence.

However, within a year the Dutch operation was ended when it had become public knowledge that a "Western Intelligence Agency" had hacked Russian systems allowing them to monitor APT29's activities as well as hacking into CCTV through which they could identify faces. Unnamed U.S. intelligence sources had briefed *The Washington Post* in late March/early April 2017.[278] This authorized but off-the-record press leak revealed the methods Dutch intelligence were employing and this appears to have "ruined their operation" causing "great anger in The Hague and Zoetermeer" (where the MIVD and AIVD are based).[279]

It was said this made the MIVD and AIVD more cautious in sharing intelligence. This caution increased after the November 2016 election which saw Donald Trump elected president. The only conclusion that can be drawn is that this disclosure led the SVR to place countermeasures which cut access to the goldmine.[280] This was a goldmine that could have continued to be mined. With it, more intelligence would likely have been gleaned and other attacks mitigated or prevented. At this time, Russian interference – and denialism that Russian influence played a part in the results of the 2016 U.S. presidential election (analyzed in Chapter 4) – was already a major domestic (and international) political issue.

275 "Cyber Threats: Perspectives from the NSA and FBI," March 21, 2017, https://www.aspeninstitute.org/events/cyber-threats-perspectives-nsa-fbi/, accessed 22 July 2023.

276 Michael N. Schmitt, "Grey Zones in the International Law of Cyberspace," *Yale Journal of International Law Online*, Vol. 42, No. 2 (May 2017), pp. 2–3.

277 Modderkolk, "Dutch agencies provide crucial intel."

278 Ellen Nakashima, "New details emerge about 2014 Russian hack of the State Department: It was 'hand to hand combat,'" (April 3, 2017), https://www.washingtonpost.com/world/national-security/new-details-emerge-about-2014-russian-hack-of-the-state-department-it-was-hand-to-hand-combat/2017/04/03/d89168e0-124c-11e7-833c-503e1f6394c9_story.html, accessed 22 July 2023.

279 van Rosenthal, "Dutch intelligence first to alert U.S. about Russian hack."

280 Modderkolk, "Dutch agencies provide crucial intel."

President-elect Donald Trump categorically refused to acknowledge that Russian interference might have affected the course and outcome of the election, thereby tarnishing his against-the-odds victory.[281] In March 2017 he tweeted, "The Democrats made up and pushed the Russian story as an excuse for running a terrible campaign."[282] When the USIC drew their conclusions, instead of supporting them, instead he frequently praised Russia, Russian policies, and President Putin.[283] In November 2017, on his way back from a summit in the Vietnamese city of Da Nang, Trump told reporters interviewing him onboard Air Force One of his personal belief. Trump told them that he accepted President Putin's word that Russia did not meddle in the 2016 U.S. election: "Every time he [Putin] sees me he says, 'I didn't do that,' and I really believe that."[284]

In December 2017, it was reported that denialism of the "objective reality" that Russia intervened was causing "historic turmoil" in the White House leading to a reluctance to show the President any new intelligence on Russian interference.[285] In February 2018, President Trump told CBS's *Face The Nation* "Knowing something about hacking, if you don't catch a hacker … in the act, it's very hard to say who did the hacking. With that being said, I'll go along with Russia. It could

281 "Who will win the presidency?" (November 8, 2016), https://projects.fivethirtyeight.com/2016-election-forecast/, accessed 24 July 2023.

282 Cody Derespina, "Trump: Russia story is 'FAKE NEWS and everyone knows it!'" (March 20, 2017), https://www.foxnews.com/politics/trump-russia-story-is-fake-news-and-everyone-knows-it, accessed 24 July 2023. See also Andrew S. Ross and Damian J. Rivers, "Discursive Deflection: Accusation of 'Fake News' and the Spread of Mis- and Disinformation in the Tweets of President Trump," *Social Media + Society*, Vol. 4, Issue 2 (April–June 2018), pp. 1–12.

283 Tom Porter, "How Do I Love Thee? A Short History of Trump's Praise for Putin" (November 11, 2017), https://www.newsweek.com/heres-all-times-trump-has-praised-putin-708859, accessed 24 July 2023.

284 James Clapper commented, ""The fact that the President would take Putin at his word over that of the intelligence community is quite simply unconscionable" whilst John McCain, the Republican chairman of the Senate Armed Services Committee, remarked "There's nothing 'America First' about taking the word of a KGB colonel over that of the American intelligence community." Steve Holland and Denis Pinchuk, "Trump says he trusts Putin's denials of election meddling" (November 11, 2017), https://www.reuters.com/article/us-apec-summit-usa-russia-idUSKBN1DB04N. Ryan Goodman and John Sipher, "Taking Putin's Word For It. Trump wants to believe both the Russian president's denial of election meddling, and the conclusions of his own intelligence agencies. But he can't have it both ways" (November 12, 2017), https://www.theatlantic.com/international/archive/2017/11/trump-putin-election-asia/545666/, both accessed 24 July 2023.

285 "How Trump's Russia interference doubts impact national security" (December 14, 2017), https://www.cbsnews.com/video/how-trumps-russia-interference-doubts-impact-national-security/, accessed 24 July 2023.

have been China. It could have been a lot of different groups."[286] These denials were pressurizing the FBI, its director James Comey, the Department of Justice, and the USIC into strengthening the case that Russia interfered. These domestic political pressures likely underlay the deliberate leak on the American side that Russian interference was discovered by a Western ally independently of the USIC prior to the election (and to defend the conclusions the USIC had drawn).

This defense of the USIC in the midst of a politicized vortex and competing narratives, also laid the building blocks for the Mueller inquiry. Congressional hearings were beginning to examine the extent of Russian involvement, the FBI was beginning its investigations, and out of this the Department of Justice would appoint Robert Mueller as Special Counsel on May 17, 2017.[287] The influence of Russia on the election of Donald J. Trump as 45th president has since become one of the most controversial and most debated episodes in recent U.S. history. The wake of this political turbulence continues to be felt (including through the 2024 presidential election).

The Dutch operation was initiated (in major part) by the downing of MH17 by a Russian Buk missile over eastern Ukraine. Though involvement continues to be denied, direct Russian government participation was subsequently demonstrated by investigative journalists from Bellingcat and by the Joint Investigation Team (JIT) led by the Dutch government. This was accomplished through a mixture of Open Source Intelligence (OSINT), SIGINT, Satellite Intelligence (SATINT), telemetry data, hacked Russian databases, and forensic investigation. Three Russians and one Ukrainian were subsequently prosecuted *in abstentia.*[288] All were found guil-

---

286 Face the Nation, "Trump in 2017 on Russian hacking: 'It could have been China'" (February 16, 2018), https://www.cbsnews.com/news/trump-in-2017-on-russian-hacking-it-could-have-been-china/, accessed 24 July 2018.

287 Kevin Johnson, "DNC cyber attack by Russia highlighted delayed response, FBI chief says" (March 21, 2017), https://www.usatoday.com/story/news/politics/2017/03/21/dnc-cyber-attack-russia-highlighted-delayed-response-fbi-chief-says/99455634/, accessed January 21 2018. "FBI Director James Comey and NSA Director Admiral Michael Rogers testified at a House Select Intelligence Committee hearing on Russian interference in the 2016 presidential election" (March 20, 2017), https://www.c-span.org/video/?425087-1/russian-election-interference, accessed 23 July 2023.

288 They are Igor Girkin, a former FSB colonel who was commander of the army of the self-proclaimed Donetsk People's Republic; Sergey Dubinskiy, a former military officer of the GRU (a deputy to Girkin and head of the intelligence service of the DPR; Oleg Pulatov, a former GRU Spetznaz and a deputy to Dubinskiy; and Leonid Kharchenko, a Ukrainian separatist and commander of a combat unit in the Donetsk region. Prosecution and Trial, https://www.prosecutionservice.nl/topics/mh17-plane-crash/prosecution-and-trial. Eliot Higgins, "MH17 – The Open Source Evidence" (October 8, 2015), https://www.bellingcat.com/news/uk-and-europe/2015/10/08/mh17-the-open-source-evidence/; The criminal investigation by the Joint Investigation Team (JIT), https://

ty.[289] The Netherlands separately expelled two SVR officers working under official cover as part of a substantial espionage network in December 2020.[290] However, Russian official cover operations (out of their diplomatic service) are still ongoing.[291]

17 The GRU: Its institutes and military units

More widely, in October 2018 seven operatives of the GRU were charged by a U.S. Department of Justice Grand Jury as part of an international effort to "name and shame" Russia. Many of the same operatives were also charged by the office of U.S. Special Counsel, Robert Mueller, in a July 2018 indictment. They are charged with hacking into around forty anti-doping agencies and sporting organizations including the World Anti-Doping Authority (WADA) and the International Olympic Committee (IOC). The indictments also charged them with hacking other targets including the nuclear power company Westinghouse, the OPCW, and Spiez Chemical Laboratory, a Swiss lab working with the OPCW.[292] Not all are hackers.[293] However, all were trained by the GRU's research institutes.

---

www.prosecutionservice.nl/topics/mh17-plane-crash/criminal-investigation-jit-mh17. All accessed 22 July 2023.

289 Girkin (who goes by the *nom de guerre* Strelkov ("Shooter")) was arrested in July 2023 but by his former employers, the FSB, and charged with inciting extremism. Unrelatedly, "Strelkov" had overstepped the mark in his ultranationalist criticisms of Russia's military failings in Ukraine and attacks on the military leadership. This included criticizing Putin on Telegram. Strelkov is also widely suspected of being involved fighting Chechen separatists and being one of the leaders of "Little Green Men" in Crimea in 2014 prior to his involvement in the Donbas. Douglas Busvine and Veronika Melkozerova, "Pro-war nationalist and Putin scourge Igor Girkin held on extremism charges" (July 21, 2023), https://www.politico.eu/article/pro-war-vladimir-putin-critic-igor-girkin-strelkov-arrested-russia-ukraine/, accessed 22 July 2023.

290 Anonymous, "Netherlands expels two Russians after uncovering 'espionage network'" (December 10, 2020), https://www.bbc.co.uk/news/world-europe-55258790, accessed 22 July 2023.

291 Eelco Bosch van Rosenthal and Ben Meindertsma, "This is what we know about the Russian spies in the Netherlands" (October 14, 2022), https://nos.nl/artikel/2448320-dit-weten-we-over-de-russische-spionnen-in-nederland, "Nieuwsuur Zo achterhaalden we de identiteit van 17 Russische spionnen" (October 15, 2022), https://www.youtube.com/watch?v=b39P4WKlwu4, accessed 22 July 2023.

292 "U.S. Charges Russian GRU Officers with International Hacking and Related Influence and Disinformation Operations," https://www.justice.gov/opa/pr/us-charges-russian-gru-officers-international-hacking-and-related-influence-and, and Bill Chappell and Carrie Johnson, "U.S. Charges 7 Russian Intelligence Officers with Hacking 40 Sports and Doping Groups" (October 4, 2018), https://www.npr.org/2018/10/04/654306774/russian-cyber-unit-accused-of-attacking-opcw-chemical-wea

The GRU's headquarters in "The Aquarium" is ringed by research institutes affiliated to the intelligence services. One of these is run by the FSB: the Kvant Research Institute (aka "Quantum"), where the first Soviet computers were developed. It was taken over by the FSB in 2008 and lies near the industrial zone in Khovrino district in northwest Moscow. It is five stories high, ringed with a barbed wire fence, with its lower floor windows painted over. It is said to conduct work of "national importance."[294]

Other research institutes are run by Russia's GRU and MOD. They include cyber training centers at the Cherepovets Higher Military School of Radio Electronics and Alexander Mozhaysky Military Space Academy. Alexey Morenets, accused of the attempted hack of the OPCW, trained there. Others include the Defense Ministry's 46th Central Research Institute (Military Unit 54726). There is also the Center for Special Studies on Moscow's Svoboda Street. This analyzes exploits and searches for vulnerabilities in computer networks. The Center for Special Studies has been hiring staff who can locate network vulnerabilities and are able to use exploits against them.[295] This is where Evgeny Serebryakov worked (one of the GRU officers who tried to hack into the OPCW building).[296]

Military Unit 26165 (based at the Khamovnichesky barracks complex near the Kremlin) meanwhile, is one of the GRU's main cyberespionage units. The Khamovnichesky barracks also houses the GRU's 85th Central Research Center (GTsSS – *Glavni Centar za Specijalne Službe*/Main Center for Special Services). This initially studied and practiced cryptography but has long now concentrated on cyberespionage.[297] Its main base is located at 20 Komsomol'skiy Prospekt in Moscow. Military Unit 74455 is/was located at 22 Kirova Street, Khimki, Moscow.

---

pons-watchdog. Arrest warrants have been issued by the FBI, but this is more an attempt to "name and shame." GRU Hacking to Undermine Anti-Doping Efforts, https://www.fbi.gov/wanted/cyber/gru-hacking-to-undermine-anti-doping-efforts. All accessed 7 January 2019.

293 Bellingcat, "305 Car Registrations" (October 4, 2018).

294 Turovsky, "Russian armed cyberforces." The Kvant Research Institute is also mentioned in connection with sanctioned individuals by the U.S Treasury. Treasury Sanctions Russian Federal Security Service Enablers, June 11, 2018, https://home.treasury.gov/news/press-releases/sm0410, accessed 21 July 2023.

295 Sheera Frenkel, "New Report Lifts Curtain On Russia's Construction Of Powerful 'Cyber-army'" (November 7, 2016), https://www.buzzfeednews.com/article/sheerafrenkel/new-report-lifts-curtain-on-russias-construction-of-powerful, accessed 30 November 2016.

296 Egloff and Smeets, "Publicly Attributing Cyber Attacks: A Framework," p. 521.

297 PROFILE: GRU CYBER AND HYBRID THREAT OPERATIONS, https://assets.publishing.service.gov.uk/media/687a0d96a52cca025ef5be89/Profile-GRU-cyber-and-hybrid-threat-operations.pdf. "unidade militar 26165", https://www.opensanctions.org/entities/NK-4QuWKcAhpWZCgqBKvefro7/. Both accessed 19 July 2025.

This building is referred to as "the Tower" within the GRU. The 18th Central Research Center works here on communications electronics. All of these specialist centers and groups also have links to cyberespionage and cyberwarfare activities specializing in various hacking techniques.[298]

The GRU also runs Military Unit 54777 (72nd Special Service Center). This is mainly used for psychological operations, including Internet-based mis/dis and mal-information operations. These encompass socio-political influence operations against foreign targets.[299] Unit 54777 was formed in 1994 but its heritage dates back to the Soviet Union where it was tasked with monitoring dissent within the Red Army. It is housed on the second floor of the Aquarium. As part of its psychological operations, Unit 54777 is accused of running two "public diplomacy organizations" supporting Russian expatriates, InfoRos and the Institute of the Russian Diaspora. These have been accused of promoting Russian intervention in Ukraine and conducting "legal aid" work for Russian expats in countries including Syria, Yemen, and Libya (all being conflict zones where Russian forces have intervened).[300] This saw hashtags #IstandwithPutin and #IstandwithRussia trending on Twitter (now rebranded X) as the Ukraine War began.[301] As part of a series of U.S. government sanctions against Russian elites InfoRos, and three other Russian organizations, were designated as "propagating Russian intelligence services-directed content" by the U.S. Treasury in April 2021.[302]

Unit 26165 at the Khamovnichesky barracks has been tied to the "hack and leak" of Emmanuel Macron's e-mails in May 2017 and were a "base of operations" for the infamous Democratic National Committee (DNC) "hack and leak" of 2016 analyzed in Chapter 4. Military Unit 26165 and Unit 74455 were named in a July 2018 U.S. Grand Jury indictment and the March 2019 Mueller Report. Both were tied to the GRU.[303] The leakers used the personas "DCLeaks" and "Guccifer 2.0" (the latter of which also purported the hack was conducted by a "lone wolf" Ro-

---

298 Turovsky, "What is the GRU?"

299 Andrew S. Bowen, Russian Cyber Units (updated February 2, 2022), https://crsreports.congress.gov/product/pdf/IF/IF11718, accessed 1 July 2023.

300 Andrei Soldatov and Michael Weiss, "Inside Russia's Secret Propaganda Unit. Newly discovered documents reveal the role of a secret Russian intelligence section called Unit 54777 in propaganda and espionage operations" (December 7, 2020), https://newlinesmag.com/reportage/inside-russias-secret-propaganda-unit/, accessed 21 July 2023.

301 Carl Miller and Jeremy Reffin, "#IstandwithRussia – Anatomy of a Pro-Kremlin Influence Operation" (March 8, 2022), https://www.isdglobal.org/digital_dispatches/istandwithrussia-anatomy-of-a-pro-kremlin-influence-operation/, accessed 21 July 2023.

302 Treasury Sanctions Russians Bankrolling Putin and Russia-Backed Influence Actors (March 3, 2022), https://home.treasury.gov/news/press-releases/jy0628, accessed 21 July 2023.

303 Mueller Report Volume I, pp. 36–41.

manian who was claiming credit).[304] The July 2018 indictment named twelve Russian intelligence officers belonging to the GRU along with the addresses of the military facilities where they worked.[305] It has been suggested by Russian news sources that FSB agents were bribed $10 million for "outing" them to the FBI.[306]

These Russian news sources had been briefed by unnamed officials who pointed the finger at Colonel Sergei Mikhailov as the recipient of the $10 million. It was mentioned in the introduction that he was the former head of the FSB's Center 18 (Unit 64829) who had been sentenced in early 2019 for passing classified information to Western intelligence. The investigations began in December 2016 and were undertaken not by the FSB but by the GRU and the case featured "competing narratives" and "score settling" between the GRU and FSB. This saw Mikhailov arrested during a meeting and a sack placed on his head as he was led out of the room. Whilst he got a 22-year sentence for committing treason, with another "middleman" (Ruslan Stoyanov) sentenced to 14 years, the others implicated with the case (all tied to the FSB) struck plea deals in return for their cooperation.[307]

Other FSB officers were arrested, including Dmitriy Dokuchavev (a subordinate of Mikhailov), along with "Internet entrepreneur", Georgiy Fomchenkov. It seems unlikely Mikhailov acted alone. He had complex ties through cut-outs dating back to 2011 involving cooperation with the FBI through a cybercriminal turned Internet entrepreneur named Pavel Vrublevskiy who founded the PayPal-like Chronopay. It is believed this bribe could have elicited the exposure of the simultaneous GRU-directed operation by APT28/"Fancy Bear" and at the time of his arrest, there was deep underlying conflict with the GRU. This had seen the FSB employ a cybercriminal hacking group with the moniker "Shaltay Boltay" (Russian for Humpty Dumpty) who were also operating under the cover of the hacktivist group Anonymous.

---

304 The original Guccifer, Marcel Lazăr Lehel, was a Romanian hacker and cybercriminal who was extradited to the U.S. in 2016 but served the majority of his seven-year sentence in a Romanian prison. Catalin Cimpanu, "Hacker Guccifer, who exposed Clinton private email server, ready for US prison sentence" (October 24, 2018), https://www.zdnet.com/article/hacker-guccifer-who-exposed-clinton-private-email-server-ready-for-us-prison-sentence/, accessed 10 May 2019.

305 https://www.justice.gov/file/1080281/download, accessed 2 January 2018.

306 "Гостайна раскрылась за $10 млн Дела обвиняемых в измене офицеров ФСБ дошли до суда" (October 5, 2018), https://www.kommersant.ru/doc/3760232 and "Чей медведь? Как связано дело полковника ФСБ Сергея Михайлова с разоблачением офицеров ГРУ и кибергруппировки Fancy Bear" (October 8, 2018), https://www.novayagazeta.ru/articles/2018/10/06/78097-chey-medved?utm_source=yxnews. Both accessed 8 January 2019.

307 Mike Eckel, "In Moscow Treason Trial, A Major Scandal For Russian Security Agency" (February 27 2019), https://www.rferl.org/a/russia-hacker-mikhailov-stoyanov-fsb-scandal-for-russian-security-agency/29794092.html, accessed 8 August 2025.

This group's *modus operandi* included hacking and leaking stolen information (intelligence) from compromised accounts of prominent Russian business and political leaders. This included Kseniya Bolshakova, the secretary to the head of the construction department of Russia's Ministry of Defense (MOD). They were then instructed to publicize classified information found during the breach to embarrass the MOD and the FSB's own head of the DVKR, General Colonel Aleksandr Bezverkhniy. This prompted Defense Minister Sergei Shoigu to order an investigation which contributed to Mikhailov's arrest for state treason in December 2016. The chief of the TsIB at the time was also "dismissed under a cloud and sent into retirement".[308] It is also worth noting that despite the cybersecurity industry (and resultantly government agencies) unhelpfully adopting their own naming conventions for APTs and other state-affiliated threat actors, identified individuals associated with Russian groups show up repeatedly in multiple cases.[309]

In July 2025 further evidence of named individuals and Russian intelligence sub-groups came to light after the British government sanctioned almost two dozen Russians as well GRU Units 29155, 26165 and 74455 in order for their leadership to be held accountable for the actions of those under their command. The British government could not ascertain whether the three groups coordinated but did note that Unit 29155 is the 161st Specialist Training Center (TsPS), containing the cyber sub-unit designated "Cadet Blizzard". 18 of those sanctioned were GRU intelligence officers. Two more were linked previously to the FSB and Wagner Group but were now leaders the Africa Corps/African Initiative.

Funded by Russia and employing Russian intelligence officers for influence operations in Africa, Unit 29155 also organized a delegation of bloggers and journalists to visit Mariupol, illegally occupied by Russia, in what was described as a a press tour. Coordinating closely with the FBI, NATO, and the EU further details were also provided as part of the July 2025 sanctions. Unit 26165 had targeted Yulia Skripal's e-mail with X-Agent malware in 2013. It had also conducted online reconnaissance of shelters housing civilians in Mariupol and Kharkiv the day before Russian artillery struck and killed civilians on March 16 2022. In the earth

---

308 Riehle, *The Russian FSB*, pp. 74–75.

309 Andy Greenberg, "This Is the New Leader of Russia's Infamous Sandworm Hacking Unit. Evgenii Serebriakov now runs the most aggressive hacking team of Russia's GRU military spy agency. To Western intelligence, he's a familiar face" (March 15, 2023), https://www.wired.com/story/russia-gru-sandworm-serebriakov/, accessed 18 March 2024.

above the Mariupol Theatre shelter had been written "дети" (Russian for children). The message was large enough to seen from the air.[310]

18 Conclusion

Cyberespionage has proven much more cost effective than traditional spycraft, but traditional spycraft has not melted away. Far from it. It continues to be used as Russia's intelligence agencies have employed cyber allied to hard military power in their near abroad to advance their defense and foreign policy aims. Whether we think of them as extensions of Cold War-era active measures, or as part of Russia's hybrid warfare strategy or hybrid intelligence, the value and efficacy is the same. It has been a cost-effective method to reestablish Russia as a major global power and counterbalance NATO and EU expansion into former Soviet territory following the end of the Cold War and the breakup of the bipolar international system. During the 1990s this saw Russia deprioritized by Western intelligence. This gave the Kremlin opportunities to strategize and push back.

Since his first election in 2000, and especially after his return as president in 2012, Vladimir Putin has "unleashed increasingly powerful intelligence agencies in campaigns of domestic repression and external destabilisation, appearing to genuinely want to revise the structures of the international order."[311] Since 2012, Kremlin aims have been to divide and deter NATO and the EU from confronting Russian foreign adventurism enabled by "hybrid warfare." The Donbas conflict prior to February 2022 is a good illustration of how Russia was adept at operations in the "gray zone"; especially in creating plausible deniability over its use of armed force and intervention.

From 2019 to 2022 "passportization" (offers of fast track Russian passports and a form of lawfare) had been a means to create a pretext for intervention (or false flag) and then invasion as part of its suite of hybrid warfare activities as well as a means of further destabilization.[312] Pro-Russian factions were in evidence and Russia capitalized and exploited these to destabilize the region whilst

---

310 Policy paper Profile: GRU cyber and hybrid threat operations (July 18 2025), https://www.gov.uk/government/publications/profile-gru-cyber-and-hybrid-threat-operations/profile-gru-cyber-and-hybrid-threat-operations. accessed 6 August 2025.

311 Galeotti, "Putin's Hydra," p. 2.

312 Fabian Burkhardt, Cindy Wittke, Elia Bescotti, and Maryna Rabinovych, "Russian Military Build-up Around Ukraine – Part 2," *Russian Analytical Digest*, No. 277 (February 23, 2022), https://www.research-collection.ethz.ch/bitstream/handle/20.500.11850/533782/RAD277.pdf?sequence=3, accessed 6 January 2023.

denying they provided direct military support despite ample evidence of regular soldiers, *spetsnaz*-GRU troops, and GRU operatives on the ground. None of these wore Russian uniforms or insignia and were instead, like in Crimea, "Little Green Men."[313] Åtland argues this made it a "blended conflict"; neither exclusively intrastate nor unambiguously interstate.[314]

Some of the same tactics used in Crimea and the Donbas are also present in other parts of the former Soviet Union, including Moldova and its breakaway province of Transnistria, where there are Russian peacekeepers and where the Kremlin continues to exert pressure.[315] They had also been used in Georgia.[316] Within these regions, the Kremlin has actively fermented separatism, ethnonationalism towards Russia, and fostered political tensions with the host state.[317] Counters to Russian adventurism required action, confrontation, or accommodation. A clear warning that instead of being deterred, they were being emboldened was given in 2014 when Russia annexed Crimea. Through inaction over Crimea, the West quiescently chose accommodation.

Crimea is important not only in historical and cultural terms but as a strategic asset. It is seen by the Kremlin as an unsinkable aircraft carrier granting port and basing facilities on the Black Sea and providing a gateway to the Mediterranean. Since Russian occupation in 2014, major investments have been made in Crimea to build-up industrial, transport and logistics, energy and water infrastructure on

313 Tor Bukkvoll, "Why Putin Went to War. Ideology, Interests and Decision-Making in the Russian Use of Force in Crimea and Donbas," *Contemporary Politics*, Vol. 22, Issue 3, pp. 275–276.
314 Kristian Åtland, "Destined for Deadlock? Russia, Ukraine, and the Unfulfilled Minsk Agreements," *Post-Soviet Affairs*, Vol. 36, No. 2 (January 2020), pp. 122–139.
315 https://md.usembassy.gov/national-security-council-coordinator-for-strategic-communications-john-kirby-commented-on-russian-attempts-to-destabilize-moldova/, accessed 16 March 2023. Sarah Rainsford, "European leaders boost Moldova in face of 'relentless' Russia" (August 27, 2025), https://www.bbc.co.uk/news/articles/cx2xzng4rwro. Oana Marocico & Seamus Mirodan, "How Russian-funded fake news network aims to disrupt election in Europe – BBC investigation" (September 21, 2025), https://www.bbc.co.uk/news/articles/c4g5kl0n5d2o. Both accessed 22 September 2025. Russian peacekeepers are also present in the disputed territory of Nagorno-Karabakh between Azerbaijan and Armenia. Cory Welt and Andrew S. Bowen, Azerbaijan and Armenia: The Nagorno-Karabakh Conflict, Congressional Research Service (January 7, 2021), https://apps.dtic.mil/sti/pdfs/AD1147494.pdf, accessed 11 November 2023.
316 Fabian Burkhardt, Cindy Wittke, and Elia Bescotti, "TCUP Report: Passportization, diminished citizenship rights, and the Donbas vote in Russia's 2021 Duma elections" (January 2022), p. 5, https://huri.harvard.edu/files/huri/files/idp_report_3_burkhardt_et_al.pdf?m=1642520438, accessed 21March 2023.
317 Adam Potočňák and Miroslav Mares, "Donbas Conflict: How Russia's Trojan Horse Failed and Forced Moscow to Alter Its Strategy," *Problems of Post-Communism*, Vol. 70, Issue 4 (October 2023), pp. 341–351.

the peninsula. This is in addition to the massive Kerch bridges linking Crimea to Krasnodar Krai on the Sea of Azov (with Krasnodar Krai also an important base for the Black Sea Fleet). The bridges have been the subject of regular Ukrainian attacks. Between 2016 and 2020, 14 keels were laid down in Crimea's shipyards. These included Karakurt-class cruise missile corvettes and modular patrol ships. Most noteworthy are two 40,000-ton (Project 23900) helicopter-carrier amphibious assault ships (LHDs).

These can operate beyond the range of coastal artillery and some missile systems giving the Russian Navy "an unparalleled capability to carry out surprise, blitzkrieg amphibious missions" and for performing fleet command-and-control (C2) management that the Black Sea Fleet has lacked since the Moskva was sunk.[318] The two delayed Project 23900 LHDs are not projected to become operational until after 2028. During the Cold War (and for centuries before) the Mykolaiv shipyards were "the jewel in the crown of Soviet naval construction" and among the chief reasons why Russia attempted to control the Kherson-Mykolaiv axis in 2022.[319] In addition, plans are underway for developing the tourist potential of occupied Ukraine including the Port of Yalta in occupied Crimea.[320] Across this southern theater, some early Russian gains were reversed in the oblasts of Kherson and Zaporizhia with both Russian and Ukrainian counterattacks repelled as Russia tried to take and hold ground. As an ongoing war at the time of writing, territorial gains and losses can change even if a peace settlement is brokered with the course of the war followed in great detail by the Institute for the Study of War.[321]

In March 2009, when then U.S. Secretary of State, Hillary Clinton, presented Russian Foreign Minister Sergei Lavrov with a symbolic red button it was hoped this would lead to more stable and peaceful relations. The Kremlin instead shifted its posture and changed gear. This was a year after Russia's invasion of Georgia and ending of the decade-long Second Chechen War in the North Cauca-

318 Ihor Kabanenko, "Arsenal of Empire: Russian Naval Construction in Crimea and Its Implications for Black Sea Security" (June 3 2022), https://jamestown.org/program/an-arsenal-of-empire-russian-naval-construction-in-crimea-and-implications-for-black-sea-security/, accessed 19 August 2025.

319 Kabanenko, "Arsenal of Empire".

320 Paul Conroy, Eloise Herdegen, and Karolina Hird, "Russian Occupation Update" (August 6 2025), accessed 19 August 2025, https://understandingwar.org/sites/default/files/Russian%20Occupation%20Update%2C%20August%207%2C%202025%20PDF.pdf.

321 https://understandingwar.org/, accessed 19 August 2025.

sus.[322] Driven by bitterness over the collapse of the Soviet Union, Russia's demise as a superpower, and Western expansion to its borders, after this time Putin instead began to challenge the architecture of not just the new world order that had been ushered in by the end of the Cold War but also the post-1945 global order.[323]

In the intervening years, Russian cyberespionage campaigns have been a low-cost operational arm of Russian policy financially and politically. Through to February 2022 and the invasion of Ukraine, they had proved to be highly effective. Built on active measures, they offered Russia asymmetric tools of foreign and security policy which could not be gained by traditional intelligence gathering or through conventional force modernization and the use of military force.[324] This includes modernization of their nuclear forces which repeat the zero-sum game schooled during the Cold War.[325] The nuclear card has been increasingly played because Russia's conventional forces have been hollowed out by "embezzlement from top to bottom, and corruption in terms of false reporting, sleaze, cynicism and brutality."[326]

This is not to discount Russia's military, but its limitations and effectiveness have been systematically demonstrated in Ukraine alongside a system of top-down command and control that has impeded military performance and created friction. The decision to invade Ukraine was founded on a belief "that if the door was kicked in the whole building would collapse."[327] It was also based on inflated and politized intelligence that Russian forces would be greeted with flowers and cheering crowds as they "liberated" Eastern Ukraine.[328] Russia's intelligence direc-

---

322 Mikhail Zygar, "The Russian Reset That Never Was: How Palace Intrigues in the Kremlin, the Death of Qaddafi, and War in Ukraine Ushered in a New Era of Mistrust between Russia and the United States under Obama," *Foreign Policy*, December 9, 2016.

323 Galeotti, "(Mis)Understanding Russia's two 'hybrid wars,'" p. 1.

324 Scott Boston, Michael Johnson, Nathan Beauchamp-Mustafaga, and Yvonne K. Crane, "Assessing the Conventional Force Imbalance in Europe. Implications for Countering Russian Local Superiority" (2018), https://www.rand.org/pubs/research_reports/RR2402.html, accessed 7 January 2019.

325 Despite nuclear saber-rattling, nuclear use scenarios are not strategies that can lead to success. Hans M. Kristensen and Robert S. Norris, "Russian Nuclear Forces, 2018," *Bulletin of the Atomic Scientists*, Vol. 74, Issue 3 (April 2018), pp. 185–195.

326 Robert Dalsjö, Michael Jonsson and Johan Norberg, "A Brutal Examination: Russian Military Capability in Light of the Ukraine War," *Survival*, Vol. 64, No. 3 (June–July 2022), pp. 13–14.

327 Dalsjö, Jonsson and Norberg, "A Brutal Examination," pp. 13–14.

328 Taras Kuzio, "Imperial Nationalism as the Driver Behind Russia's Invasion of Ukraine," *Nations and Nationalism*, Vol. 29, Issue 1 (January 2023), pp. 35–36. Mark Galeotti, "Spooks in the Kremlin. The Dangers of Putin's Unhealthy Reliance on Russian Intelligence," *Foreign Policy*, No. 232 (Spring 2019), pp. 17–19.

tors, Sergei Naryshkin (SVR), Igor Kostyukov (GRU), and Alexander Bortnikov (FSB) told Putin what he wanted to hear. This institutionalized confirmation bias downplayed or filtered out more realistic assessments.[329]

For rank-and-file Russian citizens, this is portrayed as a "Special Military Operation." It is what the Kremlin wants them to hear. Protests are met with force and opposition has been systematically and methodically stifled and silenced with only the veneer of representative democracy remaining. This has enabled a one party state led by United Russia and embedded the rule not only of Putin, but a system of corruption, cronyism, and patronage. Russian intelligence is also known to contract work to the private sector to counter domestic discord and threats to the system. In March 2023, some 5,000 Russian documents were leaked from NTC Vulkan, a Moscow-based cybersecurity company with contracts with Russia's military and intelligence agencies. These contained plans, operations, and connections between Russian intelligence and sub-contractors from 2016 to 2021.[330] They appear to show links between Russia's military, the military research institutes, and the MVD (*Ministerstvo Vnutrennikh Del*/Ministry of Internal Affairs), in domestic surveillance projects.[331] These measures are in addition to state media propaganda, and the System of Operative-Investigative Measures (SORM) which allows Russia's intelligence agencies and police to lawfully intercept and record landline and cell phone telecommunications.[332]

Whether one sees Russia's invasion as the descendent of hybrid warfare and active measures since 2014 (and before), the Ukraine War was a major step

329 Huw Dylan, David V. Gioe, and Elena Grossfeld, "The Autocrat's Intelligence Paradox: Vladimir Putin's (Mis)Management of Russian Strategic Assessment in the Ukraine War," *British Journal of Politics and International Relations*, Vol. 25, Issue 3 (August 2023), pp. 385–404.

330 Luke Harding, Stiliyana Simeonova, Manisha Ganguly, and Dan Sabbagh, "'Vulkan files' leak reveals Putin's global and domestic cyberwarfare tactics" (March 30, 2023), https://www.theguardian.com/technology/2023/mar/30/vulkan-files-leak-reveals-putins-global-and-domestic-cyberwarfare-tactics, accessed 15 July 2023.

331 In the Soviet Union, the KGB was also tasked with monitoring their own military who viewed the KGB with suspicion from the time of Stalin's purges. Robert W. Pringle, "SMERSH: Military Counterintelligence and Stalin's Control of the USSR," *International Journal of Intelligence and CounterIntelligence*, Vol. 21, Issue 1 (January 2008), pp. 122–134. Until the Putin era, "Russia's army and its secret police did not just hate each other; they viewed the world through different lenses." Andrei Soldatov, "Cyberwarfare leaks show Russian army is adopting mindset of secret police" (March 30, 2023), https://www.theguardian.com/technology/2023/mar/30/cyberwarfare-leaks-show-russian-army-is-adopting-mindset-of-secret-police, accessed 15 July 2023.

332 Andrei Soldatov and Irina Borogan, "Russia's Surveillance State," *World Policy Journal*, Vol. 30, Issue 23 (Fall 2013), pp. 23–30. SORM is run by Center 12 (the Center for Operational Technical Measures (*Tsentr Operativno Tekhnicheskikh Meropriyatiy*, TsOTM)) within the FSB. It too has KGB antecedents. Riehle, *The Russian FSB*, pp. 60–61, 91–92.

change. Without minimizing the cost of life that has followed, it was a major policy shift from one which had brought success without crossing the threshold into unequivocal interstate conflict. Previously, this had seen Putin and his Kremlin advisors exploit the gray zone to considerable effect. Through the use of cyberespionage and the Wagner Group, it was the "Gerasimov doctrine" in action. Already, the 4Ds of Russian information warfare: dismiss, distort, distract, and dismay should have been joined by a fifth – disruption. Chapters 2–4 will demonstrate the scale of this disruption.

Western counterintelligence has seen successes. The Dutch government went public with declarations of blame and expelled four GRU officers who were caught red-handed in the attempted breach of the OPCW in April 2018 following the attempted assassination of Sergey and Yulia Skripal and use of chemical weapons by Russia's ally Syria.[333] Their remarkable penetration of the SVR's APT29/"Cozy Bear" also deserves credit as does their sharing of key intelligence with their American counterparts. The Swiss also went public after taking their time conducting technical analysis of the Russian "hack and leak" attacks on the IOC and WADA.[334] This is "a major departure from previous practice" with "potentially substantial implications for state handling of cyber conflict."[335]

However, diplomatic expulsions and naming and shaming as the FBI has attempted did not deter Russia and, according to Keir Giles, does not work.[336] Whilst this might degrade capabilities and capacity (often followed by tit-for-tat expulsions), this appears to have had minimal impact and they simply deny everything (a "look over there" defense). Riehle suggests the exposure of their operations could be an indication that their covert tradecraft has deteriorated post-Cold War or the leadership has become less concerned with hiding responsibility.

---

333 Anthony Deutsch and Stephanie van den Berg, "Dutch government says it disrupted Russian attempt to hack chemical weapons watchdog" (October 4, 2018), https://www.reuters.com/article/us-britain-netherlands-russia/dutch-government-says-it-disrupted-russian-attempt-to-hack-chemical-weapons-watchdog-idUSKCN1ME14X accessed 16 December 2018.

334 John Revill, "Swiss investigate alleged Russian cyber attack on World Anti-Doping Agency" (September 15, 2018), https://www.reuters.com/article/us-swiss-russia/swiss-investigate-alleged-russian-cyber-attack-on-world-anti-doping-agency-idUSKCN1LV0B5, accessed 16 December 2018.

335 Keir Giles and Kim Hartmann, '"Silent Battle" Goes Loud: Entering a New Era of State-Avowed Cyber Conflict,' p. 23. See also Gil Baram and Udi Sommer, "Covert or not Covert: National Strategies During Cyber Conflict," both in Tomáš Minárik, Siim Alatalu, Stefano Biondi, Massimiliano Signoretti, Ihsan Tolga and Gábor Visky (eds.), *2019 11th International Conference on Cyber Conflict: Silent Battle* (Tallinn: CCD COE Publications, 2019), pp. 197–212.

336 https://www.fbi.gov/wanted/cyber, accessed 15 October 2023. Giles, *Russia's War on Everybody*, pp. 91–96.

Both are likely true.[337] Russia's intelligence agencies running these campaigns are not "ten feet tall." They have serious weaknesses. They are "often divided, competitive, and poorly tasked." Moreover, "They are certainly not in charge of the Kremlin, but nor is the Kremlin wholly adept at managing them."[338] Still, neither of these scenarios is comforting and the FSB, GRU, and SVR have also shown in their "brutal competition between them ... forays into crime, and their willingness to take extreme measures, even targeted killings."[339]

This means, that despite shared priorities, the FSB, GRU, and SVR, engage in periodic turf wars and fierce competition. This leads them to attempt "to outper-

---

337 Riehle, *Russian Intelligence*, p. 213.

338 Galeotti, "Putin's Hydra," p. 2.

339 Galeotti, "Putin's Hydra," p. 2. Those conducted by the GRU have been described above (especially that of Unit 29155). For the FSB wetwork is suspected of being conducted by "Department V" (V for Vympel) and their Alpha *Spetsnaz*, whilst the SVR has "an elite operational unit known as Zaslon [Shield or Screen]" (officially referred to as Directorate-A and Directorate-V) but the extent of their current portfolio is uncertain. Thought to have been formed in 1997 before becoming operational in 1998, Zaslon are trained for missions outside of Russia. They have allegedly been deployed to multiple war zones including Iraq and Afghanistan, with a more permanent presence in Syria protecting the Assad regime and Russian interests before his brutal regime fell in December 2024. According to Galeotti, Zaslon numbers around 280 personnel (approximately the size of a Russian battalion) and their portfolio ranges from hostage-rescue to assassination missions. Whilst they can wear their distinctive uniforms, they are also suspected of deploying as civilians or donning the uniforms of other units, including embassy security details. Riehle and others also suggest their portfolio (possibly their primary role) includes the protection of Russian embassy staff and government officials (including high value targets) traveling in dangerous locations. They are also believed to be involved in evacuation and extraction missions. These include extracting personnel and incriminating documents and equipment. However, the extent of their portfolio, deployments, and mission parameters remains uncertain and even their very existence has been regularly denied. Mark Galeotti, "Russia's 'Zaslon' Military Operators Are So Shadowy They Make Ninjas Look Like Amateurs" (May 19 2013), https://www.businessinsider.com/russian-zaslon-special-operations-2013-5?IR=T. Ahmed Hassan, "Zaslon: Russia's Most Secretive Unit" (March 10 2025), https://greydynamics.com/zaslon-russias-most-secretive-unit/, accessed 2 September 2025. Riehle, *Russian Intelligence*, pp. 64–65, 207–209. Andrew S. Bowen, Russian Military Intelligence: Background and Issues for Congress (November 15 2021), https://apps.dtic.mil/sti/trecms/pdf/AD1157209.pdf, p. 13. Accessed 3 August 2025. Andrew S. Bowen, Russia's Foreign Intelligence Services (January 3 2025), https://www.congress.gov/crs_external_products/IF/PDF/IF12865/IF12865.1.pdf. "'V' for 'Vympel'"; "FSB's Magnificent Seven: New Links between Berlin and Istanbul Assassinations" (June 29 2020), https://www.bellingcat.com/news/uk-andeurope/2020/06/29/fsbs-magnificent-seven-new-links-between-berlin-and-istanbul-assassinations/. All accessed 3 August 2025. There is also a dedicated Vympel Spetsnaz unit assigned to Ukraine under the designation Directorate T (Taurida). Riehle, *The Russian FSB*, pp. 39–41, 84–6, 138–139.

form and embarrass rivals."[340] This is also one of the reasons, Russia's APT28 and APT29 have been seen running separate campaigns in competition (and unknown) to the other. The FSB was not previously attributed with foreign cyberespionage campaigns in anything like the same frequency. This includes major cases of cybercrime and menacing forays into critical infrastructure. This view is now changing, and the activities of the FSB's APTs are now becoming clearer alongside those of the GRU and SVR. This is the subject of Chapter 2.

340 Anonymous, "Russia's three intelligence agencies, explained" (October 12, 2018), https://themoscowproject.org/explainers/russias-three-intelligence-agencies-explained/, accessed 9 March 2020.

Chapter 2
Russia: An Advanced Persistent Threat to economies and critical infrastructure

1 Introduction

This chapter will demonstrate the extent of Russian campaigns against critical infrastructure (CI) and how they have pre-positioned within CI. It begins by discussing Russian cybercrime, its links with the state, and some of the most serious cases of cybercrime drawing on the connections between Russian organized crime/cybercriminals and Russia's intelligence community. It then moves onto in-depth case studies of some of the main CI campaigns emanating out of Russia. It finally analyzes the main tactics, techniques, and procedures (TTPs) used for attacks on or for pre-positioning against CI.

2 Russia's use of cybercriminals and "patriotic hackers"

Russian cybercriminals are part of a melting pot where "the boundaries between organized crime, intelligence operations, and state-operations have become increasingly unclear."[1] Russia's intelligence agencies have found it is convenient to use Russia's cybercriminal scene to pilfer from the West and other parts of the world. There is only one rule. Do not conduct cyberattacks within Russia or on its friends and allies, including those in its near abroad. Two actions are encouraged. Share anything interesting useful to the state and be prepared to be called upon for patriotic duties – or face prison.[2] The bulk of organized crime gangs operate out of Eastern Europe, especially former Soviet states. Many are based in Russia or have Russian ties.[3] This makes them, like the Wagner Group under

---

1 "Hybrid War as a War on Governance Interview by Octavian Manea with Dr. Mark Galeotti" (undated), https://smallwarsjournal.com/jrnl/art/hybrid-war-as-a-war-on-governance, accessed 13 January 2018.

2 Trevor McDougal, "Establishing Russia's Responsibility for CyberCrime Based on Its Hacker Culture," *Brigham Young University International Law & Management Review*, Vol. 11, Issue 2 (August 2015), pp. 59–60.

3 Paul Peachey, "Director of Europol: "Top computer graduates are being lured into cybercrime" (December 29, 2014), https://www.independent.co.uk/news/uk/crime/director-of-europol-top-computer-graduates-are-being-lured-into-cybercrime-9948990.html, accessed 4 September 2018.

https://doi.org/10.1515/9783111583464-005

the late Yevgeny Prigozhin and other proxies, useful cloaks for the Kremlin to hide behind.[4] They also provide a veil of plausible deniability to mask state involvement.[5]

For former Deputy Director of Britain's Secret Intelligence Service (SIS), Nigel Inkster, this association has seen Russia's criminal sub-state hackers become state-protected "privateers."[6] More broadly, Maurer sees that these ties "range across a spectrum: from delegation to orchestration and sanctioning."[7] If delegated, they are on a tight leash and under operational state control, effectively making them front-line troops. If orchestrated, then they are tethered but on a looser leash and can be provided with funding and tools. Sanctioning is where Russia sees cybercrime as benefiting state interests whether by tacit or active approval or by shielding them from prosecution.[8] This is illustrated in cases like the 2021 Colonial Pipeline ransomware attack in the U.S. (discussed below).[9]

This intermix is not restricted to Russia and one has to be careful of "false flags" (including through misattribution). Whilst significant advancements in cyber forensics have aided attribution, similar methodologies (known as tactics/tools, techniques, and procedures, TTPs) are capable of being used by industrial competitors, or other foreign intelligence services (who may have been provided with Russian tools and knowhow). They could also potentially be hackers/crackers or hacktivists (who draw on political or ideological rationales) with no affiliation to the state.[10] These are among the reasons why cyber forensic skills and cyber threat intelligence (CTI) are important, especially as the Russian hacking/cracking scene is highly dynamic and innovative.

---

4 Sam Jones, "Licensed to hack: the rise of the cyber privateer Russia is increasingly using criminal proxies, say western intelligence officials" (March 16, 2017), https://www.ft.com/content/21be48ec-0a48-11e7-97d1-5e720a26771b, accessed January 21 2018.

5 Wider perspectives can be found in R. B. Andrew, "State-Sponsored Militias are Coming to a Server Near You" (2013), *Foreign Policy*, http://foreignpolicy.com/2013/02/12/cyber-gang-warfare/, accessed 3 April 2017.

6 Nigel Inkster, *China's Cyber Power* (Abingdon: Routledge, 2016), p. 68. See also Tim Maurer, *Cyber Mercenaries: The State, Hackers, and Power* (Cambridge: Cambridge University Press, 2018).

7 Maurer, *Cyber Mercenaries*, p. xii.

8 Maurer, *Cyber Mercenaries*, p. xii.

9 Stephen Collinson, "Ransomware attacks saddle Biden with grave national security crisis" (June 7, 2021), https://edition.cnn.com/2021/06/07/politics/president-joe-biden-cyber-attacks-russia-putin-trump-economy/index.html, accessed 8 July 2021.

10 On hacktivism, see Jonathan Diamond, "Early Patriotic Hacking," in Jason Healey (ed.), *A Fierce Domain: Conflict in Cyberspace 1986–2002* (Vienna, VA: CSSA/Atlantic Council, 2013), pp. 136–151.

These links between criminals and the Russian state were augmented by "patriotic hackers" after the 2008 Georgian conflict. Almost contemporaneously, the second Chechen conflict added patriotic fuel to the tank. Especially after the annexation of Crimea in 2014, these were encouraged by Defence Minister Shoigu to join with Russia in his "big hunt for programmers."[11] Since at least the late 2000s, Russian intelligence has periodically used them as a source of free expert labor, recruiting them voluntarily as well as through threats of criminal prosecution. Not only does their employment provide a veneer of plausible deniability but also allows these "privateers" time and resources to develop new code or reengineer existing code. It also allows them to moonlight as cybercriminals when not in the employ of the state.

This is one of the hallmarks of Russian cybercrime in denying responsibility. It will be shown in Chapter 3 that Western cybersecurity providers struggled to determine whether cases of financial or financially motivated cybercrime were Russian state intelligence or splinter operations. This has seen them employ former cybercriminals who are suspected of moonlighting or working with cybercriminals and other proxies "to conduct operations".[12] This has been characterized as an "adhocracy" and a reinterpretation of "social contract" where cybercriminals and talented coders use their own initiative without being micromanaged by the Kremlin and Russia's "Special Services." In return, they are granted state protection under a *krysha* (roof) in return for kickbacks from the proceeds.[13] These are determinations that continue to be wrestled with. Former FBI official Leo Taddeo had "no doubt [that] Russia uses these criminal organizations to mask their state-sponsored intelligence and military operations."[14] This *modus vivendi* has been ongoing for at least a decade. Russian intelligence, partic-

---

11 Christian Esch, "Doing Putin's dirty work. The rise of Russia's GRU military intelligence service" (October 19, 2018), http://www.spiegel.de/international/world/russia-and-the-rise-of-gru-military-intelligence-service-a-1233576.html, accessed 3 January 2018. Miriam Lanskoy and Dylan Myles-Primakoff, "Power and Plunder in Putin's Russia," *Journal of Democracy*, Vol. 29, Issue 1 (January 2018), p. 81.

12 Andrew S. Bowen, Russia's Foreign Intelligence Services (January 3 2025), https://www.congress.gov/crs_external_products/IF/PDF/IF12865/IF12865.1.pdf, accessed 4 August 2025.

13 Dave Aitel, Sophia d'Antoine, Thomas Garwin, Ian Roos, Nicholas Rostow, Justin Sherman, and Abraham Wagner, 'Russia's Cyber Operations A Threat to American National Security' (2022), pp. vii–viii, 1–4, 19–20, 24–26, 29, 31 34-,48, 52–54, 58, 65, 80–81, https://margin.re/content/files/2023/01/Russia-s-Cyber-Operations---Full-Report.pdf, accessed 7 August 2023.

14 Patrick Howell O'Neill, "Russia's rise to cyberwar superpower" (February 29, 2020), https://www.dailydot.com/debug/russia-cyberwar-cyberattack-dnc-breach-history/, accessed 9 April 2020.

ularly the GRU and FSB, has even been said to "hide hackers in safe houses, so the Interior Ministry's [MVD] cybercrime investigative unit doesn't catch them."[15]

Russia has essentially become a "safe haven" for cybercrime, and other criminal activities. Hackers such as the St. Petersburg based, Petr Levashov, whose botnets earned him the moniker "the king of spam" have also been known to work against (as well as with) domestic opposition to Vladimir Putin's rule.[16] Given the nature and scale of domestic Internet surveillance in Russia, Russian authorities are aware of most cybercriminal activities taking place from within their borders.[17] The regime might cream off some of the profit from their criminal enterprises, but they appear happy just to offer them "privateer" status and protect them when in Russia and targeting foreign businesses. If and when they venture abroad and, as in Levashov's case, extradited to face justice (a rare event), the Russian government decries all knowledge and attests that Russia follows the Rule of Law.

A lack of legitimate and well-paid work for Russian hackers has directly contributed to increasing cybercrime.[18] In the late 2000s this included the Russian Business Network. Operating as a large-scale for-hire service out of St. Petersburg, it was described as "the mother of cybercrime" linked with "child pornography, corporate blackmail, spam attacks and online identity theft."[19] Identity theft includes credit card details. This not only generates direct revenue but can be sold on to target and exploit individuals and organizations. This is where cybercriminal gangs become surrogates for Russian intelligence (and other governments). This smudging of digital fingerprints obscures direct involvement.[20]

---

15 Daniil Turovsky, "It's our time to serve the Motherland." How Russia's war in Georgia sparked Moscow's modern-day recruitment of criminal hackers" (August 7, 2018), https://meduza.io/en/feature/2018/08/07/it-s-our-time-to-serve-the-motherland, accessed 7 October 2018.

16 Taken from the word robot, bots/botnets are automated applications that (among other things) are used to generate or spread mis and disinformation. "Alleged Spam Kingpin 'Severa' Extradited to US" (February 18, 2018), https://krebsonsecurity.com/2018/02/alleged-spam-kingpin-severa-extradited-to-us/, and Russian National Who Operated Kelihos Botnet Pleads Guilty to Fraud, Conspiracy, Computer Crime and Identity Theft Offenses (September 12, 2018), https://www.justice.gov/opa/pr/russian-national-who-operated-kelihos-botnet-pleads-guilty-fraud-conspiracy-computer-crime, both accessed 9 January 2019.

17 Andrei Soldatov and Irina Borogan, "Russia's Surveillance State," *World Policy Journal*, Vol. 30, Issue 3 (September 2013), pp. 23–30.

18 Maurer, *Cyber Mercenaries*, pp. 38, 40, 95, 103–106.

19 Erika Kraemer-Mbula, Puay Tang, and Howard Rush, "The Cybercrime Ecosystem: Online Innovation in the Shadows?" *Technological Forecasting & Social Change*, Vol. 80, Issue 3 (March 2013), p. 545.

20 Hearing of the House (Select) Intelligence Committee Subject: "Cybersecurity Threats: The Way Forward" November 20, 2014, https://www.nsa.gov/news-features/speeches-testimonies/Article/

The extent to which the use, reuse, or repurposing of tools, alongside techniques and procedures is a sign of Russian state involvement is a difficult judgment for the cybersecurity industry. According to a 2012 Northrop-Grumman report, Russia creates "plausible scenarios … in which freelance hackers are hired by state entities to perform network exploitation on a contract basis."[21] Northrop-Grumman's added that these "marriages of convenience" between state intelligence and sub-state cybercrime actors "typically operate in the same environment and sometime against similar classes of targets. This is an overlap that poses attribution challenges."[22] This is why Russian intelligence has also been suspected of leaking advanced tools to groups on the "Dark Net." This includes tools provided to the "Shadow Brokers."[23]

Within Russia, a great deal of cybercrime is conducted quite openly. Their main aim is stealing from the West. The Russian hacker scene is fiercely competitive with a focus on material (financial) benefits, but it also exhibits online and offline social support networks.[24] Furthermore, "Black Hat" tools and services are for sale on the "Dark Net." This includes malware for specifically tailored attacks including for phishing campaigns, industrial espionage, and insider information.[25] McAfee noted in 2018 that stolen "digital data, which drives much of the profits, will continue to be a key motivator."[26]

What has evolved is development and sales of wiperware/ransomware as-a-service (RaaS) combined with growing exposure of data on individuals and companies.[27] Ransomware encrypts company data with the means to decrypt provided only if a ransom is paid. Wiperware deletes the data but can still be accompanied

---

1620360/hearing-of-the-house-select-intelligence-committee-subject-cybersecurity-threat/, accessed 21 January 2019.

21 Bryan Krekel, Patton Adams, and George Bakos, *Occupying the Information High Ground: Chinese Capabilities for Computer Network Operations and Cyber Espionage.* Prepared for the U.S.–China Economic and Security Review Commission by Northrop Grumman Corp (McLean, VA: Northrop Grumman Corporation, March 7, 2012), p. 97, https://info.publicintelligence.net/USCC-ChinaCyberEspionage.pdf, accessed 16 April 2019.

22 Krekel, Adams, and Bakos, *Occupying the Information High Ground*, p. 94.

23 Bruce Schneier, "Who Are the Shadow Brokers? What is—and isn't—known about the mysterious hackers leaking National Security Agency secrets" (May 23, 2017), https://www.theatlantic.com/technology/archive/2017/05/shadow-brokers/527778/, accessed 8 January 2020.

24 Alexander Klimburg, "Mobilising Cyber Power," *Survival*, Vol. 53, No. 1 (February–March 2011), pp. 50–51.

25 Anonymous, "Cyber-thieves turn to 'invisible net' to set up attacks" (June 7, 2019), https://www.bbc.co.uk/news/technology-47319971, accessed 8 June 2019.

26 McAfee Labs Threats Report (December 2018), p. 4, https://www.mcafee.com/enterprise/en-us/assets/reports/rp-quarterly-threats-dec-2018.pdf, accessed 31 January 2019.

27 McAfee Labs Threats Report (December 2018), pp. 5–6.

by ransom demands and in 2019–20 reported ransomware payments increased by 300 percent. Communications between buyers and sellers is now increasingly over encrypted apps, with demands leaving specific usernames on Telegram and Wickr as points of contact.[28]

Cryptocurrencies are the default mode of payment. Difficult to trace digital transactions mean ransomware attacks are proving challenging to counter and prevent. Having evolved from sending mass and untargeted phishing e-mails, these attacks now often begin with well-crafted and plausible spear-phishing e-mails that contain malware attachments against socially engineered targets.[29] With Russia "the original home of cybercrime," ransomware is widespread and an almost untraceable and lucrative form of cyberattack.[30] It has been a growth industry in Russia offering rich rewards for relatively low risk.[31]

Another growth area for Russian cybercriminals is sales of Common Vulnerabilities and Exposures (CVE), which can be bundled with Internet browser exploit kits. These pieces of malware come in prepackaged form and include RIG, Grandsoft, Fallout, and GandCrab which can be used against well-known or newly discovered vulnerabilities.[32] GandCrab is specifically designed not to infect Russian systems. Malware is actively developed, with end users waiting for new releases, and tailored to stay one step ahead of cybersecurity industry responses. They are devised to be persistent, bypass existing defenses, and to escalate privileges giving them wider system access. This lets attackers step laterally and vertically further into breached systems and networks.[33] Corporate payers are often thought of as equivalent to ATMs.[34] Cases are publicly reported but an unknown

---

28 IOCTA Internet Organized Crime Threat Assessment 2021, pp. 21–22, 34–38, https://www.europol.europa.eu/cms/sites/default/files/documents/internet_organised_crime_threat_assessment_iocta_2021.pdf, accessed 15 June 2022.

29 See for example Anonymous, "Cyber-thieves cash in from malware" (June 9, 2015), http://www.bbc.co.uk/news/technology-33048949, and "How Ransomware Infects Computers," https://www.mcafee.com/enterprise/en-us/security-awareness/ransomware/ransomware-infections.html. Both accessed 10 November 2016.

30 Kraemer-Mbula, Tang, and Rush, "The Cybercrime Ecosystem," p. 545. IOCTA Internet Organized Crime Threat Assessment [2019], p, 4, https://www.europol.europa.eu/sites/default/files/documents/iocta_2019.pdf, accessed 30 December 2019.

31 2021 Data Breach Investigations Report, http://verizon.com/dbir/, pp. 55–57, 79–83. Verizon Data Breach Investigations Report 2022, pp. 100–103, https://www.verizon.com/business/en-gb/resources/reports/dbir/2022/, accessed 30 December 2022.

32 McAfee Labs Threats Report (December 2018), p. 5.

33 McAfee Labs Threats Report (December 2018), pp. 8–9.

34 D. H. Kass, "Riviera Beach, Florida Ransomware Attack; City Pays $600,000" (June 20, 2019), https://www.msspalert.com/cybersecurity-breaches-and-attacks/ransomware/riviera-beach-florida-malware-attack/, accessed 4 January 2020.

number (but probably a high percentage) of cases go unreported. Small-to-medium sized enterprises and corporate boards fear the reputational damage this could cause, as well as falls in their stock price among other concerns.

There is also a marketplace for Remote Desktop Protocols (RDP) through "shops" on the "Dark Net." According to one McAfee researcher, "By accessing a system via RDP, attackers can obtain almost all data stored on a system. This ... can be used for identity theft, account takeovers, credit card fraud, and extortion, etc."[35] RDPs can access hacked computer systems which could "potentially cripple cities and bring down major companies," sold on the Russian-based Ultimate Anonymity Service.[36] Through the "Dark Net" access to "multiple government systems" is also "being sold worldwide, including those linked to the United States, and dozens of connections linked to health care institutions, from hospitals and nursing homes to suppliers of medical equipment."[37]

These are real and present dangers. Hospitals have been forced to shut down their systems and turn away patients. U.S. cities and municipalities have also seen increasing ransomware attacks.[38] IBM reported in 2021 that ransomware was responsible for 23 percent of their recorded incidents. Targets included manufacturing, the energy sector (oil and gas especially), as well as law firms. The cybercriminal gangs behind the attacks also threaten to (and do) leak sensitive data if payment is not made.[39] Data theft, and who gains access to that data, is an important aspect of ransomware attacks.

---

35 John Fokker, "Organizations Leave Backdoors Open to Cheap Remote Desktop Protocol Attacks" (July 11, 2018), https://securingtomorrow.mcafee.com/other-blogs/mcafee-labs/organizations-leave-backdoors-open-to-cheap-remote-desktop-protocol-attacks/, accessed 25 July 2019.

36 Fokker, "Organizations Leave Backdoors Open" (July 11, 2018).

37 Fokker, "Organizations Leave Backdoors Open" (July 11, 2018).

38 Anna Beahm, "DCH Health System 'closed to all but most critical' new patients due to ransomware attack" (October 2, 2019), https://www.al.com/news/2019/10/dch-health-system-closed-to-all-but-most-critical-new-patients-due-to-ransomware-attack.html, accessed 2 October 2019. IOCTA Internet Organized Crime Threat Assessment [2019], pp. 15–17, Kenneth Kraszewski, "SamSam and the Silent Battle of Atlanta," in Tomáš Minárik, Siim Alatalu, Stefano Biondi, Massimiliano Signoretti, Ihsan Tolga, and Gábor Visky (eds.), *2019 11th International Conference on Cyber Conflict: Silent Battle* (Tallinn: CCD COE Publications, 2019), pp. 291–306.

39 IBM Security, X-Force Threat Intelligence Index 2021, pp. 8, 10, 30–33, 39–44, 47, https://www.ibm.com/downloads/cas/M1X3B7QG, accessed 8 January 2021.

3 Russian cybercrime: "Pinprick attacks" or cyber enabled economic warfare?

During the turbulent 1990s Russia's hacker scene developed rapidly. It became a route to easy money just as the Russian mafia was establishing itself. Russia's economic collapse in the late 1990s saw many computer programmers, IT specialists, and businesses financially ruined and out of work.[40] This heralded the growth of the Russian hacking scene with "overeducated and underemployed specialists ... [an] ideal breeding ground for hackers."[41] By now, neither economic benefits nor financial profit through cybercrime were key aims for Russian state-intelligence as they had been in the early 1990s. However, in the late 1990s and into the 2000s cybercrime continued to flourish with a *modus vivendi* between organized criminal gangs and the state.[42]

Cybercriminals with various skillsets now frequent the cyber black market (through encrypted and protected forums on the "Dark Net"). Many are effectively guns for hire and Russian cybercriminals have been detected in a large number of high-profile cases.[43] This includes ransomware and Russian intelligence-led cyberespionage campaigns. Data theft is also part of this business model. Who has access to this data, who gains access, and what it is and could be used for, are important questions to think about.

The U.S. Secret Service's appendix to Verizon's 2022 Data Breach Investigations Report (DBIR), documented an uptick in ransomware cases impacting businesses of various sizes, across industry, directly affecting critical infrastructure and national security. The most prolific of these cases originate in Russian-speaking ransomware networks. Around 74 percent of ransomware payments are Russian-affiliated and because destructive wiperware (a form of malware designed to unrecoverably delete information from computer systems) is now also being

40 Roman Dremliuga, Olga Dremliuga, and Pavel Kuznetsov, "Combating the Threats of Cybercrimes in Russia Evolution of the Cybercrime Laws and Social Concern," *Communist and Post-Communist Studies*, Vol. 53, No. 3 (September 2020), pp. 123–136.

41 John Blau, "Russia – a happy haven for hackers," http://www.computerweekly.com/feature/Russia-a-happy-haven-for-hackers, (May 2004),

42 Hedieh Nasheri, *Economic Espionage and Industrial Spying* (Cambridge: Cambridge University Press, 2005), pp. 8–9, 11.

43 Adam Shepherd, "Interpol: Dark web hacking tools are fuelling cybercrime" (September 5, 2017), http://www.itpro.co.uk/security/29391/interpol-dark-web-hacking-tools-are-fuelling-cybercrime, accessed 21 January 2018. Mike Eckel, "For Russia and U.S., Uneasy Cooperation on Cybercrime Is Now a Mess" (April 29, 2017), https://www.rferl.org/a/cyber-crime-us-russia-cooperation-mess/28459178.html, accessed November 19 2017.

masked as ransomware, this presents "a growing risk which blurs distinctions [between] politically and financially motivated cybercrimes."[44]

Many cases of cybercrime are low level nuisances or "pinprick attacks" but many are significant and orchestrated and even the pinprick attacks add up.[45] The initial gateway to ransomware and wiperware is regularly through socially engineered targets, and there have been a large number of serious cases of cybercrime that in the U.S. alone run into the hundreds of millions of dollars.[46] For example, at least a dozen global banks were targeted in a large-scale ransomware campaign from 2012 to mid-2015. This saw the personal data of over 100 million people stolen, including those of over 80 million customers from one financial institution alone. They were then subjected to "double-extortion" with a proportion leaked on the "Dark Net" as proof and a negotiating incentive for ransomware victims to pay up.[47] Cyberespionage actors "rarely, if ever, interact with the employees of the organizations they target beyond social engineering or spear phishing efforts," but cybercriminal gangs not only negotiate but now have members dedicated to it.[48]

Victims included the Bank of America (BAC), Regions Bank (RF), Canada's TD Trust, and Commercial Bank International in the United Arab Emirates. Germany's Commerzbank was also a suspected target. $900 million had been stolen by the time the attacks stopped. The multinational investment bank JPMorgan Chase was also hit early on in the same campaign. It was this attack which appears to have enabled access to the other institutions. The attack on JPMorgan exposed 76 million personal customers and 7 million businesses. The group behind it was linked to the GRU's APT28 by one reputable cybersecurity firm.[49] This could be an example of Russian intelligence directly cooperating with cybercriminals or

44 Verizon Data Breach Investigations Report 2022 (Appendix D), p. 100.

45 Kristin Shields, "Cybersecurity: Recognizing the Risk and Protecting Against Attacks," *North Carolina Banking Institute Journal*, Vol. 19, Issue 1 (January 2015), pp. 351–354.

46 Kristan Stoddart, *Cyberwarfare: Threats to Critical Infrastructure* (London: Palgrave/Springer, 2022), pp. 281–300, 353–357, 368–376, 411–413.

47 Bryson Payne and Edward Mienie, "Multiple-Extortion Ransomware: The Case for Active Cyber Threat Intelligence," in Thaddeus Eze, Lee Speakman, Cyril Onwubiko (eds.), *ECCWS 2021 20th European Conference on Cyber Warfare and Security* (Sonning Common, UK: Academic Conferences and Publishing International, 2021), pp. 331–336.

48 M-Trends 2023, Introduction, p. 76, https://mandiant.widen.net/s/dlzgn6w26n/m-trends-2023, accessed 3 August 2023.

49 Elizabeth MacDonald, "New Russian Hacks Target US Banks" (May 14, 2015), http://www.foxbusiness.com/features/2015/05/14/new-russian-hacks-target-us-banks.html, accessed January 21 2018.

GRU cyber intelligence operatives freelancing given the extent that Russian intelligence has recruited and coerced hackers from the cybercriminal underworld.[50]

Members of this cybercrime gang were subsequently indicted in a case which clearly illustrates some of the problems and scope in investigating and prosecuting Russian-centered transnational organized crime. A Russian national, Andrei Tyurin, was among those extradited and prosecuted, a rare event in itself. The "mastermind" was the Georgian-born Gery Shalon (son of Georgian politician Shota Shalelashvili). He had triple nationalities (Georgian/Israeli/Russian). Shalon's "accountant," the Israeli national, Ziv Orenstein, and Joshua Aaron, a U.S. national living in Moscow, were the other two main members. Shalon and Orenstein were arrested by Israeli police in July 2015 and in 2019 Shalon started cooperating with U.S. authorities. In January 2021 he returned to Israel a free man.[51]

Tyurin, was extradited from Georgia and handed over to U.S. authorities whilst vacationing in September 2018 (with an international arrest warrant for him). Russia had also tried to extradite Tyurin.[52] Tyurin pled guilty in Manhattan federal court in January 2021 and was sentenced to 12 years.[53] Aaron too was offered asylum by Russia but "voluntarily returned to the United States."[54] The case against them was extensive.[55] Nowhere in the indictments was the GRU's APT28/ "Fancy Bear" implicated. But absence of (public) evidence is not evidence of absence. Specifically, the malware deployed by Tyurin contained code signatures and a server previously associated with APT28.[56] U.S. intelligence suspected

---

50 The only rule appears to be "no targets can be in Russia or post-Soviet states." Putin's Asymmetric Assault on Democracy in Russia and Europe: Implications for U.S. National Security. A Minority Staff Report, Committee on Foreign Relations United States Senate, January 10, 2018, pp. 1, 157, 181–183, https://www.foreign.senate.gov/imo/media/doc/FinalRR.pdf, accessed 5 November 2019.

51 Toi Staff, "Israeli behind massive JPMorgan hack has moved to country, his father says" (January 29, 2023), https://www.timesofisrael.com/israeli-behind-massive-jpmorgan-hack-has-moved-to-country-his-father-says/, accessed 1 August 2023.

52 Bloomberg, "Mystery JPMorgan Hacker Is in U.S. Hands. What Does He Know?" (September 8, 2018), https://fortune.com/2018/09/08/jpmorgan-hacker-andrei-tyurin/, accessed 1 August 2023.

53 Russian Hacker Sentenced to 12 Years in Prison for Involvement in Massive Network Intrusions at U.S. Financial Institutions, Brokerage Firms, a Major News Publication, and Other Companies, January 7, 2021, https://www.secretservice.gov/newsroom/releases/2021/01/russian-hacker-sentenced-12-years-prison-involvement-massive-network, accessed 1 August 2023.

54 Anonymous, "Suspected JP Morgan hacker arrested after returning from Moscow" (December 14, 2016), https://www.cbsnews.com/news/joshua-samuel-aaron-suspected-jp-morgan-hacker-arrested-after-returning-from-moscow/, accessed 1 August 2023.

55 https://www.justice.gov/opa/pr/attorney-general-and-manhattan-us-attorney-announce-charges-stemming-massive-network (November 10, 2015), accessed 1 August 2023.

56 MacDonald, "New Russian Hacks Target US."

links to Russian intelligence and is one of the reasons they were keen to extradite Tyurin, the gang's hacker-for-hire.[57]

Aside from financial losses and data losses there are valid concerns that by targeting JPMorgan, infiltration of even a single financial institution indicates risks "'spilling over' into the broader financial system." This systemic risk is a potential global financial security issue because "a systemic cyberattack launched specifically to disrupt the target's financial ecosystem and therefore the real economy" can cause major financial instability.[58] Vedral makes a persuasive case that "the probability of a systemic attack is neither "zero" nor "very low"" and whilst watching the financial system burn is unlikely to serve Russian aims, reflexive large-scale cybercrime and cyberespionage attacks are part of Russia's *modus operandi.*[59]

The links between Russia's hackers, Russian hacking gangs, and the Russian government has been the subject of several books and television documentaries. None captures the whole story or has the complete picture. This chapter and book only add to the picture.[60] Russian-based gangs can appear, seemingly disappear, and then reconstitute and rebrand at pace alongside their malware. This includes gangs like REevil and "Evil Corp."[61] The 2021 USIC Annual Threat Assessment noted "Cyber threats from nation states and their surrogates will remain acute. Foreign states [including Russia] use cyber operations to steal information, influence populations, and damage industry, including physical and digital critical in-

---

57 Bloomberg, "Mystery JPMorgan Hacker Is in U.S. Hands."

58 Bobby Vedral, "The Vulnerability of the Financial System to a Systemic Cyberattack," in Tat'ána Jančárková, Lauri Lindström, Gábor Visky, and Philippe Zotz (eds.), *13th International Conference on Cyber Conflict: Going Viral* (Tallinn: NATO CCDCOE Publications, 2021), p. 95.

59 Vedral, "The Vulnerability of the Financial System to a Systemic Cyberattack," p. 98. Stoddart, *Cyberwarfare*, p. 148.

60 Misha Glenny, *Dark Market How Hackers Became the New Mafia* (London: Random House, 2011); Maurer, *Cyber Mercenaries*; Mark Galeotti, *The Vory: Russia's Super Mafia* (New Haven, CT: Yale University Press, 2018). For documentaries see for example Joe Tidy and Andrei Zakharov, "The Russian hackers being hunted by the West – BBC News" (November 19, 2021), https://www.youtube.com/watch?v=UG1lJaJsru8; ABC News In-depth, "How Cyber-Crime Has Become Organised Warfare | Four Corners (April 17, 2023), https://www.youtube.com/watch?v=4m6Ydx0TGMY. Both accessed 2 August 2023.

61 Amer Elsad and Daniel Bunce, "Ransom Cartel Ransomware: A Possible Connection With REvil" (October 14, 2022), https://unit42.paloaltonetworks.com/ransom-cartel-ransomware/; Annual Threat Assessment of the U.S. Intelligence Community, Office of the Director of National Intelligence, February 6, 2023, pp. 30–31, https://www.dni.gov/files/ODNI/documents/assessments/ATA-2023-Unclassified-Report.pdf. National Cyber Security Centre, Annual Review 2024, pp. 2, 19, https://www.ncsc.gov.uk/files/NCSC_Annual_Review_2024.pdf. All accessed 4 December 2024.

frastructure."[62] One of their methodologies is to target upstream suppliers in supply chains to bigger fish. This is what happened to the U.S. retail giant Target.

3.1 Target

Target, the second largest retail chain in the U.S. behind Walmart, was hit in late 2013 with a massive data breach through a third-party sub-contractor who was also employed by a number of other leading retailers. The hackers were able to gather up to 40 million credit and debit card details used by shoppers during the 2013 Christmas period. Brian Krebs recorded that "the stolen card data was offloaded via FTP communications to a location in Russia" but that servers in countries such as Brazil, as well as the U.S. itself, were used to "house the stolen data and that could be safely accessed by the suspected perpetrators in Eastern Europe and Russia."[63]

Target disclosed that remedial action cost them $202 million. This not only hit Target's stock price and shook customer confidence but also has led them to settle class action lawsuits with 47 states and the District of Columbia.[64] The hackers had gained access through stolen credentials from the third party, a Pennsylvania-based provider of refrigeration and HVAC systems which had been provided with external access "exclusively for electronic billing, contract submission and project management."[65] Once inside Target's systems the attackers uploaded malware to steal credit card details first via a small amount of cash registers within Target stores and, once this worked and lay undetected, they rolled out the malware across their stores throughout the U.S. This led them to harvest card details from live transactions of around 40 million separate credit and debit cards in under three weeks (November 27–December 15, 2013). The overall cost to Target

---

62 The 2022 and 2023 assessments omitted mention of transnational proxy links. Annual Threat Assessment of the U.S. Intelligence Community, Office of the Director of National Intelligence, April 9, 2021, p. 20, https://www.dni.gov/files/ODNI/documents/assessments/ATA-2021-Unclassified-Report.pdf, accessed 2 August 2023.

63 "Target Hackers Broke in Via HVAC Company" (February 14, 2017), https://krebsonsecurity.com/2014/02/target-hackers-broke-in-via-hvac-company/, accessed December 2 2017.

64 "Target Settles 2013 Hacked Customer Data Breach For $18.5 Million" (May 24, 2017), https://www.nbcnews.com/business/business-news/target-settles-2013-hacked-customer-data-breach-18-5-million-n764031, accessed December 2 2017.

65 Krebs, "Target Hackers Broke in Via HVAC Company."

was around $420 million. This included reimbursement to banks forced to reissue compromised cards and legal fees.[66]

3.2 Home Depot

Between April and September 2014 Home Depot, the world's largest home-improvement retailer with 1,977 stores across North America, also fell victim to a data breach using similar malware to that which infected Target. 56 million customers of Home Depot were affected. They had their "names, credit card numbers, expiration dates, cardholder verification values and service codes stolen."[67] Krebs described how Home Depot was hit by, "a new variant of '**BlackPOS**' (a.k.a. 'Kaptoxa')," the same malware that also was found on point-of-sale systems of Target. Card details stolen from Home Depot turned up for sale on **Rescator**, an underground cybercrime "shop" on the "Dark Net," also selling those stolen in the Target breach alongside millions of other card details.[68] Although neither the Target or Home Depot breaches were linked directly to the Russian state "it appears the cyber-attack on Home Depot may have been politically motivated and not just a means-to-an-end-theft."[69]

Krebs' technical analysis indicated ties to Russia and pro-Russian forums and at least one individual who appeared to be working out of Odessa in Ukraine (which at that time contained a significant number of Russian separatists backed by the Kremlin). On Rescator the stolen cards were being marketed in batches under the title "American Sanctions."[70] It was reported in October 2014, that "Supporting this theory is that Western sanctions against Russia were enacted around mid-March and the malware is reported to have been active since April."[71] These major breaches were touted as a wake-up call to others.[72] Over time these also form part of a series of "pinprick" attacks which weaken national economies.

---

66 In addition, upgrades to Target's chip-and-PIN facilities could cost them a further $100 million. Krebs "Target Hackers Broke in Via HVAC Company."

67 Jennifer McCartney, "The Home Depot hack: How, why and what we can learn" (October 8, 2014), http://www.techradar.com/news/internet/the-home-depot-hack-how-why-and-what-we-can-learn-1268333, accessed December 2 2017.

68 "Home Depot Hit by Same Malware as Target" (September 14, 2014), https://krebsonsecurity.com/2014/09/home-depot-hit-by-same-malware-as-target/, accessed 2 December 2017.

69 McCartney, "The Home Depot hack."

70 Krebs "Home Depot Hit by Same Malware as Target" (September 14, 2014).

71 McCartney, "The Home Depot hack."

72 Jeff John Roberts, "3 Security Breaches That Freaked Out U.S. Companies" (September 21, 2016), http://fortune.com/2016/09/21/biggest-security-breaches/, accessed 2 December 2017.

In September 2024, the DOJ revealed that in coordination with Dutch police, supported by Latvia, Germany's Federal Criminal Police Office and Britain's National Crime Agency, they had indicted two of those involved in the Target and Home Depot breaches. Both are Russian nationals: Sergey Ivanov and Timur Shakhmametov. They are charged with operating multiple cybercrime driven money laundering services and three illicit anonymized cryptocurrency exchanges (Cryptex, UAPS and PM2BTC). Ivanov aided drug traffickers and ransomware gangs operating on the Dark Net. Ivanov was also helping launder proceeds from "Carding" sites on the Dark Net (the unlawful acquisition of and trade in stolen credit and debit card information). Ivanov was a seasoned cybercriminal with a two-decade long history of advertising his services on exclusively Russian-speaking criminal forums. He also either created and/or operated the Russian payment and exchange services UAPS, PinPays, and PM2BTC. These cryptocurrency services delivered money transfer and laundering services directly to criminals and was traded around $1.15 billion. One of their carding websites, "Joker's Stash", is said to be "one of the largest known carding markets in history."[73] Despite having a bounty of $11 million on their heads, neither are likely to face extradition let alone trial. This case forms part of ongoing investigations by the U.S. Secret Service Cyber Investigative Section. Most cases of this type are handled by the FBI, so this was an unusual move.[74]

Brian Krebs also records that "Jokers Stash" also traded card details stolen from breaches at U.S. retailers, including Saks Fifth Avenue, Lord and Taylor, Bebe Stores, Hilton Hotels, Jason's Deli, Whole Foods, Chipotle, Wawa, Sonic Drive-In, the Hy-Vee supermarket chain, Buca Di Beppo, and Dickey's BBQ. In addition, in 2017 Bellingcat and Transparency International had begun to tie these money laundering networks to the Kremlin and Russian oligarchs and *siloviki.* They had also been used to launder up to $80 billion from the Russian treasury and state contracts to offshore accounts described as "The Laundromat". This included utilizing limited partnerships in Scotland, UK. There were also ties to drugs trafficking.[75]

---

73 Press Release Two Russian Nationals Charged in Connection with Operating Billion Dollar Money Laundering Services (September 26 2024), https://www.justice.gov/archives/opa/pr/two-russian-nationals-charged-connection-operating-billion-dollar-money-laundering-1, accessed 26 August 2025.

74 Press Release Two Russian Nationals Charged (September 26 2024).

75 "U.S. Indicts 2 Top Russian Hackers, Sanctions Cryptex" (September 26 2024), https://krebsonsecurity.com/2024/09/u-s-indicts-2-top-russian-hackers-sanctions-cryptex/comment-page-1/. Offshore in the UK Analysing the use of Scottish Limited Partnerships in Corruption and Money

3.3 Targets of opportunity or design?

The same year as Home Depot, APT28 targeted the Farnborough Air Show, one of Europe's two largest aviation industry events, including using malware capable of voice recording and accessing text messages targeting iOS devices.[76] From mid-2015/16, APT28 also engaged in phishing Google accounts. They were particularly interested in the accounts of Russians and nationals of former Soviet states. These also included personnel working in the U.S. and Europe, particularly in defense supply chains, as well as NGOs and journalists critical of Russia. The leadership of the Syrian opposition were also targeted. There was no direct evidence of monetary gain or economic advantage.[77]

Similarly to cybercriminals (and APT29/"Cozy Bear"), APT28/"Fancy Bear" tries to cover its tracks through bogus identities, virtual private networks, cryptocurrencies, and transaction brokers like Liberty Reserve.[78] Liberty Reserve, based in Costa Rica, was shut down in May 2013 after being widely linked to international criminal money laundering (including from Russia).[79] The GRU uses these cryptocurrencies (including Bitcoin and Perfect Money) to mask transactions and are reported to have access to significant funds.[80] The same might well be true of the SVR (and FSB).

McAfee and Intel pinpointed that for most gangs their primary motivations have been monetizing what they access and steal. This includes the resale of stolen data (where buyers will likely also find other uses). There are myriad security implications related to stolen data, including that experienced in the healthcare sector.[81] Through the reseller market they have also rented server space in multiple

---

Laundering, https://archive.transparency.org.uk/sites/default/files/pdf/publications/Offshore_In_The_UK_TIUK_June_2017.pdf. Both accessed 25 August 2025.

76 Chris Vallance, "Russian Fancy Bear hackers' UK link revealed" (November 23, 2017), http://www.bbc.co.uk/news/technology-42056555, accessed 4 December 2017.

77 "Threat Group-4127 Targets Google Accounts" (June 26, 2016), https://www.secureworks.com/research/threat-group-4127-targets-google-accounts, accessed 4 December 2017.

78 Anonymous, "Liberty Reserve digital cash chief jailed for 20 years" (May 9, 2016), http://www.bbc.co.uk/news/technology-36247289, accessed 4 December 2017.

79 Jake Halpern, "Bank of the Underworld Liberty Reserve was like PayPal for the unbanked. Was it also a global money-laundering operation?" *The Atlantic* (May 2015), https://www.theatlantic.com/magazine/archive/2015/05/bank-of-the-underworld/389555/, https://www.justice.gov/usao-sdny/pr/manhattan-us-attorney-announces-charges-against-liberty-reserve-one-world-s-largest. Both accessed 4 December 2017.

80 Vallance, "Russian Fancy Bear hackers' UK link revealed."

81 Andrew Goldsmith, "What do we know about REvil, the Russian ransomware gang likely behind the Medibank cyber attack?" (November 11, 2022), https://theconversation.com/what-do-

locations, including the UK and Pakistan. All of these pathways can make it difficult to differentiate between them and cybercriminals or to clearly identify state involvement in lucrative cybercrime enterprises. This is a sideline that sees controllers in the GRU, SVR, and FSB profiting with Kremlin backing.[82] Previously FireEye indicated that the targets for cybercriminal groups had moved from multinational corporations, where they have gained significant experience of successful intrusion methods, to lower hanging fruit. This includes companies in the supply chains of larger firms for economic gain or with contracts to governments and militaries.[83] These tactics stretch back to the 1990s.

4 Russian cyberespionage campaigns

4.1 Moonlight Maze

The earliest Russian cyberespionage campaign was Moonlight Maze in the mid–late 1990s. It first penetrated the Colorado School of Mines and from there migrated to NASA, the National Oceanic and Atmospheric Administration (NOAA), and the U.S. Navy and Air Force. Military installations and military-linked U.S. universities were also targeted with university networks used as staging posts for other intrusions.[84] It was first detected in January 1998 and ended in 1999. Whilst undetected it allowed Russia to gain access to and exfiltrate sensitive but unclassified information-intelligence and is the first evidence of an Advanced Persistent Threat (APT) group from Russia.[85] Mitigating it took a huge multi-agency effort through-

we-know-about-revil-the-russian-ransomware-gang-likely-behind-the-medibank-cyber-attack-194337, accessed 2 August 2023. "WHO reports outline responses to cyber-attacks on health care and the rise of disinformation in public health emergencies" (February 6, 2024), https://www.who.int/news/item/06-02-2024-who-reports-outline-responses-to-cyber-attacks-on-health-care-and-the-rise-of-disinformation-in-public-health-emergencies, accessed 11 May 2025.

82 Vallance, "Russian Fancy Bear hackers' UK link revealed."

83 FireEye, M-Trends 2017. A View from the Front Lines, p. 43. Accessed 31 March 2020, available from https://www.fireeye.com/current-threats/annual-threat-report/mtrends/rpt-m-trends-2017.html.

84 Adam Elkus, "Moonlight Maze," in Jason Healey (ed.), *A Fierce Domain: Conflict in Cyberspace 1986–2002* (Vienna, VGN: CSSA/Atlantic Council, 2013), pp. 152–163.

85 Christopher C. Joyner and Catherine Lotrionte, "Information Warfare as International Coercion: Elements of a Legal Framework," *European Journal of International Law*, Vol. 12, Issue 5 (December 2001), pp. 840–841.

out 1999.[86] Moonlight Maze was possibly geared towards the acquisition of military technologies, ideas and forward plans, and intellectual property (IP) theft.[87] It was also a proving ground through which Russian APTs learned to innovate, with the code base used in Moonlight Maze still being used in modified form 20 years later.[88] This campaign was successful enough for more sophisticated follow-on operations.[89]

4.2 Red October

Red October was an advanced cyberespionage campaign which used malware dubbed "Rocra." Red October was discovered by Kaspersky Lab in January 2013,[90] in conjunction with US-CERT, the Romanian CERT, and the Belarusian CERT. It had been active since at least 2007. It too was "an elusive cyber-espionage campaign targeting diplomatic, governmental and scientific research organizations in several countries."[91] It focused on targets in Eastern Europe and countries in Central Asia (most if not all former Soviet satellite nations) but was also found

86 Accessed 7 August 2023: https://nsarchive.gwu.edu/sites/default/files/documents/3173333/Document-02.pdf.

87 Edward Lucas, *Deception: The Untold Story of East-West Espionage Today* (New York: Bloomsbury, 2012), pp. 54, 57, 114–115, 176.

88 Kim Zetter, "New Evidence Links a 20-Year-Old Hack on the US Government to a Modern Attack Group" (April 4, 2017), https://www.vice.com/en/article/vvk83b/moonlight-maze-turla-link, accessed 7 August 2017.

89 Juan Andres Guerrero-Saade, Daniel Moore, Costin Raiu, and Thomas Rid, "Penquin's Moonlit Maze. The Dawn of Nation-State Espionage" (April 3, 2017), https://www.ridt.co/d/jags-moore-raiu-rid.pdf, accessed 7 August 2023.

90 Kaspersky itself, one of the world's most widely used cyber security providers, has itself been accused of cooperation with the Kremlin. Carol Matlack, Michael Riley, and Jordan Robertson, "The Company Securing Your Internet Has Close Ties to Russian Spies" (March 20, 2017), https://www.bloomberg.com/news/articles/2015-03-19/cybersecurity-kaspersky-has-close-ties-to-russian-spies. Iain Thompson, "Kaspersky Lab hits back at Bloomberg's Russian spy link hit piece" (March 19, 2015), https://www.theregister.co.uk/2015/03/19/kaspersky_lab_denies_its_handinglove_with_russian_security_services/. "DHS Statement on the Issuance of Binding Operational Directive 17–01" (September 13, 3017), https://www.dhs.gov/news/2017/09/13/dhs-statement-issuance-binding-operational-directive-17-01. All accessed 16 September 2017.

91 "Kaspersky Lab Identifies Operation 'Red October,' an Advanced Cyber-Espionage Campaign Targeting Diplomatic and Government Institutions Worldwide," accessed 15 September 2016, http://www.kaspersky.co.in/about/news/virus/2013/Kaspersky_Lab_Identifies_Operation_Red_October_an_Advanced_Cyber_Espionage_Campaign_Targeting_Diplomatic_and_Government_Institutions_Worldwide. See also the work of individuals such as Arno Reuser, http://arnoreuser.com/.

in other locations including Western Europe and North America. Technical analysis indicated Russian origins (including the rendering of Cyrillic fonts), and it was noteworthy in highlighting growing computer forensics and analysis capabilities as an aid for law enforcement and attribution.[92]

The primary objective of Red October was to harvest sensitive information useful to Russian intelligence. This included "geopolitical intelligence, credentials to access classified computer systems, and data from personal mobile devices and network equipment."[93] Targets included diplomatic missions including embassies and consulates and research institutions in trade, energy, nuclear and aerospace sectors. Kaspersky monitored Red October from November 2, 2012 to January 10, 2013. During this period Kaspersky found over 55,000 connections from 250 infected Internet Protocol (IP) addresses (which identify devices connected to the Internet), registered in 39 countries. The volume of these connections and their wide geographical spread are hallmarks of "Botnets," such as those designed by the "king of spam." These run background processes through programs or applications (Apps) on infected computers.

Victims were targeted by spear-phishing e-mails crafted to look like legitimate e-mails from trusted sources but with a link embedded within them or file attachment that runs malicious code when clicked. These TTPs are in widespread use. These particular spear-phishing attacks included customized Trojan malware which exploited vulnerabilities inside Microsoft Office and Microsoft Excel.[94] Rocra/Red October used a multi-functional attack platform with a modular architecture which used "extensions and malicious files designed to quickly adjust to different systems' configurations" and used them to gather information-intelligence from infected machines.[95]

This was an attack pattern not previously seen by Kaspersky in prior campaigns of cyberespionage. These characteristics included a unique "resurrection" module: using an Adobe Reader plug-in and Microsoft Office files which gave Red October a "foolproof way to regain access to a target system if the main malware body is discovered and removed, or if the system is patched."[96] Advanced crypto-

92 The Cyrillic alphabet is the basis of the Russian language and various related alphabets used across Eastern Europe and north and central Asia. "Kaspersky Lab Identifies Operation 'Red October.'"

93 "Kaspersky Lab Identifies Operation 'Red October.'"

94 "Trojan.Dropper," https://www.symantec.com/security_response/writeup.jsp?docid=2002-0827 18-3007-99, accessed 15 September 2016.

95 "Kaspersky Lab Identifies Operation 'Red October.'"

96 "Kaspersky Lab Identifies Operation 'Red October.'"

graphic spying modules were also employed to defeat cryptographic systems including Acid Cryptofiler (used since 2011 by organizations including NATO, the European Union, European Parliament, and European Commission). Red October could target and reacquire access to remote workstations, mobile devices (including smartphones with different operating systems), configuration information from routers and switches connected to Internet-facing Enterprise Networks and recover deleted files from removable disk drives.[97] These were then used as entry pathways into additional systems. This used stolen credentials to guess passwords or phrases for further access privileges. Red October generated over 60 domain names and had a number of server hosting locations in various countries (mainly Germany and Russia) employed as proxies to disguise the location of the "mothership" control server.[98]

The group behind the attack was identified as the GRU's APT28/"Fancy Bear".[99] As well as its social engineering lures, efficient credential phishing, use of zero-days (previously unknown vulnerabilities) and exploit tools, including highly evolved malware, it is also known to stage false flag operations.[100] They are also suspected of targeting high profile individuals.[101] These highly valuable zero-days (in Microsoft Office, Java, Adobe Flash Player, Windows Operating Systems) were used alongside infected USB sticks to access air-gapped machines in defense industry organizations.

As in the case of Stuxnet, the joint U.S.-Israeli cyberespionage operation against Iran's Natanz nuclear enrichment facility during the Obama administration, these are examples of the reach hacking groups can have behind the security defenses of organizations where security is a part of their core business or is their core business.[102] Its sophistication is worth further consideration. Red October has

97 "Kaspersky Lab Identifies Operation 'Red October.'" John Leyden, "'Red October' has been spying on World Leaders for 5 years – researchers," http://www.theregister.co.uk/2013/01/14/red_october_cyber_espionage/, accessed 16 September 2016.

98 "Kaspersky Lab Identifies Operation 'Red October,'"

99 "Who is Fancy Bear?" (September 12, 2018), https://www.crowdstrike.com/blog/who-is-fancy-bear/, accessed 10 December 2018.

100 Feike Hacquebord, "Two Years of Pawn Storm Examining an Increasingly Relevant Threat," https://documents.trendmicro.com/assets/wp/wp-two-years-of-pawn-storm.pdf, accessed 10 December 2018.

101 Kelly Jackson Higgins, "Microsoft Sinkholes 6 Fancy Bear/APT28 Internet Domains" (August 21, 2018), https://www.darkreading.com/attacks-breaches/microsoft-sinkholes-6-fancy-bear-apt28-internet-domains/d/d-id/1332628, accessed 20 December 2018.

102 Darren Pauli, "Russian 'Pawn Storm' expands, rains hell on NATO, air-gapped PCs. Group cooks zero days, malware modules, and hacks anything it likes," http://www.theregister.co.uk/2015/

many of the hallmarks of a state-sponsored attack, especially given that it took a good amount of traditional espionage to target the embassies and research institutions. Red October used and carefully crafted spear-phishing e-mails in local languages that appeared to originate from an individual known to the recipient alongside tailor-made malware.[103]

4.3 "Dragonfly"

"Dragonfly," was an advanced cyberespionage campaign with ample funding which began as far back as 2010.[104] It initially targeted aviation and defense companies in the U.S. and Canada and then moved into the energy sector early in 2013.[105] It was reported to have infected more than 1,000 energy companies in North America and Europe and between 2,500 and 2,800 in total. "Dragonfly" has also been found in other industries such as pharmaceuticals and academia looking for gateway (and persistent) access into facilities.[106] It was an unusual operation because it appears to involve hackers from the FSB (specifically Military Unit 71330/Center 16[107]) and GRU (through the TsNIIKhM research institute) working in tandem.[108]

12/07/op_pawn_storm/, accessed 16 September 2016. On zero-days see Stoddart, *Cyberwarfare*, pp. 171–172, 231–233.

103 "Cyberwarfare, Crime and Security (Eugene Kaspersky, Mikko Hypponen, and Dan Dubno) | DLD13," https://www.youtube.com/watch?v=2BJ_aB4fuOQ, "A Visionairs Keynote," http://dld-conference.com/events/a-visionairs-keynote, and Fredric Lardinois, "Eugene Kaspersky and Mikko Hypponen Talk Red October and the Future of Cyber Warfare at DLD," https://techcrunch.com/2013/01/21/eugene-kaspersky-and-mikko-hypponen-talk-red-october-and-the-future-of-cyber-warfare-at-dld/. All accessed 16 September 2016.

104 Nell Nelson (SANS Institute), "The Impact of Dragonfly Malware on Industrial Control Systems" (January 18, 2016), p.5, https://www.sans.org/reading-room/whitepapers/ICS/impact-dragonfly-malware-industrial-control-systems-36672, "Energetic Bear — Crouching Yeti Kaspersky Lab Global Research and Analysis Team," p. 40 https://media.kasperskycontenthub.com/wp-content/uploads/sites/43/2018/03/08080817/EB-YetiJuly2014-Public.pdf, "Dragonfly," https://attack.mitre.org/groups/G0035/, all accessed 5 October 2018.

105 Stephen Blank and Younkyoo Kim, "Economic Warfare a la Russe: The Energy Weapon and Russian National Security Strategy," *The Journal of East Asian Affairs*, Vol. 30, Issue 1 (Spring/Summer 2016), pp. 1–39.

106 Joel T. Langhill, "Defending Against the Dragonfly Cyber Security Attacks" (December 10, 2014), p. 3. Previously available from https://www.controlglobal.com/assets/15WPpdf/150311-Belden-DragonflyCybersecurity.pdf, accessed 5 October 2018. "Energetic Bear — Crouching Yeti," p. 3.

107 Known variously as "Dragonfly," "Berzerk Bear," "Energetic Bear," and "Crouching Yeti" amongst other names. https://attack.mitre.org/groups/G0035/, accessed 8 August 2023.

However, there is some disagreement whether the energy sector was the prime target.[109] Langhill's thorough study claims the pharmaceutical sector was the prime target. Eric Byers, another expert in Industrial Control Systems (ICS), believed that "Dragonfly" was directed at intellectual property theft.[110] Although "Dragonfly" began in 2010, it was not discovered until 2013 when they were given away by spear phishing.[111] It was a targeted campaign, not one driven by opportunism.[112]

The first phase of the attack was reconnaissance. This was accomplished through OSINT. To gain access they employed spear-phishing e-mails containing seemingly legitimate links to retrieve documents. To accomplish this, they had hijacked legitimate websites to spread malware (known as watering hole attacks). These websites contained exploitation kits and trojan installers which were "planted on compromised vendor sites."[113] These spear-phishing e-mails first targeted companies in the supply chain to the main targets. This was an information-intelligence gathering phase which was used to locate more important targets who used these suppliers in one or more sectors. They crafted e-mails which offered ICS utilities and drivers which contained the exploitation malware. Once installed this provided a greater reach into now infected companies. Mesa Imaging in Belgium, eWon in Germany, and MB Connect Line in Switzerland were the first of the compromises. Each were Small to Medium sized Enterprises (SMEs) with around 50 employees at the time.[114]

This was between February and June 2013.[115] The "Dragonfly" group owned and operated the servers hosting the websites and their malware was then

---

108 Four Russian Government Employees Charged in Two Historical Hacking Campaigns Targeting Critical Infrastructure Worldwide, March 24 2022), https://www.justice.gov/opa/pr/four-russian-government-employees-charged-two-historical-hacking-campaigns-targeting-critical, accessed 8 August 2023.

109 "Energetic Bear — Crouching Yeti," p. 38. Langhill, "Defending Against the Dragonfly," pp. 6–7.

110 Langhill, "Defending Against the Dragonfly," pp. 4–8, 20.

111 Nelson (SANS Institute), "The Impact of Dragonfly," p. 5.

112 Alert TA18–074 A, March 16, 2018, https://www.cisa.gov/news-events/alerts/2018/03/15/russian-government-cyber-activity-targeting-energy-and-other-critical, accessed 8 August 2023.

113 "Backdoor:W32/Havex," https://www.f-secure.com/v-descs/backdoor_w32_havex.shtml, accessed 4 October 2018.

114 Langhill, "Defending Against the Dragonfly," pp. 4–8.

115 Langhill suggests, "Logic would suggest it is much easier to compromise a small business' web servers than it would be to perform a similar attack against much larger corporations. Bigger organizations typically invest heavily in security for their public-facing cyber assets and normally do not depend on open-source software for their website CMS." Langhill, "Defending Against the Dragonfly," pp. 6–7.

used to infect target computers, gather information-intelligence from them, using them to infiltrate company networks. These are similar TTPs to cybercriminals. TTPs often include phishing and targeted spear phishing and redirection to infected websites/"watering holes."[116] The second phase was the malware and the use of a Remote Access Trojan/Tool (RAT) which gave them administrative privileges and far greater access. The RAT, dubbed Havex, was used to gather system information, including Microsoft Outlook address books and what files and programs were installed, whilst a Trojan was used to upload the stolen data, download new files, and then run them on infected computers.[117]

In December 2016 these attacks were publicly attributed through a joint U.S. Department of Homeland Security (DHS) and Federal Bureau of Investigation (FBI) investigation published by US-CERT. The attribution was to Russia's civilian and military intelligence services (the SVR and GRU – APT 29/"Cozy Bear" first and then APT 28/"Fancy Bear" from Spring 2016).[118] "Dragonfly" was estimated to have infected around 2,000 critical infrastructure sites, mainly in the U.S. and Europe.[119] Havex, which has been in existence since 2013, has been used for other attacks on CI.[120]

The third phase, begun in May 2013, used hacked versions of legitimate ICS software they had located on vendor websites, but which now also contained the Havex code. Havex allowed the "Dragonfly" group to examine and exfiltrate network details and harvest further contact details. Havex also scanned for ICS and other networked devices and gathered information on them.[121] Havex was used as a means for other malware to infect the compromised computers and provided an "open backdoor." This included Karagany malware, which could take

116 Chris Bing, "An old foe's footprints muddle the mystery around group responsible for energy sector hacks" (July 12, 2017), https://www.cyberscoop.com/us-nuclear-hack-russia-energetic-bear-fireeye-phishing-watering-hole/, accessed 20 December 2017.

117 Bing, "An old foe's footprints."

118 Reference Number: JAR-16–20296 A December 29, 2016 Grizzly Steppe – Russian Malicious Cyber Activity, https://www.us-cert.gov/sites/default/files/publications/JAR_16-20296A_GRIZZLY%20STEPPE-2016-1229.pdf, accessed 8 October 2018.

119 "Havex," https://www.cyber.nj.gov/threat-profiles/ics-malware-variants/havex, accessed 5 October 2018.

120 Alastair Stevenson, "Fresh threat to critical infrastructure found in Havex malware," http://www.v3.co.uk/v3-uk/news/2356410/fresh-threat-to-critical-infrastructure-found-in-havex-malware, accessed 27 September 2014. See also Swati Khandelwal, "Stuxnet-like "Havex" Malware Strikes European SCADA Systems," http://thehackernews.com/2014/06/stuxnet-like-havex-malware-strikes.html, accessed 27 September 2014. Langhill, "Defending Against the Dragonfly," p. 2.

121 Object Linking and Embedding/Open Platform Communication. For detailed information see https://www.opcconnect.com/, accessed 5 October 2018.

screenshots, collect passwords, and alter operating systems. Another module employed by "Dragonfly" could decrypt passwords stored by web browsers and search for SCADA software.[122] "Dragonfly" became far less active from April 2014, but Idaho National Laboratory (IHL) reported in 2016 that unless properly mitigated its "complexity and range of access ... could produce future effects."[123]

"Dragonfly" was a cyberespionage campaign that also gave Russia a foothold in critical infrastructure sectors that enable cyberwarfare. This was discussed in detail and at length in *Cyberwarfare: Threats to Critical Infrastructure.*[124] A concerted attack on just one sector of critical infrastructure, particularly electric power generation and distribution, could prove life threatening and produce mass casualty events. It can also produce unanticipated and unpredictable cascade effects to other sectors.[125]

The Internet is the main vehicle for global connectivity, but it is one of many forms of connectivity including intranets (seen in a wide variety of facilities and home networks). For industries this includes Operational Technology (OT). OT sits alongside IT/ICT systems and networks and controls physical processes and devices throughout industry and across critical infrastructure. OT includes Industrial Control Systems (ICS) and Supervisory Control and Data Acquisition (SCADA) systems. ICS controls processes whilst SCADA provides the ability to manage and access remote devices. Attacks on SCADA systems, ICS, and the field devices they control and monitor "can disrupt and damage critical infrastructural operations, cause major economic losses, contaminate [the] ecological environment and ... claim human lives."[126] As in the case of "Dragonfly," the steps between these capabilities moving from cyberespionage and into undeclared war-fighting tools

122 "Dragonfly: Western Energy Companies Under Sabotage Threat" (June 30, 2014), https://www.symantec.com/connect/blogs/dragonfly-western-energy-companies-under-sabotage-threat?inid=us_ghp_hero2_dragonfly, accessed 16 December 2018.

123 Cyber Threat and Vulnerability Analysis of the U.S. Electric Sector Prepared by: Mission Support Center, Idaho National Laboratory August 2016, p. 4, https://www.energy.gov/sites/prod/files/2017/01/f34/Cyber%20Threat%20and%20Vulnerability%20Analysis%20of%20the%20U.S.%20Electric%20Sector.pdf, accessed 12 August 2019.

124 Stoddart, *Cyberwarfare.*

125 Cyber Security Building Resilience Reducing Risk conference, Chatham House, London (May 19–20, 2014) attended by author. See also Chris Keeling, Waking Shark II: Desktop Cyber Exercise: Report to Participants, 12 November 2013, https://www.bba.org.uk/wp-content/uploads/2014/02/Banking_3192106_v_1_Waking-Shark-II-Report-v1.pdf.pdf, accessed 6 April 2020.

126 Bonnie Zhu, Anthony Joseph, and Shankar Sastry, "A Taxonomy of Cyber Attacks on SCADA Systems," 2011 IEEE International Conferences on Internet of Things, and Cyber, Physical and Social Computing, p. 380, https://ieeexplore.ieee.org/stamp/stamp.jsp?tp=&arnumber=6142258, accessed 21 July 2019.

capable of kinetic destruction qualifying as cyberwarfare under international law are small.[127] Code that can be weaponized for destruction is a short step from "Dragonfly."

"Dragonfly" was primarily interested in intelligence gathering and establishing persistence in foreign energy infrastructure as a precursor for future sabotage campaigns, or as a stage in cyber-kinetic attacks. Havex in particular was an intelligence gathering tool but "payloads" that attempt to control connected hardware were not found.[128] This would be an escalatory step.[129] Through "Dragonfly" and other cyberespionage campaigns, vast amounts of seemingly disconnected data, allied to OSINT and gathered by APTs, can compromise the security of entire systems. "Dragonfly" was "Offense in Depth" because of the "diversified arsenal of attack vectors it employed."[130] Security solutions at the time would not have worked against "Dragonfly."

Eric Byres remarked that although the creators of "Dragonfly" did not design it to be destructive, it was "trivial" to alter the code to make it destructive.[131] "Dragonfly" concentrated on legacy systems running Windows XP which can no longer be patched and is still widely used in industry. One of the first targets, Ewon, as a supplier to industry had over a million global connections despite its small size, demonstrating the value in compromising just a single supplier. As a provider of remote support, they might also very well have been connected to ICS networks. The ICS themselves were vulnerable if "DragonFly" had gone further. This could have led to "denial of service events that may include complete loss of view or control of real-time data."[132] Havex was run in a "Sandbox" test environment with ICS hosts and found that it could cause "vital services to crash (such as Windows Explorer) rendering the host useless" with Havex also possessing a resurrection module which persisted after rebooting the system.[133] This access meant that any user could initiate potentially damaging attacks on physical systems and processes. It was also found to be harvesting sensitive information, including passwords, to be used to gain unauthorized access to critical

---

127 Michael N. Schmitt (ed.), *Tallinn Manual 2.0 on the International Law Applicable to Cyber Operations* (New York: Cambridge University Press, 2017).

128 "Havex Hunts For ICS/SCADA Systems," https://www.f-secure.com/weblog/archives/00002718.html, accessed 5 October 2018.

129 Maurer, *Cyber Mercenaries*, pp. 154–155.

130 Langhill, "Defending Against the Dragonfly," p. 2.

131 Eric Byres quoted in Langhill, "Defending Against the Dragonfly," p. 23.

132 Langhill, "Defending Against the Dragonfly," p. 22.

133 Langhill, "Defending Against the Dragonfly," p. 22.

systems. These compromises also provided remote access through suppliers and maintenance companies.[134]

Anti-virus systems and Intrusion Detection Systems (IDS) had not detected "Dragonfly's" activities. It is also highlighting a worrying trend with trusted product suppliers targeted.[135] This is upstream targeting of industry through the supply chain. Specifically targeted by "Dragonfly" were ICS managing electrical, water, oil, gas, and data systems. Symantec came to believe that "Dragonfly's" main purpose was espionage with "the capability to mount sabotage operations that could have disrupted energy supplies across a number of European countries."[136] Moreover, the malware deployed was unique and delivered a framework for future attacks. It had the ability to generate further malicious processes and establish persistence, even though the initial user was unauthorized to install or update applications.[137] Concerns around this and other cyberespionage campaigns, and the potential for destructive acts of cyberwarfare, were well-founded with "Dragonfly 2.0" and other related campaigns emerging in 2015.

4.4 TV5 Monde and BlackEnergy: Testing the water?

The April 2015 attack on TV5 Monde, a national French television channel, targeting e-mail, administrative, and critical hardware was one such case. The damage was estimated at €5 million as well as millions more invested annually for remedial cybersecurity measures to try and prevent future attacks.[138] It was disguised as an attack by the "Cyber Caliphate," but cyber forensics revealed Russian origins. It has been speculated that it was a means to test cyber capabilities and assess Western intelligence abilities and responses.[139] APT 28/"Fancy Bear" (specifi-

134 Langhill, "Defending Against the Dragonfly," p. 23.
135 Charlie Hart, 'Troubling' rise in supply chain cyber attacks" (April 13, 2021), https://www.cips.org/supply-management/news/2021/april/troubling-rise-in-supply-chain-cyber-attacks/, accessed 10 August 2023.
136 Anonymous, Energy firms hacked by "cyber-espionage group Dragonfly," (July 1, 2014), http://www.bbc.co.uk/news/technology-28106478, accessed 15 July 2014.
137 Langhill, "Defending Against the Dragonfly," p. 21.
138 Ben Buchanan and Michael Sulmeyer, "Russia and Cyber Operations: Challenges and Opportunities for the Next U.S. Administration" (December 13, 2016), pp. 3–4, https://carnegieendowment.org/2016/12/13/russia-and-cyber-operations-challenges-and-opportunities-for-next-u.s.-administration-pub-66433, accessed 28 January 2018.
139 Buchanan and Sulmeyer, "Russia and Cyber Operations," p. 4.

cally the group "Pawn Storm") was subsequently identified.[140] False flags and attempts at plausible deniability or misdirection remain a problem in cyber breach forensics (a well-known hallmark of Russian cyberespionage operations).[141] Worse was to follow.

4.5 BlackEnergy: "Lights Out"

In December 2015 Ukraine was subjected to a major cyberattack which tested its responses. Ukraine had already experienced serious Russian pressure, leading to the annexation of Crimea in 2014. Further north in eastern Ukraine, the Donbas, military intelligence and active measures were employed, alongside arms shipments, and relatively small numbers of regular and mercenary soldiers alongside a campaign of destabilization and public diplomacy.[142] Throughout the 2010s Ukraine had experienced cyberattacks and destabilization campaigns from Russia. These included information warfare operations, as well as disruptive cyberattacks on government, military, telecommunications systems and many other intrusions or breaches in Ukraine's private sector, including critical infrastructure.[143]

For years previously, Russia has been a determined user of cyberespionage both for intelligence gathering and for "preparation of the battlefield" in Ukraine and in the West.[144] More targeted cyberattacks have been seen since 2014. These include energy, transport, and banking sectors as well as Ukrainian elections.[145] There is also evidence that Russia's GRU "Fancy Bear" APT used a "trojan" (malware disguised as legitimate to infect a host) against Ukraine's military. This trojan, X-Agent, seen in other cyberattack campaigns, infected an Android application

140 John Leyden, "Russia's to blame for pro-ISIS megahack on French TV network. APT28 crew left their fingerprints all over this one" (June 10, 2015), http://www.theregister.co.uk/2015/06/10/russian_trolls_staged_tv5monde_megahack_shocker/, accessed 18 November 2017.

141 Thomas Rid, *Cyber War Will Not Take Place* (London: Hurst, 2013), p. 76.

142 Roy Allison, "Russian 'Deniable' Intervention in Ukraine: How and Why Russia Broke the Rules," *International Affairs*, Vol. 90, Issue 6 (November 2014), pp. 1255–1297.

143 Michael Connell and Sarah Vogler, "Russia's Approach to Cyber Warfare," Center for Naval Analyses, Occasional Paper, March 2017, p. 19, https://www.cna.org/cna_files/pdf/DOP-2016-U-014231-1Rev.pdf, accessed 9 January 2018.

144 Jen Weedon, "Beyond 'Cyber War': Russia's Use of Strategic Cyber Espionage and Information Operations in Ukraine," in Kenneth Geers (ed.), *Cyber War in Perspective: Russian Aggression against Ukraine* (Tallinn: NATO CCD COE Publications, 2015).

145 Andy Greenberg, "Everything We Know About Russia's Election-Hacking Playbook" (June 9, 2017), https://www.wired.com/story/russia-election-hacking-playbook/, accessed 27 March 2023.

developed by a Ukrainian military officer for an artillery piece.[146] In July 2014 a successful Ukrainian offensive was blunted by a separatist counter-offensive with, it is alleged, support from Russian artillery (something Russian officials denied) because of X-Agent.[147] In 2025, the British government stated that the development of X-Agent was led by Sergey Morgachev supported by Aleksey Lukachev, Ivan Yermakov, Sergey Vasyuk and Artem Malyshev. All worked for Unit 26165.[148] Russian cyberespionage in Ukraine includes wiperware masquerading as cybercriminal ransomware attacks, most notably NotPetya in 2017.[149]

This progressive drumbeat intensified after Revolution of Dignity/Euromaidan in 2014. There was then a step change into cyber-physical attacks in 2015 and 2016 when Ukraine became the first nation to experience a cyberattack which took down part of its power grid. This was through malware known as BlackEnergy which has evolved into a campaign spanning almost a decade. BlackEnergy's origins date back to 2007 and its use as a botnet primarily for Distributed Denial of Service (DDoS) attacks.[150] It was authored by one or more Russian hackers gaining notoriety in 2008 during the short-lived Russia-Georgian conflict in 2008. By 2010, this had evolved into BlackEnergy 2.0.[151] It was speculated that BlackEnergy 2.0 was designed for cybercriminals operating in Russia and Ukraine based on an analysis of its codebase. These included modules containing code which could hijack banking sessions and steal banking credentials.[152]

It continued to be refined with BlackEnergy 3.0 used to precision-target three regional power distribution companies through external attack leading to power cuts at Christmas 2015 in the Ivano-Frankivsk region of Western Ukraine.[153] Al-

146 Adam Meyers, "Danger Close: Fancy Bear Tracking of Ukrainian Field Artillery Units" (December 22, 2016), https://www.crowdstrike.com/blog/danger-close-fancy-bear-tracking-ukrainian-field-artillery-units/, accessed 27 March 2023.

147 "Bellingcat Report – Origin of Artillery Attacks on Ukrainian Military Positions in Eastern Ukraine Between 14 July 2014 and 8 August 2014" (February 17, 2015), https://www.bellingcat.com/news/uk-and-europe/2015/02/17/origin-of-artillery-attacks/, accessed 27 March 2023.

148 Policy paper Profile: GRU cyber and hybrid threat operations, https://www.gov.uk/government/publications/profile-gru-cyber-and-hybrid-threat-operations/profile-gru-cyber-and-hybrid-threat-operations (July 18 2025), accessed 20 July 2025.

149 https://www.justice.gov/opa/press-release/file/1328521/download, pp. 16–23.

150 Jose Nazario, "BlackEnergy DDoS Bot Analysis" (October 2007), http://atlas-public.ec2.arbor.net/docs/BlackEnergy+DDoS+Bot+Analysis.pdf, accessed 11 January 2019.

151 Joe Stewart, "BlackEnergy Version 2 Threat Analysis" (March 3, 2010), https://www.secureworks.com/research/blackenergy2, accessed 11 January 2019.

152 Stewart, "BlackEnergy Version 2 Threat Analysis."

153 Natalia Zinets, "Ukraine charges Russia with new cyber attacks on infrastructure" (February 15, 2017), http://www.reuters.com/article/us-ukraine-crisis-cyber/ukraine-charges-russia-with-new-cyber-attacks-on-infrastructure-idUSKBN15U2CN, accessed 7 September 2017.

though it lasted only 3 – 6 hours, 225,000 customers were affected.[154] Ukraine's Security Service (the SBU) immediately and publicly blamed Russia's security services.[155] Western experts were less certain.[156]

BlackEnergy 3.0 was spread by unsuspecting users clicking on plausible spear-phishing e-mails with attachments which asked their targets to enable macros (files that enable further functionality).[157] Once in BlackEnergy migrated into the SCADA distribution management system which allocated electric power. The attackers also attempted to delay restoration by means of wiperware which "took multiple substations offline and disabled backup power from two distribution centers simultaneously" whilst automated telephone calls (robocalls) temporarily prevented customers from reporting outages. This likely took "months of reconnaissance and planning."[158] It was widely believed that BlackEnergy originated from Russia's underground hacker community with the original authored by "Cr4sh" of the hacker group "Hellknights Crew."[159] Over time, it was developed and refined into a very sophisticated cyberespionage toolkit.[160]

Like Stuxnet, it is a proof of concept for cyber-physical operations with Ukraine a proving ground or "laboratory" for Russian cyberespionage and cyberwar-

154 "Cyber-Attack against Ukrainian Critical Infrastructure," Industrial Control Systems Cyber Emergency Response Team, February 25, 2016, accessed at https://ics-cert.us-cert.gov/alerts/IR-ALERT-H-16-056-01, 28 June 2016. The activities of ICS-CERT and related organizations provide a valuable protective barrier.

155 Pavel Polityuk, "Ukraine to probe suspected Russian cyber attack on grid" (December 31, 2015), https://www.reuters.com/article/us-ukraine-crisis-malware/ukraine-to-probe-suspected-russian-cyber-attack-on-grid-idUSKBN0UE0ZZ20151231?feedType=RSS. See also "TLP: White Analysis of the Cyber Attack on the Ukrainian Power Grid Defense Use Case March 18, 2016," p. iv, https://ics.sans.org/media/E-ISAC_SANS_Ukraine_DUC_5.pdf. Both accessed 19 January 2018.

156 Kim Zetter, "Inside the Cunning, Unprecedented Hack of Ukraine's Power Grid" (March 3, 2016), https://www.wired.com/2016/03/inside-cunning-unprecedented-hack-ukraines-power-grid/. Kim Zetter, "Everything We Know About Ukraine's Power Plant Hack," (January 20, 2016), https://www.wired.com/2016/01/everything-we-know-about-ukraines-power-plant-hack/. Both accessed 16 November 2017.

157 Norton Santos, "BlackEnergy APT Malware" (March 23, 2016), https://community.rsa.com/thread/186012, accessed 11 January 2019.

158 Cyber Threat and Vulnerability Analysis of the U.S. Electric Sector, p. 11.

159 "BlackEnergy and the Ukraine: Signals vs. Noise" (January 12, 2016), https://threatvector.cylance.com/en_us/home/blackenergy-and-the-ukraine-signals-vs-noise.html, accessed 11 January 2019.

160 "BlackEnergy and the Ukraine: Signals vs. Noise." Rafiullah Khan, Peter Maynard, Kieran McLaughlin, David Laverty, and Sakir Sezer, "Threat Analysis of BlackEnergy Malware for Synchrophasor based Real-time Control and Monitoring in Smart Grid," Proceedings of the 4th International Symposium for ICS & SCADA Cyber Security Research 2016, p. 10. Available from https://dl.acm.org/doi/proceedings/10.5555/3015643, accessed 30 January 2017.

fare tools, potentially portable worldwide.[161] These escalating attacks arguably began against Estonia in 2007, were used in Georgia in 2008, and have been used systematically against Ukraine since at least 2010.[162] Because it is "'highly modular' with functionality varying in deployment to different victims," this makes "it difficult to determine its future impact in the electricity industry."[163] In this respect, Russian and Ukrainian grids are similar through a shared history and border with related infrastructure and networks in Russia. To those involved in mitigating BlackEnergy, this attack inevitably also revealed Russian vulnerabilities.[164]

The group involved were subsequently identified as "Sandworm."[165] "Sandworm" (GRU Unit 74455) is now reportedly led by Evgeny Serebryakov (affiliated to APT28/"Fancy Bear"). He was part of the team indicted by the U.S. Department of Justice for the attempted hack on the Organisation for the Prohibition of Chemical Weapons (OPCW) in April 2018 (described in Chapter 1). During investigations, his computer equipment revealed he had travelled widely. This included the 2016 Olympics in Rio de Janeiro where he was photographed at events. He also travelled to an anti-doping conference in Lausanne, Switzerland. There he had targeted officials investigating Russian doping.[166] Following the OPCW operation the Dutch and British governments attributed "Sandworm" and the BlackEnergy attacks to Russia's GRU.[167] The post-breach investigation that followed determined

161 Andy Greenberg, "How an Entire Nation Became Russia's Test Lab for Cyberwar" (June 20, 2017), https://www.wired.com/story/russian-hackers-attack-ukraine/, accessed January 20, 2018.

162 Andrew Osborn and Pavel Polityuk, "Russia prepares reprisals against Ukraine over Crimea blackout" (November 24, 2015), https://www.reuters.com/article/us-ukraine-crisis-crimea-idUSKBN0TD1NI20151124, accessed 28 February 2020.

163 Cyber Threat and Vulnerability Analysis of the U.S. Electric Sector, p. 5.

164 This is based on private discussions.

165 John Hultquist, "Sandworm Team and the Ukrainian Power Authority Attacks" (January 7, 2016), https://www.fireeye.com/blog/threat-research/2016/01/ukraine-and-sandworm-team.html, accessed January 20, 2018. The most complete reporting on Sandworm to date is Andy Greenberg, *Sandworm: A New Era of Cyberwar and the Hunt for the Kremlin's Most Dangerous Hackers* (New York: Doubleday, 2019).

166 Andy Greenberg, "This Is the New Leader of Russia's Infamous Sandworm Hacking Unit. Evgenii Serebriakov now runs the most aggressive hacking team of Russia's GRU military spy agency. To Western intelligence, he's a familiar face" (March 15, 2023), https://www.wired.com/story/russia-gru-sandworm-serebriakov/, accessed 18 March 2024. They were released out of concerns regarding Russian reprisals, including expelling or arresting Dutch diplomats despite also facing possible extradition to the U.S. Greenberg, "This Is the New Leader."

167 Reckless campaign of cyber attacks by Russian military intelligence service exposed (October 4, 2018), https://www.ncsc.gov.uk/news/reckless-campaign-cyber-attacks-russian-military-intelligence-service-exposed, accessed 10 January 2019.

it involved skill, stealth, and months of planning. First this required network reconnaissance allied to social engineering to gain access credentials before the operation began.[168] These have become hallmarks of Russia's intelligence agencies (as well as other APTs).[169]

BlackEnergy was highly targeted. No two SCADA systems are precisely alike. Most are bespoke or multi-year custom builds, and the attackers studied the various distribution management systems used by each of Ukraine's power companies (and also by Russian power companies). Other exploits and methods were specific to Ukraine. Although specific, BlackEnergy is also "proof of concept" and could well be used against the U.S. and elsewhere according to multiple cyber security experts.[170] Although power was quickly restored, the circuit breakers had to be controlled manually and in the U.S. power stations have more limited manual backup.[171]

The economic consequences are unknown but soon after it was estimated that a more widespread attack on the north-eastern United States could amount to "$243 billion, or in a worst-case scenario, nearly $1 trillion" worth of damage even if it was possible to restore essential systems within 24 hours (with weeks for the rest).[172] If one excludes wiperware attacks (especially Shamoon), the 2015 BlackEnergy attack was only the third-ever known case of malicious code purpose-built to disrupt physical systems outside of computer laboratories. The first was Stuxnet.[173] The second was at a German steel mill in 2014.[174] The fourth followed a year later.

---

168 Zetter, "Inside the Cunning."

169 Andy Greenberg, "Your Guide to Russia's Infrastructure Hacking Teams" (July 12, 2017), https://www.wired.com/story/russian-hacking-teams-infrastructure/, accessed 20 January 2018.

170 Andy Greenberg, "'Crash Override': The Malware That Took Down a Power Grid" (June 12, 2017), https://www.wired.com/story/crash-override-malware/, accessed 19 January 2018.

171 Zetter, "Inside the Cunning."

172 Jeff St. John, "Cyberattack on US Power Plants Could Cause $1T in Economic Damage. Lloyd's of London games out 'improbable, but not impossible' threat of hacking, power-plant sabotage" (July 10, 2015), https://www.greentechmedia.com/articles/read/cyber-attack-on-u-s-power-plants-could-cause-1t-in-economic-damage#gs.YIxYghI. Boris Zilberman, "Don't Underestimate Economic Side of Russia's Cyber Warfare" (June 26, 2018), https://www.fdd.org/analysis/2018/06/26/dont-underestimate-economic-side-of-russias-cyber-warfare/. Both accessed 11 January 2019.

173 Robert M. Lee, Michael J. Assante, and Tim Conway, "ICS CP/PE (Cyber-to-Physical or Process Effects) case study paper – German Steel Mill Cyber Attack" (December 30, 2014), https://ics.sans.org/media/ICS-CPPE-case-Study-2-German-Steelworks_Facility.pdf, accessed 20 January 2018.

174 R. A. Becker, "Cyber Attack on German Steel Mill Leads to 'Massive' Real World Damage" (January 8, 2015), https://www.pbs.org/wgbh/nova/article/cyber-attack-german-steel-mill-leads-massive-real-world-damage/, accessed 11 April 2023.

4.6 "Industroyer"/"CrashOverride"

There was also a minor power outage in December 2016 in Kyiv, following a fortnight-long series of cyberattacks. This bore "many of the same technical hallmarks" of the 2015 attack and another show of capability which could have gone further.[175] The SBU again blamed Russia.[176] This lesser known attack saw malware dubbed "Industroyer" or "CrashOverride" used which was "far more advanced than the general-purpose tools" used in 2015.[177] It could degrade power grids, scan and map ICS environments, and cause shutdowns to relays requiring a manual reset. In addition, although it was designed to affect the electric grid in Ukraine it could be re-engineered to affect multiple sectors of CI.[178] There was disquiet from parts of the cybersecurity industry that "this was a large-scale test" also deployable worldwide.[179]

As ICS/SCADA systems operate with different protocols and equipment in different regions and different sites it could be precisely targeted. It was not designed for espionage but to induce power outages, in this case for a few days at worst. Dragos attributed the attack to the GRU's "Sandworm" group and assessed it was also designed to be portable to other countries outside of Ukraine. This is because "Industroyer"/"CrashOverride" is "not unique to any particular vendor or configuration and instead leverages knowledge of grid operations and network communications to cause impact; in that way, it can be immediately re-purposed in Europe and portions of the Middle East and Asia", or the North American grid with some retailoring.[180] Industroyer 2.0 has been used in the Ukraine War.[181]

---

175 Dan Goodin, "Hackers trigger yet another power outage in Ukraine For the second year in a row, hack targets Ukraine during one of its coldest months" (January 11, 2017), https://arstechnica.com/information-technology/2017/01/the-new-normal-yet-another-hacker-caused-power-outage-hits-ukraine/, accessed 19 January 2018.

176 Pavel Polityuk, "Ukraine points finger at Russian security services in recent cyber attack" (July 1, 2017), https://www.reuters.com/article/us-cyber-attack-ukraine/ukraine-points-finger-at-russian-security-services-in-recent-cyber-attack-idUSKBN19M39P, accessed 19 January 2018.

177 Dan Goodin, "Found: 'Crash Override' malware that triggered Ukrainian power outage. Attack tools can be used against a broad range of electric grids around the world" (June 12, 2017), https://arstechnica.com/information-technology/2017/06/crash-override-malware-may-sabotage-electric-grids-but-its-no-stuxnet/, accessed January 20, 2018.

178 "Alert (TA17–163 A) CrashOverride Malware" (July 27, 2017), https://www.us-cert.gov/ncas/alerts/TA17-163A, accessed 7 October 2018.

179 "Industroyer: Biggest malware threat to critical infrastructure since Stuxnet" (June 12, 2017), https://www.eset.com/int/industroyer/, accessed 7 October 2018.

180 "Crashoverride Analysis of the Threat to Electric Grid Operations," pp. 4–5, https://dragos.com/blog/crashoverride/CrashOverride-01.pdf, accessed 7 October 2018.

181 M-Trends 2023, p. 55.

4.7 Bugdrop

Bugdrop is another piece of sophisticated malware discovered in early 2017, again predominantly in Ukraine and especially in the self-declared separatist regions of Donetsk and Luhansk.[182] It was designed to take screenshots, as well as documents and passwords and record audio through connected microphones. It too was primarily used to target the energy sector. It again used social engineering to lure targets into installing malware. Its aim was cyber-reconnaissance to collect intelligence on targets in critical infrastructure, as well as media and scientific research institutes. Although there was no damage "identifying, locating and performing reconnaissance on targets is usually the first phase of operations with broader objectives."[183] The technical analysis pointed to a nation-state, but the technical cybersecurity community did not attribute to Russia or any other actor.[184] There are many examples of Russian activities in the energy sector outside of Ukraine especially when the "Dragonfly" group reemerged after a brief hiatus.

4.8 "Dragonfly 2.0"

The "Dragonfly" campaign reappeared in December 2015 as "Dragonfly 2.0." The campaign began in December 2015 with fake New Year's Eve invitations aimed at over 100 companies across Europe from Ireland to Turkey as well as in the U.S.[185] These targeted government facilities and multiple critical infrastructure sectors, including energy, nuclear, water, aviation, and critical manufacturing sectors as well as commercial facilities. The first part of the campaign was again aimed at companies in the supply chains of the main targets. These were targeted for credentials and gateway access. They again used many common TTPs such as spear-phishing e-mails (sent from compromised legitimate accounts) and the use of watering-hole domains. This was aimed at gathering credentials such as pass-

182 "Operation BugDrop: CyberX Discovers Large-Scale Cyber-Reconnaissance Operation Targeting Ukrainian Organizations" (February 15, 2017), https://cyberx-labs.com/blog/operation-bugdrop-cyberx-discovers-large-scale-cyber-reconnaissance-operation/, accessed 16 December 2018.
183 "Operation BugDrop."
184 Lily Hay Newman, "A Mysterious Group Has Ties to 15 Years of Ukraine-Russia Hacks" (May 19, 2023), https://www.wired.com/story/red-stinger-ukraine-russia-espionage-hackers/, accessed 12 August 2023.
185 Robert Hackett, "Hackers Have Penetrated Energy Grid, Symantec warns" (September 6, 2017), https://fortune.com/2017/09/06/hack-energy-grid-symantec/, accessed 30 September 2017.

words and then conducting open-source and network reconnaissance for host-based exploitation used to target ICS and specifically CI.

These critical infrastructure targets were deliberately targeted and were not simply targets of opportunity. During the reconnaissance phase they looked for network and organizational relationships along with ICS components and capabilities within these organizations. These relationships would, alongside OSINT as well as Social Media Intelligence (SOCMINT), help craft plausible spear-phishing e-mails. This included a high-resolution picture used by a human resources website which when expanded displayed control systems equipment models and status information in the background. Company websites themselves were also hijacked through their source code. This enabled "Dragonfly 2.0" to install malware on legitimate websites. Attempts were also made to access webmail and VPN connections. Successful spear-phishing e-mails, and the use of password-cracking code, helped them to gather valid credentials. Compromised trade and industrial websites were then used as "watering holes" used to exploit the access they had now gained.

"Dragonfly 2.0," according to Symantec, "appears to be interested in both learning how energy facilities operate and also gaining access to operational systems themselves, to the extent that the group now potentially has the ability to sabotage or gain control of these systems should it decide to do so."[186] Symantec added that intelligence-gathering normally precedes cyber sabotage. This is where information is gathered and assembled, and credentials harvested (which can also be used in later campaigns). These were features of both the Stuxnet and Shamoon cyberattacks. This is why the original "Dragonfly" campaign was now being reassessed as an exploratory campaign. "Dragonfly 2.0" was part of a noticeable evolutionary turn towards accessing and manipulating Operational Technology systems.[187] The OT side of businesses is what can lead to disruptive and destructive real world effects as described in *Cyberwarfare: Threats to Critical Infrastructure.*[188]

---

186 "Dragonfly: Western energy sector targeted by sophisticated attack group" (October 20, 2017), https://www.symantec.com/blogs/threat-intelligence/dragonfly-energy-sector-cyber-attacks, accessed 23 September 2018.

187 "Dragonfly: Western energy sector targeted by sophisticated attack group"; Jose Pagliery, "The inside story of the biggest hack in history" (August 5, 2015), https://money.cnn.com/2015/08/05/technology/aramco-hack/index.html; Stephen Jewkes and Jim Finkle, "Saipem says Shamoon variant crippled hundreds of computers" (December 12, 2018), https://www.reuters.com/article/us-cyber-shamoon-idUSKBN1OB2FA. All accessed 23 September 2018.

188 Stoddart, *Cyberwarfare*, pp. 147–225.

"Dragonfly 2.0" employed widely available malware and no "zero days" and instead adopted techniques which depended on gathering credentials to gain network access. Their use of "living-off-the-land" tools (where an attacker uses tools that are already present in penetrated systems) might "indicate a lack of resources" or "be an attempt to deliberately thwart attribution."[189] Equally, this could be a cost-effective test to prove the art of the possible "should it choose to do so."[190] Both the FBI and DHS assisted around a dozen private energy companies in the U.S. in mitigating the breaches (attacks are commonplace, breaches are not) they had been witnessing from around May 2017.[191] This also extended to nuclear power plants. This included the Wolf Creek nuclear power plant in Kansas in summer 2017 which powers up to 800,000 homes.[192] Like many other critical infrastructure sites, especially nuclear facilities, it operates as "an island" cut off from the Internet mainland with only physical (not electronic) routes in (known as an air-gapped system). As at Natanz, which Stuxnet infiltrated, this segmentation is designed to protect control systems from external interference.[193]

It was reported that both former and current U.S. government officials were concerned that this campaign was reconnaissance for vulnerabilities. This could primarily be for economic motives or ransomware in the same way that WannaCry and Petya/NotPetya malware were designed for financial gain but the dangers of ransomware are far outweighed by the disruptive and destructive potential.[194] A joint statement released by the FBI/DHS stated "There is no indication of a threat to public safety, as any potential impact appears to be limited to administrative and business networks."[195] In off-the-record conversations with *The*

189 "Dragonfly: Western energy sector targeted by sophisticated attack group." "What are living off the land (LOTL) attacks?" (February 22, 2023), https://www.crowdstrike.com/cybersecurity-101/living-off-the-land-attacks-lotl/, accessed 13 August 2023.

190 "Dragonfly: Western energy sector targeted by sophisticated attack group."

191 Using Lockheed-Martin's Cyber Kill Chain model which is widely used to analyze, discuss, and dissect serious cyberattacks. This analyzes the following campaign elements: reconnaissance, weaponization, delivery, exploitation, installation, command, and control.

192 Caroline Baylon with Roger Brunt and David Livingstone, "Chatham House Report: Cyber Security at Civil Nuclear Facilities Understanding the Risks" (September 2015), https://www.chathamhouse.org/sites/default/files/field/field_document/20151005CyberSecurityNuclearBaylonBruntLivingstoneUpdate.pdf, accessed 17 September 2018.

193 Max Londberg, "Russia infiltrated Kansas nuclear plant's business network, FBI and DHS say" (March 16, 2018), https://www.kansascity.com/news/local/article205581509.html, accessed 17 September 2018.

194 Stoddart, *Cyberwarfare*, pp. 376–378.

195 Michael Riley, Jennifer A Dlouhy, and Bryan Gruley, "Russians Are Suspects in Nuclear Site Hackings, Sources Say" (July 7, 2017), https://www.bloomberg.com/news/articles/2017-07-07/russians-are-said-to-be-suspects-in-hacks-involving-nuclear-site, accessed 19 December 2017.

Washington Post, NSA officials attributed this 2017 campaign to the FSB.[196] The US-CERT named the perpetrators as "Energetic Bear," who were linked with the original "Dragonfly," without attributing this group to Russia or a Russian agency.[197]

As *Wired* reported, this poses a frequently asked question: "Which of the Kremlin's hackers groups attempted the power grid intrusions?" Top of *Wired*'s list was "Sandworm" closely followed by a lesser known group, "Palmetto Fusion," which *Wired* suspected might be the dormant "Energetic Bear." Technical analysis by the cybersecurity community shows variance in their techniques whilst sharing many common tactics and procedures such as social engineering and spear phishing. Once in, it is common to see Russian groups move laterally through breached networks for information-intelligence gathering, the planting of exploits, or exfiltration of documents and files.[198]

Whether this case is explained by separate FSB, GRU, or SVR operations, changes in the makeup of the groups involved, cross group collaborations, temporary involvement of cybercriminal "privateers," or the evolution of TTPs or orders from the Kremlin is unclear. Perhaps it is enough to attribute with high confidence that these operations are the work of Russian intelligence and are not a false flag. A number of current and former policymakers and many from NATO would take this view.[199] This demonstrates the limits of public knowledge regarding Russia's intelligence agencies, what the lines of communication and authority to and from the Kremlin are, and how we assess Russia's cyber strategy and campaigns. These are areas of analysis and debate this book has tried to move forward.

For the U.S., and other nations, this is the kind of campaign which could lead to the disruption of power supplies. It was concerning enough to see a general alert distributed to utilities companies.[200] The affected sectors were energy, water, aviation, nuclear, and critical manufacturing. In some cases they had already com-

---

196 Ellen Nakashima, "U.S. officials say Russian government hackers have penetrated energy and nuclear company business networks" (July 8, 2017), https://www.washingtonpost.com/world/national-security/us-officials-say-russian-government-hackers-have-penetrated-energy-and-nuclear-company-business-networks/2017/07/08/bbfde9a2-638b-11e7-8adc-fea80e32bf47_story.html?utm_term=.7823f4ef2368, accessed 20 December 2017.

197 US-CERT, Alert (TA17–293 A) Advanced Persistent Threat Activity Targeting Energy and Other Critical Infrastructure Sectors (October 23, 2017), https://www.us-cert.gov/ncas/alerts/TA17-293A. See also Yonathan Klijnsma, "New Insights into Energetic Bear's Watering Hole Attacks on Turkish Critical Infrastructure" (November 2, 2017), https://www.riskiq.com/blog/labs/energetic-bear/. Both accessed 20 December 2017.

198 Greenberg, "Your Guide to Russia's Infrastructure Hacking Teams."

199 Privately at least.

200 Riley, Dlouhy, and Gruley, "Russians Are Suspects in Nuclear Site Hackings, Sources Say."

promised networks.[201] These included choke points of the power supply with attempts to establish backdoors on plant systems for later use.[202] There had also been breaches in conventional power plants which could lead to regional effects if they can be exploited. When these campaigns are looked at alongside the attacks in Ukraine as it looks like methodologies are being tested. This increases the possibility that a major attack "is very, very possible," including by migrating from the front-facing IT side of businesses to OT.[203] Clearly, the implications and security repercussions go much further than economic consequences or cyber-enabled economic warfare. This is obviously a worry and a U.S. Department of Defense Science Board Task Force specifically mentioned Havex and BlackEnergy as concerns after they were discovered in the U.S. electrical grid.[204]

US-CERT indicated in a March 2018 alert that a joint investigation by DHS and the FBI had discovered that this campaign had been able to manipulate systems running Microsoft Windows to take screenshots on systems across the network.[205] US-CERT added they: "accessed workstations and servers on a corporate network that contained data output from control systems within energy generation facilities. The threat actors accessed files pertaining to ICS or supervisory control and data acquisition (SCADA) systems ... targeted and copied profile and configuration information for accessing ICS systems on the network ... [as well as copying] configuration information on accessing ICS systems."[206]

---

201 The alert added, "Historically, cyber threat actors have targeted the energy sector with various results, ranging from cyber espionage to the ability to disrupt energy systems in the event of a hostile conflict. Historically, threat actors have also targeted other critical infrastructure sectors with similar campaigns." US-CERT, Alert (TA17–293 A).

202 Riley, Dlouhy, and Gruley, "Russians Are Suspects in Nuclear Site Hackings, Sources Say."

203 Riley, Dlouhy, and Gruley, "Russians Are Suspects in Nuclear Site Hackings, Sources Say." This is in line with other separate cases and findings. Kristan Stoddart, Kevin Jones, Hugh Soulsby, Andrew Blyth, Peter Eden, Peter Burnap, and Yulia Cherdantseva, "Live Free or Die Hard: U.S.–UK Cybersecurity Policies," *Political Science Quarterly* Vol. 131, Issue 4 (December 2016), pp. 803–842.

204 Department of Defense. Defense Science Board Task Force on Cyber Deterrence, February 2017, p. 7, https://www.armed-services.senate.gov/imo/media/doc/DSB%20CD%20Report%202017-02-27-17_v18_Final-Cleared%20Security%20Review.pdf, accessed 1 December 2018.

205 Alert (TA18–074 A) Russian Government Cyber Activity Targeting Energy and Other Critical Infrastructure Sectors, March 15, 2018, https://www.us-cert.gov/ncas/alerts/TA18-074A, accessed 17 September 2018.

206 Alert (TA18–074 A) March 15, 2018.

4.9 Colonial Pipeline

Concerns that Russian cyberespionage could shut down or damage CI have been evident for years. What has been less evident is the capability for Russian cybercriminals to do the same. Whilst Russia's criminal underworld is widely suspected of working with the Russian state and Russian intelligence, the May 2021 ransomware attack on the key U.S. energy supplier Colonial Pipeline leads to some challenging questions.[207] Based in Alpharetta, Georgia, Colonial Pipeline operates onshore pipes and piping systems that supply oil and petroleum from Houston on the Gulf of Mexico across the U.S. eastern seaboard and eastern U.S. carrying 45 percent of the gasoline, diesel, and kerosene to the automotive and aviation industry as well as home heating oil.[208]

Colonial Pipeline was forced to shut down its entire system for six days following the attack. The group claiming responsibility was "DarkSide," a cybercrime gang believed to operate from Russia.[209] "DarkSide's" attack had major real time effects on suppliers and motorists from Atlanta to Tennessee, cascading all the way up the east coast to New York. It led to panic buying and fuel shortages in multiple states. Cascading effects were felt not only for motorists and gas stations, but also in the wider economy and under considerable pressure Colonial Pipeline paid up. It cost them $4.4 million in Bitcoin. Although Colonial Pipeline received a decryption tool in return it is unclear what happened to the 100 gigabytes of data "DarkSide" had access to.[210]

---

207 And the largest U.S. oil pipeline company. Andy Greenberg, "The Colonial Pipeline Is a New Extreme for Ransomware" (May 8, 2021), https://www.wired.com/story/colonial-pipeline-ransomware-attack/, accessed 31 July 2023.

208 Jack Beerman, David Berent, Zach Falter, and Suman Bhunia, "A Review of Colonial Pipeline Ransomware Attack," 2023 IEEE/ACM 23rd International Symposium on Cluster, Cloud and Internet Computing Workshops (CCGridW), p. 10. Available from https://www.computer.org/csdl/proceedings/ccgridw/2023/1OUmVoAlwru, accessed 1 November 2023.

209 Renee Dudley and Daniel Golden, "The Colonial Pipeline Ransomware Hackers Had a Secret Weapon: Self-Promoting Cybersecurity Firms" (May 24, 2021), Propublica/MIT Technology Review, pp. 7–8, https://energyrights.info/sites/default/files/artifacts/media/pdf/the_colonial_pipeline_ransomware_hackers_had_a_secret_weapon_self-promoting_cybersecurity_firms_-_propublica.pdf, accessed 31 July 2023.

210 Anonymous, "US fuel pipeline hackers 'didn't mean to create problems'" (May 10, 2021), https://www.bbc.co.uk/news/business-57050690, accessed 31 July 2023. Collin Eaton and Dustin Volz, "Colonial Pipeline CEO Tells Why He Paid Hackers a $4.4 Million Ransom. Joseph Blount says he needed to quickly restore service after cyberattack threatened East Coast supply" (May 19, 2021), https://www.wsj.com/articles/colonial-pipeline-ceo-tells-why-he-paid-hackers-a-4-4-million-ransom-11621435636?mod=breakingnews, accessed 31 July 2023.

Their entry point was suspected to be a Virtual Private Network (VPN) linked to a dormant user account (potentially a previous employee). With no multi-factor authentication (MFA) in place, all that was needed was the password and username. When they cracked this, the VPN gave "DarkSide" access to Colonial Pipeline's network.[211] "DarkSide" penetrated the IT network and did not appear to migrate to the more critical Operation Technology (OT) network.[212] Colonial Pipeline may have taken preventive measures when they learned of the attack but did not do so not ahead of time, meaning they might also have got lucky.[213]

As detailed in *Cyberwarfare: Threats to Critical Infrastructure*, migration to the OT network would have been much more serious. This controls, monitors, and displays pressures, flow rates, leaks as well as a whole host of other safety critical features. Accessing the OT network could have led to "DarkSide" being able to override safety shutdown features, sabotaging key systems, potentially causing oil spills, fires, and explosions. Malware called Triton/Trisis was already available which could have caused these effects with a little development and the Department of Justice had indicted a GRU officer for a previous attack using this malware.[214]

Aside from the immediate and cascading economic and motoring impacts, the U.S. government likely saw the broader danger signs.[215] Immediately a wide series of government agencies were involved in mitigations. This included the Department of Energy.[216] In the aftermath the Cybersecurity and Infrastructure Security Agency (CISA) founded two new bodies. A Joint Ransomware Task Force (JRTF) was set up with the FBI alongside a Joint Cyber Defense Collaborative (JCDC) which brought together a standing community of public and private cybersecurity sector expertise. CISA also created the website stopransomware.gov.[217] These were all positive remedial actions but the Colonial Pipeline case calls into question a number of issues:

211 The attack was preventable with MFA and more stringent cybersecurity hygiene.

212 Beerman et al., "A Review of Colonial Pipeline Ransomware Attack," p. 8.

213 Anonymous, "US fuel pipeline hackers 'didn't mean to create problems.'"

214 Stoddart, *Cyberwarfare*, pp. 4, 14, 20–22, 106, 147–148, 160–161, 167, 194, 234, 237, 244, 259, 317–318.

215 Paul W. Parfomak and Chris Jaikaran, Colonial Pipeline: The DarkSide Strikes, https://crsreports.congress.gov/product/pdf/IN/IN11667, accessed 3 August 2023.

216 Colonial Pipeline Cyber Incident, https://www.energy.gov/ceser/colonial-pipeline-cyber-incident, accessed 31 July 2023.

217 The Attack on Colonial Pipeline: What We've Learned & What We've Done Over the Past Two Years (May 7, 2023), https://www.cisa.gov/news-events/news/attack-colonial-pipeline-what-weve-learned-what-weve-done-over-past-two-years, accessed 30 July 2023.

- To what extent was their federal regulator sufficiently aware of cybersecurity threats facing private owner-operators like Colonial Pipeline?
- Was there a failure in the Information Sharing and Analysis Center (ISAC), which is designed to promote cooperation and intelligence-information sharing between the federal government and private sector owner-operators of critical infrastructure?[218]
- Should federal government and state government agencies become more directly engaged with private industry and the networks that control critical infrastructure?[219]

The attack had major socio-political implications but "DarkSide" claimed "We do not participate in geopolitics, [*sic*] do not need to tie us with a defined government."[220] Despite this disclaimer, they have acted as cover or as a proxy for affiliates which could plausibly include the SVR/GRU and their hacking units.[221] "DarkSide" are one of a number of cybercrime groups to offer ransomware-as-a-service (RaaS) and more broadly paying ransomware incentivizes cybercriminals.[222] They could also be an incentive to Russian intelligence, a useful proxy, and a weapon against economic and other sanctions levied on Russia. Before they disappeared, "DarkSide" and their affiliates had pocketed at least $90 million from running RaaS operations. This included two companies in the energy industry who paid ransoms of between $1.25 million and $6 million. "DarkSide" could also not be trusted not to leak or pass on ransomed data, regardless of whether the ransom was paid or not.[223] As the Colonial Pipeline attack happened, another potentially more significant case was breaking.

---

218 These did not get a mention in Blount's testimony to the U.S. Senate. Hearing before the United States Senate Committee on Homeland Security & Governmental Affairs, June 8 2021, Testimony of Joseph Blount, President and Chief Executive Officer Colonial Pipeline Company, https://www.hsgac.senate.gov/wp-content/uploads/imo/media/doc/Testimony-Blount-2021-06-08.pdf, accessed 31 July 2023.
219 The ISAC system is covered in Stoddart, *Cyberwarfare*, pp. xxvi, 323, 327.
220 "US fuel pipeline hackers 'didn't mean to create problems.'"
221 Beerman et al., "A Review of Colonial Pipeline Ransomware Attack," pp. 10–11.
222 "DarkSide" advertised their services on the "Dark Net," where they also describe their victims and release stolen data if companies refuse to pay. This can affect stock market prices and can be used to profit by short-sellers. Dudley and Golden, "The Colonial Pipeline Ransomware Hackers Had a Secret Weapon," pp. 7–8.
223 Cyber insurers would sometimes act as intermediaries. Dudley and Golden, "The Colonial Pipeline Ransomware Hackers," pp. 8–9.

4.10 SolarWinds

In September 2019 APT29/"Fancy Bear" began a cyberespionage campaign that hit at least nine U.S. government agencies and around one hundred private-sector organizations. The campaign was an upstream supply chain attack on a hitherto little-known network management company called SolarWinds based in Austin, Texas. Its software is widely used on U.S. federal government and private industry systems to monitor network activity. They first compromised SolarWinds through the VPN of an employee in late January 2019. This gave them beachhead access to SolarWinds' network. After this first breach, they remained dormant for over two months. Then in February malicious code was inserted into a suite of SolarWinds products called Orion – a monitoring and management software platform designed to simplify ICT administration at-scale.[224] This trojanized code was also inserted into a library file (.dll) subsequently included in one of the periodic updates to Orion. This code was a RAT which gave the SVR a backdoor into the networks and systems of SolarWinds' clients, with more than one backdoor created. Almost 18,000 clients received the update, from a total client base of 33,000.[225]

Recognizing its value for espionage, APT29 then targeted high-value customers. This included federal government agencies. Through the undiscovered RAT, this led them to breach Microsoft cloud platforms. This gave them increased network access, including access to unclassified systems of the federal government.[226] Over the summer and fall of 2020, SolarWinds was contacted by the U.S. Justice Department who had discovered rogue traffic in their network and were trying to figure out how their systems had been compromised. They were not alone. The Department of Defense, Department of Homeland Security, and U.S. Treasury had also unknowingly been compromised. So too had some of America's leading technology and cybersecurity companies, including Intel, Cisco, and Palo Alto Networks. FireEye, which would be called in by SolarWinds to help, was also on the list.[227]

---

224 SolarWinds Orion Platform Features, https://www.solarwinds.com/orion-platform/use-cases, accessed 30 July 2023.

225 SolarWinds Cyberattack Demands Significant Federal and Private-Sector Response (infographic), April 22, 2021, https://www.gao.gov/blog/solarwinds-cyberattack-demands-significant-federal-and-private-sector-response-infographic. Kim Zetter, "The Untold Story of the Boldest Supply-Chain Hack Ever" (May 2, 2023), https://www.wired.com/story/the-untold-story-of-solarwinds-the-boldest-supply-chain-hack-ever/. Both accessed 30 July 2023.

226 GAO, SolarWinds Cyberattack.

227 It later transpired that the FBI had come close to detecting what was happening in spring 2020 and had passed on information that rogue traffic had been discovered which was traced back to SolarWinds. Zetter, "The Untold Story of the Boldest Supply-Chain Hack Ever."

FireEye had never before seen a serious breach of its own systems. Its founder and CEO, Kevin Mandia, was informed on November 20 and soon after began reaching out to the National Security Agency and other government agencies. His colleague, Charles Carmakal, simultaneously approached former FireEye employees now working for Microsoft. As a key global cybersecurity provider, FireEye held intelligence of much value to the SVR. The hunter had suddenly become the hunted. This was described by Microsoft's head of Threat Intelligence as a "holy shit" realization.[228] From November to December, FireEye (now Mandiant) was called in to investigate the compromise at SolarWinds and on December 12/13, 2020 gave their technical analysis. It was only then that SolarWinds notified government authorities.[229]

Microsoft and CISA immediately responded. Alongside other industry partners, they managed to prevent APT29 from gaining further network access. CISA issued an emergency directive to mitigate the threat and deployed a software tool called Sparrow which detects malicious activity in Microsoft Azure/Office 365 cloud services. APT29's campaign was so serious, any federal systems that had installed the Orion update had to be disconnected or powered down.[230] This was both challenging and highly complex. In addition, CISA was asking affected U.S. government agencies if any COVID vaccine research labs were among the victims. Foreign governments were also asking whether this affected them, as were critical infrastructure owner-operators.[231]

APT29 had employed exceptional technical skill and tradecraft to cover their tracks, including searching compromised e-mail accounts for indications they had been discovered whilst wiping logs that could have given them away. Characterized by Carmakal as a "top-tier adversary," remediation meant sifting through Orion's 18,000 files containing 14 gigabytes of code and data as well as discovering and reanalyzing APT29's methods and new server locations.[232]

This chain of events led the National Security Council to activate the Cyber Unified Coordination Group (UCG). This is an inter-agency group including officials from the Office of the Director of National Intelligence, FBI, and CISA, supported

228 Zetter, "The Untold Story of the Boldest Supply-Chain Hack Ever."
229 GAO, SolarWinds Cyberattack.
230 GAO, SolarWinds Cyberattack. On why accessing Azure is important see M-Trends 2023, pp. 78–85.
231 SolarWinds had over 320,000 customers in 190 countries, including 499 of the Fortune 500. The SolarWinds Cyberattack: Key Takeaways, January 29, 2021, https://www.rpc.senate.gov/policy-papers/the-solarwinds-cyberattack, accessed 31 July 2023. Zetter, "The Untold Story of the Boldest Supply-Chain Hack Ever."
232 Zetter, "The Untold Story of the Boldest Supply-Chain Hack Ever."

by the NSA and is responsible for coordinating government-wide cyber responses. The UCG publicly pointed the finger at Russia in early January. On April 15, 2021, the NSA, CISA, and the FBI jointly confirmed the SVR was responsible. Mitigations through software patching were ongoing as late as April 2021.[233] By this time SolarWinds had also called in a law firm, DLA Piper, to oversee their internal investigation as well as CrowdStrike for further technical analysis and support. This was all during the COVID-19 pandemic crossing from the Trump administration to the transition and early presidency of Joe Biden. In this critical period the SVR/APT29 had lain undetected for eight months.[234]

Congress subsequently convened multiple hearings worried not only by the campaign itself, but by the risks associated with supply chain attacks; especially on government contractors.[235] The Senate's main intelligence committee also held emergency hearings. It is still not known what was stolen and neither House has a complete picture of the full impact, except perhaps in classified settings. What is known is that the campaign was premeditated, carefully planned and actioned, and extremely complex with malware and techniques that had never been encountered before.[236] It was also extremely costly. Aside from the intelligence losses, the Senate estimated remedial actions could cost up to $100 billion. They were also concerned as time went on "whether there may be more sinister objectives in addition to espionage, such as inserting backdoor access into key government agencies, major IT and cybersecurity companies, critical infrastructure like the electric grid, and nuclear storage facilities."[237] One U.S. government official remarked, "The speed with which an actor can move from espionage to degrading or disrupting a network is at the blink of an eye, and a defender cannot move at that speed."[238]

The SolarWinds attack was serious enough for the Biden administration to impose financial sanctions and diplomatic expulsions on Russia. What appeared

233 GAO, SolarWinds Cyberattack.

234 Zetter, "The Untold Story of the Boldest Supply-Chain Hack Ever."

235 S.Hrg. 117–478 – Understand and Responding to the SolarWinds Supply Chain Attack: The Federal Perspective 117th Congress (2021–2022), March 18, 2021, May 11, 2021, https://www.congress.gov/event/117th-congress/senate-event/329328/text, accessed 31 July 2023.

236 Zetter, "The Untold Story of the Boldest Supply-Chain Hack Ever."

237 The SolarWinds Cyberattack: Key Takeaways.

238 Dustin Volz, "In Punishing Russia for SolarWinds, Biden Upends U.S. Convention on Cyber Espionage," *Wall Street Journal* (April 19, 2021), https://www.wsj.com/articles/in-punishing-russia-for-solarwinds-biden-upends-u-s-convention-on-cyber-espionage-11618651800, accessed 30 July 2023.

most concerning was the scale of the campaign.[239] This went beyond previously accepted cyberespionage boundaries further raising the prospect of cyberespionage attacks turning from intelligence exfiltration to destruction. In going public the Biden administration had high confidence from the USIC that the SVR was behind the campaign.[240]

The defender, in this case SolarWinds, has been accused of lax security practices but in APT29 they had a tier-1 adversary who with subtle and difficult to detect alternations to a small part of the codebase library of Orion managed to infiltrate multiple government departments and global companies, including one of the best-in-class cybersecurity firms in FireEye. APT29 was stealthy. They lay dormant after the first compromise in late January 2019 where they had gained a foothold into SolarWinds' network. Their hackers then returned in March, before going dark again for six months. During that time, they were developing expertise on Orion's source code. They also tested whether alternations would be detected through a benign code injection prior to the full attack. APT29 were also identified in attacks on cloud servers in 2022 directed at members of NATO.[241]

5 Enduring unease

There remain lingering concerns that even after a "brain drain" from Russia resulting from the Ukraine War, the SVR and GRU (as well as the FSB) might still be finding other ways and means to compromise other key providers through indirect supply chain attacks.[242] More widely, a 2023 report indicated a 742 percent increase in supply chain attacks from 2020 to 2023.[243] The cyberespionage/cyberwarfare dangers posed by Russia were also highlighted by the Vulkan leaks of March 2023. NTC Vulkan, a Moscow-based cybersecurity company with contracts with Russia's military and intelligence agencies is one of a wide number of private firms with government contracts.

239 Marcus Willett, "Lessons of the SolarWinds Hack, *Survival*, Vol. 63, No. 2 (April–May 2021), pp. 7–26.

240 Volz, "In Punishing Russia for SolarWinds."

241 Mike Harbison and Peter Renals, "Russian APT29 Hackers Use Online Storage Services, DropBox and Google Drive" (July 19, 2022), https://unit42.paloaltonetworks.com/cloaked-ursa-online-storage-services-campaigns/, accessed 24 October 2024.

242 Zetter, "The Untold Story of the Boldest Supply-Chain Hack Ever."

243 8th Annual State of the Software Supply Chain Sonatype's industry-defining research on the rapidly changing landscape of open source (2023), https://www.sonatype.com/resources/2023-software-supply-chain-report, accessed 30 July 2023.

The leaks showed plans, operations, and links between Russian intelligence and sub-contractors from 2016 to 2021.[244] What they also appear to show is connections between Russia's military (and the military research institutes described in Chapter 1), as well as the MVD in projects which were useful for domestic surveillance.[245] They also revealed that Vulkan was contracted by the SVR, through Military Unit 33949, to work on multiple projects.[246] Separately, an April 2023 report also indicates that Russian "patriot hackers" might have penetrated a Canadian gas distribution firm and could have the ability to control valve pressure, cause explosions, disable alarms, and even begin emergency shut-down of procedures. It is believed that although they may be receiving instructions from the FSB, they were working in tandem with the GRU and SVR (and this involvement cannot be ruled out).[247] Although Russia's intelligence agencies are known to compete, since the Ukraine War they have also coordinated.[248] In the Ukraine War APT28 has been the lead Russian threat actor.[249]

However, Mandiant's 2023 M-Trends Report indicated how the Ukraine War was leaving Russian affiliated cybercriminals to either choose sides or shut down their operations altogether. This has seen Ukrainian, and Ukrainian-supporting cybercrime gangs operating in Russia and Eastern Europe, split down politico-nationalist lines. The war has also sparked a revival of hacktivism as well as the use of false hacktivist personas by the GRU (trumpeted by Russian state media not as cover operations but examples of patriotism). Throughout the war Russia has continued to target Ukrainian critical infrastructure through cyberattacks and air-delivered weapons and since the invasion Ukraine has become the primary

---

244 Luke Harding, Stiliyana Simeonova, Manisha Ganguly, and Dan Sabbagh, "'Vulkan files' leak reveals Putin's global and domestic cyberwarfare tactics" (March 30, 2023), https://www.theguardian.com/technology/2023/mar/30/vulkan-files-leak-reveals-putins-global-and-domestic-cyberwarfare-tactics, accessed 15 July 2023.

245 In the Soviet Union, the KGB was also tasked with monitoring their own military who viewed the KGB with suspicion from the time of Stalin's purges. Robert W. Pringle, "SMERSH: Military Counterintelligence and Stalin's Control of the USSR," *International Journal of Intelligence and CounterIntelligence*, Vol. 21, Issue 1 (January 2008), pp. 122–134. Until the Putin era, "Russia's army and its secret police did not just hate each other; they viewed the world through different lenses." Andrei Soldatov, "Cyberwarfare leaks show Russian army is adopting mindset of secret police" (March 30, 2023), https://www.theguardian.com/technology/2023/mar/30/cyberwarfare-leaks-show-russian-army-is-adopting-mindset-of-secret-police, accessed 15 July 2023.

246 Harding et al., "'Vulkan files' leak."

247 Kim Zetter, "Leaked Pentagon Document Claims Russian Hacktivists Breached Canadian Gas Pipeline Company" (April 9, 2023), https://zetter.substack.com/p/leaked-pentagon-document-claims-russian, accessed 30 July 2023.

248 M-Trends 2023, p. 61.

249 M-Trends 2023, p. 56.

focus of Russian cyberattacks.[250] Even if or when a peaceful resolution emerges, the above cases should provide ample warning of Russian capabilities and intent. In addition, Russia appears to have engaged in severing undersea cables (as well as being accused of sabotaging the Nord Stream pipeline). Not only do these telecommunication cables form part of the backbone infrastructure, they are part of the Sea Lines of Communication (SLOC) and could be subject to compromise.[251] Their cyberespionage campaigns into CI are also ongoing. This includes a threat actor first identified in April 2022 which Dragos has termed Chernovite. This is fielding potentially destructive modular malware called Pipedream which is directed at ICS.[252]

Media and industry reports and industry insiders have long been warning of the dangers.[253] There is an awareness that Russian state hackers potentially have the foothold needed to manipulate or shut down power plants.[254] What appears to be missing is political motivation.[255] These campaigns could be reconnaissance for a future attack and not just industrial espionage. This might have been the assumption back in 2013 "given the importance of Russia's oil and gas industry" but after two years spent analyzing the first "Dragonfly" campaign Russian hackers had been tied "to hundreds of attacks on energy grid and oil and gas pipeline operators in the United States and Europe."[256] In December 2017 when Triton was

250 M-Trends 2023, Introduction, pp. 4, 6–12, 53–64.

251 Bradford Dismukes, "The Return of Great-Power Competition—Cold War Lessons about Strategic Antisubmarine Warfare and Defense of Sea Lines of Strategic Antisubmarine Warfare and Defense of Sea Lines of Communication," *Naval War College Review*, Vol. 73, No. 3 (Summer 2020), pp. 1–27. Douglas Guilfoyle, Tamsin Phillipa Paige, and Rob McLaughlin, "The Final Frontier of Cyberspace: The Seabed Beyond National Jurisdiction and the Protection of Submarine Cables," *International & Comparative Law Quarterly*, Vol. 71, Issue 3 (July 2022), pp. 657–696.

252 "PIPEDREAM Malware and the CHERNOVITE Threat Group Dragos Intelligence Briefing" (April 26, 2022), https://hub.dragos.com/on-demand/pipedream-malware-chernovite-activity-group, "Tool: PIPEDREAM", https://apt.etda.or.th/cgi-bin/listgroups.cgi?t=PIPEDREAM. Both accessed 11 May 2025.

253 Alert (TA18–074 A) March 15, 2018.

254 Nicole Perlroth and David E. Sanger, "Cyberattacks Put Russian Fingers on the Switch at Power Plants, U.S. Says," *New York Times*, March 15, 2018, https://www.nytimes.com/2018/03/15/us/politics/russia-cyberattacks.html.

255 Perlroth and Sanger, "Cyberattacks Put Russian Fingers on the Switch at Power Plants, U.S. Says."

256 Perlroth and Sanger, "Cyberattacks Put Russian Fingers on the Switch at Power Plants, U.S. Says." Ciaran Martin, "'Cyber security: fixing the present so we can worry about the future'. An address to the Times Tech Summit" (November 15, 2017), https://www.ncsc.gov.uk/news/cyber-security-fixing-present-so-we-can-worry-about-future, accessed on 17 November 2017. Alexander J. Martin, "'Russia government hackers attacking critical national infrastructure in UK and US'"

discovered researchers pointed out this attacked "the last line of automated safety defense for industrial facilities, designed to prevent equipment failure and catastrophic incidents such as explosions or fire."[257] Triton was "specifically traced … to Russia's Central Scientific Research Institute of Chemistry and Mechanics, located in the Nagatino-Sadvoniki district of Moscow."[258]

6 Cyberwar: Russian critical infrastructure vulnerabilities

Russian officials involved with critical infrastructure are concerned about escalating an offensive cyber "shooting match." Alarms are regularly raised "But only after there's some real major catastrophe" but also operatives do not always recognize when they see a problem.[259] Instead, they believe that cyber security breaches, including on air-gapped critical infrastructure systems, are usually criminal attempts at extortion.[260]

To compound matters, years of under-investment have led to what industry insiders describe as "the retro world of the Russian power grid."[261] It is reported that the power generation and distribution sector (the most important of all sectors of critical infrastructure because it affects all others) is tremendously inefficient. It is a legacy of Soviet-era central planning and in need of at least $750 billion of investment and modernization. This could take two decades or more. It has changed little since it was first laid down in the 1950s and 1960s. Decades old legacy wiring is still prevalent. Most Russian cities continued to be served by district

---

(April 16, 2019), https://news.sky.com/story/russia-government-hackers-attacking-critical-national-infrastructure-in-uk-and-us-11334028, accessed 28 September 2019.

257 Andrea Carcano, "Black Hat: Understanding TRITON, The First SIS Cyber Attack" (August 8, 2018), https://www.nozominetworks.com/2018/08/08/blog/black-hat-understanding-triton-the-first-sis-cyber-attack/. Blake Johnson, Dan Caban, Marina Krotofil, Dan Scali, Nathan Brubaker, and Christopher Glyer, "Attackers Deploy New ICS Attack Framework 'TRITON' and Cause Operational Disruption to Critical Infrastructure" (December 14, 2017), https://www.fireeye.com/blog/threat-research/2017/12/attackers-deploy-new-ics-attack-framework-triton.html. Both accessed 10 January 2019.

258 Lili Hay Newman, "Russia Linked to Disruptive Industrial Control Malware" (October 23, 2018), https://www.wired.com/story/triton-malware-russia-industrial-controls/, accessed 10 January 2019.

259 Sasha Baranovskaya, "Moscow's cyber-defense How the Russian government plans to protect the country from the coming cyberwar" (July 19, 2017), https://meduza.io/en/feature/2017/07/19/moscow-s-cyber-defense, accessed 28 December 2017.

260 Baranovskaya, "Moscow's cyber-defense."

261 David Ferris, "Russia's power grid, held together with spit and grit" (December 18, 2014), https://www.eenews.net/stories/1060010742, accessed 28 February 2020.

systems and around 60 percent of CI is owned and operated by the state alongside most of the electricity transmission infrastructure. During the late 1990s and early 2000s, electrical demand increased during waves of economic boom and bust cycles. This included plug loads from domestic consumer products like televisions and refrigerators. It also increased in ways Soviet planners never anticipated including new restaurants, shopping centers, theaters, and illuminated signage.

This leads to a seesaw of demand that the power distribution grid cannot cope well with. These problems affect Russia's major cities less because they have had money and resources poured into them. These have been upgraded with modern digital switching systems and other pieces of equipment. This includes Moscow and St. Petersburg. Smaller cities, let alone outlying towns and villages or the more remote areas of central Russia with vast and sparsely populated areas, are a relic of the 1960s and 1970s. Russian power plants and transmission lines, visible on Google Earth, clearly indicate the scale of the problems. Moreover, most transmission lines were installed inefficiently. Instead of moving West and East, they instead prioritized the Western, NATO-facing half of the country, stretching down into Kazakhstan and the Caucasus. This means remote areas such as Siberia and the far East, home to 20 million people, are unconnected to the nationwide power grid. These areas often rely on diesel generators with the fuel having to be driven in on trucks, shipped by boat, or flow in by helicopter. Into the mid-2010s, electrical operators were still using paper maps and marker pens to track developments on the electrical grid and telephone calls made to place orders for electricity supplies.[262]

Moreover, climate change notwithstanding, repairs and upgrades can only take place in these vast and often inhospitable areas during the summer months of May to October. Operations during the harsh Russian winters are much more difficult (including costly and labor intensive repairs). This means the priorities are to patch where needed to avoid potential blackouts, not to make improvements. Electrical blackouts would pose a threat to life to those but the most hardy and resourceful. 85 percent of the equipment Russia relies on is foreign, and overwhelmingly Western. This also means Russians need to be trained to install and maintain it by Western companies. This is one of the reasons why Russia has been trying to develop a version of the open-source Linux operating system (Astra Linux) in accelerating efforts since 2022. It is also trying to replace Western software and hardware and replace it with Russian technology as well as purchas-

262 Ferris, "Russia's power grid, held together with spit and grit."

ing Chinese-made systems.[263] This means that critical infrastructure is an area where economic sanctions have teeth. Prior to the major series of sanctions imposed after the invasion of Ukraine in February 2022, it was already expensive for Russian businesses to buy Western equipment given the relative decline in the ruble. Given that much of Russia's economy rests on its massive hydrocarbon base, economic and travel sanctions affect Russia's ability to maintain existing facilities and pipelines and restrict their ability to exploit new opportunities brought about by climate change and new methods of extraction. It also effects oil and gas prices and Russia's ability to trade these commodities has an outsized effect on the economy.

Since 2014, and sanctions imposed following the annexation of Crimea, China and Chinese firms began to step into the Russian market to fill the breach. Cheap oil and gas in Russia have also seen the Kremlin underinvest in renewable energy. However, this underinvestment is also driven in part by a lack of natural sunlight and freezing temperatures across large swathes of Russia (especially during the Russian winter).[264] Northern Russia has less sunlight throughout large parts of the year than parts of the south. Moreover, the best wind generation capacity is near the Arctic Circle. This is over a thousand miles away from Russia's major population centers concentrated in the west of the country.[265] These factors have meant sluggish and erratic investments in solar, wind, geothermal energy, and biofuels.[266]

Attacking the power grid would affect Russian civilians, especially in the Russian winter (potentially gravely).[267] As was suggested in *Cyberwarfare: Threats to Critical Infrastructure*, this would likely breach the Law of Armed Conflict which would influence the Rules of Engagement.[268] To partially address these issues and the "shoot back" abilities Russia faces, the FSB-run cybersecurity organizations, GosSOPKA and Gov-CERT, were established in 2015. Gov-CERT is intended as a perimeter defense against CI attacks and in November 2016 it was expanded to

---

263 Dave Aitel, Sophia d'Antoine, Thomas Garwin, Ian Roos, Nicholas Rostow, Justin Sherman, and Abraham Wagner, 'Russia's Cyber Operations A Threat to American National Security' (2022), pp. viii, 83–88, https://margin.re/content/files/2023/01/Russia-s-Cyber-Operations---Full-Report.pdf, accessed 7 August 2023.

264 Ferris, "Russia's power grid, held together with spit and grit."

265 Ferris, "Russia's power grid, held together with spit and grit." Ksenia Isaeva and Daria Gonzales, "How do Russians live without the sun for 40 days in a row?" (February 29, 2018), https://www.rbth.com/multimedia/pictures/2016/02/29/polar-night-40-days_571553, accessed 28 February 2020.

266 Ferris, "Russia's power grid, held together with spit and grit."

267 Ferris, "Russia's power grid, held together with spit and grit."

268 Stoddart, *Cyberwarfare*, pp. 53–78.

include ten state agencies. Response centers had already been established at Rostec (a state-controlled holding company specializing in defense and arms) and Russia's Central Bank, combined with data sharing between critical infrastructure owner-operators and the FSB.[269] In July 2016 Russia also established a cyber defense center at Rostec, which consolidated strategically important industries under Kremlin control. It reports to the FSB.[270] In 2018 a National Coordination Center for Computer Incidents (NKTsKI) was founded. This is said to have evolved from the KGB's Eighth Chief Directorate which was responsible for communications security and encryption. It is designed to better coordinate, protect, and mitigate cyberattacks in a similar way to America's Cybersecurity and Infrastructure Security Agency (CISA), which was also established in 2018.[271] This was a reactive response to a significant number of attacks. Former FSB Deputy Director Dmitry Shalkov told the State Duma that attacks included the financial services sector in November 2016 targeting, amongst others, Sberbank, Alfa-Bank, and the Bank of Moscow.[272] However, these were simple DDoS attacks, not a major threat. Far more threatening has been alleged intrusions into the Russian power grid by U.S. Cyber Command under National Security Presidential Memoranda 13 which gave USCYBERCOM increased autonomy to act.[273] If cyber operations were to be conducted offensively against Russian critical infrastructure this would certainly have major effects.

Instead, U.S. incursions into Russia's power grid have been used both as a deterrent and signaling tool.[274] In a similar vein, there has been no visible discussion

269 Nathan Hodge, "The 'Putin list': A Who's Who of Russia's political and business elite" (January 30, 2018), https://edition.cnn.com/2018/01/30/europe/putin-list-russia-oligarchs-intl/index.html, accessed 8 January 2019. Baranovskaya, "Moscow's cyber-defense."

270 Damien Sharkov, "Russian State Arms Contractor Launches Cyber Defence Center," (November 7, 2016), http://www.newsweek.com/russian-state-arms-contractor-launches-cyber-defence-center-517915, accessed 29 December 2017.

271 Kevin P. Riehle, *The Russian FSB* A concise history of the Federal Security Service (Washington DC: Georgetown University Press, 2024) pp. 48–51. Stoddart, *Cyberwarfare*, pp. 105–106.

272 Baranovskaya, "Moscow's cyber-defense."

273 Ivan Nechepurenko, "Kremlin Warns of Cyberwar After Report of U.S. Hacking Into Russian Power Grid" (June 17, 2019), https://www.nytimes.com/2019/06/17/world/europe/russia-us-cyberwar-grid.html; Matthew Choi, "Trump slams NYT report on U.S. cyberattacks against Russia" (June 15, 2019); https://www.politico.com/story/2019/06/15/trump-nyt-report-cyber-attacks-russia-1365852; Edward Moyer, "US Cyber Command powers up attacks against Russia's electrical grid" (June 15, 2019), https://www.cnet.com/news/us-cyber-command-powers-up-attacks-against-russias-electrical-grid/. All accessed 4 October 2019.

274 David E. Sanger and Nicole Perlroth, "U.S. Escalates Online Attacks on Russia's Power Grid" (June 15, 2019), https://www.nytimes.com/2019/06/15/us/politics/trump-cyber-russia-grid.html, accessed 30 September 2019.

by Western governments that they view Russian and Chinese pre-positioning in Western critical infrastructure as anything other than holding sectors (including electricity) "at risk." Exploration of issues arising from mutual or self-deterrence merits closer examination.[275] It has been pointed out that Russia has thought through the implications of a disruptive and potentially destructive cyberwar, and this is why it started making *defensive* preparations alongside its wide and deep *offensive* forays into critical infrastructure. This includes defending sites such as nuclear power plants, military factories, logistics, and supply systems that could cause environmental, financial, and social disruption or damage.[276] Attacks on critical infrastructure, especially in the energy sector, can be used strategically for politico-military effects. This includes attacks by Russia on critical infrastructure in former Soviet republics. This was tried in Ukraine as a precursor and adjunct to the invasion. This took a huge and coordinated effort between Western and Ukrainian agencies to blunt.[277] These activities in cyberspace also need to be set in the broader context of domestic politics, foreign and defense policies, and the means and aims of the Russian Federation.[278]

7 Common Tactics, Techniques and Procedures (TTPs) and responses

Governments across the developing world are becoming increasingly aware of the kinds of cyber activities emanating out of Russia backed by detailed analysis from cybersecurity professionals in the private sector. For Europe and the United States,

---

275 Adam Segal, "China and the Power Grid: Hacking and Getting Hacked" (December 3, 2014), https://www.cfr.org/blog/china-and-power-grid-hacking-and-getting-hacked; Joe Cheravitch, "Cyber Threats from the U.S. and Russia Are Now Focusing on Civilian Infrastructure" (July 23, 2019), https://www.rand.org/blog/2019/07/cyber-threats-from-the-us-and-russia-are-now-focusing.html. Both accessed 28 February 2020. Brandon Valeriano, Benjamin Jensen, and Ryan C. Maness, *Cyber Strategy: The Evolving Character of Power and Coercion* (New York: Oxford University Press, 2018). Alex Wilner, "Cyber Deterrence and Critical-Infrastructure Protection: Expectation, Application, and Limitation," *Comparative Strategy*, Vol. 36, No. 4 (November 2017), pp. 309–318.

276 Daniil Turovsky, "Moscow's cyber-defense. How the Russian government plans to protect the country from the coming cyberwar" (July 19, 2017), https://meduza.io/en/feature/2017/07/19/moscow-s-cyber-defense, accessed 8 January 2019.

277 Stoddart, *Cyberwarfare*, pp. 189–198.

278 This includes the occupation of the Zaporizhzhia nuclear power plant. This turned it "into a tool for coercion" through placing it at risk and turning it into a base of military operations. Ali Alkis and Bethany Goldblum, "Lessons from Zaporizhzhia: How to protect reactors against 'nuclear piracy'" (September 20, 2023), https://thebulletin.org/2023/09/lessons-from-zaporizhzhia-how-to-protect-reactors-against-nuclear-piracy/, accessed 15 November 2023.

Russian attacks especially aimed at the energy and water utilities sectors of CI are a genuine cause of concern. The targeted reconnaissance they are engaging in begins with attempts to compromise the IT side of business networks. This helps them map corporate structures and computer networks and identify key individuals and nodes for current or future exploitation. In the initial reconnaissance phase "social engineering" (SE) and other elements of HUMINT are used to identify and exploit their targets; often beginning with simple phishing or spear-phishing campaigns. These can leverage HUMINT and the clandestine practices of Russia's intelligence services using widespread SE methods. This also include the use and utilization of SOCMINT in common with other state and non- or sub-state actors like criminals and terrorists.[279] This is used to aid technical means of infiltration and exploitation.

Migration across to Operational Technology (OT) networks which run ICS and SCADA is both much more complicated and more threatening. Both the front (Internet) facing IT corporate networks and the access privileged world of OT means that inroads can be found and exploited for espionage or sabotage. Causing a blackout has not been seen outside of Ukraine nor one over an extended period. We have not (yet) seen Russia triggering an explosion or breaching a dam. Outside of Ukraine, we are seeing non-damaging (but highly costly and disruptive) persistent and long-term campaigns of operations. These have been ongoing since the early mid-1990s with Moonlight Maze.

Gaining digital access to targets often requires time, as does developing a capability that can have a tailored effect on the target. Nations like Russia that desire bespoke offensive capabilities, therefore, often need to launch their intrusions early.[280] Attribution had been problematic from a technical standpoint as well as politically, but as computer forensics has advanced, attribution has increased (although "false flags" can still be generated). If or when cyber intrusions are detected, immediate costs are incurred in terms of remedial action. This includes the immediate attention of the in-house IT department or buying in expertise from an external contractor.[281] This might also involve notifying law enforcement or central government. However, it is widely recognized that many private compa-

---

279 Sir David Omand, Jamie Bartlett, and Carl Miller, "Introducing Social Media Intelligence (SOCMINT)," *Intelligence and National Security*, Vol. 27, Issue 6 (December 2012), pp. 801–823.
280 Buchanan and Sulmeyer, "Russia and Cyber Operations," p. 3.
281 This can also lead them to identify a need to upgrade software or hardware or employ hard to find cybersecurity specialists. Whilst there are financial costs attached to this, this is designed to improve security and prevent or mitigate future breaches and could instead lead to cost savings over the medium to long term.

nies will not report breaches for fear of reputational harm and the potential damage this can do for business confidence and stock prices.[282]

More fundamentally, Russia's actions are undermining the Rule of Law because of a *modus vivendi* between cybercrime and the state leading to "no risks or repercussions to hacking companies in the West," with attackers finding safe harbor in countries without extradition treaties with the U.S., such as Russia, North Korea, and Iran. This means that "'Until we can impose some risk, some deterrence, these intrusions are here to stay.'"[283] "Naming and shaming," sanctions, travel bans, and placing suspected Russian cybercriminals and intelligence operatives under national and international arrest warrants has been fairly ineffective against Russian cyberespionage. However, the use of offensive cyber against Russia as a future deterrent might be provocative and escalatory.

8 Conclusion

Cyberwarfare is no longer only a theoretical construct. "Cyberwar Will Not Take Place" declared Thomas Rid in 2013. For Rid what we were witnessing was orchestrated strategic campaigns of cyberespionage, disinformation, and non-violent sabotage. Rid suggested these were decreasing risk and the resort to armed force with the catastrophic uses of cyber against critical infrastructure a fiction.[284] This chapter has shown that by attacking critical infrastructure through the means and methods described above, cyberwarfare is no fiction and is crossing the threshold into attacks that could qualify as armed force. Ukraine has been Russia's laboratory and battlefield. Whilst "The nightmare of cyberattacks crippling critical infrastructure systems still has the sound of science fiction to most Americans ... in Ukraine, this nightmare is real."[285] The Colonial Pipeline and Solar-

282 Detailed analysis of these issues can be found in "The Economic Impact of Cybercrime and Cyber Espionage," Center for Strategic and International Studies/McAfee, July 2013, https://www.csis.org/analysis/economic-impact-cybercrime-and-cyber-espionage, accessed 31 March 2020. In the European Union, the General Data Protection Regulation (GDPR) and Network and Information Security Directive (NIS Directive) are purposely designed to legally mandate intrusion and breach reporting and the raising of cybersecurity standards for critical infrastructure protection.

283 Robert Hackett and Anna Teregulova, "FireEye CEO: Businesses Are 'Getting Sucker Punched' in Cyberspace" (March 22, 2017), http://fortune.com/2017/03/22/fireeye-ceo-kevin-mandia-cyber-attack/, accessed December 2 2017.

284 Rid, *Cyber War Will Not Take Place*, pp. xiv and 3–4.

285 Alina Polyakova, "The next Russian attack will be far worse than bots and trolls" (March 22, 2018), https://www.brookings.edu/blog/order-from-chaos/2018/03/22/the-next-russian-attack-will-be-far-worse-than-bots-and-trolls/amp/, accessed 30 September 2019.

Winds cybercrime and cyberespionage cases portend to this potential as do Russian efforts at defending their vulnerable sectors and sites.[286] In late 2024, Britain's National Cyber Security Centre's annual review warned of ongoing attempts at cyber-kinetic attacks on CI.[287]

Even financially motivated cybercrime from Russia, arguably a form of cyber-enabled economic warfare, is undermining companies, industries, and national economies.[288] These attacks have turned into long-term systematic campaigns. Additionally, in the "gray zone" between war and peace, cyberespionage has shown that critical infrastructure is not a taboo target during peacetime and Russia, and many other nations before them, have shown it is certainly a wartime target. Russia's cyberespionage campaigns have not crossed the threshold into destructive cyberwarfare, but they are indicators of geopolitical and socioeconomic conflict. What cyberespionage has developed is "the capability to remotely access and disrupt … control systems in the event of hostilities. Thus, it is possible that the Kremlin is adopting a hold-at-risk approach against U.S. and allied critical civilian infrastructure in order to influence perceived adversaries and deter unwelcome behavior."[289] This might be a form of deterrence but, as in other politico-military domains, it is both a shield and a sword that adds to the security dilemma.

Attacks against power grids in particular are a demonstration of capability and a show of force. They are also being used for intimidation, gauging responses, and signaling. Attacks on electrical supplies are built on recognition that electrical energy is fundamental to the functioning of society and economies. The success of, and responses to these campaigns, will set the tone for the Russian attacks in the future. Russia is continuing to actively access the business networks of major energy companies, including in the nuclear industry. Furthermore, offensive cyber weapons being used against the West's energy sector are based on those tested against the Ukraine – a non-NATO member.[290] James Clapper, when Director of National Intelligence, said "in the event of a military conflict or geo-political crisis

---

286 Stoddart, *Cyberwarfare*, pp. 189–198. M-Trends 2023, pp. 53–64.

287 As well as "malicious activity targeting UK institutions and individuals, including Parliamentarians." National Cyber Security Centre, Annual Review 2024, pp. 25–26, 63. This is said to be the work of the FSB's Center 18. Oscar Rosengren, "The FSB: Russia's Federal Security Service" (October 9 2024), https://greydynamics.com/the-fsb-russias-federal-security-service/, accessed 22 August 2025.

288 Vedral, "The Vulnerability of the Financial System to a Systemic Cyberattack," p. 96.

289 Connell and Vogler, "Russia's Approach to Cyber Warfare," p. 28.

290 Ellen Nakashima, "Russia has developed a cyberweapon that can disrupt power grids, according to new research" (June 12, 2017), https://www.washingtonpost.com/world/national-security/russia-has-developed-a-cyber-weapon-that-can-disrupt-power-grids-according-to-new-research/2017/06/11/b91b773e-4eed-11e7-91eb-9611861a988f_story.html, accessed 7 September 2017.

with Russia, some U.S. critical infrastructure networks will be at risk."[291] To Congress he specifically named "critical infrastructures such as electric power grids, urban mass-transit systems, air-traffic control, and oil and gas distribution networks."[292] In addition, General Mark Dempsey, a former Chairman of the Joint Chiefs of Staff, has discussed "a Russian military doctrine known as Strategic Operations to Destroy Critical Infrastructure Targets (SODCIT)."[293]

SODCIT remains a closely guarded secret but it dates from at least 2014 and originated in publications by Russian military officials. Designed to update existing (essentially post-Cold War) concepts of military deep strikes, SODCIT includes cyber as an attack vector but extends beyond cyber operations. As a strategic doctrine, SODCIT is not designed only for war-fighting in a single scenario (e.g. Ukraine or against the United States). It is predicated on pre-nuclear/non-nuclear use and escalation control favorable to Russia. Its broad aims are to degrade or damage the military, economic, and political-administrative assets of an adversary. This also embraces civilian targets including electrical power generation and distribution sites, transport networks and hubs, ports, and civilian communications targets. SODCIT also includes industrial and administrative buildings, hydrocarbon facilities, and chemical sites. Military targets include intelligence, surveillance and reconnaissance sites as well as conventional and strategic nuclear forces. Further targets include troop formations, airfields, armaments depots, space-based assets, and communications nodes. All fall into detailed designated categories. SODCIT is also designed to affect the quality of life and lower civilian, military, and political morale. The psychological impact is intended to be more debilitating than the material damage and designed to undermine the will to fight or resist. It is also aimed at cascading these effects to supportive allies. SODCIT has a Western focus and is designed to be utilized in cross/multi-domain operations using all kinetic and non-kinetic (e.g. cyber) capabilities at Russia's disposal.[294]

---

291 Remarks as delivered by The Honorable James R. Clapper Director of National Intelligence "National Intelligence, North Korea, and the National Cyber Discussion" International Conference on Cyber Security Fordham University, January 7, 2015 https://www.dni.gov/index.php/newsroom/speeches-interviews/speeches-interviews-2015/item/1156-remarks-as-delivered-by-dni-james-r-clapper-on-national-intelligence-north-korea-and-the-national-cyber-discussion-at-the-international-conference-on-cyber-security, accessed 28 September 2019.

292 John P. Carlin, "Detect, Disrupt, Deter: A Whole-of-Government Approach to National Security Cyber Threats," *Harvard National Security Journal*, Vol. 7 (2016), p. 408, https://lawfare.s3-us-west-2.amazonaws.com/staging/2016/Carlin%20FINAL.pdf, accessed 28 September 2019.

293 Putin's Asymmetric Assault, p. 63.

294 Michael Kofman, Anya Fink, Dmitry Gorenburg, Mary Chesnut, Jeffrey Edmonds, and Julian Waller, "Russian Military Strategy: Core Tenets and Operational Concepts" (August 2021), Center

The cyberattacks attributed to the Russian government or actors connected to Russia span multiple sectors and targets have included successful penetrations of the business networks of companies in supply chains and industry giants. Even within governments and industries used to constant risk management and mitigation, and managing large budgets, they have not always been equipped to deal effectively with intrusions or data breaches. The last decade has convincingly proven that nation states or entities controlled by them are not shy to use cyberspace against other nation states. The threat in cyberspace is by no means a uniquely American issue. It is not specific to any nation or sector but rather reflects the motivation and capabilities of the adversaries.[295] Each of the cyber campaigns described in this chapter were attributed to Russia. For targets in former Soviet states and for many in the West, Russia is becoming the go-to suspect.

Russian APTs gain access through tried and trusted technical TTPs. After obtaining access, they conduct network reconnaissance, move laterally, gather, and then exfiltrate information. Thus far, against Industrial Control Systems and SCADA, outside of Ukraine's critical infrastructure attacks, they have stopped there. Should they actively go further or cause accidents by miscalculation or error this might elicit a response beyond just "naming and shaming," expulsions or sanctions. This could cross NATO's threshold, articulated in the Tallinn Manuals, constituting an armed attack. This would permit the law of self-defense to apply and, potentially, for Article 5 to be invoked.[296]

Western, and western-aligned governments have been proactively searching for deterrent strategies and mitigation means for government systems, their militaries, and for ways to support private industry who, in many cases, own and operate critical infrastructure facilities. These sets of important issues were among the key themes of *Cyberwarfare: Threats to Critical Infrastructure.*[297] To counter these campaigns large corporations, particularly in critical infrastructure sectors

---

for Naval Analysis, DRM-2021-U-029755-Final, pp. 68–71, https://www.cna.org/archive/CNA_Files/pdf/russian-military-strategy-core-tenets-and-operational-concepts.pdf. Dave Johnson, "Russia's Conventional Precision Strike Capabilities, Regional Crises, and Nuclear Thresholds", Livermore Papers on Global Security No. 3, Lawrence Livermore National Laboratory Center for Global Security Research February 2018, pp. 131, 35–36, 48, 52–55, 60, 71, 75, 81–87, 90, https://www.osti.gov/servlets/purl/1424635. Both accessed 4 August 2025. Riehle, *Russian Intelligence*, pp. 177–186.

295 P. W. Singer, Prepared Testimony and Statement for the Record at the hearing on "Cyber Warfare in the 21st Century: Threats, Challenges, and Opportunities" Before the House Armed Services Committee March 1, 2017, http://docs.house.gov/meetings/AS/AS00/20170301/105607/HHRG-115-AS00-Wstate-SingerP-20170301.pdf, accessed on 5 January 2018.

296 Schmitt (ed.), *Tallinn Manual 2.0*, pp. 25–26, 38–38, 126, 135–141, 342–354, 373–400.

297 Stoddart, *Cyberwarfare*, pp. 18, 25–27, 37, 47–48, 55, 60, 65, 68, 71–73, 76, 79, 83–86, 113, 122, 127–128, 144–146, 154, 199, 233, 304, 384, 390, 401–406, 423, 428.

such as financial services, have also been setting up their own monitoring, response, and information sharing mechanisms as well as finding opportunities for cross-sector and international information exchange and cooperation.

Holding Western critical infrastructure at-risk, alongside Russia's active measures of mis and disinformation campaigns to influence public and political opinion through to election interference all fit the controversial "Gerasimov doctrine" and notions of "hybrid warfare." Since 2016, Russia stands accused by the U.S. intelligence community of direct and sustained interference in the U.S. political process. Elsewhere, Russia also stands accused of attempting to influence a wide variety of elections and referenda, influencing the UK's Brexit vote and the political center of a large number of other target states all within the design that weakening the EU is likely to benefit Russia and indirectly dilute NATO's effectiveness.[298] To anyone that doubts Russia intervened, the two chapters that follow aim to dispel that doubt beginning with Britain's 2016 Brexit referendum.

---

298 Numbers vary but there are suggestions that at least 27 nations have experienced meddling by Russia in their political process. Oren Dorell, "Alleged Russian political meddling documented in 27 countries since 2004" (September 7, 2017), https://eu.usatoday.com/story/news/world/2017/09/07/alleged-russian-political-meddling-documented-27-countries-since-2004/619056001/, accessed 9 January 2019.

Chapter 3
Russian election interference: The UK and Brexit

1 Introduction

Russian election and foreign political interference through active measures campaigns has Cold War and pre-Cold War antecedents.[1] This includes targeting European elections campaigns.[2] This can be interpreted as a "wedge strategy" for "hybrid interference" that involves clandestine diplomacy, geoeconomics, and disinformation. However, for reasons set out throughout, it is referred to in this book not as "hybrid interference" but as a crucial aspect of Russia's hybrid warfare strategy against the West.[3] Under Vladimir Putin these campaigns have been resuscitated and reenergized. Since 2013 Russia has employed a wide variety of targeted cyberespionage campaigns and operations to divide and sow confusion in the West and to support individuals, political parties, and issues that align with Kremlin views. Britain has long been a target of Russian active measures and covert action stretching back to the Russian Revolution and into the Cold War.

Prior to the 2016 Brexit referendum, Russia supported the Scottish independence movement led by the Scottish National Party (SNP), and similar movements in regions including Catalonia, up until the SNP made it clear they would rejoin the European Union (EU). For Russia, these secessionist movements weakened Western Europe and provided a degree of moral equivalence and false legitimacy to the March 2014 annexation referendum in Crimea and demands for more autonomy by pro-Russian separatists in the regions of Donetsk and Luhansk.[4] So when Scotland voted to remain part of the UK in a September 2014 independence

---

1 Richard Norton-Taylor, "Zinoviev letter was dirty trick by MI6" (February 4, 1999), https://www.theguardian.com/politics/1999/feb/04/uk.politicalnews6, accessed 9 March 2020. Nor was this exclusive to Russia. Rhodri Jeffreys-Jones, *In Spies We Trust: The Story of Western Intelligence* (Oxford: Oxford University Press, 2013).

2 Vaili Mitrokhin and Christopher Andrew, *The Mitrokhin Archive: The KGB and Europe and the West* (London: Gardners Books, 2000).

3 Mikael Wigell, "Hybrid interference as a wedge strategy: a theory of external interference in liberal democracy", *International Affairs*, Vol. 95, Issue 2 (March 2019), pp. 255–275.

4 David Leask, "How Russia Is Prodding Scotland Toward Independence" (February 18, 2020), https://foreignpolicy.com/2020/02/18/scotland-independence-russia-putin-ukraine-propaganda/. Anonymous, "Russia 'set to U-turn on support for Scottish independence'" (May 11, 2017), https://www.scotsman.com/news/politics/russia-set-to-u-turn-on-support-for-scottish-independence-1449947. Both accessed 16 August 2023.

https://doi.org/10.1515/9783111583464-006

referendum, Russian trolls sowed doubts on social media regarding the result and seeded calls for a revote.[5] Some of the groundwork for Russia's interference in the June 2016 Brexit referendum may also have been laid during the Scottish referendum as well as the 2015 UK-wide general election.[6]

In the UK, general elections and referenda are conducted (as in all but a small handful of countries), by secret ballot. This is handwritten in-person, and hand counted on paper. Tellers count the votes by hand overseen by local election officials, with returning officers publicly announcing the results.[7] As a result, directly tampering with election results is difficult. Instead, Russia has been meddling during election and referenda campaigns, especially in marginal votes and constituencies, in attempts to affect the way people vote.[8] This is enabled because "The age where electoral activity was conducted through traditional print media, canvassing and door knocking, is rapidly vanishing. Instead it is dominated by digital and social media. They are now the source from which voters get most of their information and political messaging."[9] Leading up to the 2016 Brexit referendum, most informed opinion believed that Britain would vote to remain a member of the European Union (EU) on June 23, 2016.[10] Instead 51.9 percent voted to leave

5 Ben Nimmo, "#ElectionWatch: Scottish Vote, Pro-Kremlin Trolls" (December 13, 2017), https://medium.com/dfrlab/electionwatch-scottish-vote-pro-kremlin-trolls-f3cca45045bb, accessed 16 August 2023. Eugene Kondratov and Elisabeth Johansson-Nogués, "Russia's Hybrid Interference Campaigns in France, Germany and the UK: A Challenge against Trust in Liberal Democracies?" *Geopolitics*, Vol. 28, Issue 5 (November 2023), pp. 2177–2180.

6 Intelligence and Security Committee of Parliament, Russia HC 632, July 21, 2020, pp. 13–14. http://isc.independent.gov.uk/news-archive/21july2020, accessed 29 December 2020. Kim Sengupta, "Russia accused of launching hacking campaign during UK general election" (February 14, 2017), https://www.independent.co.uk/news/uk/politics/uk-general-election-russia-hacked-cyber-attack-a7580076.html, accessed 13 November 2019.

7 Guidance and resources for (Acting) Returning Officers administering a UK Parliamentary election in Great Britain, https://www.electoralcommission.org.uk/i-am-a/electoral-administrator/uk-parliamentary-general-election-great-britain, accessed 18 December 2019.

8 Joshua A. Tucker, Andrew Guess, Pablo Barberá, Cristian Vaccari, Alexandra Siegel, Sergey Sanovich, Denis Stukal, and Brendan Nyhan, "Social Media, Political Polarization, and Political Disinformation: A Review of the Scientific Literature" (March 2018), p. 17, https://www.hewlett.org/wp-content/uploads/2018/03/Social-Media-Political-Polarization-and-Political-Disinformation-Literature-Review.pdf, accessed 17 November 2019.

9 House of Lords, Select Committee on Democracy and Digital Technologies, Report of Session 2019–21, Digital Technology and the Resurrection of Trust, June 29, 2020, p. 6, https://committees.parliament.uk/publications/1634/documents/17731/default/, accessed 23 August 2023.

10 Daniel Dunford and Ashley Kirk, "How right or wrong were the polls about the EU referendum?" (June 27, 2016), https://www.telegraph.co.uk/news/2016/06/24/eu-referendum-how-right-or-wrong-were-the-polls/, Anonymous, "EU Referendum: How the bookies got it so wrong over Brexit" (June 24, 2016), https://www.independent.co.uk/news/uk/politics/eu-referendum-brexit-

against 48.1 percent to remain.[11] The turnout was 72.2 percent, and it has since been termed the biggest democratic vote in British history.[12]

2 The background to Brexit

From the founding of the European Economic Community through the 1957 Treaty of Rome onwards there have long been Europhile and Eurosceptic trends in British politics.[13] Deepening political and economic integration, calls for an EU defense force, and concerns over immigration and the strain this was placing on essential services were amongst the most pressing issues at the heart of the Brexit referendum. These also feature in many European elections and have become socio-political issues tied to national identity.[14] Calls for a referendum were persistently made from within the Conservative Party and by the UK Independence Party (UKIP).[15] Then Conservative Prime Minister, David Cameron, "never wanted to leave the EU, but he put this promise in the Tory manifesto and when they won

how-the-bookies-got-eu-referendum-odds-so-wrong-40-million-bet-a7100856.html. Both accessed 5 December 2019.

11 "EU Referendum Results," https://www.bbc.co.uk/news/politics/eu_referendum/results, accessed 4 November 2019.

12 Although there have been higher turnouts and more votes cast in other referenda and elections. Joël Reland, "The EU referendum wasn't quite the largest democratic exercise in UK history" (April 18, 2019), https://fullfact.org/europe/eu-referendum-not-largest-democratic-exercise/, accessed 3 November 2019.

13 Balanced and thorough accounts are provided by Stephen George, *An Awkward Partner: Britain in the European Community* (Oxford: Oxford University Press, 3rd edition 1998), and in Tim Shipman's books *ALL OUT WAR: The Full Story of Brexit* (London: William Collins, 2017) and *Fall Out: A Year of Political Mayhem* (London: William Collins, 2018). James Walker, "Traditional media more responsible for Brexit vote than Facebook, says Nick Clegg" (June 24, 2019), https://pressgazette.co.uk/traditional-media-more-responsible-for-brexit-vote-than-facebook-says-nick-clegg/, accessed 29 November 2019.

14 Sara B. Hobolt, "The Brexit Vote: A Divided Nation, a Divided Continent," *Journal of European Public Policy*, Vol. 23, Issue 9 (September 2016), pp. 1259–1277. Jonathan Lis, "Brexiters' scaremongering about a European army is just another of their lies" (January 25, 2019), https://www.theguardian.com/commentisfree/2019/jan/25/brexiters-european-army-myths-franco-german, accessed 26 January 2019.

15 This has now become the Reform Party and it has made ground on the three main political parties.

the [2015] election, he followed through with it. The rise of anti-EU feeling was demonstrated ... by UKIP winning 3.8 million votes (12.6 %)."[16]

Cameron campaigned for Britain to remain in the EU and only agreed to a referendum to satisfy demands from the entrenched and vocal Eurosceptic wing of his party – the European Research Group (ERG) and to try and neuter UKIP as a political force (drawing Conservative voters).[17] The official *Vote Leave* campaign was led by Boris Johnson, then a Conservative Member of Parliament (MP) and subsequently Prime Minister, with *Britain Stronger in Europe* the official remain campaign. There were wider sets of pressures at work too. Nationalists in Northern Ireland have long campaigned, and many did so bloodily during The Troubles, for a united Ireland. Northern Ireland (56 to 44 percent) voted to remain in the EU. In Scotland, the Scottish Nationalist Party (SNP) had been carving out a majority but in the 2014 referendum on Scottish independence 55.5 percent voted to remain part of a United Kingdom.[18] Scotland also strongly voted to remain in the EU (62 to 38 percent). In Wales prior to Brexit there has been little widespread support for independence with Plaid Cymru a minority nationalist party. In the 2016 Brexit referendum Wales (52.5 to 47.5 percent) and England (53.4 to 46.6 percent) voted to leave.[19]

The results in Scotland and Northern Ireland led to strengthened calls for independence and reunification respectfully.[20] These conditions made the issue of Brexit and particularly the 2016 Brexit referendum "the ideal target of a Kremlin influence operation."[21] The June 2016 Brexit referendum result has since cast a

---

16 Phil Haigh, "Why did David Cameron call a referendum on Brexit?" (December 11, 2018), https://metro.co.uk/2018/12/11/david-cameron-call-referendum-brexit-8231803/, accessed 18 December 2019.

17 The ERG was formed in 1993 to oppose to the Maastricht Treaty which created the European Union out of the European Community and laid the foundations of the Euro. This is detailed in the BBC series *Inside Europe: Ten Years of Turmoil*, https://www.bbc.co.uk/programmes/b0c1rjj7, accessed 9 December 2019.

18 The SNP subsequently lost its majority in the 2024 UK General Election to the Labour Party which itself had previously long held a majority in Scotland. Gerry Hassan, "The UK General Election in Scotland: The End of an Era, Age of Ultra-Competition or Interregnum?" *The Political Quarterly*, Vol. 96, Issue 1 (January/March 2025), pp. 102–110.

19 "EU Referendum Results."

20 Therese Raphael, "Boris Johnson Love Bombs the Other Union. As Brexit pulls the United Kingdom apart, the prime minister is struggling to keep it together" (August 9, 2019), https://www.bloomberg.com/opinion/articles/2019-08-09/scottish-independence-irish-reunification-brexit-helps-both, accessed 4 November 2019.

21 Veronika Špalková, "Influence of Russian disinformation operation: Specific examples in data and numbers," Kremlin Watch Program (2018), p. 6, https://www.europeanvalues.net/wp-content/

long shadow over British politics up until the COVID-19 pandemic beginning in Spring 2020. Although many in the country were already longstanding Eurosceptics, pre-election polls strongly indicated that Britain would choose to remain. This narrowed considerably heading towards the day of the referendum.[22]

3 Russian state media messaging

In the lead up to the referendum Russian media outlets were highly active. Between them, Russia Today and Sputnik produced more anti-EU content than the either the official Vote Leave and non-official Leave.EU campaigns. Indeed, Russia's state-run channels were able to create 134 million impressions during the Brexit campaign.[23] The study of impressions are a whole sub-field of study embracing multiple disciplines including marketing and psychology. Studies suggest that impressions, especially first impressions, are long-lasting.[24] In relation to social media, impressions are the number of times content is displayed and an impression made. Content does not need to be clicked on to create an impression. These impressions matter and interrelate to issues that include media literacy, critical thinking education and skill levels, social and behavioral psychology, and other factors. These factors are analyzed over the next two chapters and the conclusion. Between January 1, 2016 and June 23, 2016 RT and Sputnik published 261 media stories on the UK's Brexit referendum with clear anti-EU sentiment.[25] Moreover, social media posts by these two channels "spiked on the day of the referendum," and both increased their Twitter posts appreciably "which

uploads/2019/02/Influence-of-Russian-Disinformation-Operations-Specific-examples-in-data-and-numbers.pdf, accessed 4 November 2019.

22 "EU referendum poll tracker" (June 22, 2016), https://www.bbc.co.uk/news/uk-politics-eu-referendum-36271589, accessed 13 November 2019.

23 Špalková, "Influence of Russian disinformation operation," p. 4.

24 See for example Georgs Mote, Janis Vanags, Ineta Geipele, and James Bowen, "Impression Management: Impression Conceptual Definition and Model", *Recent Advances in Business Administration* Proceedings of the 6th WSEAS International Conference on BUSINESS ADMINISTRATION (ICBA '12) Harvard, Cambridge, USA January 25–27, 2012 (Harvard, MA: WSEAS Press, 2012, pp. 149–153.

25 "Brexit poll: Almost half of Europeans want own vote on leaving EU" (May 10, 2016), https://www.rt.com/news/342500-brexit-poll-european-union/. For commentary see Ben Nimmo, "Putin's Media Are Pushing Britain For The Brexit" (February 12, 2016), http://www.interpretermag.com/putins-media-are-pushing-britain-for-the-brexit/, and "89up releases report on Russian influence in the EU referendum" (February 10, 2018), http://89up.org/russia-report, all accessed 5 November 2019.

matched the surge in Russian bot activity on the day."[26] Vote Leave garnered 287,000 engagements through Twitter (allied to Facebook and Instagram posts and advertisements) and RT and Sputnik a combined 263,000.[27]

The total cost of this messaging campaign is estimated around £4 million and "No other state controlled media outlet came close to social exposure of Russian media compared to other major foreign state-funded media outlets."[28] As foreign media outlets their content, both broadcast and online, was not regulated by UK government-approved bodies including the Office of Communications (Ofcom), the independent press regulator (IMPRESS), or the Independent Press Standards Organisation (IPSO).

Meanwhile, Russia's automated Twitter bots and botnets created and shared coordinated pro-leave content closely aligned to leave campaign messaging. This amounted to a third of all leave-related hashtags. These bots were subsequently recycled for other election campaigns in Europe and the United States. They were specifically used "to engage in harassment and hate speech in political conversations, generally contributing to a climate of polarization and enmity in online political discussions."[29] Part of their *modus operandi* was (and remains) creating and disseminating "fake news" stories. Not all of these are believed to be Kremlin sponsored, some Russian groups "are just in it for the money. Because social media is a largely unregulated medium, supported and driven by advertising ..."[30]

Since the referendum the UK Electoral Commission, the Information Commissioner's Office (ICO), the Department of Culture, Media and Sport (DCMS), and the Intelligence and Security Committee (ISC) have each examined evidence that Russia interfered in the 2016 Brexit referendum. According to a U.S Congress report this:

> only begun to come into sharper focus as subsequent elections around the world revealed common elements—false or inflammatory stories circulated by bots and trolls, allegations of cyber hacking, stories in Russian state-sponsored media outlets playing up fears of migration and globalization, and allegations of corrupt foreign influence on political parties and candidates—that suggested a possible Russian hand. The Kremlin has long aimed to undermine European integration and the EU, in addition to its aims to sow confusion and under-

26 "89up releases report on Russian influence in the EU referendum."
27 Špalková, "Influence of Russian disinformation operation," p. 6.
28 "Putin's Brexit? The influence of Kremlin media & bots during the 2016 UK EU referendum" (February 16, 2018), https://www.slideshare.net/89up/putins-brexit-the-influence-of-kremlin-media-bots-during-the-2016-uk-eu-referendum, accessed 5 November 2019.
29 Tucker et al., "Social Media, Political Polarization, and Political Disinformation," p. 24.
30 Tucker et al., "Social Media, Political Polarization, and Political Disinformation," p. 24.

mine confidence in democratic processes themselves, making Brexit a potentially appealing target.[31]

The ICO cautioned: "We may never know whether individuals were unknowingly influenced to vote a certain way in either the UK EU referendum or in the US election campaigns. But we do know that personal privacy rights have been compromised by a number of players and that the digital electoral ecosystem needs reform."[32]

The ICO's "Investigation into the use of data analytics in political campaigns" was their most complex to date and the catalyst for strengthening legal protections in the UK under an updated Data Protection Act (2018) with the ICO working with their counterparts in Canada, the U.S., and further afield. Their November 2018 report was one of the first deep dives beneath the surface of "the nature of the relationship between social media platforms, political parties and campaigns and data brokers in respect of the use of personal data for political purposes" in modern election campaigning.[33] Russian anti-EU/Leave state messaging through RT and Sputnik was only one prong of a multi-armed strategic active measures campaign.

4 The Internet Research Agency and influence operations in Europe

Russia also leveraged the Internet Research Agency (IRA), a "private" firm headed by Yevgeny Prigozhin based in St. Petersburg as a proxy actor, working under the direction of the Kremlin to support Russian government interests.[34] Using the IRA and other proxy/front organizations provides a layer of plausible deniability to cloak the Kremlin from some of their intelligence-led active measures campaigns. Since 2016 the IRA's involvement has placed a spotlight on disinformation cam-

31 Putin's Asymmetric Assault on Democracy in Russia and Europe: Implications for U.S. National Security. A Minority Staff Report, Committee on Foreign Relations United States Senate, January 10, 2018, p. 116, https://www.foreign.senate.gov/imo/media/doc/FinalRR.pdf, accessed 5 November 2019.

32 ICO, Investigation into the use of data analytics in political campaigns. A report to Parliament 6 November 2018, p. 4, https://ico.org.uk/media/action-weve-taken/2260271/investigation-into-the-use-of-data-analytics-in-political-campaigns-final-20181105.pdf, accessed 20 November 2019.

33 ICO, Investigation into the use of data analytics in political campaigns, p. 16.

34 Mick Krever and Anna Chernova, "Wagner chief admits to founding Russian troll farm sanctioned for meddling in US elections" (February 14, 2023), https://edition.cnn.com/2023/02/14/europe/russia-yevgeny-prigozhin-internet-research-agency-intl/index.html, accessed 15 August 2023.

paigns as a tactic of hybrid warfare and the operational use of the controversial "Gerasimov doctrine."

The GRU and SVR (and from 2022 the FSB) lead Russian active measures against the West on a wide variety of targets, but the IRA also played a significant role. This includes "trolling" with comments that inflame opinion, fanning populist right-wing politicians and opinions, as part of orchestrated mis and disinformation campaigns and propaganda. This has sown distrust in mainstream political parties and institutions (including mainstream media), eroding democracy itself into an age of "post-truth" politics.[35] This has contributed to polarization and the politicization of social, cultural, and public policy issues that have increased distrust in traditional institutions of liberal democracies. The key enabler has been through weakly regulated and unmediated Western social media platforms which simultaneously provide instant one-to-one and one-to-many channels of communication and discourse.[36] These Kremlin-led campaigns have become an ongoing feature of Russia's domestic and foreign policy since the early 2000s.[37]

The IRA was established in St. Petersburg in 2013. When it was at its height it resembled a multi-tooled marketing agency employing around a thousand staff "in round-the-clock influence operations."[38] Ukrainian and Russian citizens were its initial targets before its focus and capacity grew to encompass European and American objectives. The IRA was funded by Prigozhin through Concord, a company which lists catering among its businesses.[39] Prigozhin spent the majority of his 20s in prison for robbery, fraud, and prostitution. His road to Damascus started with hotdog stands in St. Petersburg, Putin's hometown, which grew

35 This aligns with Russian *maskirovka.* Keir Giles, *Russia's War on Everybody And What It Means For You* (London: Bloomsbury, 2024), pp.137–146.

36 Kondratov and Johansson-Nogués, "Russia's Hybrid Interference Campaigns," pp. 5–8.

37 Philip N. Howard, Bharath Ganesh, Dimitra Liotsiou, John Kelly, and Camille François, "The IRA, Social Media and Political Polarization in the United States, 2012–2018," https://int.nyt.com/data/documenthelper/534-oxford-russia-internet-research-agency/c6588b4a7b940c551c38/optimized/full.pdf, and Anonymous, "Inside the Internet Research Agency's lie machine," https://www.economist.com/briefing/2018/02/22/inside-the-internet-research-agencys-lie-machine. Both accessed 9 January 2019.

38 Renee DiResta, Kris Shaffer, Becky Ruppel, David Sullivan, Robert Matney, Ryan Fox, Jonathan Albright, and Ben Johnson, "The Tactics & Tropes of the Internet Research Agency," p. 6, https://cdn2.hubspot.net/hubfs/4326998/ira-report-rebrand_FinalJ14.pdf, accessed 27 August 2019.

39 https://www.justice.gov/file/1035477/download, pp. 6–7, accessed 2 September 2019.

into a catering business whose clients included the Kremlin (and why Prigozhin was dubbed "Putin's chef").[40]

Prigozhin was one of 13 Russians linked to the IRA indicted by the U.S. Department of Justice in February 2018 (and placed on the international sanctions list).[41] Prior to the Russo-Ukraine War he was a relative unknown in Russia despite close ties to the Kremlin and Russian military through the Wagner Group. On a budget of around $25 million the IRA "reached 126 million people on Facebook, at least 20 million users on Instagram, 1.4 million users on Twitter, and uploaded over 1,000 videos to YouTube."[42] The IRA's "troll farm" was run out of a nondescript building in St. Petersburg's northwestern Primorsky District. The trolls were paid between $550 and $777 a month for 12-hour shifts constantly producing hundreds of comments designed to create the appearance of genuine engagement and debate. They sometimes coordinated on the same forums.[43]

They were trained to target a variety of divisive social and political issues in the target state. The IRA itself no longer operates but these activities are ongoing. The content can first appear off-topic to entice engagement, but quickly turns polemical to incite debate and division and "rock the boat." Their aims outside of their near abroad are not guided by overt support of Russian interests and views but to covertly stoke domestic division and discord in the target state. The same tactics have been used throughout Western Europe mainly focusing on national and societal fault lines, including issues within the EU. When their fake accounts have been identified and removed (especially by Facebook and Twitter) the IRA were believed to have dedicated teams to fight back.[44] Through automated bots and botnets disinformation can spread virally "quickly amplifying a false story's reach and profile and making it trend on social media platforms."[45] A 2016 NATO study observed some common traits. These were: posting unsupported information; posting links without comment; seeding or perpetuating conspir-

---

40 Greg Myre, "'Putin's Chef' Has His Fingers In Many Pies, Critics Say" (January 30, 2019), https://www.npr.org/2019/01/30/685622639/putins-chef-has-his-fingers-in-many-pies-critics-say?t=1566819541250, accessed 26 August 2019.

41 https://www.justice.gov/file/1035477/download.

42 DiResta et al., "The Tactics & Tropes of the Internet Research Agency," p. 6.

43 Todd C. Helmus, Elizabeth Bodine-Baron, Andrew Radin, Madeline Magnuson, Joshua Mendelsohn, William Marcellino, Andriy Bega, and Zev Winkelman, "Russian Social Media Influence Understanding Russian Propaganda in Eastern Europe" (2018), RAND Corporation, p. 22, https://www.rand.org/content/dam/rand/pubs/research_reports/RR2200/RR2237/RAND_RR2237.pdf, accessed 25 October 2019.

44 Putin's Asymmetric Assault, p. 45.

45 Putin's Asymmetric Assault, p. 45.

acy theories; off-topic comments (indicating human interaction); and finally repeating content through "three phases: luring, taking the bait and hauling in."[46]

5 How did Russia meddle in the Brexit referendum? Social media data analysis

89up, a campaigns agency who worked for the pro-EU remain side and were commissioned by the DCMS inquiry may have been the first to critically analyze some of the raw data. Using data from Twitter's application programming interface (API), Facebook's API, Buzzsumo (a research and monitoring tool), and other methods of scraping data from the Internet their findings indicated that:

- Russian state media in the UK had almost the same social media impact as the two main official Leave campaigns.
- Russian state media had a significantly larger impact on Twitter than the two official Leave campaigns combined, suggesting the potential work of bots.
- Russian state media interference in the EU referendum campaign had a value estimated at between £1,455,500 – £4,140,000.
- [Confirmed] Russian bots delivered 10,000,000+ potential Twitter impressions during the EU referendum, with a reach nearly ⅓ of the Leave.EU account.[47]

Twitter (now X, following Elon Musk's 2022 takeover) matters because not only do users view content, they also discuss what they see and retweet content from other platforms. On mobile devices such as smartphones, Twitter was one of the main conduits for dissemination. According to Ofcom smartphones promote "passive news consumption." This seeding and dissemination was hiding in plain sight during the referendum and "Russian state media propaganda through Facebook and Twitter led to significant online traction."[48]

89up's CEO, Mike Harris, pointed out that their content was highly misleading. This included grossly exaggerated, fabricated, or bogus stories from RT and Sputnik on refugees in Europe and immigration into the UK, that the CIA helped create the EU, and that MI5 was influencing the referendum. Through Twitter this propaganda had three times more impact than both the official Leave campaigns com-

46 Robert Szwed, Framing of the Ukraine–Russia Conflict in Online and Social Media (May 2016), pp. 58–60, 122, https://www.stratcomcoe.org/framing-ukraine-russia-conflict-online-and-social-media, accessed 4 November 2019.

47 "Putin's Brexit?" (February 16, 2018).

48 "89up releases report on Russian influence in the EU referendum."

bined.[49] Its two mainstream media outlets, Sputnik and Russia Today (RT), had offices in the UK in London and Edinburgh.[50] Both are part of a wider state-owned media conglomerate called *Rossiya Segodnya.*[51] In the leadup to the referendum both ran hundreds of misleading news articles which were seeded and amplified through social media.[52]

Whether and how much RT and Sputnik paid Facebook and Twitter for their Brexit-only content remains unknown. When Facebook was asked by the DCMS about Russian content they were told "no work has been done by Facebook to look for Russian activity around the EU referendum ... [or] other fake accounts and pages that could be linked to Russian-backed agencies and which were active during the EU referendum ..."[53] Twitter, in response to a request from the UK's Electoral Commission, noted only that "Among the accounts that we have previously identified as likely funded from Russian sources, we have thus far identified one account – @RT_com – which promoted referendum-related content during the regulated period."[54]

What is illuminating is how their output compares with other international media organizations. 89up assessed:

Russia

- RT– Leave: 73 % Neutral: 21 % Remain: 6 %
- Sputnik – Leave: 58 % Neutral: 38 % Remain: 4 %

France

- France 24 – Leave: 2 % Neutral: 38 % Remain: 60 %

---

49 "89up releases report on Russian influence in the EU referendum."

50 The Edinburgh bureau chief, Oxana Brazhnik, was previously a political adviser to Putin's deputy chief of staff, Vyacheslav Volodin. She denied there was any connection or that the move was designed to "encourage the break up of the UK at a time when the SNP is pressing for a second independence referendum in the aftermath of Brexit." Anonymous, "Russian-backed Sputnik TV channel lands in Edinburgh" (August 25, 2016), https://www.scotsman.com/news/politics/russian-backed-sputnik-tv-channel-lands-in-edinburgh-870723, accessed 15 August 2023. Both offices closed in 2021.

51 The head of *Rossiya Segodnya*, Dmitry Kiselev, has been described as the Kremlin's "propagandist-in-chief." Tom Parfitt, "Russia launches 'Sputnik' media offensive to counter US propaganda" (November 10, 2014), https://www.telegraph.co.uk/news/worldnews/europe/russia/11221511/Russia-launches-Sputnik-media-offensive-to-counter-US-propaganda.html, accessed 15 August 2023.

52 "89up releases report on Russian influence in the EU referendum."

53 Rory Cellan-Jones, "Facebook and Twitter: Nine Russian Brexit ads found by inquiries" (December 13, 2017), https://www.bbc.co.uk/news/technology-42342216, accessed 5 November 2019.

54 Cellan-Jones, "Facebook and Twitter."

USA

- PBS – Leave: 25 % Neutral: 50 % Remain: 25 %.

RT and Sputnik's content peaked on the day of the referendum, June 23, 2016.[55] RT's reporting overwhelmingly sided towards leave. They quoted and interviewed "a disproportionate number of Leave campaigners" and ran stories based on unchallenged "comments by prominent British Eurosceptics such as Nigel Farage and Patrick Minford" with an estimated UK audience over the referendum period from 20 to 26 June of 926,000.[56]

156,000 Russian accounts switched their attention to Brexit after previously confining themselves to posting about subjects like the conflict in Ukraine as the referendum approached. This included 45,000 messages in the final 48 hours.[57] These original and retweeted posts contained #Brexit and it was believed these were seen hundreds of millions of times. Between May 24 and August 17, 2016, 20 percent of 28.6 million #Brexit-related tweets were from Twitter bots.[58] These were all leave supporting with hashtags like "ReasonsToLeaveEU."[59]

The searching question is what effect did Russian/IRA messaging have on the result? Research has indicated that bots were more influential upon "leavers" than "remainers" consistent with the "echo chamber effect." This is where people are exposed to like-minded self-reinforcing views within online community spaces. Echo chambers amplify and reinforce pre-existing beliefs and ideas through the information being communicated. Whilst the effects are not uniform across people, social media users appear more liable to believe and embrace opinions that align with their own. This includes "fake news," whilst distancing themselves from mainstream media and official sources. These sources might contradict their be-

55 Russian influence in political campaigns (July 2018), https://publications.parliament.uk/pa/cm201719/cmselect/cmcumeds/363/36308.htm, accessed 29 November 2019.

56 Kondratov and Johansson-Nogués, "Russia's Hybrid Interference Campaigns," p. 11.

57 Alexi Mostrous, Mark Bridge, and Katie Gibbons, "Russia used Twitter bots and trolls 'to disrupt' Brexit vote" (November 15, 2017), https://www.thetimes.co.uk/article/russia-used-web-posts-to-disrupt-brexit-vote-h9nv5zg6c. accessed 5 November 2019.

58 "Research suggests bots generated social media stories during EU Referendum" (November 22, 2017), https://www.swansea.ac.uk/press-office/news-archive/2017/researchsuggestsbotsgeneratedsocialmediastoriesduringeureferendum.php, accessed 5 November 2019.

59 This was followed by posts after the referendum with messages including "Brits MADE UK Great Again," and anti-immigration rhetoric including "Algerian illegally in Britain attacked 8 women in ten days! Send the Muslim back to EU! #BrexitVote" and "I hope UK after #BrexitVote will start to clean their land from muslim [*sic*] invasion!" and "7 more dead in London because of climate change. Oh, wait, nope, it's Islamic terrorism again. #London Attacks." Kondratov and Johansson-Nogués, "Russia's Hybrid Interference Campaigns," p. 2178.

liefs and resultantly, "information polarisation is increased, which makes reaching consensus on important public issues more difficult."[60]

Separate studies also showed how fake IRA accounts, such as "Texas Lone Star" (@SouthLoneStar), were subsequently used as part of broader anti-Islamic and anti-immigration messaging in mainstream media. Whilst Twitter suspended 2,752 of these IRA accounts in the wake of the 2016 U.S. presidential election this was believed to be the tip of the iceberg. Despite their suspension "Archives of the now deleted Russian accounts show they included people purporting to be a US Navy veteran, a Tennessee Republican and a Texan patriot – all tweeting in favour of Brexit."[61] These posts included @TEN_GOP who quoted Nigel Farage on Fox News speaking about Brexit and Donald Trump: "What you've seen this year is just ordinary, decent people, the little people, who've said 'We've had enough. We want change.'" @WadeHarriot, claiming to be a former member of the U.S. Navy, "retweeted criticisms of 'leftists' for 'trying to subvert #Brexit' and predictions of '#Brexit #Frexit #Grexit.'" Putin commented the day after the result "We closely followed the voting but never interfered or sought to influence it." Michael McFaul, a former U.S. ambassador to Russia, called it "a giant victory for Putin's foreign policy objectives."[62]

After 2016, Facebook and Twitter made efforts to close down IRA operations on their platforms, but it is a game of whac-a-mole.[63] Other similar proxies like Glavset, Teka, and the Federal News Agency have also been used by the Kremlin as the IRA reduced their profile having been placed under the spotlight. Increased awareness means remaining undetected is more difficult, but bots and botnets can still be purchased cheaply to disseminate content, including that produced by RT and Sputnik or amplifying corners of the web where conspiracies abound.[64]

---

60 "Research suggests bots generated social media stories during EU Referendum." Their study can be found in Yuriy Gorodnichenko, Tho Pham, and Oleksandr Talavera, "Social media, sentiment and public opinions: Evidence from #Brexit and #USElection," https://eml.berkeley.edu/~ygorodni/Brexit_Election.pdf, accessed 5 November 2019.

61 Robert Booth, Matthew Weaver, Alex Hern, Stacee Smith, and Shaun Walker, "Russia used hundreds of fake accounts to tweet about Brexit, data shows" (November 14, 2017), https://www.theguardian.com/world/2017/nov/14/how-400-russia-run-fake-accounts-posted-bogus-brexit-tweets, accessed 5 November 2019.

62 Booth et al., "Russia used hundreds of fake accounts to tweet about Brexit, data shows."

63 Tucker et al., "Social Media, Political Polarization, and Political Disinformation," p. 37.

64 Diana Pilipenko, "Facebook must 'follow the money' to uncover extent of Russian meddling" (October 9, 2017), https://www.theguardian.com/commentisfree/2017/oct/09/facebook-russian-meddling-investigation. Jack Stubbs, "Russian operatives sacrifice followers to stay under cover on Facebook" (October 24, 2019), https://www.reuters.com/article/us-facebook-accounts-russia/rus

Without referencing the Brexit vote, then Prime Minister Theresa May publicly stated in November 2017 that Russia had "mounted a sustained campaign of cyber-espionage and disruption"; a point reiterated by Ciaran Martin then head of Britain's National Cyber Security Centre (NCSC).[65] The Information Commissioner's Office (ICO) grasped that technological developments and the uptake in social media consumption "have been so rapid that many voters are unaware of the scale and context in which they are being targeted."[66] Supporting the ICO's findings is a February 2019 report, the result of an 18-month long investigation on disinformation and "fake news," conducted by a cross-party group of MPs sitting as part of a Select Committee of the Department of Culture, Media and Sport (DCMS).

This DCMS Select Committee were critical of social media companies and especially Facebook, whose CEO Mark Zuckerberg refused to appear before the committee. The DCMS were scathing: "some malicious forces use Facebook … to disseminate hate speech and propaganda of all kinds, and to influence elections and democratic processes—much of which Facebook, and other social media companies, are either unable or unwilling to prevent."[67] The policing of content across social media platforms and the ways technology permits users to disseminate and access information has become a hot topic issue. However, even in the context of combatting external influence, policing content has implications regarding free speech, freedom of expression, and free assembly. For social media platforms and governments around the world, where the boundaries lie are subjective judgments.[68]

The Interim Report by the DCMS claimed Facebook was reluctant to look into IRA influence on its platforms until pressure from the Mueller inquiry forced their hand. Until this point they had barely scratched the surface of the role

---

sian-operatives-sacrifice-followers-to-stay-under-cover-on-facebook-idUSKBN1X3224. Both accessed 12 November 2019.

65 Anonymous, "UK cyber-defence chief accuses Russia of hack attacks" (November 15, 2017), https://www.bbc.co.uk/news/technology-41997262, accessed 5 November 2019. These messaging campaigns continued post-Brexit as the government had still to decide the mode of exiting the EU. Kondratov and Johansson-Nogués, "Russia's Hybrid Interference Campaigns," pp. 2179–2180.

66 ICO, Investigation into the use of data analytics in political campaigns, p. 18.

67 House of Commons Digital, Culture, Media and Sport Committee Disinformation and 'fake news': Final Report, 14 February 2019, p. 5, https://publications.parliament.uk/pa/cm201719/cmselect/cmcumeds/1791/1791.pdf, accessed 15 February 2019.

68 Joey D'Urso and Marianna Spring, "General Election 2019: The Facebook influencers you've never heard of" (November 27, 2019), https://www.bbc.co.uk/news/blogs-trending-50479877, Joey D'Urso and Marianna Spring, "How a misleading story about Lib Dem leader Jo Swinson's husband went viral" (November 5, 2019), https://www.bbc.co.uk/news/blogs-trending-50160148. Both accessed 29 November 2019.

played by the IRA as Russia's primary actor in the lead-up to the 2016 Brexit referendum. They had been "reluctant" to conduct an internal study but as "Facebook knows its system better than anyone else ... [it] should not be passively reacting to outside concerns before they carry out their own research and take action."[69]

6 The 2020 Intelligence and Security Committee Report and the body politik

Russia's role in 2016 and in UK politics more generally were also examined in a report by the Intelligence and Security Committee (ISC). Its release was controversially delayed prior to the December 2019 General Election, which returned Boris Johnson's Conservative Party to power with an 80-seat majority.[70] The ISC is in a privileged position with members having access to top secret intelligence, but its reports can only be published with approval from the Prime Minister. For reasons which are unclear, this approval was delayed by Prime Minister Johnson.[71] The ISC's chairman at the time, Dominic Grieve MP, called the reasons provided by the government for withholding the ISC report "bogus" because it had already received prior approval for release and required only Prime Minister Johnson's signature. Grieve, a former Attorney General who left the Conservative Party over Brexit, added it was in the public interest to release the 50-page report.[72] The former head of MI5, Jonathan Evans, also called for it to be released.[73]

---

69 House of Commons Digital, Culture, Media and Sport Committee Disinformation and 'fake news': Interim Report (July 24, 2018), p. 46, https://publications.parliament.uk/pa/cm201719/cmselect/cmcumeds/363/363.pdf, accessed 25 July 2018. The findings of the DCMS were similar to those found in a Canadian government inquiry. Democracy under threat: Risks and solutions in the era of disinformation and data monopoly. Report of the Standing Committee on Access to Information, Privacy and Ethics (December 2018), https://www.ourcommons.ca/Content/Committee/421/ETHI/Reports/RP10242267/ethirp17/ethirp17-e.pdf, accessed 20 November 2019.

70 Tom Harper and Caroline Wheeler, "Labour asks about Dominic Cummings' years working in Russia. A whistleblower has prompted questions on vetting the PM's top adviser" (November 3, 2019), https://www.thetimes.co.uk/edition/news/labour-asks-about-dominic-cummings-years-working-in-russia-vl6d0w62z, accessed 4 November 2019, "Why won't the government release the Russia report? James O'Brien asks the experts" (November 14, 2019), https://www.youtube.com/watch?v=jZYR7n2gpOU&feature=youtu.be, accessed 29 November 2019.

71 Deborah Haynes, "Russia report row: Dominic Grieve accuses PM of using No 10 'to spread propaganda and disinformation'" (November 6, 2019), https://news.sky.com/story/russia-report-row-dominic-grieve-accuses-pm-of-using-no-10-to-spread-propaganda-and-disinformation-11855996, accessed 30 November 2019.

72 Haynes, "Russia report row."

There was plenty of press speculation on the delay. This included the extent of Russian influence upon the British establishment and successive UK governments. These investigations include whether the Kremlin and Russian oligarchs built a network of parliamentarians and other influencers and employed lawyers to deter or shut down investigative journalists.[74] It included allegations that Russian intelligence had been cultivating links within the Conservative Party, including through individual donations from Russians. These include Sergey Nalobin, the First Secretary in the Russian Embassy's political section in London, who had alleged ties with the SVR.[75] Other donors include the wife of a former Russian deputy finance minister and the Conservative Friends of Russia, a group made up of Russian expats living in London.[76] In addition, it has been alleged that research roles in the House of Commons were being targeted. Other Russians were seeking British citizenship and were accused of hiring public relations companies to "cleanse reputations."[77] In July 2025, under part 4 of the National Security Act (2023), a new Foreign Influence Registration Scheme (FIRS) came into force. This mandated registration if conducting "political influence activities in the UK" or related activities. It "specified foreign power-controlled organisations

---

73 Anonymous, "General election 2019: No 10 denies suppressing Russia interference report" (November 5, 2019), https://www.bbc.co.uk/news/uk-politics-50300551, accessed 6 November 2019. Intelligence and Security Committee Report on Russia Hansard Volume 667: debated on Tuesday, 5 November 2019, https://hansard.parliament.uk/Commons/2019-11-05/debates/AABC4DE9-4D70-4937-9AF5-D58CE7B0601D/IntelligenceAndSecurityCommitteeReportOnRussia, accessed 16 May 2021.

74 Nina dos Santos, "UK inquiry was warned of Russian infiltration, leaked testimony shows" (November 11, 2019), https://edition.cnn.com/2019/11/08/uk/uk-russia-inquiry-intelligence-security-committee-gbr-intl/index.html, accessed 30 November 2019. Haroon Siddique, "English courts get new powers to dismiss Slapp cases against reporters" (July 20, 2022), https://www.theguardian.com/media/2022/jul/20/english-courts-get-new-powers-to-dismiss-slapp-cases-against-reporters, accessed 16 August 2023.

75 Dan Sabbagh and Luke Harding, "PM accused of cover-up over report on Russian meddling in UK politics" (November 4, 2019), https://amp.theguardian.com/politics/2019/nov/04/no-10-blocks-russia-eu-referendum-report-until-after-election, accessed 30 November 2019. Nalobin's links to Russian intelligence were further examined in the podcast series "Sergei & the Westminster Spy Ring". It described it as ""the biggest spy story since the Cambridge five". Separately, Nalobin's family "are said to have connections to the ... FSB." Fiona Sturges, "Podcast review — Sergei & the Westminster Spy Ring investigates a 'hostile influence campaign'" (January 6 2025), https://www.ft.com/content/5990fd02-5541-48f2-88f7-45235bacfbde. "Sergei & the Westminster Spy Ring", https://www.globalplayer.com/podcasts/42L25Z/. Both accessed 6 August 2025.

76 Carole Cadwalladr, "Brexit, the ministers, the professor and the spy: How Russia pulls strings in UK" (November 4, 2017), https://www.theguardian.com/politics/2017/nov/04/brexit-ministers-spy-russia-uk-brexit, accessed 9 December 2019.

77 dos Santos, "UK inquiry was warned of Russian infiltration."

must register any 'relevant activities' that they carry out themselves in the UK." . This was specifically directed to Russia and Iran.[78] Until the enactment of this legislation, the UK did "not have a single, comprehensive counter-espionage law". Instead, UK government legislation had "developed in a piecemeal way", with "relevant criminal offences ... set out in three key statutes: the Official Secrets Act 1911, the Official Secrets Act 1920, and the Official Secrets Act 1939".[79]

If this is the case, it was not illegal to be a foreign agent in the UK. This contributed to calls for a new Espionage Act modelled on the U.S. Foreign Agents Registration Act (FARA).[80] A new act, similar to FARA, was finally proposed in May 2021.[81] It was subsequently enacted as the National Security Act (2023).[82] In July 2025, under part 4 of the National Security Act (2023), a new Foreign Influence Registration Scheme (FIRS) came into force. This mandated registration if conducting "political influence activities in the UK" or related activities. It "specified [that] foreign power-controlled organisations must register any 'relevant activities' that they carry out themselves in the UK." . This was specifically directed to Russia and Iran.[83] Until the enactment of this legislation, the UK did "not have a single, comprehensive counter-espionage law". Instead, UK government legislation had "developed in a piecemeal way", with "relevant criminal offences ... set out in three key statutes: the Official Secrets Act 1911, the Official Secrets Act 1920, and the Official Secrets Act 1939".[84]

The ISC report was eventually released in July 2020 but only after an attempt was made by the Johnson government to install its favored candidate, Christopher Grayling MP, as its chairman failed.[85] The report is based on evidence from Britain's main intelligence services, MI5 (the Security Service), MI6 (the Secret Intel-

78 Foreign Influence Registration Scheme (updated July 25 2025), https://www.gov.uk/government/collections/foreign-influence-registration-scheme, accessed 6 August 2025.

79 UK Government Considers New Foreign Agents Registration Act" (July 30 2020), https://www.cov.com/-/media/files/corporate/publications/2020/07/uk-government-considers-new-foreign-agents-registration-act.pdf, accessed 6 August 2025.

80 Russia HC 632, pp. 33–34.

81 Open consultation, Legislation to counter state threats, May 13, 2021, https://www.gov.uk/government/consultations/legislation-to-counter-state-threats, accessed 16 May 2021.

82 National Security Act 2023, https://bills.parliament.uk/bills/3154, accessed 16 August 2023.

83 Foreign Influence Registration Scheme (updated July 25 2025), https://www.gov.uk/government/collections/foreign-influence-registration-scheme, accessed 6 August 2025.

84 "UK Government Considers New Foreign Agents Registration Act" (July 30 2020), https://www.cov.com/-/media/files/corporate/publications/2020/07/uk-government-considers-new-foreign-agents-registration-act.pdf, accessed 6 August 2025.

85 Camilla Tominey, "Chris Grayling quits intelligence committee after losing the chance for chairman's role in coup," August 28, 2020, https://www.telegraph.co.uk/news/2020/08/28/chris-grayling-quit-intelligence-committee-losing-chance-chairmans/, accessed 29 December 2020.

ligence Service or SIS), and Government Communications Headquarters (GCHQ). It spoke of Russia posing a significant threat to the UK. This included espionage, interference in democratic processes, and serious crime.[86] The ISC noted that British intelligence agencies "appeared determined to distance themselves from any suggestion that they might have a prominent role in relation to the democratic process itself," instead each government department and agency treated the question like a "hot potato."[87] Bearing in mind this reluctance, the agencies called for increasing "burden sharing" between the "Five Eyes" partners and NATO members to tackle Russian threats.[88]

Like the DCMS, the ISC was also critical of social media companies who had failed to spot or failed to act on covert hostile state use of their platforms by Russia (and capable of being used by many other states). The ISC however described Russian interference in the Brexit referendum as allegations and, rather than discuss any intelligence that was accrued on these activities, instead talked of "Open source studies [that] have pointed to the preponderance of pro-Brexit or anti-EU stories on RT and Sputnik, and the use of 'bots' and 'trolls.'"[89]

It appears MI5 was not tasked to investigate or counter Russia's influence, even with prior warnings that Russia sought to influence the 2014 Scottish independence referendum. This is supported by evidence submitted to the DCMS inquiry by Simon Milner, Facebook's then Policy Director for the UK, Middle East, and Africa. Milner had stated to the DCMS inquiry: "Unlike the US election, we have still not been furnished with any intelligence reports from the UK authorities to suggest that there was direct Russian interference using Facebook in the Brexit Referendum."[90] The ISC did indicate that Britain's longstanding Joint Intelligence Committee (JIC) was aware this had taken place but in carefully couched language the ISC recorded the UK government "had not seen or sought evidence of success-

86 Russia HC 632, p. 19.

87 Russia HC 632, pp. 10–11. The agencies include MI5, MI6, GCHQ, the NCSC, supported by the work of the Joint Intelligence Organisation (JIO) and National Security Secretariat (NSS) in the Cabinet Office; Defence Intelligence (DI) in the Ministry of Defence; and the Office for Security and Counter-Terrorism (OSCT) in the Home Office. Russia HC 632, pp. iii–iv. The ISC felt overall responsibility should fall to MI5 but why MI5 was chosen over MI6, or the NCSC/GCHQ, was not clear. Russia HC 632, p. 11.

88 Russia HC 632, pp. 37–39.

89 Russia HC 632, pp. 11–13.

90 Digital, Culture, Media and Sport Committee Oral evidence: Fake News – 8 February 2018 (George Washington University, Washington DC), HC 363, https://data.parliament.uk/writtenevidence/committeeevidence.svc/evidencedocument/digital-culture-media-and-sport-committee/fake-news/oral/78195.html, accessed 23 August 2023.

ful interference in UK democratic processes or any activity that has had a material impact on an election, for example influencing results."[91] The ISC made clear:

> [the UK's intelligence agencies] nonetheless have capabilities which allow them to 'stand on the shoulders' of open source coverage: for example, GCHQ might attempt to look behind the suspicious social media accounts which open source analysis has identified to uncover their true operators (and even disrupt their use), or SIS might specifically task an agent to provide information on the extent and nature of any Russian influence campaigns.[92]

No retrospective assessment of Russian interference in the referendum was provided by the UK Intelligence Community and it is doubtful one was requested by the government. The ISC noted this stood in stark contrast to both classified and unclassified reports into Russian interference by the American intelligence community on the 2016 U.S. presidential election.[93] The divisiveness of Brexit, which contributed to the resignation of two Conservative Prime Ministers, David Cameron and Theresa May, and the election of a third, Boris Johnson, whose "oven ready" Brexit deal was a significant factor in the 2019 election is a major contributory factor. As importantly, Russian influence could have called into question the Brexit referendum.

7 Russian financing and Brexit

British campaign laws restrict expenditures by political parties but not donations to them. There are "fit and proper person" tests to determine that donations come from legitimate sources. These are declared by the main political parties and, in the case of Brexit, had to be declared by the two official sides of the campaign – Vote Leave and Britain Stronger in Europe. Organizations wishing to donate must be registered in the UK and individuals must be on the UK electoral role and there are strict spending limits.[94] However, foreign companies incorporated in Britain or the EU conducting business in the UK are permitted to donate.[95]

91 Russia HC 632, pp. 11–13.
92 Russia HC 632, p. 14.
93 Russia HC 632, p. 14.
94 The Political Parties, Elections and Referendum Act 2000, chapter II, c. 41, http://www.legislation.gov.uk/ukpga/2000/41/pdfs/ukpga_20000041_en.pdf, accessed 13 November 2019.
95 Alina Polyakova, Marlene Laruelle, Stefan Meister, and Neil Barnett, Foreword by Radosław Sikorski, "The Kremlin's Trojan Horses. Russian Influence in France, Germany, and the United Kingdom, 3rd edition," The Atlantic Council (November 2016), p. 25, https://www.atlanticcouncil.org/in-depth-research-reports/report/kremlin-trojan-horses/, accessed 18 November 2019.

As of August 2025 this remains the case, even as Sir Keir Starmer's Labour government has expressed the need to review donation rules to political parties.[96]

This line of reasoning led to questions regarding the origins of funds channeled to official and unofficial "Leave" campaigns.[97] The concern was that Russian financial contributions were being "used to curry favor with political heavyweights and parties, to shape party positions/platforms in the UK, and to exert power through London's powerful financial markets."[98] This form of influencing through political funding is much wider than the UK alone but for wealthy Russians, directly or indirectly tied to oligarchs and the Kremlin, it is a method of advancing Russian interests.[99] These interests also include alleviating or removing economic sanctions and travel bans initiated after the illegal annexation of Crimea in 2014, those by the U.S. Department of Justice (DOJ) after 2016, which widened after the Skripal poisonings in Salisbury, UK in March 2018 and Russian invasion of Ukraine in 2022.

In Europe especially, but also in North America, Russian money is being actively used to help sow and spread division for their own perceived national interests. Ed Lucas who specializes in Russian cyberespionage, testified to the DCMS that this has "created lobbies in this country who are extremely unhappy at the thought of relations with Russia going downhill, and you get those lobbies exercising power in all the political powers."[100] As part of these lobbying efforts questions have been asked of how the leave campaign and prominent leavers are financed.[101] Nigel Farage was the torch bearer for Brexit. As a Member of the

---

96 Foreign political donations in the UK, https://commonslibrary.parliament.uk/foreign-political-donations-in-the-uk/, accessed 6 August 2025.

97 Putin's Asymmetric Assault, p. 117.

98 Vera Zakem, Paul Saunders, Umida Hashimova, and P. Kathleen Hammerberg, "Mapping Russian Media Network: Media's Role in Russian Foreign Policy and Decision-Making," CNA (January 2018), p. 41, https://www.cna.org/cna_files/pdf/DRM-2017-U-015367-3Rev.pdf, accessed 18 November 2019.

99 Polyakova et al., "The Kremlin's Trojan Horses."

100 Russian influence in political campaigns (July 2018).

101 DCMS Disinformation and 'fake news': Interim Report, pp. 48–50. Arron Banks, edited by Isabel Oakeshott, *The Bad Boys of Brexit: Tales of Mischief, Mayhem & Guerrilla Warfare in the EU Referendum Campaign* (London: Biteback Publishing, 2017). Anonymous, "Nigel Farage's funding secrets revealed" (May 16, 2019), https://www.channel4.com/news/nigel-farages-funding-secrets-revealed. Investigation into payments made to Better for the Country and Leave.EU (October 11, 2019), https://www.electoralcommission.org.uk/who-we-are-and-what-we-do/our-enforcement-work/investigations/investigation-payments-made-better-country-and-leaveeu. See also the "The Banks Files: How Brexit 'bad boy' Arron Banks was eyeing a massive Russian gold deal" (March 5, 2019), https://www.channel4.com/news/the-banks-files-how-brexit-bad-boy-arron-banks-was-eyeing-a-massive-russian-gold-deal. All accessed 29 November 2019.

European Parliament (MEP) he led the UK Independence Party (UKIP) during the referendum. He was not affiliated to the official Vote Leave campaign headed by Boris Johnson and instead fronted the unofficial lobby Leave.EU. Immigration fears were one of the core pillars of their platform. As UKIP shifted to the right after he stepped down as leader, he formed the Brexit Party.[102] This has since become Reform, which Farage leads.

Leave.EU coordinated with another unofficial group, BeLeave, during the referendum.[103] Leave.EU targeted "persuadable" leave voters through microtargeting.[104] This used fears of uncontrolled immigration and unaccountable EU bodies.[105] There have been persistent claims of Russian connections, including direct contacts and financing of prominent leavers.[106] These claims led the award-winning investigative journalist Carole Cadwalladr to be sued for defamation.[107] The case was litigated.[108] Cadwalladr won her case eventually but at great personal cost "where my career, my reputation, my finances, even my home was on the line."[109] Concerns of potential litigation are the reason why more open-

---

102 Anonymous, "Nigel Farage launches Brexit Party ahead of European elections" (April 12, 2019), https://www.bbc.co.uk/news/uk-politics-47907350, accessed 18 December 2019.

103 DCMS Disinformation and "fake news': Final Report, p. 43.

104 DCMS Disinformation and "fake news': Interim Report, p. 41. ICO, Investigation into the use of data analytics in political campaigns, pp. 46–49.

105 Decca Aitkenhead, "Nigel Farage: 'They say I'm toxic. Quite the opposite'" (May 20, 2016), https://www.theguardian.com/politics/2016/may/20/nigel-farage-ukip-eu-referendum-interview-vote-leave-brief-every-day, accessed 12 December 2019. Ed Caesar, "The chaotic triumph of Arron Banks, the 'Bad Boy of Brexit,'" (March 18, 2019) https://www.newyorker.com/magazine/2019/03/25/the-chaotic-triumph-of-arron-banks-the-bad-boy-of-brexit.

106 Molly Scott Cato, "Arron Banks," https://badboysofbrexit.com/2017/12/22/arron-banks/, accessed 17 December 2019. Banks, *The Bad Boys of Brexit*, no page numbers are provided and takes the form of a chronology. The date was November 6, 2015 in a passage entitled "Sampling Stalin's vodka." "The Banks Files" (March 5, 2019); Caesar, "The chaotic triumph of Arron Banks." For more on "the bad boys of Brexit" see https://badboysofbrexit.com/; Alastair Sloan and Iain Campbell, "How did Arron Banks afford Brexit" (October 19, 2017), https://www.opendemocracy.net/en/dark-money-investigations/how-did-arron-banks-afford-brexit/. All accessed 28 November 2019.

107 Freddy Mayhew, "Judge denies opinion claim over tweet in libel battle between Carole Cadwalladr and Arron Banks" (December 12, 2019), https://pressgazette.co.uk/judge-denies-opinion-claim-over-tweet-in-libel-battle-between-carole-cadwalladr-and-arron-banks/, accessed 17 December 2019.

108 Anonymous, "Carole Cadwalladr ordered to pay £1.2 m costs in Arron Banks libel trial" (May 19, 2023), https://www.bbc.co.uk/news/uk-65644475, accessed 17 August 2023.

109 Carole Cadwalladr, "This is what a digital coup looks like" (April 2025), https://www.ted.com/talks/carole_cadwalladr_this_is_what_a_digital_coup_looks_like/transcript, accessed 13 May 2025.

source evidence naming individuals and detailing these connections were omitted from the final text of this chapter.

8 Follow the money

Britain, and London in particular, has been home to capital from Russia. Prime real estate has been purchased, investments made in London's financial markets, and international sanctions circumvented. This was detailed in a House of Commons Foreign Affairs Committee report, "Moscow's Gold: Russian Corruption in the UK."[110] It showed how and why London was a preferred destination for many Russian oligarchs to hide their assets and launder the proceeds of corruption or questionable business deals. Through to the invasion of Ukraine, this saw £100 billion of Russian money coming into the UK via financial dealings through the City of London, property purchases, and investments in various businesses.[111]

These UK assets were insulated from domestic corruption and political change within Russia. Within the UK, wealthy Russians and their assets enjoy legal protections and up to the invasion of Ukraine were mostly welcomed as inward investment. A blind eye was turned to how this wealth was accumulated. Roman Borisovich, a Russian anti-corruption campaigner, argues the oligarch system has plundered Russia's natural wealth. Prior to 2022, earnings were swiftly moved abroad to insulate them from endemic and systematic corruption at all levels of the Russian state. Borisovich asserts this was often deposited in British offshore territories before entering the UK. This offshore laundromat means Russian wealth "doesn't sit under a palm tree in the Cayman Islands; it is invested in stocks, shares, bonds, properties, yachts, planes and reputation laundering."[112] This saw London dubbed "Moscow-on-Thames," and is part of the global laundromat outlined below. The House of Commons Foreign Affairs Committee was unequivocal: "The use of London as a base for the corrupt assets of Kremlin-connected individuals is now clearly linked to a wider Russian strategy and has implications for our national security."[113]

Oligarchs owe a debt to the Kremlin for the transfer of state assets and resources into private hands. In return they support Kremlin interests or fall

110 House of Commons Foreign Affairs Committee, Moscow's Gold: Russian Corruption in the UK, Eighth Report of Session 2017–19 (May 15, 2018), https://publications.parliament.uk/pa/cm201719/cmselect/cmfaff/932/932.pdf, accessed 11 December 2019.

111 Moscow's Gold, pp. 4–5, 8–14.

112 Moscow's Gold, pp. 5–7, 17–18.

113 Moscow's Gold, p. 10.

from grace and favor.[114] Since fresh sanctions and travel bans were introduced in 2018 in the wake of the Skripal poisoning, Russian demand for property in the UK, especially London, fell by 75 percent after visas of Russian oligarchs regularly travelling to or residing in the UK were revoked.[115] However, in cases of suspected money laundering the police (nationally and internationally) lack the ability and resources to investigate fully and, even if they prosecute, Russia does not extradite its own citizens.[116] A complicating factor is how to determine legitimately earned money and that gained through criminal entanglements and corruption. The *modus vivendi* between the state and corruption and kickbacks "means that every clampdown on a 'businessman' or their cash is an attack on the foundations of Russia's political system."[117] This can produce diplomatic ripple effects harmful to bilateral relations.

The sheer scale and number of companies involved in moving money out of Russia was described in 2018 U.S. Congressional report as "staggering." From 2004 to 2013 alone, an average of $100 billion dollars left annually, totaling over $1 trillion. In addition, "An exhaustive investigation by the Organized Crime and Corruption Reporting Project (OCCRP) tracked over $20 billion in illicit money that travelled from 19 Russian banks to 5,140 companies with accounts at 732 banks in 96 countries, including nearly every country in the EU."[118] A 2015 report by

---

114 Mary Dejevsky, "The weird world of Boris Berezovsky: Alexander Litvinenko's inquest has provided an intriguing insight into the dead tycoon" (March 18, 2015), https://www.independent.co.uk/news/world/europe/the-weird-world-of-boris-berezovsky-alexander-litvinenkos-inquest-has-provided-an-intriguing-insight-10117927.html; "Boris Berezovsky's witness statement – full text" (November 2, 2011), https://www.theguardian.com/world/interactive/2011/nov/02/boris-berezovsky-witness-statement-full. Both accessed 11 December 2019.

115 Melissa Lawford, "Why are the Russians leaving London?" (October 25, 2019), https://www.ft.com/content/8685683e-d2b8-11e8-9a3c-5d5eac8f1ab4, accessed 10 December 2019.

116 Alex Perry, "Organised crime in the UK is bigger than ever before. Can the police catch up?" (November 22, 2018), https://www.theguardian.com/uk-news/2018/nov/22/uk-organised-crime-can-police-catch-up-national-crime-agency-lynne-owens, accessed 10 December 2019. Moscow's Gold, pp. 19–24.

117 Peter Hobson, "How Europe Became a Russian Gangster Playground" (May 12, 2016), https://www.themoscowtimes.com/2016/05/12/how-europe-became-a-russian-gangster-playground-a52842, accessed 12 November 2019. The FSB houses a unit dealing with internal corruption designated the Economic Counterintelligence Service (SEK – *Sluzhba Ekonomicheskoy Kontrrazvedki*), part of the broader Internal Security Directorate (USB). The current head of the DKRO is Aleksey Komkov (a previous head of the USB) who replaced Sergey Korolev when he was promoted to first deputy to the FSB's director in 2022. Through to 2019, the DKRO was run by the career KGB-era counterintelligence officer, Aleksandr Zhomov. Kevin P. Riehle, *The Russian FSB A concise history of the Federal Security Service* (Washington DC: Georgetown University Press, 2024), pp. 32–33.

118 Putin's Asymmetric Assault, p. 57.

Deutsche Bank recorded that $1.5 billion was entering the UK monthly without being recorded in official statistics. Half was from Russia.[119] As part of the investigation resulting from the Panama and Paradise papers disclosures of 2016 and 2017 centered on international money laundering, the International Consortium of Investigative Journalists (ICIJ) found "a clandestine network operated by Putin associates" that had moved around $2 billion through banks and offshore companies.[120]

Bill Browder, a U.S. hedge fund manager who saw $230 million of assets disappear (and his lawyer Sergei Magnitsky arrested and die in custody) after the offices of his firm Hermitage Capital were raided by Russia's Interior Ministry (the MVD) believed that much more should have been done to investigate the sources of this "dirty money."[121] Instead, tax havens, shell corporations, dummy holdings, tax loopholes, the cooperation of banks, law firms, and specialist lawyers helped make the "ill-gotten gains of corrupt Russian officials and other bad actors around the world" remain "anonymous and hidden from public sight."[122] Prior to 2022 and much more wide-ranging restrictions, Russian oligarchs were still evading sanctions.[123]

Given the multinational players, some at the apex of the political system and the legal and financial worlds, and the complexity of these financial arrangements, efforts to trace (let alone prosecute) the sources of this "dirty money" by law enforcement (whether national or international) are extremely difficult. The scale "far outweighs the response, particularly in prime destinations for illicit funds."[124] In addition, Russian organized crime gangs in Europe largely operate with or are behind indigenous European gangs. These are also used to cloak "state-sponsored intelligence and military operations."[125] Directorate K of the FSB's "Fourth Service" is where corrupt money is hidden, laundered and reinvest-

119 Hobson, "How Europe Became a Russian Gangster Playground."

120 Jake Bernstein, Petra Blum, Oliver Zihlmann, David Thompson, Frederik Obermaier, and Bastian Obermayer, "The Panama Papers. All Putin's Men: Secret Records Reveal Money Network Tied To Russian Leader" (April 3, 2016), https://www.icij.org/investigations/panama-papers/20160403-putin-russia-offshore-network/, accessed 13 April 2019. Moscow's Gold, pp. 21–24.

121 Hobson, "How Europe Became a Russian Gangster Playground."

122 Putin's Asymmetric Assault, p. 58.

123 Daniel Balint-Kurti et al., "Leaked Emails Reveal How Putin's Friends Dodged Sanctions With Help of Western Enablers" (June 20, 2023), https://www.occrp.org/en/rotenberg-files/leaked-emails-reveal-how-putins-friends-dodged-sanctions-with-help-of-western-enablers, accessed 18 August 2023.

124 Putin's Asymmetric Assault, p. 58.

125 Patrick Howell O'Neill, "Russia's rise to cyberwar superpower" (February 29, 2020), https://www.dailydot.com/debug/russia-cyberwar-cyberattack-dnc-breach-history/, accessed 9 April 2020.

ed offshore. This includes the proceeds of criminal enterprises and cuts from corrupt bankers. In this respect, it competes with Directorate M. Directorate M has also been implicated in corruption and money laundering.

The FSB's "Sixth Service" of the Internal Security Directorate (USB), dubbed "Sechin's Spetsnaz" is also part of these interagency rivalries demanding their cut or kickback.[126] For Mark Galeotti, the Putin regime is the "upperworld" face of Russia's criminal underworld.[127] Whilst part of the FSB's remit is anti-corruption, it is also accused of extortion and controlling business activities. If business owners refuse to "share', the FSB can seize or dismantle the company. Even more concerning are reports that officers from the FSB have also been accused of torture and other human rights violations.[128] Of the $1.5 billion of unrecorded money that entered Britain much of it looked "superficially clean."[129] This was "a boon for real estate agents, lawyers, and luxury service providers in the West."[130] This included £180 million worth of properties purchased through offshore companies whilst British banks stood accused of funneling $740 million of an estimated $20 billion of money moved out of Russia between 2010 and 2014. This flight of capital out of Russia and into the West was linked to money laundering implicating 500 "Russian oligarchs, bankers, or individuals with connections to the FSB."[131] The FSB and SEB are deeply enmeshed in this shadow economy.[132] Russian money laundering is international, systemic, and ongoing.[133]

In the wake of the Skripal poisoning the British government did act. In May 2016, an anti-corruption summit was hosted where 43 governments and six inter-

---

126 Riehle, *The Russian FSB*, pp. 86–89, 124.

127 Mark Galeotti, "CRIMINTERN: How the Kremlin Uses Russia's Criminal Networks in Europe," European Council on Foreign Relations policy brief, https://www.ecfr.eu/page/-/ECFR208_-_CRIMINTERM_-_HOW_RUSSIAN_ORGANISED_CRIME_OPERATES_IN_EUROPE02.pdf, accessed 12 November 2019.

128 Ben Smith, "Russian intelligence services and special forces" House of Commons Library, Briefing Paper Number CBP 8430, 30 October 2018, p. 4, https://researchbriefings.files.parliament.uk/documents/CBP-8430/CBP-8430.pdf, accessed 18 August 2025.

129 Hobson, "How Europe Became a Russian Gangster Playground."

130 Putin's Asymmetric Assault, p. 58. For a wider look see Misha Glenny, *McMafia A Journey Through the Global Criminal Underworld* (London: Vintage, 2018).

131 Putin's Asymmetric Assault, pp. 117–118. Organized Crime and Corruption Reporting Project, "The Russian Laundromat" (March 20, 2017), https://www.occrp.org/en/laundromat/the-russian-laundromat-exposed/, accessed 14 November 2019.

132 The Dossier Center, "Lubyanka federation: How the FSB determines the politics and economics of Russia" (October 5 2025), https://www.atlanticcouncil.org/in-depth-research-reports/report/lubyanka-federation/, accessed 22 August 2025.

133 "The Troika Laundromat," https://www.occrp.org/en/troikalaundromat/, accessed November 14, 2019.

national organizations made 648 commitments towards greater transparency and accountability to combat corruption.[134] Britain also established beneficial ownership registers for "**persons who ultimately own or control an asset** (for example, a property or a company) and benefit from it."[135] Traction requires global cooperation and EU states in the G7 as well as the U.S. and Canada began to enact similar legislation. This was supported by the work of the intergovernmental Financial Action Task Force (FATF) and was followed by an EU declaration that all member states also had to adopt these protocols by January 2020.[136]

In addition, the UK's Criminal Finances Act (2017) is directed at individuals and organizations who have "unexplained wealth" with powers to freeze assets, issue disclosure orders, and mount prosecutions in cases of suspected money laundering.[137] This applies to UK citizens and non-nationals. It also applies to offshore financial service providers and offshore financial advisors, trustees, accountants, law firms, and professional indemnity insurers. All were deemed potentially "high risk." Those breaching the law face onerous compliance requirements and unlimited fines.[138] Zamira Hajiyeva, the wife of the former chairman of the International Bank of Azerbaijan was the first to be prosecuted under the UK's Unexplained Wealth Order (UWO).[139] Additionally the UK and EU have also adopted FATF recommendations on politically exposed persons (PEPs). PEPs are individuals (and family members) holding, or who have held, public office making them potentially susceptible to bribery or corruption. In the UK this is regulated by the Financial Conduct Authority (FCA).[140]

---

134 Putin's Asymmetric Assault, p. 120.

135 Original emphasis. "Registers of Beneficial Ownership" (August 7, 2019), https://researchbriefings.parliament.uk/ResearchBriefing/Summary/CBP-8259#fullreport, accessed 14 November 2019.

136 Registers of beneficial ownership, 06 April 2022. https://commonslibrary.parliament.uk/research-briefings/cbp-8259/; FATF Guidance Politically Exposed Persons (Recommendations 12 and 22), https://www.fatf-gafi.org/content/dam/fatf-gafi/guidance/Guidance-PEP-Rec12-22.pdf, both accessed 18 August 2023.

137 Criminal Finances Act 2017, http://www.legislation.gov.uk/ukpga/2017/22/contents/enacted, accessed 14 November 2017.

138 "The UK Criminal Finances Act 2017: implications for offshore financial providers" (April 23, 2018), https://www.kennedyslaw.com/thought-leadership/article/the-uk-criminal-finances-act-2017-implications-for-offshore-financial-providers, accessed 14 November 2019.

139 Dominic Casciani, "Woman who spent £16 m in Harrods revealed" (October 10, 2018), https://www.bbc.co.uk/news/uk-45812210, accessed 14 November 2019.

140 Anti-money laundering. Politically exposed persons (December 19, 2019), https://www.lawsociety.org.uk/topics/anti-money-laundering/peps; Lara Keay, "What are PEPs and are banks allowed to close their accounts?" (July 20, 2023), https://news.sky.com/story/what-are-peps-and-are-banks-allowed-to-close-their-accounts-12923419. Both accessed 18 August 2023.

9 Russian influence in Britain: "Bermuda Triangle stuff"?

In spite of these forward steps, Prime Minister Boris Johnson asserted ahead of the 2019 General Election there was no evidence of Russian interference in UK politics. Johnson termed this "Bermuda Triangle stuff."[141] The evidence presented by the DCMS, testimony to the ISC, a large number of Russia watchers, and by U.S. Congress, suggests otherwise. Instead, there are longstanding accusations that Russia has invested in agents or networks of influence (also referred to as trojan horses) in British politics. This adds weight to the argument that powerful Russian interests have been used to further Kremlin designs in the UK.[142] In addition and like in the U.S. and many other Western nations, the priority accorded to counterterrorism since 9/11 diminished the capacity and ability of British intelligence to respond to renewed state-level threats, especially Russia and China.[143] They also needed political instruction to investigate, including Russian involvement in Brexit. Instead, its politically and electorally charged nature meant instead that it was treated as a hot potato that no government department or intelligence agency wanted to handle.

As a result, whether Russia tipped the scales towards Brexit remains largely unexplored from within government (publicly at least). Even if Russia's role was marginal and indecisive, Brexit fits their agenda to divide target states and weaken the EU and NATO. The debates over Brexit that followed became a corrosive issue in British politics from the June 2016 referendum through to the "Brexit election" of December 2019. This included what form it should take and if there should have been a second confirmatory referendum. The mode of exit fed public uncertainty and even after the decisive election victory for the ruling Conservative government, the terms of Brexit increased concerns for Northern Ireland's loyalist parties, with renewed calls for reunification with the Republic of Ireland. In Scotland, the SNP revived calls for another Scottish independence referendum and re-

141 Anonymous, "General election 2019: Boris Johnson quizzed on Russia, flooding and his children" (November 15, 2019), https://www.bbc.co.uk/news/election-2019-50433574. "Boris Johnson dismisses Russian concerns as 'Bermuda triangle stuff'" (November 22, 2019), https://news.sky.com/video/share-11867604. Both accessed 29 November 2019.

142 Polyakova et al., "The Kremlin's Trojan Horses," pp. 20–24. Carole Cadwalladr, "Boris Johnson and the Lebedevs: How I exposed the prime minister's defining scandal" (July 16, 2022), https://www.theguardian.com/politics/2022/jul/16/carole-cadwalladr-boris-johnson-lebedevs-prime-ministers-defining-scandal, accessed 18 August 2023.

143 Russia HC 632, pp. 15–28. This also applies legislatively, pp. 34–36.

joining the EU.[144] Whether or not this division was part of Russia's gambit in 2016, it is part of Russia's playbook and achieved "policy paralysis by sowing confusion, stoking fears, and eroding trust in Western and democratic institutions."[145]

Russia was not the only actor sowing confusion, stoking fears, and stoking Brexit. A relatively small UK company, Cambridge Analytica, and its "parent company" SCL Elections, funded by Steve Bannon and the alt-right in the United States, were also micro-targeting voters they dubbed "persuadables" to vote for Brexit using social media platforms and the wider Internet. Like Russia, they too would also play a significant role in the 2016 Brexit campaign and U.S. presidential election.[146] Cambridge Analytica has since been investigated and their work made into the Netflix documentary *The Great Hack.*[147] One of the strands of the investigations by the DCMS and ICO was whether Russia had access to Cambridge Analytica's datasets.[148] SCL/Cambridge Analytica and the Leave.EU and Vote Leave campaigns were at pains to distance themselves from one another in the resultant scandal.[149] Leave.EU was fined a total of £120,000 by the Information Commissioner over their use of personal data and breaches of UK electoral law.[150]

---

144 Gianfranco Baldini and Nicola Chelotti, "The Brexit Effect: Political Implications of the Exit of the United Kingdom from the European Union," *International Political Science Review*, Vol. 43, Issue 3 (June 2022), pp. 319–328. See also other articles in this special issue on Brexit.

145 Helmus et al., "Russian Social Media Influence Understanding Russian Propaganda in Eastern Europe" p. 7.

146 "4 Aggregate IQ," https://publications.parliament.uk/pa/cm201719/cmselect/cmcumeds/1791/179107.htm, accessed 26 November 2019.

147 https://www.netflix.com/title/80117542, accessed 14 November 2019.

148 DCMS Disinformation and "fake news': Final Report, pp. 45–56, 73. "Brexit Brief: Article 50," https://www.instituteforgovernment.org.uk/brexit/brexit-brief-article-50, accessed 23 November 2019.

149 Carole Cadwalladr, "Robert Mercer: The big data billionaire waging war on mainstream media" (February 26, 2017), https://www.theguardian.com/politics/2017/feb/26/robert-mercer-breitbart-war-on-media-steve-bannon-donald-trump-nigel-farage; Sam Knight, "Life inside S.C.L., Cambridge Analytica's parent Company" (March 26, 2018), https://www.newyorker.com/news/letter-from-the-uk/life-inside-scl-cambridge-analyticas-parent-company. Both accessed 6 December 2019.

150 Anonymous, "Brexit: Leave.EU and Arron Banks' firm fined £120,000 over data breaches" (February 1, 2019), https://www.bbc.co.uk/news/uk-politics-47087440, accessed 29 November 2019. Voter profiling and targeting is a growing business which has become mainstream in addition to lobbying firms, focus groups, and political "spin doctors." In 2018, 48 countries experienced "organized media manipulation" by either domestic political actors or through foreign interference. Samantha Bradshaw and Philip N. Howard, "Challenging Truth and Trust: A Global Inventory of Organized Social Media Manipulation" (2018), http://comprop.oii.ox.ac.uk/research/cybertroops2018/, accessed 26 November 2019.

Concerns that Russia influenced the Brexit vote on the side of leave alongside other well publicized election interfering events across Europe and America have led to calls to reform the British electoral system. This led to a parliamentary select committee proposing "stronger checks for online donations, clearer records on digital spending and information about who is behind adverts" amongst other safeguards.[151] This is very unlikely to prove enough because what the Russian's helped pioneer is now becoming a mainstream electoral business.

10 Conclusion

The ruling Conservative government suggested in 2019 that although Russia has tried to interfere in British elections and the Brexit referendum there is no evidence that it materially affected the way people voted.[152] This was despite four investigations by the Information Commissioner's Office, the National Crime Agency and, most thoroughly and publicly, by the Select Committee of the Department for Culture Media and Sport, as well as for the delayed report published in 2020 by the Intelligence and Security Committee.[153] There has never been an independent inquiry along the lines of the Robert Mueller inquiry in the United States to look retrospectively at Russian interference in the 2016 Brexit referendum campaign. The ISC recommended a retrospective investigation but even this does not go far enough.

Successive UK government ministers instead skirted around the issue. Instead, and partly because they did not ask or task British intelligence to look, there has been a repeated refrain that government ministers have seen "'no evidence' of Russia successfully interfering with the Brexit vote."[154] This is a line of defense that stretches credibility. Dodging or delaying a deep dive into this issue undermines UK democracy and national sovereignty by giving a pass to foreign interference because it is politically damaging, disadvantageous, divisive to a government

151 Anonymous, "MPs call for laws to protect elections against online interference" (July 2, 2019), https://www.bbc.co.uk/news/uk-politics-48834193, accessed 27 September 2019.

152 DCMS Disinformation and 'fake news': Final Report, pp. 68–72.

153 Whilst the DCMS, "a small Whitehall policy department," "holds primary responsibility for disinformation campaigns," many other government agencies have cross-cutting remits. This includes the Electoral Commission which "has responsibility for the overall security of democratic processes." Russia HC 632, pp. 10–11.

154 Deborah Haynes, "Sky Views: UK has a duty to investigate potential Russian interference" (March 24, 2019), https://news.sky.com/story/sky-views-britain-has-a-duty-to-investigate-potential-russian-interference-11673887, accessed 29 November 2019.

that made Brexit its central policy plank, and because it has remained politically divisive to successive governments.[155] The campaign they undertook demonstrates to Vladimir Putin and the Kremlin how division can be sown (cost effectively). It is a demonstration of hybrid warfare and the "Gerasimov doctrine" in action.

Although progressive laws have been enacted, whether they are robust enough to deal with transnational social media driven mis and disinformation campaigns is open to question.[156] This includes the Online Safety Act (2023).[157] The current regulatory system is designed for the analog age and needs a fundamental overhaul working with technology and social media companies, not only in the UK but internationally and transnationally.[158] Transparency over paid political adverts, including watermarks on platforms like Facebook, are a step forward but these need the full compliance and appropriate resources devoted to them by social media companies.[159] Twitter (now X) banned political adverts and took a clear stand before they were controversially taken over by Elon Musk.[160] Google has agreed to flag paid political advertisements, but they can still appear without an ad disclaimer.[161] Google's rules vary by region.[162]

155 "Boris Johnson dismisses Russian concerns as 'Bermuda triangle stuff'."

156 Elections Act 2022, https://bills.parliament.uk/bills/3020/publications. Significant changes proposed to UK elections – Electoral Commission responds, July 5, 2021, https://www.electoralcommission.org.uk/media-centre/significant-changes-proposed-uk-elections-electoral-commission-responds, both accessed 19 August 2023.

157 Online Safety Act, https://bills.parliament.uk/bills/3137, accessed 24 August 2023.

158 Amol Rajan, "Who will regulate digital political ads?" (August 9, 2019), https://www.bbc.co.uk/news/entertainment-arts-49278999; "Transparent digital campaigning," https://www.electoralcommission.org.uk/who-we-are-and-what-we-do/changing-electoral-law/transparent-digital-campaigning, both accessed 29 November 2019.

159 Editorial, "The Guardian view on political advertising: Time to regulate it, Mr Zuckerberg" (November 1, 2019), https://www.theguardian.com/commentisfree/2019/nov/01/the-guardian-view-on-political-advertising-time-to-regulate-it-mr-zuckerberg?CMP=Share_iOSApp_Other, accessed 30 November 2019.

160 Lauren Feiner, "Twitter bans political ads after Facebook refused to do so" (October 30, 2019), https://www.cnbc.com/2019/10/30/twitter-bans-political-ads-after-facebook-refused-to-do-so.html. Josh Meyer, "Amid Elon Musk's Twitter changes, why 2024 presidential election threats now pose bigger risk" (July 19, 2023), https://eu.usatoday.com/story/news/politics/2023/07/19/elon-musk-twitter-changes-2024-election-risks/70269226007/. Both accessed 29 November 2019.

161 Dave Lee, "Google to restrict political adverts worldwide" (November 21, 2019), https://www.bbc.co.uk/news/technology-50498166, accessed 29 November 2019. Alex Lee, "Why is Google hiding one of the UK's biggest political advertisers?" (November 28, 2019), https://www.wired.co.uk/article/google-uk-general-election-ads-best-for-britain, accessed 29 November 2019.

162 "Political Content," https://support.google.com/adspolicy/answer/6014595?hl=en, accessed 19 August 2023.

Meta (previously Facebook) has its own guidelines.[163] Their updated self-regulating guidelines have not prevented unlabeled or mislabeled political advertising slipping through.[164] Mis and disinformation is also replete on the platform (further evidenced during the COVID-19 pandemic). Despite a greater use of artificial intelligence (AI), Meta has only moderately improved its ability to remove or correct mis and disinformation. These technical fixes still cannot comprehensively and accurately determine intentions or meaning; especially combined with the surrounding social reality and cultural and political contexts.[165] Moderating these platforms is ultimately driven by opinions and is always likely to suffer from subjective bias. This is not helped by social media algorithms, designed to keep users engaged by showing them information designed to increase their engagement. These generate filter bubbles (personalized content), and lead to echo chambers (online environments that reinforce existing views and promote confirmation bias).[166]

Mis and disinformation remain an ever-present issue and both are often shared across platforms, even when fact checking correctives are issued. This includes sharing on more intimate platforms like WhatsApp (owned by Meta).[167] Whilst warning messages are sometimes accompanied by fact-checked research, mis and disinformation is not removed and continues to circulate. False information warnings are seen as a solution both on Meta and Twitter/X.[168] They are not a solution. Instead, they are an abrogation of responsibility and one of the reasons

---

163 "About ads about social issues, elections or politics," https://www.facebook.com/business/help/167836590566506, accessed 19 August 2023.

164 "Samples of ads misclassified by Facebook," https://cybersecurityfordemocracy.org/missed-ads, accessed 19 August 2023.

165 Jay Jennings and Natalie Jomini Stroud, "Asymmetric Adjustment: Partisanship and Correcting Misinformation on Facebook," *New Media & Society*, Vol. 25, Issue 7 (July 2023), pp. 1501–1521. Jack Andersen and Sille Obelitz Søe, "Communicative Actions We Live By: The Problem with Fact-Checking, Tagging or Flagging Fake News – The Case of Facebook," *European Journal of Communication*, Vol. 35, Issue 2 (April 2020), pp. 126–139.

166 Samuel C. Rhodes, "Filter Bubbles, Echo Chambers, and Fake News: How Social Media Conditions Individuals to Be Less Critical of Political Misinformation," *Political Communication*, Vol. 39, Issue 1 (January 2022), pp. 1–22.

167 Patrícia Rossini, Jennifer Stromer-Galley, Erica Anita Baptista, and Vanessa Veiga de Oliveira, "Dysfunctional Information Sharing on WhatsApp and Facebook: The Role of Political Talk, Cross-Cutting Exposure and Social Corrections," *New Media & Society*, Vol. 23, Issue 8 (August 2021), pp. 2430–2451.

168 Jordan Harner, Lydia Ray, and Florence Wakoko-Studstill, "An Investigation of the Effectiveness of Facebook and Twitter Algorithm and Policies on Misinformation and User Decision Making," *Journal of Systemics, Cybernetics and Informatics*, Vol. 20, No. 5 (2022), pp. 118–137.

why national and international regulation needs consideration.[169] Their responsibilities to human content moderators are also questionable.[170] As a result, social media also continues to leave itself open to attack by hostile state actors from Russia.[171]

Meta now provides web-based public searches of who is advertising and who pays for adverts.[172] This "falls into the same trap as existing broadcast TV and radio attribution rules since the identification of the front organization sponsor does nothing to reveal who is really behind the ad."[173] Whilst Meta is making efforts to put additional measures in place to deal with mis and disinformation for political purposes, this is firefighting not prevention.[174] Their business model, connecting like-minded people into groups produces huge swathes of personal data, and the ways that information is being consumed by developed societies through technology makes it a prime target for Russia.[175] The denials by more junior Facebook executives to the DCMS inquiry that Russia intervened in Brexit were described as "misleading" and "simply not true," led them to the conclusion that either they had not been briefed by Facebook's senior executives or they had deliberately misled the committee.[176]

---

169 These were part of 45 recommendations in a scathing report on the influence of social media and UK government responses issued by the UK's upper parliamentary chamber, the House of Lords, in June 2020. Digital Technology and the Resurrection of Trust, pp. 125–130.

170 Anna D. Gibson, "What Teams Do: Exploring Volunteer Content Moderation Team Labor on Facebook," Social Media + Society, Vol. 9, No. 3 (July–September 2023), pp. 1–10. Anonymous, "Facebook moderation firm Cognizant quits" (October 31, 2019), https://www.bbc.co.uk/news/technology-50247540; Chris Vallance, "Firm regrets taking Facebook moderation work" (August 16, 2023), https://www-bbc-com.cdn.ampproject.org/c/s/www.bbc.com/news/technology-66465231.amp. Both accessed 19 August 2023.

171 Kondratov and Johansson-Nogués, "Russia's Hybrid Interference Campaigns." Ben Riley-Smith and Jack Maidment, "Russia 'tops list of suspects' in cyber attack which exposed data of 40 m UK voters" (August 8, 2023), https://www.telegraph.co.uk/news/2023/08/08/election-watchdog-cyber-attack-hostile-actors/, accessed 19 August 2023.

172 "What is the Meta Ad Library and how do I search it?" https://www.facebook.com/help/259468828226154, accessed 22 August 2023.

173 Tom Wheeler, "Mark Zuckerberg's call for internet rules only goes part way" (April 3, 2019), https://www.brookings.edu/blog/techtank/2019/04/03/mark-zuckerbergs-call-for-internet-rules-only-goes-part-way/; Rory Cellan-Jones, "Online political ads 'need law change'" (May 6, 2019), https://www.bbc.co.uk/news/business-48174817, both accessed 2 October 2019.

174 Anonymous, "Facebook reveals preparations for UK election" (October 21, 2019), https://www.bbc.co.uk/news/technology-50128055, accessed 29 November 2019.

175 Andrew Dawson and Martin Innes, "How Russia's Internet Research Agency Built its Disinformation Campaign," *The Political Quarterly*, Vol. 90, No. 2 (April–June 2019), pp. 245–256.

176 DCMS Disinformation and 'fake news': Final Report, p. 72.

There has been continual debate since *whether* Russia interfered in the 2016 Brexit referendum. That debate needs to move on to *how* the Kremlin interfered and *what effect* it had. That they interfered is based not on "'intentions', 'possibilities' or 'assumptions', but rather hard data and practically irrefutable evidence."[177] The effects of Russian interference are difficult to measure but is *the* most important question. Given Russia's target list, all elections and all types of democratic voting systems Russia is targeting are under threat. It is particularly important in narrow votes. Those on the winning side aided by Russian interference should not be turning a blind eye to external interference. In commenting on the UK's 2024 general election result, Sergei Lavrov ironically remarked "Unlike the British government, we do not meddle in domestic matters." This followed reports of Russian bots supporting the newly formed Reform Party (the successor to UKIP).[178]

In Britain, coordinated efforts to call out Russian hybrid warfare through targeted political disinformation were placed on the backburner due to the divisive issue they helped fan.[179] An Ipsos Mori poll found that a third of Britons admit to having been fooled by a "fake news" story.[180] Reported Russian influence on Western elections is dismissed by the Kremlin as a fabrication. Even after investigations by Britain's Intelligence and Security Committee, the DCMS, the FBI, the Mueller inquiry, and a whole raft of high-profile media reporting demonstrating the extent of Russia's influence operations, this was sidelined and marginalized by the winning side on both sides of the Atlantic. Brexit supporters, and supporters of President Trump, now see this narrative in terms of a conspiracy theory of liberals and the left and not as coordinated and orchestrated mis and disinformation

177 Špalková, "Influence of Russian disinformation operation," p. 6.

178 "'I don't care" says Russian foreign minister Sergei Lavrov about election of Keir Starmer" (July 5, 2024), https://news.sky.com/video/i-dont-care-says-russian-foreign-minister-sergei-lavrov-about-election-of-keir-starmer-13173722; "Investigation reveals content posted by bot-like accounts on X has been seen 150 million times ahead of the UK elections" (July 2, 2024), https://www.globalwitness.org/en/campaigns/digital-threats/investigation-reveals-content-posted-bot-accounts-x-has-been-seen-150-million-times-ahead-uk-elections/. For wider appreciation see Sam Stockwell, Megan Hughes, Phil Swatton, and Katie Bishop, "AI-Enabled Influence Operations: The Threat to the UK General Election Briefing Paper," https://cetas.turing.ac.uk/publications/ai-enabled-influence-operations-threat-uk-general-election, all accessed 6 July 2024.

179 Russian influence in political campaigns (July 2018).

180 Mike Wright, "Facebook takes down 130 pages linked to first 'fake news' network" (March 7, 2019), https://www.telegraph.co.uk/news/2019/03/07/facebook-takes-130-pages-linked-first-fake-news-network-uncovered/.

campaigns designed to advance the interests of a revisionist foreign government serving Russian interests and foreign policy goals.[181]

Whilst these debates remain vituperative and highly politicized, policymakers, lawmakers, and the general public cannot lose sight of Russia's role and their agenda. Part of this agenda is to sow disharmony and it is succeeding.[182] Foreign propaganda has long been a tool of political influence (and for some, espionage) but in an age of global interconnection, 24-hour news, and social media it has, as Chinese theorists forecast and understood during the 1990s and into the 2000s, renewed purpose and capabilities.[183] As Chapter 4 will explore and make clear, a number of the players revealed in the Brexit interventions were also players in the U.S. in 2016 and Brexit was used by the IRA to advance secessionist sentiment in America.[184]

---

181 Brendan O'Neill, "Can we finally put the Russia-Brexit conspiracy to bed?" (July 21, 2020), https://www.spectator.co.uk/article/can-we-finally-put-to-bed-the-russia-brexit-conspiracy/, accessed 23 August 2023.

182 Tom Sanders, "Fake news outlet which spread lies about Southport stabbings has links to Russia" (August 1, 2024), https://metro.co.uk/2024/08/01/russian-linked-fake-news-outlet-spread-lies-southport-attacks-21341702/, "The far right, disinformation and the Southport riot | The News Agents" (August 1, 2024), https://www.youtube.com/watch?v=KApvOew48FQ; Lauren Shirreff, "The obscure Russian-linked 'news' outlet fuelling violence on Britain's streets" (August 3, 2024), https://www.telegraph.co.uk/news/2024/08/03/obscure-russian-linked-news-outlet-fuelling-violence/. All accessed 4 September 2024.

183 Timothy L. Thomas, *Dragon Bytes: Chinese Information Warfare Theory and Practice* (Fort Leavenworth, KS: Foreign Military Studies Office, 2004). Timothy L. Thomas, *Decoding the Virtual Dragon: Critical Evolutions in the Science and Philosophy of China's Information Operations and Military Strategy* (Fort Leavenworth, KS: Foreign Military Studies Office, 2007). Timothy L. Thomas, *Three Faces of the Cyber Dragon: Cyber Peace Activist, Spook, Attacker* (Fort Leavenworth, KS: Foreign Military Studies Office, 2012).

184 DiResta et al., "The Tactics & Tropes of the Internet Research Agency," pp. 71–72.

Chapter 4
Russian interference in the 2016 U.S. presidential election

1 Introduction

Russian meddling in the 2016 U.S. presidential elections and similar attempts on other Western elections is now well documented.[1] This has been a long-standing espionage practice and Russia is not the only perpetrator. But under the rule of Vladimir Putin Russia is not only the most active but also the most "successful" state conducting active measures campaigns. They demonstrate fundamental political resolve and patterns outlined in the "Gerasimov doctrine" and subsequent Russian military pronouncements. These active measures are fundamentally interwoven into Russia's wider "hybrid warfare" strategy and their political, military, cyber, and economic goals.

How the "Gerasimov doctrine" was utilized in Russia's playbook for the 2016 U.S. election was directly pointed to by Hillary Clinton in her 2018 book, *What Happened*, as "psychological and information warfare."[2] Russian meddling in the 2016 elections in the U.S. and Europe also clearly indicates the lengths Russia is prepared to go to advance its perceived interests. Bill Priestap, then Assistant Director of the Counterintelligence Division at the Federal Bureau of Investigation (FBI), made this interwoven Russian approach clear in June 2017:

> Russia's 2016 Presidential election influence effort was its boldest to date in the United States. Moscow employed a multi-faceted approach intended to undermine confidence in our democratic process. Russia's activities included efforts to discredit Secretary Clinton and to publicly contrast her unfavorably with President Trump. This Russian effort included the weaponization of stolen cyber information, the use of Russia's English-language state

---

1 For example, the January 2017 report by the Director of National Intelligence, "Background to 'Assessing Russian Activities and Intentions in Recent US Elections': The Analytic Process and Cyber Incident Attribution," https://www.dni.gov/files/documents/ICA_2017_01.pdf and Michael H. Fuchs, Carolyn Kenney, Anna Perina, and Francesca VanDoorn, "Why Americans Should Care About Russian Hacking" (February 14, 2017), https://cdn.americanprogress.org/content/uploads/2017/02/13093554/RussianHackingWhyItMatters-brief.pdf. Both accessed 21 January 2018.
2 Hillary Rodham Clinton, *What Happened* (New York: Simon & Schuster, 2018), pp. 331–332.

https://doi.org/10.1515/9783111583464-007

> media as a strategic messaging platform, and the mobilization of social media bots and trolls to spread disinformation and amplify Russian messaging.[3]

This chapter focuses on the two most well-known and extensively debated Russian efforts in the 2016 U.S. presidential race: the hacking and subsequent leaking of information from the Clinton campaign and the Democratic Party and the use of social media to spread information to influence the election. There was also a third strand which sought to hack online voting systems which had far more limited success. The sum of these actions point to an integrated intelligence-led and politically-directed strategic campaign, combining cyber, influence, psychological, and information operations.

2 Active measures

As Chapter 3 made clear, Russian election meddling is not only targeting the U.S. and is not the only policy agenda in Russia's information warfare toolbox, but it has become controversial and contested. That Russia intervened in 2016 is extremely well documented. This picture is informed by multiple searching and detailed investigations. This includes those of the FBI, especially their Crossfire Hurricane investigation into potential ties between the Trump campaign team and Russia. Further investigations by the U.S. intelligence community (USIC) were also conducted. Investigations were also initiated by the Senate Select Committee on Intelligence (SSCI), leading to the appointment and subsequent report by Special Prosecutor, Robert Mueller, and multifarious hearings held on Russian interference and influence. Further research was conducted through investigative journalism, academic study, and by third-party researchers. This includes in-house analysis made public by companies targeted by Russia – most notably Facebook (now Meta). There is a counter narrative that this is all a "witch hunt" driven by the Democratic Party and perpetrated by U.S. intelligence and their friends and allies.[4] What follows supports the first hypothesis which demonstrates that

---

3 Statement of Bill Priestap Assistant Director Counterintelligence Division Federal Bureau of Investigation Select Committee on Intelligence United States Senate "Assessing Russian Activities and Intentions in Recent Elections" (June 21, 2017), https://www.intelligence.senate.gov/sites/default/files/documents/os-bpriestap-062117.pdf, accessed 10 January 2018.

4 This counter narrative includes Dan Bongino, D. C. McAllister, and Matt Palumbo, *Spygate: The Attempted Sabotage of Donald J. Trump* (New York: Post Hill Press, 2018); Jason Chaffetz, *The Deep State: How an Army of Bureaucrats Protected Barack Obama and Is Working to Destroy the Trump Agenda* (New York: Broadside Books, 2018), Jason Chaffetz, *Power Grab: The Liberal Scheme to*

the concerns and involvement of the FBI, federal government, and the USIC and their "Five Eyes" partners were in defense of U.S. democracy, not some "deep state" underminer of it.

The election interference perpetrated in the U.S. in 2015–16 is perhaps the best documented case of Russian cyberespionage through active measures to date. It demonstrates the seemingly unlimited scope of Russian actions where virtually any targets are legitimate, highlighting attack patterns evident in previous campaigns against corporations, organizations, and governments. These include the use of social engineering, laying low to gather information and credentials, patiently mapping networks and accessing data, retaining contact with remote operatives, and being opportunistic and reactive in using what has been gathered.[5] When it was ordered and who originated and developed these plans is unclear, but the USIC has firmly pointed to who greenlit it.

In the Fall of 2016, during the midst of election campaigning, the U.S. intelligence community were reporting their findings. According to the *Washington Post*, Barack Obama was handed a CIA intelligence report based on Russian government sources indicating that Vladimir Putin had issued specific instructions to damage or defeat Hillary Clinton, Obama's Secretary of State and the Democratic nominee for president, and help elect Donald Trump to the White House.[6] The report was characterized by James Clapper, then Director of National

---

Undermine Trump, the GOP, and Our Republic (New York: Broadside Books, 2019); Dan Bongino, *Exonerated: The Failed Takedown of President Donald Trump by the Swamp* (New York: Post Hill Press, 2019); Gregg Jarrett, *Witch Hunt: The Story of the Greatest Mass Delusion in American Political History* (New York: Broadside Books, 2019), Kenneth P. Vogel and David Stern, "Ukrainian efforts to sabotage Trump backfire Kiev officials are scrambling to make amends with the president-elect after quietly working to boost Clinton" (January 11, 2017), https://www.politico.com/story/2017/01/ukraine-sabotage-trump-backfire-233446, accessed 26 November 2019.

5 These and other techniques were detailed and described in *Cyberwarfare*. For example, social engineering was described as a well-established set of techniques which exploit human psychology. It is used as a gateway for technical hacking and gaining access to individuals and the computer systems they use. This is then used by attackers to migrate across "internal systems, and organizations, the data they hold, and is also used to access physical sites and buildings". Kristan Stoddart, *Cyberwarfare: Threats to Critical Infrastructure* (London: Palgrave/Springer, 2022), pp. 282–300.

6 Greg Miller, Ellen Nakashima, and Adam Entous, "Obama's secret struggle to punish Russia for Putin's election assault" (June 23, 2017), https://www.washingtonpost.com/graphics/2017/world/national-security/obama-putin-election-hacking/, accessed 7 October 2018. Katelyn Polantz, Kara Scannell, Kevin Liptak, Allison Main, Caroline Kelly, David Shortell, and Evan Perez, "Highlights from the new Mueller FBI investigation documents" (January 3, 2020), https://edition.cnn.com/2020/01/02/politics/mueller-investigation-documents/index.html, accessed 28 January 2020.

Intelligence (DNI), as "a landmark product—among the most important ever produced by US intelligence."[7]

During Putin's time as a relatively low-level field agent in the KGB's First Chief Directorate (responsible for foreign intelligence) he was "expected to spend 25 percent of his time conceiving and implementing" active measures.[8] What to do vexed the Obama administration because whatever the U.S. Intelligence Community and White House did or did not do about this revelation could be viewed as political interference in the election in favor Hillary Clinton.[9] It is possible the Obama administration was wary of overt interjection at this stage and subsequent publicity because of the Hatch Act, which prohibits government employees from using their positions to influence political elections.[10]

Although aspects of Russia's operation appear to have been recognized early resulting in public and private warnings to the campaigns of both candidates this was not geared towards a specific threat. Both the 2008 and 2012 election cycle had seen cyber threats.[11] Clapper added that the USIC wanted to remain impartial both to avoid perceived bias to one or other of the candidates but what transpired during the campaign made it uncomfortable to hold that line.[12] In former FBI Di-

---

7 James R. Clapper with Trey Brown, *Facts and Fears: Hard Truths from a Life in Intelligence* (New York: Viking Press, 2018), p. 4.

8 Steve Abrams, "Beyond Propaganda: Soviet Active Measures in Putin's Russia," *Connections: The Quarterly Journal,* Vol. 15, No. 1 (Winter 2016), p. 16. ABC News, "Trump/Russia: Follow the money (1/3) | Four Corners" (June 17, 2018), https://www.youtube.com/watch?v=XwvjkJXaIJE&feature=youtu.be, accessed 30 November 2019. "Active Measures," https://www.imdb.com/title/tt8135494/, accessed 20 January 2020.

9 Brett Velicovich, "Why didn't Obama do more to counter Russia's interference in our election?" (March 31, 2019), https://www.foxnews.com/opinion/why-didnt-obama-do-more-to-counter-russias-interference-in-our-election, accessed 27 September 2019.

10 Todd Carney, "Establishing a United Nations Convention to Stop Foreign Election Interference," *Loyola University Chicago International Law Review,* Vol. 17, Issue 1 (January 2021), pp. 21–56, esp. pp. 43–44.

11 Dustin Volz and Mark Hosenball, "Hackers target presidential campaigns: U.S. spy chief" (May 18, 2016), https://www.reuters.com/article/us-usa-election-hackers-idUSKCN0Y929G; Shawn Henry, "I worked for the FBI. The midterms could be hacked, but here's the bigger threat" (November 6, 2018), https://edition.cnn.com/2018/11/05/perspectives/fbi-mid-term-elections-hack/index.html, both accessed 28 September 2019.

12 Clapper and Brown, *Facts and Fears*, pp. 312–400. Former senior intelligence officials like Michael Hayden, unencumbered from these bounds, were worried about the activities of the Russians and the Trump administration. Michael V. Hayden, *The Assault on Intelligence: American National Security in an Age of Lies* (New York: Penguin, 2018), pp. 43–76, 79–80, 104–112, 140–143, 189–218.

rector James Comey's view, the FBI and the USIC moved slowly but attentively because polling and pollsters were indicating Trump would lose the election.[13]

These and other subjects became part of the investigations conducted by Special Counsel, Robert Mueller.[14] The FBI investigations, and the issues that prompted it, have been highly controversial.[15] According to the March 2019 Mueller Report, two days after Trump was elected president on November 8, 2016 "Russian officials told the press that the Russian government had maintained contacts with Trump's 'immediate entourage' during the campaign." Hope Hicks, the Trump campaign spokesperson, denied this.[16] This question was raised again in mid-December by John Podesta, the Clinton campaign chairman and:

> The same day, incoming Chief of Staff Reince Priebus appeared on Fox News Sunday and declined to say whether the President-Elect accepted the intelligence community's determination that Russia intervened in the election. When asked about any contact or coordination between the Campaign and Russia, Priebus said, "Even this question is insane. Of course we didn't interface with the Russians ... this whole thing is a spin job" and said, "the real question is, why the Democrats ... are doing everything they can to delegitimize the outcome of the election?"[17]

The Mueller Report found there was no direct collusion and this baseline defense and continuous references to a "witch hunt" that followed, replayed almost nonstop over the next four years.

The joint assessment of the CIA, FBI, and NSA in January 2017 was that they had "high confidence" Russia intervened in the 2016 presidential election and

---

13 James Comey, *A Higher Loyalty: Truth, Lies, and Leadership* (New York: Flatiron Books, 2018), pp. 190–191.

14 Garrett M. Graff, "A complete guide to all 17 (known) Trump and Russia investigations" (December 17, 2018), https://www.wired.com/story/mueller-investigation-trump-russia-complete-guide/, accessed 8 January 2018.

15 Peter W. Stevenson, "Bob Woodward on Trump-Watergate Comparisons 'Let's see what the evidence is'" (May 10, 2017), https://www.washingtonpost.com/news/the-fix/wp/2017/05/10/bob-woodward-on-trump-watergate-comparisons-lets-see-what-the-evidence-is/?outputType=amp. Dylan Scott, Tara Golshan, and Jeff Stein, "'Don't forget we still have all the Hillary activity': GOP reacts to Manafort charges" (October 30, 2017), https://www.vox.com/policy-and-politics/2017/10/30/16571678/paul-manafort-indictment-mueller-investigation-republican-reaction. Both accessed 27 January 2020. Special Counsel Robert S. Mueller, III, Report On The Investigation Into Russian Interference In The 2016 Presidential Election Volume I of II (March 2019), pp. 2, 180–181, https://www.justice.gov/storage/report.pdf, accessed 2 September 2019.

16 Special Counsel Robert S. Mueller, III, Report On The Investigation Into Russian Interference In The 2016 Presidential Election Volume II of II (March 2019), p. 21, https://www.justice.gov/storage/report_volume2.pdf, accessed 2 September 2019.

17 Mueller Report Volume II, pp. 21–22.

sought to damage the campaign of Hillary Clinton and promote the Trump campaign.[18] This assessment was also motivated by personal animosity between Putin and Hillary Clinton with the preference for Donald Trump stemming from "Trump's stated policy to work with Russia" and "what they saw as his Russia-friendly positions on Syria and Ukraine" as well as Trump's business interests in Russia.[19] When it appeared that Clinton was becoming a heavy favorite to win, "the Russian influence campaign focused more on undercutting Secretary Clinton's legitimacy and crippling her presidency from its start, including by impugning the fairness of the election."[20]

2.1 "Hack and leak" and covert and overt propaganda

What was new about this campaign was Russia's "hack and leak" tactics and its highly targeted use of American social media platforms to influence the electorate. This active measures campaign also blended covert intelligence operations, with overt messaging/propaganda by Russian government agencies, state-funded mainstream media outlets, third-party intermediaries, and Russian social media "trolls" (especially the Internet Research Agency).[21] Guided by their established use in Ukraine, these campaigns "are multifaceted and designed to be deniable because they use a mix of agents of influence, cutouts, front organizations, and false-flag operations."[22]

Informed by Russian intelligence, these "hack and leak" tactics were complemented with "intrusions into US state and local electoral boards; and overt propaganda" and intelligence collected on U.S. primary campaigns, think tanks, and lobbying groups as movers and shakers of future policy.[23] WikiLeaks was chosen as the main outlet to leak Russian hacking "because of its self-proclaimed reputation

18 DNI "Assessing the Russian Activities and Intentions in Recent US Elections," January 6, 2017, p. 1.
19 DNI "Assessing the Russian Activities and Intentions in Recent US Elections," January 6, 2017, pp. 1–2.
20 DNI "Assessing the Russian Activities and Intentions in Recent US Elections," January 6, 2017, pp. 1–2. Clinton's own views of this period can be found in Clinton, *What Happened*, pp. 325–366.
21 DNI "Assessing the Russian Activities and Intentions in Recent US Elections," January 6, 2017, p. 2.
22 DNI "Assessing the Russian Activities and Intentions in Recent US Elections," January 6, 2017, p. 2.
23 DNI "Assessing the Russian Activities and Intentions in Recent US Elections," January 6, 2017, p. 2.

for authenticity."[24] Its founder, Julian Assange, had pre-existing contacts and a broadcasting contract with RT (previously Russia Today) – long suspected to be a Kremlin propaganda platform and a "soft power" defense against Western media's "anti-Russian" reporting.[25]

The Clinton campaign team, and Democratic Congressional Campaign Committee (DCCC) and Democratic National Committee (DNC) were each subjected to cyberattacks which breached their systems. As Chapter 1 showed, the U.S. intelligence community had been informed by their Dutch counterparts in the summer of 2015 this was happening. The extent to which this was acted on, or why it was not acted on sooner is uncertain, but it damaged the Clinton campaign.[26] It is worth noting that the DNC is a private nonprofit organization and not a government body where the U.S. government can directly intervene. The DNC had cybersecurity defenses, including filters and firewalls to prevent against known spam, phishing, and malware attacks, but against a determined and well-resourced nation-state APT they were a sitting duck.[27] They were also considered by senior members of the USIC to be a legitimate foreign intelligence target.[28]

In September 2015 an FBI Special Agent called the DNC to warn them. He repeatedly called back in the weeks and months that followed but the FBI's approach remained low-key (despite their Washington DC offices being a half mile apart). The Obama White House appeared to be slow moving in deciding a course of action and reluctant to involve the intelligence community. It is also likely the seriousness and scope of Russian operations was underestimated. Importantly, the DNC did not inform the DCCC they had been compromised. They are housed

24 DNI "Assessing the Russian Activities and Intentions in Recent US Elections," January 6, 2017, p. 3.

25 Monika L. Richter, "What We Know about RT (Russia Today)" (September 10, 2017), https://www.europeanvalues.net/wp-content/uploads/2017/09/What-We-Know-about-RT-Russia-Today-1.pdf; Matthew Kupfer, "How Russia and WikiLeaks Became Allies Against the West. Some claim WikiLeaks is working for the Kremlin. The reality is hardly so simple" (March 16, 2017), https://www.themoscowtimes.com/2017/03/16/how-russia-and-wikileaks-became-allies-against-the-west-a57443. Both accessed 4 September 2019.

26 Eelco Bosch van Rosenthal, "Dutch intelligence first to alert U.S. about Russian hack of Democratic Party" (January 25, 2018), https://nos.nl/nieuwsuur/artikel/2213767-dutch-intelligence-first-to-alert-u-s-about-russian-hack-of-democratic-party.html, accessed 22 July 2023.

27 Eric Lipton, David E. Sanger, and Scott Shane, "The Perfect Weapon: How Russian Cyberpower Invaded the U.S." (December 13, 2016), https://www.nytimes.com/2016/12/13/us/politics/russia-hack-election-dnc.html, accessed 23 July 2023.

28 "Cyber Threats: Perspectives from the NSA and FBI" (March 21, 2017), https://www.aspeninstitute.org/events/cyber-threats-perspectives-nsa-fbi/, accessed 22 July 2023.

in the same building on Capitol Hill, and the DCCC had also been compromised by this point.[29]

It was not until April 2016 that the private cybersecurity company Crowd-Strike was called in to help. It is reported that only then were the FBI and NSA to become involved.[30] By this time seven months had passed. Even then, Russian intelligence still maintained access until at least June.[31] In mid-June, the DNC decided to go public but by then it was too late. The first hacked e-mails began to be leaked by "Guccifer 2.0" the day after.[32] The USIC believed this was a GRU operation conducted by APT28/"Fancy Bear." No mention was made of the SVR and APT29/"Cozy Bear."[33] This is despite strong evidence it was APT29/"Cozy Bear" that had first breached the DNC.[34]

The 2019 Mueller Report evidenced GRU involvement. It detailed that Russia's GRU Military Unit 26165 had two departments devoted to malware development and spear phishing. A third was devoted to Bitcoin mining (Bitcoin was used to pay for servers, websites, and equipment through which the GRU sought to cover their tracks). Military Unit 74455 "separately hacked computers belonging to state boards of elections, secretaries of state, and U.S. companies" providing election software and hardware. They also assisted Unit 26165 in leaking to Wikileaks, publicizing the releases, and through "publication of anti-Clinton content on social media accounts operated by the GRU."[35]

The GRU was known for pursuing specific targets for months in order to compromise them. Once inside, the GRU deploys malware tools to maintain persistent access whilst moving laterally and vertically through and across networks. This spear phishing has involved sending repeating bespoke messages for over a year to high-value individuals until one succeeds and the bait is swallowed. This was one of the prime methods used to gain access into the Clinton campaign,

---

29 Lipton et al., "The Perfect Weapon."
30 David E. Sanger and Eric Schmitt, "Spy Agency Consensus Grows That Russia Hacked D.N.C." (July 26, 2016), https://www.nytimes.com/2016/07/27/us/politics/spy-agency-consensus-grows-that-russia-hacked-dnc.html, accessed 23 July 2023.
31 DNI "Assessing the Russian Activities and Intentions in Recent US Elections," January 6, 2017, p. 2.
32 Lipton et al., "The Perfect Weapon." The original Guccifer is the Romanian Marcel Lazar.
33 DNI "Assessing the Russian Activities and Intentions in Recent US Elections," January 6, 2017, p. 2.
34 van Rosenthal, "Dutch intelligence first to alert U.S. about Russian hack," Lipton et al., "The Perfect Weapon."
35 Mueller Report Volume I, p. 37.

DNC, and DCCC.[36] When CrowdStrike undertook the incident response for the hack on the DNC in June 2016, they promptly identified both APT28 and APT29 on the network. CrowdStrike argued that both "Fancy Bear" and "Cozy Bear" had attempted "to target our customers in the past and know them well."[37] Their analysis appears at odds with the Mueller Report and a July 2018 U.S. Grand Jury indictment which identified these two groups as the GRU's Military Units 26165 and 74455.[38]

2.2 Hacking online voting systems

Separately, there was a hacking attempt of the online voting systems of U.S. states. This included Unit 74455 sending spear-phishing e-mails to public officials administrating the elections and companies providing voting technology. It met with limited success.[39] As part of the wider post-mortem this was the subject of a series of Congressional hearings. Richard Burr, the Republican chairman of the Select Committee on Intelligence, saw that America was "woefully unprepared" and was caught "flatfooted" and this "helped Moscow to potentially build detailed knowledge of how our elections work ... with the goal of undermining our system."[40] Committee Vice Chair, Democratic Senator Mark Warner, also pointed out "Less well understood ... is the intelligence community's conclusion that they also secured and maintained access to elements of multiple U.S. State and local electoral boards."[41]

Despite widespread attempts, only two intrusions in Arizona and Illinois were detected. There, they got into the voter registration databases but made no changes. Up to 21 American states are suspected to have been in the crosshairs.

---

36 Leo Kelion "Why Windows hack is being blamed on Russia-linked group" (November 6, 2016), http://www.bbc.co.uk/news/technology-37847070, accessed 2 November 2016.

37 Dmitri Alperovitch, "Bears in the Midst: Intrusion into the Democratic National Committee" (June 14, 2016), https://www.crowdstrike.com/blog/bears-midst-intrusion-democratic-national-committee/, accessed 13 October 2016.

38 Mueller Report Volume II, pp. 36–41.

39 Mueller Report Volume I, pp. 49–51.

40 Russian Interference in the 2016 U.S. Elections Hearing before the Select Committee on Intelligence of the United States Senate, Wednesday, June 21, 2017, p. 1, https://www.intelligence.senate.gov/sites/default/files/hearings/Russian%20Interference%20in%20the%202016%20U.S.%20Elections%20S.%20Hrg.%20115-92.pdf, accessed 21 September 2019.

41 Russian Interference in the 2016 U.S. Elections Hearing before the Select Committee on Intelligence, p. 3.

Eighteen are known to have been targeted.[42] Although the voting systems are varied and decentralized, "states may be vulnerable when it comes to the defense of voter registration and voter history databases."[43] The Department for Homeland Security (DHS) was confident Russia was not successful and would not be successful in future elections. This is because of multiple checks and redundancies; the diversity of systems at state and federal level; air-gapped voting machines with no Internet connection; pre-election testing; "and processes for media, campaign, and election officials to check, audit, and validate results."[44] However, "multiple elements of election infrastructure remain potentially vulnerable to cyber intrusions" and "The risk … varies from county to county, between types of devices used, and among processes used by polling stations."[45]

The Multi-State Information Sharing and Analysis Center (MS-ISAC) and National Cybersecurity and Communications Center (NCCIC) are on hand to advise states but there are still many ways to hack voting machines. Many are only updated when absolutely necessary and "Voting infrastructure desperately needs vetting from hackers" as well as dedicated funding.[46] Contemporaneously the GRU was also going after firms supplying software for voter registration (useful for spear-phishing ruses) and were able to access details of 500,000 voters through a website attack on a state board of elections.[47]

42 Senate Intel Committee Releases Unclassified 1st Installment in Russia Report, Updated Recommendations on Election Security, Tuesday, May 8, 2018, https://www.intelligence.senate.gov/press/senate-intel-committee-releases-unclassified-1st-installment-russia-report-updated, accessed 21 September 2019.

43 Russian Interference in the 2016 U.S. Elections Hearing before the Select Committee on Intelligence, p. 3.

44 Russian Interference in the 2016 U.S. Elections Hearing before the Select Committee on Intelligence, p. 10.

45 Russian Interference in the 2016 U.S. Elections Hearing before the Select Committee on Intelligence, p. 10.

46 A Congressional Task Force on Election Security reported on these protections in a detailed report in January 2018, https://homeland.house.gov/imo/media/doc/TFESReport.pdf; Lily Hay Newman, "At DefCon, the Biggest Election Threat Is Lack of Funding" (August 10, 2018), https://www.wired.com/story/defcon-election-threat-funding/; Donie O'Sullivan and Sarah Mucha, "Hackers bring stark warning about election security to Capitol Hill ahead of midterms" (September 27, 2018), https://edition.cnn.com/2018/09/27/politics/hackers-warning-midterm-elections/index.html, all accessed 21 September 2019.

47 https://www.justice.gov/file/1080281/download, pp. 25–26, accessed 9 September 2019.

2.3 Hacking the DCCC, DNC, and Clinton campaign team

By mid-March 2016 Unit 26165 had breached the DCCC and DNC. They also continued targeting the Clinton campaign team through e-mail accounts. Their initial social engineering forays involved searches of websites belonging to the Democratic Party (or affiliated to the party). After this open source intelligence gathering, hundreds of spear-phishing e-mails were then sent to work on personal e-mail accounts. Through this they gained access to numerous members of the Clinton campaign, from junior volunteers to informal Clinton Campaign advisors and to John Podesta, the campaign chairman, and a DNC employee.[48]

Alongside campaign communications and documents, the GRU also gained access to the DCCC network over a period of weeks using spear-phished credentials gathered through e-mails. They then followed tried and trusted tactics, techniques, and procedures (TTPs) which allowed them to move laterally and vertically in the network. They eventually gained system administrator privileges which gave them unrestricted network access. Once inside the DCCC they moved laterally through virtual private network (VPN) connections, again using stolen credentials, into the DNC network from April 18 to June 8, 2016. They used purpose-built malware dubbed "X-Agent," "X-Tunnel," and "Mimikatz." "X-agent" allowed them to log keystrokes and take screenshots and gather further data. "X-Tunnel" encrypted and exfiltrated the data back to servers controlled by the GRU.[49] "Mimikatz" enabled, disabled, and removed privileges, exported security certificates and could disable security and log-on services.[50]

Through "X-Agent" they captured login details and screenshots which they sent to their proxy servers and access to the DCCC allowed them to steal credentials of a user who had access to the DNC network. Exfiltration required them to compress the files. They then used "X-Tunnel," which provides a VPN-type connection, through to their servers. After they had exfiltrated files they attempted to cover their tracks by deleting event logs, login history, and corroborating files. Eventually they were caught. CrowdStrike disabled "X-Agent" and attempted to exclude them from the DNC's network. However, the GRU then began deploying countermeasures and researched CrowdStrike's reporting of "X-Agent" and "X-Tunnel." These countermeasures meant the GRU teams were able to maintain ac-

48 Mueller Report Volume I, p. 37.
49 Mueller Report Volume I, pp. 38–39.
50 "Hacktool.Mimikatz" (June 21, 2018), https://www.symantec.com/security-center/writeup/2012-042615-3731-99, accessed 16 September 2019.

cess through a Linux version of "X-Agent" and the DNC's use of third-party Cloud services.

The stolen information was leaked to (and released by) Wikileaks in July 2016 where (at the time of writing) it is still available on their searchable Internet database.[51] The now closed GRU-registered website DCLeaks was also used to release hacked e-mails from personal accounts. This included personally identifying information such as prior political jobs, financial information (including files on fundraising), and internal correspondence on the Clinton Campaign. Also released were a small number of e-mails from Grand Old Party (GOP/Republican Party) members. Russian-controlled Facebook pages were used to publicize these hacks under the guise of leaks.[52]

The DCLeaks site alone, which purported to have been established by American hacktivists, had 1 million visitors before it was closed. A DCLeaks Facebook page and Twitter account was also set up, along with other accounts which promoted DCLeaks. This included a WordPress blog claiming to be written by "Guccifer 2.0." The "Guccifer 2.0" persona was also used to release hacked documents in a series of blog posts and was offered to "The Smoking Gun" which, after verifying them, published them on its website on June 15, 2016. "Guccifer 2.0" also spoke via Twitter to a member of the Trump campaign team about the leaks.[53] A candidate for Congress even got in touch with "Guccifer 2.0" and was sent documents on their opponent. The GRU was also proactively sending stolen data to a number of other individuals and organizations (including The Hill) as well as conspiring with Wikileaks which released 50,000 documents from GRU hacks.[54]

CrowdStrike's 2016 analysis of the DNC hack not only highlights how social engineering tactics were used to gain entry into the systems of the DNC (common to many other groups) but also reveals that underneath the surface of what some considered to be criminals, hacktivists, or script kiddies was Russian intelligence. Specifically, this was the SVR ("Cozy Bear") and GRU ("Fancy Bear") separately engaging in active measures and espionage. CrowdStrike noted that both APT28/"Fancy Bear" and APT29/"Cozy Bear" engage in extensive political and economic

51 https://wikileaks.org/, accessed 5 September 2023.

52 Mueller Report Volume I, pp. 41–42.

53 Mueller Report Volume I, pp. 43–44 and Anonymous, "DNC Hacker Releases Trump Oppo Report. 'Guccifer 2.0' claims credit for illegal breach" (June 15, 2016), http://www.thesmokinggun.com/documents/crime/dnc-hacker-leaks-trump-oppo-report-647293 and William Bastone, "Roger Stone's Russian Hacking 'Hero' Trump loyalist communicated with 'Guccifer 2.0,'" http://www.thesmokinggun.com/documents/investigation/roger-stone-and-guccifer-913684, both accessed 5 September 2019.

54 https://www.justice.gov/file/1080281/download, accessed 9 September 2019.

cyberespionage. APT29/"Cozy Bear" had also penetrated the unclassified networks of the White House, State Department, and U.S. Joint Chiefs of Staff. Both groups have also targeted companies across the defense industrial base, including defense ministries. They have been found operating in Western Europe, Brazil, Canada, China, Georgia, Iran, Japan, Malaysia, and South Korea as well as the United States. Meanwhile, both groups stood accused by Microsoft of hitting second order targets including political advisers, journalists, as well as organizations linked to political activism in Central Asia. Amidst all this activity, what stood out in the DNC hack was the lack of deconfliction between APT28 and APT29 and the GRU and SVR. This competition saw them separately breach the same systems and steal identical credentials. This is not something generally observed in the West because this can compromise operations.[55]

3 Active measures: "Project Lakhta" and IRA and attempts to influence U.S. voters

Their "hack and leak" operation was allied to a Russian active measures campaign which included propaganda and dis/misinformation, destabilization attempts, and election interference.[56] Active measures (as well as covert action) can also include assistance to foreign political factions or individuals or even the overthrow (or supporting an attempted overthrow) of a regime.[57] The distinctions between covert action and active measures can be blurry. For Russia, active measures are rooted in practices honed by the KGB and GRU during the Cold War. In a world of massive digital interconnections, the means of conducting these operations have changed but there remain "strikingly close parallels ... between the 'ends' and 'ways' of the Soviet active measures playbook and the 'malign influence' of Putin's Russia."[58] These have many historical antecedents, but their modern iteration includes hacking politically connected individuals and organizations and the generation of "fake news" stories for political effect.[59]

55 Alperovitch, "Bears in the Midst." Kelion "Why Windows hack is being blamed on Russia-linked group."

56 Darien Pun, "Rethinking Espionage in the Modern Era," *Chicago Journal of International Law*, Vol. 18, No. 1 (Summer 2017), pp. 353–391.

57 Now widely referred to as regime change.

58 Abrams, "Beyond Propaganda," p. 9.

59 John Sipher, "Western Covert Action and Russian Active Measures: Hypocrisy or Divergent Values?" (January 22, 2019), https://www.justsecurity.org/62324/western-covert-action-russian-active-measures/, accessed 10 March 2020.

The attempts to influence voters and public opinion were outsourced to the St. Petersburg-based Internet Research Agency (IRA). In the lead up to the Republican National Congress' hard-fought decision to support Donald Trump as the GOP candidate against Hillary Clinton, the IRA consistently supported his nomination over the other candidates including Ted Cruz, Marco Rubio, and Jeb Bush.[60] During the presidential election the IRA developed and actively ran social media accounts purporting to be fellow citizens engaging in conversations and content sharing. Their focus was often on politically charged and divisive issues including race, culture, immigration, LGBT issues, and gun rights. 470 fake Russian Facebook accounts and Facebook pages were identified and $100,000 in advertising had been spent by the IRA. These were designed to amplify socially and politically divisive messages to voters across the ideological spectrum. Almost 4,000 Twitter IRA-connected accounts were also identified. These reached 677,775 voters who either followed these accounts or liked and retweeted content during the election.[61]

This was a widespread operation. Detailed research by Oxford University's Oxford Internet Institute (OII), commissioned by the SSCI showed that through social media the IRA reached tens of millions of U.S. users from 2013 to 2018. From 2015 to 2017 over 30 million liked and shared IRA Facebook and Instagram posts with family and friends. They also reacted to them and commented on the content. IRA posts and paid advertising were geared around significant dates in the U.S. political calendar, and actively responded to live domestic and international events and crises. Their activities increased from the Democratic and Republican National Conventions in July 2016 through to voting day in November 2016. This included the third of the Democratic primary debates and sixth Republican primary debate in January 2016 as well as the late September presidential candidate debate between Hillary Clinton and Donald Trump. Activity also peaked on December 29–30 as President Obama announced responses to Russia's election interference.[62]

---

60 Renee DiResta, Kris Shaffer, Becky Ruppel, David Sullivan, Robert Matney, Ryan Fox, Jonathan Albright, and Ben Johnson, "The Tactics & Tropes of the Internet Research Agency," pp. 79–82, https://cdn2.hubspot.net/hubfs/4326998/ira-report-rebrand_FinalJ14.pdf, accessed 27 August 2019.
61 David V. Gioe, Michael S. Goodman, and Alicia Wanless, "Rebalancing Cybersecurity Imperatives: Patching the Social Layer," *Journal of Cyber Policy*, Vol. 4, No. 1 (March 2019), p. 124.
62 Philip Howard, Bharath Ganesh, Dimitra Liotsiou, John Kelly, and Camille François, "The IRA, Social Media and Political Polarization in the United States, 2012–2018," Computational Propaganda Research Project, University of Oxford (2018), pp. 3, 12, https://comprop.oii.ox.ac.uk/wp-content/uploads/sites/93/2018/12/The-IRA-Social-Media-and-Political-Polarization.pdf, accessed 9 April 2019.

The OII's analysis demonstrated that Russian interference had begun in 2013 (ahead of the annexation of Crimea). They first focused on Twitter but then their efforts "quickly evolved into a multi-platform strategy involving Facebook, Instagram, and YouTube amongst other platforms."[63] Additional analysis by New Knowledge (now Yonder) of Austin, Texas, also commissioned by the SSCI, noted the massive amplification Russia was able to gain. Through Facebook the IRA reached 126 million people. Utilizing botnets, they posted 10.4 million tweets on Twitter. On Instagram they reached 20 million users. They also uploaded over 1,000 videos on YouTube. Russia had learned to conduct these campaigns on their own population to manufacture consent. It then used them to stir up dissent in their "sphere of influence" in their near abroad, especially Ukraine. Now, through the U.S.'s own indigenous social media platforms, they were able "to wage a propaganda war."[64]

The campaign included waves of false reports ranging from explosions at chemical plants to shootings and an outbreak of the Ebola virus. This was a sophisticated operation which "didn't just doctor screenshots from CNN; they also created fully functional clones of the websites of ... [local] TV stations and newspapers."[65] IRA operators were trained on "the nuances of American social polemics on tax issues, LGBT rights, the gun debate, and more ... their job was to incite [Americans] further and try to 'rock the boat.'"[66] Their aims were not guided by trying to turn Americans toward Russia but "to set Americans against their own government: to provoke unrest and discontent."[67]

3.1 Implementing "Project Lakhta"

Members of the IRA also traveled undercover to the United States to gather intelligence for their activities. There they bought and used equipment and rented server space to help conceal Russian involvement whilst avoiding detection by

63 Howard *et al.*, "The IRA, Social Media and Political Polarization in the United States, 2012–2018," p. 3.

64 "The Disinformation Report" (December 17, 2018), https://www.newknowledge.com/articles/the-disinformation-report/, accessed 26 August 2019.

65 Adrian Chen, "The Agency," https://www.nytimes.com/2015/06/07/magazine/the-agency.html?_r=0, accessed 27 August 2019.

66 Putin's Asymmetric Assault on Democracy in Russia and Europe: Implications for U.S. National Security A Minority Staff Report, Committee on Foreign Relations United States Senate, January 10, 2018, p. 45, https://www.foreign.senate.gov/imo/media/doc/FinalRR.pdf, accessed 5 November 2019.

67 Putin's Asymmetric Assault, p. 45.

counterintelligence agencies and law enforcement. Their activities, and those of the wider IRA, were funded by Yevgeny Prigozhin using various shell companies through his firm Concord. This included contacting and paying U.S. social media users to disparage or promote candidates. The IRA employed hundreds to carry out these tasks and had a budget of millions of dollars. It was a well-structured organization with a management team and dedicated departments. It had departments for graphics, data analysis, search-engine optimization, IT, and a finance department which budgeted and allocated funds and payments. Their aim was "to sow discord in the U.S. political system, including the 2016 U.S. presidential election."[68]

"Organic posting" was their main method of engagement. This mainly targeted African American and Hispanic voters. They sought to mislead them by misrepresenting voting procedures and suggesting boycotting the elections. This was an attempt to dilute opposition through voter suppression especially towards those more likely to vote for Democratic nominee, Hillary Clinton. In addition, those identified as being on the extreme right were encouraged to be confrontational with "sensationalist, conspiratorial, and other forms of junk political news and misinformation" but this was also spread "to voters across the political spectrum."[69]

African Americans were specifically targeted by the IRA with messages intended to sow distrust and division. Attempts were also made to redirect voters to third-party candidates whilst discouraging voter turnout through messages like "stay home on Election Day, your vote doesn't matter." To this was added messaging which played on distrust of the federal government and Washington elites. Messages also promoted secessionist movements in Texas and California. In fomenting these grass roots movements, secessionism was sometimes equated to Brexit.[70] In addition, conservatives and those on the right were being courted through messaging on issues including support of the military, policing (especially against the Black Lives Matter movement), Second Amendment (gun) rights, and underlying themes of patriotism and concerns over immigration.[71]

From the beginning of the presidential primaries to the election itself, pro-Donald Trump and anti-Hillary Clinton sentiments were being disseminated. Posts supporting Julian Assange and Wikileaks and denigrating then FBI Director,

---

68 https://www.justice.gov/file/1035477/download, accessed 26 August 2019.
69 Howard et al., "The IRA, Social Media and Political Polarization in the United States, 2012–2018," p. 3.
70 DiResta et al., "The Tactics & Tropes of the Internet Research Agency," pp. 8–9.
71 Howard et al., "The IRA, Social Media and Political Polarization in the United States, 2012–2018," p. 18.

James Comey, were also evident. This also included messages immediately prior to the leak from the DNC by Wikileaks on October 5, 2016. Distrust of mainstream media reporting was also a theme advanced by the IRA. The SSIC commissioned report by New Knowledge identified three broad groups had been targeted. These were African Americans, and left and right-leaning voters, with messaging "designed to influence individuals and to shape narratives."[72] As well as this, websites were created directing unsuspecting users to Russian-created content and automated content, including contemporaneous news events. Real world groups such as United Muslims of America, Cop Block, Black Guns Matter, and L for Life were also used. This was believed to be "an attempt to loosely backstop an identity if a curious individual did a Google Search, or to piggyback on an established brand."[73]

The IRA's YouTube videos carried anti-Hillary Clinton content. Google, YouTube's parent company, confirmed these had come from Gmail addresses affiliated to the IRA. They were linked to multiple social media accounts across platforms with advertising "clickbait" used to drive traffic to IRA Facebook pages. The pages had inflammatory content designed to outrage. The IRA particularly targeted right-wing and conservative voters with messaging designed to encourage this demographic to get behind the Trump campaign. Meanwhile, undecided floating voters (especially African Americans) were instead encouraged to think about boycotting the election and prompted to think cynically about whether to turn out to vote (a form of voter suppression). Repetitive slogans were introduced with messaging designed to cast doubt on the ability to change established political institutions through processes like elections. This included concerns whether structural inequalities faced by African Americans would be served through an establishment candidate like Hillary Clinton. The IRA diverted this demographic by negatively representing issues such as policing and spotlighting cases of police violence, wealth divides and poverty, as well as disproportionate levels of incarceration.[74]

Meanwhile, three sets of messages were being promoted to right-wing/right-leaning voters and conservatives. These were anti-immigration slogans blended with patriotic messaging and how liberals were appeasing immigrants and ethnic minorities (non-white) at the expense of U.S. citizens. This "othering" was used to reinforce Trump's campaign messaging about immigration concerns, open borders, and the wall he planned to build on the Mexican–American border. This

72 DiResta et al., "The Tactics & Tropes of the Internet Research Agency," p. 13.
73 DiResta et al., "The Tactics & Tropes of the Internet Research Agency," p. 13.
74 Howard et al., "The IRA, Social Media and Political Polarization in the United States, 2012–2018," p. 18.

led to "divisive, and at times prejudiced and bigoted, statements about minorities, particularly Muslims."[75]

Whilst efforts were made to split the vote of groups more likely to support the election of Hillary Clinton by promoting third party candidates, "What is clear is that all of the messaging clearly sought to benefit the Republican Party – and specifically, Donald Trump."[76] OII's research, based on the same data set provided by Facebook, Twitter, and Google/YouTube to the SSCI (made available to them and the team from New Knowledge) found that Trump was most mentioned in messaging to right-wing and conservative voters. Groups of voters that were more likely to vote for Clinton over Trump were targeted with messaging to dismay, distract, confuse, and discourage them from voting. In essence, "While the IRA strategy was a long-term one, it is clear that activity between 2015 and 2016 was designed to benefit President Trump's campaign."[77]

A February 2018 indictment by the Department of Justice (DOJ) revealed the name of the Kremlin/IRA operation as "Project Lakhta."[78] "Project Lakhta" was funded through Concord. Dubbed "Putin's chef" as his firm – Concord – catered to the Kremlin, Prigozhin was the founder, or was fronting funds, to the IRA through companies affiliated to Concord. Fourteen separate bank accounts were used by "Project Lakhta" to try to conceal sources of funding.[79] Mikhail Bystrov was the IRA's general director and Mikhail Burchik the executive director. Burchik oversaw operational planning, infrastructure, and personnel.

Aleksandra Krylova was a scout who traveled to the U.S. in 2014 to gather intelligence. She was followed by Sergey Polozov, the manager of the IRA's IT department who oversaw the procurement of U.S. servers and other computer equipment. Anna Bogacheva headed their data analysis group and worked on translation. The head of translation, Maria Bovda, also visited the U.S. Her husband, Robert Bovda, the deputy head of translation, also tried to visit but was denied a visa. Dzheykhun Aslanov, who oversaw many of the operations targeting the 2016 U.S. presidential election, was also named in a February 2018 DOJ indictment as was Vadim Podkopaev and Gleb Vasilchenko, who were responsible for posting, monitoring, and updating social media content. Irina Kaverzina worked

75 Howard et al., "The IRA, Social Media and Political Polarization in the United States, 2012–2018," pp. 18–19.

76 Howard et al., "The IRA, Social Media and Political Polarization in the United States, 2012–2018," p. 19.

77 Howard et al., "The IRA, Social Media and Political Polarization in the United States, 2012–2018," p. 19.

78 https://www.justice.gov/file/1035477/download, p. 4.

79 https://www.justice.gov/file/1035477/download, pp. 6–7.

on the IRA's translation team and Vladimir Venkov posted, monitored, and updated social media content. The IRA's translation department was not simply substituting Russian to English. It included analytics of the platforms being used and produced graphical content for greatest effect.[80]

On their missions to the U.S., they purchased cameras, SIM cards, and cell phones they would discard after use (known as burner or drop phones). They also planned an exit strategy should they be caught. Krylova and Bogacheva traveled throughout the U.S. visiting Nevada, California, New Mexico, Colorado, Illinois, Michigan, Louisiana, Texas, and New York, and reported back what they found on their return. Another unnamed suspect traveled to Atlanta, Georgia, in November 2014. They were communicating with Americans to find out what and where best to target. On one visit in May 2016 they even arranged for someone to stand in front of the White House to hold up a placard on Prigozhin's birthday which read "Happy 55th Birthday Dear Boss."[81]

Back home in St. Petersburg, IRA operatives were working round-the-clock shifts to develop content and post to correlate with U.S. time zones. According to the February 2018 indictment this began with Facebook and Instagram groups and pages. These attracted hundreds of thousands of followers. This included "Secured Borders," "Blacktivist," "Army of Jesus," and "Heart of Texas." Adverts were then purchased to further the reach of these groups. Twitter accounts were created alongside these activities with one, "Tennessee GOP," purporting to be an official state Republican group. This alone attracted 100,000 followers. These online groups mutually supported and fed off one another whilst VPNs were used to make it appear these were being posted from within the U.S. to cover their Russian origins. They also used fake IDs to open PayPal accounts to make purchases.

At some point, through either an intelligence operation or leak from within Russia, the FBI gained access to the IRA's internal communications. This showed how the IRA were directing their campaign against Hillary Clinton and supporting Donald Trump (including against other Republican presidential candidates). This was not detected and from February 2016 IRA operatives were told to ramp up their posts and engagements, including allegations of voter fraud by the Democratic Party. At one campaign rally they promoted through the "United Muslims of America" account they persuaded an unwitting U.S. attendee to hold up a sign depicting Hillary Clinton which read "I think Sharia Law will be a powerful new direction of freedom." Further rallies were promoted including "March for Trump" in June 2016 and "Down with Hillary" the following month. Money was

80 https://www.justice.gov/file/1035477/download, pp. 13–23. Mueller Report Volume I, pp. 19–20.
81 https://www.justice.gov/file/1035477/download, p. 7.

even offered for Americans to attend, and an attempt was made to persuade a volunteer for the Trump campaign in New York to provide signs and placards. Other unwitting individuals were paid to dress up as Hillary Clinton in a prison uniform at Trump rallies in Florida.[82]

In early October 2018 the DOJ charged the chief accountant of "Project Lakhta," Elena Khusyaynova, with funding political interference, including the November 2016 presidential election and November 2018 midterm elections. These included payment to activists for advertisements, the promotion of news stories on social media platforms, registration of domain names, and the purchase of proxy servers. Her annual budget was estimated at $10 million with $35 million having been spent to date, including for operations outside the U.S., for "information warfare against the United States."[83] To what extent did this relatively small investment make an historic difference?

3.2 Did Russian interference make a difference to the election result?

In his opening statement on the influence social media had during the 2016 election SSCI Chairman Richard Burr stated:

> Even with the benefit of numbers and what can be calculated and measured, this is an incredibly complex story. We can look at the amount of money spent, the number of ads purchased, and draw conclusions about priorities. We can look at the divisive content of the ads and the pages that they directed people towards, the number of tweets and retweets, and the manipulated search results, and draw inferences about the intent of the information operation. What we cannot do, however, is calculate the impact that foreign meddling in social media had on this election, nor can we assume that it must be the explanation for an election outcome that many didn't expect.[84]

This calculation is difficult to assess but swing states with a history of passing from Republican to Democrat control and back again were especially targeted. This included Colorado, Florida, Iowa, Michigan, Minnesota, Nevada, New Hamp-

82 https://www.justice.gov/file/1035477/download, pp. 13–23.

83 Russian National Charged with Interfering in U.S. Political System, October 19, 2018, https://www.justice.gov/opa/pr/russian-national-charged-interfering-us-political-system; Alyza Sebenius and Kartikay Mehrotra, "Microsoft Data Shows Hackers Still Targeting U.S. Elections" (July 17, 2019), https://www.bloomberg.com/news/articles/2019-07-17/state-backed-hackers-still-targeting-u-s-elections-microsoft. Both accessed 2 September 2019.

84 Open Hearing: Social Media Influence in the 2016 U.S. Election before the United States Senate Select Committee on Intelligence, November 1, 2017, https://www.intelligence.senate.gov/hearings/open-hearing-social-media-influence-2016-us-elections#, accessed 21 September 2019.

shire, North Carolina, Ohio, Pennsylvania, Virginia, Wisconsin as well as "new" swing states of Arizona, Georgia, Maine, and Utah.[85]

Going into the election, most opinion polls, pollsters and professional psephologists believed (by sizable margins) that Hillary Clinton would be the 45th President of the United States. A post-election analysis by Nate Silver, then head of the widely respected polling and analytics company FiveThirtyEight, partly explained this failure of prediction on high uncertainty throughout the campaign due to large numbers of undecided voters.

Although Clinton won the popular vote by over 2.8 million votes, she lost the Electoral College 304 to 227. Silver contends that the mainstream media did not anticipate pre- or post-election, the effects a decline in African American turnout would have on the Clinton vote and focused instead on potential gains from Hispanic voters. Furthermore, major news organizations also failed to recognize the importance of FBI Director James Comey's letter to Congress on October 28, 2016 in their post-election reporting. This had indicated that the FBI was reopening its investigation into Hillary Clinton's use of a personal e-mail server for official State Department use. This was a pivotal interjection after which polling shifted towards Trump. It particularly resonated with late undecided voters who "broke strongly toward Trump in the final two weeks of the campaign, amid a news cycle dominated by discussion of the Comey letter and the WikiLeaks hack of Democratic emails."[86]

Clinton herself put significant blame for her loss on Comey's "misguided letter" with a section of her 2018 book, *What Happened*, focusing on "The Comey Effect."[87] Silver's initial post-mortem emphasized that mainstream media reporting might have heightened Trump's chances, but did not evaluate the role played by social media.[88] However, in a subsequent blog Silver directly addressed the question of Russian interference. He downplayed its significance pointing to a wide variety of factors, including the Comey letter, the use of the moniker "Crooked Hillary," and frequent chants of "lock her up." This drove home the message she was

---

85 Howard et al., "The IRA, Social Media and Political Polarization in the United States, 2012–2018," p. 21.

86 Nate Silver, "The Real Story of 2016" (January 19, 2017), https://fivethirtyeight.com/features/the-real-story-of-2016/, accessed 1 September 2019. Amy Watson, "Share of adults who trust news media most of the time in selected countries worldwide as of February 2019" (last updated July 1, 2019), https://www.statista.com/statistics/308468/importance-brand-journalist-creating-trust-news/, accessed 8 October 2019.

87 Clinton, *What Happened*, pp. 348, 403–407.

88 For a critique of Silver's approach see David Sumpter, *Outnumbered: From Facebook and Google to Fake News and Filter-bubbles – The Algorithms That Control Our Lives* (New York: Bloomsbury Sigma, 2018), chapter 8.

untrustworthy.[89] It was a line of attack also leveraged by Russia, and Clinton herself said "The controversy over my emails quickly cast a shadow over our efforts and threw us into a defensive crouch from which we never fully recovered."[90] For Silver, these "easier-to-prove effects" were more damaging, leaving him "fairly agnostic" about Russia's campaign.[91]

At this time, the extent of Russian interference was only starting to be revealed. The same day Silver filed his report the DOJ indicted 13 members of the IRA. The indictment revealed in some detail how Russia had sought to suppress voter turnout, especially among African Americans. Russia's messaging also included widespread allegations of voter fraud.[92] This might have been decisive. Clinton herself believed this critical, and called out the Trump campaign for misdirecting voters with "fake news" using "some of the same tactics as the Russians, including ... under-the-radar Facebook attacks."[93] "Fake news" stories were the 20 top performing during the election cycle. These generated 8.7 million engagements through shares, reactions, and commentary.[94] Under these conditions Russian messaging could have been "mistaken for background noise." For Silver, Russian engagement was potentially enough "to swing the election by 0.8 percentage points toward Trump – not a high hurdle to clear because 0.8 points isn't much at all."[95]

That the IRA was successful in messaging many millions of American voters raises a great many questions. If and how they influenced voters or were successful in swaying swing voters, splitting the vote, or dissuading targeted groups like African Americans or Hispanics from exercising their vote requires systematic and wide-ranging study. These are important areas of study for the future, especially as election strategists and influencers use many of the same tools and tactics

89 Nate Silver, "How Much Did Russian Interference Affect The 2016 Election? It's hard to say" (February 15, 2018), https://fivethirtyeight.com/features/how-much-did-russian-interference-affect-the-2016-election/, accessed 1 September 2019.

90 Clinton, *What Happened*, p. 72. The e-mail "scandal" is further discussed on pp. 11, 71–74, 86, 120, 122, 219–223, 289–323, 364, 403–406, 468. On the FBI's initial investigation and the reopening of it see Comey, *A Higher Loyalty*, pp. 161–187, 192–208, 238–239.

91 Silver, "How Much Did Russian Interference Affect The 2016 Election?"

92 https://www.justice.gov/file/1035477/download.

93 Clinton, *What Happened*, p. 419.

94 Joshua A. Tucker, Andrew Guess, Pablo Barberá, Cristian Vaccari, Alexandra Siegel, Sergey Sanovich, Denis Stukal, and Brendan Nyhan, "Social Media, Political Polarization, and Political Disinformation: A Review of the Scientific Literature" (March 2018), pp. 37–38, https://www.hewlett.org/wp-content/uploads/2018/03/Social-Media-Political-Polarization-and-Political-Disinformation-Literature-Review.pdf, accessed 17 November 2019.

95 Silver, "How Much Did Russian Interference Affect The 2016 Election?" See also Clinton, *What Happened*, pp. 377–426.

as the Russians and social media is increasingly at least as influential as traditional print and mainstream broadcast media in a trend that is only appearing to go in one direction.[96] Trump was unequivocal on Twitter: "The vote was not affected" but, as one senior British journalist asked, "How can he know? How can anyone be sure? And why is this question not being asked more loudly?"[97]

Mis and disinformation aimed at groups, constituencies, and interests of the left and right has been the subject of study by the OII and New Knowledge but what cannot be gauged from their studies is the effect this had on voter intentions, especially amongst key constituents in battleground states and particularly with undecided and swing voters. At one level, as consumers of this targeted content, people can fact check (as mainstream organizations increasingly do) but increasingly they rely on social media as reputable information sources. In growing numbers, social media has already become the primary source for news and current affairs. In 2018, almost 64.5 percent of Internet users saw breaking news on social media, including Facebook, Twitter, YouTube, Snapchat, and Instagram.[98] Why is this?

A polarized and politized mainstream media landscape often does not help sift fact from opinion, and soundbites and headline grabbers are more easily disseminated and consumed than substantive content and informed debate, even if this is reflective of the lack of consensus between Republicans and Democrats.[99] Relatedly, traditional print media is in decline. Since 2007 American newspaper journalists have halved. Out of 3,000 counties in the U.S., two-thirds no longer have a daily local newspaper. This is a trend replicated worldwide. It is not because there is decreasing appetite for news, but because news is being brought to them by social media platforms, instant notifications, or shared by friends and family. This is especially true of the big two of Facebook (Meta) and Google (Alphabet). These now claim the lion's share of advertising revenue that previous-

96 Elisa Shearer and Amy Mitchell, "Broad agreement in U.S. – even among partisans – on which news outlets are part of the 'mainstream media'" (May 7, 2021), https://www.pewresearch.org/short-reads/2021/05/07/broad-agreement-in-u-s-even-among-partisans-on-which-news-outlets-are-part-of-the-mainstream-media/, accessed 18 March 2024.

97 Deborah Haynes, "Sky Views: We need to know if Russia's interference won Trump the election" (April 21, 2019), https://news.sky.com/story/sky-views-we-need-to-know-if-russias-interference-won-trump-the-election-11699677, accessed 4 October 2019.

98 Nicole Martin, "How Social Media Has Changed How We Consume News" (November 30, 2018), https://www.forbes.com/sites/nicolemartin1/2018/11/30/how-social-media-has-changed-how-we-consume-news/#54fd33b93c3c, accessed 16 September 2019.

99 Alison Dagnes, *Super Mad at Everything All the Time. Political Media and Our National Anger* (New York: Palgrave: 2019). Tucker et al., "Social Media, Political Polarization, and Political Disinformation," pp. 49–53.

ly was the mainstay of print and television journalism. The advertising revenue that supported an independent press from the early nineteenth century onwards is now under threat as a result.[100]

The rise and increasing use of social media has also led to debates over media literacy and the ability or inability of segments of the population to discern between fact, fiction, and opinion. This has been one of the contributory factors behind what is being described as a legitimacy crisis facing traditional institutions in established democracies like the United States.[101] Social media has helped empower populists and populism and is a propellant for partisan opinions (and many other things). This is eating away at some of the core roots and branches of democracy and "Without this crisis ... Putin's options for political war would be vastly more limited."[102] These trends invite searching socio-political questions related to information consumption in the age of the Internet, social media, 24-hour news, and the role and responsibilities of social media companies and news outlets, including the mainstream media. In this "hearts and minds" battle the United States was *the* prime target for this form of active measures and with the most to lose.[103] *How* Russia accomplished "Project Lakhta" is easier to dissect as a result of the two detailed studies commissioned by the SSCI and the Mueller Report.

3.3 Facebook and Instagram

Russia had 187 million "engagements" on Instagram through targeting 20 million users. Although this far exceeded Facebook's 76.5 million, Facebook reached 126 million people. Instagram use by the IRA appears to have grown as media report-

---

100 Matt Stoller, "The great break-up of Big Tech is finally beginning" (September 9, 2019), https://openmarketsinstitute.org/op-eds-and-articles/great-break-big-tech-finally-beginning/, accessed 6 October 2019.

101 Carolien van Ham, Jacques Thomassen, Kees Aarts, and Rudy Andeweg (eds.), *Myth and Reality of the Legitimacy Crisis: Explaining Trends and Cross-National Differences in Established Democracies* (Oxford: Oxford University Press, 2017).

102 Mark Galeotti, "(Mis)Understanding Russia's two 'hybrid wars,'" *Critique & Humanism*, Vol. 59, No. 1 (2018), pp. 7–8. Reprinted in https://www.eurozine.com/misunderstanding-russias-two-hybrid-wars/?pdf, accessed 3 January 2018. These issues are further explored in David Runciman, *How Democracy Ends* (London: Profile Books, 2018) and Carl Miller, *The Death of the Gods: The New Global Power Grab* (London: William Heinemann, 2018).

103 Joel Brenner, "How Obama Fell Short on Cybersecurity: Under the President's Proposals, We'll Remain America the Vulnerable" (January 21, 2015), http://www.politico.com/magazine/story/2015/01/state-of-the-union-cybersecurity-obama-114411.html#ixzz3PjrwwEnf, accessed 24 January 2015.

ing on Russian operations on Facebook and Twitter spread.[104] Analysis requested by the Senate Select Committee on Intelligence found that Instagram (which had been purchased by Facebook in 2012) became a meaningful front for the IRA's influence operations. However, this was played down in Congressional testimony from Facebook's senior executives although Sheryl Sandberg, Facebook's then Chief Operating Officer, did admit the IRA had "posted about 120,000 pieces of content."[105]

New Knowledge's report commissioned by the SSCI was categorical in its assessments of the IRA's use of the social media ecosystem. Their analysis concluded that the IRA functioned almost like a digital marketing agency. They essentially had a "brand" they marketed on these platforms. This brand included memes or tropes, made up of pictures, icons, lyrics, and catchphrases (which are widespread and understood). These were easily and readily shared as part of their dissemination strategy, and this helped them build and shape their "advertising" to build up their cross-platform presence and strategic messaging and grow their audience. This was aided by likes, comments, and link-sharing as well as paid adverts and partnerships. These were "media mirages: interlinked information ecosystems designed to immerse and surround targeted audiences ... using digital marketing best practices, even evolving their Facebook Page logos and typography over time."[106]

Automation, including the use of "bots" built upon algorithms, data harvesting, big-data analytics, and micro-profiling were all in evidence. These were all features of IRA social media campaigns throughout the West as part of the wider Kremlin-orchestrated active measures campaign of mis and disinformation. Using the IRA provided a cloak of plausible deniability. Moreover, creating and disseminating divisive content also reflected, and was used to support, pre-existing views.[107] Facebook's Ads Manager software tool, which plays a key part of

---

104 DiResta et al., "The Tactics & Tropes of the Internet Research Agency," p. 42.

105 Hearing before the United States Senate Select Committee on Intelligence September 5, 2018, Testimony of Sheryl Sandberg Chief Operating Officer, Facebook, https://www.intelligence.senate.gov/sites/default/files/documents/os-ssandberg-090518.pdf, p. 2. Questions for the Record Senate Select Committee on Intelligence Hearing on Foreign Influence Operations Using Social Media, September 17, 2018, https://www.intelligence.senate.gov/sites/default/files/documents/Facebook%20Questions%20for%20the%20Record.pdf. Both accessed 20 September 2023.

106 DiResta et al., "The Tactics & Tropes of the Internet Research Agency," pp. 7. 50–61. On this ecosystem see Martin Moore, *Democracy Hacked: Political Turmoil and Information Warfare in the Digital Age* (London: Oneworld, 2018).

107 Gillian Warner-Søderholm, Andy Bertsch, Everlyn Sawe, Dwight Lee, Trina Wolfe, Josh Meyer and Uepati Normann Fatilua, "Who Trusts Social Media?" *Computers in Human Behavior*, Vol. 81 (April 2018), pp. 303–315 and "Number of social network users worldwide from 2010 to 2021 (in

its business model, then allowed them to target voters based on their interests and engagement on the platform.[108]

The IRA segmented these voters based on race, ethnicity, and other identifiers using their interests and location to target these groups. This messaging on Facebook and Instagram was used to expose U.S. voters to distracting or deliberate dis and misinformation, including content on external websites. Much of this was designed to provoke anger, annoyance, or cynicism. It especially appealed to what became Trump's base of support and sought to disenchant or disaffect potential Clinton voters and suppress turnout.[109]

Although the groups they established on Facebook were small in number, the content of these pages (targeting mainly African Americans and conservatives) reached approximately 31 million users. It was liked by almost 39 million (showing evidence of sharing), eliciting 3.5 million comments and nearly 5.4 million emoji reactions.[110] The Mueller Report indicated the IRA groups were still active until they began to be deactivated by Facebook from mid-2017. Facebook's own investigations showed that by then they had amassed hundreds of thousands of followers. The "United Muslims of America" page had over 300,000 followers, "Don't Shoot Us" over 250,000, "Being Patriotic" more than 200,000, and "Secured Borders" over 130,000.[111]

Christians were also targeted, including through the fabricated "Army of Jesus" account, which purported to preach Christian values. Emphasis was also placed on immigration and played on concerns of Muslim immigrants and terrorism. These groups lauded patriotism and were positive about those serving in the military. Anti-immigration rhetoric also mirrored and reflected Trump campaign rhetoric from early to mid-2016 as his primary campaign geared up. The Black Lives Matter movement was invoked as a threat as were many other real and fictious groups. Around 338,300 people saw rallies announced on Facebook. 62,500 planned to attend. As far is known no member of the IRA or Russian operative attended the real-world protests they promoted.[112]

billions)" (August 14, 2019 and regularly updated), https://www.statista.com/statistics/278414/number-of-worldwide-social-network-users/, accessed 1 September 2019.

108 For more detail see Sumpter, *Outnumbered.*

109 Howard et al., "The IRA, Social Media and Political Polarization in the United States, 2012–2018," p. 32.

110 Howard et al., "The IRA, Social Media and Political Polarization in the United States, 2012–2018," p. 32.

111 Mueller Report Volume I, p. 26.

112 Scott Shane, "How Unwitting Americans Encountered Russian Operatives Online" (February 18, 2018), https://www.nytimes.com/2018/02/18/us/politics/russian-operatives-facebook-twitter.html,

It is difficult to discern how many of the 76.5 million engagements across 3.3 million Facebook page followers – broken down as 30.4 million shares, 37.6 million likes, 3.3 million comments, and 5.2 million reactions to these pages of content – were from genuine voters and how many were generated by the IRA. What can be discerned is the "content that garnered the most Likes was Being Patriotic (Right-targeted; 6.3 million Likes) ... most comments ... Stop All Invaders (Right-targeted, 773,305 comments), most reactions ... Blacktivist (Black-targeted, 1.4 million reactions), most shares ... [and] Heart of Texas (Right-targeted, 4.8 million shares)."[113] Facebook's General Counsel, Colin Stretch, believed around 126 million people had viewed IRA content in the two years from 2014 to 2016.[114] The Select Committee on Intelligence concluded that 66 percent of messaging by the IRA raised racial issues which targeted African Americans.[115]

3.4 Facebook and damage limitation

In the wake of the 2016 election, Facebook played down its role in facilitating the IRA. After the DOJ's February 2018 indictment of IRA members, Facebook's vice president for advertising, Rob Goldman, used Twitter to claim, "I have seen all of the Russian ads and I can say very definitively that swaying the election was *NOT* the main goal." This was retweeted by President Trump.[116] A white paper, "Information Operations and Facebook" co-authored by Alex Stamos, Facebook's then Chief Security Officer, also played down their role. It recognized that social media (and Facebook particularly) reaches and potentially influences its global audience and has no historical parallel. But in addition to the positive benefits of the interconnections Facebook extolls, it also generates openings for malicious actors to exploit it for information operations.[117]

accessed 1 September 2019 and Howard et al., "The IRA, Social Media and Political Polarization in the United States, 2012–2018," p. 34.

113 DiResta et al., "The Tactics & Tropes of the Internet Research Agency," p. 21.

114 Mueller Report Volume I, p. 15. See also Open Hearing: Social Media Influence in the 2016 U.S. Election.

115 Report of the Select Committee on Intelligence United States Senate on Russian Active Measures Campaigns and Interference in the 2016 Election Volume 2: Russia's Use of Social Media with Additional Views (October 2019), https://www.intelligence.senate.gov/sites/default/files/documents/Report_Volume2.pdf, accessed 10 October 2019.

116 Shane, "How Unwitting Americans Encountered Russian Operatives Online."

117 Jen Weedon, William Nuland, and Alex Stamos, "Information Operations and Facebook," pp. 3–4, https://about.fb.com/wp-content/uploads/2017/04/facebook-and-information-operations-v1.pdf, accessed 26 August 2019, and Alexander J. Martin, "Facebook's security chief warns 'not all

Stamos et al. termed these “false amplifiers” and set them in the historical context of foreign influence operations stretching back to antiquity. They also tackled the use of the term “fake news” which it said “has emerged as a catch-all phrase to refer to everything from news articles that are factually incorrect to opinion pieces, parodies and sarcasm, hoaxes, rumors, memes, online abuse, and factual misstatements by public figures.”[118] What Facebook found was networks of these politically-motivated “false amplifiers” and “financially-motivated fake accounts ... sometimes ... commingling,” and exhibiting similar behaviors to authentic accounts.[119] These “curated accounts” presented “authentic characteristics with well-developed online personas.”[120] Illustrating the IRA’s *modus tollens*, Yevgeny Prigozhin, said of these charges: “Americans are very impressionable people. They see what they want to see. If they want to see the devil – let them see one.”[121]

The IRA’s skilled efforts displayed features found in Chinese theories of Social Psychological War potentially imported into Russia and reflected in the “Gerasimov doctrine.”[122] Facebook saw how Russian efforts had been directed to promoting or denigrating a specific cause or issue, sowing distrust in political institutions and spreading confusion. This was allied to coordinated or repeated comments and coordinated “likes” and reactions through groups or pages which masked their underlying purpose mixed with legitimate and unrelated content. These were sown to “spread sensationalistic or heavily biased news or headlines, often distorting facts to fit a narrative.”[123]

Facebook did not believe automated “bots” were used. Instead coordinated groups were responsible based on the language skills needed alongside basic knowledge of the political environment. Instead, it was believed that lesser-skilled

voices equal’” (June 2, 2018), https://news.sky.com/story/facebooks-security-chief-warns-not-all-voices-equal-11392482, accessed 30 September 2019.

118 Weedon et al., “Information Operations and Facebook,” p. 4.

119 Greg Myre, “‘Putin’s Chef’ Has His Fingers In Many Pies, Critics Say” (January 30, 2019), https://www.npr.org/2019/01/30/685622639/putins-chef-has-his-fingers-in-many-pies-critics-say?t=1566819541250, accessed 26 August 2019. Weedon et al., “Information Operations and Facebook,” p. 8.

120 Weedon et al., “Information Operations and Facebook,” p. 8.

121 Myre, “‘Putin’s Chef’ Has His Fingers In Many Pies, Critics Say.”

122 Timothy L. Thomas, *Decoding the Virtual Dragon. Critical Evolutions in the Science and Philosophy of China’s Information Operations and Military Strategy* (Fort Leavenworth, KS: Foreign Military Studies Office, 2007); Dai Qingmin, *New Perspectives on War* (Beijing: PLA Publishing House, 2008).

123 Weedon et al., “Information Operations and Facebook,” p. 9.

Russians could have been employed for guidance on content and outlines.[124] Bots were used however, but perhaps not widely (or at all) on Facebook. Not all were Russian. 3.8 million tweets were believed generated by bots in the final month of the 2016 election (meaning around 20 percent were computer generated).[125]

What Facebook did admit is that it was a conduit for pointing to the leaks from the DNC and used to amplify and spread them. However, Facebook's report, and subsequent actions, sought to minimize their responsibility. Facebook's conclusion was that the public needed better media literacy and critical thinking skills to be able to distinguish mis and disinformation and manipulated debates. This is of value by helping "netizens" and the wider public understand the motivations and frame of reference for foreign actors (and many others) who post/repost false or fake news or misinformed opinion. In regard to the DNC/DNCC "leaks," it also includes questioning the reasons behind publishing and pushing leaked or stolen data (often spun for political effect).[126] The development of these analytical skills is rooted in education and awareness. However, it is also a post-mortem case of Facebook executives being wise only after the event and evidence that the platform was growing out of their control.

In Spring 2016, a subordinate of Stamos had raised the issue of Russian interference on Facebook with him. A team led by Stamos then began to uncover IRA activities. They had to start from scratch. They had no policies, procedures, or resources dedicated to mis and disinformation. Even then, Facebook's founder Mark Zuckerberg was skeptical of Russian interference as was Sheryl Sandberg. Nevertheless, both agreed that a group called "Project P" (for propaganda) should be set up.[127] "Project P"'s internal investigations led in September 2017 to a public review by Stamos on adverts placed on Facebook by Russia. What it found was ads as well as accounts focused on discussing and amplifying divisive social and political issues. These ranged across the political spectrum. Subjects included LGBT issues, immigration, and gun control rights and debates. A quarter of the ads were geographically targeted.[128] This self-discovery led Facebook to begin closing accounts

124 Weedon et al., "Information Operations and Facebook," p. 9.

125 Tucker et al., "Social Media, Political Polarization, and Political Disinformation," pp. 24–25, 32.

126 Weedon et al., "Information Operations and Facebook," p. 12.

127 Sheera Frenkel, Nicholas Confessore, Cecilia Kang, Matthew Rosenberg, and Jack Nicas, "Delay, Deny and Deflect: How Facebook's Leaders Fought Through Crisis" (November 14, 2018), https://www.nytimes.com/2018/11/14/technology/facebook-data-russia-election-racism.html?action=click&module=Top%20Stories&pgtype=Homepage, accessed 28 November 2019.

128 Alex Stamos, "An Update On Information Operations On Facebook" (September 6, 2017), https://newsroom.fb.com/news/2017/09/information-operations-update/, accessed 26 August 2019.

attributed to the IRA between August and September 2017. However, then IRA recreated them under different aliases.[129]

Since 2016 the use, and uses, of social media to spread mis and disinformation and target swing voters and key demographics through targeted advertising embroiled Facebook and Twitter most. Facebook, and its board, faced searching questions from government and the media. Zuckerberg told senators in April 2018 that Facebook was now in an "arms race" with Russia over these fake accounts.[130] Zuckerberg admitted, "We were too slow to spot and respond to Russian interference, and we're working hard to get better."[131] Separately but relatedly, Zuckerberg was also called before Congress to explain how data harvested from millions of Facebook users across the world was used "to profile and target them with political messages and misinformation, without their knowledge or consent."[132] This was the result of another controversy resulting from user access sold for almost $1 million to the controversial UK-based third party elections firm Cambridge Analytica.[133]

3.5 Twitter and local and mainstream media

During the U.S. presidential election cycle, 14 million people also engaged with IRA-run Twitter accounts using 3,841 false personas. The original content they created led to 72,801,807 engagements. This does not include retweeted content amplified by these accounts but does include the use of "Newsbots" (automated programs designed to deliver content on chosen topics). These accounts were

129 Howard et al., "The IRA, Social Media and Political Polarization in the United States, 2012–2018," pp. 9–12.

130 Anonymous, "Zuckerberg: Facebook In 'Arms Race' With Russia-Backed Groups" (April 10, 2018), https://www.rferl.org/a/zuckerberg-russia-election/29157227.html, accessed 28 September 2019.

131 Sara Salinas, "Congress releases Mark Zuckerberg's prepared testimony ahead of Wednesday's hearing" (April 10, 2018), https://www.cnbc.com/2018/04/09/congress-released-mark-zuckerbergs-prepared-testimony-ahead-of-wednesdays-hearing.html, accessed 22 May 2020.

132 Carole Cadwalladr, "Cambridge Analytica a year on: 'a lesson in institutional failure'" (March 17, 2019), https://www.theguardian.com/uk-news/2019/mar/17/cambridge-analytica-year-on-lesson-in-institutional-failure-christopher-wylie, accessed 30 September 2019. Both Zuckerberg and Sandberg were heavily briefed by lobbying firms hired by Facebook before their appearances and a public relations strategy mapped out. Frenkel et al., "Delay, Deny and Deflect."

133 Brennan Weiss, "New details emerge about Steve Bannon's ties to Cambridge Analytica" (March 24, 2018), https://www.businessinsider.com/steve-bannon-ties-to-cambridge-analytica-facebook-data-run-deep-2018-3?r=US&IR=T, accessed 30 September 2019.

registered through proxy servers based in the U.S. and Europe. They not only masked their Russian origins but made the persona appear authentic. A substantial number originated at IP addresses in Venezuela and the home of the IRA in St. Petersburg. These accounts spent a good deal of time retweeting posts and Facebook and Instagram helped develop deeper relationships between senders and recipients. They were essentially manufacturing and recycling content through social media platforms, using continuous looped reinforcement of content and messages.[134]

Mainstream political figures were taken in by the IRA's Twitter accounts. This included former Ambassador Michael McFaul, veteran Republican lobbyist Roger Stone, Fox News anchor Sean Hannity, and people affiliated to the Trump campaign, including Donald Trump himself. Also taken in were Donald J. Trump Jr., Eric Trump, Kellyanne Conway, Michael Flynn, and Michael Flynn Jr. These were often tweets containing allegations of voter fraud and mishandling of classified information by Hillary Clinton. Retweets and engagements by the Trump campaign team were then flagged to IRA account followers.[135] This lent credibility to these Russian-originated posts and posters. According to the Mueller Report, the Twitter accounts included @TEN_GOP (claiming to be an unofficial account of the Tennessee Republican Party; @jenn_abrams (a Virginian Trump supporter with 70,000 followers); @Pamela_Moore13 (a Texan Trump supporter with 70,000 followers); and @America:_1st_ (an anti-immigration persona with 24,000 followers).[136] @TEN_GOP had more followers than the real Tennessee Republican Party account and Kellyanne Conway and Donald Trump Jr. both retweeted posts from this fake account.[137]

Twitter was also used to help organize protests and rallies, including those on different sides of the same issue. These were allied to Facebook groups such as the "Heart of Texas" and "United Muslims of America" and included protests in Texas in May 2016.[138] The IRA-controlled accounts claimed they could not attend themselves as they had a scheduling conflict or were in another part of the U.S. at the time. IRA operatives would engage with the most fervent supporters of these events to encourage them to coordinate them. The IRA contacted local media

---

134 DiResta et al., "The Tactics & Tropes of the Internet Research Agency," pp. 18–20.

135 Mueller Report Volume I, pp. 15, 28, 35. See also Gillian Cleary, "Twitterbots: Anatomy of a Propaganda Campaign" (June 5, 2019), https://www.symantec.com/blogs/threat-intelligence/twitter bots-propaganda-disinformation, accessed 26 September 2019.

136 Mueller Report Volume I, p. 27.

137 The Tennessee Republican party asked them to take it down repeatedly. Open Hearing: Social Media Influence in the 2016 U.S. Election.

138 DiResta et al., "The Tactics & Tropes of the Internet Research Agency," p. 25.

(as these were likely to be more trusted than nationwide media outlets) to publicize these events and would post videos and photographs of rallies and protests to their accounts. Not all of these events took place. When they did, they varied in size but some attracted hundreds.[139]

The IRA targeted both right- and left-leaning voters with thousands of tweets and were adept at creating and using faked news stories and disinformation, leveraging local news outlets, playing on the theme that mainstream news and media could not be trusted. The OII's analysis of IRA Twitter data:

> shows a long and successful campaign that resulted in false accounts being effectively woven into the fabric of online US political conversations right up until their suspension. These embedded assets each targeted specific audiences they sought to manipulate and radicalize, with some gaining meaningful influence in online communities after months of behavior designed to blend their activities with those of authentic and highly engaged US users.[140]

Immediately prior to the election, IRA messaging alleging voter fraud and encouraging a grass roots uprising against the federal government were posted as part of the anti-Hillary Clinton lobby, a cornerstone built up (or upon) distrust of the DOJ, Department of Homeland Security (DHS), FBI, White House, and Obama administration. Posts targeted at "right-leaning" voters frequently denigrated mainstream media and the U.S. Intelligence Community and painted them as untrustworthy. They simultaneously eulogized about Donald Trump whilst aiming criticisms at Conservative rivals including senators Lindsey Graham and John McCain.[141]

The IRA consistently targeted local communities to generate support for events and rallies and played on concerns and promises including employment opportunities in rust-belt states and pro-police and pro-law enforcement pages linked to the Second Amendment and gun rights content. The IRA understood the concerns of the audience it was targeting, and content was not only tailored to them, it resonated with them. Advertising and merchandizing augmented the political messaging and although their overall advertisement spend was low, they were able to reach a mass audience with over 100,000 followers using only two dozen Facebook and Instagram accounts. Through just 109 Twitter accounts

139 Mueller Report Volume I, pp. 29–33. Zacchary Ritter and Priscilla Standridge, "Interaction with Local Media Tied to Trust in Local News" (September 12, 2019), https://news.gallup.com/opinion/gallup/266675/interaction-local-media-tied-trust-local-news.aspx, accessed 8 October 2019. This formed part of the February 2018 indictment of the IRA. https://www.justice.gov/file/1035477/download, p. 4.

140 Howard et al., "The IRA, Social Media and Political Polarization in the United States, 2012–2018," p. 27.

141 DiResta et al., "The Tactics & Tropes of the Internet Research Agency," p. 25.

(purporting to be legitimate news organizations) the IRA reached 660,335 followers. These "news accounts" were automated and nearly identical in content and included stories from local news outlets.[142] Not only were these spawned in Russia, but their tweets were also imported into Russian state media outlets including RT and Sputnik.[143] These "Russian state-sponsored media outlets" were the "'white propaganda' component" reinforcing the "symbiotic, mutually supporting system of disinformation."[144] Strategic messaging from RT included:

> an English-language video called 'Julian Assange Special: Do WikiLeaks Have the E-mail That'll Put Clinton in Prison?"... an exclusive interview with Assange entitled "Clinton and ISIS Funded by the Same Money." RT's most popular video on Secretary Clinton, "How 100% of the Clintons' "Charity" Went to ... Themselves," [which] had more than 9 million views on social media platforms. RT's most popular English language video about the President-elect, called "Trump Will Not Be Permitted To Win," featured Assange and had 2.2 million views.[145]

Mainstream media has been increasingly accused of becoming politicized and biased, not only in Russia but across the West, especially on politically-charged issues and during the election, U.S. reporting was increasingly seen to be growing more partisan and divisive.[146] Mainstream media content, television in particular, has long been seen as an important tool for the Russian state under Putin. RT's Editor in Chief, Margarita Simonyan, stated in 2016 that "the word 'propaganda' has a very negative connotation, but indeed, there is not a single international foreign TV channel that is doing something other than promotion of the values of the country that it is broadcasting from."[147]

These values not only change over time, but mainstream media content has become part of the fuel for large sections of voters who have growing mistrust in government, traditional media reporting, and choose to place more faith in

---

142 Press release, "Russian Trolls Relied on Local News More than Fake News in 2016 Presidential Election, New Analysis Finds" (November 19, 2018), https://www.nyu.edu/about/news-publications/news/2018/november/russian-trolls-relied-on-local-news-more-than-fake-news-in-2016-.html, accessed 8 October 2019.

143 Clinton, *What Happened*, p. 350.

144 Abrams, "Beyond Propaganda," p. 18.

145 DNI "Assessing the Russian Activities and Intentions in Recent US Elections," p. 4.

146 Travis N. Ridout (ed.), *New Directions in Media and Politics*, Second Edition (New York: Routledge, 2019); Paul Statham and Hans-Jörg Trenz (eds.), *The Politicization of Europe: Contesting the Constitution in the Mass Media* (London: Routledge: 2012),; Karen Akerlof, Katherine E. Rowan, Dennis Fitzgerald, and Andrew Y. Cedeno, "Communication of Climate Projections in US Media Amid Politicization of Model Science," *Nature Climate Change*, Vol. 2 (2012), pp. 648–654.

147 DNI "Assessing the Russian Activities and Intentions in Recent US Elections," p. 8.

new media (including social media) not only in the U.S. but globally.[148] Russia harnessed this. Up until 2022 and the invasion of Ukraine, RT broadcast in over 100 countries, and RT's YouTube channel "reached a record 7 billion views ... far surpassing the total number of views of BBC, CNN, Al Jazeera and Euronews" with more than 10 million subscribers.[149] RT's Twitter account also had 2.9 million followers and its Facebook page 5.7 million.[150]

The IRA also used Twitter to advance conspiracy theories including "Pizzagate," (a belief that a pizzeria was at the center of a child trafficking ring involving senior Democrats first spread on users of 4Chan and later perpetuated by the QAnon movement) the "globalist" agenda and the work of George Soros, anti-vaccination beliefs, and pseudoscience claims. Some of the most bizarre, and easily refutable, theories were ones aimed at African American communities. These included that Wolfgang Amadeus Mozart was Black, Shakespeare's plays had been written by a Black woman, and the Statue of Liberty was initially intended to be a black woman.[151] Anti-immigration and anti-Muslim rhetoric from IRA accounts continued through to at least November 2018 and was widely shared.[152] Facebook too saw continued Russian activity on its platform.[153] Other platforms including Vine, Gab, Meetup, VKontakte, LiveJournal, Reddit, Tumblr, Pinterest, and Medium were all also targeted. Video games were also targets for Russia (including Pokémon Go), browser extensions, and music apps. All were ranked and listed by Google's web crawling algorithms and are gamed by those (such as the IRA) who want to maximize publicity for their content. Google/Alphabet, YouTube, Facebook, and Twitter all make analytics available to amplify content and generate user engagement.[154]

---

148 2019 Edelman Trust Barometer Global Report, https://www.edelman.com/sites/g/files/aatuss191/files/2019-02/2019_Edelman_Trust_Barometer_Global_Report.pdf, accessed 4 September 2019.

149 "RT number one TV news network on YouTube with record 7 billion views," https://www.rt.com/about-us/press-releases/record-7-billion-views-rt/, accessed 25 September 2019.

150 Both accessed 25 September 2019: https://twitter.com/rt_com?lang=en; https://www.facebook.com/RTnews/.

151 DiResta et al., "The Tactics & Tropes of the Internet Research Agency," pp. 34–38, 66, 70.

152 DiResta et al., "The Tactics & Tropes of the Internet Research Agency," p. 24.

153 Heather Kelly, Julia Horowitz, and Donie O'Sullivan, "Facebook takes down 652 pages after finding disinformation campaigns run from Iran and Russia" (August 21, 2018), https://money.cnn.com/2018/08/21/technology/facebook-disinformation-iran-russia/index.html, accessed 1 October 2019.

154 https://analytics.twitter.com/about, https://analytics.facebook.com/; https://creatoracademy.youtube.com/page/course/analytics-series; https://analytics.google.com/analytics/web/provision/?authuser=0#/provision, all accessed 24 September 2019.

3.6 The reaction of social media companies

Twitter, Facebook, and Alphabet, the parent company of Google, were each accused of providing incomplete data sets to the SSCI. They were also accused of potentially misrepresenting evidence or evading scrutiny in Congressional statements.[155] When they appeared before the SSCI in November 2017 it was put to senior executives:

> many of us on this Committee have been raising this issue since the beginning of this year, and our claims were frankly blown off by the leaderships of your companies, dismissed, said, there's no possibility, nothing like this happening, nothing to see here. It bothers me, if you're really committed to trying to work with us to resolve this, that it took until this Committee continually went at you, and it was July and early August when you made your first presentations. And, candidly, your first presentations were less than sufficient and showed in my mind a lack of resources, a lack of commitment, and a lack of genuine effort. Candidly, your companies know more about Americans in many ways than the United States government does. And the idea that you had no idea any of this was happening strains your credibility.[156]

The OII were also critical of the way the social media platforms provided data to the SSCI. This made interrogating the data more difficult. The OII suggested that social media platforms need to be more open to researchers. This would allow legitimate research to better analyze how their platforms are reflecting significant movements and trends in public life. One of the ways social media platforms can do this is through improving access to their Application Programming Interfaces (APIs). For major universities Twitter used to grant access to a series of their APIs but then withdrew access. This made scrutiny and analysis more difficult (even for basic social scientific research).

The data Twitter provided to the SSCI did, however, cover activity in multiple languages. Facebook only provided English language activity and their API was very limited. No API was provided for Instagram. Facebook only disclosed a small number of pages revealing organic post data and chose not to disclose data from suspected IRA accounts or groups. For unclear reasons, Google supplied data in a format that was not machine-readable when it could have used standard machine readable file formats and useable advertising text and spreadsheets. In-

155 DiResta et al., "The Tactics & Tropes of the Internet Research Agency," pp. 5–6.
156 Open Hearing: Social Media Influence in the 2016 U.S. Election.

stead, these were provided as images and pdfs as though their submission would be printed out on paper.[157]

Whilst Google, in the wake of criticism levied at social media platforms and sites including YouTube did introduce greater transparency of political advertising and a searchable website for paid political content, nevertheless, social media providers have had longstanding problems tracking content on their platforms and in responding to content queries. Since 2016 Google adopted policies which ban non-U.S. citizens from running U.S. election ads.[158] Facebook also launched a similar transparency initiative but does not flag news reports as political advertising leaving ways to repackage political messaging.[159] Facebook's policies are still flawed.[160] Their current guidelines leave room for interpretation.[161] Through to its takeover by Elon Musk, Twitter published transparency reports since 2012 but, like Facebook and YouTube, it also faced longstanding criticism over how it moderated user posts and how posts were removed or accounts permanently or temporarily disabled for violating in-house content guidelines.[162] Content deregulation has been policy since Twitter was taken over by Musk during 2022 and rebranded as X.[163]

As these companies bite into the market share of broadcast television for political (and all other) advertising, how they are regulated and how they police

157 Howard et al., "The IRA, Social Media and Political Polarization in the United States, 2012–2018," pp. 40–41.

158 Open Hearing: Social Media Influence in the 2016 U.S. Election.

159 Emily Glazer and Patience Haggin, "Google's Tool to Tame Election Influence Has Flaws" (July 17, 2019), https://www.wsj.com/articles/google-archive-of-political-ads-is-fraught-with-missing-content-delays-11563355800, accessed 24 September 2019.

160 Bill Chappell, "Researchers explain why they believe Facebook mishandles political ads" (December 9, 2021), https://www.npr.org/2021/12/09/1062516250/researchers-explain-why-they-believe-facebook-mishandles-political-ads, accessed 21 September 2023.

161 About ads about social issues, elections or politics, https://www.facebook.com/business/help/167836590566506?id=288762101909005, accessed 21 September 2023.

162 https://transparency.twitter.com/en.html; "The Santa Clara Principles On Transparency and Accountability in Content Moderation," https://santaclaraprinciples.org/; Kurt Wagner, "Twitter says it's getting better at detecting abusive tweets without your help" (April 16, 2019), https://www.vox.com/2019/4/16/18410931/twitter-abuse-update-health-technology-harassment, all accessed 24 September 2019.

163 Barbara Ortutay, "US says Elon Musk should not be immune to testifying about the former Twitter" (September 12, 2023), https://abcnews.go.com/Business/wireStory/us-elon-musk-immune-testifying-former-twitter-103135605, accessed 17 September 2023.

their content remains a germane question.[164] Government regulation remains light touch. In the U.S. alone digital political advertising was projected to hit $3.3 billion in the U.S. in 2020. In 2016 it was $1.4 billion. By contrast $4.4 billion was spent on political advertising on broadcast TV in 2016 and around $5 billion in 2020 and 2022. Television advertising might still be king, but its market share is decreasing in the face of online competition.[165] These represent longer term trends and issues.[166] Russia (and for that matter any state or state-backed organization with sufficient resources and expertise) can use social media and the wider bandwidth provided by the Internet and Internet apps (as well as state media) to mount a campaign against another state or region. This might be used to sow division, to interfere in elections but it has wider applications and intents.[167] Russia also leveraged Wikileaks. Should Julian Assange ever appear before American courts, his role and the role of Wikileaks in the 2016 presidential election will be under renewed scrutiny.

3.7 Julian Assange and Wikileaks

Julian Assange (an Australian national) is as divisive and controversial as the website he founded, Wikileaks. Assange, like his website, divides opinion. To his supporters he is a campaigning journalist championing free speech and holding governments to account. To his detractors, he is "he is a publicity-seeker who has endangered lives by putting a mass of sensitive information into the public

164 Courtney C. Radsch, "Platformization and Media Capture: A Framework for Regulatory Analysis of Media-Related Platform Regulations," *UCLA Journal of Law & Technology*, Vol. 28, No. 2 (Winter 2023), pp. 175–223.

165 Glazer and Haggin, "Google's Tool to Tame Election Influence Has Flaws"; "Political advertising spending in the United States election cycles from 2014 to 2022, by medium," https://www.statista.com/statistics/1182087/political-advertising-spending-election-cycle-by-medium-united-states/; "Digital political advertising spending in the United States from 2008 to 2020," https://www.statista.com/statistics/309592/online-political-ad-spend-usa/, both accessed 17 September 2023.

166 Ed Stein, "What's in the Executive Order on Election Interference?" (September 19, 2018), https://www.lawfareblog.com/whats-executive-order-election-interference; Lawrence Norden and Daniel I. Weiner, "U.S. Elections Are Still Not Safe From Attack. Congress Can Change That If It Acts Fast" (July 23, 2019), https://www.foreignaffairs.com/articles/russia-fsu/2019-07-23/us-elections-are-still-not-safe-attack, both accessed 24 September 2019.

167 Peter Pomerantsev, "The Kremlin's Information War," *Journal of Democracy*, Vol. 26, No. 4 (October 2015), pp. 40–50.

domain" who continues to be a "useful idiot" for Russia.[168] After the release of leaked U.S. "war logs" from Iraq, the "Afghan War Diary", and diplomatic cables by Bradley (now Chelsea) Manning to Wikileaks in early 2010 he feared extradition to the U.S. Hillary Clinton, then Secretary of State, said at the time the releases were "an attack on the international community" with the DOJ and Pentagon examining charges "under the Espionage Act, which could lead to decades in jail."[169]

From 2012, he was living under an arrest warrant from Sweden on sexual assault allegations. He was granted asylum by Ecuador whilst living in London, England whilst being "America's public enemy number one."[170] Assange spent the next seven years in the Ecuadorian embassy in Knightsbridge. With the threat of extradition hanging over him there was an aborted plot by Russian agents to extract him on Christmas Eve 2017.[171] With this background in mind and with supportive comments from then candidate Trump, he said to members of Wikileaks in November 2015, "[w]e believe it would be much better for GOP to win ... Dems +Media+liberals woudl [*sic*] then form a block to reign in their worst qualities ... With Hillary in charge, GOP will be pushing for her worst qualities., dems+media +neoliberals will be mute ... She's a bright, well connected, sadisitic [*sic*] sociopath."[172]

During his residence in the Ecuadorian embassy, Wikileaks continued to release leaked U.S. government files including CIA documents, dubbed "Vault 7," in March 2017. These releases continued even after Assange's Internet access had been cut-off.[173] Following a change of government in Ecuador in April 2019

---

168 Anonymous, "Julian Assange: Campaigner or attention-seeker?" (May 23, 2019), https://www.bbc.co.uk/news/world-11047811; Brian Ross and Paul Blake, "Fugitive Assange Backs Trump in Questioning Russia's Election Hacking Role" (January 4, 2017), https://abcnews.go.com/International/fugitive-assange-backs-trump-questioning-russias-election-hacking/story?id=44540371, accessed 16 September 2019.

169 David Samuels, "The Shameful Attacks on Julian Assange" (December 3, 2010), https://www.theatlantic.com/international/archive/2010/12/the-shameful-attacks-on-julian-assange/67440/, accessed 16 September 2019.

170 David Leigh and Luke Harding, *Wikileaks Inside Julian Assange's War on Secrecy* (London: Guardian Books: 2013), pp. 5, 227–239.

171 Stephanie Kirchgaessner, Dan Collyns, and Luke Harding, "Revealed: Russia's secret plan to help Julian Assange escape from UK" (September 21, 2018), https://www.theguardian.com/world/2018/sep/21/julian-assange-russia-ecuador-embassy-london-secret-escape-plan, accessed 16 September 2019.

172 Mueller Report Volume I, p. 44.

173 Ewen MacAskill, Sam Thielman, and Philip Oltermann, "WikiLeaks publishes 'biggest ever leak of secret CIA documents'" (March 7, 2017), https://www.theguardian.com/media/2017/mar/07/wikileaks-publishes-biggest-ever-leak-of-secret-cia-documents-hacking-surveillance, accessed 16 September 2019.

his asylum status was revoked. He was then dragged out of the embassy by police in the glare of the media. In May 2019 Assange was charged by the DOJ with 18 counts of illegally obtaining, receiving, and disclosing classified information. He remained in Belmarsh prison for breaching bail conditions relating to the charges with U.S. extradition hearings ongoing.[174] Sweden had dropped its investigation in November 2019.[175] In a plea deal negotiated between the United States, United Kingdom, and Australia, he was eventually released in June 2024 and returned to Australia.[176]

The Mueller Report painted Wikileaks as an organization which wanted to directly involve itself in the election and oppose Hillary Clinton's run for president. Because of this (alongside previous leaks and commentary) it became a beacon and a cipher for the GRU to release information they felt would damage Clinton's election chances.[177] The Mueller Report also paints the picture of a Trump campaign team seeing Wikileaks releases on Clinton and the Democrats in a positive light. Whilst the sections on Wikileaks are heavily redacted, the Mueller report hints at coordination between Wikileaks releases and the Trump campaign but leaves it unclear whether the timing of the releases was a unilateral decision by Wikileaks or coordinated. This includes the release of the first set of e-mails exfiltrated by the GRU from the office of John Podesta an hour after the *Washington Post* ran a potentially damaging story on Trump based on the *Access Hollywood* tape where he allegedly said that he could grab women "by the pussy" because "when you're a star, they let you do it."[178]

---

174 Esther Addley, "The seven-year itch: Assange's awkward stay in the embassy" (April 11, 2019), https://www.theguardian.com/media/2019/apr/11/how-ecuador-lost-patience-with-houseguest-julian-assange; Anonymous, "Julian Assange to stay in prison over absconding fears," https://www.bbc.co.uk/news/uk-49689167; WikiLeaks Founder Julian Assange Charged in 18-Count Superseding Indictment (May 23, 2019), https://www.justice.gov/opa/pr/wikileaks-founder-julian-assange-charged-18-count-superseding-indictment; Ben Doherty, "Julian Assange 'dangerously close' to US extradition after losing latest legal appeal" (June 9, 2023), https://www.theguardian.com/media/2023/jun/09/julian-assange-dangerously-close-to-us-extradition-after-losing-latest-legal-appeal. All accessed 21 September 2023.

175 Anonymous, "Julian Assange: Sweden drops rape investigation" (November 19, 2019), https://www.bbc.co.uk/news/world-europe-50473792, accessed 21 September 2023.

176 Vincent Hooper, "Julian Assange's Release: a victory for press freedom or a perilous precedent?" (25 June 2024), https://www.spectator.com.au/2024/06/julian-assanges-release-a-victory-for-press-freedom-or-a-perilous-precedent/, accessed 15 May 2025.

177 Mueller Report Volume I, pp. 44–49.

178 Mueller Report Volume I, pp. 51–62. Gabrielle Bruney, "Billy Bush Says 'Everybody' at NBC Knew About the Donald Trump Access Hollywood Tape" (September 9, 2019), https://www.esquire.com/entertainment/tv/a28970882/billy-bush-donald-trump-access-hollywood-tape-interview/, accessed 17 September 2019. Clinton, *What Happened*, pp. 347–348.

The hack on John Podesta was about to be released by Wikileaks and the Mueller investigation and media reports looking into these issues questioned whether members of the Trump campaign team knew about this in advance through communications with Assange. Those on Trump's team interested in Wikileaks releases included Paul Manafort, Trump's sometime campaign chairman, Rick Gates (Manafort's deputy), and Roger Stone, the veteran Republican political operative. Stone was subsequently indicted by Mueller in January 2019 on seven counts including making false statements to the House Intelligence Committee about contacts with WikiLeaks during the campaign and tampering with a witness who could have discredited his story.[179]

It is alleged there were e-mail communications between Stone and former Infowars contributor Jerome Corsi two months prior to the second batch of releases (e-mails which the Mueller investigation says were subsequently deleted by Corsi). It is alleged that Stone asked Corsi in late July–early August 2016 to approach Wikileaks directly telling him "Get to [Assange] [a]t Ecuadorian Embassy in London and get the pending [Wikileaks] emails." According to court documents Corsi immediately forwarded this e-mail request to a contact in London. Corsi then allegedly told Stone, "Word is friend in embassy plans 2 more dumps ... Impact planned to be very damaging ... Time to let more than [the Clinton Campaign chairman] to be exposed as in bed w[ith] enemy if they are not ready to drop HRC [Hillary Rodham Clinton]." The go-between or bagman Corsi contacted is alleged to be Ted Malloch, a London-based academic who was aiming to become the U.S. ambassador to the EU in the Trump administration.[180]

---

179 Katelyn Polantz, "Judge won't dismiss Roger Stone case, but allows him to see unredacted Mueller docs" (August 1, 2019), https://edition.cnn.com/2019/08/01/politics/roger-stone-mueller/index.html, accessed 16 September 2019. See also Executive Session Permanent Select Committee on Intelligence, U.S. House of Representatives, Washington, D.C. Interview of: Glenn Simpson, Tuesday, November 14, 2017, pp. 112–115, https://docs.house.gov/meetings/IG/IG00/20180118/106796/HMTG-115-IG00-20180118-SD002.pdf, accessed 18 September 2019.

180 https://assets.documentcloud.org/documents/5302125/Draft-Jerome-Corsi-statement-of-offense.pdf. William Cummings, "'I did not intentionally lie': Roger Stone associate Jerome Corsi rejects Mueller deal" (November 26, 2018), https://eu.usatoday.com/story/news/politics/2018/11/26/jerome-corsi-rejects-mueller-deal/2114836002/; Anna Schecter, "Mueller has emails from Stone pal Corsi about WikiLeaks Dem email dump 'Word is (Julian Assange) plans 2 more dumps ... Impact planned to be very damaging,' Jerome Corsi said in email to Stone, say draft court documents" (November 27, 2018), https://www.nbcnews.com/politics/justice-department/mueller-has-emails-stone-pal-corsi-about-wikileaks-dem-email-n940611; Pierre Thomas, Ali Dukakis, and James Gordon Meek, "Mueller's agents asked about Roger Stone, Trump supporter says" (May 28, 2018), https://abcnews.go.com/Politics/muellers-agents-asked-roger-stone-trump-supporter/story?id=55450667 and Nick Cohen, "Farage finds Ukip awful. So what about his more sinister friends?"

Another figure to emerge in this story is Nigel Farage, then leader of the UK Independence Party (UKIP). He too was suggested as a go-between to speak with Assange and allegedly visited him in the Ecuadorian embassy in March 2017 – the same month Wikileaks released the "Vault 7" files leaked from the CIA.[181] Farage and Trump were, and remain, public supporters of one another and the policies they stand for, and Farage was "an open campaigner for President Donald Trump in the run up to the American election."[182]

Trump said at the time of the leaks, that his campaign team believed the DNC themselves did the "hacking."[183] Hours later GRU officers targeted Clinton's personal office with spear-phishing e-mails. They again breached the DNC and copied databases but this time they went further. The GRU went after state and local election boards, through a SQL injection attack which scanned for website vulnerabilities. In Illinois they managed to gain access to a database of 1 million registered voters and were in the process of exfiltrating the database when they were stopped. These activities continued throughout the election.[184]

4 Election results, the end of the Obama administration, and transition

Trump won the November 2016 election with 306 electoral votes to Clinton's 232 with a record 137.5 million Americans voting in the election (61.4 percent of the voting population). Black voter turnout decreased from a high of 66.6 percent in 2012, to 59.6 percent in 2016. White turnout increased from 64.1 percent to 65.3 per-

(December 8, 2018), https://www.theguardian.com/commentisfree/2018/dec/08/nigel-farage-ukip-awful-more-sinister-friends-ted-malloch. All accessed 17 September 2019.

181 Farage did meet with Assange according to reports but what was said are a mystery. Carole Cadwalladr, "Who is the real Nigel Farage … and why won't he answer my questions?" (November 25, 2018), https://www.theguardian.com/politics/2018/nov/25/why-wont-nigel-farage-answer-my-brexit-questions; Carole Cadwalladr, "When Nigel Farage met Julian Assange" (April 23, 2017), https://www.theguardian.com/politics/2017/apr/23/when-nigel-farage-met-julian-assange; and Cyrus Farivar, "Man who allegedly gave Vault 7 cache to WikiLeaks busted by poor opsec" (June 19, 2018), https://arstechnica.com/tech-policy/2018/06/ex-cia-engineer-indicted-on-several-new-charges-connected-to-vault-7-leak/. All accessed 17 September 2019.

182 Anonymous, "Nigel Farage gave Julian Assange data on USB stick, US congressional enquiry hears" (January 20, 2018), https://www.france24.com/en/20180120-usa-uk-nigel-farage-julian-assange-secret-meetings-congressional-enquiry, accessed 17 September 2019.

183 Eric Bradner, "Trump: DNC hacked itself" (June 16, 2016), https://edition.cnn.com/2016/06/15/politics/dnc-hack-donald-trump/index.html, accessed 9 September 2019.

184 Mueller Report Volume I, pp. 49 – 51.

cent. Latino turnout remained largely the same.[185] Trump "remade the battleground-state map by punching successfully through a wall of blue states that had been carried by Democrats for decades."[186] In 2012 only two states, Florida and Ohio, were decided by 2 percentage points or less. In 2016 this applied to six states (the rustbelt states of Pennsylvania, Michigan, Ohio, Iowa, and Wisconsin – along with Florida).[187]

The extent to which "Project Lakhta" contributed to a Trump victory remains an open, highly charged, and germane question. It was Russia's intention through the coordinated activities of the IRA and Russian intelligence to suppress voter turnout favorable to Clinton and the Democrats and mobilize the Trump vote. The Mueller Report revealed that:

> As soon as news broke that Trump had been elected President, Russian government officials and prominent Russian businessmen began trying to make inroads into the new Administration. They appeared not to have preexisting contacts and struggled to connect with senior officials around the President-Elect ... those efforts entailed both official contact through the Russian Embassy in the United States and outreaches—sanctioned at high levels of the Russian government-through business rather than political contacts ... [leading to a] flurry of Russian activity.[188]

At the top of their list were the sanctions imposed on Russia in the wake of Ukrainian intervention and annexation of Crimea in 2014 as well as possible further sanctions as Russia's 2016 election interference was coming to light.[189]

In the interregnum prior to Trump's January 2017 inauguration, there followed a five-month long debate amongst the Obama administration that secretly discussed a range of options to deter Russia from future influence campaigns and

---

185 Jens Manuel Krogstad and Mark Hugo Lopez, "Black voter turnout fell in 2016, even as a record number of Americans cast ballots" (May 12, 2017), https://www.pewresearch.org/fact-tank/2017/05/12/black-voter-turnout-fell-in-2016-even-as-a-record-number-of-americans-cast-ballots/; and Thom File, "Voting in America: A Look at the 2016 Presidential Election" (May 10, 2017), https://www.census.gov/newsroom/blogs/random-samplings/2017/05/voting_in_america.html. Both accessed 17 September 2019.

186 David Catanese, "The 10 Closest States in the 2016 Election" (November 14, 2016), https://www.usnews.com/news/the-run-2016/articles/2016-11-14/the-10-closest-states-in-the-2016-election, accessed 17 September 2019.

187 "An Evaluation of 2016 Election Polls in the U.S.," https://www.aapor.org/Education-Resources/Reports/An-Evaluation-of-2016-Election-Polls-in-the-U-S.aspx; and Dan McLaughlin, "The Real Reason Trump Won: Part 2 of 4" (January 11, 2017), https://www.nationalreview.com/2017/01/real-reason-trump-won-he-flipped-big-battleground-states/. Both accessed 17 September 2019.

188 Mueller Report Volume I, p. 144.

189 Mueller Report Volume I, pp. 146–173.

potential forms of reprisal. This included disclosing CIA intelligence to embarrass the Putin administration and Kremlin, cyberattacks on Russian infrastructure, and "sanctions that officials said could 'crater' the Russian economy."[190] In the end limited sanctions were chosen. Additionally, 35 Russian official cover intelligence agents were expelled. A number were suspected of active involvement in "Project Lakhta." Two Russian compounds were closed in September 2017 and fresh sanctions imposed in March 2018.[191]

5 A drink in a London bar overseen by a pair of "Five Eyes"

Russian interference in the 2016 U.S. presidential election started to come to light in mid-2016. This coincided with the hack on the DNC released to Wikileaks by "Guccifer 2.0" in June 2016. As Chapter 1 showed, this was a fake persona operated by the GRU's Unit 26165 at the Khamovnichesky barracks. Wikileaks published their hacks immediately with further releases in October and November. In July the FBI was tipped off by a friendly government that George Papadopoulos, a foreign policy advisor brought into the Trump campaign, had told them the Trump campaign had been approached by representatives of the Russian government with damaging information on Hillary Clinton. This prompted the FBI to open an inquiry on July 31, 2016, which led to the Mueller investigation.[192]

Which friendly government tipped off the Obama administration has not been officially confirmed but over drinks at a London bar an Australian diplomat is alleged to have heard from Papadopoulos that thousands of Clinton campaign e-mails were in Russia's possession. That diplomat reported Papadopoulos' claim through diplomatic channels but did not lend it much credence at the time. Papadopoulos was something of an unknown being young and inexperienced. Around this time Robert Hannigan, then Director of Britain's GCHQ, visited Washington. There he briefed CIA director John Brennan. Hannigan is reported to have told Brennan of intercepted communications between members of Trump's campaign team and Russian sources. What these intercepts contained is unknown but

190 Miller et al., "Obama's secret struggle."

191 Miller et al., "Obama's secret struggle." Sophie Tatum and Laura Koran, "Smoke spotted coming from Russian consulate ahead of facility closure" (September 2, 2017), https://edition.cnn.com/2017/09/01/politics/russia-consulate-san-francisco-smoke/index.html. "Treasury Sanctions Russian Cyber Actors for Interference with the 2016 U.S. Elections and Malicious Cyber-Attacks" (March 15, 2018), https://home.treasury.gov/news/press-releases/sm0312. Both accessed 18 September 2018.

192 Mueller Report Volume I, p. 1.

after the DNC hack was attributed to Russia, Australia reconsidered what Papadopoulos had said and told their American opposite numbers.[193]

The Australian diplomat was later revealed by Papadopoulos as Australia's High Commissioner to the UK, Alexander Downer. Papadopoulos believed he had been set-up by Australian intelligence in order to pass this discussion onto their U.S. counterparts and "Five Eyes" partner.[194] In September 2019 it was revealed that the late Sir Charles Farr, then Chair of Britain's Joint Intelligence Committee, "assisted" Downer.[195] This chain of events was the potential spark that set off the Mueller investigation. It has become part of the "Witch Hunt" and "deep state" narrative involving, as Downer said, "a kind of a ASIS-ASIO-MI6-MI5-FBI-CIA-Ukrainian Government conspiracy to bring down the Trump administration."[196] In Summer 2019, Trump had explored withholding military aid to Ukraine unless they investigated Hunter Biden, the son of then-Democratic presidential rival Joe Biden, and his involvement with the Ukrainian energy company Burisma.[197] In September 2019 Trump requested an investigation from the Australian

193 Jane Meyer, "Christopher Steele, the Man Behind the Trump Dossier How the ex-spy tried to warn the world about Trump's ties to Russia." (March 5, 2018), https://www.newyorker.com/magazine/2018/03/12/christopher-steele-the-man-behind-the-trump-dossier, accessed 19 September 2019.

194 Andrew Probyn and Matthew Doran, "What happened when Trump campaign aide George Papadopoulos sat down with Australian diplomat Alexander Downer" (September 23, 2018), https://www.abc.net.au/news/2018-09-22/george-papadopoulos-alexander-downer-meeting-what-happened/10286868; Matthew Bevan and Ruby Jones, "The drink that started the Mueller investigation: George Papadopoulos and Alexander Downer tell us everything" (May 23, 2019), https://www.abc.net.au/news/2019-05-24/mueller-investigation-george-papadopoulos-alexander-downer-speak/11107712. Both accessed 1 October 2019. George Papadopoulos, *Deep State Target: How I Got Caught in the Crosshairs of the Plot to Bring Down President Trump* (New York: Diversion Books, 2019), pp. 73–80.

195 Deborah Haynes, "British intelligence involved in Trump election probe, sources say" (October 2, 2019), https://news.sky.com/story/british-intelligence-involved-in-trump-election-probe-sources-say-11825044; Patrick Wintour and Luke Harding, "William Barr discussed FBI Russia inquiry with UK intelligence" (October 1, 2019), https://www.theguardian.com/us-news/2019/oct/01/william-barr-us-attorney-general-discussed-mueller-inquiry-uk-intelligence. Both accessed 2 October 2019.

196 Downer went onto say "it's a little bit sad that people take that kind of thought seriously." An increasing number do take it seriously. Bevan and Jones, "The drink that started the Mueller investigation."

197 Paul LeBlanc, Jim Acosta, Jeremy Diamond, and Kaitlan Collins, "Trump ordered hold on military aid days before call with Ukrainian President, senior administration officials say" (September 24, 2019), https://edition.cnn.com/2019/09/23/politics/trump-ukraine-military-aid-call/index.html, accessed 21 September 2023.

government led by Prime Minister Scott Morrison.[198] Despite repeated allegations that this is all a "Witch Hunt" to constrain or bring down his presidency this did not stop the inchoate investigation sparked by America's "Five Eyes" partners. It was not for want of trying.

6 The Mueller Inquiry: A "Witch hunt"?

Soon after coming into office Trump had a private dinner with FBI Director Comey where he asked for his loyalty. For Comey "the demand was like Sammy the Bull's Cosa Nostra induction ceremony – with Trump, in the role of the family boss, asking me if I had what it takes to be a 'made man.'"[199] On February 13, 2017 President Trump asked his National Security Advisor Michael Flynn to resign because he had lied to Vice President Pence regarding phone calls made to Russia's U.S. Ambassador, Sergey Kislyak, discussing Russian sanctions President Obama had announced in late December 2016.[200] The following day Trump asked Comey in a one-on-one meeting whether this might precipitate the end of the investigation saying to Comey, "I hope you can see your way clear to letting this go, to letting Flynn go."[201] When the FBI's investigation into Russian interference was publicly announced on March 20, 2017, "In the days and weeks that followed, the President contacted Comey and other intelligence agency leaders and asked them to push back publicly on the suggestion that the President had any connection to Russia's election-interference efforts in order to 'lift the cloud' of the ongoing investigation."[202] The cloud did not lift and Comey became a target.

It was suggested by the President that rank-and-file members of the FBI and DOJ had lost confidence in Comey and his decision to fire him was based on recommendations by Deputy Attorney General Rod Rosenstein.[203] Comey was fired whilst giving a speech to FBI agents in Los Angeles on May 9, 2017. Two days later Trump was interviewed by NBC and gave his account of Comey's firing.

198 Evan Perez and Paul LeBlanc, "Trump pressed Australian Prime Minister to help with Justice review of Russia probe origins" (September 30, 2019), https://edition.cnn.com/2019/09/30/politics/trump-mueller-barr-australia/index.html, accessed 1 October 2019.

199 Comey, *A Higher Loyalty*, pp. 237–239.

200 Azadeh Ansari and Angela Dewan, "How Michael Flynn lost his job in 23 days" (February 14, 2017), https://edition.cnn.com/2017/02/14/politics/michael-flynn-resigns-timeline/index.html, accessed 18 September 2019.

201 Mueller Report Volume II, pp. 24, 34–36, 39–41, 44–48.

202 Mueller Report Volume II, pp. 48, 55–61.

203 Mueller Report Volume II, pp. 48–54, 62–77, 107–113.

He told Lester Holt of NBC that "[t]he FBI has been in turmoil" and "regardless of recommendation, I was going to fire Comey knowing there was no good time to do it … And in fact, when I decided to just do it, I said to myself – I said, you know, this Russia thing with Trump and Russia is a made-up story. It's an excuse by the Democrats for having lost an election that they should've won."[204] For Comey, "the administration … chose to defame me" and charges that the FBI was in turmoil and poorly led "were lies, plain and simple."[205]

In a meeting with Russian Foreign Minister Sergey Lavrov and Ambassador Kislyak in the Oval Office, Trump told them "I just fired the head of the F.B.I. He was crazy, a real nut job. I faced great pressure because of Russia. That's taken off … I'm not under investigation."[206] The morning after, when it was being reported that Trump had asked for Comey's loyalty, Trump claimed "When James Clapper himself, and virtually everyone else with knowledge of the witch hunt, says there is no collusion, when does it end?"[207] By now there was deep-seated animosity between Trump and Comey.[208] The FBI continued its investigations even after Comey was fired.[209]

The investigations led directly to the appointment of Special Counsel, Robert Mueller, in May 2017 by Rosenstein. President Trump "reacted negatively," saying privately, "that it was the end of his presidency" and "I'm fucked."[210] He instead wanted Attorney General, Jeff Sessions, to have oversight of the investigation and have Special Counsel Mueller removed. According to the Mueller Report Trump then "engaged in efforts to curtail the Special Counsel's investigation and prevent the disclosure of evidence to it, including through public and private contacts with potential witnesses."[211] Sessions, who himself had also been under investigation (and was exonerated), recused himself from the investigation and resigned on November 7, 2018, the day after the midterm elections.[212]

Three congressional committees were then set up to look into the issues of Russian interference. These were initiated by the House Permanent Select Com-

---

204 Mueller Report Volume II, p. 73.

205 Comey, *A Higher Loyalty*, p. 275.

206 Mueller Report Volume II, pp. 24, 34–36, 39–41, 44–48.

207 Mueller Report Volume II, p. 74.

208 Mueller Report Volume II, p. 72.

209 Ian Schwartz, "Andrew McCabe: Trump's Own Words Prompted Probe, He Spoke About The FBI 'In A Derogatory Way'" (February 18, 2019), https://www.realclearpolitics.com/video/2019/02/18/andrew_mccabe_trumps_own_words_prompted_probe_he_spoke_about_the_fbi_in_a_derogatory_way.html, accessed 1 October 2010.

210 Mueller Report Volume II, p. 78.

211 Mueller Report Volume I, p. 8 and Volume II, pp. 77–98, 113–120.

212 Mueller Report Volume I, pp. 197–198.

mittee on Intelligence (HPSCI), the Senate Select Committee on Intelligence (SSCI), and the Senate Judiciary Committee (SJC) alongside the Mueller inquiry. Throughout its 18-month duration (and to this day) it was characterized as a "Witch hunt" by President Trump and his supporters.[213] By this time, two agencies of the USIC both assessed the DNC/DNCC "hack and leak" had originated with the Russian government. The Mueller inquiry forensically examined the evidence and despite finding there had been contacts with Russian government officials, pronounced there was no direct collusion between Trump campaign officials and Russia.[214] Although media speculation regarding the meeting between Russian representatives and senior Trump campaign officials on June 9, 2016 at Trump Tower in New York was also pointed to as collusion no such evidence was found by the Mueller inquiry. Instead, despite money laundering dirt on the Clintons being dangled by Russian intermediaries, the main focus of the meeting appears to have been on sanctions levied on Russia under the Magnitsky Act and anti-Russian adoption laws.[215]

---

213 Alex Pappas and Judson Berger, "Tight-lipped Mueller faces GOP ire over probe's handling, as hearing retreads Russia report" (July 24, 2019), https://www.foxnews.com/politics/mueller-in-capitol-hill-testimony-says-no-trump-russia-conspiracy-no-trump-exoneration-on-obstruction, accessed 18 September 2019.

214 Mueller Report Volume I, pp. 83–103, 120–123, 185, 192–194; and Sharon LaFraniere, David D. Kirkpatrick, Andrew Higgins, and Michael Schwirtz, "A London Meeting of an Unlikely Group: How a Trump Adviser Came to Learn of Clinton 'Dirt'" (November 10, 2017), https://www.nytimes.com/2017/11/10/us/russia-inquiry-trump.html. Meyer, "Christopher Steele, the Man Behind the Trump Dossier." Oliver Laughland and Martin Pengelly, "Trump-Russia: FBI believed Carter Page 'collaborated and conspired' with Moscow" (July 22, 2018), https://www.theguardian.com/us-news/2018/jul/22/trump-administration-releases-carter-page-wiretap-documents. All accessed 6 September 2019.

215 Sergei Magnitsky was a tax advisor to hedge fund manager Bill Browder who was arrested in 2009 in Moscow and died in pre-trial detention. He had alleged that Russian police and tax authorities had attempted to steal $230 million in taxes paid by Browder's Moscow-based investment firm, Hermitage Capital. As the *New Yorker* reported, this was pursued by Browder for years afterwards. He actively lobbied for a law to hold those responsible to account. This lobbying eventually led to the Magnitsky Act. This was passed by Congress in 2012 and "sanctions Russian human-rights violators and other officials implicated in corruption and abuse-of-power cases … and has been a subject of furious preoccupation for Putin ever since." Browder remains an active Kremlin critic. Joshua Yaffa, "How Bill Browder became Russia's most wanted man" (August 13, 2018), https://www.newyorker.com/magazine/2018/08/20/how-bill-browder-became-russias-most-wanted-man. One of Browder's business associates, Alexander Perepilichnyy, who supported the allegations levied by Browder, mysteriously collapsed and died whilst out jogging near his mansion in Surrey near London in November 2012. Jim Reed and Louis Lee Ray, "Alexander Perepilichnyy possible MI6 links to stay secret" (September 8, 2018), https://www.bbc.co.uk/news/uk-45548975. Both accessed 19 September 2019.

7 Indictments and prosecutions

When reports first began to surface about the activities of the IRA, e-mails and data were destroyed and IRA employees began to delete some of their social media accounts. This accelerated after Facebook announced on September 6, 2017 that they were cooperating with the Mueller inquiry and had handed over the findings of their internal investigation. This led the IRA's Irina Kaverzina to say in a personal e-mail "We had a slight crisis here at work: the FBI busted our activity (not a joke). So, I got preoccupied with covering tracks together with the colleagues" and admitting "I created all these pictures and posts, and the Americans believed that it was written by their people."[216]

In July 2018 a dozen members of the GRU were indicted by Mueller. The Netyksho indictment, named after the Russian military officer then commanding Unit 26165, Viktor Netyksho, saw them charged with hacking the DCCC and DNC during the 2016 election and conspiring to leak the stolen cache of e-mails and documents to Wikileaks through the guise of "Guccifer 2.0" and "DCLeaks." Also indicted were Boris Antonov, Dmitriy Badin, Anatliy Kovalev, Nikolay Kozachek, Aleksey Lukashev, Artem Malyshev, Sergey Morgachev, Aleksandr Osadchuk, Aleksey Potemkin, Ivan Yermakov, and Pavel Yershov.[217] The FBI describes them as "at large" but in reality, they know there is no chance of extradition under a Putin government. Instead, by going public, the FBI is attempting to dispel any suggestion this was not a Russian government sanctioned operation and an attempt to "name and shame."

Ten American citizens have either been prosecuted or reached plea deals with the Special Counsel.[218] Although collusion with Russia was not proven, a number of Trump campaign members were charged with making false statements and obstructing justice. Some of these concerned contacts with Russian personas such as "Guccifer 2.0" and Wikileaks.[219] Paul Manafort, Rick Gates, and Michael Flynn were found to have violated the Foreign Agents Registration Act (FARA), but Mu-

216 https://www.justice.gov/file/1035477/download, p. 24.

217 https://www.justice.gov/file/1080281/download, accessed 21 September 2023.

218 Andrew Prokop, "All of Robert Mueller's indictments and plea deals in the Russia investigation" (March 22, 2019), https://www.vox.com/policy-and-politics/2018/2/20/17031772/mueller-indictments-grand-jury, accessed 16 September 2019.

219 Mueller Report Volume I, pp. 194–195. Katelyn Polantz, "Justice Department drops criminal case against Michael Flynn" (May 7, 2020), https://edition.cnn.com/2020/05/07/politics/michael-flynn-prosecution/index.html. Polantz, "Judge won't dismiss Roger Stone case." Jacob Ogles, "Roger Stone to enjoy last Thanksgiving as free man in Orange Park" (November 27, 2019), https://floridapolitics.com/archives/312285-roger-stone-to-enjoy-last-thanksgiving-as-free-man-in-orange-park, accessed 7 May 2020.

eller's inquiry "did not find evidence likely to prove beyond a reasonable doubt that Campaign officials such as Paul Manafort, George Papadopoulos, and Carter Page acted as agents of the Russian government – or at its direction, control, or request."[220]

Prior to the release of the full report, Mueller issued a synopsis of its findings which was seized upon on by politicians on both sides of the aisle, and President Trump himself, as exonerating him.[221] What was concluded, and stated at the outset, was "Although the investigation established that the Russian government perceived it would benefit from a Trump presidency and worked to secure that outcome, and that the [Trump] Campaign expected it would benefit electorally from information stolen and released through Russian efforts, the investigation did not establish that members of the Trump Campaign conspired or coordinated with the Russian government in its election interference activities."[222] Of the president himself the Mueller Report was less clear. In remarks seized on by the mainstream media, by Congress, commentators, and by the president himself it was stated, "this report does not conclude that the President committed a crime, it also does not exonerate him" and left open the possibility of future charges.[223] Trump's ties to Russia were also implied in the controversial Steele Dossier.

8 The Steele dossier

In January 2017 a dossier on Trump by Christopher Steele, a former senior British intelligence officer with MI6/SIS, was leaked by Buzzfeed. Steele ran the Russia desk for MI6 in London and oversaw MI6's investigation of the assassination of Alexander Litvinenko with polonium-210 in 2006. He had credibility in the intel-

---

220 Mueller Report Volume I, p. 183 and Volume II, pp. 120–133, D-1-D-6. Page was a short-lived foreign policy advisor. On his role and the role of others talking with Russian intelligence agents see David Gioe, "Cyber Operations and Useful Fools: The Approach of Russian Hybrid Intelligence," *Intelligence and National Security*, Vol. 33, No. 7 (December 2018), pp. 954–973.

221 Michael Collins, John Fritze, and David Jackson, "Trump claims 'total exoneration' from Mueller summary despite lack of answers on obstruction" (March 24, 2019), https://eu.usatoday.com/story/news/politics/2019/03/24/mueller-report-white-house-claims-vindication-ag-barrs-summary/3261486002/, accessed 27 January 2020.

222 Mueller Report Volume I, pp. 1–2.

223 Mueller Report Volume II, pp. 2, 159–182. Sonam Sheth, "US spies say Trump's G7 performance suggests he's either a 'Russian asset' or a 'useful idiot' for Putin" (August 29, 2019), https://www.businessinsider.com/spies-react-trump-g7-summit-russian-asset-2019-8?r=US&IR=T, accessed 27 September 2019.

ligence community on both sides of the Atlantic.[224] Its existence had been an inside secret in Washington since the summer.[225] The dossier was raw intelligence with 16 separate reports, totaling 35 pages recording what Steele and Fusion GPS (a commercial research consultancy, which includes opposition research) were told.[226] The Steele dossier put forward that the Kremlin had been "cultivating, supporting, and assisting TRUMP for at least 5 years. Aim, endorsed by PUTIN, has been to encourage splits and divisions in [the] western alliance."[227] It claimed that Russia has *kompromat* on Trump which included salacious details.[228] Oleg Kalugin, a former head of counterintelligence for the KGB, separately acknowledged *kompromat* on Trump exists with a file on him opened when he married his first wife, Ivana (a Czech national), dating back to 1978.[229]

Steele reported his findings to the FBI as a matter of national security.[230] During the transition officials in the Obama administration were reportedly reluctant to pursue it because of the Hatch Act. It was only after the DNC hack by Russia that the FBI met again with Steele and "asked him for everything he had." This he duly supplied along with a further report in October 2016.[231] The Mueller Report detailed that President-Elect Trump and the incoming Administration was informed of its contents at the time and he was briefed by intelligence officials. They were informed of the USIC's assessment that Russia had meddled in the 2016 pres-

224 Meyer, "Christopher Steele, the Man Behind the Trump Dossier."
225 Ken Bensinger, Miriam Elder, and Mark Schoofs, "These Reports Allege Trump Has Deep Ties To Russia" (January 10, 2017), https://www.buzzfeednews.com/article/kenbensinger/these-reports-allege-trump-has-deep-ties-to-russia, accessed 10 September 2019.
226 Fusion GPS had sub-contracted investigations to Steele's company, Orbis Business Intelligence. Sarah Grant and Chuck Rosenberg, "The Steele Dossier: A Retrospective" (December 14, 2018), https://www.lawfareblog.com/steele-dossier-retrospective, accessed 17 September 2019.
227 https://www.documentcloud.org/documents/3259984-Trump-Intelligence-Allegations.html, accessed 9 September 2019.
228 https://www.documentcloud.org/documents/3259984-Trump-Intelligence-Allegations.html. See also Rosalind S. Helderman and Tom Hamburger, "Who is 'Source D'? The man said to be behind the Trump-Russia dossier's most salacious claim" (March 29, 2017), https://www.washingtonpost.com/politics/who-is-source-d-the-man-said-to-be-behind-the-trump-russia-dossiers-most-salacious-claim/2017/03/29/379846a8-0f53-11e7-9d5a-a83e627dc120_story.html, accessed 9 September 2019.
229 Craig Unger, "When a Young Trump Went to Russia" (August 15, 2018), https://newrepublic.com/article/150646/young-trump-went-russia, accessed 16 January 2020. See also Craig Unger, *American Kompromat: How the KGB Cultivated Donald Trump, and Related Tales of Sex, Greed, Power, and Treachery* (New York: Penguin Random House, 2021), p. 86.
230 Glenn Simpson interview, Permanent Select Committee on Intelligence, November 14, 2017, pp. 23–27, 60–62 and Meyer, "Christopher Steele, the Man Behind the Trump Dossier."
231 Meyer, "Christopher Steele, the Man Behind the Trump Dossier."

idential election. At the end of this briefing Trump was privately briefed on the Steele dossier by FBI director James Comey. According to the Mueller Report:

> The President-Elect stated that he thought highly of Comey, looked forward to working with him, and hoped that he planned to stay on as FBI director. Comey responded that he intended to continue serving in that role. Comey then briefed the President-Elect on the sensitive material in the Steele reporting. Comey recalled that the President-Elect seemed defensive, so Comey decided to assure him that the FBI was not investigating him personally. Comey recalled he did not want the President-Elect to think of the conversation as a 'J. Edgar Hoover move.[232]

Trump campaign officials implicated in the Steele dossier immediately denied its validity and contents including President Trump himself.[233] On Twitter, Trump described Steele as a "lowlife" and the dossier "phony & discredited paid for by Crooked Hillary & the DNC ..."[234]

From the beginning, the credibility of Steele's sources, and by extension, the dossier itself have been called into question. A sequence of investigations and lawsuits followed. This included the December 2019 Horowitz Report, resulting from the FBI's Crossfire Hurricane investigation, relating to four members of the Trump campaign team (George Papadopoulos, Carter Page, Paul Manafort, and Michael Flynn) and whether they had coordinated knowingly or unwittingly with Russian government. Steele was one of the FBI's sources.

Horowitz levelled criticisms at both the FBI and DOJ over flawed evidence submitted to the Foreign Intelligence Surveillance Court (FISC) in their applications to investigate and surveil the four as part of the wider Russia investigation.[235] Horowitz saw evidence that Steele might have artificially inflated the "raw intelligence."[236] This included false evidence of cooperation between the

232 Mueller Report Volume II, pp. 27–28.

233 Mueller Report Volume II, p. 23. Bensinger et al., "These Reports Allege Trump Has Deep Ties To Russia."

234 https://twitter.com/realdonaldtrump/status/1028347518822825984?lang=en, accessed 18 September 2019.

235 Office of the Inspector General U.S. Department of Justice, Review of Four FISA Applications and Other Aspects of the FBI's Crossfire Hurricane Investigation, December 2019 revised, https://www.justice.gov/storage/120919-examination.pdf, accessed 19 July 2023.

236 Jeremy Diamond, "Intel report: Putin directly ordered effort to influence election" (January 6, 2017), https://edition.cnn.com/2017/01/06/politics/intelligence-report-putin-election/; and Katelyn Polantz and Marshall Cohen, "7 new things we learned from the Horowitz report," https://edition.cnn.com/2019/12/09/politics/horowitz-reports-new-things/index.html, both accessed 19 July 2023.

Kremlin and Trump campaign team.[237] Special Counsel John Durham's investigation and report into the FBI's handling of President Trump's ties to Russia found that Steele's primary source repeatedly lied to the FBI. It also found that Steele's sources were being fed (dis)information by Clinton supporters. The Senate's Select Committee on Intelligence also investigated Russia's active measures campaigns, with a focus on Russian election interference in 2016.[238] It too indicated that Steele's report might have contained Russian disinformation.[239]

Despite these major reservations, an alleged CIA mole lends credence to elements of the Steele dossier. In September 2019 CNN broke the story of a high-level covert source that had to be extracted from Russia by the CIA in July 2017.[240] The following day Russian media named the alleged spy as Oleg Smolenkov. Smolenkov worked for Yury Ushakov, a foreign policy aide to President Putin within the Presidential Administration. Smolenkov was well placed inside the Kremlin with direct access to Putin and top secret documents.[241]

According to *The New York Times* he had been cultivated and then recruited as a mid-level official who rose up the ranks to become a highly prized CIA mole. The CIA started to worry that media reporting regarding Russian involvement and decision-making would give away their asset. Fearing for his safety, and with emerging concerns regarding his trustworthiness, Smolenkov was offered the

---

237 Marshall Cohen, "The Steele Dossier: A reckoning" (November 1, 2021), https://edition.cnn.com/2021/11/18/politics/steele-dossier-reckoning/index.html, accessed 19 July 2023.

238 Russian Active Measures Campaigns and Interference in the 2016 U.S. Election Volume 5: Counterintelligence Threats and Vulnerabilities, Report 116-XX, August 2020, United States Senate Select Committee on Intelligence, https://www.intelligence.senate.gov/sites/default/files/documents/report_volume5.pdf, accessed 19 July 2023.

239 Jeremy Herb, Marshall Cohen, and Katelyn Polantz, "Bipartisan Senate report details Trump campaign contacts with Russia in 2016, adding to Mueller findings" (August 20, 2023), https://edition.cnn.com/2020/08/18/politics/senate-intelligence-report-russia-election-interference-efforts/index.html, accessed 19 July 2023.

240 Jim Sciutto, "Exclusive: US extracted top spy from inside Russia in 2017" (September 10, 2019), https://edition.cnn.com/2019/09/09/politics/russia-us-spy-extracted/index.html; Greg Miller and Adam Entous, "Declassified report says Putin 'ordered' effort to undermine faith in U.S. election and help Trump" (January 6, 2017), https://www.washingtonpost.com/world/national-security/intelligence-chiefs-expected-in-new-york-to-brief-trump-on-russian-hacking/2017/01/06/5f591416-d41a-11e6-9cb0-54ab630851e8_story.html; and Ken Dilanian and Tatyana Chistikova, "Possible Russian spy for CIA now living in Washington area" (September 10, 2019), https://www.nbcnews.com/news/us-news/possible-ex-russian-spy-cia-living-washington-area-n1051741. All accessed 10 September 2019.

241 Anonymous, "Russia-US espionage: Details emerge of 'extracted spy'" (September 10, 2019), https://www.bbc.co.uk/news/world-us-canada-49651576; and Sciutto, "Exclusive: US extracted top spy from inside Russia in 2017."

chance of extraction from Russia. He initially refused, reasoning he needed to protect his family, but after more public revelations the CIA pressed him again and he agreed to leave. With it, the CIA lost an important asset within the walls of the Kremlin. What Smolenkov told the CIA was that the order to interfere in the election came from President Putin himself. This was a key part of the CIA's assessment that Putin had aimed to see Trump elected and personally ordered the hack and leak of the DNC/DCCC to discredit the Clinton campaign.[242]

9 Conclusion

Russia's systematic active measures campaigns against the U.S. during the 2016 American presidential election had three interrelated strands. The first tried to hack online voting systems with limited success. The second hacked and then leaked information held by the Clinton campaign team and Democratic Congressional Campaign Committee (DCCC) and Democratic National Committee (DNC). The third was a "sweeping and sustained social influence operation consisting of various coordinated disinformation tactics aimed directly at US citizens, designed to exert political influence."[243] This was a multi-year coordinated mis and disinformation campaign orchestrated at the highest levels by the Kremlin and Russian intelligence. Roger Stone, who was indicted by Mueller for communicating with "Guccifer 2.0" and Wikileaks with prior knowledge of the "hack and leak," has described his political strategy as "Admit nothing, deny everything, launch counterattack."[244] This same tactic is used by the Kremlin for all its espionage activities and covert actions/active measures, including those conducted during the 2016 presidential election campaign.[245]

In an October 2018 indictment, DOJ prosecutors working for Robert Mueller directly referred to Russian interference as "information warfare" that moved from a general effort in 2014/15 to undermine the U.S. electoral system to a "tar-

242 Julian E. Barnes, Adam Goldman, and David E. Sanger, "C.I.A. Informant Extracted From Russia Had Sent Secrets to U.S. for Decades" (September 9, 2019), https://www.nytimes.com/2019/09/09/us/politics/cia-informant-russia.html?action=click&module=Top%20Stories&pgtype=Homepage, accessed 10 September 2019.

243 DiResta et al., "The Tactics & Tropes of the Internet Research Agency," p. 4.

244 Jeffrey Toobin, "The Dirty Trickster" (May 23, 2008), https://www.newyorker.com/magazine/2008/06/02/the-dirty-trickster, accessed 9 September 2019.

245 The connections between members of the Trump campaign team were examined in the documentary *Active Measures*. "Active Measures," https://www.imdb.com/title/tt8135494/, accessed 20 January 2020.

geted operation" that by early 2016 was actively lobbying for Donald Trump's election and disparaging Hillary Clinton. They squarely laid this operation on the GRU. President Trump has remained skeptical that Russia intervened, especially through "hacking and leaks," with K. T. McFarland the only member of the campaign team to contemporaneously go on record calling out Russian interference.[246] The "hack and leak" side of their operation, using the personas "DCLeaks" and "Guccifer 2.0," first targeted Clinton's campaign chairman, John Podesta, and then the Democratic Congressional Campaign Committee (DCCC) itself and the Democratic National Committee (DNC). These were then sent to Wikileaks who then published them. Whistleblowing sites like Wikileaks and investigative sites like Bellingcat might well be long-term outlets for "hacks and leaks" but where these leaks come from and for what purpose they serve are important questions to ask.

Russia also sought to exploit divisions in the underbelly of American society to affect the election outcome in favor of Donald Trump. Through the Internet Research Agency they exploited divisions in American society fueling America's "culture wars" on issues such as the civilian–military divide, gun control, religion, race, and immigration, alongside secessionist movements.[247] They targeted and profiled people and interest groups on the left and right and played to particular audiences for amplification, including "alt-right" conspiracy sites like Alex Jones' Infowars and Breitbart.[248] The usefulness of the IRA and similar organs as a "privateer" proxy has not stopped. Despite negative publicity at the time, platforms including Facebook/Meta, Instagram, Twitter/X, and other forms of social media continue to grow.[249]

Despite a vast array of evidence there was skepticism of Russian interference from the outset of the investigation from many Republican members of Congress

246 Mueller Report Volume I, p. 171.

247 Gioe et al., "Rebalancing Cybersecurity Imperatives: Patching the Social Layer," p. 124.

248 Nick Fox, "The Alex Jones Presidency" (May 25, 2018), https://www.nytimes.com/2018/05/25/opinion/trump-alex-jones-conspiracy.html; Pema Levy, "How Russia Can Spend Money to Influence the 2020 Election–Legally" (June 11, 2019), https://www.motherjones.com/politics/2019/06/how-russia-can-spend-money-to-influence-the-2020-election-legally/; "Alex Jones Of 'Infowars,' Conspiracy Theories, And Trump Campaign (Full) | Megyn Kelly | NBC News" (June 19, 2017), https://www.youtube.com/watch?v=-HzOqZeX3Yk. All accessed 16 September 2019.

249 Warner-Søderholm et al., "Who Trusts Social Media?" pp. 303–315 and "Number of social network users worldwide from 2010 to 2021 (in billions)" (August 14, 2019 and regularly updated), https://www.statista.com/statistics/278414/number-of-worldwide-social-network-users/, accessed 1 September 2019.

and Trump himself before and after he became president.[250] Skepticism had also been directed at a mainstream liberal-leaning press as generators of "fake news" for perpetuating a Democratic Party driven "witch hunt" and a "deep state" in cahoots with the U.S. Intelligence Community and foreign friends and allies. However past and serving members of the USIC have concluded on multiple separate occasions that Russia interfered in the 2016 U.S. presidential election and continues to try to meddle in U.S. politics. President Trump muddied these waters by casting doubt on the case laid out by the USIC. This includes remarks made during and after the Trump–Putin summit in Helsinki in July 2018 where he appeared to take Putin's word that Russia did not interfere over well-founded USIC conclusions.[251]

Many column inches, television commentary, and congressional committee time (much of it centered around the Mueller inquiry) have been devoted to Russian interference in 2016. Those claiming to have the "inside story" can tell this only from the U.S. perspective.[252] Unless and until a more complete record of the Russian side, and other foreign actors, comes to light what remains to be discovered remains conjecture. Russia did not stand still. They continued to leverage what they learned in 2016 to influence the 2020 election.[253] Further developments in artificial intelligence (and quantum computing) forbode a much wider series of attacks on elections and other areas of critical infrastructure in the future.[254] Top-down government initiatives like extending the remit of the State Department's Global Engagement Center (GEC) to counter "foreign state and non-state propaganda and disinformation" are welcome but inchoate at best.[255]

Due to its politically-charged nature, the Mueller investigation and March 2019 report has generated at least as much heat and light as the Watergate scandal

---

250 Sophie Tatum, "Report: CIA's Brennan criticized some lawmakers' grasp of Russian interference" (August 25, 2017), https://edition.cnn.com/2017/08/24/politics/cia-memos-john-brennan-congress/index.html, accessed 16 September 2019.

251 Katie Rogers, "Trump-Putin Summit Is Over. The Head-Scratching? Not So Much" (July 16, 2018), https://www.nytimes.com/2018/07/16/world/europe/trump-putin-summit-helsinki.html, accessed 30 September 2019.

252 Michael Isikoff and David Corn, *Russian Roulette: The Inside Story of Putin's War on America and the Election of Donald Trump* (New York: Twelve, 2018).

253 Treasury Escalates Sanctions Against the Russian Government's Attempts to Influence U.S. Elections, April 15, 2021, https://home.treasury.gov/news/press-releases/jy0126, accessed 2 August 2023.

254 Alina Polyakova, "The next Russian attack will be far worse than bots and trolls" (March 22, 2018), https://www.brookings.edu/blog/order-from-chaos/2018/03/22/the-next-russian-attack-will-be-far-worse-than-bots-and-trolls/amp/, accessed 30 September 2019.

255 Putin's Asymmetric Assault, pp. 149 – 150.

which heralded the end of the Nixon presidency in the early 1970s.[256] For all the light it, alongside media reporting and House enquiries, sheds on the machinations between official and non-official representatives of the Kremlin and the Trump campaign team, it has also contributed to a great deal of smoke and mirrors, competing narratives, and motivations, producing a parallax view of events.[257] There were also ongoing investigations.[258]

Although the Mueller investigation did not find that members of the Trump campaign team knew that they were communicating with members of Russia's IRA, "The president ... has spent much of his time feuding with, and occasionally directly condemning, the US intelligence community – the so-called 'deep state.'"[259] Comey's epilogue in his 2018 book, *A Higher Loyalty*, warned "Donald Trump's presidency threatens much of what is good in this country."[260] Impeachment proceedings against him lengthened the shadow cast by Russian interference in 2016.[261] In the meantime U.S. government officials knew that Russia was gearing up for the 2020 presidential election and 2024 election.[262] America was much more prepared this time to combat Russian efforts to sway its election process. This applied in the 2020 election of President Joe Biden and the (re)election of President Donald J. Trump in November 2024. Both were a clear choice made by the American people and by American democracy.

---

256 Bob Woodward, *Fear: Trump in the White House* (New York: Simon & Schuster, 2018), 27–30, 60–71, 80–87, 164, 172–174, 197–198, 330, 345, 349; Michael Wolff, *Fire and Fury: Inside the Trump White House* (New York: Henry Holt, 2018), pp. 24, 37–39, 41, 95–107, 151–154, 168, 190–191, 212, 218–221, 236–242, 244–245, 253–262, 271–272, 278–279, 283, 303, 307–308.

257 Russian Interference in the 2016 Election, https://www.govtrack.us/congress/oversight/2-russian-interference-2016, accessed 23 September 2019.

258 Madeleine Carlisle and Olivia Paschal, "After Mueller: The Ongoing Investigations Surrounding Trump" (March 22, 2019), https://www.theatlantic.com/politics/archive/2019/03/after-mueller-ongoing-investigations-trump/585376/. Lisa Desjardins, "Trump faces 4 investigations. Here's where they stand" (March 22, 2023), https://www.pbs.org/newshour/politics/your-guide-to-all-of-the-investigations-into-trump. Both accessed 30 March 2023.

259 Mueller Report Volume I, p. 175 and Anonymous, "Russia-US espionage: Details emerge of 'extracted spy'."

260 Comey, *A Higher Loyalty*, pp. 237–239.

261 Donnie O'Sullivan, "Facebook: Russian trolls are back. And they're here to meddle with 2020," https://edition.cnn.com/2019/10/21/tech/russia-instagram-accounts-2020-election/index.html, accessed 23 October 2019.

262 Gretchen Frazee, "Read Fiona Hill's full testimony in the impeachment inquiry" (November 8, 2019), https://www.pbs.org/newshour/politics/read-the-transcript-of-fiona-hills-full-testimony-in-the-impeachment-probe, accessed 29 November 2019.

Final conclusions

Russia has not been a status quo power since its adversities of the 1990s. Against the West, Russia's aims are not designed for a westwards military invasion.[1] Any serious contemplation of physical intervention in the West or an invasion of a NATO ally risks direct war with the NATO alliance. Nevertheless, despite being overmatched by NATO in every category of power, Russia's actions and adventurism over the past 25 years mean direct threats might not be off the table and assumes that Russia is a rational actor.[2] It also assumes that NATO will continue with American support and will not splinter. Russia's economy and defense budget is dwarfed by NATO.[3] Currently, Russia poses side order threats beneath direct military intervention which are also real and material. President Vladimir Putin and the decision-makers clustered around him have used this "gray zone" beneath the level of outright intervention and conflict to advance perceived Russian interests and challenge the West, liberal-democracy, and the Rule of Law. Along the way this has seen Russia withdraw from a series of nuclear and arms control and limitation treaties as well as the Conventional Armed Forces in Europe (CFE) treaty and reach back to its Soviet past.

This includes using cyberespionage and information warfare/influence operations as a form of active measures. This is part of a wider suite of hybrid warfare activities, including the use of proxy and paramilitary forces (especially the Wagner Group), and traditional spycraft.[4] The main aim has been to divide the Western alliance (focused on NATO and European Union), challenge the liberal order,

---

1 Richard Sakwa, "'New Cold War' or Twenty Years' Crisis? Russia and International Politics," *International Affairs*, Vol. 84, No. 2 (2008), pp. 241–267.

2 Dana H. Allin, "Ukraine: The Shock of Recognition," *Survival*, Vol. 64, No. 2 (April–May 2022), p. 207.

3 Russia's defense budget is estimated at between $62.2 and $65.9 billion. The U.S. budget alone is $801 billion. For NATO as a whole it is $1,175 billion or almost 18 times that of Russia. Whilst overall spending is not a measure of effectiveness or deployable combat power, across the five domains of war various official assessments and the assessments of organizations including the Stockholm International Peace Research Institute (SIPRI), and International Institute for Strategic Studies point to this overmatch. Anthony H. Cordesman and Paul Cormarie, "NATO Force Planning and the Impact of the Ukraine War" (October 24, 2022), https://www.csis.org/analysis/nato-force-planning-and-impact-ukraine-war. Siemon T. Wezeman "Russia's military spending: Frequently asked questions" (undated), https://www.sipri.org/commentary/topical-backgrounder/2020/russias-military-spending-frequently-asked-questions. Both accessed 22 October 2023.

4 Jack Watling, Oleksandr V. Danylyuk, and Nick Reynolds, "The Threat from Russia's Unconventional Warfare Beyond Ukraine, 2022–24," February 2024, pp. 14–25, https://static.rusi.org/SR-Russian-Unconventional-Weapons-final-web.pdf, accessed 5 May 2025.

https://doi.org/10.1515/9783111583464-008

and divide member states. This has included exploiting or creating wedge issues between citizens and undermining trust in governments and state institutions. They have been supporting and fanning political divisions, nationalism, and secessionist movements, and mining the bedrock of Western liberal-democracy since Putin's return to the presidency in 2012. This has shaken their foundations, helped demoralize their citizens, and has been destabilizing the Western alliance whilst distracting member states from Russia's wider aims. Whilst technological changes, and especially the rise of the Internet and social media, have been major factors enabling Russian information warfare, Russia has also been a beneficiary of globalization, increased free trade, and more open borders. This has seen travel between (and within) nations become much easier in the post-1991 world than was possible during the Cold War. These are among the marked differences when looking at the conduct and character of Russia's designs and actions if seeing these through the intelligence studies lens as a continuation or mutation of active measures or one (as this book argues) that is better conceived of through the lens of hybrid warfare. This also applies to those who also see antecedents of hybrid warfare in millennia-old counterinsurgency (COIN) campaigns.[5]

Putin's greatest foreign policy successes came in 2014–16 when it annexed Crimea from Ukraine, and then interfered in Britain's Brexit referendum and the U.S. presidential elections. This interference was through orchestrated political influence campaigns involving propaganda and manipulation of Western social media users whilst leveraging mainstream media platforms. Whether it was successful in tilting both results as they intended cannot be proven and is disputed.[6] However, it is legitimate to ask that if these two Russian campaigns were unsuccessful then why does Russia continue not only to conduct these campaigns throughout Europe but also export them in support of regimes in central Africa and to influence the political landscape of South Africa and India?[7]

In 2016, the Kremlin's campaigns also showed it was capable of dividing, demoralizing, and distracting UK and U.S. intelligence communities, their governments, and deceiving their populations. Scores of other attempts were made. As

5 Kristan Stoddart with Christian Kaunert and Kiril Avramov (eds.), *Hybrid Warfare: Western and non-Western definitions, concepts, and regional case studies* (Quantico, VA: Marine Corps University Press, 2026).

6 Those who dispute this and the effectiveness of social media to influence opinion, including the idea of impressions, include Thomas Rid. Thomas Rid, *Active Measures The Secret History of Disinformation and Political Warfare* (New York: Farrar, Straus and Giroux), p. 431.

7 UK exposes sick Russian troll factory plaguing social media with Kremlin propaganda (1 May 2022), https://www.gov.uk/government/news/uk-exposes-sick-russian-troll-factory-plaguing-social-media-with-kremlin-propaganda.

detailed in the introduction, prior to 2014, these were concentrated on former Soviet states of Russian near abroad as distant as central Asia.[8] These campaigns stretch into the Balkan states of Montenegro, Serbia, through to Bulgaria and Hungary and the Nordic states of Sweden, Denmark, Norway as well as Finland. They have been seen in The Netherlands, France, Germany, Spain, and Italy. Between 2004 and 2017, at least 27 European and North American countries experienced Russian influence campaigns.[9] This might be an underestimate.[10] In Europe alone, ongoing evidence strongly shows increasing cases. In addition, as well as Afghanistan, at least 10 African nations have seen non-military interventions, including disinformation campaigns.[11]

These foreign influence campaigns followed domestic campaigns used to silence opposition politicians, government, and policy critics, and investigations of corruption. This has seen the end of press freedoms in Russia with newspapers compelled to follow the Kremlin worldview and agenda presented on state-controlled television. Not toeing the line sees them placed under legal restrictions, experience harassment, whilst putting them at odds with their audiences, who mainly receive news through television.[12] This has left them with three choices:

---

8 Todd C. Helmus, Elizabeth Bodine-Baron, Andrew Radin, Madeline Magnuson, Joshua Mendelsohn, William Marcellino, Andriy Bega, and Zev Winkelman, "Russian Social Media Influence. Understanding Russian Propaganda in Eastern Europe" (2018), RAND Corporation, pp. 2–3, https://www.rand.org/content/dam/rand/pubs/research_reports/RR2200/RR2237/RAND_RR2237.pdf, accessed 25 October 2019.

9 Putin's Asymmetric Assault on Democracy in Russia and Europe: Implications for U.S. National Security. A Minority Staff Report, Committee on Foreign Relations United States Senate, January 10, 2018, pp. 65–97, 99–139, https://www.foreign.senate.gov/imo/media/doc/FinalRR.pdf, accessed 5 November 2019.

10 Nomaan Merchant, "US: Russia spent $300M to covertly influence world politics" (September 13, 2022), https://apnews.com/article/russia-ukraine-putin-biden-politics-presidential-elections-03d0ae84fb34833b78b1753d0a9602db. Department Press Briefing – September 13, 2022, https://www.state.gov/briefings/department-press-briefing-september-13-2022/. Both accessed 2 November 2023.

11 House of Commons Foreign Affairs Committee, Guns for gold: The Wagner Network exposed, Seventh Report of Session 2022–23, 18 July 2023, pp. 9–16, 69–70, 74–75, https://committees.parliament.uk/publications/41073/documents/200048/default/. See also Guns for gold: the Wagner Network exposed, https://committees.parliament.uk/committee/78/foreign-affairs-committee/news/196695/guns-for-gold-the-wagner-network-exposed/. Both accessed 26 July 2023.

12 Vasily Gatov, "How the Kremlin and the Media Ended Up in Bed Together" (March 11, 2015), https://www.themoscowtimes.com/2015/03/11/how-the-kremlin-and-the-media-ended-up-in-bed-together-a44663. Vera Zakem, Paul Saunders, Umida Hashimova, and P. Kathleen Hammerberg, "Mapping Russian Media Network: Media's Role in Russian Foreign Policy and Decision-Making," CNA (January 2018), https://www.cna.org/cna_files/pdf/DRM-2017-U-015367-3Rev.pdf. Both accessed 18 November 2019.

conform, close, or exile. Those who do not conform face threats and intimidation, or imprisonment. Some have also been assassinated.[13]

These attempts to influence have been focused on civil society, elections, political parties, and cultural institutions. These tools of soft power are also part of Russia's 4Ds of information warfare: dismiss, distort, distract, and dismay. When challenged it dismisses critics, distorts the facts, and distracts from the facts on the ground and its overall policy aims. These are attempts to dismay its critics and challengers and has become predictable.[14] More importantly, a fifth – disruption, needs to be added. This not only includes activities in the domain of information warfare, but also in relation to economic cyberespionage and critical infrastructure. Following the invasion of Ukraine in February 2022, a sixth D needs to be included – destruction.

1 Hybrid warfare

The invasion, and Russian actions and activities in the years leading up to it, needs setting in the context of hybrid warfare. Ukraine has long been a prime target. Whether or not one sees this as the manifestation of the "Gerasimov doctrine," interventions in its near abroad are an assertion of Russia's historic great power status and an attempt to rebuild a "sphere of influence" over the post-Soviet states of Ukraine, Belarus, and those of Eurasia. It has also attempted to regrow its influence over former Soviet states which are now part of the European Union (EU) and NATO.[15]

Under Putin Russian policy has been steadily, sometimes brutally, consolidating its influence over Belarus and disputed territories in the North Caucasus, espe-

13 Putin's Asymmetric Assault, p. 31. Shaun Walker, "The murder that killed free media in Russia" (October 5, 2016), https://www.theguardian.com/world/2016/oct/05/ten-years-putin-press-kremlin-grip-russia-media-tightens, accessed 25 October 2019. This might also be extended to nationals outside of their near abroad. Katie Bo Lillis, Natasha Bertrand and Frederik Pleitgen, "Exclusive: US and Germany foiled Russian plot to assassinate CEO of arms manufacturer sending weapons to Ukraine" (July 11, 2024), https://edition.cnn.com/2024/07/11/politics/us-germany-foiled-russian-assassination-plot?cid=ios_app, accessed 12 July 2024.

14 Ben Nimmo, "Anatomy of an Info-War: How Russia's Propaganda Machine Works, and How to Counter It" (May 19, 2015), https://www.stopfake.org/en/anatomy-of-an-info-war-how-russia-s-propaganda-machine-works-and-how-to-counter-it/, accessed 2 April 2023.

15 Mark Galeotti, "(Mis)Understanding Russia's Two 'Hybrid Wars,'" *Critique & Humanism*, Vol. 59, No. 1 (2018), p. 2.

cially Chechnya.[16] Framing these as counterterrorism operations, this has included targeting Chechen separatist leaders for assassination. It is believed their kill list had nineteen names on it. Three failed but the remainder succeeded. Twelve of these were in Turkey (including Abdulvakhid Edilgeriev and Abdullah Bukhari), three in Ukraine, two in Austria (including Mamikhan Umarov), with one each in Germany (Zelimkhan Khangoshvili), the United Arab Emirates, and Qatar.[17] In 2008 it also invaded Georgia in the Southern Caucasus. This saw Georgia sever ties with Moscow. These attitudes are shaped by its loss of superpower status after the fall of communism and the embrace of the EU and NATO by many of its former Soviet republics during the 1990s and 2000s.[18] During the 1990s Russia was at its weakest and unable to resist Western encroachment and for Russian nationalists and the political elites that were forming (or re-forming) this was viewed through the lens of the security dilemma and a zero-sum game. Since then, NATO/EU encroachment has been portrayed as threatening politically, economically, and militarily to Russia's security and national interests.

In addition, Russia's list of allies is thin. It supported the regime of Bashar Al Assad in Syria, developed a "tactical entente" with Islamist Iran, and found common cause with President Nicolás Maduro in Venezuela. It also exerts power and influence over two of its former satellites in Belarus and Georgia. Alignments with likeminded or anti-Western regimes are frequently accompanied by arms sales. Russia's relationship, perhaps rapprochement, with China is more difficult to assess but in this and other cases power politics and marriages of convenience are at work.[19] Economic interests and development are also at work. This includes fric-

---

16 Watling, Danylyuk, and Reynolds, "The Threat from Russia's Unconventional Warfare Beyond Ukraine, 2022–24," pp. 26–32.

17 The names and the outlines of the cases can be found alongside mention of opponents of the Assad regime targeted for assassination in Syria as well as Ukrainian targets inside Ukraine in Kevin P. Rielhe, *Russian Intelligence: A Case-Based Study of Russian Services and Missions Past and Present* (Bethesda, MD: National Intelligence Press, 2022), pp. 91–101, 208–209. Kevin P. Riehle, *The Russian FSB A concise history of the Federal Security Service* (Washington DC: Georgetown University Press, 2024), pp. 84–86.

18 Derek Averre, "NATO Expansion and Russian National Interests," *European Security*, Vol. 7, Issue 1 (January 1998), pp. 10–54, Edward P. Joseph, "NATO Expansion: The Source of Russia's Anger?" (May 1, 2014), https://nationalinterest.org/feature/nato-expansion-the-source-russias-anger-10344, accessed 25 February 2020.

19 This well captured by Oriana Skylar Mastro, "Sino-Russian Military Alignment and Its Implications for Global Security," *Security Studies*, Vol. 33, No. 2 (2024), pp. 254–290. Jon Grevatt, "China, Russia approve 2021–25 road map to increase military co-operation" (November 24, 2021), https://www.janes.com/defence-news/news-detail/china-russia-approve-202125-road-map-to-increase-military-co-operation. China has also been supplying microelectronics and machine tools to Russia as the Ukraine War progressed. Aamer Madhani, "U.S. intelligence shows China is surging

tion over China's Belt and Road Initiative in the former Soviet states of Central Asia and into the European Union.[20] Also in play are balance of power and balance of threat calculations where weak/weaker states will bind themselves to a stronger power.[21] According to Britain's Intelligence and Security Committee (ISC), "its poor national brand and lack of long-term global friends appear to feed its enormous risk appetite – perhaps on the basis that it thinks it has nothing to lose."[22]

This is a nation that remains a nuclear superpower and uses nuclear saber rattling as part of its foreign and security policy. It also assumed the seat of the Soviet Union on the UN Security Council. In most other indexes, Russia has fallen behind Western states and is dwarfed by the Chinese economy and military. Its conventional military size and capabilities have fallen sharply from the Soviet era.[23] They are potent but have been hollowed out by systemic and endemic corruption. This is reflected in Russia's military performance from the beginnings of the Ukraine War. Where it has done well to offset these relative weaknesses, is to use cyberespionage allied to traditional spycraft as a force multiplier. This, alongside conventional munitions and drones, has been an arena for defense innovation visible in Ukraine.[24]

Their cyberespionage and traditional intelligence operations under Putin utilize "hybrid warfare." Russia's use is described by RAND as "a broad range of subversive instruments, many of which are nonmilitary, to further Russian national

---

equipment sales to Russia to help war effort in Ukraine, AP says" (April 12, 2024), https://www.pbs.org/newshour/world/u-s-intelligence-shows-china-is-surging-equipment-sales-to-russia-to-help-war-effort-in-ukraine-ap-says. Both accessed 24 October 2024.

20 Andreea Brinza, "Putin's War Has Killed China's Eurasian Railway Dreams" (March 1, 2022), https://foreignpolicy.com/2022/03/01/belt-road-initiative-new-eurasian-land-bridge-china-russia-poland/, accessed 11 May 2025.

21 Clément Therme, "Iran and Russia in the Middle East: Toward a Regional Alliance?" *Middle East Journal*, Vol. 72, No. 4 (Autumn 2018), pp. 549–562. Andrew Kydd, "Switching Sides: Changing Power, Alliance Choices and US–China–Russia Relations," *International Politics*, Vol. 57, Issue 5 (October 2020), pp. 855–884.

22 Intelligence and Security Committee of Parliament, Russia HC 632, 21 July 2020, p. 1. https://isc.independent.gov.uk/wp-content/uploads/2021/01/20200721_HC632_CCS001_CCS1019402408-001_ISC_Russia_Report_Web_Accessible.pdf, accessed 29 December 2020.

23 Gerhard Mangott, "Farewell to Russia: The Decay of a Superpower," in Heinz Gärtner, Adrian Hyde-Price and Erich Reiter (eds.), *Europe's New Security Challenges* (London: Lynne Rienner, 2000) pp. 385–388.

24 "Tactical Unit Combat Control System 'Kropyva,'" https://logika.ua/en/automation-systems/, accessed 11 May 2025.

interests."[25] This also reflects the controversial "Gerasimov doctrine," which outlined using nonmilitary means to achieve strategic ends. Cyberespionage is a key element to try and achieve these ends and being used to further Russia's foreign and security policy goals and the Kremlin's revisionist agenda. This includes the use of *dezinformatsiya* (disinformation) as well as hacking and then leaking information-intelligence stolen from a variety of governmental and non-state agencies, including the World Anti-Doping Authority (WADA) and Organisation for the Prohibition of Chemical Weapons (OPCW). These illustrate that where they have been unable to access systems remotely, they have physically traveled to high value targets to hack locally.

Although there is little to no possibility of Russia extraditing those suspected, through forensic intelligence-led operations, nations such as the United States and Netherlands have "named and shamed" which has led to expulsions and some prosecutions allied to financial and travel sanctions. Western counterintelligence has also had successes. Independently of governments and their intelligence agencies, so too has the crowdsourced Open Source Intelligence (OSINT) organization Bellingcat which has outed Russian intelligence operations involved in assassination attempts abroad and much more still, including helping establish the chain of events that led to the downing of MH17 in 2014. Russia's Wagner Group has also been exposed in operations abroad, especially in conflict zones including the Central African Republic (CAR), Libya, Mozambique, Mali, and Sudan. They also intervened in Syria to prop up the regime of President Bashar al-Assad. Where they operate is often accompanied by reports (denied by the Kremlin) of human rights violations. A 2023 British Foreign Affairs Committee report remarked, "The brutality of Wagner fighters when offering military services is notorious and well-documented, violating the norms of international law and taking the lives of civilians."[26] Whether that brutality is tempered by Wagner's infusion into Russia's military structure, including through the Africa Corps, is doubtful.[27]

In conflict zones and on the "virtual battlefield," information warfare and cyberwarfare capable of "armed attack" are used alongside traditional means and

---

25 Christopher S. Chivvis, "Understanding Russian 'Hybrid Warfare' And What Can Be Done About It" (March 2017), p. 1, https://www.rand.org/content/dam/rand/pubs/testimonies/CT400/CT468/RAND_CT468.pdf, accessed 25 January 2020.

26 To which was later added "Wagner fighters have left behind a trail of atrocities in virtually all theatres where they have operated, with limited accountability." Guns for gold, pp. 21, 52.

27 Mark Galeotti, "Siloviki at War: The Russian Security Community Since February 2022," *Russian Analytical Digest*, No. 323 (January 2025), p. 8, https://css.ethz.ch/content/dam/ethz/special-interest/gess/cis/center-for-securities-studies/pdfs/russiananalyticaldigest-323.pdf, accessed 27 April 2025.

modern tools of warfare.[28] Russia has embraced these as a strategy to advance their interests.[29] So far Russia's intelligence-led activities in cyberspace have not crossed the threshold where they have been deemed to qualify as an armed attack or the use of force by NATO under the Tallinn Manuals. Instead, Russia has benefited from playing in what is described by militaries and policymakers as the "gray zone" beneath this threshold. This takes place both on the "virtual battlefield" described throughout this book and in war and conflict zones such as Ukraine where Russia has deployed both regular and irregular forces. This includes situations, like in Ukraine in 2014, where Russian forces stripped away their insignia prior to crossing the border to become irregular "little green men." Mark Galeotti is one of a number of informed commentators and policymakers who believe "The West finds itself in a new 'hot peace' in which many consider Russia not just as an irritant or challenge, but as an outright threat."[30]

2 Russia's elites and foreign policy

Putin has led the Russian Federation for two decades after "flip-flopping with Dmitry Medvedev for a brief stint as prime minister before returning to the presidency through a slick interpretation of the Russian constitution."[31] Although there has been opposition to his rule this has been systematically suppressed through the kinds of strategic messaging and disinformation campaigns seen in the West. Worse still, opponents of Putin are often faced with a choice of conforming to the system, exile abroad, or imprisonment. A number of those in exile, chiefly émigrés or double agents, have been assassinated or seen attempts made on their lives. This includes the brazen attempt on double agent Sergei Skripal. Not only did Putin remain president of the Russian Federation following Russia's last presidential election in 2024, but the embedded *siloviki* network will almost

---

28 Christian Enemark, *Armed Drones and the Ethics of War: Military Virtue in a Postheroic Age* (Abingdon: Routledge, 2013).

29 Peter R. Mansoor, "Introduction: Hybrid Warfare in History," in Williamson Murray and Peter R. Mansoor (eds.), *Hybrid Warfare: Fighting Complex Opponents from the Ancient World to the Present* (New York: Cambridge University Press, 2012), pp. 1–3.

30 Mark Galeotti, "Putin's Hydra: Inside Russia's Intelligence Services," p. 1, https://www.ecfr.eu/page/-/ECFR_169_-_PUTINS_HYDRA_INSIDE_THE_RUSSIAN_INTELLIGENCE_SERVICES_1513.pdf, accessed 2 January 2018.

31 Steve Abrams, "Beyond Propaganda: Soviet Active Measures in Putin's Russia," *Connections: The Quarterly Journal*, Vol. 15, No. 1 (Winter 2016), p. 17.

certainly outlive the Putin era.[32] In this eventuality, active measures are likely to continue.[33]

Under Putin, Russia has become an autocratic kleptocracy. That process began under his predecessor, Boris Yeltsin, with antecedents stretching back to the Soviet era with echoes in Tsarist Russia. There were green shoots of democracy in the 1990s, but these shoots have always been nipped in the bud with opposition parties restricted and domestic opposition killed, poisoned, or imprisoned. Ethnic nationalism is also a feature of Putin's Russia and "used to either annex or destabilize other countries."[34] Putin is also driven by revanchism and a desire to restore the former Soviet Union or for a Russian sphere of influence over the post-Soviet states of its near abroad. With it comes superpower status alongside the United States and China.

Putin and those around him use nationalism to promote regime loyalty, as a tool to achieve cohesiveness, and to justify Russia's great power ambitions.[35] Their brand of nationalism has also been used to denigrate opponents and draw support to their vision of Russia and Russia's place at the top table of nations.[36] Against this backdrop, since the late 2000s their cyber campaigns have been driven by a desire for Russia to reassert itself as a major global power with concerns of NATO and EU expansion into former Soviet territory major drivers for Putin and the *siloviki*. Much of this is directed by the Kremlin, in particular the Presidential Administration and Security Council headed by Vladimir Putin, and Russian intelligence.

3 Russia's intelligence agencies: A force multiplier?

The Introduction began by outlining and characterizing Russia's fall as a superpower, how it has changed since Vladimir Putin assumed the presidency in 2000, and what it is seeking to accomplish through its active measures campaigns,

32 Keir Giles, *Moscow Rules What Drives Russia to Confront the West* (Washington DC: Brookings, 2019), pp. 71–99.

33 Abrams, "Beyond Propaganda," p. 17. See also Reid Standish, "'Russia's Political Transition Has Arrived Ahead of Schedule'" (January 15, 2020), https://foreignpolicy.com/2020/01/15/russia-political-transition-ahead-schedule-putin-government-resign-constitution/, accessed 25 January 2020.

34 "Contextualizing Putin's 'On the Historical Unity of Russians and Ukrainians,'" https://huri.harvard.edu/news/putin-historical-unity, accessed 3 April 2021. See also Serhii Plokhy, *Lost Kingdom: The Quest for Empire and the Making of the Russian Nation* (New York: Basic Books, 2017).

35 Giles, *Moscow Rules*, 1–25.

36 "Contextualizing Putin's 'On the Historical Unity of Russians and Ukrainians.'"

especially through cyberespionage. It showed that the rise of *siloviki* ("strong men") like Putin and the oligarchs who became rich on the privatization of Russia's natural resources has been accompanied by an organized crime network that supports them in exchange for favor and protection. Putin also set about coordinating and refocusing Russia's intelligence agencies both to support his domestic power base and to conduct foreign intelligence operations against a "besieged" Russia, denied its rightful place among the top table of nations.

By the 1970s and 1980s, HUMINT, and much wider areas of intelligence-gathering and exploitation were being changed by technological research and development. Technological developments were being refined and developed at an increasingly rapid pace in line with Moore's Law. Moore's Law is the maxim that computer capacity doubles every two years leading to the onwards and accelerating drive of ICT innovation and maturation. This would lead to more technological intelligence gathering, processing, and sharing. This included geospatial intelligence through satellites (SATINT) and a significant expansion in open source intelligence (OSINT). Following Russia's "decade of catastrophe" during the 1990s Putin, a former KGB colonel, saw the intelligence agencies as tools to help reassert Russia's "great power" status.[37]

With training still conducted at former KGB locations like "The Conservatory," contemporary Russian operations reflect their KGB ancestry but also their adaptation to the modern world. This includes active measures operations and campaigns using "gray zone" hybrid warfare tactics which involve mis and disinformation campaigns and widespread campaigns of election interference (reaching an apotheosis in 2016).[38] Patriotism plays a major part in these state activities as it can with cybercriminal hackers. This includes targeting Western companies for direct and indirect monetary gain which some consider to be Cyber Enabled Economic Warfare. Russian cybercrime is rampant against the West. The Target and Home Depot cases provide two major examples.

Russia's state-backed use of cyberattacks has the capacity to produce systemic consequences for the international financial system whether intentional or through unintended consequences.[39] The relationship between the *siloviki*, Russian hackers, and the Russian mafia (the *Vory*), is not only in evidence in cybers-

37 Andrei Shleifer and Daniel Treisman, "A Normal Country: Russia After Communism," *Journal of Economic Perspectives*, Vol. 19, No. 1 (Winter 2005), pp. 151–153.

38 Keir Giles, *Russia's War on Everybody And What It Means For You* (London: Bloomsbury, 2024), pp. 132–142.

39 Bobby Vedral, "The Vulnerability of the Financial System to a Systemic Cyberattack," in Tat'ána Jančárková, Lauri Lindström, Gábor Visky, and Philippe Zotz (eds.), *13th International Conference on Cyber Conflict: Going Viral* (Tallinn: NATO CCDCOE Publications, 2021), pp. 95–110.

pace campaigns but on the ground.[40] If they are uncooperative, they are frequently made an offer they cannot refuse: serve the state or face jail.[41] Russian organized crime is closely entwined with state political interests. Britain's Government Communications Headquarters (GCHQ) informed the UK's ISC, that *"intelligence now ... shows the links between serious and organised crime groups and Russian state activity"* with increasing evidence of *"serious and organised crime ... being connected at high levels of Russian state and Russian intelligence,"* in a *"symbiotic relationship."*[42]

This symbiosis is accompanied to varying degrees by traditional foreign intelligence gathering and espionage. These are the mainstay of the SVR and a feature of GRU operations. The FSB is more concerned with domestic surveillance and order, but its power and portfolio now extend beyond Russia. Chapter 2 discussed how cybercrime is leveraged by Russia's three main intelligence agencies, the FSB, GRU, and SVR. It also closely examined how, where, and when its intelligence agencies and cybercriminal proxy actors were targeting critical infrastructure.

The SVR, Russia's foreign intelligence service, and the GRU, Russia's military intelligence agency, are also heavily involved in traditional spycraft. From 2022 and the invasion of Ukraine, the FSB's remit has extended into this murky realm. Through their "Fifth Service", they have primarily concentrated on Russia's near abroad.[43] These agencies (or "Special Services") also compete with one another displaying division, duplication, and rivalry.[44] Dutch intelligence assessed that the operators of APT29 ("Cozy Bear") are the SVR.[45] Meanwhile, the GRU is

---

40 CrowdStrike, 2018 Global Threat Report Blurring the Lines Between Statecraft and Tradecraft, p. 19. https://www.crowdstrike.com/resources/reports/2018-crowdstrike-global-threat-report-blurring-the-lines-between-statecraft-and-tradecraft/, accessed 31 March 2020.

41 Karina Orlova, "The KGB is back. The Siloviki Coup in Russia" (September 21, 2016), https://www.the-american-interest.com/2016/09/21/the-siloviki-coup-in-russia/; Louise Shelley, "A tangled web: Organized crime and oligarchy in Putin's Russia" (November 15, 2018), https://warontherocks.com/2018/11/a-tangled-web-organized-crime-and-oligarchy-in-putins-russia/. Both accessed 24 February 2020. See also Mark Galeotti, *The Vory: Russia's Super Mafia* (New Haven, CT: Yale University Press, 2018), pp. 109–272.

42 Original emphasis. Russia HC 632, 21 July 2020, p. 5.

43 Jack Watling, "The Kaleidoscopic Campaigning of Russia's Special Services" (September 20, 2022), https://www.rusi.org/explore-our-research/publications/commentary/kaleidoscopic-campaigning-russias-special-services, accessed 29 April 2025.

44 Galeotti, "Putin's Hydra," p. 3.

45 Eelco Bosch van Rosenthal, "Dutch intelligence first to alert U.S. about Russian hack of Democratic Party" (January 25, 2018), https://nos.nl/nieuwsuur/artikel/2213767-dutch-intelligence-first-to-alert-u-s-about-russian-hack-of-democratic-party.html; Dmitri Alperovitch, "Bears in the Midst: Intrusion into the Democratic National Committee," https://www.crowdstrike.com/blog/bears-midst-intrusion-democratic-national-committee/; Huib Modderkolk, "Dutch agencies pro-

running APT28 ("Fancy Bear"), which among other things, has collected intelligence on defense and geopolitical issues. Both have been known to run competing operations, including those conducted against the U.S. Democratic National Committee in 2016 during the U.S. presidential elections.[46] Both "Cozy Bear" and "Fancy Bear" "engage in extensive political and economic espionage."[47] Russia has also ventured into pre-positioning in critical infrastructure with a growing capacity to conduct destructive cyberwarfare.

4 Russian cyberespionage into critical infrastructure and cyberwar

A year before his appointment as Minister of Defense, Sergei Shoigu publicly articulated his belief in cyberespionage as a force multiplier. Shoigu argued that cyber was gaining the capacity to become "weapons of mass destruction ... We have already come close to that ... shown by hackers from different countries," who "can get to anything."[48] As was made clear in-depth in *Cyberwarfare: Threats to Critical Infrastructure*, code can be weaponized and through cyberespionage and growing connectivity and the expansion of the Internet is being actively exploited. It is already a massive attack surface and still growing. This is compounded by the increasing use of Self-Monitoring Analysis and Reporting Technology (SMART) devices, which has developed and deepened further the Internet of Things (IoT), along with 4G and 5G cellular technologies and mobile applications. Alongside these developments, the growing convergence between the Operational Technologies that control critical infrastructure sites and Internet-facing Information (Communication) Technologies is providing increasing gateway access.[49]

vide crucial intel about Russia's interference in US-elections" (January 25, 2018), https://www.volkskrant.nl/wetenschap/dutch-agencies-provide-crucial-intel-about-russia-s-interference-in-us-elections~b4f8111b/; Elizabeth Lea Vos, "Dutch 'Cozy Bear' Farce Does Not Show DNC Emails Were Hacked By Russians" (January 26, 2018), https://www.zerohedge.com/news/2018-01-26/dutch-cozy-bear-farce-does-not-show-dnc-emails-were-hacked-russians. All accessed 4 March 2020.

46 Alperovitch, "Bears in the Midst."

47 Alperovitch, "Bears in the Midst."

48 Daniil Turovsky, "What is the GRU? Who gets recruited to be a spy? Why are they exposed so often? Here are the most important things you should know about Russia's intelligence community" (November 6, 2018), https://meduza.io/en/feature/2018/11/06/what-is-the-gru-who-gets-recruited-to-be-a-spy-why-are-they-exposed-so-often, accessed 26 December 2018.

49 Kristan Stoddart, *Cyberwarfare: Threats to Critical Infrastructure* (London: Palgrave/Springer, 2022), pp. 1–25, 31–32, 147–430.

As an autocracy and with the rule of law bent to serve state interests, its intelligence agencies are able to act quickly to exploit the cyber domain. This allows Russia to act "without constraint or consideration ... and the fusion of government and business allow it to leverage all its intelligence, military and economic power at the same time to pose an all-encompassing security threat."[50] The Kremlin sees "foreign policy as a zero-sum game" where "any actions it can take which damage the West are fundamentally good for Russia." As in Soviet times "It is also seemingly fed by paranoia, believing that Western institutions such as NATO and the EU have a far more aggressive posture towards it than they do in reality." In believing "an undemocratic 'might is right' world order plays to its strengths," its actions "undermine the Rules Based International Order – whilst nonetheless benefitting from its membership of international political and economic institutions."[51]

There is ongoing debate whether or not Russia is "impulsive and opportunistic," or "consistent and clear," as James R. Clapper questioned when U.S. Director of National Intelligence (DNI).[52] They are opportunistic in cybercrime, especially outright theft through fraud and in ransomware campaigns. But when the totality of their operations is considered, especially in campaigns of election interference, against critical infrastructure, and because of the links between Russia's government and organized crime networks, orchestration and goals are apparent. The goals are to steal from the West, protect those who stole, and pre-position and test (in Ukraine and beyond) vulnerabilities in critical infrastructure. To assist these aims, the Kremlin seeks to destabilize and divide Western governments and see "how much Moscow can provoke its adversaries before they respond."[53]

Drawing on the controversial "Gerasimov doctrine," hybrid tactics have been used to divide and destabilize the West and have been actively used in Ukraine from at least 2014.[54] Chapter 2 detailed how Russian cyberespionage began with the multi-year "Moonlight Maze" campaign in the mid-1990s when Russia was in turmoil. This was aimed at technology acquisition and intellectual property

50 Russia HC 632, 21 July 2020, p. 1.
51 Russia HC 632, 21 July 2020, p. 1.
52 Greg Miller, "As Russia reasserts itself, U.S. intelligence agencies focus anew on the Kremlin," *Washington Post* (September 14, 2016), https://www.washingtonpost.com/world/national-security/as-russia-reasserts-itself-us-intelligence-agencies-focus-anew-on-the-kremlin/2016/09/14/cc212c62-78f0-11e6-ac8e-cf8e0dd91dc7_story.html, accessed 17 June 2019.
53 Miller, "As Russia reasserts itself."
54 General of the Army Valery Gerasimov, Chief of the General Staff of the Russian Federation Armed Forces, "The Value of Science Is in the Foresight New Challenges Demand Rethinking the Forms and Methods of Carrying out Combat Operations," *Military Review* (January–February 2016), p. 24.

(IP) theft. Since then, they have gone after diplomatic, governmental, and scientific research organizations (through the "Red October" campaign), aviation and defense companies, pharmaceuticals and energy companies, and IP theft ("Dragonfly") before moving further into cyber reconnaissance and then into cyber-physical attacks against critical infrastructure.

The BlackEnergy campaign which targeted Ukraine took out part of their power grid in December 2015. This was followed by "Industoyer"/"CrashOverride" in 2016 which led to power cuts in Ukraine's capital Kyiv. "Dragonfly 2.0" of 2015 was a much wider campaign which targeted industries and commercial companies across multiple CI sectors. This was designed to probe how energy facilities operate and how to gain access to Operational Technology networks and systems after penetrating the IT side of businesses (mainly through socially engineered spear phishing).[55] The attack on Colonial Pipeline also demonstrated that Russian cybercriminals operating independently can disrupt or damage critical infrastructure. The SolarWinds attack demonstrated that government agencies are vulnerable to upstream supply chain attacks. It also showed Russia to be a tier-1 adversary in cyberspace.[56]

These attacks have turned into long-term and systematic campaigns directed from the Kremlin and sometimes including freelance, co-opted cyber criminals, or "patriotic hackers" operating as proxies or privateers. They are potentially able to hold Western critical infrastructure at-risk. Return fire, across the spectrum of cyber and into kinetic politico-military operations carries risks of escalation and back channels exist to try and limit this.[57] This is an important part of the diplomatic toolbox. As Britain's ISC report of 2020 pointed out:

> In the case of Russia, the potential for escalation is particularly potent: the Russian regime is paranoid about Western intelligence activities and "*is not able to treat objectively*" international condemnation of its actions. It views any such moves as Western efforts to encourage internal protest and regime change. The risk is compounded by limitations on UK engagement with the Russian government at official and political levels, making deciphering Russian leadership intent even more difficult.[58]

---

55 "Dragonfly: Western energy sector targeted by sophisticated attack group" (October 20, 2017), accessed 23 September 2018: https://www.symantec.com/blogs/threat-intelligence/dragonfly-energy-sector-cyber-attacks.

56 The SolarWinds Cyberattack (January 29, 2021), https://www.rpc.senate.gov/policy-papers/the-solarwinds-cyberattack, accessed 11 November 2023.

57 Russia HC 632, 21 July 2020, pp. 41–42.

58 Russia HC 632, 21 July 2020, p. 30.

5 Russian cyber doctrine

Western APTs also pose cyber threats facing Russia and this has prompted the Kremlin to react. In November 2016 Russia's information security policy was updated in an attempt to bolster CI. They also aimed to instill cooperation between national sectors to guard against the same range of cybersecurity threats they face from Western nations (where conversely Russia is the most active player alongside China).[59] Another stated aim was to build cybersecurity cooperation through the Shanghai Cooperation Organization (SCO) and Collective Security Treaty Organization (CSTO).[60]

Russia's wider (unclassified/public) foreign and security policy was simultaneously updated in late November 2016 and provides considerable insight into their doctrine and intentions. The 2016 strategy update uses the term information in two ways (which might be an attempt to confuse the audience): influence/propaganda and information security. Influence is always a priority, and cyber operations feed into this. Influence operations are a fundamental goal under Putin. Although this is mainly directed against foreign states, information is also weaponized domestically. Externally, social media is the main conduit for dissemination through skewed news stories, partisan opinions, or straight out disinformation. These are coordinated information operations serving politico-military ends. It allowed Prigozhin's IRA, alongside Russia's two main state-run and intelligence agency-led Advanced Persistent Threat (APT) groups to become Advanced Persistent Manipulators (APMs) too. A little less than a year before his 2023 assassination Prigozhin boasted of Russia's involvement. In response to direct ques-

---

59 Nikolai Litovkin, "What is the updated Russian cyber-security doctrine about?" (December 7, 2017), https://www.rbth.com/defence/2016/12/07/what-is-the-updated-russian-cyber-security-doctrine-about_654407, accessed 31 December 2017.

60 The SCO, formed in 2001, is comprised of the People's Republic of China, the Kyrgyz Republic, the Russian Federation, the Republic of Tajikistan, and the Republic of Uzbekistan. The CSTO is a military and political organization which grew out of the loose federation of the Commonwealth of Independent States formed after the collapse of the Soviet Union, founded by Armenia, Kazakhstan, Kyrgyzstan, Russia, Tajikistan, and Uzbekistan with Azerbaijan, Belarus, and Georgia joining in 1994. Azerbaijan, Georgia, and Uzbekistan left in 2012. Belarus, Kyrgyzstan, Tajikistan, Kazakhstan, and Russia are also members of the Eurasian Economic Union (EEU, also referred to by the acronym EAEU). Janko Šćepanović, "20 Years of Russia's Institutionalism in Eurasia. What is Russia trying to accomplish with the CSTO, SCO, and EAEU?" (December 26, 2019), https://thediplomat.com/2019/12/20-years-of-russias-institutionalism-in-eurasia/; "The Shanghai Cooperation Organisation," http://eng.sectsco.org/about_sco/. Both accessed 28 February 2020. Malina Kaszuba, "The Collective Security Treaty Organization (CSTO) in the Foreign Policy of the Russian Federation," *The Copernicus Journal of Political Studies*, No. 1 (2019), pp. 141–153.

tions, Prigozhin said "Gentlemen, we have interfered, are interfering and will interfere. Carefully, precisely, surgically and in our own way, as we know how to do."[61]

Furthermore, Russia does not necessarily distinguish between civilian and military, political and economic tools, and therefore the public or private nature of a target can be secondary to their objective.[62] This has been a contributory factor behind the infodemic affecting the West and the growth of "fake news" (a term which has taken on other meanings partly as a result of Russia).[63] This includes false reporting on people and events, heightened in Internet echo chambers where like-minded views are reinforced. This has led to the term "fake news" and its use to pour scorn over traditional television and print mainstream media reporting that challenges or undermines existing viewpoints and beliefs.[64] These are allied to the brush fires that can be stoked through "fake news" at distance from within Russia.

Russia's strategy (or "doctrine") is part of a wider pattern of active measures to advance perceived state interests. In the realm of destabilization campaigns and politico-military operations Russian Defense Minister Sergei Shoigu, who has been touted as a potential successor to Vladimir Putin, stated in early 2017 that "information troops" were tasked with "intelligent, effective propaganda." Shoigu did not shed light on their numbers or makeup, their targets, or activities. However, Russia's former military commander-in-chief, General Yuri Baluyevsky, claimed that information warfare (*informatsionnaya voyna*) "can be much more important than victory in a classical military conflict, because it is bloodless, yet the impact is overwhelming and can paralyze all of the enemy state's power structures."[65]

---

61 Perhaps referencing his moniker as "Putin's chef," he also told these were ongoing efforts when remarking "During our pinpoint operations, we will remove both kidneys and the liver at once." Reuters, "Russia's Prigozhin admits interfering in U.S. elections" (November 7, 2022), https://www.reuters.com/world/us/russias-prigozhin-admits-interfering-us-elections-2022-11-07/, accessed 15 November 2023.

62 Litovkin, "What is the updated Russian cyber-security doctrine about?"

63 Speech of Vice President Věra Jourová on countering disinformation amid COVID-19 "From pandemic to infodemic," June 4, 2020, https://ec.europa.eu/commission/presscorner/api/files/document/print/es/speech_20_1000/SPEECH_20_1000_EN.pdf, accessed 23 August 2023.

64 Kim Andersen, Adam Shehata, and Dennis Andersson, "Alternative News Orientation and Trust in Mainstream Media: A Longitudinal Audience Perspective," *Digital Journalism*, Vol. 11, Issue 5 (2023), pp. 833–852. Gordon Pennycook and David G. Rand, "Lazy, Not Biased: Susceptibility to Partisan Fake News is Better Explained by Lack of Reasoning than by Motivated Reasoning," *Cognition*, Vol. 188 (July 2019), pp. 39–50.

65 Anonymous, "Russian military admits significant cyber-war effort," (February 23, 2017), http://www.bbc.co.uk/news/world-europe-39062663. See also Mark Hollingsworth, "Silent strongman

These views share distinct similarities with Chinese thinking. They might also reflect changes in Russian strategic culture, which according to Reznikova, Hryhorenko, and Myronenko, was fundamentally shaped by the legacy of the USSR and Russia's imperial past. In turn, Russia's war on Ukraine has molded Ukraine's strategic culture from seeking accommodation with Russia into one founded on a marked shift embracing Euro-Atlantic values, collective security, and the objective of NATO and EU membership, resilience, and national unity.[66]

Valerii Gerasimov, Russia's long-serving Chief of the General Staff, in his annual speech to the Russian Academy of Military Science in March 2019, outlined the underlying rationale behind the creation in 2016 of a more integrated system designed to protect Russia critical infrastructure and information security. Gerasimov believed this would improve preparedness in terms of any early cyber aggression, especially attempts at destabilization to "create an atmosphere of chaos and uncontrollability."[67] He added, portentously, the promise that cyber holds for Russia as a type of weapon. Gerasimov saw an information sphere which lacked clearly defined national borders which "provides opportunities for remote, covert influence not only on critical information infrastructures, but also on the population of the country. This directly impacts the state's national security."[68] According to Connell and Vogler, Russia's employment of cyberespionage and information warfare "blurs the separation between peacetime and wartime … [with a] relatively low bar for employing cyber in ways that U.S. decision makers are likely to view as threatening and escalatory in nature." [69] This has important implications.

Sergey Shoigu is the real force behind Russia's military aggression" (December 5, 2015), *The Spectator*, http://www.spectator.co.uk/2015/12/silent-strongman-sergey-shoigu-is-the-real-force-behind-russias-military-aggression/. Both accessed 27 February 2017.

66 Olga Reznikova, Oleksandr Hryhorenko, and Viacheslav Myronenko, "Transformation of the Strategic Culture of Ukraine under the Influence of the Russian Threat," *Politologija*, Vol. 116, No. 4 (2024), pp. 59–108.

67 "Special Despatch No. 7943," https://www.memri.org/reports/russian-first-deputy-defense-minister-gerasimov-our-response-based-active-defense-strategy, accessed 26 October 2019.

68 "Special Despatch No. 7943."

69 Michael Connell and Sarah Vogler, "Russia's Approach to Cyber Warfare," Center for Naval Analyses, Occasional Paper, March 2017, pp. 27–28, https://www.cna.org/cna_files/pdf/DOP-2016-U-014231-1Rev.pdf, accessed 9 January 2018.

6 "The largest intelligence failure since 9/11": The GWOT, Arab Spring, and deprioritizing Russia

From 2012 onwards, when Putin became president once again, Russian cyberespionage campaigns began to become purposeful, coordinated, and targeted. Western intelligence appears to have been blindsided. China's rise saw discussion of a pivot to Asia emerge and many more actors and regions were being prioritized during both Obama administrations (2007–2017).[70] Under his predecessor, George W. Bush, 9/11 had been a turning point for the United States Intelligence Community (USIC). This saw counterterrorism prioritized followed by the invasion of Afghanistan a month later in October 2001, and Iraq in 2003 following false intelligence of an active program to develop Weapons of Mass Destruction (WMD). This became part of a Global War on Terror (GWOT) that saw cooperation with Russia.[71]

The occupation of Iraq lasted until December 2011 when the withdrawal of U.S.-led forces began to fuel and release long-standing religious and ethnic tensions in the Middle East. This was one of the contributory factors behind the Arab Spring revolts that spread from Tunisia in late 2010 to encompass Libya, Egypt, Yemen, Syria, and Bahrain. Major protests also occurred in Morocco, Iraq, Algeria, Lebanon, Jordan, Kuwait, Oman, and Sudan. Insurgencies, instability, and civil wars have followed.[72] These took focus away from Russia. At the height of the Cold War 40 percent or more of the U.S. intelligence budget was devoted to the Soviet Union. By 2016, it was nearer 10 percent with no plans to return to Cold War levels. During the Obama Administration this led the Chairman of the U.S. House Intelligence Committee, Devin Nunes, to term "The failure to understand Putin's plans and intentions ... the largest intelligence failure since 9/11."[73]

9/11 also provides another salutary lesson in respect to the renewed threat from Russia. The intelligence needed to prevent these terrible attacks was disassembled in a sea of information. Just 20 years on, our increasingly highly networked world has increased this volume of information-intelligence by orders of

---

70 David Shambaugh, "Assessing the US 'Pivot' to Asia," *Strategic Studies Quarterly*, Vol. 7, No. 2 (Summer 2013), pp. 10–19.
71 Tuomas Forsberg and Graeme Herd, "Russia and NATO: From Windows of Opportunities to Closed Doors," *Journal of Contemporary European Studies*, Vol. 23, No. 1 (2015), pp. 41–57.
72 Andrew Flibbert, "The Arab World: Grappling with Multiple Consequences," in Mohammed Ayoob and Etga Ugur (eds.), *Assessing the War on Terror* (Boulder, CO: Lynne Rienner, 2013), pp. 93–112.
73 Miller, "As Russia reasserts itself."

magnitude, further altering intelligence gathering, operations, and processing.[74] Russia (alongside China) has learned to exploit these growing interconnections. Finding better ways of sifting through information for intelligence, managing information overload, and locating better ways to find future needles in the haystack after 9/11 has proved to be difficult. Whilst improving intelligence analysis, intelligence sharing, and judgments might be proving successful in counterterrorism, this has left doors open for Russia and China. After 9/11, the need-to-share as well as the need-to-know provoked greater intelligence sharing. This also carries risks of their own as undetected U.S. insiders including Edward Snowden, Bradley Manning, and Jack Teixeira have shown.[75] Increasing intelligence gathering and analysis, and greater intelligence sharing are not a panacea for intelligence failures.

Prior to the 2003 invasion of Iraq, the West's vast capabilities had not discerned intentions or facts on the ground. HUMINT can often be a key guide to plans and intentions, but it can also lead to intelligence failures with major repercussions for international security. Even a single individual can prove damaging. In the case of Iraq this was a self-admitted liar codenamed "Curveball." "Curveball," Rafid Ahmed Alwan al-Janabi, was a disaffected Iraqi who invented fake intelligence on Saddam Hussein's WMD program, and his testimony became a key part of the case for the Second Gulf War in 2003. "Curveball" reinforced preexisting IC beliefs that Iraq had a WMD program at a time of heightened suspicion.[76] "Curveball" is a reminder of the risks of politicized intelligence and how this can lead to false positives. Mistaken and politicized intelligence prior to Russia's invasion of Ukraine, telling Putin and decision-makers in the Security Council what they wanted to hear and not what they needed to know is a further remainder. This grossly inflated pro-Russian sentiment and led to the belief that Russian forces would be greeted with flowers and cheering crowds for "liberating" Ukraine from fictitious neo-Nazis. Politized intelligence carries dangers all of its

---

74 Avi Tal and David Siman-Tov, "HUMINT in the Cybernetic Era: Gaming in Two Worlds," *Military and Strategic Affairs*, Vol. 7, No. 3 (2015), p. 95.

75 Helene Cooper and Eric Schmidt, "Ukraine War Plans Leak Prompts Pentagon Investigation. Classified documents detailing secret American and NATO plans have appeared on Twitter and Telegram" (April 6, 2023), https://www.nytimes.com/2023/04/06/us/politics/ukraine-war-plan-russia.html. Emma L. Briant, "How Social Media Incentives Helped Drive the Discord Leaks" (May 1, 2023), https://techpolicy.press/how-social-media-incentives-helped-drive-the-discord-leaks/. Both accessed 10 July 2023.

76 John Prados, "The Record on Curveball Declassified Documents and Key Participants Show the Importance of Phony Intelligence in the Origins of the Iraq War" (November 5, 2007), https://nsarchive2.gwu.edu/NSAEBB/NSAEBB234/, accessed 27 January 2020.

own.[77] Simultaneously, not acting on intelligence of Russian political influence, election interference, and destabilization campaigns for domestic political reasons is equally dangerous.

7 Election interference

Chapters 3 and 4 were case studies on election interference. They both took place in 2016 and conceivably tilted the results. Chapter 3 concentrated on Britain's 2016 Brexit referendum and Chapter 4 on the 2016 U.S. presidential election – two narrow victories for campaigns Russia actively and covertly supported (Britain exiting the European Union and the election of Donald Trump over Hillary Clinton). Intelligence-led foreign political influence campaigns are not new but what was new was Russia's coordinated state intelligence use and uses of social media for strategic messaging.[78] That they were effective raises troubling questions.

To those who might doubt whether they were effective (or how effective), former CIA and National Security Agency director General Michael Hayden called it "the most successful covert influence campaign in recorded history" and former Director of National Intelligence, James Clapper, commented how "They must be congratulating themselves for having exceeded their wildest expectations with a minimal expenditure of resources."[79] Since renewed Russian election interference operations first began in 2004 upwards of 38 nations have been targets spanning four continents; Europe, North America, Africa, and Asia. There are also suspicions that the Wagner Group conducted operations in Latin America.[80] As well as cyberespionage/information warfare influenced campaigns, money has been covertly siphoned to foreign political parties, officials, and politicians. Some of

77 Taras Kuzio, "Imperial Nationalism as the Driver Behind Russia's Invasion of Ukraine," *Nations and Nationalism*, Vol. 29, Issue 1 (January 2023), pp. 35–36. Mark Galeotti, "Spooks in the Kremlin. The Dangers of Putin's Unhealthy Reliance on Russian Intelligence," *Foreign Policy*, No. 232 (Spring 2019), pp. 17–19.

78 On the breadth of foreign political influence/election intervention over time (including by the United States) see Dov H. Levin, *Meddling in the Ballot Box: The Causes and Effects of Partisan Electoral Interventions* (New York: Oxford University Press, 2020).

79 David Gioe, "Cyber Operations and Useful Fools: The Approach of Russian Hybrid Intelligence," *Intelligence and National Security*, Vol. 33, No. 7 (December 2018), p. 955.

80 "Guns for Gold," p. 9.

this remains undetected.[81] These are active measures campaigns which increasingly leverage social media to significant effect.

These are designed to shape and influence foreign governments, their decision-making and decision-makers, and their populations. These can be overt in the form of bilateral and multilateral trade and security deals, including through security organizations such as the Shanghai Cooperation Organisation (SCO), Commonwealth of Independent States (CIS), and Collective Security Treaty Organization (CSTO). They can also be covert or semi-covert. These seek to conceal Russian influence, including using shell companies to hide the original source of funding. Shell companies have also been used to evade sanctions and include payments for flags of convenience for Russia's "shadow fleet" of commercial vessels. These were detailed as part of the 2021 Pandora Papers disclosures. This followed earlier leaked disclosures in the 2016 Panama Papers and 2017 Paradise Papers. They showed, among other things, how offshore companies were being used to hide Russian money, assets, and business deals, which were designed to conceal the true owners and ultimate beneficiaries. Through secretive and complex legal and financial arrangements they avoided scrutiny and taxes.[82]

The degree of anonymity these arrangements provides also reflects Russian active measures more widely. False flags and proxies are used to cloak Russian involvement. These were features of the two case studies of election interference/political influence campaigns in the UK and U.S. that were Chapters 3 and 4. This included the use of the St. Petersburg based Internet Research Agency (IRA) with funding channeled through Yevgeny Prigozhin, the head of the Wagner Group with close ties to the Kremlin. They were adept at exploiting wedge issues which mined pre-existing cracks in society as well as trying to fund and exploit agents of influence. The results have arguably and demonstrably deepened societal divisions and increased political polarization on issues such as nationalism, culture, identity politics, and immigration. The IRA, as well as the GRU and SVR used Western social media to target sections of their electorates rapidly and

---

81 Kylie Atwood, Michael Conte, and Devan Cole, "Russia has spent over $300 million on influencing foreign elections since 2014, US officials say" (September 13, 2022), https://edition.cnn.com/2022/09/13/politics/russia-foreign-elections-influence/index.html, accessed 5 November 2023.

82 James Oliver, Will Dahlgreen, James Melley, and Andy Verity, "Criminals and sanctions-busters exploiting UK secrecy loophole" (November 2, 2023), https://www.bbc.co.uk/news/uk-67276289; ICIJ, "Giant Leak of Offshore Financial Records Exposes Global Array of Crime and Corruption" (April 3, 2016), https://www.icij.org/investigations/panama-papers/20160403-panama-papers-global-overview/; "An ICIJ Investigation. Paradise Papers" (undated), https://www.icij.org/investigations/paradise-papers/. All accessed 5 November 2023.

pro-actively and reactively at scale.[83] In the U.S. presidential election these coordinated efforts were allied to the hacking and leaking of documents following separate breaches of the Democratic Congressional Campaign Committee (DCCC) and Democratic National Committee (DNC).

American society was already highly polarized and politically fractured but Russian election interference in 2016 also "created a crisis of confidence in the legitimacy of outcomes and the electoral process, and exacerbated social fissures – all worthy Russian goals even if the Kremlin did not have a direct electoral impact."[84] The use of propaganda to incite or promote division and destabilization was also a feature of the Brexit referendum and other European elections or referenda including in France, Italy, Germany, Spain (especially in the Catalonian referendum of 2017), Ukraine, the Balkans, and Turkey.[85] Russia's political influence campaigns continue through to the present. This included efforts to influence Moldova's referendum on EU membership, the Romanian presidential election, and the 2024 U.S. presidential elections.[86]

---

83 Disinformation. A Primer in Russian Active Measures and Influence Campaigns. Hearings before the Select Committee on Intelligence United States Senate 30 March 2017, pp. 2–3, https://www.intelligence.senate.gov/sites/default/files/documents/os-trid-033017.pdf, accessed 20 January 2020. See also Thomas Rid, *Active Measures: The Secret History of Disinformation and Political Warfare* (New York: Farrar, Straus and Giroux, 2020).

84 Gioe, "Cyber Operations and Useful Fools," p. 956.

85 Andrew Dawson and Martin Innes, "The Internet Research Agency in Europe 2014–2016), Crime & Security Research Institute, Cardiff University (May 2019), https://static1.squarespace.com/static/57875c16197aea2902e3820e/t/5cd14804104c7bb3cafeaa06/1557219339758/The+Internet+Research+Agency+In+Europe+2014-2016.pdf, accessed 28 August 2019.

86 Justice Department Leads Efforts Among Federal, International, and Private Sector Partners to Disrupt Covert Russian Government-Operated Social Media Bot Farm (July 9, 2024), https://www.justice.gov/opa/pr/justice-department-leads-efforts-among-federal-international-and-private-sector-partners; "US Elections Integrity Hub," https://www.tiktok.com/transparency/en-us/us-election-hub; EUvsDisinfo, https://euvsdisinfo.eu/?s=Moldova; Catherine Belton, "American creating deepfakes targeting Harris works with Russian intel, documents show" (October 24, 2024), https://www.washingtonpost.com/world/2024/10/23/dougan-russian-disinformation-harris/; Joint ODNI, FBI, and CISA Statement, https://www.cisa.gov/news-events/news/joint-odni-fbi-and-cisa-statement-1; Stephen McGrath, "Romania's top court annuls first round of presidential vote won by far-right candidate" (December 6, 2024), https://apnews.com/article/romania-election-president-georgescu-court-585e8f8f3ce7013951f5c7cf4054179b. All accessed 5 November 2024.

8 An Advanced Persistent Manipulator: The Kremlin's use of proxies and soft power

From St. Petersburg, the Internet Research Agency (IRA) played a major role in election interference as part of a wider Kremlin messaging strategy demonstrating the use of proxy sub-state actors. Outside of the IRA, Russia has cultivated agents of influence inside foundations, think tanks, companies, and organizations as well as with individuals who share a similar or related national or world view. Whether knowingly or unwittingly, these individuals are cultivated as agents of influence. They are seen by Russia as "useful idiots" (or "sock puppets"). This has seen Russia embrace figures from the political right but also some from the left or center if it serves their purpose.

This adds another layer of soft power. It has been accompanied by accusations that Russian money is used to fund these "useful idiots" as well as organizations and movements.[87] This has seen "cooperation agreements" between Putin's United Russia party and the Freedom Party in Austria, Jobbik in Hungary, the Lega Nord (Northern League) in Italy, the Marine Le Pen led National Front in France (now rebranded National Rally), and *Alternative für Deutschland* (AfD) in Germany. All are Conservative/far-right nationalist/populist parties. It has also seen "a menagerie of right wing, nationalist groups in Europe and further abroad" both "embraced and cultivated."[88] There has been widespread and systematic reporting that through Russian bank loans the Russian government has funneled money to these parties and other influential organizations.[89] Oligarchs connected to the Kremlin have also been linked with funding organizations and political parties as well as individuals, less for overt or covert influence but because their views align or are useful to the Kremlin.[90]

For example, they repeat the Kremlin line that sees the EU project in terminal decline, NATO an aggressor, and Russia as besieged with strong nationalist leaders needed.[91] Russia understands, as Sun Tzu put forth in *The Art of War*, "If sovereign

---

87 Douglas Rushkoff, "How We All Became Russia's 'Useful Idiots,'" https://medium.com/team-human/how-we-all-became-russias-useful-idiots-4df90bf9dea0, accessed 25 January 2020.

88 Putin's Asymmetric Assault, pp. 47, 50.

89 Cory Welt, "Russia: Background and U.S. Policy," Congressional Research Service, August 21, 2017, p. 29, https://fas.org/sgp/crs/row/R44775.pdf, accessed 12 November 2019.

90 Andrew Rettman, "Illicit Russian billions pose threat to EU democracy" (April 21, 2017), https://euobserver.com/foreign/137631, accessed 12 November 2019.

91 Martin Kragh and Sebastian Åsberg, "Russia's Strategy for Influence Through Public Diplomacy and Active Measures: The Swedish Case," *Journal of Strategic Studies*, Vol. 40, Issue 6 (2017), pp. 773–816. Giles, *Moscow Rules*, pp. 35–68.

and subject are in accord, put division between them. Attack him where he is unprepared, appear where you are not expected."[92] Russian active measures have also been seen in the Nordic states and they offer an interesting case study for combating mis and disinformation campaigns and active measures.[93] Kremlin mis and disinformation campaigns appear to have little traction throughout the Nordic states whereas in cases including Britain and the United States they did gain considerable traction. The Nordic states are not immune but their resistance to infection has been built up over decades of influence operations, in addition to government backed initiatives that teach critical thinking skills from an early age and by fostering trust in government and institutions.[94]

The 2018 Senate Select Committee on Intelligence (SSCI)-commissioned report, "The Tactics & Tropes of the Internet Research Agency" (detailed in Chapter 4) said Russian interference was "designed to exploit societal fractures, blur the lines between reality and fiction, erode our trust in media entities and the information environment, in government, in each other, and in democracy itself."[95] Not only did the USIC appear blindsided, the Obama administration also appeared to be caught in the headlights of a dilemma. Actively countering "Project Lahkta" could be seen as weaponizing the USIC and Justice Department to favor the Clinton campaign and Democratic Party. Instead, "Project Lahkta" pursued its "objectives with innovative skill, scope, and precision. With at least some of the Russian government's goals achieved in the face of little diplomatic or other pushback."[96] Russia has not stood still on seeding and spreading disinformation.[97]

---

92 Sun Tzu, *The Art of War*, translated by John Minford (London: Penguin, 2009), p. 102.

93 Flemming Splidsboel Hansen, Robert van der Noordaa, Øystein Bogen, and Henrik Sundbom, "The Kremlin's Trojan Horse Russian Influence in Denmark, The Netherlands, Norway, and Sweden" (December 2018), http://pure.diis.dk/ws/files/2553319/The_Kremlins_Trojan_Horses_3.pdf, accessed 7 November 2019. For a still wider look see Alicia Wanless, "One Strategy Democracies Should Use to Counter Disinformation" (March 28, 2022), https://carnegieendowment.org/2022/03/28/one-strategy-democracies-should-use-to-counter-disinformation-pub-86734, accessed 21 September 2023.

94 Putin's Asymmetric Assault, pp. 109–112.

95 Renee DiResta, Kris Shaffer, Becky Ruppel, David Sullivan, Robert Matney, Ryan Fox, Jonathan Albright, and Ben Johnson, "The Tactics & Tropes of the Internet Research Agency," pp. 99–100, https://cdn2.hubspot.net/hubfs/4326998/ira-report-rebrand_FinalJ14.pdf, accessed 27 August 2019.

96 DiResta et al., "The Tactics & Tropes of the Internet Research Agency," pp. 99–100.

97 Grace Cooper, "Leaks reveal how Russia's foreign intelligence agency conducts disinformation campaigns in the West" (July 8, 2024), accessed 24 October 2024: https://pressway.org.uk/news/295784-leakc_reveal_how_russiaefs_foreign_intelligence_agency_conducts_disinformation_campaigns_in_the_west.

9 Information Warfare through social media: From political spin to "fake news"

The extent to which the Kremlin was behind orchestrated campaigns to see Donald Trump elected and for Britain to exit the European Union is clear. What is less clear is why they had such effects. This lends itself to further studies of socio-psychological effects on targeted populations. This includes research on issues used to exploit biases, tendencies, and trends regarding voters and voting intentions (well understood by pollsters and "spin doctors" in the world of electioneering). If the intent has been to enhance pre-existing discord and division these campaigns have fully fulfilled Kremlin designs.[98] Social media provided under the radar "direct contact" to actively "shape public opinion to sow or exploit social divisions" in efforts "to undermine Western societies and institutions."[99] This is an ongoing effort.[100]

Richard Burr, the Republican Senator who chaired the SSCI commented during a November 2017 hearing on Social Media Influence in the 2016 U.S. Elections contested that with 60 percent of the U.S population using Facebook alone, "A foreign power using that platform to influence how Americans see and think about one another is as much a public policy issue as it is a national security concern."[101] In the wake of excoriating questioning from the U.S. Senate, Facebook's responses were described as "virtue signaling."[102] The U.S. Joint Chiefs of Staff took up the issue saying: "The ability of social networks in cyberspace to incite popular support (whether factually based or not) and to spread ideology is not ge-

98 Samuel C. Wooley and Philip N. Howard (eds.), *Computational Propaganda: Political Parties, Politicians, and Political Manipulation on Social Media* (New York: Oxford University Press, 2019).
99 Eugene Kondratov and Elisabeth Johansson-Nogués, "Russia's Hybrid Interference Campaigns in France, Germany and the UK: A Challenge against Trust in Liberal Democracies?" *Geopolitics*, Vol. 28, Issue 5 (November 2023), p. 2170.
100 Ben Nimmo, "Anatomy of an Info-War: How Russia's Propaganda Machine Works, and How to Counter It (May 19, 2015), https://www.stopfake.org/en/anatomy-of-an-info-war-how-russia-s-propaganda-machine-works-and-how-to-counter-it/, accessed 18 March 2024.
101 Burr added, "Crafting an elegant policy solution that is effective, but not overly burdensome, demands good faith and partnership between companies and this Committee." Open Hearing: Social Media Influence in the 2016 U.S. Election before the United States Senate Select Committee on Intelligence, November 1, 2017, https://www.intelligence.senate.gov/hearings/open-hearing-social-media-influence-2016-us-elections#, accessed 21 September 2019.
102 John Naughton, "Has Mark Zuckerberg's total control of Facebook turned into a liability?" (September 25, 2021), https://www.theguardian.com/commentisfree/2021/sep/25/mark-zuckerberg-facebook-senate-hawley-thiel-cambridge-analytica, accessed 23 August 2023.

ographically limited, and the continued proliferation of IT has profound implications for the joint force and US national security."[103]

The reach social media provides into the minds of individuals, groups, and whole populations is only gradually being recognized.[104] Russia (as well as China) might well be further ahead in understanding the advantages this remote reach provides and the implications. This includes influencing public opinion domestically and for foreign intelligence agency-led campaigns.[105] Alex Younger, Chief of Britain's Secret Intelligence Service/MI6, claims "when your defences as a country are being probed on multiple fronts at the same time, it can be difficult to see the totality of what your opponent is trying to do. Security in the hybrid world is therefore all about who can partner to the greatest effect."[106] This includes the defensive perimeter and capabilities of the "Five Eyes" group – led by the U.S. and UK alongside Canada, Australia, and New Zealand. However, even with their vast networks and resources, they have struggled to limit Russian and Chinese espionage in a changing world with much of their focus on counterterrorism and regional threats.[107] Meanwhile the responsibility of democratic governments to regulate or legislate social media content and its uses has been slow to arrive.

Western social media was used during 2016 to target the electorate on both sides of the Atlantic. During the U.S. presidential election, Twitter was the first to be targeted. Twitter reached 677,775 voters.[108] As this started to be recognized, the IRA moved over to Facebook and Instagram. On Instagram, 20 million users were engaged. Facebook 126 million people.[109] This included micro-profiling vot-

---

103 Joint Publication 3–12 Cyberspace Operations Joint Chiefs of Staff (June 8, 2018), p. II-6, https://www.jcs.mil/Portals/36/Documents/Doctrine/pubs/jp3_12.pdf?ver=2018-07-16-134954-150, accessed 6 April 2020.

104 Joshua A. Tucker, Andrew Guess, Pablo Barberá, Cristian Vaccari, Alexandra Siegel, Sergey Sanovich, Denis Stukal, and Brendan Nyhan, "Social Media, Political Polarization, and Political Disinformation: A Review of the Scientific Literature" (March 2018), pp. 18–21, https://www.hewlett.org/wp-content/uploads/2018/03/Social-Media-Political-Polarization-and-Political-Disinformation-Literature-Review.pdf, accessed 17 November 2019.

105 Many other countries are also engaged in these practices as well as untold numbers of private companies, organized criminal gangs, hacking collectives, and lone wolves.

106 "MI6 'C' speech on fourth generation espionage" (December 3, 2018), https://www.gov.uk/government/speeches/mi6-c-speech-on-fourth-generation-espionage, accessed 7 August 2019.

107 Michael J. Sulick, *American Spies: Espionage against the United States from the Cold War to the Present* (Washington: Georgetown University Press, 2013), pp. 8–9. See also David Wise, *Spy: The Inside Story of How the FBI's Robert Hanssen Betrayed America* (New York: Random House, 2002).

108 David V. Gioe, Michael S. Goodman, and Alicia Wanless, "Rebalancing Cybersecurity Imperatives: Patching the Social Layer," *Journal of Cyber Policy*, Vol. 4, No. 1 (March 2019), p. 124.

109 DiResta et al., "The Tactics & Tropes of the Internet Research Agency," p. 42.

ers down to the individual. Facebook was particularly culpable via Facebook's own and publicly available analytical tools. This was used to actively target voters – especially in swing regions.[110] This saw Facebook's creator and CEO, Mark Zuckerberg and Sheryl Sandberg, Facebook's longstanding former Chief Operating Officer (and former Clinton administration official and Google employee), both subject to public criticism.[111] This included ignoring warning signs and concealing problems from public view. They were also accused of handing off security and policy decisions to subordinates.[112] By abdicating its responsibilities in these areas, "Facebook's strategy has the ability to push its problems into the shadows."[113] It is from the shadows that Russia emerged in February 2022 when, after annexing Crimea in 2014 as well as destabilizing Ukraine's eastern Donbas region, it attempted a full-scale invasion.

10 The Ukraine War

To almost all other outside observers, save for Russia's few remaining allies, this was a blatant attempt to overturn a democratically-elected government and install a puppet regime by force. Its invasion of a fellow Slavic state with sympathetic Russian factions was supported by Belarus and Syria.[114] According to Giles, it

---

110 Rowland Manthorpe, "Sky Views: Why Mark Zuckerberg won't ban political ads on Facebook" (October 31, 2019), https://news.sky.com/story/sky-views-why-mark-zuckerberg-wont-ban-political-ads-on-facebook-11849805, accessed 30 November 2019. See also Chang Sup Park and Barbara K. Kaye, "Applying News Values Theory to Liking, Commenting and Sharing Mainstream News Articles on Facebook," *Journalism*, Vol. 24, No. 3 (2023), pp. 633–653.

111 Sandberg stood down as COO in August 2022 but remained a board member at Meta.

112 Sheera Frenkel, Nicholas Confessore, Cecilia Kang, Matthew Rosenberg, and Jack Nicas, "Delay, Deny and Deflect: How Facebook's Leaders Fought Through Crisis" (November 14, 2018), https://www.nytimes.com/2018/11/14/technology/facebook-data-russia-election-racism.html?action=click&module=Top%20Stories&pgtype=Homepage, accessed 28 November 2019. Joshua Boyd, "The History of Facebook: From BASIC to Global Giant" (January 25, 2019), https://www.brandwatch.com/blog/history-of-facebook/; Dave Lee, "Mark Zuckerberg, missing in inaction" (November 16, 2018), https://www.bbc.co.uk/news/technology-46231284. All accessed 28 November 2019.

113 Dave Lee, "Facebook may be 'pivoting' to something worse" (July 2, 2019), https://www.bbc.co.uk/news/technology-48835250, accessed 3 July 2019. See also Diana Bossio, Terry Flew, James Meese, Tama Leaver, and Belinda Barnet, "Australia's News Media Bargaining Code and the Global Turn Towards Platform Regulation," *Policy and Internet*, Vol. 14, Issue 1 (March 2022), pp. 136–150.

114 Jonathan Haslam, "H-Diplo Essay 420- Commentary Series on Putin's War: 'Russia Attacks Ukraine: A Post Mortem for Putin?'" (March 17, 2022), https://networks.h-net.org/node/28443/discussions/9948394/h-diplo-essay-420-commentary-series-putin%E2%80%99s-war-%E2%80%9Crussia-at

was "the result of Western powers not wishing to stand up to Putin."[115] Giles adds the invasion was "uncoordinated, unprepared and underequipped" with both rank-and-file soldiers and their field commanders finding themselves isolated among a hostile population (which they did not expect), and "bewildered and disorientated" with little to no provision for resupply.[116]

From the north Belarus had been a staging ground for Russia's army and air force under the pretext of a joint military exercise. Syria encouraged volunteers to fight for Russia as well as providing diplomatic support. Belarus is ruled by President Alexander Lukashenko and Syria (until December 2024) by President Bashar al-Assad. Both are (or in Assad's case were), authoritarian leaders like Putin who owe/owed the survival of their respective regimes to Russian interventions.[117] Patronage and loyalty are features of the Putin regime. China, which is a complicated geopolitical "partner" of Russia, is well aware of the risks of escalation and under President Xi has steered a line between tacit support for Russia whilst calling for an end to hostilities.[118]

The invasion was the culmination of years of pressure on Ukraine following the Revolution of Dignity/Euromaidan protests in late 2013 and early 2014 which deposed Ukraine's pro-Russia president Victor Yanukovych.[119] Euromaidan was a blow to Putin and the Kremlin and their hopes that Ukraine would voluntarily align with Russia and not seek to join the European Union (and certainly not NATO). Yanukovych (widely viewed as a pro-Russian proxy) fled to Russia during Euromaidan.[120] During the interregnum following Yanukovych's flight and fresh elections Crimea was annexed.[121]

---

tacks, accessed 1 April 2022. Two other authoritarian states, North Korea and Eritrea, also voted with Russia in the United Nations.

115 Giles, *Russia's War on Everybody*, p. 121.

116 Giles, *Russia's War on Everybody*, p. 123.

117 Kimberly Marten, "Whither Wagner? The Consequences of Prigozhin's Mutiny and Demise," *Survival*, Vol. 65, No. 5 (October–November 2023), pp. 45–64.

118 Nigel Gould-Davies, "Putin's Strategic Failure," *Survival*, Vol. 64, No. 2 (April–May 2022), pp. 7–16.

119 Leonid Peisakhin, "Euromaidan revisited: Causes of regime change in Ukraine one year on," Wilson Center, Kennan Cable, No. 5 (February 2015), https://www.files.ethz.ch/isn/188792/5-kennan%20cable-Peisakhin.pdf, accessed 30 March 2022. Ukraine's troubled post-Soviet history, some of which mirrors other former Soviet republics and Russia itself, is well captured in Taras Kuzio, "Ukraine's Orange Revolution. The Oppositions Road to Success," *Journal of Democracy*, Vol. 16, No. 2 (April 2005), pp. 117–130.

120 Miriam Lanskoy and Dylan Myles-Primakoff, "Power and Plunder in Putin's Russia," *Journal of Democracy*, Vol. 29, No. 1 (January 2018), p. 81.

121 Jeffrey Mankoff, "Russia's Latest Land Grab: How Putin Won Crimea and Lost Ukraine," *Foreign Affairs*, Vol. 93, No. 3 (May/June 2014), pp. 60–68.

Influence operations had laid the groundwork for Russian ground forces when they intervened in late February 2014. Some were on heightened combat readiness for the closing of the Sochi Winter Olympics. This included GRU Spetsnaz special forces who, stripped of insignia and blending in as local militia as so-called "Little Green Men," blockaded Ukrainian military bases. On March 16 a sham referendum was held and by March 24 Ukraine had evacuated its forces. Russian forces were restrained and there were few fatalities. Both sides wanted to avoid bloodshed. That had not been the case in Chechnya or Georgia in 2008.[122]

Unlike the 2004 Orange Revolution, the trigger for Euromaidan and Crimea's annexation was not "stolen elections, but by the stolen dream" of an Association Agreement with the EU.[123] The subsequent presidential election was won by Petro Poroshenko who signed the Association Agreement with the EU in June 2014.[124] Poroshenko took steps to align Ukraine with EU values through institutional and cultural reforms. These also fostered a stronger sense of Ukrainian nationalism whilst partially dealing with significant corruption, cronyism, and the power of Ukraine's oligarchs.[125] This continued to stymie Ukraine's ambitions for EU membership.[126] Ahead of the 2019 presidential election, Poroshenko warned that "Russian meddling to influence Ukraine's elections is well under way."[127] This was in evidence.[128] In the 2019 presidential elections Poroshenko lost to Volodymyr Zelenskyy, a former comedian with no political experience.

---

122 Charles K. Bartles and Roger N. McDermott, "Russia's Military Operation in Crimea Road – Testing Rapid Reaction Capabilities," *Problems of Post-Communism*, Vol. 61, No. 6 (November/December 2014), pp. 55, 59.

123 Yuriy Matsiyevsky, "Revolution Without Regime Change," *Communist and Post-Communist Studies*, Vol. 51, No. 4 (December 2018), p. 350. Michael McFaul, "Ukraine Imports Democracy: External Influences on the Orange Revolution," *International Security*, Vol. 32, No. 2 (Fall 2007), pp. 45–83.

124 Roy Allison, "Russian 'Deniable' Intervention in Ukraine: How and Why Russia Broke the Rules," *International Affairs*, Vol. 90, Issue 6 (November 2014), p. 1272.

125 Elżbieta Olzacka, "The Development of Ukrainian Cultural Policy in the Context of Russian Hybrid Aggression Against Ukraine," *International Journal of Cultural Policy*, Vol. 30, No. 2 (2023), 141–157.

126 Joanna Rohozinska and Vitaliy Shpak, "Ukraine's Post-Maidan Struggles: The Rise of an 'Outsider' President," *Journal of Democracy*, Vol. 30, No. 3 (July 2019), pp. 33–47.

127 Pavel Polityuk with Tatiana Ustinova, "Exclusive: Ukraine says it sees surge in cyber attacks targeting election" (January 25, 2019), https://www.reuters.com/article/us-ukraine-cyber-exclusive/exclusive-ukraine-says-it-sees-surge-in-cyber-attacks-targeting-election-idUSKCN1PJ1KX, accessed 27 March 2023.

128 Ihor Hurak and Paul D'Anieri, "The Evolution of Russian Political Tactics in Ukraine," *Problems of Post-Communism*, Vol. 69, No. 2 (March 2022), pp. 121–132.

Putin's infamous 2021 pre-invasion essay contained no mention of self-determination for Ukraine, only Russia's desire to determine Ukraine's future. Putin believed Western nations orchestrated a coup in Euromaidan, "aimed at turning Ukraine into a barrier between Europe and Russia, a springboard against Russia" where "Radical nationalist groups [and neo-Nazis] served as its battering ram."[129] Russia's response was to actively support pro-Russian separatists in the Donbas and annex Crimea. As Crimea had experienced, the Donbas was being destabilized from within and without by a mixture of propaganda, lawfare (including passportization), direct interventions, and Russian-inspired military action.[130] At the same time, it was fomenting Russian nationalism and identity politics in the self-declared Peoples Republics of Donetsk and Luhansk (DPR and LPR).[131]

Kremlin intervention and support for these separatist forces led to a "frozen conflict" and thousands dying for little gain on either side.[132] Ukraine and Russia entered talks in June 2014 to try to broker an agreement. Begun in the margins of the commemorations marking the 70th anniversary of D-Day, the "Normandy format" led to the Minsk Protocol and Memorandum in September 2014 ("Minsk I") and Package of Measures in February 2015 ("Minsk II"). A Trilateral Contact Group (TCG) was additionally brokered through the United Nations and the Organization for Security and Cooperation in Europe (OSCE).[133]

Neither Minsk I nor Minsk II provided stability or an end to the fighting in the Donbas with the Russian-backed breakaway DPR and LPR separatists. The last prewar meetings were held in Paris in January 2022 and Berlin on February 10. Immediately prior to the invasion on February 21 the two leaders of the self-pro-

129 en.kremlin.ru/events/president/news/66181, accessed 3 April 2022.

130 Fabian Burkhardt, Cindy Wittke, and Elia Bescotti, "TCUP Report: Passportization, diminished citizenship rights, and the Donbas vote in Russia's 2021 Duma elections" (January 2022), pp. 6–20, https://www.huri.harvard.edu/sites/g/files/omnuum4931/files/huri/files/idp_report_3_burkhardt_et_al.pdf, accessed 21 March 2023.

131 Jaroslava Barbieri, "Raising Citizen-Soldiers in Donbas: Russia's Role in Promoting Patriotic Education Programmes in the Donetsk and Luhansk Peoples" Republics," *Ethnopolitics*, Vol. 23, No. 5 (2023), 515–536..

132 Group think is described as "a result of the individuals involved being too similar in background (homogeneity) and not often enough in contact with alternative groups (insulation)." Tor Bukkvoll, "Why Putin Went to War: Ideology, Interests and Decision-Making in the Russian Use of Force in Crimea and Donbas," *Contemporary Politics*, Vol. 22, Issue 3 (June 2016), p. 274.

133 Kristian Åtland, "Destined for Deadlock? Russia, Ukraine, and the Unfulfilled Minsk Agreements," *Post-Soviet Affairs*, Vol. 36, No. 2 (March 2020), pp. 122–139. https://peacemaker.un.org/sites/peacemaker.un.org/files/UA_150212_MinskAgreement_en.pdf, https://press.un.org/en/2015/sc11785.doc.htm, accessed 15 March 2023.

claimed republics, both "perceived as puppets of the Kremlin," called for referendums on joining Russia and in a public ceremony in the Kremlin, Russia recognized the DPR and the LPR. On September 30, 2022 the Duma ratified their annexation into Russia, an illegal act under the UN Charter.[134] Less than 10 percent of Donbas residents had voted.[135] Simultaneously Russia also declared it had "annexed" the Kherson and Zaporizhzhia oblasts, neither of which it controlled.[136]

Ukraine is a target for politico-military and economic reasons.[137] As a non-NATO/EU member it was also being used to test the limits and responses to Russian actions as it has across its near abroad, and more distantly across four continents. Russia's war aims in Ukraine appear to have been a blitzkrieg military invasion, a swift collapse of Ukrainian resistance and the Ukrainian government, and the installation of a pro-Russian puppet regime. More widely it appears that the Kremlin saw an opportunity.

Angela Merkel, who had been German Chancellor since 2005, had retired with Olaf Scholz succeeding her. U.S. president Joe Biden had barely been in office a year (dogged by large sections of the American population believing the 2020 presidential had been stolen and with his son, Hunter Biden, implicated in business deals in Ukraine). British Prime Minister Boris Johnson was facing calls to resign (eventually resigning in September 2022). France's Emmanuel Macron was facing re-election and had tried but failed to avert Russia's invasion. Italy had another new leader. Giorgia Meloni had spent a career in opposition and (like Zelenskyy) was untested in high office. More widely, EU countries were facing migration pressures even before the war and these had become hot topic electoral issues. This number would be added to as refugees from Ukraine fled the war. In addition, Britain had "Brexited" the EU and Poland, a state which has become pivotal in its

134 Andrew Lohsen and Pierre Morcos, "Understanding the Normandy Format and Its Relation to the Current Standoff with Russia" (February 9, 2022), https://www.csis.org/analysis/understanding-normandy-format-and-its-relation-current-standoff-russia, accessed 15 March 2023. Oleksiy Gnatiuk and Sergei Basik, "Performing Geopolitics of Toponymic Solidarity: The Case of Ukraine," *Norwegian Journal of Geography*, Vol. 77, Issue 1 (February 2023), pp. 1–15.

135 Fabian Burkhardt, Cindy Wittke, and Elia Bescotti, "TCUP Report,", pp. 8–9.

136 Sanctions in response to Putin's illegal annexation of Ukrainian regions (September 30, 2022), https://www.gov.uk/government/news/sanctions-in-response-to-putins-illegal-annexation-of-ukrainian-regions, accessed 21 March 2023.

137 Keir Giles, "Russia and Its Neighbours: Old Attitudes, New Capabilities," in Kenneth Geers (ed.), *Cyber War in Perspective: Russian Aggression Against Ukraine* (Tallinn: NATO CCD COE Publications, 2015), pp. 19–28.

support for Ukraine, was facing a wave of Euroscepticism (a trend seen across Europe).[138] Zelenskyy himself was thought a moveable obstacle.

Despite high reliance on Russian gas and oil, Putin also decided to invade despite the threat of economic sanctions. Putin, the *siloviki* around him, and any restraining influence the oligarchs might have had, had not been deterred by Western responses prior to February 2022. This included responses to Russia's invasion of Georgia in 2008, the brutal pacification of Chechnya from 1999 to 2009, and Crimean annexation in 2014. Instead, Putin had become emboldened by Western "appeasement."[139] This was not lost on Zelenskyy when he told the Munich security conference five days before the invasion "Has our world completely forgotten the mistakes of the 20th century? ... Where does appeasement policy usually lead to?"[140]

This said, if NATO became or becomes directly involved on the battlefield there are deep-seated fears that this could lead to World War III. This world war would be fought by major (nuclear-armed) powers. President Putin is well aware of the potency when he publicly ordered Russia's nuclear alert level to be raised immediately prior to Russia's invasion. Since then, nuclear signaling has been a feature of Russian diplomacy and domestic propaganda.[141] Even if this is saber-rattling it raised the stakes to heights not seen since the 1962 Cuban Missile Crisis.[142] Like in Cuba, there are also risks that sub-ordinates and proxy forces might exceed their authority, countermand orders, rebel, or act on their own initiative (or through a breakdown of the chain-of-command). Miscalculation and spillover are part of the fog of war. Whilst a deliberate armed attack on a NATO member "would appear manifestly foolish" it presupposes that Putin and Russia's leadership are rational actors and have complete control of Russia's armed forces and proxies at all times.[143] Prigozhin's mutiny is a reminder of the possibilities this might not always be the case.

---

138 Quinton Mayne and Alexia Katsanidou, "Subnational Economic Conditions and the Changing Geography of Mass Euroscepticism: A Longitudinal Analysis," *European Journal of Political Research*, Vol. 62, Issue 3 (August 2023), pp. 742–760.

139 A sentiment also expressed in Giles, *Moscow Rules*, pp. 159–174.

140 Suzanne Lynch, Lili Bayer, and Jacopo Barigazzi, "'Oh my God, it's really happening'" (February 24, 2023), https://www.politico.eu/article/ukraine-invasion-war-russia-zelenskyy-putin-one-year-on-michel-stoltenberg/, accessed 13 April 2023.

141 Alexander K. Bollfrass and Stephen Herzog, "The War in Ukraine and Global Nuclear Order," *Survival*, Vol. 64, No. 4 (August–September 2022), pp. 7–32.

142 Stephen Blank, "How Ukraine Reveals Russian Nuclear Strategy," *Defense & Security Analysis*, Vol. 39, Issue 3 (May 2023), pp. 353–368. Vipin Narang and Scott D. Sagan (eds.), *The Fragile Balance of Terror: Deterrence in the New Nuclear Age* (Ithaca: Cornell University Press, 2022).

143 Allin, "Ukraine: The Shock of Recognition," p. 207.

Ukraine is still an active war zone at the time of writing with widely reported and well-evidenced reports of war crimes being committed by Russia.[144] One of the most egregious war crimes has been the abduction and attempted resettlement of Ukrainian children separated from their families by the fighting. In addition, the UN's Human Rights Office has reported large-scale human rights violations (including "unimaginable suffering on millions of children").[145] In addition, Russian occupation authorities have also stand accused of indoctrinating Ukrainian children through military-patriotic programs which valorize the Soviet Union and Russian history. In addition, deported Ukrainian children are indoctrinated at Russian summer camps.[146] As an occupying force Russia is (putatively) legally bound by international law/international humanitarian law, including the Geneva Conventions and Hague Conventions that form the Law of Armed Conflict (LOAC).[147] António Guterres, the UN Secretary General, said in March 2023 after visiting Ukraine: "The position of the United Nations, which I have consistently expressed, is crystal clear: Russia's invasion of Ukraine is a violation of the UN Charter and international law."[148] For Putin, "true sovereignty of Ukraine is possible only in partnership with Russia … And what Ukraine will be – it is up to its citizens to decide."[149] They have decided, and that decision is for Ukraine to remain an independent state. Since the invasion, for many inside and outside Uk-

---

144 Report on the human rights situation in Ukraine 1 February–31 July 2023 (October 4, 2023), https://www.ohchr.org/sites/default/files/documents/hrbodies/hrcouncil/coiukraine/23-10-04-OHCHR-36th-periodic-report-ukraine-en.pdf, accessed 11 November 2023.

145 Office of the UN High Commissioner for Human Rights, The impact of the armed conflict and occupation on children's rights in Ukraine, 24 February 2022 – 31 December 2024, https://ukraine.ohchr.org/sites/default/files/2025-04/2025-03-21%20OHCHR%20Report%20on%20Children%27s%20Rights%20in%20Ukraine.pdf, accessed 8 August 2025.

146 Paul Conroy, Eloise Herdegen, and Karolina Hird, "Russian Occupation Update" (August 6 2025), accessed 19 August 2025, https://understandingwar.org/sites/default/files/Russian%20Occupation%20Update%2C%20August%207%2C%202025%20PDF.pdf.

147 Page Wilson, "The Myth of International Humanitarian Law," *International Affairs*, Vol. 93, Issue 3 (May 2017), pp. 563 – 579, "What is International Humanitarian Law?" https://www.icrc.org/en/doc/assets/files/other/what_is_ihl.pdf. See also related discussions on Customary International Law such as "Customary Law," https://www.icrc.org/en/war-and-law/treaties-customary-law/customary-law, "Customary International Law," https://www.law.cornell.edu/wex/customary_international_law. All accessed 29 February 2020. Maurizio D'Urso, "The Cyber-Combatant: A New Status for a New Warrior," in Ludovica Glorioso and Anna-Maria Osula (eds.), *1st Workshop on Ethics of Cyber Conflict Proceedings* (CCDCOE: Tallinn, 2014), pp. 41 – 48.

148 https://www.un.org/sg/en/content/sg/press-encounter/2023-03-08/secretary-generals-press-encounter-kyiv-ukraine-delivered, accessed 20 March 2023.

149 en.kremlin.ru/events/president/news/66181.

raine, Zelenskyy has become a lightning rod standing up for freedom and self-determination.[150]

For Putin, Russia was more sinned against than sinner in relation to Ukraine. Whether or not a new Cold War has emerged, an historic "Russia problem" has been revived.[151] Whilst Russia's invasion was not inevitable, "nor was it unforeseeable."[152] Even if Russia prevails and wins a military victory, "will it prove to be pyrrhic?"[153] Could it result in Putin being unseated? What happens in Ukraine will likely shape Russia's future and help shape the future of European and global security. Russia could also plausibly wither from the outside in.

11 Winning the war but losing the peace?

Russia's 143 million people ranked ninth in terms of the global population in 2022 with around 193 ethnic groups and distinct regions.[154] 75 percent live in European Russia. The remaining 25 percent in Asian Russia, often in sparsely populated and remote regions. South in the Caucasus, Russia has periodically intervened to try and prevent the Balkanization of its territory. This included two Chechen wars in the 1990s and early to mid-2000s and intervention in Georgia in 2008. For these reasons and to shore up his system of government, in the years since Vladimir Putin was first elected president in 2000, Russia's political system has grown more authoritarian.[155]

Despite sporadic anti-government protests and some domestic opposition, there remain dormant threats to Putin's rule amid crackdowns and restrictions. They are accompanied by outside reporting, Kremlin critics, and pro-democracy appeals from Russian émigrés supplemented by Western commentators. Democracy promotion is however a threat to the ruling elite whose wealth and power

150 Jessica Pisano, "How Zelensky Has Changed Ukraine," *Journal of Democracy*, Vol. 33, No. 3 (July 2022), pp. 5–13.

151 Sakwa, "'New Cold War' or Twenty Years' Crisis?" p. 263.

152 T. G. Otte, "H-Diplo Essay 416 Commentary Series on Putin's War: 'Zeitenwende: Russia's War against Ukraine and the End of the Thirty Years' Holiday'" (March 11, 2022), https://issforum.org/essays/PDF/E416.pdf, accessed 1 April 2022.

153 Haslam, "H-Diplo Essay 420."

154 "Population, total – Russian Federation," https://data.worldbank.org/indicator/SP.POP.TOTL?locations=RU, accessed 11 November 2023.

155 Timothy Frye and Ekaterina Borisova, "Elections, Protest and Trust in Government: A Natural Experiment from Russia," BOFIT Discussion Papers 9 (2016), https://www.econstor.eu/bitstream/10419/212852/1/bofit-dp2016-009.pdf, "Russia," https://freedomhouse.org/report/freedom-world/2019/russia. Both accessed 25 February 2020.

was made during the 1990s and the first two decades of the 2000s. Since then, Russian domestic order and power is shaped by personal self-interest and politico-economic aggrandizement.

The regime of President Putin, orchestrated through the Presidential Administration and Security Council in the Kremlin, is widely accused of corruption and self-aggrandizement supported by Russia's powerful clans of oligarchs and the criminal underworld. The groundwork for both was laid in the 1990s by his predecessor, Boris Yeltsin.[156] In sum a system has been evolved which rests on a belief that it is the people who serve the state, not a government serving its people.[157] This includes the foreign and security policymaking ministries which, like the Russian *Duma*, apply policy dictated by the Presidential Administration and Security Council with limited discussion.[158]

State media repeats the government narrative and Internet access to foreign news sources has been increasingly restricted. Domestic opposition is severely limited and has been systematically and increasingly strangled since 2000. Putin has frequently opined of "Russophobia" and an "anti-Russia project." Russia not only has a relatively small population compared with the West and People's Republic of China, it also has few friends and allies. Its cultural influence is limited to its border states. This is combined with systemic corruption and cronyism in public and democratic institutions and use of the Rule of Law as an arm of the state and political authority.[159]

Aside from military force, economic sanctions have been the main lever used to try and restrain and penalize the Kremlin. Since the Ukraine war, economic and travel sanctions have included removing Russia's central bank and other major banks from the SWIFT clearing system and curtailing its ability to sell oil and gas. Kremlin blackmail through cutting supplies from the controversial Nord Stream pipelines (before supplies were terminated) was one of the concerns in terms of Western European imports of cheap and available Russian gas.[160] West-

---

156 Edward Lucas, *Deception: The Untold Story of East-West Espionage Today* (New York: Bloomsbury, 2012), p. 62.

157 Alexis A. Blanc, Alyssa Demus, Sandra Kay Evans, Michelle Grisé, Mark Hvizda, Marta Keep, Natasha Lander, and Krystyna Marcinek, "The Russian General Staff Understanding the Military's Decisionmaking Role in a 'Besieged Fortress,'" (2023), Rand Corporation, p. 100, https://www.rand.org/content/dam/rand/pubs/research_reports/RRA1200/RRA1233-7/RAND_RRA1233-7.pdf, accessed 30 June 2023.

158 Galeotti, "Putin's Hydra," pp. 1–2.

159 Russia HC 632, 21 July 2020, p. 1.

160 László Á. Kóczy, Dávid Csercsik, and Balázs R. Sziklai, "Nord Stream 2: A Prelude to War," *Energy Strategy Reviews*, Vol. 44 (November 2022), pp. 1–9. Riehle, *The Russian FSB*, pp. 120–121.

ern firms have also exited Russia. This has seen drains on Russia's foreign currency reserves, foreign direct investment, and a retraction of the Russian economy. However, they have also been circumvented in a variety of ways. Whether they work as a restraining mechanism is uncertain and needs to be allied to wider diplomatic and policy levers.[161]

12 The end of history and the clash of civilizations: Could Putin have been deterred?

Russia's policies and campaigns have become a long train running and one that might have been derailed or diverted at various junctions prior to February 2022. Policy choices were made by Western leaders, and options not acted on, in attempts to restrain Russia. To what extent were Western intelligence agencies warning about Russian actions and the threats they posed? What policy choices were available and which options taken? Were at least two key Western governments, the United States and United Kingdom, immobilized by disunity and division aided by Russian external influence campaigns? Should the West have done more to oppose Russia prior to the invasion of Ukraine?

In Ukraine, the menace that Russia has become has been laid bare. The pathways that resulted in the Ukraine War began to be paved three decades before. In 1993, then CIA Director James Woolsey remarked, "we have slain a large dragon, but we live now in a jungle filled with a bewildering variety of poisonous snakes. And in many ways the dragon was easier to keep track of."[162] In the thirty years since, the snakes have evolved and metastasized and many other new security threats have emerged or mutated. The world is also now more fractured and multipolar with a new bipolar competitor to the United States and Western order in China. The Russian Federation also seeks "great power" status alongside China and the United States and whilst it is not the Soviet Union 2.0, it has once more become a dragon to contend with. Nevertheless, Russian intelligence and its military operations have significant weaknesses that can, and have been, exploited. Bribery using the MICE framework is among them.

When Francis Fukuyama famously hypothesized that the collapse of the Soviet Union and Eastern European communism in 1989–1991 marked the end of his-

---

161 Cory Welt, Kristin Archick, Rebecca M. Nelson, and Dianne E. Rennack, U.S. Sanctions on Russia (January 18, 2022), https://crsreports.congress.gov/product/pdf/R/R45415, accessed 11 November 2023.

162 Quoted in David Kilcullen, *The Dragons and the Snakes: How the Rest Learned to Fight the West* (New York: Oxford University Press, 2020), p. 11.

tory, Russia was in disarray. In a separate hypothesis, Samuel Huntingdon contended this seismic change foreshadowed a clash of civilizations.[163] Russia has since become a revived threat with great power ambitions. It is not the dragon it once was, but Russia is one of the key drivers behind renewed contestation of the liberal international order.[164] Conversely, Zbigniew Brzezinski cautioned in 1994 that attempts to recreate the Soviet Union and preserve the Russian Federation by "coercion and/or economic subsidy would condemn Russia not only to dictatorship but to poverty."[165]

9/11 did not mean that the focus on nations and regions of interest melted away and intelligence, and (as the Kremlin experienced in Ukraine) its politicization, certainly played a considerable role in the decision of U.S.-led coalition forces to invade Afghanistan and Iraq in 2001 and 2003.[166] By this time the old rival, Russia, had now began to reorganize and reassert itself following the demise and death of Boris Yeltsin and the rise of Vladimir Putin (which saw their intelligence agencies renewed).[167] Soviet intelligence activities during the Cold War were well honed and have experienced a renaissance in the Russian Federation under Vladimir Putin, including their use of espionage/cyberespionage and active measures. It also continued to handle a number of trusted insiders within a variety of

---

163 Francis Fukuyama, "The End of History," *The National Interest*, No. 16 (Summer 1989), pp. 3–18; Francis Fukuyama, *The End of History and the Last Man* (New York: Free Press, 1992); Samuel P. Huntingdon, "The Clash of Civilizations," *Foreign Affairs* Vol. 72, No. 3 (Summer 1993), pp. 22–49; Samuel P. Huntingdon, *The Clash of Civilizations and the Remaking of World Order* (New York, Simon & Schuster, 1996). Both Fukuyama and Huntingdon have reassessed and revised their original theses and they remain subjects of active debate. Francis Fukuyama, "The 'End of History' 20 Years Later," *New Perspectives Quarterly*, Vol. 27, Issue 1 (Winter 2010), pp. 7–10; Samuel P. Huntingdon, "The Clash of Civilizations Revisited," *New Perspectives Quarterly*, Vol. 30, Issue 4 (October 2013), pp. 46–54.

164 Paul Kennedy, *Rise and Fall of the Great Powers: Economic Change and Military Conflict from 1500–2000* (New York: Random House, 1988); John J. Mearsheimer, *The Tragedy of Great Power Politics* (New York: Norton, 2001).

165 Zbigniew Brzezinski, "The Premature Partnership," *Foreign Affairs*, Vol. 73, No. 2 (March–April 1994), p. 72.

166 See for example Brian Jones, *Failing Intelligence: The True Story of How We Were Fooled into Going to War in Iraq* (London: Biteback Publishing, 2010). The 2016 Chilcot Report, available from http://www.iraqinquiry.org.uk/, accessed 20 April 2017; Robert Jervis, "Reports, Politics, and Intelligence Failures: The Case of Iraq," *Journal of Strategic Studies*, Vol. 29, No. 1 (February 2006), pp. 3–52, Peter Gill and Mark Pythian, *I*ntelligence in an Insecure World, second edition (Cambridge: Polity Press, 2012), pp. 153–166.

167 Lucas, *Deception*, pp. 52–53. Hedieh Nasheri, Economic Espionage and Industrial Spying (Cambridge: Cambridge University Press, 2005), pp. 8–9, 11; Iosif Androulidakis Fragkiskos and Emmanouil Kioupakis, Industrial Espionage and Technical Surveillance Counter Measurers (New York: Springer, 2016).

government agencies most of whom appeared to spy for the money on offer. Russia has also mounted widespread active measures campaigns on European and U.S. elections. Because of partisan divisiveness between Republicans and Democrats these core issues are getting lost in the United States.[168]

The 2016 U.S. Intelligence World Threat Assessment indicated, "Russia is assuming a more assertive cyber posture based on its willingness to target critical infrastructure systems and conduct espionage operations even when detected and under increased public scrutiny … and continuing preparation of the cyber environment for future contingencies."[169] Senator Richard Blumenthal warned during Senate Armed Services Committee hearings in May 2017 that, "the Russians will continue to attack us … as long as they are not made to pay a price or … as long as the benefits outweigh the price that they pay."[170] Meanwhile China has not lost its focus. Others have warned of the comparisons with the pre-World War II, "long peace," era of the 1930s.[171]

During hearings of the Senate Subcommittee on Cybersecurity in March 2018, Senator Bill Nelson pointedly questioned, "We conduct information operations in support of commanders at the tactical level. Putin and other adversaries are coming at us at the strategic level in so-called peacetime. I'm afraid that we are ceding the playing field."[172] That might well be an accurate assessment, and whilst much of what Russia does in the field of cyberespionage is illegal under national laws, it is permissible under international law, even if "unlawful when appraised against general principles of international law."[173] Traditional standalone espionage too is legal under international law.[174]

168 David Shortell, "FBI director: Russia is the 'most aggressive actor' in election interference" (July 19, 2018), https://edition.cnn.com/2018/07/18/politics/wray-russia-meddling-contrast-trump/index.html, accessed 30 September 2019.

169 Worldwide Threat Assessment of the US Intelligence Community, James R. Clapper Director of National Intelligence, February 9, 2016, p. 6, https://www.dni.gov/files/documents/SASC_Unclassified_2016_ATA_SFR_FINAL.pdf, accessed 13 December 2018.

170 Committee on Armed Services United States Senate. Hearing to receive testimony on cyber policy, strategy and organization Thursday May 11, 2017, p. 71, https://www.armed-services.senate.gov/imo/media/doc/17-45_05-11-17.pdf, accessed 16 December 2017.

171 Among them is Keir Giles. Keir Giles, *Who Will Defend Europe? An Awakened Russia and a Sleeping Continent* (London: Hurst, 2024), pp. 1–11.

172 United States Senate, Cyber Posture of the Services, Tuesday March 13, 2018, p. 6, https://www.armed-services.senate.gov/imo/media/doc/18-25_03-13-18.pdf, accessed 3 December 2018.

173 Russell Buchan, "The International Legal Regulation of State-Sponsored Cyber Espionage," in Anna-Maria Osula and Henry Rõigas (eds.), *International Cyber Norms: Legal, Policy & Industry Perspectives* (Tallinn: NATO CCDCOE Publications, 2016), p. 68.

Regardless of these general principles of international law all nations, and the various sub-state actors within them, are likely to engage in traditional espionage and cyberespionage as much as their capabilities and political appetite will permit. As Darien Pun describes: "States have an interest in maintaining confidentiality regarding their abilities. There is the fundamental value of surprise in any activity involving national security and defense. The problem then is, if multiple countries believe they have the advantage in this field or could have the advantage, no one has an incentive to stop developing more espionage capabilities."[175] This makes finding legal remedies, compliance, and binding enforcement mechanisms extremely difficult and where considerations of ethics and morality take a backseat to perceived national security interests. At the same time, states and their intelligence agencies have also provided or constructed ethical justifications for espionage activities. This is often centered around two primary ethical frameworks: deontology (a universal moral law mostly associated with the philosopher Immanuel Kant) and consequentialism where the ends are seen to justify the means.[176]

For cybercriminals few targets appear out of reach or ethically off-limits and in parts of Eastern Europe cybercriminal activity is rife (especially in some former Soviet states and especially in Russia). A number of these have ties to Russian organized crime working "in the grey zones" which produces a "symbiosis between the Russian state" and organized crime.[177] This is why this effectively not only turns these sub-state hackers into state-protected "privateers" by sanctioning their activities but also leads to orchestration and delegation.[178] These lend the

---

174 Geoffrey B. Demarest, "Espionage in International Law", *Denver Journal of International Law & Policy*, Vol. 24, No. 2 (Spring 1996), pp. 321–348. Jared Beim, "Enforcing a Prohibition on International Espionage," *Chicago Journal of International Law*, Vol. 18, No. 2 (2018), pp. 647–672.

175 Darien Pun, "Rethinking Espionage in the Modern Era," *Chicago Journal of Internal Law*, Vol. 18, No. 1 (Summer 2017), pp. 369–372.

176 These issues are well covered by David L. Perry, *Partly Cloudy: Ethics in War, Espionage, Covert Action, and Interrogation* second edition (Lanham, MD: Rowman & Littlefield, 2016), esp. pp. 1–20 and 101–234.

177 Sam Jones, "Licensed to hack: The rise of the cyber privateer. Russia is increasingly using criminal proxies, say western intelligence officials" (March 16, 2017), https://www.ft.com/content/21be48ec-0a48-11e7-97d1-5e720a26771b, accessed 21 January 2018.

178 Nigel Inkster, "China's Cyber Power," *Adelphi*, Vol. 55, Issue 456 (2015), p. 68. See also Tim Maurer, *Cyber Mercenaries: The State, Hackers, and Power* (Cambridge: Cambridge University Press, 2018), p. xii.

Kremlin (and other likeminded governments) "plausible deniability" through sowing confusion and the ability to generate "false flags" to cloud direct attribution.[179]

A significant number of cybercrime cases involving or directly implicating the Kremlin and Russian actors have been subjected to in-depth investigations. These investigations can include intelligence from agencies like the NSA which are "capable of combining signals and human intelligence to attribute such an incident and determine whether it was a false flag operation or not."[180] This is far from straightforward. Complicating the picture politically and strategically is that cybercriminals from Russia, Eastern Europe, and other parts of the world employ similar tactics, techniques, and procedures (TTPs) which can also be leveraged by other actors. This can include cyberespionage by industrial competitors in other countries, some of which might be operating hand-in-glove with their host state through their foreign intelligence services (FIS) or hired, co-opted, or freelancing.[181] Cyberspace and growing global interconnectivity (globalization) was one of the results of the end of the Cold War.

The end of the Cold War was not the end of history as Francis Fukuyama's much debated, much admired, and much maligned thesis suggested.[182] Instead, "History has returned" and with it, major interstate war.[183] Russia has visited the type of destruction on Ukraine not seen since the Yugoslav civil wars of the 1990s, and on a scale reminiscent of the opening of World War II. It has left millions displaced and tens of thousands homeless. Many have lost family members. Some have lost everyone and everything. Whilst war crimes have been perpetrated, many ordinary Russians have been conscripted to fight and lost their lives too. They are told they are fighting Nazis and defending the motherland. If this is believed, it is little or no comfort to Russia's dead or wounded soldiers and their

---

179 Florian Egloff, "Cybersecurity and the Age of Privateering" (October 16, 2017), http://carnegieendowment.org/2017/10/16/cybersecurity-and-age-of-privateering-pub-73418,, accessed 21 January 2018. Joe Devanny, Ciaran Martin, and Tim Stevens, "On the Strategic Consequences of Digital Espionage," *Journal of Cyber Security Technology*, Vol. 6, Issue 3 (2021), pp. 429–450. Mohiuddin Ahmed and Matthew Gaber, "An investigation on cyber espionage ecosystem," *Journal of Cyber Security Technology*, forthcoming.

180 Tim Maurer, "When States Pretend to Be Terrorists or Hacktivists in Cyberspace" (April 18, 2017), http://carnegieendowment.org/2017/04/18/when-states-pretend-to-be-terrorists-or-hacktivists-in-cyberspace-pub-68703, accessed 21 January 2018.

181 FireEye, "M-Trends 2017 A View From the Front Lines," p. 43. Available from https://www.fireeye.com/current-threats/annual-threat-report/mtrends/rpt-m-trends-2017.html, accessed 31 March 2020. Jonathan Diamond, "Early Patriotic Hacking," in Jason Healey (ed.), *A Fierce Domain: Conflict in Cyberspace 1986–2002* (Vienna, VA: CSSA/Atlantic Council, 2013), pp. 136–151.

182 Fukuyama, "The End of History?" pp. 3–18, Fukuyama, *The End of History and the Last Man.*

183 Otte, "H-Diplo Essay 416."

families. An unknown number of returning servicemen also experience post-traumatic stress disorder with very limited support.[184] Western support has poured into Ukraine. Beyond outright security reasons, this support is also seen in terms of Western values and democracy. This may be, as former German Chancellor Olaf Scholz pondered, a *Zeitenwende* – a watershed moment.[185]

Scholz was directly referring to German military and strategic support for Ukraine. It was also a call to arms for NATO and EU members to continue support for Ukraine. This book has made clear that NATO members and other like-minded nations have to be better prepared against Russia's comprehensive approach to "hybrid warfare" that combines cyber, influence operations, destabilization efforts, information warfare, lawfare, financial bribery, and corruption, as well as the use of military and paramilitary force.[186] This is especially important because NATO members have been targets. Keir Giles has long been vocal in making this case, including in his 2024 book *Who Will Defend Europe?*[187]

Russia has been sowing distrust and disinformation that tug at the threads which connect Western societies and their institutions and keep communities together. Russia has purposefully and nefariously become home to Advanced Persistent Manipulators through orchestrated social media campaigns allied to their own propaganda. Especially through social media, the Kremlin are picking at the knots that bind us as nations.[188] This is being used both to promote Kremlin messages and narratives whilst providing dis/mis/and mal-information to users.

184 Javier G. Cuesta, "The battle Russia has not yet fought: The mental health of its war veterans" (October 6 2024), https://english.elpais.com/international/2024-10-06/the-battle-russia-has-not-yet-fought-the-mental-health-of-its-war-veterans.html, accessed 30 August 2025. This includes Russian *Spetsnaz.* Riehle, *Russian Intelligence*, p. 266. This also mirrors the experiences of Soviet servicemen returning from the Soviet occupation of Afghanistan in the 1980s who, in the midst of a perceived defeat, had similar experiences to Vietnam veterans. Jan Claas Behrends, ""Some call us heroes, others call us killers." Experiencing violent spaces: Soviet soldiers in the Afghan War", *Nationalities Papers*, Vol. 43 Issue 5 (September 2015), pp. 719–734. Mark Boulton, *Failing Our Veterans: The G.I. Bill and the Vietnam Generation* (New York: New York University Press, 2014).

185 Policy statement by Olaf Scholz, Chancellor of the Federal Republic of Germany and Member of the German Bundestag, 27 February 2022 in Berlin, https://www.bundesregierung.de/breg-en/news/policy-statement-by-olaf-scholz-chancellor-of-the-federal-republic-of-germany-and-member-of-the-german-bundestag-27-february-2022-in-berlin-2008378, accessed 12 November 2023.

186 Lawfare is using "law as a substitute for traditional military means" or similarly "the use of law as a weapon of war against a military adversary." Major General Charles J. Dunlap, "Lawfare Today: A Perspective," *Yale Journal of International Affairs*, Vol. 3, Issue 1 (Winter 2008), pp. 146154 and David Luban, "Carl Schmitt and the Critique of Lawfare," *Case Western Reserve Journal of International Law*, Vol. 43, Issue 1 (2010), pp. 457–471.

187 Giles, *Who Will Defend Europe?*

188 Kondratov and Johansson-Nogués, "Russia's Hybrid Interference Campaigns," p. 2170.

This has led to a war on truth and honesty. There are now earnest debates questioning whether we are entering a post-truth world. Ill-informed opinions are also used to denigrate political opponents and entrench views.

This is further spun out by satellite constituencies of think tanks, influencers, opinion shapers, digital electioneering companies, and professional marketing outfits. Domestically, with election integrity under sustained and deep-seated challenge in the United States, truth and honestly should not be a casualty in this battle of ideas in a quest for power and a victory at all costs mentality. If not, established democracies and transitional democracies alike risk becoming like Russia. Part of the way to renew the social contract could be in "comprehensive governmental or independent investigations into the nature and scope of Russian government interference."[189] Alongside, more robust government intervention through strengthened regulation and legislation for social media companies should be on the table. This needs to be thought through and thoroughly debated.

Government intervention in social media leaves governments and legislators open to partisan attacks from opposition politicians and political parties. Moreover, without political consent and support from an already skeptical civil society this also has the capacity to be seen as government overreach into personal freedoms, especially freedom of expression, and a gateway into the surveillance state and "Big Brother."[190] Bearing in mind Russian political influence campaigns, it is vital to inform the public to gain and maintain public support. This applies equally to social media platforms who currently self-police and do not appear to welcome scrutiny, challenge, and interventions. This would be a social media contract for the information age and an adjunct component of the social contract between citizen and state. Improving media and digital literacy are two key components, allied to the promotion of critical thinking skills through education programs.[191] These platforms have been key components of Russia's campaigns of political influence, destabilization, and election interference. They are components of Russian active measures and part of a wider strategy of hybrid warfare.

Crimea demonstrated the potency of "hybrid warfare" combining cyber, information, influence, lawfare, and economic operations, as well as the use of military

189 Putin's Asymmetric Assault, p. 159.
190 Kondratov and Johansson-Nogués, "Russia's Hybrid Interference Campaigns," pp. 2186–2187.
191 Some of this thinking is evidenced in a June 2020 report by the UK's House of Lords, House of Lords, Select Committee on Democracy and Digital Technologies, Report of Session 2019–21, Digital Technology and the Resurrection of Trust, 29 June 2020, p. 16–124, https://committees.parliament.uk/publications/1634/documents/17731/default/, accessed 23 August 2023.

and paramilitary force. It led to a "seamless transition from peace to conflict."[192] The road to war from February 2014 to February 2022 was replete with further and wider examples of these activities in Ukraine (and far beyond). Russia succeeded with Crimea and its success emboldened Kremlin ambitions. In a prescient 1994 article, Zbigniew Brzezinski, cautioned Western leaders of "the open assertion of Russian territorial claims to portions of Ukraine."[193] Euromaidan/the Revolution of Dignity had demonstrated that Ukraine was now moving West and turning away from Russia as had all of the former states of Eastern Europe except Belarus. It is only when the Kremlin's risk-averse foreign policy oversteps as it did in annexing Crimea in 2014, the attempted assassination of Sergey Skripal in 2018, and in the Ukraine invasion from 2022, that Russia has paid a price.

Brzezinski saw thirty years ago: "Regrettably, the imperial impulse remains strong and even appears to be strengthening. This is not only a matter of political rhetoric. Particularly troubling is the growing assertiveness of the Russian military in the effort to retain or regain control over the old Soviet empire."[194] A 2020 report by Britain's Intelligence and Security Committee indicated, "The dissolution of the USSR was a time of hope in the West. In the 1990s and early 2000s, Western thinking was, if not to integrate Russia fully, at least to ensure that it became a partner. By the mid-2000s, it was clear that this had not been successful." Instead, "Russia under President Putin had moved from potential partner to established threat."[195]

---

192 Kristin Ven Bruusgaard, "Crimea and Russia's Strategic Overhaul," *Parameters*, Vol. 44, No. 3 (2014), p. 1.

193 Brzezinski, "The Premature Partnership," p. 74.

194 Brzezinski, "The Premature Partnership," p. 72.

195 Russia HC 632, 21 July 2020, p. 1.

Bibliography

Books

Applebaum, A., *Autocracy, Inc: The Dictators Who Want to Run the World* (New York: Penguin, 2025).

Andrew, C. and Mitrokhin, V., T*he Mitrokhin Archive The KGB in Europe and the West* (London: Allen Lane/Penguin Press, 1999).

Andrew, C. and Mitrokhin, V., *The Mitrokhin Archive II The KGB in the World* (London: Penguin Press, 2018).

Åslund, A., *Russia's Crony Capitalism: The Path from Market Economy to Kleptocracy* (New Haven, CT: Yale University Press, 2019).

Askerov, A., Brooks, S., and Tchantouridzé, L., *Post-Soviet Conflicts: The Thirty Years' Crisis* (London: Lexington Books, 2020).

Ayoob, M. and Ugur, E. (eds.), *Assessing the War on Terror* (Boulder, CO: Lynne Rienner, 2013).

Balmaceda, M. M., *Energy Dependency, Politics and Corruption in the Former Soviet Union: Russia's Power, Oligarchs' Profits and Ukraine's Missing Energy Policy, 1995–2006* (Abingdon: Routledge, 2007).

Banks, A., edited by Oakeshott, I., *The Bad Boys of Brexit: Tales of Mischief, Mayhem & Guerrilla Warfare in the EU Referendum Campaign* (London: Biteback Publishing, 2017).

Bongino, D., *Exonerated: The Failed Takedown of President Donald Trump by the Swamp* (New York: Post Hill Press, 2019).

Bongino, D., McAllister, D. C., and Palumbo, M., *Spygate: The Attempted Sabotage of Donald J. Trump* (New York: Post Hill Press, 2018).

Boulton, M., *Failing Our Veterans: The G.I. Bill and the Vietnam Generation* (New York: New York University Press, 2014).

Born, H. and Caparini, M. (eds), *Democratic Control of Intelligence Services: Containing Rogue Elephants* (Abingdon: Routledge, 2007).

Chaffetz, J., *The Deep State: How an Army of Bureaucrats Protected Barack Obama and Is Working to Destroy the Trump Agenda* (New York: Broadside Books, 2018).

Chaffetz, J., *Power Grab: The Liberal Scheme to Undermine Trump, the GOP, and Our Republic* (New York: Broadside Books, 2019).

Clapper, J. R., with Brown, T., *Facts and Fears: Hard Truths from a Life in Intelligence* (New York: Viking Press, 2018).

Clinton, H. R., *What Happened* (New York: Simon & Schuster, 2018).

Comey, J., *A Higher Loyalty: Truth, Lies, and Leadership* (New York: Flatiron Books, 2018).

Corera, G., *Intercept: The Secret History of Computers and Spies* (London: Weidenfeld & Nicolson, 2016).

Dagnes, A., *Super Mad at Everything All the Time. Political Media and Our National Anger* (New York: Palgrave: 2019).

Dehghantanha, A., Conti, M., and Dargahi, T. (eds.), *Cyber Threat Intelligence* (Cham, Switzerland: Springer Nature, 2018).

Derrig, R., *The New Haven School: American International Law* (Oxford: Oxford University Press, 2025).

Dieckhoff, A., Jaffrelot, C., and Massicard, E. (eds.), *Contemporary Populists in Power* (Cham, Switzerland: Palgrave/Springer Nature, 2022).

https://doi.org/10.1515/9783111583464-009

Dugin, A., *The Foundations of Geopolitics: Russia's Geopolitical Future* (Moscow: Arktogeya, 1997).

Eze, T., Speakman, L., and Onwubiko, C. (eds.), *ECCWS 2021 20th European Conference on Cyber Warfare and Security* (Sonning Common, UK: Academic Conferences and Publishing International, 2021).

Enemark, C., *Armed Drones and the Ethics of War: Military Virtue in a Postheroic Age* (Abingdon: Routledge, 2013.

Felshtinky, Y., and Litvinenko, A., *Blowing Up Russia: Terror from Within* (New York: Encounter Books, 2007).

Fiorentini, G., and Peltzman, S. (eds.), *The Economics of Organised Crime* (Cambridge: Cambridge University Press, 1995).

Fragkiskos, I. A., and Kioupakis, E., *Industrial Espionage and Technical Surveillance Counter Measurers* (New York: Springer, 2016).

Fridman, O., *Russian "Hybrid Warfare": Resurgence and Politicisation* (New York: Oxford University Press, 2018).

Fukuyama, F., *The End of History and the Last Man* (New York: Free Press, 1992).

Futter, A., *Hacking the Bomb: Cyber Threats and Nuclear Weapons* (Washington DC: Georgetown University Press, 2018).

Galeotti, M., *The Vory: Russia's Super Mafia* (New Haven, CT: Yale University Press, 2018).

Gärtner, H., Hyde-Price, A., and E. Reiter (eds.), *Europe's New Security Challenges* (Boulder: Lynne Rienner, 2001).

Geers, K. (ed.), *Cyber War in Perspective: Russian Aggression against Ukraine* (Tallinn: CCD COE Publications, 2015).

George, S., *An Awkward Partner: Britain in the European Community* (Oxford: Oxford University Press, 3rd edition 1998).

Giles, K., *Moscow Rules. What Drives Russia to Confront the West* (Washington DC: Brookings, 2019).

Giles, K., *Russia's War on Everybody and What It Means For You* (London: Bloomsbury, 2024).

Giles, K., *Who Will Defend Europe? An Awakened Russia and a Sleeping Continent* (London: Hurst, 2024).

Gill, P., and Pythian, M., *Intelligence in an Insecure World*, second edition (Cambridge: Polity Press, 2012).

Glenny, M., *Dark Market How Hackers Became the New Mafia* (London: Random House, 2011).

Glenny, M., *McMafia A Journey Through the Global Criminal Underworld* (London: Vintage, 2018).

Glorioso, L., and Osula, A.-M. (eds.), 1st Workshop on Ethics of Cyber Conflict Proceedings (CCDCOE: Tallinn, 2014).

Greenberg, A., *Sandworm: A New Era of Cyberwar and the Hunt for the Kremlin's Most Dangerous Hackers* (New York: Doubleday, 2019).

Hayden, M. V., *The Assault on Intelligence: American National Security in an Age of Lies* (New York: Penguin, 2018).

Healey, J. (ed.), *A Fierce Domain: Conflict in Cyberspace 1986–2002* (Vienna, VGN: CSSA/Atlantic Council, 2013).

Hecker, S.S., *Doomed to Cooperate: How American and Russian Scientists Joined Forces to Avert Some of the Greatest Post-Cold War Nuclear Dangers* (Los Alamos: Bathtub Row Press, 2016).

Henderson, J., and Ferguson, A., *International Partnership in Russia: Conclusions from the Oil and Gas Industry* (London: Palgrave Macmillan, 2014).

Herman, E. S., and Chomsky, N., *Manufacturing Consent: The Political Economy of the Mass Media* (London: Vintage Books, 1994).

Higgins, E., *We Are Bellingcat: An Intelligence Agency for the People* (London: Bloomsbury, 2022).
Hoffman, D. E., *The Billion Dollar Spy: A True Story of Cold War Espionage and Betrayal* (New York: Doubleday, 2015).
Hoffman, F. G., *Conflict in the 21st Century: The Rise of Hybrid Wars* (Arlington VA: Potomac Institute for Policy Studies, 2007).
Inkster, N., *China's Cyber Power* (Abingdon: Routledge, 2016).
Huntingdon, S. P., *The Clash of Civilizations and the Remaking of World Order* (New York, Simon & Schuster, 1996).
Isikoff, M., and Corn, D., *Russian Roulette: The Inside Story of Putin's War on America and the Election of Donald Trump* (New York: Twelve, 2018).
Jančárková, T., Lindström, L., Visky, G., and Zotz, P. (eds.), *13th International Conference on Cyber Conflict: Going Viral* (Tallinn: NATO CCDCOE Publications, 2021).
Jarrett, G., *Witch Hunt: The Story of the Greatest Mass Delusion in American Political History* (New York: Broadside Books, 2019).
Jeffreys-Jones, R., *In Spies We Trust: The Story of Western Intelligence* (Oxford: Oxford University Press, 2013).
Jones, B., *Failing Intelligence: The True Story of How We Were Fooled into Going to War in Iraq* (London: Biteback Publishing, 2010).
Kaldor, M., *New and Old Wars: Organized Violence in a Global Era Third Edition* (Cambridge: Polity Press, 2012).
Kello, L., *The Virtual Weapon and International Order* (New Haven, CT: Yale University Press, 2017).
Kennedy, P., *Rise and Fall of the Great Powers: Economic Change and Military Conflict from 1500–2000* (New York: Random House, 1988).
Kilcullen, D., *The Dragons and the Snakes: How the Rest Learned to Fight the West* (New York: Oxford University Press, 2020).
Klimburg, A., *The Darkening Web: The War for Cyberspace* (New York: Penguin 2017).
Krepinevich, A. F., *The Origins of Victory: How Disruptive Military Innovation Determines the Fates of Great Powers* (New Haven CT: Yale University Press, 2023).
Kuzio, T., *Russian Nationalism and the Russian-Ukrainian War: Autocracy-Orthodoxy-Nationality* (Abingdon: Routledge, 2022).
Leigh, D., and Harding, L., *Wikileaks: Inside Julian Assange's War on Secrecy* (London: Guardian Books: 2013).
Ledeneva, A. V., *How Russia Really Works: The Informal Practices That Shaped Post-Soviet Politics and Business* (Ithaca: Cornell University Press, 2006).
Levin, D. H., *Meddling in the Ballot Box: The Causes and Effects of Partisan Electoral Interventions* (New York: Oxford University Press, 2020).
Litvinenko, A., *Lubyanka Criminal Group* (Dnìpropetrovs'k: Grani, 2002).
Lucas, E., *Deception: The Untold Story of East-West Espionage Today* (New York: Bloomsbury, 2012).
Maurer, T., *Cyber Mercenaries: The State, Hackers, and Power* (Cambridge: Cambridge University Press, 2018).
Mearsheimer, J. J., *The Tragedy of Great Power Politics* (New York: Norton, 2001).
Miller, C., *The Death of the Gods: The New Global Power Grab* (London: William Heinemann, 2018).
Minárik, T., Jakschis, R., and Lindström, L. (eds), *2018 10th International Conference on Cyber Conflict CyCon X: Maximising Effects* (Tallinn: CCD COE Publications, 2018).
Minárik, T., Alatalu, S., Biondi, S, Signoretti, M., Tolga, I., and Visky, G. (eds.), *2019 11th International Conference on Cyber Conflict: Silent Battle* (Tallinn: CCD COE Publications, 2019).

Mitrokhin, V., *KGB lexicon: The Soviet Intelligence Officer's Handbook* (London: Frank Cass, 2002).

Mitrokhin, V., and Andrew, C., *The Mitrokhin Archive: The KGB and Europe and the West* (London: Gardners Books, 2000).

Moore, M., *Democracy Hacked: Political Turmoil and Information Warfare in the Digital Age* (London: Oneworld, 2018).

Murray, W., and Mansoor, P. R. (eds.), *Hybrid Warfare: Fighting Complex Opponents from the Ancient World to the Present* (New York: Cambridge University Press, 2012).

Narang, V., and Sagan, S. D. (eds.), *The Fragile Balance of Terror: Deterrence in the New Nuclear Age* (Ithaca: Cornell University Press, 2022).

Nasheri, H., *Economic Espionage and Industrial Spying* (Cambridge: Cambridge University Press, 2005).

Osula A.-M., and Rõigas, H. (eds.), *International Cyber Norms: Legal, Policy & Industry Perspectives* (Tallinn: NATO CCDCOE Publications, 2016).

Papadopoulos, G., *Deep State Target: How I Got Caught in the Crosshairs of the Plot to Bring Down President Trump* (New York: Diversion Books, 2019).

Plokhy, S., *Lost Kingdom: The Quest for Empire and the Making of the Russian Nation* (New York: Basic Books, 2017).

Phythian, M., *Understanding the Intelligence Cycle* (Abingdon: Routledge, 2013).

Podins, K., Stinissen, J., and Maybaum, M. (eds.), *5th International Conference on Cyber Conflict Proceedings* (Tallinn: CCD COE Publications, 2013).

Pringle, R. W., *Historical Dictionary of Russian and Soviet Intelligence* (Lanham, MA: Scarecrow Press, 2006)

Qiao, L., and Wang, X., *Unrestricted Warfare* (Beijing: People's Liberation Army Literature and Arts Publishing House, 1999).

Qingmin, D., *New Perspectives on War* (Beijing: PLA Publishing House, 2008).

Perry, D.L., *Partly Cloudy: Ethics in War, Espionage, Covert Action, and Interrogation* second edition (Lanham, MD: Rowman & Littlefield, 2016).

Radchenko, S., *To Run the World: The Kremlin's Cold War Bid for Global Power* (Cambridge: Cambridge University Press, 2024).

Recent Advances in Business Administration Proceedings of the 6th WSEAS International Conference on BUSINESS ADMINISTRATION (ICBA '12) Harvard, Cambridge, USA January 25 – 27, 2012 (Harvard, MA: WSEAS Press, 2012).

Richards, J., *The Art and Science of Intelligence Analysis* (Oxford: Oxford University Press, 2011).

Rid, T., *Active Measures: The Secret History of Disinformation and Political Warfare* (New York: Farrar, Straus and Giroux, 2020).

Rid, T., *Cyber War Will Not Take Place* (London: Hurst, 2013).

Ridout, T. N. (ed.), *New Directions in Media and Politics*, Second Edition (New York: Routledge, 2019).

Riehle, K. P., *Russian Intelligence: A Case-Based Study of Russian Services and Missions Past and Present* (Bethesda, MD: National Intelligence Press, 2022).

Riehle, K.P., *The Russian FSB A Concise History of the Federal Security Service* (Washington, DC: Georgetown University Press, 2024).

Runciman, D., *How Democracy Ends* (London: Profile Books, 2018).

Sakwa, R., *Putin and the Oligarch: The Khodorkovsky-Yukos Affair* (London: IB Tauris, 2014).

Schmitt, M. N. (ed.), *Tallinn Manual 2.0 on the International Law Applicable to Cyber Operations* (New York: Cambridge University Press, 2017).

Shipman, T., *ALL OUT WAR: The Full Story of Brexit* (London: William Collins, 2017).

Shipman, T., *Fall Out: A Year of Political Mayhem* (London: William Collins, 2018).
Slipchenko, V. and Gareev, M., *Budushchaya voyna* (Future War) (Moscow: Polit.ru Ob"edinennoye Gumarnitarnoye Izdatelstvo, 2005).
Smyth, R., *Elections, Protest, and Authoritarian Regime Stability: Russia 2008–2020* (Cambridge: Cambridge University Press, 2020).
Statham, P., and Trenz, H. J. (eds.), *The Politicization of Europe: Contesting the Constitution in the Mass Media* (London: Routledge: 2012).
Stoddart, K., *Cyberwarfare: Threats to Critical Infrastructure* (London: Palgrave/Springer, 2022).
Stoddart, K. with Kaunert, C. and Avramov, K. (eds.), *Hybrid Warfare: Western and non-Western definitions, concepts, and regional case studies* (Quantico, VA: Marine Corps University Press, 2025)
Sulick, M. J., *American Spies: Espionage against the United States from the Cold War to the Present* (Washington: Georgetown University Press, 2013).
Sumpter, D., *Outnumbered: From Facebook and Google to Fake News and Filter-bubbles – The Algorithms That Control Our Lives* (New York: Bloomsbury Sigma, 2018).
Tzu, S., *The Art of War*, translated by John Minford (London: Penguin, 2009).
Taylor, B., *State Building in Putin's Russia: Policing and Coercion After Communism* (New York: Cambridge University Press, 2011).
Thomas, T. L., *Dragon Bytes: Chinese Information Warfare Theory and Practice* (Fort Leavenworth, KS: Foreign Military Studies Office, 2004).
Thomas, T. L., *Decoding the Virtual Dragon: Critical Evolutions in the Science and Philosophy of China's Information Operations and Military Strategy* (Fort Leavenworth, KS: Foreign Military Studies Office, 2007).
Thomas, T. L., *Three Faces of the Cyber Dragon: Cyber Peace Activist, Spook, Attacker* (Fort Leavenworth, KS: Foreign Military Studies Office, 2012).
Unger, C., *American Kompromat: How the KGB Cultivated Donald Trump, and Related Tales of Sex, Greed, Power, and Treachery* (New York: Penguin Random House, 2021).
Urban, M., *The Skripal Files: Putin, Poison and the New Spy War* (London: Macmillan, 2018).
Valeriano, B., Jensen, B., and Maness, R. C., *Cyber Strategy: The Evolving Character of Power and Coercion* (New York: Oxford University Press, 2018).
van Ham, C., Thomassen, J., Aarts, K., and Andeweg, R. (eds.), *Myth and Reality of the Legitimacy Crisis: Explaining Trends and Cross-National Differences in Established Democracies* (Oxford: Oxford University Press, 2017).
von Clausewitz, C., *On War*, edited and translated by Michael Howard and Peter Paret (Oxford: Oxford University Press, 1997).
von Clausewitz, C., *Principles of War*, translated by Hans Wilhelm Gatkze (Harrisburg PA: Military Service Publishing, 1942).
van Creveld, M., *The Transformation of War* (New York: Free Press 1991).
White (ed.), S., *Politics and the Ruling Group in Russia* (New York: Palgrave Macmillan, 2008).
Wise, D., *Spy: The Inside Story of How the FBI's Robert Hanssen Betrayed America* (New York: Random House, 2003).
Wolff, M., *Fire and Fury: Inside the Trump White House* (New York: Henry Holt, 2018).
Wooley, S. C., and Howard, P. N. (eds.), *Computational Propaganda: Political Parties, Politicians, and Political Manipulation on Social Media* (New York: Oxford University Press, 2019).
Woodward, B., *Fear: Trump in the White House* (New York: Simon & Schuster, 2018).

Book chapters

Anderson, A., "Organised crime, mafia and governments," in Fiorentini, and Peltzman (eds.), *The Economics of Organised Crime.*

Baram, G., and Sommer, U., "Covert or not Covert: National Strategies During Cyber Conflict," in Minárik, Alatalu, Biondi, Signoretti, Tolga, and Visky (eds.), *2019 11th International Conference on Cyber Conflict: Silent Battle.*

Buchan, R., "The International Legal Regulation of State-Sponsored Cyber Espionage," in Osula and Rõigas (eds.), *International Cyber Norms: Legal, Policy & Industry Perspectives.*

Campbell, L., and Lord, N., "Following the Money: Illicit Financial Flows and SDG," in Blaustein, Fitz-Gibbon, Pino, and White (eds.), *The Emerald Handbook on Crime, Justice and Sustainable Development.*

D'Urso, M., "The Cyber-Combatant: A New Status for a New Warrior," in Glorioso and Osula (eds.), *1st Workshop on Ethics of Cyber Conflict Proceedings.*

Diamond, J., "Early Patriotic Hacking," in Healey (ed.), *A Fierce Domain.*

Elkus, A., "Moonlight Maze," in Healey (ed.), *A Fierce Domain.*

Flibbert, A., "The Arab World: Grappling with Multiple Consequences," in Ayoob and Ugur (eds.), *Assessing the War on Terror.*

Giles, K., "Russia and Its Neighbours: Old Attitudes, New Capabilities," in Geers (ed.), *Cyber War in Perspective: Russian Aggression Against Ukraine.*

Giles, K., and Hartmann, K., "'Silent Battle' Goes Loud: Entering a New Era of State-Avowed Cyber Conflict," in Minárik, Alatalu, Biondi, Signoretti, Tolga, and Visky (eds.), *2019 11th International Conference on Cyber Conflict: Silent Battle.*

Gill, P., "Democratic and Parliamentary Accountability of Intelligence Services After 9/11", in Born and Caparini (eds.), *Democratic Control of Intelligence Services: Containing Rogue Elephants.*

Hartmann, K., and Steup, C., "The Vulnerability of UAVs to Cyber Attacks – An Approach to the Risk Assessment," in Podins, Stinissen, and Maybaum (eds.), *5th International Conference on Cyber Conflict Proceedings.*

Hartmann, K., and Giles, K., "Net Neutrality in the Context of Cyber Warfare," in Minárik, Jakschis, and Lindström (eds), *2018 10th International Conference on Cyber Conflict CyCon X: Maximising Effects.*

Kraszewski, K., "SamSam and the Silent Battle of Atlanta." in Minárik, Alatalu, Biondi, Signoretti, Tolga, and Visky (eds.), *2019 11th International Conference on Cyber Conflict: Silent Battle.*

Mangott, G., "Farewell to Russia: The Decay of a Superpower," in Gärtner, Hyde-Price, and Reiter (eds.), *Europe's New Security Challenges.*

Mansoor, P. R., "Introduction: Hybrid Warfare in History," in Murray and Mansoor (eds.), *Hybrid Warfare: Fighting Complex Opponents from the Ancient World to the Present.*

Mote, G., Vanags, J., Geipele, I., and Bowen, J., "Impression Management: Impression Conceptual Definition and Model", *Recent Advances in Business Administration* Proceedings of the 6th WSEAS International Conference on BUSINESS ADMINISTRATION (ICBA '12) Harvard, Cambridge, USA January 25 – 27, 2012 (Harvard, MA: WSEAS Press, 2012).

Payne, B., and Mienie, E., "Multiple-Extortion Ransomware: The Case for Active Cyber Threat Intelligence," in Eze, Speakman, and Onwubiko (eds.), *ECCWS 2021 20th European Conference on Cyber Warfare and Security.*

Posado, T., "From Chávez to Maduro: From Delegative Democracy to De-Democratization," in Dieckhoff, Jaffrelot, and Massicard (eds.), *Contemporary Populists in Power.*

Schneider, E., "The Russian Federal Security Service under President Putin", in White (ed.), *Politics and the Ruling Group in Russia.*

Vedral, B., "The Vulnerability of the Financial System to a Systemic Cyberattack," in Jančárková, Lindström, Visky, and Zotz (eds.), *13th International Conference on Cyber Conflict: Going Viral.*

Weedon, J., "Beyond 'Cyber War': Russia's Use of Strategic Cyber Espionage and Information Operations in Ukraine," in Geers, K., (ed.), *Cyber War in Perspective: Russian Aggression against Ukraine.*

Zeb, R., "Hybrid or No Hybrid, War is War" in Stoddart et al (eds.), *Hybrid Warfare: Western and non-Western definitions, concepts, and regional case studies.*

Journal articles

Abrams, S., "Beyond Propaganda: Soviet Active Measures in Putin's Russia." *Connections: The Quarterly Journal*, Vol. 15, No. 1.

Ahmed, M., & Gaber, M., "An Investigation on Cyber Espionage Ecosystem." *Journal of Cyber Security Technology*, forthcoming.

Aimeur, E., Sabrine Amri, & Giles Bassard, "Fake news, disinformation and misinformation in social media: a review", *Social Media Analysis and Mining*, Vol. 13, Article No. 30 (2023).

Akerlof, K., Rowan, K. E., Fitzgerald, D., and Cedeno, A. Y., "Communication of Climate Projections in US Media Amid Politicization of Model Science." *Nature Climate Change*, Vol. 2.

Allin, D. H., "Ukraine: The Shock of Recognition." *Survival*, Vol. 64, No. 2.

Allison, R., "Russian 'Deniable' Intervention in Ukraine: How and Why Russia Broke the Rules." *International Affairs*, Vol. 90, Issue 6.

Allison, R., "Russia and Syria: Explaining Alignment with a Regime in Crisis." *International Affairs*, Vol. 89, No. 4.

Andersen, J. and Søe, S. O., "Communicative Actions We Live By: The Problem with Fact-Checking, Tagging or Flagging Fake News – The Case of Facebook." *European Journal of Communication*, Vol. 35, Issue 2.

Andersen, K., Shehata, A., & Andersson, D., "Alternative News Orientation and Trust in Mainstream Media: A Longitudinal Audience Perspective." *Digital Journalism*, Vol. 11, Issue 5.

Andrew, R. B., "State-Sponsored Militias are Coming to a Server Near You." *Foreign Policy*, http://foreignpolicy.com/2013/02/12/cyber-gang-warfare/.

Åslund, A., "How Vladimir Putin Rose to the Top." *The International Economy*, http://www.international-economy.com/TIE_Sp19_Aslund.pdf.

Åtland, K., "Destined for Deadlock? Russia, Ukraine, and the Unfulfilled Minsk Agreements." *Post-Soviet Affairs*, Vol. 36, No. 2.

Averre, D., "NATO Expansion and Russian National Interests." *European Security*, Vol. 7, Issue 1.

Baldini, G., and Chelotti, N., "The Brexit Effect: Political Implications of the Exit of the United Kingdom from the European Union." *International Political Science Review*, Vol. 43, Issue 3.

Barbieri, J., "Raising Citizen-Soldiers in Donbas: Russia's Role in Promoting Patriotic Education Programmes in the Donetsk and Luhansk Peoples' Republics." *Ethnopolitics*, Vol. 23, No. 5.

Bartles, C. K., and McDermott, R. N., "Russia's Military Operation in Crimea Road – Testing Rapid Reaction Capabilities." *Problems of Post-Communism*, Vol. 61, No. 6.

Beerman, J., Berent, D., Falter, A., and Bhunia, S., "A Review of Colonial Pipeline Ransomware Attack." 2023 IEEE/ACM 23rd International Symposium on Cluster, Cloud and Internet

Computing Workshops (CCGridW). Available from https://www.computer.org/csdl/proceedings/ccgridw/2023/1OUmVoAlwru.

Behrends, J.C., ""Some call us heroes, others call us killers." Experiencing violent spaces: Soviet soldiers in the Afghan War", *Nationalities Papers*, Vol. 43 Issue 5.

Beim, J., "Enforcing a Prohibition on International Espionage." *Chicago Journal of International Law*, Vol. 18, No. 2.

Beliakova, N., and Timofeeva, Z., "Religious Symbolism and Political Resistance: Navalny's Martyr Narrative in the Russian Opposition." *Religions*, Vol. 16, Issue 1.

Bjola, C., "Diplomatic Leadership in Times of International Crisis: The Maverick, the Congregator and the Pragmatist." *The Hague Journal of Diplomacy*, Vol. 10, Issue 1.

Blank, S., "How Ukraine Reveals Russian Nuclear Strategy." *Defense & Security Analysis*, Vol. 39, Issue 3.

Blank, S., and Kim, Y., "Economic Warfare a la Russe: The Energy Weapon and Russian National Security Strategy." *The Journal of East Asian Affairs*, Vol. 30, Issue 1.

Bøås, M., and Strazzari, F., "Governance, Fragility and Insurgency in the Sahel: A Hybrid Political Order in the Making." *The International Spectator*, Vol. 55, No. 4.

Bollfrass, A. K., and Herzog, S., "The War in Ukraine and Global Nuclear Order." *Survival*, Vol. 64, No. 4.

Bossio, D., Flew, T., Meese, J., Leaver, T., and Barnet, B., "Australia's News Media Bargaining Code and the Global Turn Towards Platform Regulation." *Policy and Internet*, Vol. 14, Issue 1.

Bouchet, N., "Russia's 'Militarization' of Colour Revolutions." *Policy Perspectives*, Vol. 4, No. 2.

Braguinsky, S., "Postcommunist Oligarchs in Russia: Quantitative Analysis." *The Journal of Law and Economics*, Vol. 52, No. 2.

Braw, E., "Wagner's Revolt May Weaken Russia's Draft." https://foreignpolicy.com/2023/06/26/wagner-revolt-russia-conscription-ukraine-war/.

Brinza, A., "Putin's War Has Killed China's Eurasian Railway Dreams." https://foreignpolicy.com/2022/03/01/belt-road-initiative-new-eurasian-land-bridge-china-russia-poland/

Brockmeier, S., Stuenkel, O., and Tourinho, M., "The Impact of the Libya Intervention Debates on Norms of Protection." *Global Society*, Vol. 30, No. 1.

Brzezinski, Z., "The Premature Partnership." *Foreign Affairs*, Vol. 73, No. 2.

Bremmer, I., and Charap, S., "The Siloviki in Putin's Russia: Who They Are and What They Want." *The Washington Quarterly*, Vol. 30, Issue 1.

Brown, I., "Data Protection: The New Technical and Political Environment." *Computers & Law*, Vol. 20, No. 6.

Budnitsky, S. and Jia, L., "Branding Internet sovereignty: Digital media and the Chinese–Russian cyberalliance", *European Journal of Cultural Studies*, Vol. 21, Issue 5.

Bukkvoll, T., "Why Putin Went to War: Ideology, Interests and Decision-Making in the Russian Use of Force in Crimea and Donbas." *Contemporary Politics*, Vol. 22, Issue 3.

Burkhardt, F., Wittke, C., Bescotti, E., and Rabinovych, M., "Russian Military Build-up Around Ukraine – Part 2." *Russian Analytical Digest*, No. 277. https://www.research-collection.ethz.ch/bitstream/handle/20.500.11850/533782/RAD277.pdf?sequence=3.

Burkle, F. M., Goniewicz, K., and Khorram-Manesh, A., "Bastardizing Peacekeeping and the Birth of Hybrid Warfare." *Prehospital and Disaster Medicine*, Vol. 37, No. 2.

Carlin, J. P., "Detect, Disrupt, Deter: A Whole-of-Government Approach to National Security Cyber Threats." *Harvard National Security Journal*, Vol. 7. https://lawfare.s3-us-west-2.amazonaws.com/staging/2016/Carlin%20FINAL.pdf.

Carney, T., "Establishing a United Nations Convention to Stop Foreign Election Interference." *Loyola University Chicago International Law Review*, Vol. 17, Issue 1.

Charap, S., "The Ghost of Hybrid War." *Survival*, Vol. 57, No. 6.

Charbonneau, B., "Counter-Insurgency Governance in the Sahel." *International Affairs*, Vol. 97, No. 6.

Chekov, A. D., Makarycheva, A. V., Solomentseva, A. M., Suchkov, M. A., and Sushentsov, A. A., "War of the Future: A View from Russia." *Survival*, Vol. 61, Issue 6.

Cheloukhine, S., Kalkayeva, N., Khvedelidze, T., and Bizhanova, A. R., "Corruption in Russian Law Enforcement." *Communist and Post-Communist Studies*, Vol. 53, No. 1.

Cormac, R., and Aldrich, R. J., "Grey is the New Black: Covert Action and Implausible Deniability." *International Affairs*, Vol. 94, Issue 3.

Cunliffe, K. S., "Cyber-Enabled Tradecraft and Contemporary Espionage: Assessing the Implications of the Tradecraft Paradox on Agent Recruitment in Russia and China." *Intelligence and National Security*, Vol. 38, No. 7.

Cunliffe, K. S., "Hard Target Espionage in the Information Era: New Challenges for the Second Oldest Profession." *Intelligence and National Security*, Vol. 36, No. 7.

Davies, C. M., "The Ukraine Conflict, Economic–Military Power Balances and Economic Sanctions." *Post-Communist Economies*, Vol. 28, Issue 2.

Dalsjö, R., Jonsson, M., and Norberg, J., "A Brutal Examination: Russian Military Capability in Light of the Ukraine War." *Survival*, Vol. 64, No. 3.

Dawson, A., and Innes, M., "How Russia's Internet Research Agency Built its Disinformation Campaign." *The Political Quarterly*, Vol. 90, No. 2.

Demarest, G.B., "Espionage in International Law", *Denver Journal of International Law & Policy*, Vol. 24, No 2.

Desgrais, N., Guichaoua, Y., and Lebovich, A., "Unity is the Exception. Alliance Formation and Deformation Among Armed Actors in Northern Mali." *Small Wars & Insurgencies*, Vol. 29, No. 4.

Devanny, J., Martin, C., and Stevens, T., "On the Strategic Consequences of Digital Espionage." *Journal of Cyber Security Technology*, Vol. 6, Issue 3.

Dismukes, B., "The Return of Great-Power Competition—Cold War Lessons about Strategic Antisubmarine Warfare and Defense of Sea Lines of Strategic Antisubmarine Warfare and Defense of Sea Lines of Communication." *Naval War College Review*, Vol. 73, No. 3.

Dremliuga, R., Dremliuga, O., and Kuznetsov, P., "Combating the Threats of Cybercrimes in Russia Evolution of the Cybercrime Laws and Social Concern." *Communist and Post-Communist Studies*, Vol. 53, No. 3.

Dudley, R., and Golden, D., "The Colonial Pipeline Ransomware Hackers Had a Secret Weapon: Self-Promoting Cybersecurity Firms." Propublica/MIT Technology Review. https://energyrights.info/sites/default/files/artifacts/media/pdf/the_colonial_pipeline_ransomware_hackers_had_a_secret_weapon_self-promoting_cybersecurity_firms_-_propublica.pdf.

Dunlap, C. J., "Lawfare Today: A Perspective." *Yale Journal of International Affairs*, Vol. 3, Issue 1.

Dylan, H., Gioe, D. V., and Grossfeld, E., "The Autocrat's Intelligence Paradox: Vladimir Putin's (Mis) Management of Russian Strategic Assessment in the Ukraine War." *British Journal of Politics and International Relations*, Vol. 25, Issue 3.

Dylan, H., Gioe, D. V., and Richterova, D., "Western Agencies Offer an Open Door for Russian Defectors." https://foreignpolicy.com/2023/07/26/western-intelligence-recruit-russian-defectors/.

Egloff, F. J., and Smeets, M., "Publicly Attributing Cyber Attacks: A Framework." *Journal of Strategic Studies*, Vol. 46, No. 3.

Farbman, S., "Telegram, "Milbloggers' and the Russian State." *Survival*, Vol. 65, No. 3.

Forsberg, T., and Herd, G., "Russia and NATO: From Windows of Opportunities to Closed Doors." *Journal of Contemporary European Studies*, Vol. 23, No. 1.

Frye, T., Reuter, O. J., and Szakonyi, D., "Vote Brokers, Clientelist Appeals, and Voter Turnout: Evidence from Russia and Venezuela." *World Politics*, Vol. 71, No. 4.

Fukuyama, F., "The End of History." *The National Interest*, No. 16.

Fukuyama, F., "The 'End of History' 20 Years Later." *New Perspectives Quarterly*, Vol. 27, Issue 1.

Galeotti, M., "I'm Sorry for Creating the 'Gerasimov Doctrine.'" *Foreign Policy*, March 5, 2018, https://foreignpolicy.com/2018/03/05/im-sorry-for-creating-the-gerasimov-doctrine/.

Galeotti, M., "Hybrid, ambiguous, and non-linear? How new is Russia's 'new way of war'?", *Small Wars and Insurgencies*, Vol. 27, No. 2

Galeotti, M., "(Mis)Understanding Russia's Two 'Hybrid Wars.'" *Critique & Humanism*, Vol. 59, No. 1. Reprinted in https://www.eurozine.com/misunderstanding-russias-two-hybrid-wars/?pdf.

Galeotti, M., "Putin's Spies and Security Men: His Strongest Allies, His Greatest Weakness." *Russian Analytical Digest*, No. 173.

Galeotti, M., "Spooks in the Kremlin. The Dangers of Putin's Unhealthy Reliance on Russian Intelligence." *Foreign Policy*, No. 232.

Galeotti, M., "The Mythical 'Gerasimov Doctrine' and the Language of Threat." *Critical Studies on Security*, Vol. 7, No. 2.

Giacomo, C., and Bugos, S., "Putin Calls Up Reservists, Renews Nuclear Threat." *Arms Control Today*, Vol. 52, Issue 8.

Gibson, A. D., "What Teams Do: Exploring Volunteer Content Moderation Team Labor on Facebook." Social Media + Society, Vol. 9, No. 3.

Gioe, D. V., "Cyber Operations and Useful Fools: The Approach of Russian Hybrid Intelligence." *Intelligence and National Security*, Vol. 33, No. 7.

Gioe, D. V., Goodman, M. S., and Wanless, A., "Rebalancing Cybersecurity Imperatives: Patching the Social Layer." *Journal of Cyber Policy*, Vol. 4, No. 1.

Gioe, D. V., Goodman, M. S., and Frey, D. S., "Unforgiven: Russian Intelligence Vengeance as Political Theater and Strategic Messaging." *Intelligence and National Security*, Vol. 34, No. 4.

Gnatiuk, O., and Basik, S., "Performing Geopolitics of Toponymic Solidarity: The Case of Ukraine." *Norwegian Journal of Geography*, Vol. 77, Issue 1.

Gobbin, N., and Merlevede, B., "The Russian Crisis: A Debt Perspective." *Post-Communist Economies* 12, issue 2.

Goodman, M.S., Frey, D., and Gioe, D., "Alexei Navalny poisoning: what theatrical assassination attempts reveal about Vladimir Putin's grip on power in Russia." https://theconversation.com/alexei-navalny-poisoning-what-theatrical-assassination-attempts-reveal-about-vladimir-putins-grip-on-power-in-russia-145664.

Gould-Davies, N., "Putin's Strategic Failure." *Survival*, Vol. 64, No. 2.

Greene, S. A., "Editor's Introduction." *Russian Politics & Law*, Vol. 55, Issue 2.

Grinin, L. E., "The Role of an Individual in History: A Reconsideration." *Social Evolution & History*, Vol. 9, No. 2.

Guilfoyle, D., Paige, T. P., and McLaughlin, R., "The Final Frontier of Cyberspace: The Seabed Beyond National Jurisdiction and the Protection of Submarine Cables." *International & Comparative Law Quarterly*, Vol. 71, Issue 3.

Harner, J., Ray, L., and Wakoko-Studstill, F., "An Investigation of the Effectiveness of Facebook and Twitter Algorithm and Policies on Misinformation and User Decision Making." *Journal of Systemics, Cybernetics and Informatics*, Vol. 20, No. 5.

Hassan, G., "The UK General Election in Scotland: The End of an Era, Age of Ultra-Competition or Interregnum?" *The Political Quarterly*, Vol. 96, Issue 1.

Hill, F., "Putin: The One-Man Show the West Doesn't Understand." *Bulletin of the Atomic Scientists*, Vol. 72, No. 3.

Hobolt, S. B., "The Brexit Vote: A Divided Nation, a Divided Continent." *Journal of European Public Policy*, Vol. 23, Issue 9.

Hurak, I., and D'Anieri, P., "The Evolution of Russian Political Tactics in Ukraine." *Problems of Post-Communism*, Vol. 69, No. 2.

Huntingdon, S. P., "The Clash of Civilizations." *Foreign Affairs* Vol. 72, No. 3.

Huntingdon, S. P., "The Clash of Civilizations Revisited." *New Perspectives Quarterly*, Vol. 30, Issue 4.

Ingesson, T., and Andersson, M., "Clandestine Communications in Cyber-Denied Environments Numbers Stations and Radio in the 21st Century." *Journal of Policing, Intelligence and Counter Terrorism*, Vol. 19, No. 2.

Inkster, N., "China's Cyber Power." *Adelphi*, Vol. 55, Issue 456.

Jennings, J., and Stroud, N. J., "Asymmetric Adjustment: Partisanship and Correcting Misinformation on Facebook." *New Media & Society*, Vol. 25, Issue 7.

Jervis, R., "Reports, Politics, and Intelligence Failures: The Case of Iraq." *Journal of Strategic Studies*, Vol. 29, No. 1.

Johnston, A. I., "Thinking about Strategic Culture." *International Security*, Vol. 19, No. 4 (Spring 1995).

Joyner, C. C., and Lotrionte, C., "Information Warfare as International Coercion: Elements of a Legal Framework." *European Journal of International Law*, Vol. 12, Issue 5.

Kaczmarski, M., "Domestic Power Relations and Russia's Foreign Policy." *Demokratizatsiya*, Vol. 22, No. 3.

Kaltseis, M., "Cold and Distant or Hearty and Human? The Visual Portrayal of Vladimir Putin on Russian Television." *Media Literacy and Research*, Vol. 2, Issue 2.

Kappel, R., "Russia and Africa: The Invasion of Ukraine Leads to the Next Major Crisis." *Strategic Review for Southern Africa*, Vol. 44, No. 1.

Kaszuba, M., "The Collective Security Treaty Organization (CSTO) in the Foreign Policy of the Russian Federation." *The Copernicus Journal of Political Studies*, No. 1.

Khan, R., Maynard, P., McLaughlin, K., Laverty, D., and Sezer, S., "Threat Analysis of BlackEnergy Malware for Synchrophasor based Real-time Control and Monitoring in Smart Grid." Proceedings of the 4th International Symposium for ICS & SCADA Cyber Security Research 2016. https://dl.acm.org/doi/proceedings/10.5555/3015643.

Kipp, J. W., "Book Review Vladimir Slipchenko and Makhmut Gareev. *Future War.*" *Journal of Slavic Military Studies*, Vol. 20, Issue 1.

Klimburg, A., "Mobilising Cyber Power." *Survival*, Vol. 53, No. 1.

Kóczy, L. A., Csercsik, D., and Sziklai, B. R., "Nord Stream 2: A Prelude to War." *Energy Strategy Reviews*, Vol. 44.

Kofman, M., and Rojansky, M., "What Kind of Victory for Russia in Syria?" *Military Review.*

Kondratov, E., and Johansson-Nogués, E., "Russia's Hybrid Interference Campaigns in France, Germany and the UK: A Challenge against Trust in Liberal Democracies?" *Geopolitics*, Vol. 28, Issue 5.

Kragh, M., and Umland, A., "Putinism beyond Putin: The Political Ideas of Nikolai Patrushev and Sergei Naryshkin in 2006–20." *Post-Soviet Affairs*, Vol. 39, Issue 5.

Kragh, M., and Åsberg, S., "Russia's Strategy for Influence Through Public Diplomacy and Active Measures: The Swedish Case." *Journal of Strategic Studies*, Vol. 40, Issue 6.

Kraemer-Mbula, E., Tang, P., and Rush, H., "The Cybercrime Ecosystem: Online Innovation in the Shadows?" *Technological Forecasting & Social Change*, Vol. 80, Issue 3.

Kraj, K., "The System of Military Higher Education in the Russian Federation." *Bezpieczeństwo. Teoria i Praktyka*, Yearbook 2019, No. 3.

Kristensen, H. M., and Norris, R. S., "Russian Nuclear Forces, 2018." *Bulletin of the Atomic Scientists*, Vol. 74, Issue 3.

Kristensen, H. M., Korda, M., & Reynolds, E., "Russian Nuclear Weapons, 2023." *Bulletin of the Atomic Scientists*, Vol. 79, No. 3.

Kubicek, P., "The Commonwealth of Independent States: An Example of Failed Regionalism?" *Review of International Studies*, Vol. 35, Issue 1.

Kunertova, D., "The War in Ukraine Shows the Game-Changing Effect of Drones Depends on the Game." *Bulletin of the Atomic Scientists*, Vol. 79, No. 2.

Kuzio, T., "Imperial Nationalism as the Driver Behind Russia's Invasion of Ukraine." *Nations and Nationalism*, Vol. 29, Issue 1.

Kuzio, T., "Nationalism and Authoritarianism in Russia: Introduction to the Special Issue." *Communist and Post-Communist Studies*, Vol. 49, Issue 1.

Kuzio, T., "Ukraine's Orange Revolution. The Oppositions Road to Success." *Journal of Democracy*, Vol. 16, No. 2.

Kydd, A., "Switching Sides: Changing Power, Alliance Choices and US–China–Russia Relations." *International Politics*, Vol. 57, Issue 5.

Lanskoy, M., and Myles-Primakoff, D., "Power and Plunder in Putin's Russia." *Journal of Democracy*, Vol. 29, No. 1.

Libman, A. & Yakovlev, A., "A Centralist Approach to Regional Development: The Case of the Russian Ministry for the Development of the Far East", *Europe-Asia Studies*, Vol. 73, No. 6.

Lin, H., "Russian Cyber Operations in the Invasion of Ukraine." *Cyber Defense Review*, Vol. 7, No. 4.

Lipma, M., "How Putin Silences Dissent Inside the Kremlin's Crackdown." *Foreign Affairs*, Vol. 95, No. 3.

Lopes, C., "The Untamed Impact of a Faraway Shock: Africa and the War in Ukraine." *Strategic Review for Southern Africa*, Vol. 44, No. 1.

Luban, D., "Carl Schmitt and the Critique of Lawfare." *Case Western Reserve Journal of International Law*, Vol. 43, Issue 1.

Lynch, D., "'The enemy is at the gate': Russia after Beslan", *International Affairs*, Vol. 80, Issue 1.

Mackinnon, A., and Gramer, R., "Russian Mercenaries Staged Atrocities in Mali, France Says. The French military watched what appeared to be Wagner operatives attempting a false-flag operation to discredit the West." https://foreignpolicy.com/2022/04/26/russian-mercenaries-staged-atrocities-mali-france-says/.

Mankoff, J., "Russia's Latest Land Grab: How Putin Won Crimea and Lost Ukraine." *Foreign Affairs*, Vol. 93, No. 3.

Marten, K., "Whither Wagner? The Consequences of Prigozhin's Mutiny and Demise." *Survival*, Vol. 65, No. 5.

Masoud, T., "The Arab Spring at 10: Kings or People?" *Journal of Democracy*, Vol. 32, No. 1.

Massicot, D., "What Russia Got Wrong. Can Moscow Learn from Its Failures in Ukraine?' (March/April 2023), https://www.foreignaffairs.com/ukraine/what-russia-got-wrong-moscow-failures-in-ukraine-dara-massicot.

Masterson, J., "Novichok Used in Russia, OPCW Finds." *Arms Control Today*, Vol. 50, Issue 9.

Mastro, O. S., "Sino-Russian Military Alignment and Its Implications for Global Security." *Security Studies*, Vol. 33, No. 2.

Matsiyevsky, Y., "Revolution Without Regime Change." *Communist and Post-Communist Studies*, Vol. 51, No. 4.

Mayne, Q., and Katsanidou, A., "Subnational Economic Conditions and the Changing Geography of Mass Euroscepticism: A Longitudinal Analysis." *European Journal of Political Research*, Vol. 62, Issue 3.

McDermott, R. N., "Does Russia Have a Gerasimov Doctrine?" *Parameters*, Vol. 46, No. 1.

McDougal, T., "Establishing Russia's Responsibility for CyberCrime Based on Its Hacker Culture." *Brigham Young University International Law & Management Review*, Vol. 11, Issue 2.

McFaul, M., "Russia's Road to Autocracy." *Journal of Democracy*, Volume 32, No. 4.

McFaul, M., "Ukraine Imports Democracy: External Influences on the Orange Revolution." *International Security*, Vol. 32, No. 2.

McGlynn, J., and Garner, I., "Russia's War Crime Denials Are Fuel for More Atrocities. In Moscow's myths, Russia is always the victim." https://foreignpolicy.com/2022/04/23/propaganda-russia-atrocity-bucha/.

Meakins, J. I., "Squabbling Siloviki: Factionalism Within Russia's Security Services." *International Journal of Intelligence and CounterIntelligence*, Vol. 31, Issue 2.

Mensah, A. N. A. and Aning, K., "Russia Resurgent? Untangling the Role and Meaning of Moscow's Proxies in West Africa and the Sahel." *Strategic Review for Southern Africa*, Vol. 44, No. 1.

Mijares, V. M., "Soft Balancing the Titans: Venezuelan Foreign-Policy Strategy Toward the United States, China, and Russia." *Latin American Policy*, Vol. 8, No. 2.

Mišík, M., "The EU Needs to Improve Its External Energy Security." *Energy Policy*, Vol. 165.

Mommen, A., "Boris Nemtsov, 1959–2015 The Rise and Fall of a Provincial Democrat." *Demokratizatsiya: The Journal of Post-Soviet Democratization*, Volume 24, No. 1.

Monaghan, A., "Putin's Way of War: The 'War' in Russia's 'Hybrid Warfare.'" *Parameters*, Vol. 45, No. 4.

Olzacka, E., "The Development of Ukrainian Cultural Policy in the Context of Russian Hybrid Aggression Against Ukraine." *International Journal of Cultural Policy*, Vol. 30, No. 2.

Omand, D., "Understanding Putin's Russia: a continuing challenge for Western intelligence", *Intelligence and National Security*, Vol. 39, No. 3.

Orlova, A.V., ""Digital Sovereignty," Anonymity and Freedom of Expression: Russia's Fight to Re-Shape Internet Governance", *UC Davis Journal of International Law & Policy*, Vol. 26, Issue 2.

Ng, L. H. Z., Moffitt, J. D., and Carley, K. M., "Coordinated through a Web of Images: Analysis of Image-based Influence Operations from China, Iran, Russia, and Venezuela." ICWSM-2022 workshop proceedings. https://arxiv.org/pdf/2206.03576.pdf.

Nisioti, A., Loukas, G., Mylonas, A., and Panaousis, E., "Forensics for Multi-Stage Cyber Incidents: Survey and Future Directions." *Forensic Science International: Digital Investigation*, Vol. 44.

Nocetti, J., "Contest and Conquest: Russia and Global Internet Governance." *International Affairs*, Vol. 91, Issue 1.

Norden, L., and Weiner, D. I., "U.S. Elections Are Still Not Safe From Attack Congress Can Change That If It Acts Fast." https://www.foreignaffairs.com/articles/russia-fsu/2019-07-23/us-elections-are-still-not-safe-attack.

Omand, D., Bartlett, J., and Miller, C., "Introducing Social Media Intelligence (SOCMINT)." *Intelligence and National Security*, Vol. 27, Issue 6.

Paneyakh, E., "Faking Performance Together: Systems of Performance Evaluation in Russian Enforcement Agencies and Production of Bias and Privilege." *Post-Soviet Affairs*, Vol. 30, Nos. 2–3.

Park, C. S., and Kaye, B. K., "Applying News Values Theory to Liking, Commenting and Sharing Mainstream News Articles on Facebook." *Journalism*, Vol. 24, No. 3.

Pennycook, G., and Rand, D. G., "Lazy, Not Biased: Susceptibility to Partisan Fake News is Better Explained by Lack of Reasoning than by Motivated Reasoning." *Cognition*, Vol. 188.

Petersson, B., and Petersson, E., "Coveted, Detested and Unattainable? Images of the US superpower Role and Self-Images of Russia in Russian Print Media Discourse." *International Journal of Cultural Studies*, Vol. 14, Issue 1.

Petrov, N., "The Elite New Wine into Old Bottles?" *Russian Politics & Law*, Vol. 55, Issue 2.

Pisano, J., "How Zelensky Has Changed Ukraine." *Journal of Democracy*, Vol. 33, No. 3.

Pomerantsev, P., "The Kremlin's Information War." *Journal of Democracy*, Vol. 26, No. 4.

Potočňák, A., and Mares, M., "Donbas Conflict: How Russia's Trojan Horse Failed and Forced Moscow to Alter Its Strategy." *Problems of Post-Communism*, Vol. 70, Issue 4.

Pringle, R. W., "SMERSH: Military Counterintelligence and Stalin's Control of the USSR." *International Journal of Intelligence and CounterIntelligence*, Vol. 21, Issue 1.

Pun, D., "Rethinking Espionage in the Modern Era." *Chicago Journal of Internal Law*, Vol. 18, No. 1.

Radsan, A. J., "The Unresolved Equation of Espionage and International Law." *Michigan Journal of International Law*, Vol. 28, Issue 3.

Radsch, C. C., "Platformization and Media Capture: A Framework for Regulatory Analysis of Media-Related Platform Regulations." *UCLA Journal of Law & Technology*, Vol. 28, No. 2.

Reisman, W. M., Wiessner, S., & Willard, A.R., "The New Haven School: A Brief Introduction", *Yale Journal of International Law*, Vol. 32: 575.

Renz, B., "Russia and 'Hybrid Warfare.'" *Contemporary Politics*, Vol. 22, Issue 3.

Reuter, O. J., and Remington, T. F., "Dominant Party Regimes and the Commitment Problem: The Case of United Russia." *Comparative Political Studies*, Vol. 42, No. 4.

Reznikova, O., Hryhorenko, O., and Myronenko, V., "Transformation of the Strategic Culture of Ukraine under the Influence of the Russian Threat." *Politologija*, Vol. 116, No. 4.

Rhodes, S. C., "Filter Bubbles, Echo Chambers, and Fake News: How Social Media Conditions Individuals to Be Less Critical of Political Misinformation." *Political Communication*, Vol. 39, Issue 1.

Rohozinska, J., and Shpak, V., "Ukraine's Post-Maidan Struggles: The Rise of an 'Outsider' President." *Journal of Democracy*, Vol. 30, No. 3.

Ross, A. S., and Rivers, D. J., "Discursive Deflection: Accusation of 'Fake News' and the Spread of Mis- and Disinformation in the Tweets of President Trump." *Social Media + Society*, Vol. 4, Issue 2.

Rossini, P., Stromer-Galley, J., Baptista, E. A., and de Oliveira, V. V., "Dysfunctional Information Sharing on WhatsApp and Facebook: The Role of Political Talk, Cross-Cutting Exposure and Social Corrections." *New Media & Society*, Vol. 23, Issue 8.

Sakwa, R., "'New Cold War' or Twenty Years' Crisis? Russia and International Politics." *International Affairs*, Vol. 84, No. 2.

Sakwa, R., and Webber, M., "The Commonwealth of Independent States, 1991–1998: Stagnation and Survival." *Europe-Asia Studies*, Vol. 51, No. 3.

Salamey, I., "Post-Arab Spring: Changes and Challenges." *Third World Quarterly*, Vol. 36, No. 1.

Saleem, Z. b., Khan, I., and Khurshid, Z., "The Fall of Bashar al-Assad: Implications for Syria and the Broader Middle East", *Dialogue Social Science Review*, Vol. 2, No. 5.

Schmitt, M. N., "Grey Zones in the International Law of Cyberspace." *Yale Journal of International Law Online*, Vol. 42, No. 2.

Scott, L., "Secret Intelligence, Covert Action and Clandestine Diplomacy." *Intelligence and National Security*, Vol. 19, No. 2.

Semukhina, O., "The Evolution of Policing in Post-Soviet Russia: Paternalism versus Service in Police. Officers' Understanding of their Role." *Communist and Post-Communist Studies*, Vol. 51, Issue 3.

Sempijja, N., and Eyita-Okon, E., "Examining the Effectiveness of the EU Security-Development Strategy in Tackling Instability in the Sahel: The Case for an Alternative Strategy?" *South African Journal of International Affairs*, Vol. 29, No. 2.

Sethi, M., "Nuclear Overtones in the Russia-Ukraine War." *Arms Control Today*, Vol. 52, Issue 5.

Seyedfarshi, A., "French Interventionism in the Age of R2P: A Critical Examination of the Case of Mali." *Creighton International and Comparative Law Journal*, Vol. 7, Issue 1.

Shambaugh, D., "Assessing the US 'Pivot' to Asia." *Strategic Studies Quarterly*, Vol. 7, No. 2.

Shields, K., "Cybersecurity: Recognizing the Risk and Protecting Against Attacks." *North Carolina Banking Institute Journal*, Vol. 19, Issue 1.

Shleifer, A., and Treisman, D., "A Normal Country: Russia After Communism." *Journal of Economic Perspectives*, Vol. 19, No. 1.

Skak, M., "Russian Strategic Culture: The Role of Today's *Chekisty*." *Contemporary Politics*, Vol. 22, Issue 3.

Slider, D., "How United is United Russia? Regional Sources of Intra-party Conflict." *Journal of Communist Studies and Transition Politics*, Vol. 26, Issue 2.

Smeets, M., "The Challenges of Military Adaptation to the Cyber Domain: A Case Study of the Netherlands." *Small Wars & Insurgencies*, Vol. 34, Issue 7.

Smith, H., "Russia as a Great Power: Status Inconsistency and the Two Chechen Wars." *Communist and Post-Communist Studies*, Vol. 47, Issues 3–4.

Smyth, R., "Vladimir Putin plans to win Russia's parliamentary election no matter how unpopular his party is." https://theconversation.com/vladimir-putin-plans-to-win-russias-parliamentary-election-no-matter-how-unpopular-his-party-is-160078.

Soldatov, A., and Borogan, I., "Russia's Surveillance State." *World Policy Journal*, Vol. 30, Issue 3.

Slipchenko, V., "Information Resources and Information Confrontation: Their Evolution, Role, and Place in Future War." *Armeyskiy Sbornik* (Army Journal), No. 10.

Standish, R., "'Russia's Political Transition Has Arrived Ahead of Schedule.'" https://foreignpolicy.com/2020/01/15/russia-political-transition-ahead-schedule-putin-government-resign-constitution/.

Stoddart, K., Jones, K., Soulsby, H., Blyth, A., Eden, P., Burnap, P., and Cherdantseva, Y., "Live Free or Die Hard: U.S.–UK Cybersecurity Policies." *Political Science Quarterly* Vol. 131, Issue 4.

Stoddart, K., "Russia's Cyber Campaigns and the Ukraine War: From the 'Gray Zone' to the 'Red Zone', *Applied Cybersecurity & Internet Governance*, Vol. 3, No. 1.

Stout, M., "Covert Action in the Age of Social Media." *Georgetown Journal of International Affairs*, Vol. 18, No. 2.
Sukhankin, S., "Wagner Group in Libya: Weapon of War or Geopolitical Tool?" *Terrorism Monitor*, Vol. 11, Issue 13.
Tal, A. and Siman-Tov, D., "HUMINT in the Cybernetic Era: Gaming in Two Worlds." *Military and Strategic Affairs*, Vol. 7, No. 3.
Tang, S., "The Security Dilemma: A Conceptual Analysis." *Security Studies*, Vol. 18, Issue 3.
Therme, C., "Iran and Russia in the Middle East: Toward a Regional Alliance?" *Middle East Journal*, Vol. 72, No. 4.
Thomas, T., "Thinking Like a Russian Officer: Basic Factors and Contemporary Thinking on the Nature of War." https://community.apan.org/wg/tradoc-g2/fmso/m/fmso-monographs/194971.
Thomas, T.L., "Russia's Information Warfare Structure: Understanding the Roles of the Security Council, FAPSI, the State Technical Commission and the Military", *European Security*, Vol.7, No. I.
Tkacheva, T., and Golosov, G.V., "United Russia's Primaries and the Strength of Political Machines in the Regions of Russia: Evidence from the 2016 Duma Elections." *Europe-Asia Studies*, Vol. 71, Issue 5.
Tokbaeva, D., "Media Entrepreneurs and Market Dynamics: Case of Russian Media Markets." *Journal of Media Management and Entrepreneurship*, Vol. 1, Issue 1.
Triesman, D., "Putin's Silovarchs." *Orbis*, Vol. 51, Issue 1.
van der Vet, F., "'When They Come for You': Legal Mobilization in New Authoritarian Russia." *Law & Society Review*, Vol. 52, Issue 2.
Ven Bruusgaard, K., "Crimea and Russia's Strategic Overhaul." *Parameters*, Vol. 44, No. 3.
Wagner, T. D., Mahbub, K., Palomar, E., and Abdallah, A. E., "Cyber Threat Intelligence Sharing: Survey and Research Directions." *Computers & Security*, Vol. 87.
Warner, M., "A Matter of Trust: Covert Action Reconsidered", *Studies in Intelligence*, Vol. 63, No. 4.
Warner-Søderholm, G., Bertsch, A., Sawe, E., Lee, D., Wolfe, T., Meyer, J., and Fatilua, U. N., "Who Trusts Social Media?" *Computers in Human Behavior*, Vol. 81.
Way, L., "The Real Causes of the Color Revolutions." *Journal of Democracy*, Vol. 19, No. 3.
Wiswesser, S. M., "Potemkin on the Dnieper: The Failure of Russian Airpower in the Ukraine War." *Small Wars & Insurgencies*, Vol. 34, Issue 7.
Wigell, M., "Hybrid Interference as a Wedge Strategy: A Theory of External Interference in Liberal Democracy." *International Affairs*, Vol. 95, Issue 2.
Wigell, M., and Vihma, A., "Geopolitics versus Geoeconomics: The Case of Russia's Geostrategy and Its Effects on the EU," *International Affairs*, Vol. 92, Issue 3.
Willett, M., "Lessons of the SolarWinds Hack, *Survival*, Vol. 63, No. 2.
Wilner, A., "Cyber Deterrence and Critical-Infrastructure Protection: Expectation, Application, and Limitation." *Comparative Strategy*, Vol. 36, No. 4.
Wilson, P., "The Myth of International Humanitarian Law." *International Affairs*, Vol. 93, Issue 3.
Zhu, B., Joseph, A., and Sastry, S., "A Taxonomy of Cyber Attacks on SCADA Systems." 2011 IEEE International Conferences on Internet of Things, and Cyber, Physical and Social Computing. https://ieeexplore.ieee.org/stamp/stamp.jsp?tp=&arnumber=6142258.
Zoubir, Y. H., "The Protracted Civil War in Libya: The Role of Outside Powers." *Insight Turkey*, Vol. 22, No. 4.

Zygar, M., “The Russian Reset That Never Was: How Palace Intrigues in the Kremlin, the Death of Qaddafi, and War in Ukraine Ushered in a New Era of Mistrust between Russia and the United States under Obama.” *Foreign Policy*, December 9, 2016.

Mainstream news sources (newspaper reports, magazines and periodicals)

Abeshouse, B., “Troll factories, bots and fake news: Inside the Wild West of social media.” https://www.aljazeera.com/blogs/americas/2018/02/troll-factories-bots-fake-news-wild-west-social-media-180207061815575.html.

ABC News, “Trump/Russia: Follow the money (1/3) | Four Corners.” https://www.youtube.com/watch?v=XwvjkJXaIJE&feature=youtu.be.

ABC News In-depth, “How Cyber-Crime Has Become Organised Warfare | Four Corners.” https://www.youtube.com/watch?v=4m6YdxOTGMY.

Addley, E., “The seven-year itch: Assange’s awkward stay in the embassy.” https://www.theguardian.com/media/2019/apr/11/how-ecuador-lost-patience-with-houseguest-julian-assange.

Aitkenhead, D., “Nigel Farage: ‘They say I’m toxic. Quite the opposite.’” https://www.theguardian.com/politics/2016/may/20/nigel-farage-ukip-eu-referendum-interview-vote-leave-brief-every-day.

“Alex Jones Of ‘Infowars,’ Conspiracy Theories, And Trump Campaign (Full) | Megyn Kelly | NBC News.” https://www.youtube.com/watch?v=-HzOqZeX3Yk.

Anonymous, “Alexander Litvinenko was ‘a paid consultant’ for MI6.” https://www.bbc.co.uk/news/uk-31096849.

Anonymous, “Alexander Litvinenko: Profile of murdered Russian spy.” https://www.bbc.co.uk/news/uk-19647226.

Anonymous, “Antler baths and isolation. As Putin approaches 70, investigative journalists look into the state of his health.” https://meduza.io/en/feature/2022/04/01/antler-baths-and-isolation.

Anonymous, “Bellingcat Names Second GRU Agent In Failed Montenegrin Coup.” https://www.rferl.org/a/montenegro-bellingcat-coup-/29616265.html.

Anonymous, “Boris Berezovsky.” https://www.telegraph.co.uk/news/worldnews/europe/russia/9950088/Boris-Berezovsky.html.

Anonymous, “Brexit: Leave.EU and Arron Banks’ firm fined £120,000 over data breaches.” https://www.bbc.co.uk/news/uk-politics-47087440.

Anonymous, “Carole Cadwalladr ordered to pay £1.2 m costs in Arron Banks libel trial.” https://www.bbc.co.uk/news/uk-65644475.

Anonymous, “Cyber-thieves cash in from malware.” http://www.bbc.co.uk/news/technology-33048949.

Anonymous, “Cyber-thieves turn to ‘invisible net’ to set up attacks.” https://www.bbc.co.uk/news/technology-47319971.

Anonymous, “Darya Dugina: Daughter of Putin ally killed in Moscow blast.” https://www.bbc.co.uk/news/world-europe-62621509.

Anonymous, Energy firms hacked by “cyber-espionage group Dragonfly.” http://www.bbc.co.uk/news/technology-28106478.

Anonymous, "EU Referendum: How the bookies got it so wrong over Brexit." https://www.independent.co.uk/news/uk/politics/eu-referendum-brexit-how-the-bookies-got-eu-referendum-odds-so-wrong-40-million-bet-a7100856.html.

Anonymous, "Facebook moderation firm Cognizant quits." https://www.bbc.co.uk/news/technology-50247540.

Anonymous, "Facebook reveals preparations for UK election." https://www.bbc.co.uk/news/technology-50128055.

Anonymous, "Full report: Skripal Poisoning Suspect Dr. Alexander Mishkin, Hero of Russia." https://www.bellingcat.com/news/uk-and-europe/2018/10/09/full-report-skripal-poisoning-suspect-dr-alexander-mishkin-hero-russia/.

Anonymous, "General election 2019: Boris Johnson quizzed on Russia, flooding and his children." https://www.bbc.co.uk/news/election-2019-50433574.

Anonymous, "General election 2019: No 10 denies suppressing Russia interference report." https://www.bbc.co.uk/news/uk-politics-50300551.

Anonymous, "How Russian bots appear in your timeline." https://www.bbc.co.uk/news/technology-41982569.

Anonymous, "'I consider the president a war criminal.' An escaped Federal Guard communications officer speaks about Putin's obsession with secrecy and self-preservation." https://meduza.io/en/feature/2023/04/04/i-consider-the-president-a-war-criminal.

Anonymous, "Inside the Internet Research Agency's lie machine." https://www.economist.com/briefing/2018/02/22/inside-the-internet-research-agencys-lie-machine.

Anonymous, "Julian Assange: Campaigner or attention-seeker?" https://www.bbc.co.uk/news/world-11047811.

Anonymous, "Julian Assange: Sweden drops rape investigation." https://www.bbc.co.uk/news/world-europe-50473792.

Anonymous, "Julian Assange to stay in prison over absconding fears." https://www.bbc.co.uk/news/uk-49689167.

Anonymous, "Liberty Reserve digital cash chief jailed for 20 years." http://www.bbc.co.uk/news/technology-36247289.

Anonymous, "Litvinenko poisoning and a journalist gunned down: The critics of Vladimir Putin who met untimely deaths." https://news.sky.com/story/litvinenko-poisoning-and-a-journalist-gunned-down-the-critics-of-vladimir-putin-who-met-untimely-deaths-12946525.

Anonymous, "MPs call for laws to protect elections against online interference." https://www.bbc.co.uk/news/uk-politics-48834193.

Anonymous, "Netherlands expels two Russians after uncovering 'espionage network.'" https://www.bbc.co.uk/news/world-europe-55258790.

Anonymous, "Nigel Farage gave Julian Assange data on USB stick, US congressional enquiry hears." https://www.france24.com/en/20180120-usa-uk-nigel-farage-julian-assange-secret-meetings-congressional-enquiry.

Anonymous, "Nigel Farage launches Brexit Party ahead of European elections." https://www.bbc.co.uk/news/uk-politics-47907350,

Anonymous, "Nigel Farage's funding secrets revealed." https://www.channel4.com/news/nigel-farages-funding-secrets-revealed.

Anonymous, "Profile: Mikhail Khodorkovsky." https://www.bbc.co.uk/news/world-europe-12082222.

Anonymous, "Profile: Russia's SVR intelligence agency." https://www.bbc.co.uk/news/10447308.

Anonymous, "Putin claims victory in election with no serious competition." https://www.dw.com/en/putin-claims-victory-in-election-with-no-serious-competition/a-68597661.

Anonymous, "Putin Gives GRU Boosted Role in Ukraine – Report." https://www.themoscowtimes.com/2022/05/11/putin-elevates-gru-in-ukraine-intelligence-gathering-report-a77632.

Anonymous, "Putin reappoints his prime minister, a technocrat who has kept a low political profile." https://apnews.com/article/russia-cabinet-appointment-putin-5915b06308d722e17a875892a6d1bdb5.

Anonymous, "Russian military admits significant cyber-war effort." http://www.bbc.co.uk/news/world-europe-39062663.

Anonymous, "Russia's Medvedev: 185,000 new contract soldiers have joined armed forces this year." https://www.reuters.com/world/europe/russias-medvedev-185000-new-contract-soldiers-have-joined-armed-forces-this-year-2023-07-04/.

Anonymous, "Russia 'set to U-turn on support for Scottish independence.'" https://www.scotsman.com/news/politics/russia-set-to-u-turn-on-support-for-scottish-independence-1449947.

Anonymous, "Russian-backed Sputnik TV channel lands in Edinburgh." https://www.scotsman.com/news/politics/russian-backed-sputnik-tv-channel-lands-in-edinburgh-870723.

Anonymous, "Russia-US espionage: Details emerge of 'extracted spy.'" https://www.bbc.co.uk/news/world-us-canada-49651576.

Anonymous, "Salisbury Novichok-poisoned officer Nick Bailey quits." https://www.bbc.co.uk/news/uk-england-wiltshire-54582981.

Anonymous, "Skripal Suspect Boshirov Identified as GRU Colonel Anatoliy Chepiga." https://www.bellingcat.com/news/uk-and-europe/2018/09/26/skripal-suspect-boshirov-identified-gru-colonel-anatoliy-chepiga/.

Anonymous, "Suspected JP Morgan hacker arrested after returning from Moscow." https://www.cbsnews.com/news/joshua-samuel-aaron-suspected-jp-morgan-hacker-arrested-after-returning-from-moscow/.

Anonymous, "That extra-heavy load. Instead of flying, Vladimir Putin prefers to travel around Russia by armored train (allegedly for fear of Ukrainian attack)." https://meduza.io/en/feature/2023/02/13/that-extra-heavy-load.

Anonymous, "The "Criminal Russia' Party Meduza summarizes Ilya Yashin's new report on corruption in Russia's ruling political party." https://meduza.io/en/feature/2016/08/31/the-criminal-russia-party.

Anonymous, "The Real Russia. Today. The head of Russia's GRU is dead, funny Health Ministry promos, and a 'baby murder' controversy." https://meduza.io/en/brief/2018/11/22/the-real-russia-today.

Anonymous, "Third Skripal Suspect Linked to 2015 Bulgaria Poisoning." https://www.bellingcat.com/news/uk-and-europe/2019/02/07/third-skripal-suspect-linked-to-2015-bulgaria-poisoning/.

Anonymous, "UK cyber-defence chief accuses Russia of hack attacks." https://www.bbc.co.uk/news/technology-41997262.

Anonymous, "US fuel pipeline hackers 'didn't mean to create problems.'" https://www.bbc.co.uk/news/business-57050690.

Anonymous, "Vladimir Putin: I moonlighted as a taxi driver in the 1990s." https://www.bbc.co.uk/news/world-europe-59629670.

Anonymous, "Wikileaks: Russia branded 'mafia state' in cables." https://www.bbc.co.uk/news/world-us-canada-11893886.

Anonymous, "Yevgeny Prigozhin: Who could become the new Wagner boss?" https://news.sky.com/video/yevgeny-prigozhin-who-could-become-the-new-wagner-boss-12947295.

Anonymous, "Zuckerberg: Facebook In 'Arms Race' With Russia-Backed Groups." https://www.rferl.org/a/zuckerberg-russia-election/29157227.html.

Atwood, K., Conte, M., and Cole, D., "Russia has spent over $300 million on influencing foreign elections since 2014, US officials say." https://edition.cnn.com/2022/09/13/politics/russia-foreign-elections-influence/index.html.

Ansari, A., and Dewan, A., "How Michael Flynn lost his job in 23 days." https://edition.cnn.com/2017/02/14/politics/michael-flynn-resigns-timeline/index.html.

Baranovskaya, S., "Moscow's cyber-defense How the Russian government plans to protect the country from the coming cyberwar." https://meduza.io/en/feature/2017/07/19/moscow-s-cyber-defense.

Barnes, J. E., Goldman, A., and Sanger, D. E., "C.I.A. Informant Extracted from Russia Had Sent Secrets to U.S. for Decades." https://www.nytimes.com/2019/09/09/us/politics/cia-informant-russia.html?action=click&module=Top%20Stories&pgtype=Homepage.

BBC "Tribe" series, https://www.bbc.co.uk/tribe/tribes/nenets/.

Becker, R. A., "Cyber Attack on German Steel Mill Leads to 'Massive' Real World Damage." https://www.pbs.org/wgbh/nova/article/cyber-attack-german-steel-mill-leads-massive-real-world-damage/.

Belton, C., "American creating deepfakes targeting Harris works with Russian intel, documents show." https://www.washingtonpost.com/world/2024/10/23/dougan-russian-disinformation-harris/.

Bennett, I., "'Panic' in Russia as rouble slips to symbolic mark against US dollar." https://news.sky.com/story/panic-in-russia-as-rouble-slips-to-symbolic-mark-against-us-dollar-13262344.

Bensimon, C., Vincent, E., and Le Cam, M., "France's Operation Sabre in Burkina Faso: From a quiet arrival to a bitter withdrawal. At the request of the ruling junta in Ouagadougou, French special forces have withdrawn from the West African country, marking the end of more than 20 years of military presence." https://www.lemonde.fr/en/le-monde-africa/article/2023/02/25/france-s-operation-sabre-in-burkina-faso-from-a-quiet-arrival-to-a-bitter-withdrawal_6017245_124.html.

Bevan, M., and Jones, R., "The drink that started the Mueller investigation: George Papadopoulos and Alexander Downer tell us everything." https://www.abc.net.au/news/2019-05-24/mueller-investigation-george-papadopoulos-alexander-downer-speak/11107712.

Bradner, E., "Trump: DNC hacked itself." https://edition.cnn.com/2016/06/15/politics/dnc-hack-donald-trump/index.html.

Chen, A., "The Agency." https://www.nytimes.com/2015/06/07/magazine/the-agency.html?_r=0.

Bigg, C., "Russian Police Force To Change Its Name, But Not Its Ways." https://www.rferl.org/a/russia_police_change_name_not_ways/2322433.html.

Bisset, V., and Berger, M., "Prigozhin is confirmed dead. What happened to Putin's other rivals?" https://www.washingtonpost.com/world/2023/08/24/russia-vladimir-putin-yevgeniy-prigozhin-foes/.

Bloomberg, "Mystery JPMorgan Hacker Is in U.S. Hands. What Does He Know?" https://fortune.com/2018/09/08/jpmorgan-hacker-andrei-tyurin/.

Bodner, M., "Top 3 Successes of Soviet Economic Espionage." https://themoscowtimes.com/articles/top-3-successes-of-soviet-economic-espionage-43360.

Booth, R., Weaver, M., Hern, A., Smith, S., and Walker, S., "Russia used hundreds of fake accounts to tweet about Brexit, data shows." https://www.theguardian.com/world/2017/nov/14/how-400-russia-run-fake-accounts-posted-bogus-brexit-tweets.

Borger, J., "Embassy cables: Where does diplomacy end and spying begin?" https://www.theguardian.com/world/2010/nov/28/where-diplomacy-end-spying-begin.

"Boris Berezovsky's witness statement – full text." https://www.theguardian.com/world/interactive/2011/nov/02/boris-berezovsky-witness-statement-full.

"Boris Johnson dismisses Russian concerns as 'Bermuda triangle stuff.'" https://news.sky.com/video/share-11867604.

"Brexit poll: Almost half of Europeans want own vote on leaving EU." https://www.rt.com/news/342500-brexit-poll-european-union/.

Bruney, G., "Billy Bush Says 'Everybody' at NBC Knew About the Donald Trump Access Hollywood Tape." https://www.esquire.com/entertainment/tv/a28970882/billy-bush-donald-trump-access-hollywood-tape-interview/.

Cadwalladr, C., "Boris Johnson and the Lebedevs: How I exposed the prime minister's defining scandal." https://www.theguardian.com/politics/2022/jul/16/carole-cadwalladr-boris-johnson-lebedevs-prime-ministers-defining-scandal.

Cadwalladr, C., "Brexit, the ministers, the professor and the spy: How Russia pulls strings in UK." https://www.theguardian.com/politics/2017/nov/04/brexit-ministers-spy-russia-uk-brexit.

Cadwalladr, C., "Cambridge Analytica a year on: 'a lesson in institutional failure.'" https://www.theguardian.com/uk-news/2019/mar/17/cambridge-analytica-year-on-lesson-in-institutional-failure-christopher-wylie.

Cadwalladr, C., "Robert Mercer: The big data billionaire waging war on mainstream media." https://www.theguardian.com/politics/2017/feb/26/robert-mercer-breitbart-war-on-media-steve-bannon-donald-trump-nigel-farage.

Cadwalladr, C., "When Nigel Farage met Julian Assange." https://www.theguardian.com/politics/2017/apr/23/when-nigel-farage-met-julian-assange.

Cadwalladr, C., "Who is the real Nigel Farage … and why won't he answer my questions?" https://www.theguardian.com/politics/2018/nov/25/why-wont-nigel-farage-answer-my-brexit-questions.

Caesar, E. "The chaotic triumph of Arron Banks, the 'Bad Boy of Brexit.'" https://www.newyorker.com/magazine/2019/03/25/the-chaotic-triumph-of-arron-banks-the-bad-boy-of-brexit.

Catanese, D., "The 10 Closest States in the 2016 Election." https://www.usnews.com/news/the-run-2016/articles/2016-11-14/the-10-closest-states-in-the-2016-election.

Carroll, O., "Igor Korobov: Death of Russian GRU chief latest in long line of fatal incidents surrounding agency." https://www.independent.co.uk/news/world/europe/igor-korobov-dead-russia-gru-spy-agency-sergei-skripal-yulia-salisbury-novichok-a8646856.html.

Casciani, D., "Woman who spent £16 m in Harrods revealed." https://www.bbc.co.uk/news/uk-45812210.

Cellan-Jones, R., "Facebook and Twitter: Nine Russian Brexit ads found by inquiries." https://www.bbc.co.uk/news/technology-42342216.

Cellan-Jones, R., "Online political ads 'need law change.'" https://www.bbc.co.uk/news/business-48174817.

Chappell, B., "Researchers explain why they believe Facebook mishandles political ads." https://www.npr.org/2021/12/09/1062516250/researchers-explain-why-they-believe-facebook-mishandles-political-ads.

Chappell, B., and Johnson, C., "U.S. Charges 7 Russian Intelligence Officers with Hacking 40 Sports and Doping Groups." https://www.npr.org/2018/10/04/654306774/russian-cyber-unit-accused-of-attacking-opcw-chemical-weapons-watchdog.

CNN, "'Fishy': Former DNI on Prigozhin deal with Russia." https://www.youtube.com/watch?v=JLLZ-nb_9qk.

"CNN gets rare glimpse inside Putin's secret train." https://edition.cnn.com/videos/world/2023/07/10/putin-luxury-train-matthew-chance-pkg-ac360-intl-ldn-vpx.cnn.

Cohen, M., "The Steele Dossier: A reckoning." https://edition.cnn.com/2021/11/18/politics/steele-dossier-reckoning/index.html.

Cohen, M., and Pagliery, J., "Nine months, nine prominent Russians dead." https://edition.cnn.com/2017/03/24/europe/dead-russians/index.html.

Cohen, N., "Farage finds Ukip awful. So what about his more sinister friends?" https://www.theguardian.com/commentisfree/2018/dec/08/nigel-farage-ukip-awful-more-sinister-friends-ted-malloch.

Collins, M., Fritze, J., and Jackson, D., "Trump claims 'total exoneration' from Mueller summary despite lack of answers on obstruction." https://eu.usatoday.com/story/news/politics/2019/03/24/mueller-report-white-house-claims-vindication-ag-barrs-summary/3261486002/.

Collinson, S., "Ransomware attacks saddle Biden with grave national security crisis." https://edition.cnn.com/2021/06/07/politics/president-joe-biden-cyber-attacks-russia-putin-trump-economy/index.html.

Cooper, G., "Leaks reveal how Russia's foreign intelligence agency conducts disinformation campaigns in the West." https://pressway.org.uk/news/295784-leakc_reveal_how_russiaefs_foreign_intelligence_agency_conducts_disinformation_campaigns_in_the_west.

Cooper, H., and Schmidt, E., "Ukraine War Plans Leak Prompts Pentagon Investigation. Classified documents detailing secret American and NATO plans have appeared on Twitter and Telegram." https://www.nytimes.com/2023/04/06/us/politics/ukraine-war-plan-russia.html.

Corera, G., "Long history of deep-cover 'illegals.'" http://www.bbc.co.uk/news/10452384.

Cuesta, J.G., "The battle Russia has not yet fought: The mental health of its war veterans." https://english.elpais.com/international/2024-10-06/the-battle-russia-has-not-yet-fought-the-mental-health-of-its-war-veterans.html.

Cummings, W., "'I did not intentionally lie': Roger Stone associate Jerome Corsi rejects Mueller deal." https://eu.usatoday.com/story/news/politics/2018/11/26/jerome-corsi-rejects-mueller-deal/2114836002/.

Desjardins, L., "Trump faces 4 investigations. Here's where they stand." https://www.pbs.org/newshour/politics/your-guide-to-all-of-the-investigations-into-trump.

Dejevsky, M., "The weird world of Boris Berezovsky: Alexander Litvinenko's inquest has provided an intriguing insight into the dead tycoon." https://www.independent.co.uk/news/world/europe/the-weird-world-of-boris-berezovsky-alexander-litvinenkos-inquest-has-provided-an-intriguing-insight-10117927.html.

Denisova, K., "Who is Sergey Beseda, Russian spy handler leading talks with US?." https://kyivindependent.com/sergey-beseda-russias-negotiator-in-saudi-arabia-and-his-role-in-ukraines-war/.

Derespina, C., "Trump: Russia story is 'FAKE NEWS and everyone knows it!'" https://www.foxnews.com/politics/trump-russia-story-is-fake-news-and-everyone-knows-it.

De Simone, D., "Man who spied for Russia in UK 'discussed killing journalist.'" https://www.bbc.co.uk/news/articles/c20gvl0x8yyo.

De Simone, D., and Walker, A., "Bulgarians guilty of spying for Russia in the UK." https://www.bbc.co.uk/news/articles/cx2gx52xqqpo.

Deutsch, A., and van den Berg, S., "Dutch government says it disrupted Russian attempt to hack chemical weapons watchdog." https://www.reuters.com/article/us-britain-netherlands-russia/dutch-government-says-it-disrupted-russian-attempt-to-hack-chemical-weapons-watchdog-idUSKCN1ME14X.

Dewan, A., "These are all the countries that are expelling Russian diplomats." https://edition.cnn.com/2018/03/26/europe/full-list-of-russian-diplomats-expelled-over-s-intl/index.html.

Diamond, J., "Intel report: Putin directly ordered effort to influence election." https://edition.cnn.com/2017/01/06/politics/intelligence-report-putin-election/.

Dilanian, K., and Chistikova, T., "Possible Russian spy for CIA now living in Washington area." https://www.nbcnews.com/news/us-news/possible-ex-russian-spy-cia-living-washington-area-n1051741.

Dobrokhotov, R., Grozev, C., and Weiss, M., "Unraveling Havana Syndrome: New evidence links the GRU's assassination Unit 29155 to mysterious attacks on Americans, at home and abroad." https://theins.ru/en/politics/270425.

Doherty, B., "Julian Assange 'dangerously close' to US extradition after losing latest legal appeal." https://www.theguardian.com/media/2023/jun/09/julian-assange-dangerously-close-to-us-extradition-after-losing-latest-legal-appeal.

Dorell, O., "Alleged Russian political meddling documented in 27 countries since 2004." https://eu.usatoday.com/story/news/world/2017/09/07/alleged-russian-political-meddling-documented-27-countries-since-2004/619056001/.

dos Santos, N., "UK inquiry was warned of Russian infiltration, leaked testimony shows." https://edition.cnn.com/2019/11/08/uk/uk-russia-inquiry-intelligence-security-committee-gbr-intl/index.html.

Dunford, D., and Kirk, A., "How right or wrong were the polls about the EU referendum?" https://www.telegraph.co.uk/news/2016/06/24/eu-referendum-how-right-or-wrong-were-the-polls/.

D'Urso, J., and Spring, M., "General Election 2019: The Facebook influencers you've never heard of." https://www.bbc.co.uk/news/blogs-trending-50479877.

D'Urso, J., and Spring, M., "How a misleading story about Lib Dem leader Jo Swinson's husband went viral." https://www.bbc.co.uk/news/blogs-trending-50160148.

Dutton, J., "Russia Nearly Captured Zelensky in First Few Hours of Ukraine Invasion." https://www.newsweek.com/russia-nearly-captured-zelensky-first-few-hours-ukraine-invasion-1702156.

Eaton, C., and Volz, D., "Colonial Pipeline CEO Tells Why He Paid Hackers a $4.4 Million Ransom. Joseph Blount says he needed to quickly restore service after cyberattack threatened East Coast supply." https://www.wsj.com/articles/colonial-pipeline-ceo-tells-why-he-paid-hackers-a-4-4-million-ransom-11621435636?mod=breakingnews.

Eckel, M., "For Russia and U.S., Uneasy Cooperation on Cybercrime Is Now a Mess." https://www.rferl.org/a/cyber-crime-us-russia-cooperation-mess/28459178.html.

Eckel, M., "In Moscow Treason Trial, A Major Scandal For Russian Security Agency." https://www.rferl.org/a/russia-hacker-mikhailov-stoyanov-fsb-scandal-for-russian-security-agency/29794092.html.

Editorial, "The Guardian view on political advertising: Time to regulate it, Mr Zuckerberg." https://www.theguardian.com/commentisfree/2019/nov/01/the-guardian-view-on-political-advertising-time-to-regulate-it-mr-zuckerberg?CMP=Share_iOSApp_Other.

Epatko, L., "Once a superpower, how strong is Russia now?" https://www.pbs.org/newshour/world/how-strong-is-russia-now.
Ertl, M., "Germany charges intelligence 'mole' with treason in Russia spying case." https://www.bbc.co.uk/news/world-europe-66727785.
Esch, C., "Doing Putin's dirty work. The rise of Russia's GRU military intelligence service." http://www.spiegel.de/international/world/russia-and-the-rise-of-gru-military-intelligence-service-a-1233576.html.
Escritt, T., "Who is Vadim Krasikov, Russian hitman freed from German jail in prisoner swap?." https://www.reuters.com/world/europe/vadim-krasikov-russian-hitman-sprung-german-jail-prisoner-swap-2024-08-01/.
"EU referendum poll tracker." https://www.bbc.co.uk/news/uk-politics-eu-referendum-36271589.
"EU Referendum Results." https://www.bbc.co.uk/news/politics/eu_referendum/results.
Face the Nation, "Trump in 2017 on Russian hacking: 'It could have been China.'" https://www.cbsnews.com/news/trump-in-2017-on-russian-hacking-it-could-have-been-china/.
Faulconbridge, G., and Osborn, A., "Putin demotes Cold War warrior Patrushev and raises two younger allies." https://www.reuters.com/world/europe/putin-appoints-patrushev-dyumin-kremlin-aides-2024-05-14/.
Faulconbridge, G., and Osborn, A., "Putin taps civilian economist to run defense, replacing Shoigu in surprise move." https://www.reuters.com/world/europe/putin-proposes-sacking-defence-minister-shoigu-parliament-says-2024-05-12/.
Faulconbridge, G., "What is Russia's GRU military intelligence agency?" https://uk.reuters.com/article/uk-britain-russia-gru-factbox/what-is-russias-gru-military-intelligence-agency-idUKKCN1MI27F.
"FBI Director James Comey and NSA Director Admiral Michael Rogers testified at a House Select Intelligence Committee hearing on Russian interference in the 2016 presidential election." https://www.c-span.org/video/?425087-1/russian-election-interference.
Feiner, L., "Twitter bans political ads after Facebook refused to do so." https://www.cnbc.com/2019/10/30/twitter-bans-political-ads-after-facebook-refused-to-do-so.html.
Fox, N., "The Alex Jones Presidency." https://www.nytimes.com/2018/05/25/opinion/trump-alex-jones-conspiracy.html.
Frazee, G., "Read Fiona Hill's full testimony in the impeachment inquiry." https://www.pbs.org/newshour/politics/read-the-transcript-of-fiona-hills-full-testimony-in-the-impeachment-probe.
Frenkel, S., Confessore, N., Kang, C., Rosenberg, M., and Nicas, J., "Delay, Deny and Deflect: How Facebook's Leaders Fought Through Crisis." https://www.nytimes.com/2018/11/14/technology/facebook-data-russia-election-racism.html?action=click&module=Top%20Stories&pgtype=Homepage.
Gatov, V., "How the Kremlin and the Media Ended Up in Bed Together." https://www.themoscowtimes.com/2015/03/11/how-the-kremlin-and-the-media-ended-up-in-bed-together-a44663.
Galeotti, M., "Gangster's paradise: how organised crime took over Russia." https://www.theguardian.com/news/2018/mar/23/how-organised-crime-took-over-russia-vory-super-mafia.
Glazer, E., and Haggin, P., "Google's Tool to Tame Election Influence Has Flaws." https://www.wsj.com/articles/google-archive-of-political-ads-is-fraught-with-missing-content-delays-11563355800.
Graff, G. M., "A complete guide to all 17 (known) Trump and Russia investigations." https://www.wired.com/story/mueller-investigation-trump-russia-complete-guide/.

Graff, G. M., "China's 5 Steps for Recruiting Spies." https://www.wired.com/story/china-spy-recruitment-us/?verso=true.

Graff, G. M., "Indicting 12 Russian Hackers Could Be Mueller's Biggest Move Yet." https://www.wired.com/story/mueller-indictment-dnc-hack-russia-fancy-bear/.

Grozev, C., "Russian Diplomat Who Died at Berlin Embassy is Senior Intelligence Figure's Son." https://www.bellingcat.com/news/2021/11/05/russian-diplomat-who-died-at-berlin-embassy-is-senior-intelligence-figures-son/.

Gerasimenko, O., "Russia police crisis: Burned out, disappointed and demoralised." https://www.bbc.co.uk/news/world-europe-66924404.

Greenberg, A., "'Crash Override': The Malware That Took Down a Power Grid." https://www.wired.com/story/crash-override-malware/.

Greenberg, A., "Everything We Know About Russia's Election-Hacking Playbook." https://www.wired.com/story/russia-election-hacking-playbook/.

Greenberg, A., "How an Entire Nation Became Russia's Test Lab for Cyberwar." https://www.wired.com/story/russian-hackers-attack-ukraine/.

Greenberg, A., "The Colonial Pipeline Is a New Extreme for Ransomware." https://www.wired.com/story/colonial-pipeline-ransomware-attack/.

Greenberg, A., "This Is the New Leader of Russia's Infamous Sandworm Hacking Unit. Evgenii Serebriakov now runs the most aggressive hacking team of Russia's GRU military spy agency. To Western intelligence, he's a familiar face." https://www.wired.com/story/russia-gru-sandworm-serebriakov/.

Greenberg, A., "Your Guide to Russia's Infrastructure Hacking Teams." https://www.wired.com/story/russian-hacking-teams-infrastructure/.

Gunter, J., "Sergei Skripal and the 14 deaths under scrutiny." https://www.bbc.co.uk/news/world-europe-43299598.

Hamilton, F., Brown, D., and Haynes, D., "Spy mystery: Sergei Skripal's contact with MI6 in Spain suggests links to Litvinenko case." https://www.thetimes.co.uk/article/spy-mystery-sergei-skripal-contact-with-mi6-in-spain-suggests-links-to-litvinenko-case-skripal-putin-poison-g0p2l6ptb.

Hackett, R., "Hackers Have Penetrated Energy Grid, Symantec warns." https://fortune.com/2017/09/06/hack-energy-grid-symantec/.

Hackett, R., and Teregulova, A., "FireEye CEO: Businesses Are 'Getting Sucker Punched' in Cyberspace." http://fortune.com/2017/03/22/fireeye-ceo-kevin-mandia-cyber-attack/.

Haigh, P., "Why did David Cameron call a referendum on Brexit?" https://metro.co.uk/2018/12/11/david-cameron-call-referendum-brexit-8231803/.

Harding, L., Simeonova, S., Ganguly, M., and Sabbagh, D., "'Vulkan files' leak reveals Putin's global and domestic cyberwarfare tactics." https://www.theguardian.com/technology/2023/mar/30/vulkan-files-leak-reveals-putins-global-and-domestic-cyberwarfare-tactics.

Harding, L., and Weaver, M., "Three Bulgarians suspected of spying for Russia charged in UK." https://www.theguardian.com/uk-news/2023/aug/15/three-bulgarians-suspected-of-spying-for-russia-reportedly-charged-in-uk.

Harper, T., and Wheeler, C., "Labour asks about Dominic Cummings' years working in Russia. A whistleblower has prompted questions on vetting the PM's top adviser." https://www.thetimes.co.uk/edition/news/labour-asks-about-dominic-cummings-years-working-in-russia-vl6d0w62z.

Haynes, D., "British intelligence involved in Trump election probe, sources say." https://news.sky.com/story/british-intelligence-involved-in-trump-election-probe-sources-say-11825044.

Haynes, D., "Russia report row: Dominic Grieve accuses PM of using No 10 'to spread propaganda and disinformation.'" https://news.sky.com/story/russia-report-row-dominic-grieve-accuses-pm-of-using-no-10-to-spread-propaganda-and-disinformation-11855996.

Haynes, D., "Sky Views: UK has a duty to investigate potential Russian interference." https://news.sky.com/story/sky-views-britain-has-a-duty-to-investigate-potential-russian-interference-11673887.

Haynes, D., "Sky Views: We need to know if Russia's interference won Trump the election." https://news.sky.com/story/sky-views-we-need-to-know-if-russias-interference-won-trump-the-election-11699677.

Helderman, R. S. and Hamburger, T., "Who is 'Source D'? The man said to be behind the Trump-Russia dossier's most salacious claim." https://www.washingtonpost.com/politics/who-is-source-d-the-man-said-to-be-behind-the-trump-russia-dossiers-most-salacious-claim/2017/03/29/379846a8-0f53-11e7-9d5a-a83e627dc120_story.html.

Henry, S., "I worked for the FBI. The midterms could be hacked, but here's the bigger threat." https://edition.cnn.com/2018/11/05/perspectives/fbi-mid-term-elections-hack/index.html.

Herb, J., Cohen, M., and Polantz, K., "Bipartisan Senate report details Trump campaign contacts with Russia in 2016, adding to Mueller findings." https://edition.cnn.com/2020/08/18/politics/senate-intelligence-report-russia-election-interference-efforts/index.html.

Higgins, E., "MH17 – The Open Source Evidence." https://www.bellingcat.com/news/uk-and-europe/2015/10/08/mh17-the-open-source-evidence/.

Hobson, P., "How Europe Became a Russian Gangster Playground." https://www.themoscowtimes.com/2016/05/12/how-europe-became-a-russian-gangster-playground-a52842.

Hodge, N., and Smith-Spark, L., "Igor Korobov, head of Russian military intelligence, dies age 62 – state media." https://edition.cnn.com/2018/11/22/europe/russia-gru-death-intl/index.html.

Hodge, N., "The 'Putin list': A Who's Who of Russia's political and business elite." https://edition.cnn.com/2018/01/30/europe/putin-list-russia-oligarchs-intl/index.html.

Holland, S., and Pinchuk, D., "Trump says he trusts Putin's denials of election meddling." https://www.reuters.com/article/us-apec-summit-usa-russia-idUSKBN1DB04N.

Hollingsworth, M., "Silent strongman Sergey Shoigu is the real force behind Russia's military aggression." http://www.spectator.co.uk/2015/12/silent-strongman-sergey-shoigu-is-the-real-force-behind-russias-military-aggression/.

Hooper, V. "Julian Assange's Release: a victory for press freedom or a perilous precedent?" https://www.spectator.com.au/2024/06/julian-assanges-release-a-victory-for-press-freedom-or-a-perilous-precedent/

"How Brexit could lead to a united Ireland – and wage cuts for thousands." https://www.rt.com/uk/347669-brexit-consequences-republic-ireland/.

"How Trump's Russia interference doubts impact national security." https://www.cbsnews.com/video/how-trumps-russia-interference-doubts-impact-national-security/.

"'I don't care' says Russian foreign minister Sergei Lavrov about election of Keir Starmer." https://news.sky.com/video/i-dont-care-says-russian-foreign-minister-sergei-lavrov-about-election-of-keir-starmer-13173722.

Ings, R., "The TikTokers accused of triggering an election scandal." https://www.bbc.com/articles/cqx41x3gn5zo

Inside Europe: Ten Years of Turmoil. https://www.bbc.co.uk/programmes/b0c1rjj7.

"Investigation reveals content posted by bot-like accounts on X has been seen 150 million times ahead of the UK elections." https://www.globalwitness.org/en/campaigns/digital-threats/investigation-reveals-content-posted-bot-accounts-x-has-been-seen-150-million-times-ahead-uk-elections/.

Jauvert, V., "Faux-diplomates, pseudo-journalistes, barbouzes : l'offensive des espions de Poutine en France." *Le Nouvel Observateur* (now *L'OBS*).

Jewkes, S., and Finkle, J., "Saipem says Shamoon variant crippled hundreds of computers." https://www.reuters.com/article/us-cyber-shamoon-idUSKBN1OB2FA.

Johnson, K., "DNC cyber attack by Russia highlighted delayed response, FBI chief says." https://www.usatoday.com/story/news/politics/2017/03/21/dnc-cyber-attack-russia-highlighted-delayed-response-fbi-chief-says/99455634/.

Jones, S., "Licensed to hack: The rise of the cyber privateer. Russia is increasingly using criminal proxies, say western intelligence officials." https://www.ft.com/content/21be48ec-0a48-11e7-97d1-5e720a26771b.

Jones, S., "The spy who liked me: Britain's changing secret service." https://www.ft.com/content/b239dc22-855c-11e6-a29c-6e7d9515ad15.

Keay, L., "What are PEPs and are banks allowed to close their accounts?" https://news.sky.com/story/what-are-peps-and-are-banks-allowed-to-close-their-accounts-12923419.

Kelion, L., "Why Windows hack is being blamed on Russia-linked group." http://www.bbc.co.uk/news/technology-37847070.

Kelly, H., Horowitz, J., and O'Sullivan, D., "Facebook takes down 652 pages after finding disinformation campaigns run from Iran and Russia." https://money.cnn.com/2018/08/21/technology/facebook-disinformation-iran-russia/index.html.

Kelly, L., and Trevelyan, M., "Putin visits Russian-occupied Mariupol after ICC issues arrest warrant." https://www.reuters.com/world/europe/putin-makes-surprise-trip-mariupol-first-occupied-donbas-ukraine-2023-03-19/.

Kirchgaessner, S., Collyns, D. and Harding, L., "Revealed: Russia's secret plan to help Julian Assange escape from UK." https://www.theguardian.com/world/2018/sep/21/julian-assange-russia-ecuador-embassy-london-secret-escape-plan.

Knight, S., "Life inside S.C.L., Cambridge Analytica's parent Company." https://www.newyorker.com/news/letter-from-the-uk/life-inside-scl-cambridge-analyticas-parent-company.

Korosec, K., "Meet the Russian Billionaires That Took on BP and Won." https://www.cbsnews.com/news/meet-the-russian-billionaires-that-took-on-bp-and-won/.

Krever, M., Ukraine's security service hunts the spies selling information to Russia." https://edition.cnn.com/2022/05/16/europe/ukraine-sbu-russian-spies-intl/index.html.

Krauss, C., "Russia Uses Its Oil Giant, Rosneft, as a Foreign Policy Tool," https://www.nytimes.com/2017/10/29/business/energy-environment/russia-venezula-oil-rosneft.html.

Krever, M., and Chernova, A., "Wagner chief admits to founding Russian troll farm sanctioned for meddling in US elections." https://edition.cnn.com/2023/02/14/europe/russia-yevgeny-prigozhin-internet-research-agency-intl/index.html.

Krutov, M., Dobrynin, S., Eckel, M., and Schreck, C., "Russian Wedding Photos Highlight Novichok Suspect's Security Ties." https://www.rferl.org/a/member-of-the-wedding-russian-nuptials-highlight-novichok-suspect-s-intelligence-ties/30216231.html.

Kupfer, M., "How Russia and WikiLeaks Became Allies Against the West. Some claim WikiLeaks is working for the Kremlin. The reality is hardly so simple." https://www.themoscowtimes.com/2017/03/16/how-russia-and-wikileaks-became-allies-against-the-west-a57443.

LaFraniere S., Kirkpatrick, D. D., Higgins, A., and Schwirtz, M., "A London Meeting of an Unlikely Group: How a Trump Adviser Came to Learn of Clinton 'Dirt.'" https://www.nytimes.com/2017/11/10/us/russia-inquiry-trump.html.

Laughland, O., and Pengelly, M., "Trump-Russia: FBI believed Carter Page 'collaborated and conspired' with Moscow." https://www.theguardian.com/us-news/2018/jul/22/trump-administration-releases-carter-page-wiretap-documents.

Lawford, M., "Why are the Russians leaving London?" https://www.ft.com/content/8685683e-d2b8-11e8-9a3c-5d5eac8f1ab4.

LeBlanc, P., Acosta, J., Diamond, J., and Collins, K., "Trump ordered hold on military aid days before call with Ukrainian President, senior administration officials say." https://edition.cnn.com/2019/09/23/politics/trump-ukraine-military-aid-call/index.html.

Lee, A., "Why is Google hiding one of the UK's biggest political advertisers?" https://www.wired.co.uk/article/google-uk-general-election-ads-best-for-britain.

Lee, D., "Facebook may be 'pivoting' to something worse." https://www.bbc.co.uk/news/technology-48835250.

Lee, D., "Google to restrict political adverts worldwide." https://www.bbc.co.uk/news/technology-50498166.

Lee, D., "Mark Zuckerberg, missing in inaction." https://www.bbc.co.uk/news/technology-46231284.

Lee, D., "Net neutrality rules weakened by US regulator' (14 December 2017), http://www.bbc.com/news/technology-42355666.

Lillis, K. B., Bertrand, N., and Pleitgen, F., "Exclusive: US and Germany foiled Russian plot to assassinate CEO of arms manufacturer sending weapons to Ukraine." https://edition.cnn.com/2024/07/11/politics/us-germany-foiled-russian-assassination-plot?cid=ios_app

Lipton, E., Sanger, D. E., and Shane, S., "The Perfect Weapon: How Russian Cyberpower Invaded the U.S." https://www.nytimes.com/2016/12/13/us/politics/russia-hack-election-dnc.html.

Lis, J., "Brexiters' scaremongering about a European army is just another of their lies." https://www.theguardian.com/commentisfree/2019/jan/25/brexiters-european-army-myths-franco-german.

MacAskill, E., Thielman, S., and Oltermann, P., "WikiLeaks publishes 'biggest ever leak of secret CIA documents.'" https://www.theguardian.com/media/2017/mar/07/wikileaks-publishes-biggest-ever-leak-of-secret-cia-documents-hacking-surveillance.

MacDonald, E., "New Russian Hacks Target US Banks." http://www.foxbusiness.com/features/2015/05/14/new-russian-hacks-target-us-banks.html.

Madhani, A., "U.S. intelligence shows China is surging equipment sales to Russia to help war effort in Ukraine, AP says." https://www.pbs.org/newshour/world/u-s-intelligence-shows-china-is-surging-equipment-sales-to-russia-to-help-war-effort-in-ukraine-ap-says.

Manthorpe, R., "Sky Views: Why Mark Zuckerberg won't ban political ads on Facebook." https://news.sky.com/story/sky-views-why-mark-zuckerberg-wont-ban-political-ads-on-facebook-11849805.

Marocico, O. & Mirodan, S., "How Russian-funded fake news network aims to disrupt election in Europe – BBC investigation", https://www.bbc.co.uk/news/articles/c4g5kl0n5d2o.

Martin, A. J., "Facebook's security chief warns 'not all voices equal.'" https://news.sky.com/story/facebooks-security-chief-warns-not-all-voices-equal-11392482.

Martin, A. J., "'Russia government hackers attacking critical national infrastructure in UK and US.'" https://news.sky.com/story/russia-government-hackers-attacking-critical-national-infrastructure-in-uk-and-us-11334028.

Martin, N., "How Social Media Has Changed How We Consume News." https://www.forbes.com/sites/nicolemartin1/2018/11/30/how-social-media-has-changed-how-we-consume-news/#54fd33b93c3c.

Massie, G., "Anti-war Russian FSB agents have helped thwart three assassination attempts against Zelensky, Ukraine claims." https://www.independent.co.uk/news/world/europe/russia-ukraine-zelensky-assassination-attempts-b2028963.html.

Matlack, C., Riley, M., and Robertson, J., "The Company Securing Your Internet Has Close Ties to Russian Spies." https://www.bloomberg.com/news/articles/2015-03-19/cybersecurity-kaspersky-has-close-ties-to-russian-spies.

McGrath, S., "Romania's top court annuls first round of presidential vote won by far-right candidate." https://apnews.com/article/romania-election-president-georgescu-court-585e8f8f3ce7013951f5c7cf4054179b.

Merchant, N., "US: Russia spent $300M to covertly influence world politics." https://apnews.com/article/russia-ukraine-putin-biden-politics-presidential-elections-03d0ae84fb34833b78b1753d0a9602db.

Meyer, J., "Christopher Steele, the Man Behind the Trump Dossier How the ex-spy tried to warn the world about Trump's ties to Russia." https://www.newyorker.com/magazine/2018/03/12/christopher-steele-the-man-behind-the-trump-dossier.

Meyer, J., "Amid Elon Musk's Twitter changes, why 2024 presidential election threats now pose bigger risk." https://eu.usatoday.com/story/news/politics/2023/07/19/elon-musk-twitter-changes-2024-election-risks/70269226007/.

Mikulska, A., & Hamilton, R., "Nord Stream 2: Energy Security For Europe Or Prelude To Russian Aggression In The Baltic?" https://www.forbes.com/sites/thebakersinstitute/2019/09/03/nord-stream-2-energy-security-for-europe-or-prelude-to-russian-aggression-in-the-baltic/.

Miller, G., "As Russia reasserts itself, U.S. intelligence agencies focus anew on the Kremlin." https://www.washingtonpost.com/world/national-security/as-russia-reasserts-itself-us-intelligence-agencies-focus-anew-on-the-kremlin/2016/09/14/cc212c62-78f0-11e6-ac8e-cf8e0dd91dc7_story.html.

Miller, G., and Entous, A., "Declassified report says Putin 'ordered' effort to undermine faith in U.S. election and help Trump." https://www.washingtonpost.com/world/national-security/intelligence-chiefs-expected-in-new-york-to-brief-trump-on-russian-hacking/2017/01/06/5f591416-d41a-11e6-9cb0-54ab630851e8_story.html.

Miller, G., Nakashima, E., and Entous, A., "Obama's secret struggle to punish Russia for Putin's election assault." https://www.washingtonpost.com/graphics/2017/world/national-security/obama-putin-election-hacking/.

Modderkolk, H., "Dutch agencies provide crucial intel about Russia's interference in US-elections." https://www.volkskrant.nl/wetenschap/dutch-agencies-provide-crucial-intel-about-russia-s-interference-in-us-elections~b4f8111b/.

Mortimer, C., "China to take fingerprints of all foreign travellers entering country." https://www.independent.co.uk/news/world/asia/china-fingerprints-tourist-visits-scanning-customs-a7571871.html.

Mostrous, A., Bridge, M., and Gibbons, K., "Russia used Twitter bots and trolls 'to disrupt' Brexit vote." https://www.thetimes.co.uk/article/russia-used-web-posts-to-disrupt-brexit-vote-h9nv5zg6c.

Myre, G. "'Putin's Chef' Has His Fingers In Many Pies, Critics Say." https://www.npr.org/2019/01/30/685622639/putins-chef-has-his-fingers-in-many-pies-critics-say?t=1566819541250.

Nakashima, E., "New details emerge about 2014 Russian hack of the State Department: It was 'hand to hand combat.'" https://www.washingtonpost.com/world/national-security/new-details-emerge-about-2014-russian-hack-of-the-state-department-it-was-hand-to-hand-combat/2017/04/03/d89168e0-124c-11e7-833c-503e1f6394c9_story.html.

Nakashima, E., "Russia has developed a cyberweapon that can disrupt power grids, according to new research." https://www.washingtonpost.com/world/national-security/russia-has-developed-a-cyber-weapon-that-can-disrupt-power-grids-according-to-new-research/2017/06/11/b91b773e-4eed-11e7-91eb-9611861a988f_story.html.

Nakashima, E., "U.S. officials say Russian government hackers have penetrated energy and nuclear company business networks." https://www.washingtonpost.com/world/national-security/us-officials-say-russian-government-hackers-have-penetrated-energy-and-nuclear-company-business-networks/2017/07/08/bbfde9a2-638b-11e7-8adc-fea80e32bf47_story.html?utm_term=.7823f4ef2368.

Nakashima, E., and Harris, S., "U.S. spies learned in mid-June Prigozhin was planning armed action in Russia. The intelligence fed concerns about whether Vladimir Putin would remain in power and what any instability could mean for control of Russia's nuclear arsenal." https://www.washingtonpost.com/national-security/2023/06/24/us-intelligence-prigozhin-putin/.

Naughton, J., "Has Mark Zuckerberg's total control of Facebook turned into a liability?" https://www.theguardian.com/commentisfree/2021/sep/25/mark-zuckerberg-facebook-senate-hawley-thiel-cambridge-analytica.

Nechepurenko, I., "Kremlin Warns of Cyberwar After Report of U.S. Hacking Into Russian Power Grid." https://www.nytimes.com/2019/06/17/world/europe/russia-us-cyberwar-grid.html.

Newman, L. H., "Russia Linked to Disruptive Industrial Control Malware." https://www.wired.com/story/triton-malware-russia-industrial-controls/.

Newman, L. H., "A Mysterious Group Has Ties to 15 Years of Ukraine-Russia Hacks." https://www.wired.com/story/red-stinger-ukraine-russia-espionage-hackers/.

Newman, L.H., "At DefCon, the Biggest Election Threat Is Lack of Funding." https://www.wired.com/story/defcon-election-threat-funding/.

"Nieuwsuur Zo achterhaalden we de identiteit van 17 Russische spionnen." https://www.youtube.com/watch?v=b39P4WKlwu4.

Noack, R., "How a Dutch intelligence agency secretly hacked into the Kremlin's most notorious hacking group." https://www.independent.co.uk/news/world/europe/netherlands-dutch-russia-kremlin-united-states-robert-mueller-intelligence-agencies-cozy-bear-aivd-a8181046.html.

Norton-Taylor, R., "Zinoviev letter was dirty trick by MI6." https://www.theguardian.com/politics/1999/feb/04/uk.politicalnews6.

Oliphant, R., "What is Unit 26165, Russia's elite military hacking centre?" https://www.telegraph.co.uk/news/2018/10/04/unit26165-russias-elite-military-hacking-centre/.

Oliver, J., Dahlgreen, W., Melley, J., and Verity, A., "Criminals and sanctions-busters exploiting UK secrecy loophole." https://www.bbc.co.uk/news/uk-67276289.

Ong, D., "Russian General Brutally Dies In Ukraine: 'Collected His Guts ... Back In His Belly.'" https://www.ibtimes.com/russian-general-brutally-dies-ukraine-collected-his-gutsback-his-belly-3488076.

O'Neill, B., "Can we finally put the Russia-Brexit conspiracy to bed?" https://www.spectator.co.uk/article/can-we-finally-put-to-bed-the-russia-brexit-conspiracy/.

Ortutay, B., "US says Elon Musk should not be immune to testifying about the former Twitter." https://abcnews.go.com/Business/wireStory/us-elon-musk-immune-testifying-former-twitter-103135605.

Osborn, A., "Putin names ex-bodyguard Alexei Dyumin, a potential successor, to senior role." https://www.reuters.com/world/europe/putin-makes-former-bodyguard-alexei-dyumin-secretary-state-council-says-kremlin-2024-05-29/.

Osborn, A., and Polityuk, P., "Russia prepares reprisals against Ukraine over Crimea blackout." https://www.reuters.com/article/us-ukraine-crisis-crimea-idUSKBN0TD1NI20151124.

Osborn, A., and Tsvetkova, M., "Russian police detain over 800 in opposition crackdown in Moscow." https://uk.reuters.com/article/uk-russia-politics-protests/russian-police-detain-over-800-in-opposition-crackdown-in-moscow-idUKKCN1US2MB.

O'Sullivan, D., "Facebook: Russian trolls are back. And they're here to meddle with 2020." https://edition.cnn.com/2019/10/21/tech/russia-instagram-accounts-2020-election/index.html.

O'Sullivan, D., and Mucha, S., "Hackers bring stark warning about election security to Capitol Hill ahead of midterms." https://edition.cnn.com/2018/09/27/politics/hackers-warning-midterm-elections/index.html.

Pagliery, J., "The inside story of the biggest hack in history." https://money.cnn.com/2015/08/05/technology/aramco-hack/index.html.

Pappas, A., and Berger, J., "Tight-lipped Mueller faces GOP ire over probe's handling, as hearing retreads Russia report." https://www.foxnews.com/politics/mueller-in-capitol-hill-testimony-says-no-trump-russia-conspiracy-no-trump-exoneration-on-obstruction.

Parfitt, T., "Russia launches 'Sputnik' media offensive to counter US." https://www.telegraph.co.uk/news/worldnews/europe/russia/11221511/Russia-launches-Sputnik-media-offensive-to-counter-US-propaganda.html.

Peachey, P., "Director of Europol: "Top computer graduates are being lured into cybercrime." https://www.independent.co.uk/news/uk/crime/director-of-europol-top-computer-graduates-are-being-lured-into-cybercrime-9948990.html.

Perlroth, N., and Sanger, D. E., "Cyberattacks Put Russian Fingers on the Switch at Power Plants, U.S. Says." https://www.nytimes.com/2018/03/15/us/politics/russia-cyberattacks.html.

Perez, E., and LeBlanc, P., "Trump pressed Australian Prime Minister to help with Justice review of Russia probe origins." https://edition.cnn.com/2019/09/30/politics/trump-mueller-barr-australia/index.html.

Perry, A., "Organised crime in the UK is bigger than ever before. Can the police catch up?" https://www.theguardian.com/uk-news/2018/nov/22/uk-organised-crime-can-police-catch-up-national-crime-agency-lynne-owens.

Peterson, B., "Gabbard announces plan to reorganize her agency, cut staff by half Gabbard wants to create "a leaner, faster, and more agile institution." https://abcnews.go.com/Politics/gabbard-slash-director-national-intelligence-staff-50/story?id=124819630.

Polantz, K., "Judge won't dismiss Roger Stone case, but allows him to see unredacted Mueller docs." https://edition.cnn.com/2019/08/01/politics/roger-stone-mueller/index.html.

Polantz, K., "Justice Department drops criminal case against Michael Flynn." https://edition.cnn.com/2020/05/07/politics/michael-flynn-prosecution/index.html.

Polantz, K., and Cohen, M., "7 new things we learned from the Horowitz report." https://edition.cnn.com/2019/12/09/politics/horowitz-reports-new-things/index.html.

Polantz, K., Scannell, K., Liptak, K., Main, A., Kelly, C., Shortell, D., and Perez, E., "Highlights from the new Mueller FBI investigation documents." https://edition.cnn.com/2020/01/02/politics/mueller-investigation-documents/index.html.

Polityuk, P., "Ukraine points finger at Russian security services in recent cyber attack." https://www.reuters.com/article/us-cyber-attack-ukraine/ukraine-points-finger-at-russian-security-services-in-recent-cyber-attack-idUSKBN19M39P.

Polityuk, P., "Ukraine to probe suspected Russian cyber attack on grid." https://www.reuters.com/article/us-ukraine-crisis-malware/ukraine-to-probe-suspected-russian-cyber-attack-on-grid-idUSKBN0UE0ZZ20151231?feedType=RSS.

Polityuk, P., with Ustinova, T., "Exclusive: Ukraine says it sees surge in cyber attacks targeting election." https://www.reuters.com/article/us-ukraine-cyber-exclusive/exclusive-ukraine-says-it-sees-surge-in-cyber-attacks-targeting-election-idUSKCN1PJ1KX.

Ponomarev, I. V., "In Exile, but Ready to Save Russia." https://www.nytimes.com/2015/04/16/opinion/in-exile-but-ready-to-save-russia.html.

Porter, T., "How Do I Love Thee? A Short History of Trump's Praise for Putin." https://www.newsweek.com/heres-all-times-trump-has-praised-putin-708859.

Probyn, A., and Doran, M., "What happened when Trump campaign aide George Papadopoulos sat down with Australian diplomat Alexander Downer." https://www.abc.net.au/news/2018-09-22/george-papadopoulos-alexander-downer-meeting-what-happened/10286868.

Prokop, A., "All of Robert Mueller's indictments and plea deals in the Russia investigation." https://www.vox.com/policy-and-politics/2018/2/20/17031772/mueller-indictments-grand-jury.

"Putin orders nuclear forces on high alert | AFP." https://www.youtube.com/watch?v=R4y_y84nVD0.

Rainsford, S., "European leaders boost Moldova in face of 'relentless' Russia", https://www.bbc.co.uk/news/articles/cx2xzng4rwro.

Rajan, A., "Who will regulate digital political ads?" https://www.bbc.co.uk/news/entertainment-arts-49278999.

Rakuszitzky, M., "Third Suspect in Skripal Poisoning Identified as Denis Sergeev, High-Ranking GRU Officer." https://www.bellingcat.com/news/uk-and-europe/2019/02/14/third-suspect-in-skripal-poisoning-identified-as-denis-sergeev-high-ranking-gru-officer/.

Raphael, T., "Boris Johnson Love Bombs the Other Union. As Brexit pulls the United Kingdom apart, the prime minister is struggling to keep it together." https://www.bloomberg.com/opinion/articles/2019-08-09/scottish-independence-irish-reunification-brexit-helps-both.

Rayner, G., and Bloxham, A., "'Russia spy' Anna Chapman's husband: I thought I knew her." http://www.telegraph.co.uk/news/worldnews/europe/russia/7866824/Russia-spy-Anna-Chapmans-husband-I-thought-I-knew-her.html.

Reals, T., "U.S.-Russia prisoner exchange includes Vadim Krasikov, Russian assassin serving a life sentence in Germany." https://www.cbsnews.com/news/us-russia-prisoner-swap-russians-released-include-vadim-krasikov-murder-germany/.

Reed, J., and Ray, L. L., "Alexander Perepilichnyy possible MI6 links to stay secret." https://www.bbc.co.uk/news/uk-45548975.

Regan, H., Raine, A., Tanno, S., Khalil, H., Powell, T. B., Vogt, A., and Iyer, K., "Wagner head says group standing down." https://edition.cnn.com/europe/live-news/russia-ukraine-war-news-06-24-23/h_4fba079bda68626873593a71edc1a43a.

Reuters, "Russia's Prigozhin admits interfering in U.S. elections." https://www.reuters.com/world/us/russias-prigozhin-admits-interfering-us-elections-2022-11-07/.

Reuters, "Who is Russia's Mikhail Mishustin?." https://www.reuters.com/world/europe/who-is-russias-mikhail-mishustin-2024-05-10/.

Revill, J., "Swiss investigate alleged Russian cyber attack on World Anti-Doping Agency." https://www.reuters.com/article/us-swiss-russia/swiss-investigate-alleged-russian-cyber-attack-on-world-anti-doping-agency-idUSKCN1LV0B5.

Riley, M., Dlouhy, J. A., and Gruley, B., "Russians Are Suspects in Nuclear Site Hackings, Sources Say." https://www.bloomberg.com/news/articles/2017-07-07/russians-are-said-to-be-suspects-in-hacks-involving-nuclear-site.

Riley-Smith, B., and Maidment, J., "Russia 'tops list of suspects' in cyber attack which exposed data of 40 m UK voters." https://www.telegraph.co.uk/news/2023/08/08/election-watchdog-cyber-attack-hostile-actors/.

Roberts, J. J., "3 Security Breaches That Freaked Out U.S. Companies." http://fortune.com/2016/09/21/biggest-security-breaches/.

Robbins, S., "Russia responds to GPS jamming accusations – but such instances are expected to escalate." https://news.sky.com/story/russia-responds-to-gps-jamming-accusations-but-such-instances-are-expected-to-escalate-13423288.

Rogers, K., "Trump-Putin Summit Is Over. The Head-Scratching? Not So Much." https://www.nytimes.com/2018/07/16/world/europe/trump-putin-summit-helsinki.html.

Ross, B., Madden, P., and McFee, M., "Russian spy Evgeny Buryakov deported from United States." https://abcnews.go.com/International/russian-spy-evgeny-buryakov-deported-united-states/story?id=46601947.

Roth, A., "Chelsea owner Roman Abramovich is without a UK visa." https://www.theguardian.com/world/2018/may/20/chelsea-owner-roman-abramovich-is-without-a-uk-visa.

"RT number one TV news network on YouTube with record 7 billion views." https://www.rt.com/about-us/press-releases/record-7-billion-views-rt/.

Ruddick, G., "Should Oxford and the V&A take millions from Ukrainian-born billionaire Len Blavatnik?." https://www.theguardian.com/business/2017/sep/03/len-blavatnik-oligarch-controversy-philanthropy-resignation-oxford-professor.

"Russia's 'Big Brother' Law Enters Into Force." https://www.themoscowtimes.com/2018/07/01/russias-big-brother-law-enters-into-force-a62066.

Rybałt, A., "GRU spy Andrii Derkach and his 'acquaintances' in Poland: report." https://www.polskieradio.pl/395/9766/Artykul/2988956,GRU-spy-Andrii-Derkach-and-his-%E2%80%9Cacquaintances-in-Poland-report.

Sabbagh, D., and Harding, L., "PM accused of cover-up over report on Russian meddling in UK politics." https://amp.theguardian.com/politics/2019/nov/04/no-10-blocks-russia-eu-referendum-report-until-after-election.

Salinas, S., "Congress releases Mark Zuckerberg's prepared testimony ahead of Wednesday's hearing." https://www.cnbc.com/2018/04/09/congress-released-mark-zuckerbergs-prepared-testimony-ahead-of-wednesdays-hearing.html.

Sanger, D. E., and Perlroth, N., "U.S. Escalates Online Attacks on Russia's Power." https://www.nytimes.com/2019/06/15/us/politics/trump-cyber-russia-grid.html.

Sanger, D. E., and Schmitt, E., "Spy Agency Consensus Grows That Russia Hacked D.N.C." https://www.nytimes.com/2016/07/27/us/politics/spy-agency-consensus-grows-that-russia-hacked-dnc.html.

Saprykin, Y., "20 Years of Vladimir Putin: How Russian Society Has Changed." https://www.themoscowtimes.com/2019/08/20/20-years-of-vladimir-putin-how-russian-society-has-changed-a66930.

Schwirtz, M., "Top Secret Russian Unit Seeks to Destabilize Europe, Security Officials Say." https://www.nytimes.com/2019/10/08/world/europe/unit-29155-russia-gru.html.

Sciutto, J. "Exclusive: US extracted top spy from inside Russia in 2017." https://edition.cnn.com/2019/09/09/politics/russia-us-spy-extracted/index.html.

Seibt, S., "Unit 29155, the Russian spies specialising in 'sabotage and assassinations.'" https://www.france24.com/en/europe/20210420-unit-29155-the-russian-spies-specialising-in-sabotage-and-assassinations.

Sebenius, A., and Mehrotra, K., "Microsoft Data Shows Hackers Still Targeting U.S. Elections." https://www.bloomberg.com/news/articles/2019-07-17/state-backed-hackers-still-targeting-u-s-elections-microsoft.

Sengupta, K., "Russia accused of launching hacking campaign during UK general election." https://www.independent.co.uk/news/uk/politics/uk-general-election-russia-hacked-cyber-attack-a7580076.html.

Schecter, A., "Mueller has emails from Stone pal Corsi about WikiLeaks Dem email dump 'Word is (Julian Assange) plans 2 more dumps ... Impact planned to be very damaging,' Jerome Corsi said in email to Stone, say draft court documents." https://www.nbcnews.com/politics/justice-department/mueller-has-emails-stone-pal-corsi-about-wikileaks-dem-email-n940611.

Siddique, H., "English courts get new powers to dismiss Slapp cases against reporters." https://www.theguardian.com/media/2022/jul/20/english-courts-get-new-powers-to-dismiss-slapp-cases-against-reporters.

"Skripal Suspects Confirmed as GRU Operatives: Prior European Operations Disclosed." https://www.bellingcat.com/news/uk-and-europe/2018/09/20/skripal-suspects-confirmed-gru-operatives-prior-european-operations-disclosed/.

Soldatov, A., "Cyberwarfare leaks show Russian army is adopting mindset of secret police." https://www.theguardian.com/technology/2023/mar/30/cyberwarfare-leaks-show-russian-army-is-adopting-mindset-of-secret-police.

Staff, T., "Israeli behind massive JPMorgan hack has moved to country, his father says." https://www.timesofisrael.com/israeli-behind-massive-jpmorgan-hack-has-moved-to-country-his-father-says/.

Stevenson, P. W., "Bob Woodward on Trump-Watergate Comparisons 'Let's see what the evidence is.'" https://www.washingtonpost.com/news/the-fix/wp/2017/05/10/bob-woodward-on-trump-watergate-comparisons-lets-see-what-the-evidence-is/?outputType=amp.

Stewart, W., "Exiled oligarch Boris Berezovsky was murdered because he was about to hand Putin evidence of a coup plot, claims former head of security." https://www.dailymail.co.uk/news/article-3011021/Exiled-oligarch-Boris-Berezovsky-murdered-hand-Putin-evidence-coup-plot-claims-former-head-security.html.

Pilipenko, D., "Facebook must 'follow the money' to uncover extent of Russian meddling." https://www.theguardian.com/commentisfree/2017/oct/09/facebook-russian-meddling-investigation.

Ross, B., and Blake, P., "Fugitive Assange Backs Trump in Questioning Russia's Election Hacking Role." https://abcnews.go.com/International/fugitive-assange-backs-trump-questioning-russias-election-hacking/story?id=44540371.

Sanders, T., "Fake news outlet which spread lies about Southport stabbings has links to Russia." https://metro.co.uk/2024/08/01/russian-linked-fake-news-outlet-spread-lies-southport-attacks-21341702/.

Shirreff, L., "The obscure Russian-linked 'news' outlet fuelling violence on Britain's streets." https://www.telegraph.co.uk/news/2024/08/03/obscure-russian-linked-news-outlet-fuelling-violence/.

Shortell, D., "FBI director: Russia is the 'most aggressive actor' in election interference." https://edition.cnn.com/2018/07/18/politics/wray-russia-meddling-contrast-trump/index.html.

Shuster, S., "The Russian General Who Stands to Gain Most From Wagner's Mutiny." https://time.com/6290766/zolotov-putin-prigozhin-russia-wagner/.

Solopov, M., "'An investigation loves silence' What little we know about Igor Krasnov, Russia's next attorney general." https://meduza.io/en/feature/2020/01/21/an-investigation-loves-silence.

Stubbs, J., "Russian operatives sacrifice followers to stay under cover on Facebook." https://www.reuters.com/article/us-facebook-accounts-russia/russian-operatives-sacrifice-followers-to-stay-under-cover-on-facebook-idUSKBN1X3224.

Symonds, T., "Dawn Sturgess: 'Rigorous' inquiry into Novichok death." https://www.bbc.co.uk/news/uk-england-wiltshire-60873483.

Tarasnova, D., and Smith-Spark, L., "Moscow expels diplomats from 23 more nations as Skripal case fallout widens." https://edition.cnn.com/2018/03/30/europe/russia-diplomats-retaliation-intl/index.html.

Tatum, S., "Report: CIA's Brennan criticized some lawmakers' grasp of Russian interference." https://edition.cnn.com/2017/08/24/politics/cia-memos-john-brennan-congress/index.html.

Tatum, S., and Koran, L., "Smoke spotted coming from Russian consulate ahead of facility closure." https://edition.cnn.com/2017/09/01/politics/russia-consulate-san-francisco-smoke/index.html.

"The far right, disinformation and the Southport riot | The News Agents." https://www.youtube.com/watch?v=KApvOew48FQ.

Thomas, P., Cloherty, J., and Ryan, J., "How the FBI Busted Anna Chapman and the Russian Spy Ring." http://abcnews.go.com/blogs/politics/2011/11/how-the-fbi-busted-anna-chapman-and-the-russian-spy-ring/.

Thomas, P., Dukakis, A., and Meek, J. G., "Mueller's agents asked about Roger Stone, Trump supporter says." https://abcnews.go.com/Politics/muellers-agents-asked-roger-stone-trump-supporter/story?id=55450667.

Tidy, J., "Ukraine says it is fighting first 'hybrid war.'" https://www.bbc.co.uk/news/technology-60622977.

Tidy, J., and Zakharov, A., "The Russian hackers being hunted by the West – BBC News." https://www.youtube.com/watch?v=UG1lJaJsru8.

Tominey, C., "Chris Grayling quits intelligence committee after losing the chance for chairman's role in coup." https://www.telegraph.co.uk/news/2020/08/28/chris-grayling-quit-intelligence-committee-losing-chance-chairmans/.

Toobin, J., "The Dirty Trickster." https://www.newyorker.com/magazine/2008/06/02/the-dirty-trickster.

Tucker, M., "Still standing after 260 m attacks: Inside Ukraine's cyber warfare squad." https://www.thetimes.co.uk/article/still-standing-after-260m-attacks-inside-ukraines-cyber-warfare-squad-pxkqdp3pt.

Turovsky, D., "'It's our time to serve the Motherland'. How Russia's war in Georgia sparked Moscow's modern-day recruitment of criminal hackers." https://meduza.io/en/feature/2018/08/07/it-s-our-time-to-serve-the-motherland.

Turovsky, D., “Moscow’s cyber-defense. How the Russian government plans to protect the country from the coming cyberwar.” https://meduza.io/en/feature/2017/07/19/moscow-s-cyber-defense.

Turovsky, D., “Russian armed cyberforces. How the state creates military detachments of hackers.” https://meduza.io/feature/2016/11/07/rossiyskie-vooruzhennye-kibersily.

Turovsky, D., “What is the GRU? Who gets recruited to be a spy? Why are they exposed so often? Here are the most important things you should know about Russia’s intelligence community.” https://meduza.io/en/feature/2018/11/06/what-is-the-gru-who-gets-recruited-to-be-a-spy-why-are-they-exposed-so-often.

Urban, M., “MI6 set to recruit 1,000 extra staff.” https://www.bbc.co.uk/news/uk-37434131.

van Rosenthal, E. B., “Dutch intelligence first to alert U.S. about Russian hack of Democratic Party.” https://nos.nl/nieuwsuur/artikel/2213767-dutch-intelligence-first-to-alert-u-s-about-russian-hack-of-democratic-party.html.

van Rosenthal, E. B., and Meindertsma, B., “This is what we know about the Russian spies in the Netherlands.” https://nos.nl/artikel/2448320-dit-weten-we-over-de-russische-spionnen-in-nederland.

Saito, M., and Tsvetkova, M., “The Enemy Within.” https://www.reuters.com/investigates/special-report/ukraine-crisis-russia-saboteurs/.

Shane, S., “How Unwitting Americans Encountered Russian Operatives Online.” https://www.nytimes.com/2018/02/18/us/politics/russian-operatives-facebook-twitter.html.

Sturges, F., “Podcast review — Sergei & the Westminster Spy Ring investigates a ‘hostile influence campaign’.” https://www.ft.com/content/5990fd02-5541-48f2-88f7-45235bacfbde.

“Target Settles 2013 Hacked Customer Data Breach For $18.5 Million.” https://www.nbcnews.com/business/business-news/target-settles-2013-hacked-customer-data-breach-18-5-million-n764031.

“The Banks Files: How Brexit ‘bad boy’ Arron Banks was eyeing a massive Russian gold deal.” https://www.channel4.com/news/the-banks-files-how-brexit-bad-boy-arron-banks-was-eyeing-a-massive-russian-gold-deal.

“The day in Brexit: Anti-EU feeling spreading across Europe, study finds.” https://www.rt.com/uk/345891-brexit-europe-polls-farage/.

Vallance, C., “Firm regrets taking Facebook moderation work.” https://www-bbc-com.cdn.ampproject.org/c/s/www.bbc.com/news/technology-66465231.amp.

Vallance, C., “Russian Fancy Bear hackers’ UK link revealed.” http://www.bbc.co.uk/news/technology-42056555.

Velicovich, B., “Why didn’t Obama do more to counter Russia’s interference in our election?” https://www.foxnews.com/opinion/why-didnt-obama-do-more-to-counter-russias-interference-in-our-election.

Volz, D., “In Punishing Russia for SolarWinds, Biden Upends U.S. Convention on Cyber Espionage.” https://www.wsj.com/articles/in-punishing-russia-for-solarwinds-biden-upends-u-s-convention-on-cyber-espionage-11618651800.

Volz, D., and Hosenball, M., “Hackers target presidential campaigns: U.S. spy chief.” https://www.reuters.com/article/us-usa-election-hackers-idUSKCN0Y929G.

Walker, S., “The murder that killed free media in Russia.” https://www.theguardian.com/world/2016/oct/05/ten-years-putin-press-kremlin-grip-russia-media-tightens.

Weiser, B., “Bank Employee Pleads Guilty to Conspiring to Work as Secret Russian Agent.” http://www.nytimes.com/2016/03/12/nyregion/evgeny-buryakov-russian-bank-employee-pleads-guilty-to-conspiring-to-work-as-unregistered-agent.html.

Whitehouse, K., "Russian spy busted in undercover sting gets light sentence." http://nypost.com/2016/05/25/russian-spy-busted-in-undercover-sting-gets-light-sentence/.

Wintour, P., and Harding, L., "William Barr discussed FBI Russia inquiry with UK intelligence." https://www.theguardian.com/us-news/2019/oct/01/william-barr-us-attorney-general-discussed-mueller-inquiry-uk-intelligence.

"Why won't the government release the Russia report? James O'Brien asks the experts." https://www.youtube.com/watch?v=jZYR7n2gpOU&feature=youtu.be.

Wise, D., "Closing Down the K.G.B." https://www.nytimes.com/1991/11/24/magazine/closing-down-the-kgb.html.

Wright, M., "Facebook takes down 130 pages linked to first 'fake news' network." https://www.telegraph.co.uk/news/2019/03/07/facebook-takes-130-pages-linked-first-fake-news-network-uncovered/.

Yaffa, J., "How Bill Browder became Russia's most wanted man." https://www.newyorker.com/magazine/2018/08/20/how-bill-browder-became-russias-most-wanted-man.

Zetter, K., "Everything We Know About Ukraine's Power Plant Hack." https://www.wired.com/2016/01/everything-we-know-about-ukraines-power-plant-hack/.

Zetter, K., "Inside the Cunning, Unprecedented Hack of Ukraine's Power Grid." https://www.wired.com/2016/03/inside-cunning-unprecedented-hack-ukraines-power-grid/.

Zetter, K., "Leaked Pentagon Document Claims Russian Hacktivists Breached Canadian Gas Pipeline Company." https://zetter.substack.com/p/leaked-pentagon-document-claims-russian.

Zetter, K., "New Evidence Links a 20-Year-Old Hack on the US Government to a Modern Attack Group." https://www.vice.com/en/article/vvk83b/moonlight-maze-turla-link.

Zetter, K., "The Untold Story of the Boldest Supply-Chain Hack Ever." https://www.wired.com/story/the-untold-story-of-solarwinds-the-boldest-supply-chain-hack-ever/.

Zinets, N., "Ukraine charges Russia with new cyber attacks on infrastructure." http://www.reuters.com/article/us-ukraine-crisis-cyber/ukraine-charges-russia-with-new-cyber-attacks-on-infrastructure-idUSKBN15U2CN.

Original Russian sources

Address by the President of the Russian Federation, February 24, 2022. http://en.kremlin.ru/events/president/news/67843.

en.kremlin.ru/events/president/news/66181.

General of the Army Valery Gerasimov, Chief of the General Staff of the Russian Federation Armed Forces, "The Value of Science Is in the Foresight New Challenges Demand Rethinking the Forms and Methods of Carrying out Combat Operations." *Military Review* (January–February 2016). Also in *Voenno-Promyshlenni Kurier* (VPK), "The Value of Science in Prediction." https://vpk-news.ru/sites/default/files/pdf/VPK_08_476.pdf.

Putin, V. V. (2014). Address by President of the Russian Federation, 18 March, 15:50. The Kremlin, Moscow. http://en.kremlin.ru/events/president/news/20603.

Slipchenko, V., "Information Resources and Information Confrontation: their Evolution, Role, and Place in Future War." *Armeyskiy Sbornik* (Army Journal), No. 10 (2013).

Slipchenko, V., and Gareev, M., Budushchaya voyna (Future War) (Moscow: Polit.ru Ob"edinennoye Gumarnitarnoye Izdatelstvo, 2005).

Transcripts President Events President of Russia, September 21, 2022. http://en.kremlin.ru/events/president/transcripts/statements.

"Гостайна раскрылась за $10 млн Дела обвиняемых в измене офицеров ФСБ дошли до судаÆ (October 5, 2018). https://www.kommersant.ru/doc/3760232

"Чей медведь? Как связано дело полковника ФСБ Сергея Михайлова с разоблачением офицеров ГРУ и кибергруппировки Fancy Bear" (October 8, 2018), https://www.novayagazeta.ru/articles/2018/10/06/78097-chey-medved?utm_source=yxnews

Government reports, sources, statements, and alerts

"4 Aggregate IQ." https://publications.parliament.uk/pa/cm201719/cmselect/cmcumeds/1791/179107.htm.

Advisory: APT29 targets COVID-19 vaccine development. https://media.defense.gov/2020/Jul/16/2002457639/-1/-1/0/NCSC_APT29_ADVISORY-QUAD-OFFICIAL-20200709-1810.PDF.

ALERT. Russian State-Sponsored and Criminal Cyber Threats to Critical Infrastructure. https://www.cisa.gov/news-events/alerts/2022/04/20/russian-state-sponsored-and-criminal-cyber-threats-critical.

"Alert (TA17 – 163 A) CrashOverride Malware." https://www.us-cert.gov/ncas/alerts/TA17-163A.

Alert (TA18 – 074 A) Russian Government Cyber Activity Targeting Energy and Other Critical Infrastructure Sectors. https://www.us-cert.gov/ncas/alerts/TA18-074A. and https://www.cisa.gov/news-events/alerts/2018/03/15/russian-government-cyber-activity-targeting-energy-and-other-critical.

Annual Report to Congress on Foreign Economic Collection and Industrial Espionage. https://apps.dtic.mil/sti/pdfs/ADA439091.pdf.

Annual Threat Assessment of the U.S. Intelligence Community 2021. https://www.dni.gov/files/ODNI/documents/assessments/ATA-2021-Unclassified-Report.pdf.

Annual Threat Assessment of the U.S. Intelligence Community 2023. https://www.dni.gov/files/ODNI/documents/assessments/ATA-2023-Unclassified-Report.pdf.

Background to "Assessing the Russian Activities and Intentions in Recent US Elections": The Analytic Process and Cyber Incident Attribution. https://www.dni.gov/files/documents/ICA_2017_01.pdf.

Bowen, A. S., Russian Armed Forces: Capabilities. https://crsreports.congress.gov/product/details?prodcode=IF11589.

Bowen, A. S., Russian Cyber Units. https://crsreports.congress.gov/product/pdf/IF/IF11718.

Bowen, A.S., Russia's Foreign Intelligence Services (January 3 2025), https://www.congress.gov/crs_external_products/IF/PDF/IF12865/IF12865.1.pdf.

Bowen, A. S., Russian Military Intelligence: Background and Issues for Congress. https://apps.dtic.mil/sti/pdfs/AD1157209.pdf.

Bowen, A.S., Russian Military Intelligence: Background and Issues for Congress, Updated November 15 2021. https://www.congress.gov/crs_external_products/R/PDF/R46616/R46616.7.pdf.

"Bulgarian Trio Convicted of Conspiring to Spy for Russia." https://www.cps.gov.uk/cps/news/bulgarian-trio-convicted-conspiring-spy-russia.

CIA Launches Telegram Channel. https://www.cia.gov/stories/story/cia-launches-telegram-channel/.

CIA World Factbook. https://www.cia.gov/the-world-factbook/countries/libya/.

Clapper, J. R., Statement for the Record Before the Senate Armed Services Committee. http://www.armed-services.senate.gov/imo/media/doc/Clapper_09-29-15.pdf.

Colonial Pipeline Cyber Incident. https://www.energy.gov/ceser/colonial-pipeline-cyber-incident.

Committee on Armed Services United States Senate. Hearing to receive testimony on cyber policy, strategy and organization. https://www.armed-services.senate.gov/imo/media/doc/17-45_05-11-17.pdf.

Criminal Finances Act 2017. http://www.legislation.gov.uk/ukpga/2017/22/contents/enacted.

"Cyber-Attack against Ukrainian Critical Infrastructure." https://ics-cert.us-cert.gov/alerts/IR-ALERT-H-16-056-01.

Cyber Threat and Vulnerability Analysis of the U.S. Electric Sector. https://www.energy.gov/sites/prod/files/2017/01/f34/Cyber%20Threat%20and%20Vulnerability%20Analysis%20of%20the%20U.S.%20Electric%20Sector.pdf.

Dawn Sturgess Inquiry. https://www.dawnsturgess.independent-inquiry.uk/.

Defense Intelligence Agency, Russia Military Power Building a Military to Support Great Power Aspirations, https://www.dia.mil/Portals/27/Documents/News/Military%20Power%20Publications/Russia%20Military%20Power%20Report%202017.pdf.

Democracy under threat: Risks and solutions in the era of disinformation and data monopoly. Report of the Standing Committee on Access to Information, Privacy and Ethics. https://www.ourcommons.ca/Content/Committee/421/ETHI/Reports/RP10242267/ethirp17/ethirp17-e.pdf.

Department of Defense. Defense Science Board Task Force on Cyber Deterrence. https://www.armed-services.senate.gov/imo/media/doc/DSB%20CD%20Report%202017-02-27-17_v18_Final-Cleared%20Security%20Review.pdf/

Department Press Briefing. https://www.state.gov/briefings/department-press-briefing-september-13-2022/.

"DHS Statement on the Issuance of Binding Operational Directive 17 – 01." https://www.dhs.gov/news/2017/09/13/dhs-statement-issuance-binding-operational-directive-17-01.

Digital, Culture, Media and Sport Committee Oral evidence: Fake News, 2018, HC 363. https://data.parliament.uk/writtenevidence/committeeevidence.svc/evidencedocument/digital-culture-media-and-sport-committee/fake-news/oral/78195.html.

Disinformation. A Primer in Russian Active Measures and Influence Campaigns. Hearings before the Select Committee on Intelligence United States Senate. https://www.intelligence.senate.gov/sites/default/files/documents/os-trid-033017.pdf.

Elections Act 2022. https://bills.parliament.uk/bills/3020/publications.

"Executive Order – 'Blocking the Property of Certain Persons Engaging in Significant Malicious Cyber-Enabled Activities.'" 2015. https://obamawhitehouse.archives.gov/the-press-office/2015/04/01/executive-order-blocking-property-certain-persons-engaging-significant-m.

Executive Session Permanent Select Committee on Intelligence, U.S. House of Representatives, Washington, D.C. Interview of: Glenn Simpson. https://docs.house.gov/meetings/IG/IG00/20180118/106796/HMTG-115-IG00-20180118-SD002.pdf.

Faces of Kremlin Propaganda: Margarita Simonyan, 2022. https://www.state.gov/disarming-disinformation/faces-of-kremlin-propaganda-margarita-simonyan/.

https://www.fbi.gov/wanted/cyber.

File, T., "Voting in America: A Look at the 2016 Presidential Election." https://www.census.gov/newsroom/blogs/random-samplings/2017/05/voting_in_america.html.

Foreign Influence Registration Scheme. https://www.gov.uk/government/collections/foreign-influence-registration-scheme.

Foreign political donations in the UK. https://commonslibrary.parliament.uk/foreign-political-donations-in-the-uk/.

Global Engagement Center. https://www.state.gov/wp-content/uploads/2022/01/Kremlin-Funded-Media_January_update-19.pdf.

"GRU Hacking to Undermine Anti-Doping Efforts." https://www.fbi.gov/wanted/cyber/gru-hacking-to-undermine-anti-doping-efforts.

Guidance and resources for (Acting) Returning Officers administering a UK Parliamentary election in Great Britain. https://www.electoralcommission.org.uk/i-am-a/electoral-administrator/uk-parliamentary-general-election-great-britain.

Guns for gold: The Wagner Network exposed. https://committees.parliament.uk/committee/78/foreign-affairs-committee/news/196695/guns-for-gold-the-wagner-network-exposed/.

"Havex." https://www.cyber.nj.gov/threat-profiles/ics-malware-variants/havex.

Hearing before the United States Senate Committee on Homeland Security & Governmental Affairs, Testimony of Joseph Blount. https://www.hsgac.senate.gov/wp-content/uploads/imo/media/doc/Testimony-Blount-2021-06-08.pdf.

Hearing before the United States Senate Select Committee on Intelligence, Testimony of Sheryl Sandberg Chief Operating Officer, Facebook. https://www.intelligence.senate.gov/sites/default/files/documents/os-ssandberg-090518.pdf.

Hearing of the House (Select) Intelligence Committee Subject: "Cybersecurity Threats: The Way Forward." https://www.nsa.gov/news-features/speeches-testimonies/Article/1620360/hearing-of-the-house-select-intelligence-committee-subject-cybersecurity-threat/.

https://homeland.house.gov/imo/media/doc/TFESReport.pdf.

House of Commons Digital, Culture, Media and Sport Committee Disinformation and 'fake news': Final Report. https://publications.parliament.uk/pa/cm201719/cmselect/cmcumeds/1791/1791.pdf.

House of Commons Digital, Culture, Media and Sport Committee Disinformation and 'fake news': Interim Report. https://publications.parliament.uk/pa/cm201719/cmselect/cmcumeds/363/363.pdf.

House of Commons Foreign Affairs Committee, Guns for gold: The Wagner Network exposed. https://committees.parliament.uk/publications/41073/documents/200048/default/.

House of Commons Foreign Affairs Committee Moscow's Gold: Russian Corruption in the UK Eighth Report of Session 2017–19. https://publications.parliament.uk/pa/cm201719/cmselect/cmfaff/932/932.pdf.

House of Lords, Select Committee on Democracy and Digital Technologies, Digital Technology and the Resurrection of Trust. https://committees.parliament.uk/publications/1634/documents/17731/default/.

ICO, Investigation into the use of data analytics in political campaigns A report to Parliament. https://ico.org.uk/media/action-weve-taken/2260271/investigation-into-the-use-of-data-analytics-in-political-campaigns-final-20181105.pdf.

Intelligence and Security Committee of Parliament, Russia HC 632. http://isc.independent.gov.uk/news-archive/21july2020.

Intelligence and Security Committee Report on Russia Hansard Volume 667: November 2019. https://hansard.parliament.uk/Commons/2019-11-05/debates/AABC4DE9-4D70-4937-9AF5-D58CE7B0601D/IntelligenceAndSecurityCommitteeReportOnRussia.

Investigation into payments made to Better for the Country and Leave.EU. https://www.electoralcommission.org.uk/who-we-are-and-what-we-do/our-enforcement-work/investigations/investigation-payments-made-better-country-and-leaveeu.

Johnson, D., "Russia's Conventional Precision Strike Capabilities, Regional Crises, and Nuclear Thresholds." https://www.osti.gov/servlets/purl/1424635.

Joint ODNI, FBI, and CISA Statement. https://www.cisa.gov/news-events/news/joint-odni-fbi-and-cisa-statement-1.

Joint Publication 3 – 12 Cyberspace Operations Joint Chiefs of Staff. https://www.jcs.mil/Portals/36/Documents/Doctrine/pubs/jp3_12.pdf?ver=2018-07-16-134954-150.

Martin, C., "'Cyber security: fixing the present so we can worry about the future'. An address to the Times Tech Summit." https://www.ncsc.gov.uk/news/cyber-security-fixing-present-so-we-can-worry-about-future.

https://md.usembassy.gov/national-security-council-coordinator-for-strategic-communications-john-kirby-commented-on-russian-attempts-to-destabilize-moldova/.

"MI6 'C' speech on fourth generation espionage." https://www.gov.uk/government/speeches/mi6-c-speech-on-fourth-generation-espionage.

"Minister for Europe statement: Attempted hacking of the OPCW by Russian military intelligence." https://www.gov.uk/government/speeches/minister-for-europe-statement-attempted-hacking-of-the-opcw-by-russian-military-intelligence.

National Counterintelligence Strategy of the United States of America 2020 – 2022. https://www.dni.gov/files/NCSC/documents/features/20200205-National_CI_Strategy_2020_2022.pdf.

National Cyber Security Centre, Annual Review 2024. https://www.ncsc.gov.uk/files/NCSC_Annual_Review_2024.pdf.

National Security Act 2023. https://bills.parliament.uk/bills/3154.

Nelson, R. M., *The Economic Impact of Russia Sanctions.* https://crsreports.congress.gov/product/pdf/IF/IF12092.

Norberg, J., Khan, I., and Kjellén, J., "Attrition and Regeneration: Russia's Armed Forces at War." 2023. https://www.foi.se/en/foi/reports/report-summary.html?reportNo=FOI-R--5479--SE.

Office of Naval Intelligence, The Russian Navy: A Historic Transition. https://www.oni.navy.mil/Portals/12/Intel%20agencies/russia/Russia%202015print.pdf?ver=2015-12-14-082038-923.

Office of the Inspector General U.S. Department of Justice, Review of Four FISA Applications and Other Aspects of the FBI's Crossfire Hurricane Investigation. https://www.justice.gov/storage/120919-examination.pdf.

Online Safety Act. https://bills.parliament.uk/bills/3137.

Open consultation. Legislation to counter state threats. https://www.gov.uk/government/consultations/legislation-to-counter-state-threats.

Open Hearing: Social Media Influence in the 2016 U.S. Election before the United States Senate Select Committee on Intelligence. https://www.intelligence.senate.gov/hearings/open-hearing-social-media-influence-2016-us-elections#.

Operation Ghost Stories. https://www.fbi.gov/news/stories/operation-ghost-stories-inside-the-russian-spy-case.

Parfomak, P. W., and Jaikaran, C., Colonial Pipeline: The DarkSide Strikes. https://crsreports.congress.gov/product/pdf/IN/IN11667.

Policy paper Profile: GRU cyber and hybrid threat operations. https://www.gov.uk/government/publications/profile-gru-cyber-and-hybrid-threat-operations/profile-gru-cyber-and-hybrid-threat-operations.

Policy statement by Olaf Scholz, Chancellor of the Federal Republic of Germany. https://www.bundesregierung.de/breg-en/news/policy-statement-by-olaf-scholz-chancellor-of-the-federal-republic-of-germany-and-member-of-the-german-bundestag-27-february-2022-in-berlin-2008378.

PROFILE: GRU CYBER AND HYBRID THREAT OPERATIONS, https://assets.publishing.service.gov.uk/media/687a0d96a52cca025ef5be89/Profile-GRU-cyber-and-hybrid-threat-operations.pdf.

Prosecution and Trial. https://www.prosecutionservice.nl/topics/mh17-plane-crash/prosecution-and-trial.

Putin's Asymmetric Assault on Democracy in Russia and Europe: Implications for U.S. National Security A Minority Staff Report, Committee on Foreign Relations United States Senate. https://www.foreign.senate.gov/imo/media/doc/FinalRR.pdf.

Questions for the Record Senate Select Committee on Intelligence Hearing on Foreign Influence Operations Using Social Media. https://www.intelligence.senate.gov/sites/default/files/documents/Facebook%20Questions%20for%20the%20Record.pdf.

Reckless campaign of cyber attacks by Russian military intelligence service exposed. https://www.ncsc.gov.uk/news/reckless-campaign-cyber-attacks-russian-military-intelligence-service-exposed.

Reference Number: JAR-16 – 20296 A. https://www.us-cert.gov/sites/default/files/publications/JAR_16-20296A_GRIZZLY%20STEPPE-2016-1229.pdf.

"Registers of Beneficial Ownership." https://researchbriefings.parliament.uk/ResearchBriefing/Summary/CBP-8259#fullreport.

Registers of beneficial ownership. https://commonslibrary.parliament.uk/research-briefings/cbp-8259/.

Remarks as delivered by The Honorable James R. Clapper Director of National Intelligence "National Intelligence, North Korea, and the National Cyber Discussion" International Conference on Cyber Security Fordham University. https://www.dni.gov/index.php/newsroom/speeches-interviews/speeches-interviews-2015/item/1156-remarks-as-delivered-by-dni-james-r-clapper-on-national-intelligence-north-korea-and-the-national-cyber-discussion-at-the-international-conference-on-cyber-security.

Report of the Select Committee on Intelligence United States Senate on Russian Active Measures Campaigns and Interference in the 2016 Election Volume 2: Russia's Use of Social Media with Additional Views. https://www.intelligence.senate.gov/sites/default/files/documents/Report_Volume2.pdf.

Robert Hanssen. https://www.fbi.gov/history/famous-cases/robert-hanssen.

Russia Cyber Threat Overview and Advisories. https://www.cisa.gov/topics/cyber-threats-and-advisories/advanced-persistent-threats/russia.

Russian Active Measures Campaigns and Interference in the 2016 U.S. Election Volume 5: Counterintelligence Threats and Vulnerabilities, Report 116-XX, United States Senate Select Committee on Intelligence. https://www.intelligence.senate.gov/sites/default/files/documents/report_volume5.pdf.

Russian Hacker Sentenced to 12 Years in Prison for Involvement in Massive Network Intrusions at U.S. Financial Institutions, Brokerage Firms, a Major News Publication, and Other Companies. https://www.secretservice.gov/newsroom/releases/2021/01/russian-hacker-sentenced-12-years-prison-involvement-massive-network.

Russian influence in political campaigns. https://publications.parliament.uk/pa/cm201719/cmselect/cmcumeds/363/36308.htm.

Russian Interference in the 2016 U.S. Elections Hearing before the Select Committee on Intelligence of the United States Senate. https://www.intelligence.senate.gov/sites/default/files/hearings/Russian%20Interference%20in%20the%202016%20U.S.%20Elections%20S.%20Hrg.%20115-92.pdf.

Russia's FSB malign activity: factsheet. https://www.gov.uk/government/publications/russias-fsb-malign-cyber-activity-factsheet/russias-fsb-malign-activity-factsheet.

Sanctions in response to Putin's illegal annexation of Ukrainian regions. https://www.gov.uk/government/news/sanctions-in-response-to-putins-illegal-annexation-of-ukrainian-regions.

Schwarzenberg, A. B., *Russia's Trade and Investment Role in the Global Economy.* https://crsreports.congress.gov/product/pdf/IF/IF12066.

S.Hrg. 117 – 478 — Understand and Responding to the SolarWinds Supply Chain Attack. https://www.congress.gov/event/117th-congress/senate-event/329328/text.

Senate Intel Committee Releases Unclassified 1st Installment in Russia Report. https://www.intelligence.senate.gov/press/senate-intel-committee-releases-unclassified-1st-installment-russia-report-updated.

Singer, P. W., Prepared Testimony and Statement for the Record at the hearing on "Cyber Warfare in the 21st Century: Threats, Challenges, and Opportunities" Before the House Armed Services Committee. http://docs.house.gov/meetings/AS/AS00/20170301/105607/HHRG-115-AS00-Wstate-SingerP-20170301.pdf.

Smith, B., "Russian intelligence services and special forces" House of Commons Library, Briefing Paper Number CBP 8430. https://researchbriefings.files.parliament.uk/documents/CBP-8430/CBP-8430.pdf.

Solanko, L., "Where do Russia's mobilized soldiers come from? Evidence from bank deposits." BOFIT [Bank of Finland Institute for Emerging Economies] Policy Brief 2024 No. 1 (February 21 2024), https://publications.bof.fi/bitstream/handle/10024/53281/bpb124.pdf?sequence=1&isAllowed=y.

SolarWinds Cyberattack Demands Significant Federal and Private-Sector Response (infographic). https://www.gao.gov/blog/solarwinds-cyberattack-demands-significant-federal-and-private-sector-response-infographic.

Special Counsel Robert S. Mueller, III, Report on the Investigation into Russian Interference in the 2016 Presidential Election Volume I of II. https://www.justice.gov/storage/report.pdf.

Special Counsel Robert S. Mueller, III, Report on the Investigation into Russian Interference in the 2016 Presidential Election Volume II of II. https://www.justice.gov/storage/report_volume2.pdf.

Statement of Bill Priestap Assistant Director Counterintelligence Division Federal Bureau of Investigation Select Committee on Intelligence United States Senate "Assessing Russian Activities and Intentions in Recent Elections." https://www.intelligence.senate.gov/sites/default/files/documents/os-bpriestap-062117.pdf.

"Sub-Threshold Activities, Intentions, & Indicators: Insights for MSSA in the Information Domain." https://assets.publishing.service.gov.uk/government/uploads/system/uploads/attachment_data/file/1148447/57_Functions_Excerpt_FINAL.pdf.

Switzerland's Security 2023 – Situation Report of the Federal Intelligence Service. https://www.vbs.admin.ch/en/documents/search.detail.document.html/vbs-internet/en/documents/intelligence-service/situation-reports/NDB-Lagebericht-2023-e.pdf.html.

The Attack on Colonial Pipeline: What We've Learned & What We've Done Over the Past Two Years. https://www.cisa.gov/news-events/news/attack-colonial-pipeline-what-weve-learned-what-weve-done-over-past-two-years.

The Chilcot Report. http://www.iraqinquiry.org.uk/.
The criminal investigation by the Joint Investigation Team (JIT). https://www.prosecutionservice.nl/topics/mh17-plane-crash/criminal-investigation-jit-mh17.
The Litvinenko Inquiry Report into the Death of Alexander Litvinenko, https://assets.publishing.service.gov.uk/government/uploads/system/uploads/attachment_data/file/493860/The-Litvinenko-Inquiry-H-C-695-web.pdf.
The Political Parties, Elections and Referendum Act 2000. http://www.legislation.gov.uk/ukpga/2000/41/pdfs/ukpga_20000041_en.pdf.
The SolarWinds Cyberattack. https://www.rpc.senate.gov/policy-papers/the-solarwinds-cyberattack.
The SolarWinds Cyberattack: Key Takeaways. https://www.rpc.senate.gov/policy-papers/the-solarwinds-cyberattack.
Treasury Escalates Sanctions Against the Russian Government's Attempts to Influence U.S. Elections. https://home.treasury.gov/news/press-releases/jy0126.
Treasury Sanctions Russians Bankrolling Putin and Russia-Backed Influence Actors. https://home.treasury.gov/news/press-releases/jy0628.
Treasury Sanctions Russian Cyber Actors for Interference with the 2016 U.S. Elections and Malicious Cyber-Attacks. https://home.treasury.gov/news/press-releases/sm0312.
Treasury Sanctions Russian Federal Security Service Enablers. https://home.treasury.gov/news/press-releases/sm0410.
United States Senate, Cyber Posture of the Services. https://www.armed-services.senate.gov/imo/media/doc/18-25_03-13-18.pdf.
US-CERT, Alert (TA17 – 293 A). https://www.us-cert.gov/ncas/alerts/TA17-293A.
UK exposes Russian cyber attacks. https://www.gov.uk/government/news/uk-exposes-russian-cyber-attacks.
UK exposes sick Russian troll factory plaguing social media with Kremlin propaganda. https://www.gov.uk/government/news/uk-exposes-sick-russian-troll-factory-plaguing-social-media-with-kremlin-propaganda.
Ulmishek, G.F., "Petroleum Geology and Resources of the West Siberian Basin, Russia", U.S. Geological Survey Bulletin 2201-G (2003), https://pubs.usgs.gov/bul/2201/G/B2201-G.pdf.
Welt, C., and Bowen, A. S., Azerbaijan and Armenia: The Nagorno-Karabakh Conflict. https://apps.dtic.mil/sti/pdfs/AD1147494.pdf.
Welt, C., "Russia: Background and U.S. Policy." https://fas.org/sgp/crs/row/R44775.pdf.
Welt, C., Archick, K., Nelson, R. M., and Rennack, D. E., U.S. Sanctions on Russia. https://crsreports.congress.gov/product/pdf/R/R45415.
Worldwide Threat Assessment of the US Intelligence Community 2016. https://www.dni.gov/files/documents/SASC_Unclassified_2016_ATA_SFR_FINAL.pdf.
Written evidence submitted by Professor Mark Galeotti (WGN0005). https://committees.parliament.uk/writtenevidence/108294/pdf/.

U.S. Justice Department indictments

https://assets.documentcloud.org/documents/5302125/Draft-Jerome-Corsi-statement-of-offense.pdf.
"Buryakov Complaint." Conspiracy to Act as an Unregistered Agent of a Foreign Government. https://www.justice.gov/sites/default/files/opa/press-releases/attachments/2015/01/26/buryakov-complaint.pdf.

https://www.justice.gov/opa/pr/attorney-general-and-manhattan-us-attorney-announce-charges-stemming-massive-network.
https://www.justice.gov/file/1035477/download.
https://www.justice.gov/opa/press-release/file/1328521/download.
https://www.justice.gov/file/1080281/download.
https://www.justice.gov/usao-sdny/pr/manhattan-us-attorney-announces-charges-against-liberty-reserve-one-world-s-largest.
Four Russian Government Employees Charged in Two Historical Hacking Campaigns Targeting Critical Infrastructure Worldwide. https://www.justice.gov/opa/pr/four-russian-government-employees-charged-two-historical-hacking-campaigns-targeting-critical.
Justice Department Leads Efforts Among Federal, International, and Private Sector Partners to Disrupt Covert Russian Government-Operated Social Media Bot Farm. https://www.justice.gov/opa/pr/justice-department-leads-efforts-among-federal-international-and-private-sector-partners.
Press Release Two Russian Nationals Charged in Connection with Operating Billion Dollar Money Laundering Services. https://www.justice.gov/archives/opa/pr/two-russian-nationals-charged-connection-operating-billion-dollar-money-laundering-1.
Russian Banker Sentenced in Connection with Conspiracy to Work for Russian Intelligence. https://www.justice.gov/opa/pr/russian-banker-sentenced-connection-conspiracy-work-russian-intelligence.
Russian National Charged with Interfering in U.S. Political System. https://www.justice.gov/opa/pr/russian-national-charged-interfering-us-political-system.
Russian National Pleads Guilty in Connection with Conspiracy to Work for Russian Intelligence. https://www.justice.gov/opa/pr/russian-national-pleads-guilty-connection-conspiracy-work-russian-intelligence.
Russian National Who Operated Kelihos Botnet Pleads Guilty to Fraud, Conspiracy, Computer Crime and Identity Theft Offenses. https://www.justice.gov/opa/pr/russian-national-who-operated-kelihos-botnet-pleads-guilty-fraud-conspiracy-computer-crime.
Ten Alleged Secret Agents Arrested in the United States. https://www.justice.gov/opa/pr/ten-alleged-secret-agents-arrested-united-states.
U.S. Charges Russian GRU Officers with International Hacking and Related Influence and Disinformation Operations. https://www.justice.gov/opa/pr/us-charges-russian-gru-officers-international-hacking-and-related-influence-and.
U.S. Citizens Convicted of Conspiring to Act as Illegal Agents of the Russian Government. https://www.justice.gov/archives/opa/pr/us-citizens-convicted-conspiring-act-illegal-agents-russian-government.
WikiLeaks Founder Julian Assange Charged in 18-Count Superseding Indictment. https://www.justice.gov/opa/pr/wikileaks-founder-julian-assange-charged-18-count-superseding-indictment.

Intergovernmental Organizations

Conflict prevention and resolution. https://www.osce.org/conflict-prevention-and-resolution.
Council of the EU Press release. Information manipulation in Russia's war of aggression against Ukraine: EU lists seven individuals and five entities – Consilium. https://www.consilium.

europa.eu/en/press/press-releases/2023/07/28/information-manipulation-in-russia-s-war-of-aggression-against-ukraine-eu-lists-seven-individuals-and-five-entities/,
Customary International Law such as "Customary Law." https://www.icrc.org/en/war-and-law/treaties-customary-law/customary-law.
EU imposes sanctions on state-owned outlets RT/Russia Today and Sputnik's broadcasting in the EU. https://www.consilium.europa.eu/en/press/press-releases/2022/03/02/eu-imposes-sanctions-on-state-owned-outlets-rt-russia-today-and-sputnik-s-broadcasting-in-the-eu/.
EUvsDisinfo. https://euvsdisinfo.eu/?s=Moldova.
FATF Guidance Politically Exposed Persons (Recommendations 12 and 22). https://www.fatf-gafi.org/content/dam/fatf-gafi/guidance/Guidance-PEP-Rec12-22.pdf.
IOCTA Internet Organized Crime Threat Assessment [2019]. https://www.europol.europa.eu/sites/default/files/documents/iocta_2019.pdf.
IOCTA Internet Organized Crime Threat Assessment 2021. https://www.europol.europa.eu/cms/sites/default/files/documents/internet_organised_crime_threat_assessment_iocta_2021.pdf.
Mali: New Atrocities by Malian Army, Apparent Wagner Fighters. https://www.hrw.org/news/2023/07/24/mali-new-atrocities-malian-army-apparent-wagner-fighters.
Population, total – Russian Federation. https://data.worldbank.org/indicator/SP.POP.TOTL?locations=RU.
Przetacznik, J., with Tarpova, S., "Briefing Russia's war on Ukraine: Timeline of cyber-attacks." https://www.europarl.europa.eu/RegData/etudes/BRIE/2022/733549/EPRS_BRI(2022)733549_EN.pdf.
Socioeconomic inequality in Russia (2018), https://www.europarl.europa.eu/RegData/etudes/ATAG/2018/620225/EPRS_ATA(2018)620225_EN.pdf.
Speech of Vice President Věra Jourová on countering disinformation amid COVID-19 "From pandemic to infodemic." https://ec.europa.eu/commission/presscorner/api/files/document/print/es/speech_20_1000/SPEECH_20_1000_EN.pdf.
"What is International Humanitarian Law?" https://www.icrc.org/en/doc/assets/files/other/what_is_ihl.pdf.
"WHO reports outline responses to cyber-attacks on health care and the rise of disinformation in public health emergencies." https://www.who.int/news/item/06-02-2024-who-reports-outline-responses-to-cyber-attacks-on-health-care-and-the-rise-of-disinformation-in-public-health-emergencies.

United Nations reports and the UN Charter

Eliminate nuclear weapons before they eliminate us: UN chief. https://news.un.org/en/story/2022/06/1120932.
Office of the UN High Commissioner for Human Rights, The impact of the armed conflict and occupation on children's rights in Ukraine. https://ukraine.ohchr.org/sites/default/files/2025-04/2025-03-21%20OHCHR%20Report%20on%20Children%27s%20Rights%20in%20Ukraine.pdf.
https://peacemaker.un.org/sites/peacemaker.un.org/files/UA_150212_MinskAgreement_en.pdf.
https://press.un.org/en/2015/sc11785.doc.htm.
Report on the human rights situation in Ukraine 1 February–31 July 2023. https://www.ohchr.org/sites/default/files/documents/hrbodies/hrcouncil/coiukraine/23-10-04-OHCHR-36th-periodic-report-ukraine-en.pdf.

UN chief calls for an end to 'nuclear blackmail' and risk of 'humanitarian Armageddon.' https://news.un.org/en/story/2022/09/1127961.

UN General Assembly votes to suspend Russia from the Human Rights Council. https://news.un.org/en/story/2022/04/1115782.

https://www.un.org/sg/en/content/sg/press-encounter/2023-03-08/secretary-generals-press-encounter-kyiv-ukraine-delivered.

United Nations Charter (full text), https://www.un.org/en/about-us/un-charter/full-text.

United Nations Multidimensional Integrated Stabilization Mission in the Central African Republic (MINUSCA). https://minusca.unmissions.org/en/about.

United Nations Multidimensional Integrated Stabilization Mission in Mali (MINUSMA). https://minusma.unmissions.org/en/history.

https://www.un.org/sg/en/content/sg/press-encounter/2023-03-08/secretary-generals-press-encounter-kyiv-ukraine-delivered.

Military reports

1991 Military Forces in Transition. https://archives.nato.int/uploads/r/null/1/3/137881/0300_Military_forces_in_transition_1991_ENG.pdf.

Chesnut, M., "US/NATO-Russian Strategic Stability and the War in Ukraine." CNA Occasional Paper, Russian Studies Program (2023). https://www.cna.org/reports/2023/06/US-NATO-Russian-Strategic-Stability-in-Ukraine.pdf.

Giles, K., "The Next Phase of Russian Information Warfare." NATO STRATCOM (2016). http://www.stratcomcoe.org/next-phase-russian-information-warfare-keir-giles.

Kofman, M., Fink, A., Gorenburg, M., Chesnut, M., Edmonds, J., and Waller, J., "Russian Military Strategy: Core Tenets and Operational Concepts." https://www.cna.org/archive/CNA_Files/pdf/russian-military-strategy-core-tenets-and-operational-concepts.pdf.

Medvedev, S. A., "Offense-defense theory analysis of Russian cyber capability." Monterey, California: Naval Postgraduate School (2015). http://calhoun.nps.edu/bitstream/handle/10945/45225/15Mar_Medvedev_Sergei.pdf?sequence=1.

Ratsiborynska, V., "When Hybrid Warfare Supports Ideology: Russia Today." Research Paper, NATO Defense College, Rome, No. 133 (2016).

Szwed, R., Framing of the Ukraine–Russia Conflict in Online and Social Media (May 2016). https://www.stratcomcoe.org/framing-ukraine-russia-conflict-online-and-social-media.

The Black Sea Grain Initiative: What it is, and why it's important for the world (2022). https://news.un.org/en/story/2022/09/1126811,

The Tallinn Manual. https://ccdcoe.org/research/tallinn-manual/.

Tikk, E., Kaska, K., and Vihul, L., International Cyber Incidents: Legal Considerations, NATO CCDCOE (2010), https://ccdcoe.org/sites/default/files/multimedia/pdf/legalconsiderations_0.pdf.

Zakem, V., Saunders, P., Hashimova, U., and Hammerberg, P. K., "Mapping Russian Media Network: Media's Role in Russian Foreign Policy and Decision-Making." CNA (2018). https://www.cna.org/cna_files/pdf/DRM-2017-U-015367-3Rev.pdf.

Think tank Non-governmental Organizations, and university research sources

"85e Centre principal des services spéciaux (GTsSS) de la direction générale du renseignement de l'état-major des forces armées de la Fédération de Russie (GU/GRU)." https://www.opensanctions.org/entities/NK-4QuWKcAhpWZCgqBKvefro7/.

89up releases report on Russian influence in the EU referendum. http://89up.org/russia-report.

"Alexander Bastrykin Head of Russia's Investigative Committee." https://www.occrp.org/interactives/russian-asset-tracker/en/person/15/alexander-bastrykin.

"Alexander Litvinenko's videotape transcript: protection of organized crime by FSB, part 1." https://tbcarchives.org/alexander-litvinenkos-videotape-transcript-protection-of-organized-crime-by-fsb/

An Evaluation of 2016 Election Polls in the U.S. https://www.aapor.org/Education-Resources/Reports/An-Evaluation-of-2016-Election-Polls-in-the-U-S.aspx.

"An ICIJ Investigation. Paradise Papers." https://www.icij.org/investigations/paradise-papers/.

Anti-money laundering. Politically exposed persons. https://www.lawsociety.org.uk/topics/anti-money-laundering/peps.

Africa Center for Strategic Studies, 32 Million Africans Forcibly Displaced by Conflict and Repression, 2021. https://africacenter.org/spotlight/32-million-africans-forcibly-displaced-by-conflict-and-repression/.

Aftergood, S., Russia Foreign Intelligence Service Expands. https://fas.org/publication/svr-expands/

Aitel, D., d'Antoine, S., Garwin, T., Roos, I., Rostow, N., Sherman, J., and Wagner, A., Russia's Cyber Operations. A Threat to American National Security. https://margin.re/content/files/2023/01/Russia-s-Cyber-Operations---Full-Report.pdf.

Alkis, A., and Goldblum, B., Lessons from Zaporizhzhia: How to protect reactors against "nuclear piracy." https://thebulletin.org/2023/09/lessons-from-zaporizhzhia-how-to-protect-reactors-against-nuclear-piracy/.

Amnesty International, The State of the World's Human Rights Report 2022/23. https://www.amnesty.org/en/documents/pol10/5670/2023/en/.

Anghel, V., "Why Romania Just Canceled Its Presidential Election." https://www.journalofdemocracy.org/online-exclusive/why-romania-just-canceled-its-presidential-election/

Anin, R., "Putin's Bodyguards Rewarded with Land and Power." https://www.occrp.org/en/investigations/8922-putin-s-bodyguards-rewarded-with-land-and-power.

Anonymous, "Russia's GRU: New Chief, Same Goals, 2018." https://warsawinstitute.org/russias-gru-new-chief-goals/.

Arndt, A. C., and Horovitz, L., "Nuclear rhetoric and escalation management in Russia's war against Ukraine: A Chronology." https://www.swp-berlin.org/publications/products/arbeitspapiere/Arndt-Horovitz_Working-Paper_Nuclear_rhetoric_and_escalation_management_in_Russia_s_war_against_Ukraine.pdf.

Balint-Kurti, D., et al., "Leaked Emails Reveal How Putin's Friends Dodged Sanctions With Help of Western Enablers." https://www.occrp.org/en/rotenberg-files/leaked-emails-reveal-how-putins-friends-dodged-sanctions-with-help-of-western-enablers.

Boiko, S., Davlikanova, O., Fedchyshyn, V., Kucherenko, M., Lyvch, D., Ogryzko, L., Pavytska, Y., Yashchenko, Y., "Russia 2032 Scenarios: A Decade Post Full-Scale Invasion of Ukraine Perspectives from A Neighbor Who Knows Too Well." https://sahasec.org/wp-content/uploads/2025/04/russia-Scenarious_10-4-2025-new.pdf.

"Brexit Brief: Article 50." https://www.instituteforgovernment.org.uk/brexit/brexit-brief-article-50.

Baylon, C., Brunt, R., and Livingstone, D., Chatham House Report: Cyber Security at Civil Nuclear Facilities Understanding the Risks. https://www.chathamhouse.org/sites/default/files/field/field_document/20151005CyberSecurityNuclearBaylonBruntLivingstoneUpdate.pdf.

Bernstein, J., Blum, P., Zihlmann, O., Thompson, D., Obermaier, F., and Obermayer, B., The Panama Papers. All Putin's Men: Secret Records Reveal Money Network Tied To Russian Leader. https://www.icij.org/investigations/panama-papers/20160403-putin-russia-offshore-network/.

Bertina, A., "The Rosgvardia (National Guard of Russia): Russia's Internal Guard." https://greydynamics.com/the-rosgvardia-national-guard-of-russia-russias-internal-guard/.

Blanc, A. A., Demus, A., Evans, S. K., Grisé, M., Hvizda, M., Keep, M., Lander, N., and Marcinek, K., "The Russian General Staff Understanding the Military's Decisionmaking Role in a 'Besieged Fortress.'" https://www.rand.org/content/dam/rand/pubs/research_reports/RRA1200/RRA1233-7/RAND_RRA1233-7.pdf.

Borogan, I., and Soldatov, A., "You Broke it, You Fix it—The Kremlin's Spooky Ukraine Negotiator." https://cepa.org/article/you-broke-it-you-fix-it-the-kremlins-spooky-ukraine-negotiator/.

Boston, S. Johnson, M., Beauchamp-Mustafaga, N., and Crane, Y. K., "Assessing the Conventional Force Imbalance in Europe. Implications for Countering Russian Local Superiority." https://www.rand.org/pubs/research_reports/RR2402.html.

Bradshaw, S., and Howard, P. N., "Challenging Truth and Trust: A Global Inventory of Organized Social Media Manipulation." http://comprop.oii.ox.ac.uk/research/cybertroops2018/.

Buchanan, B., and Sulmeyer, M., Russia and Cyber Operations: Challenges and Opportunities for the Next U.S. Administration. https://carnegieendowment.org/2016/12/13/russia-and-cyber-operations-challenges-and-opportunities-for-next-u.s.-administration-pub-66433.

Burns, W. J., "LIX: A world transformed and the role of intelligence." https://www.ditchley.com/programme/past-events/2020-2029/2023/lix-world-transformed-and-role-intelligence.

Carlough, M. and Harris, B., "Comparing the Size and Capabilities of the Russian and Ukrainian Militaries." https://www.cfr.org/in-brief/comparing-size-and-capabilities-russian-and-ukrainian-militaries.

Carothers, T., Is the U.S. Hypocritical to Criticize Russian Election Meddling? https://carnegieendowment.org/2018/03/12/is-u.s.-hypocritical-to-criticize-russian-election-meddling-pub-75780.

CheckFirst, "Unveiling FSB's 16th Center SIGINT Capabilities", https://checkfirst.network/decoding-secrets-through-symbols-how-military-insignia-revealed-russias-hidden-sigint-network/.

Cheravitch, J., Cyber Threats from the U.S. and Russia Are Now Focusing on Civilian Infrastructure. https://www.rand.org/blog/2019/07/cyber-threats-from-the-us-and-russia-are-now-focusing.html.

Chivvis, C. S., Understanding Russian "Hybrid Warfare" And What Can Be Done About It. https://www.rand.org/content/dam/rand/pubs/testimonies/CT400/CT468/RAND_CT468.pdf.

Committee to Protect Journalists, https://cpj.org/europe/russia/.

Connell, M., and Vogler, S., "Russia's Approach to Cyber Warfare." https://www.cna.org/cna_files/pdf/DOP-2016-U-014231-1Rev.pdf.

Conroy, P., Herdegen, E., and Hird, K., "Russian Occupation Update" (August 6 2025), https://understandingwar.org/sites/default/files/Russian%20Occupation%20Update%2C%20August%207%2C%202025%20PDF.pdf.

Cordesman, A. H., and Cormarie, P., "NATO Force Planning and the Impact of the Ukraine War." https://www.csis.org/analysis/nato-force-planning-and-impact-ukraine-war.

https://cpj.org/europe/russia/.

"Customary International Law." https://www.law.cornell.edu/wex/customary_international_law.
"Cyber Threats: Perspectives from the NSA and FBI." https://www.aspeninstitute.org/events/cyber-threats-perspectives-nsa-fbi/.
Dawson, A., and Innes, M., "The Internet Research Agency in Europe 2014 – 2016." https://static1.squarespace.com/static/57875c16197aea2902e3820e/t/5cd14804104c7bb3cafeaa06/1557219339758/The+Internet+Research+Agency+In+Europe+2014-2016.pdf.
DiResta, R., Shaffer, K., Ruppel, B., Sullivan, D., Matney, R., Fox, R., Albright, J., and Johnson, B., "The Tactics & Tropes of the Internet Research Agency." https://cdn2.hubspot.net/hubfs/4326998/ira-report-rebrand_FinalJ14.pdf.
Digital Forensic Research Lab, "Yevgeny Prigozhin: A History of Violence and Propaganda Around the World." https://dfrlab.org/2023/06/28/yevgeny-prigozhin-a-history-of-violence-and-propaganda-around-the-world/.
Djankov, S., "Russia's Economy under Putin: From Crony Capitalism to State Capitalism." https://www.piie.com/publications/policy-briefs/russias-economy-under-putin-crony-capitalism-state-capitalism.
Dresen, F. J., "The Role of State Corporations in the Russian Economy." https://www.wilsoncenter.org/publication/the-role-state-corporations-the-russian-economy.
Eastwood, B.M., "Russia's Nuclear Submarine Fleet Explained In 4 Simple Words." https://www.19fortyfive.com/2025/03/russias-nuclear-submarine-fleet-explained-in-4-simple-words/.
Egloff, F., "Cybersecurity and the Age of Privateering." http://carnegieendowment.org/2017/10/16/cybersecurity-and-age-of-privateering-pub-73418.
EUR 46/5345/2022, https://www.amnesty.org/en/wp-content/uploads/2022/03/EUR4653452022ENGLISH.pdf.
"Federal Law No. 35-FZ on counteraction against terrorism, 2006." https://ihl-databases.icrc.org/en/national-practice/federal-law-no-35-fz-counteraction-against-terrorism-2006.
Fitsanakis, J., "Revealed: Little-known Russian counterintelligence unit that targets foreigners." https://intelnews.org/2023/07/12/01-3294/.
Fomin, I., Mazaeva, M., Beketova, E., and Luzin, P., "The Prigozhin Uprising, the Aftermath, and What Comes Next." https://cepa.org/article/the-prigozhin-uprising-the-aftermath-and-what-comes-next/.
Freire, M. R., "The Russia Factor in European Security: Back to the Future." https://carleton.ca/ces/wp-content/uploads/Raquel-Freire-Policy-Brief_Russia-and-European-security-08-01-2017.docx.pdf.
Frye, T., and Borisova, E., "Elections, Protest and Trust in Government." https://www.econstor.eu/bitstream/10419/212852/1/bofit-dp2016-009.pdf.
"Russia." https://freedomhouse.org/report/freedom-world/2019/russia.
Fuchs, M. H., Kenney, C., Perina, A., and VanDoorn, F., "Why Americans Should Care About Russian Hacking." https://cdn.americanprogress.org/content/uploads/2017/02/13093554/RussianHackingWhyItMatters-brief.pdf.
Galeotti, M., "Active Measures: Russia's Covert Geopolitical Operations", Marshall Center Security Insight, https://www.marshallcenter.org/en/publications/security-insights/active-measures-russias-covert-geopolitical-operations-0.
Galeotti, M., "CRIMINTERN: How the Kremlin Uses Russia's Criminal Networks in Europe." https://www.ecfr.eu/page/-/ECFR208_-_CRIMINTERM_-_HOW_RUSSIAN_ORGANISED_CRIME_OPERATES_IN_EUROPE02.pdf.

Galeotti, M., "Putin's Hydra: Inside Russia's Intelligence Services." https://www.ecfr.eu/page/-/ECFR_169_-_PUTINS_HYDRA_INSIDE_THE_RUSSIAN_INTELLIGENCE_SERVICES_1513.pdf.

Galeotti, M., "Russia's Security Council: Where Policy, Personality, and Process Meet." https://www.marshallcenter.org/en/publications/security-insights/russias-security-council-where-policy-personality-and-process-meet-0.

Galeotti, M. "Siloviki at War: The Russian Security Community Since February 2022." https://css.ethz.ch/content/dam/ethz/special-interest/gess/cis/center-for-securities-studies/pdfs/russiananalyticaldigest-323.pdf

Galeotti, M., "The Intelligence and Security Services and Strategic Decision-Making." https://www.marshallcenter.org/mcpublicweb/mcdocs/security_insights_30_-_mark_galeotti_-_the_intelligence_and_sec_svcs_-_may_2019.pdf.

Galeotti, M., "The Law Enforcement Agencies: Russian Domestic Security and International Implications." https://www.marshallcenter.org/en/publications/security-insights/law-enforcement-agencies-russian-domestic-security-and-international-implications-0.

Giles, K., "Countering Russian Information Operations in the Age of Social Media." https://www.cfr.org/report/countering-russian-information-operations-age-social-media.

Giles, K., "Russia's 'New' Tools for Confronting the West: Continuity and Innovation in Moscow's Exercise of Power." https://www.chathamhouse.org/sites/default/files/publications/2016-03-russia-new-tools-giles.pdf.

Gorodnichenko, Y., Pham, T., and Talavera, O., "Social media, sentiment and public opinions: Evidence from #Brexit and #USElection." https://eml.berkeley.edu/~ygorodni/Brexit_Election.pdf.

Hansen, F. P., van der Noordaa, R., Bogen, Ø, and Sundbom, H., "The Kremlin's Trojan Horse Russian Influence in Denmark, The Netherlands, Norway, and Sweden." http://pure.diis.dk/ws/files/2553319/The_Kremlins_Trojan_Horses_3.pdf.

Harward, C., "Russia's Weakness Offers Leverage." https://understandingwar.org/backgrounder/russias-weakness-offers-leverage.

Hassan, A., "Zaslon: Russia's Most Secretive Unit." https://greydynamics.com/zaslon-russias-most-secretive-unit/.

Helmus, T. C., Bodine-Baron, E., Radin, A., Magnuson, M., Mendelsohn, J., Marcellino, W., Bega, A., and Winkelman, Z., "Russian Social Media Influence. Understanding Russian Propaganda in Eastern Europe." https://www.rand.org/content/dam/rand/pubs/research_reports/RR2200/RR2237/RAND_RR2237.pdf.

Howard, P., Ganesh, B., Liotsiou, D., Kelly, J., and François, C., "The IRA, Social Media and Political Polarization in the United States, 2012–2018." https://comprop.oii.ox.ac.uk/wp-content/uploads/sites/93/2018/12/The-IRA-Social-Media-and-Political-Polarization.pdf.. Also at https://int.nyt.com/data/documenthelper/534-oxford-russia-internet-research-agency/c6588b4a7b940c551c38/optimized/full.pdf.

Hüsch, P., and Jarnecki, J., "All Quiet on the Cyber Front? Explaining Russia's Limited Cyber Effects." https://www.rusi.org/explore-our-research/publications/commentary/all-quiet-cyber-front-explaining-russias-limited-cyber-effects.

Human Rights Watch, "We Had No Choice" "Filtration" and the Crime of Forcibly Transferring Ukrainian Civilians to Russia. https://www.hrw.org/report/2022/09/01/we-had-no-choice/filtration-and-crime-forcibly-transferring-ukrainian-civilians.

ICIJ, "Giant Leak of Offshore Financial Records Exposes Global Array of Crime and Corruption." https://www.icij.org/investigations/panama-papers/20160403-panama-papers-global-overview/.

Institute for the Study of War, "Russian Offensive Campaign Assessment." https://www.understandingwar.org/backgrounder/russian-offensive-campaign-assessment-may-29-2024,

Institute for the Study of War, "Ukraine Conflict Updates." https://www.understandingwar.org/backgrounder/ukraine-conflict-updates.

'International Consortium of Investigative Journalists."
https://www.icij.org/investigations/#_ga=2.33043454.1372029856.1511129892-618484866.1511129892.

International Press Institute, "Will Russia's independent journalism survive the Kremlin's crackdown?" https://ipi.media/events/will-russias-independent-journalism-survive-the-kremlins-crackdown-march-10-2022/,

International Press Institute, "One year on, Russian media survive mass repression." https://ipi.media/ipimedia/one-year-on-russian-online-media-survive-mass-repression/.

International Press Institute, "Will Russia's independent journalism survive the Kremlin's crackdown?" https://ipi.media/events/will-russias-independent-journalism-survive-the-kremlins-crackdown-march-10-2022/.

Jones, S. G., "Russia's Shadow War Against the West." https://www.csis.org/analysis/russias-shadow-war-against-west.

Joseph, E. P., "NATO Expansion: The Source of Russia's Anger?" https://nationalinterest.org/feature/nato-expansion-the-source-russias-anger-10344.

Juurvee, I., "Hybrid CoE Strategic Analysis 7 The resurrection of 'active measures': Intelligence services as a part of Russia's influencing toolbox." https://www.hybridcoe.fi/wp-content/up loads/2020/07/Strategic-analysis-7-April.pdf.

Kabanenko, I., "Arsenal of Empire: Russian Naval Construction in Crimea and Its Implications for Black Sea Security." https://jamestown.org/program/an-arsenal-of-empire-russian-naval-construction-in-crimea-and-implications-for-black-sea-security/.

Kofman, M., and Rojansky, M., "A Closer look at Russia's 'Hybrid War.'" https://www.files.ethz.ch/isn/190090/5-KENNAN%20CABLE-ROJANSKY%20KOFMAN.pdf.

Kramer, F. D., and Speranza, L.M., "Responding to Russia's 'Hybrid' Threat." http://www.atlanticcouncil.org/blogs/natosource/responding-to-russia-s-hybrid-threat.

Krogstad, J. M., and Lopez, M. H., "Black voter turnout fell in 2016, even as a record number of Americans cast ballots." https://www.pewresearch.org/fact-tank/2017/05/12/black-voter-turn out-fell-in-2016-even-as-a-record-number-of-americans-cast-ballots/.

Kaushal, S., "The Death of Gorshkov's Navy: The Future of the Russian Surface Fleet." https://www.rusi.org/explore-our-research/publications/commentary/death-gorshkovs-navy-future-russian-surface-fleet.

Laruelle, M., "Aleksandr Dugin: A Russian Version of the European Radical Right?" https://www.files.ethz.ch/isn/20571/OP294.pdf.

Latham, A., "The Russian Navy Is a Spent Force." https://www.19fortyfive.com/2025/04/the-russian-navy-is-a-spent-force/.

Lewis, J. A., "Reference Note on Russian Communications Surveillance.' https://www.csis.org/analysis/reference-note-russian-communications-surveillance.

Lobner, P., "You Need to Know About Russia's Main Directorate of Deep-Sea Research (GUGI)." https://lynceans.org/tag/military-unit-40056/.

Lohsen, A., and Morcos, P., "Understanding the Normandy Format and Its Relation to the Current Standoff with Russia." https://www.csis.org/analysis/understanding-normandy-format-and-its-relation-current-standoff-russia.

Makhanov, K., "The New Spatial Development Strategy of Russia". https://www.eurasian-research.org/publication/the-new-spatial-development-strategy-of-russia/.
Masuhr, N. and Zogg, B., 'The War in Ukraine: First Lessons', CSS Analyses in Security Policy, No. 301.
https://www.research-collection.ethz.ch/bitstream/handle/20.500.11850/540121/2/CSSAnalyse301-EN.pdf.
Maurer, T., "When States Pretend to Be Terrorists or Hacktivists in Cyberspace." http://carnegieendowment.org/2017/04/18/when-states-pretend-to-be-terrorists-or-hacktivists-in-cyberspace-pub-68703.
Medvedev, S.A.,"Offense-defense theory analysis of Russian cyber capability." http://calhoun.nps.edu/bitstream/handle/10945/45225/15Mar_Medvedev_Sergei.pdf?sequence=1.
Miller, C., "Directing Responses Against Illicit Influence Operations (D-RAIL)."
https://www.disinfo.eu/wp-content/uploads/2024/08/20240818_D-RAIL.pdf.
Miller, C., and Reffin, J., "#IstandwithRussia – Anatomy of a Pro-Kremlin Influence Operation." https://www.isdglobal.org/digital_dispatches/istandwithrussia-anatomy-of-a-pro-kremlin-influence-operation/https://minorityrights.org/country/russian-federation/.
Mizoguchi, S., "The Stability and Vulnerability of the Putin Administration in the 2021 Russian State Duma Elections." www.jiia.or.jp/en/column/2022/02/02/ENG_russia-fy2021-05.pdf.
Nimmo, B., "Anatomy of an Info-War: How Russia's Propaganda Machine Works, and How to Counter It." https://www.stopfake.org/en/anatomy-of-an-info-war-how-russia-s-propaganda-machine-works-and-how-to-counter-it/.
https://offshoreleaks.icij.org/.
Offshore in the UK Analysing the use of Scottish Limited Partnerships in Corruption and Money Laundering, https://archive.transparency.org.uk/sites/default/files/pdf/publications/Offshore_In_The_UK_TIUK_June_2017.pdf.
Organized Crime and Corruption Reporting Project, "The Russian Laundromat." https://www.occrp.org/en/laundromat/the-russian-laundromat-exposed/.
Orlova, K., "The KGB is back. The Siloviki Coup in Russia." https://www.the-american-interest.com/2016/09/21/the-siloviki-coup-in-russia/.
Paul, C., and Matthews, M., "The Russian 'Firehose of Falsehood' Propaganda Model: Why It Might Work and Options to Counter It." https://www.rand.org/pubs/perspectives/PE198.html.
Peisakhin, L., "Euromaidan revisited: Causes of regime change in Ukraine one year on." https://www.files.ethz.ch/isn/188792/5-kennan%20cable-Peisakhin.pdf.
Pry, P., "Insights into the Vulnerability of the Power System." http://mackenzieinstitute.com/insights-vulnerability-power-system/.
Polyakova, A., "The next Russian attack will be far worse than bots and trolls." https://www.brookings.edu/blog/order-from-chaos/2018/03/22/the-next-russian-attack-will-be-far-worse-than-bots-and-trolls/amp/.
Polyakova, A., and Boulègue, M., "The Evolution of Russian Hybrid Warfare: Executive Summary." https://cepa.org/comprehensive-reports/the-evolution-of-russian-hybrid-warfare-executive-summary/.
Polyakova, A., Laruelle, M., Meister, S., and Barnett, N., "The Kremlin's Trojan Horses. Russian Influence in France, Germany, and the United Kingdom, 3rd edition." https://www.atlanticcouncil.org/in-depth-research-reports/report/kremlin-trojan-horses/.

"Putin's Brexit? The influence of Kremlin media & bots during the 2016 UK EU referendum." https://www.slideshare.net/89up/putins-brexit-the-influence-of-kremlin-media-bots-during-the-2016-uk-eu-referendum.

Reichborn-Kjennerud, E. & Cullen, P., "What is Hybrid Warfare?." https://www.jstor.org/stable/pdf/resrep07978.pdf.

Reporters Without Borders, "In a new report, RSF and Truth Hounds reveal Russian strategy of bombing Ukrainian hotels to silence the press", https://rsf.org/en/new-report-rsf-and-truth-hounds-reveal-russian-strategy-bombing-ukrainian-hotels-silence-press.

"Research suggests bots generated social media stories during EU Referendum." https://www.swansea.ac.uk/press-office/news-archive/2017/researchsuggestsbotsgeneratedsocialmediastoriesduringeureferendum.php.

Ritter, Z., and Standridge, P., "Interaction with Local Media Tied to Trust in Local News." https://news.gallup.com/opinion/gallup/266675/interaction-local-media-tied-trust-local-news.aspx.

Rosengren, O., "The FSB: Russia's Federal Security Service." https://greydynamics.com/the-fsb-russias-federal-security-service/.

Royal United Services Institute (RUSI), "Cyber Operations in Ukraine: A Conversation with Victor Zhora." https://www.rusi.org/events/open-to-all/cyber-operations-ukraine-conversation-victor-zhora.

"Russia Events of 2018." https://www.hrw.org/world-report/2019/country-chapters/russia.

Salvo, D., "What Just Happened? Dismantling the Intelligence Community's Foreign Malign Influence Center." https://www.justsecurity.org/119653/wjh-dismantling-foreign-malign-influence-center/.

Segal, A., "China and the Power Grid: Hacking and Getting Hacked." https://www.cfr.org/blog/china-and-power-grid-hacking-and-getting-hacked.

Shearer, E. and Mitchell, A., "Broad agreement in U.S. – even among partisans – on which news outlets are part of the 'mainstream media.'" https://www.pewresearch.org/short-reads/2021/05/07/broad-agreement-in-u-s-even-among-partisans-on-which-news-outlets-are-part-of-the-mainstream-media/.

Significant changes proposed to UK elections – Electoral Commission responds. https://www.electoralcommission.org.uk/media-centre/significant-changes-proposed-uk-elections-electoral-commission-responds.

Silver, N., "How Much Did Russian Interference Affect The 2016 Election? It's hard to say." https://fivethirtyeight.com/features/how-much-did-russian-interference-affect-the-2016-election/.

Silver, N., "The Real Story of 2016." https://fivethirtyeight.com/features/the-real-story-of-2016/.

Sloan, A., and Campbell, I., "How did Arron Banks afford Brexit." https://www.opendemocracy.net/en/dark-money-investigations/how-did-arron-banks-afford-brexit/.

Smith, D., "How Russia Harnesses Cyberwarfare." https://www.afpc.org/publications/e-journals/cyberspace-the-new-battlefield.

Snyder, J., *The Soviet Strategic Culture: Implications for Limited Nuclear Operations* (Santa Monica: Rand, 1977).

Stanovaya, T., "The Putin Regime Cracks." https://carnegieendowment.org/files/Stanovaya_Putin_Elite-Final.pdf.

Špalková, V., "Influence of Russian disinformation operation: Specific examples in data and numbers." https://www.europeanvalues.net/wp-content/uploads/2019/02/Influence-of-Russian-Disinformation-Operations-Specific-examples-in-data-and-numbers.pdf/

Stockwell, S., Hughes, M., Swatton, P., and Bishop, K., "AI-Enabled Influence Operations: The Threat to the UK General Election Briefing Paper." https://cetas.turing.ac.uk/publications/ai-enabled-influence-operations-threat-uk-general-election.

Stoutland, P. O., and Pitts-Kiefer, S., "Nuclear weapons in the new cyber age. Report of the cyber nuclear weapons study group." https://media.nti.org/documents/Cyber_report_finalsmall.pdf.

"The Disinformation Report." https://www.newknowledge.com/articles/the-disinformation-report/.

The Dossier Center, "Governors' Affairs." https://fsb.dossier.center/gubernators/.

The Dossier Center/Atlantic Council, "Lubyanka Federation How the FSB determines the politics and economics of Russia." https://www.atlanticcouncil.org/wp-content/uploads/2020/10/FSB-Report-Printed-Final.pdf.

"The Troika Laundromat." https://www.occrp.org/en/troikalaundromat/.

"Transparent digital campaigning." https://www.electoralcommission.org.uk/who-we-are-and-what-we-do/changing-electoral-law/transparent-digital-campaigning.

"Ukraine: Apparent War Crimes in Russia-Controlled Areas Summary Executions, Other Grave Abuses by Russian Forces." https://www.hrw.org/news/2022/04/03/ukraine-apparent-war-crimes-russia-controlled-areas.

"Understanding the laws relating to 'fake news' in Russia." https://cpj.org/wp-content/uploads/2022/07/Guide-to-Understanding-the-Laws-Relating-to-Fake-News-in-Russia.pdf.

van der Meer, S., "Cyber Warfare and Nuclear Weapons: Game-changing Consequences?" https://www.swp-berlin.org/en/publication/reviving-nuclear-disarmament/.

Victor, N. M., "Gazprom: Gas Giant Under Strain." https://pesd.fsi.stanford.edu/sites/default/files/WP71,_Nadja_Victor,_Gazprom,_13Jan08.pdf.

Wanless, A., "One Strategy Democracies Should Use to Counter Disinformation." https://carnegieendowment.org/2022/03/28/one-strategy-democracies-should-use-to-counter-disinformation-pub-86734.

Watling, J. "The Kaleidoscopic Campaigning of Russia's Special Services." https://www.rusi.org/explore-our-research/publications/commentary/kaleidoscopic-campaigning-russias-special-services.

Watling, J., Danylyuk, O. V., and Reynolds, N., "The Threat from Russia's Unconventional Warfare Beyond Ukraine, 2022 – 24." https://static.rusi.org/SR-Russian-Unconventional-Weapons-final-web.pdf.

Wezeman, S. T., "Russia's military spending: Frequently asked questions." https://www.sipri.org/commentary/topical-backgrounder/2020/russias-military-spending-frequently-asked-questions.

Wheeler, T., "Mark Zuckerberg's call for internet rules only goes part way." https://www.brookings.edu/blog/techtank/2019/04/03/mark-zuckerbergs-call-for-internet-rules-only-goes-part-way/.

Wolczuk, K., et al, "What is the Eurasian Economic Union?" https://www.chathamhouse.org/2022/07/what-eurasian-economic-union.

Industry reports and policies

8th Annual State of the Software Supply Chain Sonatype's industry-defining research on the rapidly changing landscape of open source. https://www.sonatype.com/resources/2023-software-supply-chain-report.

2021 Data Breach Investigations Report. http://verizon.com/dbir/.

About ads about social issues, elections or politics. https://www.facebook.com/business/help/167836590566506 and https://www.facebook.com/business/help/167836590566506?id=288762101909005.

Alperovitch, D., "Bears in the Midst: Intrusion into the Democratic National Committee." https://www.crowdstrike.com/blog/bears-midst-intrusion-democratic-national-committee/.

https://analytics.facebook.com/.

https://analytics.google.com/analytics/web/provision/?authuser=0#/provision.

https://analytics.twitter.com/about.

APT28. https://attack.mitre.org/groups/G0007/.

APT29. https://attack.mitre.org/groups/G0016/.

APT group: APT 29, Cozy Bear, The Dukes. https://apt.etda.or.th/cgi-bin/showcard.cgi?g=APT%2029%2C%20Cozy%20Bear%2C%20The%20Dukes&n=1.

https://attack.mitre.org/groups/G0035/.

https://attack.mitre.org/versions/v7/.

Backdoor:W32/Havex. https://www.f-secure.com/v-descs/backdoor_w32_havex.shtml.

Cleary, G., Twitterbots: Anatomy of a Propaganda Campaign. https://www.symantec.com/blogs/threat-intelligence/twitterbots-propaganda-disinformation.

https://creatoracademy.youtube.com/page/course/analytics-series.

CrowdStrike, 2018 Global Threat Report Blurring the Lines Between Statecraft and Tradecraft. https://www.crowdstrike.com/resources/reports/2018-crowdstrike-global-threat-report-blurring-the-lines-between-statecraft-and-tradecraft/.

Dragonfly. https://attack.mitre.org/groups/G0035/.

Dragonfly: Western Energy Sector Targeted by Sophisticated Attack Group. https://www.symantec.com/blogs/threat-intelligence/dragonfly-energy-sector-cyber-attacks.

Dragonfly: Western Energy Companies Under Sabotage Threat. https://www.symantec.com/connect/blogs/dragonfly-western-energy-companies-under-sabotage-threat?inid=us_ghp_hero2_dragonfly.

Elsad, A., and Bunce, D., Ransom Cartel Ransomware: A Possible Connection With REvil. https://unit42.paloaltonetworks.com/ransom-cartel-ransomware/.

Energetic Bear — Crouching Yeti Kaspersky Lab Global Research and Analysis Team. https://media.kasperskycontenthub.com/wp-content/uploads/sites/43/2018/03/08080817/EB-YetiJuly2014-Public.pdf.

FireEye, APT28: A Window into Russia's Cyber Espionage Operations. https://www.fireeye.com/content/dam/fireeye-www/global/en/current-threats/pdfs/rpt-apt28.pdf.

FireEye, APT28: At the Center of the Storm Russia Strategically Evolves Its Cyber Operations. https://www.fireeye.com/blog/threat-research/2017/01/apt28_at_the_center.html.

FireEye, M-Trends 2017. A View From the Front Lines. https://www.fireeye.com/current-threats/annual-threat-report/mtrends/rpt-m-trends-2017.html.

Fokker, J., "Organizations Leave Backdoors Open to Cheap Remote Desktop Protocol Attacks." https://securingtomorrow.mcafee.com/other-blogs/mcafee-labs/organizations-leave-backdoors-open-to-cheap-remote-desktop-protocol-attacks/.

Google, "Fog of War How the Ukraine Conflict Transformed the Cyber Threat Landscape." https://services.google.com/fh/files/blogs/google_fog_of_war_research_report.pdf.

Hacquebord, F., Two Years of Pawn Storm Examining an Increasingly Relevant Threat. https://documents.trendmicro.com/assets/wp/wp-two-years-of-pawn-storm.pdf.

Harbison, M., and Renals, P., "Russian APT29 Hackers Use Online Storage Services, DropBox and Google Drive." https://unit42.paloaltonetworks.com/cloaked-ursa-online-storage-services-campaigns/.

Hart, C., 'Troubling' rise in supply chain cyber attacks. https://www.cips.org/supply-management/news/2021/april/troubling-rise-in-supply-chain-cyber-attacks/.

Crashoverride Analysis of the Threat to Electric Grid Operations. https://dragos.com/blog/crashoverride/CrashOverride-01.pdf.

FireEye, M-Trends 2017 A View From the Front Lines, https://www.fireeye.com/current-threats/annual-threat-report/mtrends/rpt-m-trends-2017.html.

Hacktool.Mimikatz. https://www.symantec.com/security-center/writeup/2012-042615-3731-99.

Havex Hunts For ICS/SCADA Systems. https://www.f-secure.com/weblog/archives/00002718.html.

Hultquist, J., Sandworm Team and the Ukrainian Power Authority Attacks. https://www.fireeye.com/blog/threat-research/2016/01/ukraine-and-sandworm-team.html.

How Ransomware Infects Computers. https://www.mcafee.com/enterprise/en-us/security-awareness/ransomware/ransomware-infections.html.

IBM Security, X-Force Threat Intelligence Index 2021. https://www.ibm.com/downloads/cas/M1X3B7QG.

Industroyer: Biggest malware threat to critical infrastructure since Stuxnet. https://www.eset.com/int/industroyer/.

Johnson, B., Caban, D., Krotofil, M., Scali, D., Brubaker, N., and Glyer, C., Attackers Deploy New ICS Attack Framework "TRITON" and Cause Operational Disruption to Critical Infrastructure. https://www.fireeye.com/blog/threat-research/2017/12/attackers-deploy-new-ics-attack-framework-triton.html.

Kaspersky Lab Identifies Operation "Red October," an Advanced Cyber-Espionage Campaign Targeting Diplomatic and Government Institutions Worldwide. http://www.kaspersky.co.in/about/news/virus/2013/Kaspersky_Lab_Identifies_Operation_Red_October_an_Advanced_Cyber_Espionage_Campaign_Targeting_Diplomatic_and_Government_Institutions_Worldwide.

Keeling, C., Waking Shark II: Desktop Cyber Exercise: Report to Participants. https://www.bba.org.uk/wp-content/uploads/2014/02/Banking_3192106_v_1_Waking-Shark-II-Report-v1.pdf.pdf.

Krekel, B., Adams, P., and Bakos, G., *Occupying the Information High Ground: Chinese Capabilities for Computer Network Operations and Cyber Espionage.* https://info.publicintelligence.net/USCC-ChinaCyberEspionage.pdf.

Langhill, J. T., Defending Against the Dragonfly Cyber Security Attacks. https://www.controlglobal.com/assets/15WPpdf/150311-Belden-DragonflyCybersecurity.pdf.

Jenkins, L., Atkins, J., and Black, D., Backchannel Diplomacy: APT29's Rapidly Evolving Diplomatic Phishing Operations. https://www.mandiant.com/resources/blog/apt29-evolving-diplomatic-phishing.

Meyers, A., Danger Close: Fancy Bear Tracking of Ukrainian Field Artillery Units. https://www.crowdstrike.com/blog/danger-close-fancy-bear-tracking-ukrainian-field-artillery-units/.

Lee, R. M., Assante, M. J., and Conway, T., ICS CP/PE (Cyber-to-Physical or Process Effects) case study paper – German Steel Mill Cyber Attack. https://ics.sans.org/media/ICS-CPPE-case-Study-2-German-Steelworks_Facility.pdf.

M-Trends 2023. https://mandiant.widen.net/s/dlzgn6w26n/m-trends-2023.

McAfee Labs Threats Report (2018). https://www.mcafee.com/enterprise/en-us/assets/reports/rp-quarterly-threats-dec-2018.pdf.

Nelson, N. (SANS Institute), The Impact of Dragonfly Malware on Industrial Control Systems. https://www.sans.org/reading-room/whitepapers/ICS/impact-dragonfly-malware-industrial-control-systems-36672.

Operation BugDrop: CyberX Discovers Large-Scale Cyber-Reconnaissance Operation Targeting Ukrainian Organizations. https://cyberx-labs.com/blog/operation-bugdrop-cyberx-discovers-large-scale-cyber-reconnaissance-operation/.

PIPEDREAM Malware and the CHERNOVITE Threat Group. Dragos Intelligence Briefing. https://hub.dragos.com/on-demand/pipedream-malware-chernovite-activity-group.

"Political Content." https://support.google.com/adspolicy/answer/6014595?hl=en.

Prepared Statement of Kevin Mandia. https://www.intelligence.senate.gov/sites/default/files/documents/os-kmandia-033017.pdf.

Propaganda in the digital age: How cyber influence operations erode trust. https://www.microsoft.com/en-us/security/business/security-insider/threat-briefs/propaganda-in-the-digital-age/.

Proska, K., Wolfram, J., Wilson, J., Black, D., Lunden, K., Kapellmann Zafra, D., Brubaker, N., McLellan, T., and Sistrunk, C., "Sandworm Disrupts Power in Ukraine Using a Novel Attack Against Operational Technology." https://www.mandiant.com/resources/blog/sandworm-disrupts-power-ukraine-operational-technology.

Roncone, G., Black, D., Wolfram, J., McLellan, T., Simonian, N., Hall, R., Prokopenkov, A., Perez, D., Aytes, L., Wahlstrom, A., "APT44: Unearthing Sandworm" (2024), https://services.google.com/fh/files/misc/apt44-unearthing-sandworm.pdf.

Santos, N., "BlackEnergy APT Malware." https://community.rsa.com/thread/186012.

Soldatov, A., and Weiss, M., Inside Russia's Secret Propaganda Unit. https://newlinesmag.com/reportage/inside-russias-secret-propaganda-unit/.

Stamos, A., An Update On Information Operations On Facebook. https://newsroom.fb.com/news/2017/09/information-operations-update/.

Stewart, J., BlackEnergy Version 2 Threat Analysis. https://www.secureworks.com/research/blackenergy2.

Tactical Unit Combat Control System "Kropyva." https://logika.ua/en/automation-systems/.

The Economic Impact of Cybercrime and Cyber Espionage. Center for Strategic and International Studies/McAfee. https://www.csis.org/analysis/economic-impact-cybercrime-and-cyber-espionage.

Threat Group-4127 Targets Google Accounts. https://www.secureworks.com/research/threat-group-4127-targets-google-accounts.

Threat Group Cards: A Threat Actor Encyclopedia APT group: APT 29, Cozy Bear, The Dukes, https://apt.etda.or.th/cgi-bin/showcard.cgi?g=APT%2029%2C%20Cozy%20Bear%2C%20The%20Dukes&n=1.

TLP: White Analysis of the Cyber Attack on the Ukrainian Power Grid Defense Use Case March 18, 2016. https://ics.sans.org/media/E-ISAC_SANS_Ukraine_DUC_5.pdf.

Tool: PIPEDREAM. https://apt.etda.or.th/cgi-bin/listgroups.cgi?t=PIPEDREAM.

https://transparency.twitter.com/en.html.

Trojan.Dropper. https://www.symantec.com/security_response/writeup.jsp?docid=2002-082718-3007-99.

Tucker, J. A., Guess, A., Barberá, P., Vaccari, C., Siegel, A., Sanovich, S., Stukal, D., and Nyhan, B., Social Media, Political Polarization, and Political Disinformation: A Review of the Scientific Literature. https://www.hewlett.org/wp-content/uploads/2018/03/Social-Media-Political-Polarization-and-Political-Disinformation-Literature-Review.pdf.

"US Elections Integrity Hub." https://www.tiktok.com/transparency/en-us/us-election-hub.
Verizon Data Breach Investigations Report 2022. https://www.verizon.com/business/en-gb/resources/reports/dbir/2022/.
What are living off the land (LOTL) attacks? https://www.crowdstrike.com/cybersecurity-101/living-off-the-land-attacks-lotl/.
What Does ICANN Do? https://www.icann.org/resources/pages/what-2012-02-25-en.
What is the Meta Ad Library and how do I search it? https://www.facebook.com/help/259468828226154.
Weedon, J., Nuland, W., and Stamos, A., Information Operations and Facebook. https://about.fb.com/wp-content/uploads/2017/04/facebook-and-information-operations-v1.pdf.
Who is Fancy Bear? https://www.crowdstrike.com/blog/who-is-fancy-bear/.
Zilberman, B., "Don't Underestimate Economic Side of Russia's Cyber Warfare." https://www.fdd.org/analysis/2018/06/26/dont-underestimate-economic-side-of-russias-cyber-warfare/.

Conferences

Cyber Security Building Resilience Reducing Risk conference, Chatham House, London (May 19–20, 2014).

Websites

2019 Edelman Trust Barometer Global Report. https://www.edelman.com/sites/g/files/aatuss191/files/2019-02/2019_Edelman_Trust_Barometer_Global_Report.pdf.
"A European Pipeline Energy infrastructure for the future." https://www.nord-stream2.com/.
"A Visionairs Keynote." http://dld-conference.com/events/a-visionairs-keynote.
"Alleged Spam Kingpin 'Severa' Extradited to US." https://krebsonsecurity.com/2018/02/alleged-spam-kingpin-severa-extradited-to-us/.
Anonymous, "Bortnikov Alexander." https://www.spisok-putina.org/en/personas/bortnikov-2/.
Anonymous, "DNC Hacker Releases Trump Oppo Report. 'Guccifer 2.0' claims credit for illegal breach." http://www.thesmokinggun.com/documents/crime/dnc-hacker-leaks-trump-oppo-report-647293.
Anonymous, "Russia's three intelligence agencies, explained." https://themoscowproject.org/explainers/russias-three-intelligence-agencies-explained/.
https://badboysofbrexit.com/.
Bastone, W., "Roger Stone's Russian Hacking 'Hero' Trump loyalist communicated with 'Guccifer 2.0.'" http://www.thesmokinggun.com/documents/investigation/roger-stone-and-guccifer-913684.
Beahm, A., "DCH Health System 'closed to all but most critical' new patients due to ransomware attack." https://www.al.com/news/2019/10/dch-health-system-closed-to-all-but-most-critical-new-patients-due-to-ransomware-attack.html.
Bernard, A., "Russian hacker group APT29 targeting diplomats." https://www.techrepublic.com/article/russian-hacker-group-apt29-targeting-diplomats/.

Bing, C., "An old foe's footprints muddle the mystery around group responsible for energy sector hacks." https://www.cyberscoop.com/us-nuclear-hack-russia-energetic-bear-fireeye-phishing-watering-hole/.

Bensinger, K., Elder, M., and Schoofs, M., "These Reports Allege Trump Has Deep Ties To Russia." https://www.buzzfeednews.com/article/kenbensinger/these-reports-allege-trump-has-deep-ties-to-russia.

Bifolchi, G., "Friends or Foes: Russia-China Relations and the FSB Intel Leaked Document." https://www.specialeurasia.com/2025/06/10/russia-china-fsb-intelligence/.

"BlackEnergy and the Ukraine: Signals vs. Noise." https://threatvector.cylance.com/en_us/home/blackenergy-and-the-ukraine-signals-vs-noise.html.

Blau, J., "Russia – a happy haven for hackers." http://www.computerweekly.com/feature/Russia-a-happy-haven-for-hackers.

Boyd, J., "The History of Facebook: From BASIC to Global Giant." https://www.brandwatch.com/blog/history-of-facebook/.

Brenner, J., "How Obama Fell Short on Cybersecurity: Under the President's Proposals, We'll Remain America the Vulnerable." http://www.politico.com/magazine/story/2015/01/state-of-the-union-cybersecurity-obama-114411.html#ixzz3PjrwwEnf.

Burkhardt, F., Wittke, C., and Bescotti, E., "TCUP Report: Passportization, diminished citizenship rights, and the Donbas vote in Russia's 2021 Duma elections." https://www.huri.harvard.edu/sites/g/files/omnuum4931/files/huri/files/idp_report_3_burkhardt_et_al.pdf.

Burton, F., "Above the Tearline: Brush Passes and Dead Drops." https://worldview.stratfor.com/article/above-tearline-brush-passes-and-dead-drops.

Busvine, D., and Melkozerova, V., "Pro-war nationalist and Putin scourge Igor Girkin held on extremism charges." https://www.politico.eu/article/pro-war-vladimir-putin-critic-igor-girkin-strelkov-arrested-russia-ukraine/.

Cadwalladr, C., "This is what a digital coup looks like." https://www.ted.com/talks/carole_cadwalladr_this_is_what_a_digital_coup_looks_like/transcript

Cancian, M., "This isn't the surprise you were expecting." https://warontherocks.com/2018/03/isnt-surprise-expecting/.

Carcano, A., "Black Hat: Understanding TRITON, The First SIS Cyber Attack." https://www.nozominetworks.com/2018/08/08/blog/black-hat-understanding-triton-the-first-sis-cyber-attack/.

Carlisle, M., and Paschal, O., "After Mueller: The Ongoing Investigations Surrounding Trump." https://www.theatlantic.com/politics/archive/2019/03/after-mueller-ongoing-investigations-trump/585376/.

Cato, M. S., "Arron Banks." https://badboysofbrexit.com/2017/12/22/arron-banks/.

Choi, M., "Trump slams NYT report on U.S. cyberattacks against Russia." https://www.politico.com/story/2019/06/15/trump-nyt-report-cyber-attacks-russia-1365852.

Cimpanu, C., "Hacker Guccifer, who exposed Clinton private email server, ready for US prison sentence." https://www.zdnet.com/article/hacker-guccifer-who-exposed-clinton-private-email-server-ready-for-us-prison-sentence/.

"Contextualizing Putin's 'On the Historical Unity of Russians and Ukrainians.'" https://huri.harvard.edu/news/putin-historical-unity.

Cryst, E., "Stoking Conflict by Keystroke." https://cyber.fsi.stanford.edu/io/news/africa-takedown-december-2020.

"Cyberwarfare, Crime and Security (Eugene Kaspersky, Mikko Hypponen, and Dan Dubno) | DLD13." https://www.youtube.com/watch?v=2BJ_aB4fuOQ.

Dettmer, J., "Russian spies rebound in Europe Critical infrastructure is a key target for Russia's intelligence gathering, the priority being to monitor 'the production and supply of Western arms to Ukraine.'" https://www.politico.eu/article/russia-spy-rebound-europe/.

Doffman, Z., "Russia's Secret Intelligence Agency Hacked: 'Largest Data Breach In Its History.'" https://www.forbes.com/sites/zakdoffman/2019/07/20/russian-intelligence-has-been-hacked-with-social-media-and-tor-projects-exposed/?sh=3bed6c3e6b11.

Dombe, A. M., "Espionage in the Era of Biometric Identity." https://www.israeldefense.co.il/en/content/espionage-era-biometric-identity.

Edwards, J., "Russia probably has more undercover 'sleeper' agents who can assassinate Western targets today than during the Cold War." https://www.businessinsider.com/illegals-of-directorate-s-russia-undercover-covert-sleeper-agents-2017-12?r=UK&IR=T.

Elliot, J. K., "Theatricality and deception: How Russia uses 'maskirovka' to shake the world." https://globalnews.ca/news/4260938/russia-strategy-maskirovka-military-politics-putin/.

Farivar, C., "Man who allegedly gave Vault 7 cache to WikiLeaks busted by poor opsec." https://arstechnica.com/tech-policy/2018/06/ex-cia-engineer-indicted-on-several-new-charges-connected-to-vault-7-leak/.

Ferris, D., "Russia's power grid, held together with spit and grit." https://www.eenews.net/stories/1060010742.

Frenkel, S., "New Report Lifts Curtain On Russia's Construction Of Powerful 'Cyberarmy.'" https://www.buzzfeednews.com/article/sheerafrenkel/new-report-lifts-curtain-on-russias-construction-of-powerful.

Mark Galeotti, "Russia's 'Zaslon' Military Operators Are So Shadowy They Make Ninjas Look Like Amateurs." https://www.businessinsider.com/russian-zaslon-special-operations-2013-5?IR=T.

Galeotti, M., "We Don't Know What to Call Russian Military Intelligence and That May Be a Problem." https://warontherocks.com/2016/01/we-dont-know-what-to-call-russian-military-intelligence-and-that-may-be-a-problem/.

Galeotti, M., "The Three Faces of Russian Spetsnaz in Syria." https://warontherocks.com/2016/03/the-three-faces-of-russian-spetsnaz-in-syria/.

Goldsmith, A., "What do we know about REvil, the Russian ransomware gang likely behind the Medibank cyber attack?" https://theconversation.com/what-do-we-know-about-revil-the-russian-ransomware-gang-likely-behind-the-medibank-cyber-attack-194337.

Goodin, D., "Found: 'Crash Override' malware that triggered Ukrainian power outage. Attack tools can be used against a broad range of electric grids around the world." https://arstechnica.com/information-technology/2017/06/crash-override-malware-may-sabotage-electric-grids-but-its-no-stuxnet/.

Goodin, D., "Hackers trigger yet another power outage in Ukraine For the second year in a row, hack targets Ukraine during one of its coldest months." https://arstechnica.com/information-technology/2017/01/the-new-normal-yet-another-hacker-caused-power-outage-hits-ukraine/.

Goodin, D., "Russia's hack of State Department was 'hand-to-hand' combat." https://arstechnica.com/tech-policy/2017/04/russias-hack-of-state-department-was-hand-to-hand-combat/.

Goodman, R., and Sipher, J., "Taking Putin's Word For It. Trump wants to believe both the Russian president's denial of election meddling, and the conclusions of his own intelligence agencies. But he can't have it both ways." https://www.theatlantic.com/international/archive/2017/11/trump-putin-election-asia/545666/.

Grant, S., and Rosenberg, C., "The Steele Dossier: A Retrospective." https://www.lawfareblog.com/steele-dossier-retrospective.

Grevatt, J., "China, Russia approve 2021–25 road map to increase military co-operation." https://www.janes.com/defence-news/news-detail/china-russia-approve-202125-road-map-to-increase-military-co-operation.

Guerrero-Saade, J. A., Moore, D., Raiu, C., and Rid, T., "Penquin's Moonlit Maze. The Dawn of Nation-State Espionage." https://www.ridt.co/d/jags-moore-raiu-rid.pdf.

Halpern, J., "Bank of the Underworld Liberty Reserve was like PayPal for the unbanked. Was it also a global money-laundering operation?" https://www.theatlantic.com/magazine/archive/2015/05/bank-of-the-underworld/389555/.

Higgins, K. J., "Microsoft Sinkholes 6 Fancy Bear/APT28 Internet Domains." https://www.darkreading.com/attacks-breaches/microsoft-sinkholes-6-fancy-bear-apt28-internet-domains/d/d-id/1332628.

"Home Depot Hit By Same Malware as Target." https://krebsonsecurity.com/2014/09/home-depot-hit-by-same-malware-as-target/.

'How the Domain Name System (DNS) Works." https://www.verisign.com/en_US/website-presence/online/how-dns-works/index.xhtml.

"Hybrid War as a War on Governance Interview by Octavian Manea with Dr. Mark Galeotti." https://smallwarsjournal.com/jrnl/art/hybrid-war-as-a-war-on-governance.

Isaeva, K., and Gonzales, D., "How do Russians live without the sun for 40 days in a row?" https://www.rbth.com/multimedia/pictures/2016/02/29/polar-night-40-days_571553.

Jenkins, D., "How Russian history and the concept of 'smuta' (turmoil) sheds light on Putin and Prigozhin – and the dangers of dissent."

https://theconversation.com/how-russian-history-and-the-concept-of-smuta-turmoil-sheds-light-on-putin-and-prigozhin-and-the-dangers-of-dissent-210289.

Kass, D. H., "Riviera Beach, Florida Ransomware Attack; City Pays $600,000." https://www.msspalert.com/cybersecurity-breaches-and-attacks/ransomware/riviera-beach-florida-malware-attack/.

https://khodorkovsky.com/.

"Kh-47M2 Kinzhal." https://missilethreat.csis.org/missile/kinzhal/.

Khandelwal, S., "Stuxnet-like 'Havex' Malware Strikes European SCADA Systems." http://thehackernews.com/2014/06/stuxnet-like-havex-malware-strikes.html.

Klijnsma, Y., "New Insights into Energetic Bear's Watering Hole Attacks on Turkish Critical Infrastructure." https://www.riskiq.com/blog/labs/energetic-bear/.

Knight, A., "GRU-SOME. This Russian Spy Agency Is in the Middle of Everything." https://www.thedailybeast.com/this-russian-spy-agency-is-in-the-middle-of-everything.

Kofman, M., "Russian Hybrid Warfare and Other Dark Arts." https://warontherocks.com/2016/03/russian-hybrid-warfare-and-other-dark-arts/.

Lardinois, F., "Eugene Kaspersky and Mikko Hypponen Talk Red October and the Future of Cyber Warfare at DLD." https://techcrunch.com/2013/01/21/eugene-kaspersky-and-mikko-hypponen-talk-red-october-and-the-future-of-cyber-warfare-at-dld/.

Leask, D., "How Russia Is Prodding Scotland Toward Independence." https://foreignpolicy.com/2020/02/18/scotland-independence-russia-putin-ukraine-propaganda/.

Levy, P., "How Russia Can Spend Money to Influence the 2020 Election—Legally." https://www.motherjones.com/politics/2019/06/how-russia-can-spend-money-to-influence-the-2020-election-legally/.

Leyden, J., "'Red October' has been spying on World Leaders for 5 years – researchers." http://www.theregister.co.uk/2013/01/14/red_october_cyber_espionage/.

Leyden, J., "Russia's to blame for pro-ISIS megahack on French TV network. APT28 crew left their fingerprints all over this one." http://www.theregister.co.uk/2015/06/10/russian_trolls_staged_tv5monde_megahack_shocker/.

Litovkin, N., "What is the updated Russian cyber-security doctrine about?" https://www.rbth.com/defence/2016/12/07/what-is-the-updated-russian-cyber-security-doctrine-about_654407.

Londberg, M., "Russia infiltrated Kansas nuclear plant's business network, FBI and DHS say." https://www.kansascity.com/news/local/article205581509.html.

Lynch, S., Bayer, L., and Barigazzi, J., "'Oh my God, it's really happening.'" https://www.politico.eu/article/ukraine-invasion-war-russia-zelenskyy-putin-one-year-on-michel-stoltenberg/.

Mayhew, F., "Judge denies opinion claim over tweet in libel battle between Carole Cadwalladr and Arron Banks." https://pressgazette.co.uk/judge-denies-opinion-claim-over-tweet-in-libel-battle-between-carole-cadwalladr-and-arron-banks/.

McCartney, J., "The Home Depot hack: How, why and what we can learn." http://www.techradar.com/news/internet/the-home-depot-hack-how-why-and-what-we-can-learn-1268333.

https://www.opcconnect.com/.

McLaughlin, D., "The Real Reason Trump Won: Part 2 of 4." https://www.nationalreview.com/2017/01/real-reason-trump-won-he-flipped-big-battleground-states/.

Miron, M., "Smersh: why Putin has reinstated Stalin's notorious and much-feared anti-spy unit." https://theconversation.com/smersh-why-putin-has-reinstated-stalins-notorious-and-much-feared-anti-spy-unit-220627.

Moyer, E., "US Cyber Command powers up attacks against Russia's electrical grid." https://www.cnet.com/news/us-cyber-command-powers-up-attacks-against-russias-electrical-grid/.

Nazario, J., "BlackEnergy DDoS Bot Analysis." http://atlas-public.ec2.arbor.net/docs/BlackEnergy+DDoS+Bot+Analysis.pdf.

https://www.netflix.com/title/80117542.

Nimmo, B., "Anatomy of an Info-War: How Russia's Propaganda Machine Works, and How to Counter It." https://www.stopfake.org/en/anatomy-of-an-info-war-how-russia-s-propaganda-machine-works-and-how-to-counter-it/.

Nimmo, B., "#ElectionWatch: Scottish Vote, Pro-Kremlin Trolls." https://medium.com/dfrlab/electionwatch-scottish-vote-pro-kremlin-trolls-f3cca45045bb.

Nimmo, B., "Putin's Media Are Pushing Britain For The Brexit." http://www.interpretermag.com/putins-media-are-pushing-britain-for-the-brexit/.

https://nsarchive.gwu.edu/sites/default/files/documents/3173333/Document-02.pdf.

Ogles, J., "Roger Stone to enjoy last Thanksgiving as free man in Orange Park." https://floridapolitics.com/archives/312285-roger-stone-to-enjoy-last-thanksgiving-as-free-man-in-orange-park.

O'Neill, P. H., "Russia's rise to cyberwar superpower." https://www.dailydot.com/debug/russia-cyberwar-cyberattack-dnc-breach-history/.

Orlova, K., "The KGB is back. The Siloviki Coup in Russia." https://www.the-american-interest.com/2016/09/21/the-siloviki-coup-in-russia/.

Paganini, P., "The Dutch intelligence service AIVD 'hacked' Russian Cozy Bear systems for years." https://securityaffairs.co/68241/intelligence/aivd-hacked-cozy-bear.html.

Pauli, D., "Russian 'Pawn Storm' expands, rains hell on NATO, air-gapped PCs. Group cooks zero days, malware modules, and hacks anything it likes." https://www.theregister.co.uk/2015/12/07/op_pawn_storm/.
Pinto, N., "The EU's imperfect choices on migration from Africa." https://www.gisreportsonline.com/r/eu-africa-migration/.
Press release, "Russian Trolls Relied on Local News More than Fake News in 2016 Presidential Election, New Analysis Finds." https://www.nyu.edu/about/news-publications/news/2018/november/russian-trolls-relied-on-local-news-more-than-fake-news-in-2016-.html.
Reland, J., "The EU referendum wasn't quite the largest democratic exercise in UK history." https://fullfact.org/europe/eu-referendum-not-largest-democratic-exercise/.
Rettman, A., "Illicit Russian billions pose threat to EU democracy." https://euobserver.com/foreign/137631.
Reuser, A., http://arnoreuser.com/.
Rushkoff, D., "How We All Became Russia's 'Useful Idiots.'" https://medium.com/team-human/how-we-all-became-russias-useful-idiots-4df90bf9dea0.
https://www.rusemb.org.uk/consnews/29.
Richter, M. L., "What We Know about RT (Russia Today)." https://www.europeanvalues.net/wp-content/uploads/2017/09/What-We-Know-about-RT-Russia-Today-1.pdf.
Risen, J., "U.S. Intelligence says Putin made a last-minute decision to invade Ukraine", https://theintercept.com/2022/03/11/russia-putin-ukraine-invasion-us-intelligence/.
Russian Interference in the 2016 Election. https://www.govtrack.us/congress/oversight/2-russian-interference-2016.
"Samples of ads misclassified by Facebook." https://cybersecurityfordemocracy.org/missed-ads.
Samuels, D., "The Shameful Attacks on Julian Assange." https://www.theatlantic.com/international/archive/2010/12/the-shameful-attacks-on-julian-assange/67440/.
Šćepanović, J., "20 Years of Russia's Institutionalism in Eurasia. What is Russia trying to accomplish with the CSTO, SCO, and EAEU?" https://thediplomat.com/2019/12/20-years-of-russias-institutionalism-in-eurasia/.
Schindler, J. R., "Putin's Espionage Offensive Against France." https://20committee.com/2014/08/02/putins-espionage-offensive-against-france/.
Schneier, B., "Who Are the Shadow Brokers? What is—and isn't—known about the mysterious hackers leaking National Security Agency secrets." https://www.theatlantic.com/technology/archive/2017/05/shadow-brokers/527778/.
Schwartz, I., "Andrew McCabe: Trump's Own Words Prompted Probe, He Spoke About The FBI 'In A Derogatory Way.'" https://www.realclearpolitics.com/video/2019/02/18/andrew_mccabe_trumps_own_words_prompted_probe_he_spoke_about_the_fbi_in_a_derogatory_way.html.
Scott, D., Golshan, T., and Stein, J., "'Don't forget we still have all the Hillary activity': GOP reacts to Manafort charges." https://www.vox.com/policy-and-politics/2017/10/30/16571678/paul-manafort-indictment-mueller-investigation-republican-reaction.
Sharkov, D., "Russian State Arms Contractor Launches Cyber Defence Center." http://www.newsweek.com/russian-state-arms-contractor-launches-cyber-defence-center-517915.
Shelley, L., "A tangled web: Organized crime and oligarchy in Putin's Russia." https://warontherocks.com/2018/11/a-tangled-web-organized-crime-and-oligarchy-in-putins-russia/.
Shepherd, A., "Interpol: Dark web hacking tools are fuelling cybercrime." http://www.itpro.co.uk/security/29391/interpol-dark-web-hacking-tools-are-fuelling-cybercrime.

Sipher, J., "Western Covert Action and Russian Active Measures: Hypocrisy or Divergent Values?" https://www.justsecurity.org/62324/western-covert-action-russian-active-measures/.
Smyth, R., "Vladimir Putin plans to win Russia's parliamentary election no matter how unpopular his party is." https://theconversation.com/vladimir-putin-plans-to-win-russias-parliamentary-election-no-matter-how-unpopular-his-party-is-160078.
SolarWinds Orion Platform Features. https://www.solarwinds.com/orion-platform/use-cases.
Sheth, S., "US spies say Trump's G7 performance suggests he's either a 'Russian asset' or a 'useful idiot' for Putin." https://www.businessinsider.com/spies-react-trump-g7-summit-russian-asset-2019-8?r=US&IR=T.
Špalková, V., "Influence of Russian disinformation operation: Specific examples in data and numbers." https://www.europeanvalues.net/wp-content/uploads/2019/02/Influence-of-Russian-Disinformation-Operations-Specific-examples-in-data-and-numbers.pdf.
Stein, E., "What's in the Executive Order on Election Interference?" https://www.lawfareblog.com/whats-executive-order-election-interference.
Stein, J., "From Moscow with Murder: Is Russia Hunting Defectors in America?" https://www.newsweek.com/russian-defectors-america-putin-russia-threat-skripal-868013.
Stevenson, A., "Fresh threat to critical infrastructure found in Havex malware." http://www.v3.co.uk/v3-uk/news/2356410/fresh-threat-to-critical-infrastructure-found-in-havex-malware.
St. John, J., "Cyberattack on US Power Plants Could Cause $1T in Economic Damage. Lloyd's of London games out 'improbable, but not impossible' threat of hacking, power-plant sabotage." https://www.greentechmedia.com/articles/read/cyber-attack-on-u-s-power-plants-could-cause-1t-in-economic-damage#gs.YIxYghI.
Stoller, M., "The great break-up of Big Tech is finally beginning." https://openmarketsinstitute.org/op-eds-and-articles/great-break-big-tech-finally-beginning/.
"Target Hackers Broke in Via HVAC Company." https://krebsonsecurity.com/2014/02/target-hackers-broke-in-via-hvac-company/.
"The UK Criminal Finances Act 2017: implications for offshore financial providers." https://www.kennedyslaw.com/thought-leadership/article/the-uk-criminal-finances-act-2017-implications-for-offshore-financial-providers.
Thompson, I., "Kaspersky Lab hits back at Bloomberg's Russian spy link hit piece." https://www.theregister.co.uk/2015/03/19/kaspersky_lab_denies_its_handinglove_with_russian_security_services/.
Tucker, P., "Russia Will Build Its Own Internet Directory, Citing US Information Warfare." http://www.defenseone.com/technology/2017/11/russia-will-build-its-own-internet-directory-citing-us-information-warfare/142822/?oref=d-river.
"UK Government Considers New Foreign Agents Registration Act." https://www.cov.com/-/media/files/corporate/publications/2020/07/uk-government-considers-new-foreign-agents-registration-act.pdf.
Unger, C., "When a Young Trump Went to Russia." https://newrepublic.com/article/150646/young-trump-went-russia.
"U.S. Indicts 2 Top Russian Hackers, Sanctions Cryptex." https://krebsonsecurity.com/2024/09/u-s-indicts-2-top-russian-hackers-sanctions-cryptex/comment-page-1/.
Vandoorne, S., and Siad, A., "Macron announces end of France's anti-terror Operation Barkhane in Africa's Sahel region." https://edition.cnn.com/2021/06/10/europe/france-sahel-operation-barkhane-end-intl/index.html.

Vogel, K. P., and Stern, D., "Ukrainian efforts to sabotage Trump backfire Kiev officials are scrambling to make amends with the president-elect after quietly working to boost Clinton." https://www.politico.com/story/2017/01/ukraine-sabotage-trump-backfire-233446,

Vos, E. L., "Dutch 'Cozy Bear' Farce Does Not Show DNC Emails Were Hacked By Russians." https://www.zerohedge.com/news/2018-01-26/dutch-cozy-bear-farce-does-not-show-dnc-emails-were-hacked-russians.

Wagner, K., "Twitter says it's getting better at detecting abusive tweets without your help." https://www.vox.com/2019/4/16/18410931/twitter-abuse-update-health-technology-harassment.

Walker, J., "Traditional media more responsible for Brexit vote than Facebook, says Nick Clegg." https://pressgazette.co.uk/traditional-media-more-responsible-for-brexit-vote-than-facebook-says-nick-clegg/.

"War and Peace in the Nuclear Age; Zero Hour; Interview with Helmut Schmidt, 1987." https://openvault.wgbh.org/catalog/V_55D8B7AC02BD4D7CA6D1E705F68A0604.

Weiss, B., "New details emerge about Steve Bannon's ties to Cambridge Analytica." https://www.businessinsider.com/steve-bannon-ties-to-cambridge-analytica-facebook-data-run-deep-2018-3?r=US&IR=T.

"**West Siberian Oil Basin.**" http://petroneft.com/operations/west-siberian-oil-basin/.

"Who will win the presidency?" https://projects.fivethirtyeight.com/2016-election-forecast/.

Zetter, K., "Security Firms Aiding Ukraine During War Could Be Considered Participants in Conflict." https://www.zetter-zeroday.com/security-firms-aiding-ukraine-during/.

Other

"305 Car Registrations May Point to Massive GRU Security Breach." https://www.bellingcat.com/news/2018/10/04/305-car-registrations-may-point-massive-gru-security-breach/.

"Active Measures." https://www.imdb.com/title/tt8135494/.

"Bellingcat Report – Origin of Artillery Attacks on Ukrainian Military Positions in Eastern Ukraine Between 14 July 2014 and 8 August 2014." https://www.bellingcat.com/news/uk-and-europe/2015/02/17/origin-of-artillery-attacks/,

Briant, E. L., "How Social Media Incentives Helped Drive the Discord Leaks." https://techpolicy.press/how-social-media-incentives-helped-drive-the-discord-leaks/.

"Digital political advertising spending in the United States from 2008 to 2020." https://www.statista.com/statistics/309592/online-political-ad-spend-usa/.

https://www.documentcloud.org/documents/3259984-Trump-Intelligence-Allegations.html.

https://www.facebook.com/RTnews/.

Grozev, C., "Balkan Gambit: Part 2. The Montenegro Zugzwang." https://www.bellingcat.com/news/uk-and-europe/2017/03/25/balkan-gambit-part-2-montenegro-zugzwang/.

Grozev, C., "Socialite, Widow, Jeweller, Spy: How a GRU Agent Charmed Her Way Into NATO Circles in Italy." https://www.bellingcat.com/news/2022/08/25/socialite-widow-jeweller-spy-how-a-gru-agent-charmed-her-way-into-nato-circles-in-italy/.

Haslam, J., "H-Diplo Essay 420- Commentary Series on Putin's War: 'Russia Attacks Ukraine: A Post Mortem for Putin?'" https://networks.h-net.org/node/28443/discussions/9948394/h-diplo-essay-420-commentary-series-putin%E2%80%99s-war-%E2%80%9Crussia-attacks.

Morris, V. R., “Grading Gerasimov: Evaluating Russian Nonlinear War Through Modern Chinese Doctrine.” https://smallwarsjournal.com/jrnl/art/grading-gerasimov-evaluating-russian-nonlinear-war-through-modern-chinese-doctrine.

Nephew, R., “Commentary: Responding to Russia.” http://energypolicy.columbia.edu/sites/default/files/CGEP%20Commentary_Responding%20to%20Russia_Nephew.pdf.

“Number of social network users worldwide from 2010 to 2021 (in billions).” https://www.statista.com/statistics/278414/number-of-worldwide-social-network-users/.

“Political advertising spending in the United States election cycles from 2014 to 2022, by medium.” https://www.statista.com/statistics/1182087/political-advertising-spending-election-cycle-by-medium-united-states/.

Otte, T. G., H-Diplo Essay 416, “Commentary Series on Putin’s War: ‘Zeitenwende: Russia’s War against Ukraine and the End of the Thirty Years’ Holiday.’” https://hdiplo.org/to/E416.

Prados, J., “The Record on Curveball Declassified Documents and Key Participants Show the Importance of Phony Intelligence in the Origins of the Iraq War.” https://nsarchive2.gwu.edu/NSAEBB/NSAEBB234/.

Rakuszitzky, M., “Second GRU Officer Indicted in Montenegro Coup Unmasked.” https://www.bellingcat.com/news/uk-and-europe/2018/11/22/second-gru-officer-indicted-montenegro-coup-unmasked/,

“Sergei & the Westminster Spy Ring.” https://www.globalplayer.com/podcasts/42L25Z/.

“The Shanghai Cooperation Organisation.” http://eng.sectsco.org/about_sco/.

“The Santa Clara Principles On Transparency and Accountability in Content Moderation.” https://santaclaraprinciples.org/.

“Special Despatch No. 7943.” https://www.memri.org/reports/russian-first-deputy-defense-minister-gerasimov-our-response-based-active-defense-strategy.

Thomas, T., “Thinking Like A Russian Officer: Basic Factors and Contemporary Thinking On the Nature of War.” https://community.apan.org/wg/tradoc-g2/fmso/m/fmso-monographs/194971.

https://twitter.com/realdonaldtrump/status/1028347518822825984?lang=en.

https://twitter.com/rt_com?lang=en.

“‘V’ for ‘Vympel’”; “FSB’s Magnificent Seven: New Links between Berlin and Istanbul Assassinations”. https://www.bellingcat.com/news/uk-andeurope/2020/06/29/fsbs-magnificent-seven-new-links-between-berlin-and-istanbul-assassinations/.

Watson, A., “Share of adults who trust news media most of the time in selected countries worldwide as of February 2019” (last updated July 1, 2019). https://www.statista.com/statistics/308468/importance-brand-journalist-creating-trust-news/.

https://wikileaks.org/.

Index of Names and Subjects

Page numbers in **bold** indicate tables in the text, and references following "n" refer to notes.

https://doi.org/10.1515/9783111583464-010